the Quinte

Bed & Breakfast
Directory
of Quality Homes

Acknowledgements

We are indebted to the Cumbria Tourist Board (CTB), Derbyshire Dales District Council (DDDC), East of England Tourist Board (EETB), Heart of England Tourist Board (HETB), Lincolnshire County Council (LCC), North West Tourist Board (NWTB), Northumbria Tourist Board (NTB), Scottish Tourist Board (SCTB), Shropshire Tourism (ST), South East England Tourist Board (SEETB), South West Tourism (SWT), Southern Tourist Board (STB), Wales Tourist Board (WTB), Worcestershire County Council (WCC), Yorkshire Tourist Board (YTB) for the use of pictures within the text.

Publisher: Davina Ludlow
Editor: Victoria Rowlands
Assistant Editor: Deidri Surtees
Administration: Josephine Woolford
Design: Zai Khan
Layout: Oliver Blackwell
Mapping: Philippa Ross
Production: Phil Cory
Research: Victoria Lippiatt

This edition edited and designed by:

Tomorrow's Guides
PO Box 7677, Hungerford RG17 0FX
Subscription sales Tel: 0800 387342
sales@tomorrows.co.uk
www.stayinstyle.com

Distribution in the UK by Portfolio

Printed in Spain

First published 1998
Fifth edition 2002

© Tomorrow's Guides Ltd 2001

ISBN 1 85890 027 1

Contents

UK Counties Map

HIGHLANDS
& ISLANDS

CENTRAL, EAST
& NORTHEAST
SCOTLAND

EDINBURGH,
GLASGOW
& SOUTHERN
SCOTLAND

NORTHUMBRIA

CUMBRIA

LANCASHIRE

YORKSHIRE

LEICESTERSHIRE,
NOTTINGHAMSHIRE
& RUTLAND

CHESHIRE,
MERSEYSIDE &
GREATER
MANCHESTER

LINCOLNSHIRE

DERBYSHIRE &
STAFFORDSHIRE

CAMBRIDGESHIRE &
NORTHAMPTONSHIRE

NORTH WALES

SHROPSHIRE

WARWICKSHIRE &
WEST MIDLANDS

NORFOLK

HEREFORD &
WORCESTER

MID-WALES

SUFFOLK

SOUTH
& SOUTHWEST
WALES

ESSEX

GLOUCESTERSHIRE

OXFORDSHIRE

BATH, BRISTOL
& NORTH EAST
SOMERSET

LONDON

SOMERSET

SURREY

KENT

CORNWALL

DEVON

DORSET

SUSSEX

WILTSHIRE

HAMPSHIRE &
ISLE OF WIGHT

BEDFORDSHIRE,
BERKSHIRE,
BUCKINGHAMSHIRE
& HERTFORDSHIRE

Introduction

Welcome to the 2002 edition of The Bed & Breakfast Directory.

Our Bed & Breakfast Directory is truly quintessential - nowhere else can you find such a concentration of quality Homes representing the best proprietor run accommodation in England, Scotland and Wales.

There are over 1,500 listings, each illustrated with a colour picture plus facts and information supplied by the owners themselves. With few exceptions you will be staying in somebody's home and your hosts will be sensitive to your needs and offer hospitality in their own unique style. In many cases they can provide dinner too, using local and home produced food.

The Bed & Breakfast Directory will help you find accommodation with facilities and services that are right for you, at a price to suit your budget. If you need to be in a particular place, you can start to plan your stay away by referring first to the applicable area/county map and then reading the entries nearest to your destination. If your first choice is unavailable, the map will show you where to find the next closest property. With so many listings we feel confident that you will easily be able to find a suitable alternative.

Tomorrow's Guides acquired the Bed & Breakfast Directory in March 2001 and for those familiar with previous editions we make no apologies for removing and replacing over 85% of the properties listed. Our aim is to provide you with a comprehensive selection of homes offering quality accommodation at a reasonable price. We have made many changes to the layout and we hope you will agree that the result is a user friendly guide to the great British tradition of 'Bed & Breakfast'.

Davina Ludlow
Publisher

How to use

Finding the right B & B home

We have divided the publication into England, Scotland and Wales. The map on page 4 details the Areas/Counties for each Country, and the Contents on page 3 provides a page reference to each Area/County, where you will find a more detailed map showing Map References for each property listed within that Area/County. You should use these Map References to locate properties within the Town or Area that you wish to stay and select your B & B from the description, prices and other information shown within the listings. Also refer to the quick reference indexes at the back which provide page references by Town and, if you are looking for a particular B & B, by Property Name.

Sequence of Entries

The listings within each Area (i.e North Wales) or within each County (i.e Cumbria) are sequenced by Town name. For multiple listings within the same Town, those in the centre of the Town will appear first in alphabetical property name order, followed by those in suburbs or adjacent villages.

Prices quoted

The prices quoted throughout our book are based on the price per person per night for two sharing a double room, which includes a full British or continental breakfast, and VAT where applicable. An extra charge is usually made for the use of a double room as a single. Reduced charges may be available for extended stays, you should check when booking. Prices are shown in British £.

Room descriptions

'Rooms' are described as follows: *Single*: 1 bed, *Double*: 1 large bed, *Twin*: 2 separate beds, *Four poster*: King or Queen size bed with canopy. 'Bathrooms' are described as follows: *Shared*: facilities are shared with some other guests, *Private*: for your own use but in an adjacent room, occasionally abbreviated to 'pb', *En-suite*: private facilities within your own bedroom suite. Again you should check the description for special features of bedrooms.

How to use

Meals

Where the B & B offers dinner, the minimum price or 'dinner available' is shown. In many cases dinner is only available by prior arrangement, so check this out when booking. You should also check the description for further information on food, specialities, etc.

Smoking

'No smoking' means no smoking anywhere in the house, 'Restricted smoking' means smoking is permitted in certain rooms, or areas of the house and you should always check with your host as to where you may smoke.

Children

We have asked our homes to clarify their policy on this often sensitive subject in one of the following ways: No children, children welcome or the minimum age at which children are welcome. If you would like to have your child in the room with you, you should check at the time of booking as to whether there is a foldaway bed, and the cost.

Dogs

'Dogs welcome' generally means that you can bring your dog, but you should always check the house rules. Only a few hosts permit dogs in bedrooms or even in the house, but are happy that your dog sleeps in your car or they can provide a kennel.

Symbols

We have resisted the temptation to use symbols and have done our best to put everything into simple English. However see 'Payment' below for the abbreviations we have used for credit cards.

Tipping

Few of your hosts would expect you to tip them, but if you have received exceptional kindness you may wish to send a thank you card.

UK Railways Network

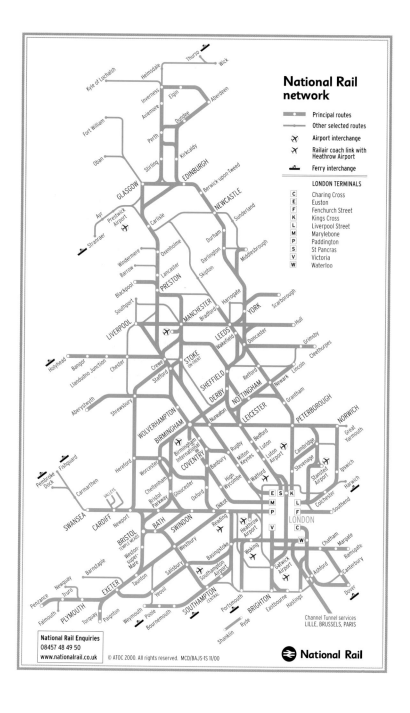

National Rail network

Principal routes	
Other selected routes	
✈	Airport interchange
✈	Railair coach link with Heathrow Airport
⚓	Ferry interchange

LONDON TERMINALS

C	Charing Cross
E	Euston
F	Fenchurch Street
K	Kings Cross
L	Liverpool Street
M	Marylebone
P	Paddington
S	St Pancras
V	Victoria
W	Waterloo

Channel Tunnel services
LILLE, BRUSSELS, PARIS

National Rail Enquiries
08457 48 49 50
www.nationalrail.co.uk

National Rail

How to use

Bookings and cancellations

Bookings should be made direct with the home by telephone, fax, email or post. A deposit may be required which is often non-refundable if you cancel at short notice and the room cannot be re-let. Your time of arrival and departure is vital information to your hosts who will do their best to meet with your requirements.

Payment

In the UK you can pay by cash or cheque drawn on a British bank with a cheque card, or in some cases by credit card. Our listings show whether credit cards are accepted (C-Cards) and which of the following cards are taken (MC Master Card, VS Visa, AE American Express, DC Diners Club). It is generally the case that if the establishment accepts credit cards, switch cards or direct debit cards will also be accepted.

Feedback

Please let us know your opinion of the accommodation that you stayed in. There is a report form at the back of the book and this should also be used to inform us of any delightful homes that you may have come across and you would like to recommend for inclusion in future editions. Feedback is essential for the integrity of our book.

www.stayinstyle.com

All homes listed are featured on our website and those that have their own E-mail addresses or Website addresses can be accessed directly from our website.

We would like to thank those who have allowed us to use their pictures on our front/back cover:

Broome Court (Broomhill, Devon), Hillside House (Burton Lazars, Leicestershire), Lamperts Cottage (Sydling St Nicholas, Dorset), and The Vauld Farm (Marden, Herefordshire)

Bath, Bristol &
Northeast Somerset

This region offers a holiday venue to suit all tastes. It is an area packed with interest and simply cries out to be revisited over and over again. Such is the appeal of this special locality, that no amount of description can do it justice. It just has to be experienced.

Bristol, in the centre of the region, is the largest town in the south west of England, a major entertainment and also communications centre since medieval times, when it claimed parity with London. Though no longer a commercial port, the docks still dominate the centre of the city, their attraction being the splendid Maritime Heritage Centre and the Bristol Industrial Museum where Brunel's magnificent steamship of 1843, 'The Great Britain', now fully restored, can be viewed. Heavy bombing during WW2 destroyed many of the medieval buildings and the city was greatly modernised in the 1950s and 60s. However the Cathedral, once the abbey church, retaining its spectacular Norman Chapter House and fine Lady Chapel, has lost none of its historical charm and is a delight to visit. There are a large number of fine Georgian houses, Queen's Square being the most impressive. Of special interest are the curious bronze pillars known as the Nails outside the exchange, where the merchants paid their accounts, hence the saying 'to pay on the nail'. As befits a city of Bristol's importance, there are theatres, concert halls, cinemas and high quality entertainment of all descriptions, as well as many famous shopping streets and the hectic life of the university.

Of course, if our Georgian heritage is an attraction, nearby Bath offers the finest Georgian architecture in the country. The Romans made Bath their headquarters in AD 44, building baths around the natural hot springs and dedicating a temple to the goddess Sulis Minerva, naming the city Aquae Sulis. To commemorate this unique period is the fascinating Roman Baths Museum. The pride of medieval Bath is its handsome monastery, whose early sixteenth century church survives today as Bath Abbey. It is renowned for its magnificent fan-vaulting and its west front. In the seventeenth century Bath became a fashionable Spa town and the centre of a culture led by Beau Nash, who for 50 years was the Master of Ceremonies here. Many of the great houses, the Circus of 1754, a circle of 30 houses noted for their famous residents of the past, and the Terrace are the work of the architect John Wood. The magnificent Pulteney Bridge was designed by Robert Adam, adding to the impressive architecture of this city

Clifton Suspension Bridge, Bristol (SWT)

The countryside in this region is as glorious a setting as the visitor will find anywhere in England. The National Trust controls Sand Point just north of Weston-super-Mare, a limestone headland which includes Castle Batch, an ancient Norman motte. The Avon Gorge Nature Reserve on the west bank of the Avon can be reached across the Clifton Suspension Bridge, a National Trust Property which includes Leigh Woods and an Iron Age hill-fort. Other sites of interest include Dyrham Park, overlooking the Severn Valley, built between 1691 and 1710 for William Blathwayt and is surrounded by 263 acres of ancient parkland with a herd of fallow deer. For the more energetic there is the eight mile Bath Skyline Walk, giving quite superb views across Bath and Dolebury Warren, some 12 miles south from Bristol where an Iron Age fort tops the barren hill, gives the most breathtaking views in the Mendips. The seaside is also well represented in this region by Weston-super-Mare, south west of Bristol, which offers in addition to all the traditional attractions, a glorious sandy bay between two protective headlands.

The region is rich in natural scenery, and such is the quality, colour and texture of the stone that even the most formal buildings seem to blend comfortably into the landscape. To the north of Bristol is the delightful Blaise Hamlet designed by John Nash in 1811 for the owner of Blaise Castle as homes for old retainers. Regarded as the most picturesque medieval hamlet in England, the cottages, each with a unique charm, are built around an undulating green and are well worth a visit. However with so much on offer the traveller is spoilt for choice. Busy days, seaside days, walking days or simply lazy days, what more could you wish for?

PLACES TO VISIT

This is a small selection of interesting places to visit. Many more are listed in our annual guide to Museums, Galleries, Historic Houses & Sites (see page 448)

Bath Abbey
Bath
Britain's last great medieval church with fan-vaulting designed by Robert and William Vertue. Its vaults are also open to the public and include Saxon and Norman sculpture.

Bristol Cathedral
College Green, Bristol
A twelfth century Norman chapter house, founded as an Augustinian Abbey but developed into a Cathedral in 1542.

Maritime Heritage Centre
Wapping Wharf, Gas Ferry Road, Bristol
Showing the development of the ship building industry within the last 200 years from wood to iron and modern steel. Also houses the SS Great Britain.

Roman Baths & Pump Room
Stall Street, Bath
Former baths, now a museum with many Roman relics and treasures.

No. 1 Royal Crescent
Bath
A representative of the finest achievements of eighteenth century architecture and the highest point of Palladian architecture in Britain. The house is restored and decorated to how it was in the eighteenth century.

Victoria Art Gallery
Bridge Street, Bath
The gallery houses Bath and North East Somerset's art collection with oil paintings from fifteenth to twentieth century, plus works of artists who lived and worked in the area.

Bath, Bristol &
Northeast Somerset

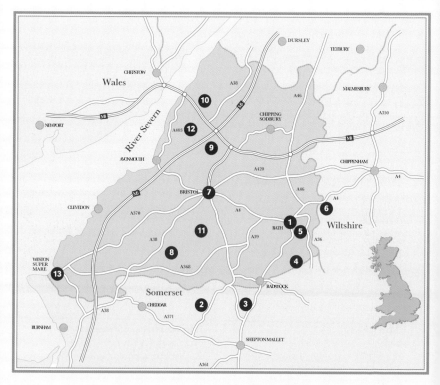

The Red Map References should be used to locate B & B properties on the pages that follow

ANCHOR FARM Combe Hay, Bath BA2 7EE   *Map Ref:* 1
Sue & Richard Saker-Harper   A369
Tel: 01225 002124 Mobile: 07703 438409

Anchor Farm is a small organic working farm in a unique rural
location, yet only 10 minutes from the beautiful City of Bath. The
excellent village pub is just a five minute walk away. Your
accommodation is a cosy self-contained suite with its own private
entrance. A delicious, healthy organic breakfast is served in the
farmhouse or on the veranda.

B & B from £28pp, Rooms 1 double en-suite, Restricted smoking,
No children or dogs, Closed Xmas & New Year

APARTMENT 1 60 Great Pulteney Street, Bath BA2 4DN   *Map Ref:* 1
Mrs Chanloo Smith *Tel:* 01225 464134 *Fax:* 01225 483663   A36
Email: chanloosmith@aptone.fsnet.co.uk

A garden apartment in one of Bath's most elegant streets. The guest
room overlooking the garden can be arranged as a double or twin
with full en-suite facilities, television and radio. The central location
gives easy access to all tourist attractions, shops and restaurants.
French and German spoken.

B & B from £30pp, Rooms 1 double en-suite, No smoking,
No children,

APSLEY HOUSE HOTEL 141 Newbridge Hill, Bath BA1 3PT   *Map Ref:* 1
David & Annie Lanz *Tel:* 01225 336966 *Fax:* 01225 425462   A431
Email: info@apsley-house.co.uk *Web:* www.apsley-house.co.uk

Apsley House Hotel, a Georgian country house was built in 1830. It
is a small privately run hotel with beautifully proportioned rooms and
pretty gardens, it stands just over one mile from the city centre, with
parking for guests' cars. The interior includes many period features.
A sumptuous breakfast is served in the delightful dining room. 5
Diamonds. Licensed Bar.

B & B from £32.50pp, Rooms 4 double, 1 four poster, 2 garden
rooms, 3 twin, 1 family, Restricted smoking, Children over 5,
No dogs, Closed Xmas

---

9 BATHWICK HILL Bath BA2 6EW   *Map Ref:* 1
Elspeth Bowman   On Bathwick Hill
Tel: 01225 460812

This is a listed Georgian family home standing in a desirable part of
Bath. Two twin bedrooms offer baths and tea/coffee facilities. A full
English breakfast is served. Guests may relax in the drawing room,
the conservatory and the garden. It is a short walk or bus trip to city
centre. Parking outside the property. Up Bathwick Hill (off A36),
Cleveland Walk on left, house on right.

B & B £25-£28pp, Rooms 2 twin with private bathrooms,
No smoking, Children over 12, No dogs, Closed Xmas

BROMPTON HOUSE St John's Road, Bath BA2 6PT   *Map Ref:* 1
The Selby Family *Tel:* 01225 420972 *Fax:* 01225 420505   A46
Email: bromptonhouse@btinternet.com *Web:* www.bromptonhouse.co.uk

Brompton House is a charming Georgian residence, it was formerly
a Rectory in 1777. Family owned and run, the accommodation is
comfortable and tastefully furnished, with en-suite bedrooms. There
is a free private car park and beautiful secluded gardens. It is 6
minutes level walk to Bath's main historic sights. A delicious choice
of English and continental breakfasts is offered.

B & B from £30pp, C-Cards MC VS AE, Rooms 2 single, 7 twin,
7 double, 1 family, No smoking, Children over 15, No dogs, Closed
Xmas & New Year

CRANLEIGH 159 Newbridge Hill, Bath BA1 3PX   *Map Ref:* 1
Tony & Jan Poole   *Tel:* 01225 310197   *Fax:* 01225 423143   A431
Email: cranleigh@btinternet.com   *Web:* www.cranleighguesthouse.com

Quietly located, minutes from the heart of Bath, Cranleigh enjoys lovely views, sunny gardens and parking. Bedrooms are en-suite and spacious, some ground floor rooms are available. Breakfasts include fresh fruit salad and scrambled eggs with smoked salmon. The Pooles will help with planning trips. An excellent place to stay for exploring Bath. There are reductions for out of season breaks. Free golf.

B & B from £33pp, C-Cards MC VS AE, Rooms 2 twin, 4 double, 2 family, all en-suite, No smoking, Children over 5, No dogs, Closed Xmas

---

DEVONSHIRE HOUSE 143 Wellsway, Bath BA2 4RZ   *Map Ref:* 1
Mrs Eileen Fermor-Harris   *Tel:* 01225 312495   *Fax:* 01225 335534   A367
Email: info@devonshire-house-bath.co.uk   *Web:* www.devonshire-house-bath.co.uk

Lovely Victorian house built in 1880. Bedrooms are fully en-suite and individually decorated with tea/coffee facilities and televisions. Breakfast is fresh fruit salad, smoked fish or traditional fare in our dining room, originally a Victorian grocers shop. Special diets catered for. Secure parking in our courtyard with the city just 12 minutes walk. 3 nights for 2 in low season.

B & B £27.50-£37.50pp, C-Cards MC VS AE, Rooms 1 double, 1 twin, 1 family, all en-suite, No smoking, Children over 6, No dogs, Open all year

---

DOLPHIN HOUSE 8 Northend, Batheaston, Bath BA1 7EN   *Map Ref:* 1
Mr & Mrs G W & A J Riley   A4
Tel / Fax: 01225 858915   *Mobile:* 07801 444521

A Georgian Grade II listed house with period furnishings and a mature terraced walled garden. There is a private suite of three rooms, also a large double room with private bathroom. All have television and tea/coffee facilities. Breakfast is served in the privacy of your own room, or on the terrace. Bath is two miles away and pubs and restaurants are close by.

B & B £25-£32.50pp, Rooms 1 double, 1 twin, 1 family, all with en-suite, No smoking, Children over 12, No dogs, Closed Xmas & New Year

---

DORIAN HOUSE 1 Upper Oldfield Park, Bath BA2 3JX   *Map Ref:* 1
Kathryn & Tim Hugh   *Tel:* 01225 426336   *Fax:* 01225 444699   A367
Email: info@dorianhouse.co.uk   *Web:* www.dorianhouse.co.uk

Enter an atmosphere of period charm in Dorian House, circa 1880. All our bedrooms feature private, en-suite bathrooms, Egyptian cotton sheets, fluffy towels, telephone, television, tea/coffee making facilities. With panoramic views overlooking Bath towards the Royal Crescent, our four-poster rooms are perfect for a celebration visit to Bath. Ten minutes walk to the Roman Baths (city centre). Licensed. Off-street parking.

B & B £34-£70pp, C-Cards MC VS, Rooms 2 twin, 2 family, 1 single, private or en-suite, No smoking, Children welcome, No dogs, Closed Xmas

---

GAINSBOROUGH HOTEL Weston Lane, Bath BA1 4AB   *Map Ref:* 1
Anna Ford   *Tel:* 01225 311380   *Fax:* 01225 447411   A4
Email: gainsborough_hotel@compuserve.com   *Web:* www.gainsboroughhotel.co.uk

Gainsborough Hotel is a spacious and comfortable country house hotel situated on high ground with nice views, near Botanical Gardens and centre. Colour satellite TV, beverage facilities, direct dial telephones and hair dryers etc. Large lounge. Friendly bar. Two sun terraces. Private car park. A warm welcome from friendly staff.

B & B £32-£48pp, C-Cards MC VS AE, Rooms 2 single, 12 twin/double, 3 family, Restricted smoking, Children welcome, No dogs, Closed Xmas & New Year

HAYDON HOUSE 9 Bloomfield Park, Bath BA2 2BY   *Map Ref:* 1
Gordon & Magdalene Ashman-Marr *Tel:* 01225 444919 *Fax:* 01225 427351 A367
Email: stay@haydonhouse.co.uk *Web:* www.haydonhouse.co.uk

Haydon house is an oasis of tranquility and elegance in a quiet residential street with unlimited free parking. Reception rooms are tastefully decorated with antiques. The Laura Ashley decorated bedrooms have en-suite facilities and offering all comforts. Innovative breakfasts are served including whiskey/rum porridge. ETB 5 Diamonds, Silver Award, AA Five Diamonds, Good Hotel Guide, Which Hotel Guide.

B & B £37.50-£49pp, C-Cards MC VS AE, Rooms 3 double, 1 twin, 1 family, all en-suite, No smoking, Children welcome, No dogs, Open all year

---

HIGHWAYS HOUSE 143 Wells Road, Bath BA2 3AL   *Map Ref:* 1
Andy & Ros Morley *Tel:* 01225 421238 *Fax:* 01225 481169 A367
Email: stay@bandbbath.co.uk *Web:* www.bandbbath.co.uk

An elegant Victorian home set in mature gardens and only ten minutes' walk from the city centre. Clean comfortable rooms with excellent beds, some king size. One triple room, a large guest lounge, double glazing and central heating throughout. Full English breakfasts, cooked to order. Off street parking and no smoking.

B & B from £30pp, C-Cards MC VS AE, Rooms 1 single, 3 double, 3 twin, all en-suite, No smoking, Children over 6, No dogs, Open all year

---

HOLLY LODGE 8 Upper Oldfield Park, Bath BA2 3JZ   *Map Ref:* 1
George Hall *Tel:* 01225 424042 *Fax:* 01225 481138 A367
Email: stay@hollylodge.co.uk *Web:* www.hollylodge.co.uk

Holly Lodge is an elegant Victorian town house set in lovely grounds with magnificent views of the city. Elegantly furnished with antiques, it is meticulously operated with fine attention to detail by George Hall. Breakfasts are superb, they are taken in the attractively presented breakfast room. This award winning house is a perfect base for touring Bath and the Cotswolds.

B & B from £40pp, C-Cards MC VS AE DC, Rooms 1 single, 4 double, 2 twin, all en-suite, No smoking, Children welcome, No dogs, Open all year

---

LAVENDER HOUSE 17 Bloomfield Park, Bath BA2 2BY   *Map Ref:* 1
Carol & Bill Huxley *Tel:* 01225 314500 *Fax:* 01225 448564 A367
Email: lavenderhouse@btinternet.com *Web:* www.lavenderhouse-bath.com

Our large Edwardian house is set in a quiet conservation area near the city centre. Each lovely guest room has television/radio, hairdryer, hospitality tray and a large, luxurious bathroom. Traditional English and speciality Cordon Vert vegetarian breakfasts. Carol, Bill and cats, Rosie and Cheeta are waiting to share their home with discerning visitors. 'A purr..fect place to be spoilt!'

B & B £35-£45pp, C-Cards MC VS, Dinner from £15, Rooms 1 single, 3 double, 1 twin, most en-suite, No smoking, Children over 8, No dogs, Closed Xmas & New Year

---

LEIGHTON HOUSE 139 Wells Road, Bath BA2 3AL   *Map Ref:* 1
Rhona Sampson *Tel:* 01225 314769 *Fax:* 01225 443079 A367
Email: welcome@leighton-house.co.uk *Web:* www.leighton-house.co.uk

Leighton House is an elegant detached Victorian House in its own large and attractive gardens. Well placed for touring the Cotswolds, Somerset and Wiltshire. Ten minutes walk to city centre. Car parking, TV, hair dryer, tea/coffee making facilities, bath and shower in every individually decorated room. King, queen or twin beds. ETC, AA 5 Diamonds, Gold Award, Premier collection and Top B&B.

B & B from £29.50pp, C-Cards MC VS AE, Rooms 4 double, 3 twin, 1 family, all en-suite, No smoking, Children over 8, No dogs, Open all year

MARLBOROUGH HOUSE 1 Marlborough Lane, Bath BA1 2NQ
Laura & Charley Dunlap *Tel:* 01225 318175 *Fax:* 01225 466127
Email: mars@manque.dircon.co.uk *Web:* www.marlborough-house.net

Map Ref: 1
A4

Marlborough House is an enchanting small hotel in the heart of Georgian Bath, exquisitely furnished with elegant antiques. We specialize in Organic Vegetarian world cuisine, with breakfast choices that include San Francisco pancakes with organic maple syrup, as well as delicate omelettes with savory mushrooms and breakfast potatoes. Our central location, gorgeous rooms and unique menu make us truly special.

B & B £32.50-£42.50pp, C-Cards MC VS, Dinner from £15, Rooms 7 single/double/twin/family, all en-suite, No smoking, Children welcome, Well behaved dogs, Open all year

MEADOWLAND 36 Bloomfield Park, Bath BA2 2BX
John & Catherine Andrew *Tel / Fax:* 01225 311079
Email: meadowland@bath92.freeserve.co.uk *Web:* www.bath.org/hotel/meadowland.htm

Map Ref: 1
A367

Elegant, non-smoking house set in secluded grounds with private car parking, providing luxury en-suite accommodation amidst a warm family atmosphere. Privacy and seclusion guaranteed, yet Meadowland is only a short walk to the city. Guests enjoy individually prepared breakfasts chosen from an extensive menu incorporating vegetarian and special diets.

B & B £37.50-£45pp, C-Cards MC VS, Rooms 2 double, 1 twin, all en-suite, No smoking, Children over 5, No dogs, Closed Xmas

NORTHWICK HOUSE North Road, Bath BA2 6HD
Veronica Metcalfe *Tel / Fax:* 01225 420963 *Mobile:* 07714 246929
Email: northwickhouse@aol.com *Web:* northwickhousebath.co.uk

Map Ref: 1
A367

You will be sure of a warm welcome to Northwick House, an unusual detached Georgian house built in 1821 and listed Grade II as being of architechtural interest. The bedrooms have far reaching views and are light, airy and comfortable with televisions, hairdryers and tea/coffee facilities. Very conveniently located with Roman Baths only five minutes by regular bus. Easy parking.

B & B £27.50-£35pp, Rooms 1 single, 1 double en-suite, 1 twin en-suite, No smoking, Children over 12, Dogs welcome, Closed Xmas & New Year

OAKLEIGH HOUSE 19 Upper Oldfield Park, Bath BA2 3JX
Jenny King *Tel:* 01225 315698 *Fax:* 01225 448223
Email: oakleigh@which.net

Map Ref: 1
10 mins walk to centre

A warm welcome awaits you at this quietly situated Victorian home overlooking Georgian Bath. The luxury rooms are en-suite with little extras to make your stay special. There is a comfortable lounge with books and games. An excellent choice of delicious breakfasts is offered. 10 minutes walk to the city centre. Private car park. Contact David and Jenny King for brochure.

B & B from £34pp, C-Cards MC VS AE DC, Rooms 2 double, 1 twin, all en-suite, No smoking, No children or dogs, Open all year

THE OLD RED HOUSE 37 Newbridge Road, Bath BA1 3HE
Chrissie Besley *Tel:* 01225 330464 *Fax:* 01225 331661 *Mobile:* 07813 399467
Email: oldredhouse@amserve.net *Web:* oldredhouse.co.uk

Map Ref: 1
A4

We hope that you will enjoy your stay at Alfred Taylor's famous Gingerbread House, which was built 100 years ago and was for many years a high class patisserie and bakers shop. Although the house retains much of its original charm, including stained glass windows, it now enjoys the unmistakable atmosphere of a warm and comfortable family home. One mile from the heart of Bath.

B & B £21-£33pp, C-Cards MC VS AE DC, Rooms 4 double, 1 twin, 1 family, all en-suite, No smoking, Children over 4, Dogs by arrangement, Closed Jan to Feb

PARADISE HOUSE 88 Holloway, Bath BA2 4PX
David & Annie Lanz   *Tel:* 01225 317723   *Fax:* 01225 482005
Email: info@paradise-house.co.uk   *Web:* www.paradise-house.co.uk

Map Ref: 1
A367

Paradise House with stunning panoramic views over the city, is an elegant Bath stone Georgian house, just 5 minutes walk from the city centre. Behind its classic and dignified exterior it conceals more than half an acre of splendid walled gardens. The delightful en-suite rooms are well equipped with TV and tea/coffee facilities. Parking. 5 Diamonds.

B & B from £35pp, Rooms 4 double, 2 four poster, 3 twin, 1 family, all en-suite, No smoking, Children welcome, No dogs, Closed Xmas

---

PICKFORD HOUSE Bath Road, Beckington, Bath BA11 6SJ
Ken & Angela Pritchard   *Tel / Fax:* 01373 830329   *Mobile:* 07885 641875
Email: AmPritchar@aol.com   *Web:* www.pickfordhouse.com

Map Ref: 1
A36

An elegant Regency style house standing on a hilltop overlooking Beckington village. Bedrooms are very comfortable, some are en-suite and all have TV and tea/coffee facilities. Angela is a talented cook, she offers an excellent 'pot luck' meal, or an extensive 'celebration' menu. The house is licensed with a wine list. In summer, visitors may be offered an 'off-the-beaten-track' pre dinner drive.

B & B from £17pp, Dinner from £14, Rooms 1 twin, 1 double, 2 double en-suite, Restricted smoking, Children welcome, Dogs by arrangement, Open all year

---

ST LEONARDS Warminster Road, Bath BA2 6SQ
Mr Tony Pugh   *Tel:* 01225 465838   *Fax:* 01225 442800
Email: stleon@dircom.co.uk

Map Ref: 1
A36

We warmly welcome you to our lovely Victorian house with breathtaking views overlooking the Avon valley, yet only 15 minutes walk into the City centre. Our home has been sympathetically restored to a very high standard with many original features, superbly appointed bathrooms, superking and king-sized beds. Lovely walks along the picturesque canal at the bottom of our garden with pub serving excellent food nearby.

B & B £29-£42.50pp, C-Cards MC VS, Rooms 2 single, 6 double, 3 twin, 2 family, all en-suite, No smoking, Children welcome, Dogs by arrangement, Closed Xmas & New Year

---

47 SYDNEY BUILDINGS Bath BA2 6DB
Ms S Johnson   *Tel:* 01225 461054   *Fax:* 01225 463033   *Mobile:* 07968 957887
Email: sydneybuildings@bigfoot.com   *Web:* www.SmoothHound.co.uk.hotels/sydney.html

Map Ref: 1
Bathwick Hill

With superb views of the Abbey and a short walk from the city centre, the house is located on a delightfully quiet street of Georgian houses. The bedrooms are luxurious and comfortable, all with TV and tea/coffee making facilities. Full English, Continental or Caribbean breakfasts are available and Mrs Johnson is happy to help her guests in any way.

B & B from £30pp, Rooms 2 double en-suite or pb, 1 twin pb, 1 single with shower, No smoking, Babies/children over 10, No dogs, Closed Xmas

---

TASBURGH HOUSE HOTEL Warminster Road, Bath BA2 6SH
David & Susan Keeling   *Tel:* 01225 425096
Email: hotel@bathtasburgh.co.uk   *Web:* www.bathtasburgh.co.uk

Map Ref: 1
M4, A36

This lovely Victorian mansion provides country comfort in a city setting, with spectacular views. Sitting in seven acres of beautiful gardens and meadowpark stretching along the Kennet and Avon Canal, there are idyllic walks into Bath. The en-suite bedrooms (including four-poster rooms) are tastefully furnished and very comfortable. Elegant drawing room, dining room and stunning conservatory. Parking, licensed, evening meals.

B & B £41-£56pp, C-Cards MC VS AE DC, Dinner £24, Rooms 1 single, 4 double/twin, 4 four-poster, 3 fam, all en-suite, No smoking, Children welcome, No dogs, Open all year

VILLA MAGDALA HOTEL Henrietta Road, Bath BA2 6LX
Roy & Lois Thwaites *Tel:* 01225 466329 *Fax:* 01225 483207
Email: office@villamagdala.co.uk *Web:* www.villamagdala.co.uk
Map Ref: 1
5 mins walk to centre

A delightful Victorian town house hotel set in its own grounds, it enjoys a peaceful location overlooking Henrietta Park, and is a few minutes level walk from the Roman Baths and Abbey. All 17 spacious rooms have en-suite bathrooms, telephone, television and tea/coffee making facilities. There is private parking. This is an ideal base for exploring Bath and the countryside.

B & B from £40pp, C-Cards MC VS AE, Rooms 12 double, 3 twin, 3 family, all en-suite, No smoking, Children over 7, No dogs, Closed Xmas

FRANKLYNS FARM Chewton Mendip, Bath BA3 4NB
Map Ref: 2
A367

Tel / Fax: 01761 241372

A cosy farmhouse in the heart of the Mendip Hills with superb views in a peaceful setting. Bedrooms are en-suite with televisions and tea/coffee facilities. Surrounded by a large garden with a tennis court and offering genuine hospitality and delicious breakfasts. Ideal for touring for Bath, Wells and Cheddar.

B & B from £20pp, Rooms 1 double, 1 twin, both en-suite, Children & dogs welcome, Open all year

RING O' ROSES Stratton Road, Holcombe, Bath BA3 5EB
Tel: 01761 232478 *Fax:* 01761 233737
Email: ringroseholcombe@tesco.net
Map Ref: 3
A367

A revitalised 17th century inn nestling in the Mendip Hills. Ring O' Roses isrenowned for its excellent food and is packed with atmosphere and antiques. It is a hidden treasure not to be missed.

B & B from £32.50pp, Rooms 8 double, all en-suite, No smoking, Open all year

HOLLYTREE COTTAGE Laverton, Bath BA2 7QZ
Julia Naismith
Tel / Fax: 01373 830786 *Mobile:* 07901 867694
Map Ref: 4
A36

17th century country house set in tranquil rural surroundings within 20 minutes drive of Bath. Top quality cuisine and lovely garden. Beautifully furnished accommodation with televisions and tea/coffee facilities in bedrooms. Visitors welcome in living rooms, conservatory and garden. Julia Naismith was employed at Bath's Holburne Art Museum and knows the area well. Ample parking and good pubs nearby.

B & B from £30pp, Dinner from £15, Rooms 2 single, 2 double, 1 twin, 1 family, all en-suite, No smoking, Children & dogs welcome, Closed Xmas

MONKSHILL Shaft Road, Monkton Combe, Bath BA2 7HL
Catherine & Michael Westlake *Tel / Fax:* 01225 833028
Email: monks.hill@virgin.net *Web:* www.monkshill.com
Map Ref: 5
A36

Five minutes from Bath lies this secluded and very comfortable Edwardian country residence surrounded by peaceful gardens and enjoying far reaching views over one of the most spectacularly beautiful parts of the Avon valley. The drawing room with its fine antiques is for the exclusive use of the guests and the spacious bedrooms enjoy magnificent views over the valley below.

B & B £32.50-£40pp, C-Cards MC VS AE, Rooms 2 double, 1 twin, most en-suite, No smoking, Children welcome, Dogs by arrangement, Closed Xmas & New Year

The Plaine, Norton St Philip near Bath

THE PLAINE Bell Hill, Norton St Philip, Bath BA2 7LT   *Map Ref:* 4
Sarah Priddle & John Webster *Tel:* 01373 834723 *Fax:* 01373 834101   A36
Email: theplaine@easynet.co.uk *Web:* www.theplaine.com   *see Photo on page 19*

The Plaine was first recorded in the Domesday Book of 1086. A family home, visitors are welcomed to beautifully presented accommodation. The bedrooms have four poster beds. Delicious breakfasts using local produce. Charming house in heart of village, stands opposite the famous George Inn. An ideal base from which to explore the interest of Bath, Wells, Longleat and the Cotswolds. Parking.

B & B £29-£36pp, C-Cards MC VS, Rooms 3 double, all en-suite, No smoking, Children welcome, No dogs, Closed Xmas

---

OWL HOUSE Lower Kingsdown Road, Kingsdown, Box SN13 8BB   *Map Ref:* 6
Anne Venus *Tel:* 01225 743883 *Fax:* 01225 744450   M4, A4
Email: venus@zetnet.co.uk *Web:* www.owlhouse.co.uk

Situated four miles from Bath with gorgeous views over the Avon Valley. Lovely rural location in a warm comfortable house in traditional Cotswold stone. Excellent English breakfasts served. The house is adjacent to the golf course surrounded by lovely walks and good pubs.

B & B £26-£32.50pp, C-Cards MC VS, Rooms 1 single, 1 double, 1 twin, 1 family, all en-suite, No smoking, Children over 8, No dogs, Open all year

---

BOX HEDGE FARM Coalpit Heath, Bristol BS36 2UW   *Map Ref:* 7
Marilyn & Bob Downes *Tel / Fax:* 01454 250786   Westerleigh Road
Email: marilyn@boxhedgefarmbandb.co.uk *Web:* www.boxhedgefarmbandb.co.uk

Box Hedge Farm is set in 200 acres of countryside on the edge of the Cotswolds, it is local to the M4 and M5 and is central for Bristol and Bath. We offer a warm family atmosphere with traditional farmhouse cooking. All the bedrooms are well equipped with a colour television and tea/coffee making facilities. We also offer self catering weekend breaks.

B & B £20-£23pp, C-Cards MC VS AE, Rooms 2 single, 2 double, 2 family, some en-suite, Restricted smoking, Open all year

---

BUTCOMBE FARM Aldwick Lane, Butcombe, Bristol BS40 7UW   *Map Ref:* 8
Tel: 01761 462380 *Fax:* 01761 462300   A38, A368
Email: info@butcombe-farm.demon.co.uk

Originally a 14th century medieval hall house, Butcombe Farm is now a beautiful manor house with en-suite bed and breakfast rooms and individual self-catering accommodation. Set in several acres amid peaceful countryside, the fantastic scenery combines perfectly with our excellent facilities. For more information, please contact Barry and Josephine Harvey.

B & B from £27pp, Rooms 3 double, 2 triple, all en-suite, No smoking, Children welcome, Closed Xmas & New Year

---

DOWNS EDGE Saville Road, Stoke Bishop, Bristol BS9 1JA   *Map Ref:* 9
Mrs Philippa Tasker *Tel / Fax:* 0117 968 3264 *Mobile:* 07885 866463   A4018
Email: welcome@downsedge

Downs Edge is situated in a superb position on the very edge of Bristol's famous Downs, an open park of some 450 acres. Furnished with fine period furniture, the house is set in magnificent gardens close to the spectacular Avon Gorge and its breathtaking views. This uniquely peaceful location is ideally situated for the City Centre, Clifton and the University.

B & B £31-£34pp, C-Cards MC VS AE, Rooms 2 single, 5 double, 1 twin, all en-suite, No smoking, Children over 6, No dogs, Closed Xmas & New Year

THE ELMS Olveston, Bristol BS35 4DR
Mr & Mrs David Moodie *Tel:* 01454 614559 *Fax:* 01454 618607
Email: b&b@theelmsmoodie.co.uk *Web:* www.theelmsmoodie.co.uk

Map Ref: 10
A38

A Georgian house in a rural area, convenient for Bristol and M4/M5 interchange. There is great emphasis on immaculate standards and green issues. Organic food served when possible. Allergy suffers are welcome and guests are requested not to use scented products. The owners are great animal and garden lovers and keep cats, dogs, hens and ornamental ducks. Tennis court available. Secure parking.

B & B £35-£40pp, Rooms 1 double with private sitting room, 1 twin, both en-suite, No smoking, No children or dogs, Open all year

---

SPRING FARM The Street, Regil, Winford, Bristol BS40 8BB
Judy & Roger Gallannaugh *Tel:* 01275 472735 *Fax:* 01275 474445
Email: springfarm@ic24.net

Map Ref: 11
A38, B3130

Spring Farm is a much loved family home where a warm welcome awaits you and with its cottage garden nestles into the peaceful North Somerset countryside. There are pretty bedrooms and a cosy sitting room with winter log fires. The delicious aga cooked breakfasts are not to be forgotten. Conveniently positioned for visiting Bristol, Bath and Wells.

B & B £22.50-£25pp, Rooms 1 single, 2 double en-suite, No smoking, Children welcome, No dogs, Closed Xmas

---

THORNBURY GOLF LODGE Bristol Road, Thornbury, Bristol BS35 3XL

Tel: 01454 281144

Map Ref: 12
A38

The old farmhouse exterior of the lodge disguises a completely refurbished interior with stunning views over the Severn Estuary and the golf courses. Thebedrooms are elegant and comfortable with en-suite baths or showers, tea/coffee making facilities and televisions. There is a licensed bar and meals are taken in the Club House restaurant.

B & B from £29pp, C-Cards MC VS, Dinner available, Rooms 3 single, all en-suite, No smoking, Children over 14, Guide dogs only, Closed Xmas

---

MOORLANDS Hutton, Weston-super-Mare BS24 9QH
Margaret Holt *Tel / Fax:* 01934 812283
Email: margaret_holt@email.com *Web:* www.guestaccom.co.uk/35.htm

Map Ref: 13
M5

Welcome to our fine Georgian house set in mature landscape gardens. Hutton village lies below the steep wooded slopes of the western Mendips which offers splendid views and walking. Log fires are an important feature of Moorlands in the winter. The pub opposite serves lovely meals. It is an excellent touring centre and pony riding for the children can also be arranged.

B & B from £20pp, C-Cards MC VS AE, Rooms 1 single, 2 twin, 2 double, 1 triple, 1 family, most ensuite, Restricted smoking, Children & dogs welcome, Open all year

---

THE SEAFARERS 12 Victoria Park, Weston-super-Mare BS23 2HZ
Francesca & Richard Day *Tel:* 01934 631178 *Fax:* 01934 414716
Email: francesca@timbertop.freeserve.co.uk *Web:* www.SmoothHound.co.uk/hotels/timbertop.html

Map Ref: 13
M5

The Seafarers is located in a leafy cul de sac close to sea front and town centre. All rooms are comfortably furnished and en-suite with bath and shower. Complimentary hot beverages, televisions, hairdryers and alarm clock radios are also provided. Breakfast times are flexible with full English breakfast served in the buffet area including strawberries and cream. On site parking.

B & B from £25pp, C-Cards MC VS, Rooms 1 single, 1 double, 1 twin, 1 family, all en-suite, Restricted smoking, Children welcome, No dogs, Open all year

Bedfordshire, Berkshire, Buckinghamshire & Hertfordshire

The Home Counties are at the very heart of England, secure in their position around the capital. It was here that the rich and famous built their homes, some of the most spectacular domestic architecture in the country. The great rolling estates, exotic gardens and countryside are cultivated and adapted to enhance the vistas of palaces and manor houses.

Bedfordshire is largely an agricultural area with the River Ouse in the north. Bedford, standing on the river, is the county town famous for its connection with the seventeenth century author of Pilgrim's Progress, John Bunyan. The town's location on the Ouse clothes it with picturesque riverside gardens and walks. Of course, no visitor to this lovely county should miss the Duke of Bedford's palatial mansion Woburn, packed with art treasures and set in its deer park or Woburn Wild Animal Kingdom, Europe's biggest drive-through safari park. Ampthill, a few miles south of Bedford is a charming town of Georgian houses and attractive cottages. Ampthill Park, landscaped by Capability Brown gives fine views over the surrounding countryside.

Luton, in the past a famous hatting town, is Bedfordshire's largest town. It has interesting walks along the River Lee and a path which follows the prehistoric Icknield Way. On the outskirts is the Woodside Farm wildfowl park, and to the south west is one of the National Trust's most unusual properties, the Whipsnade Tree Cathedral. Trees of various species have been planted in the traditional pattern of a cathedral, with grassy avenues representing the nave and transepts.

Like Bedfordshire, Berkshire is renowned for its stately homes, particularly Windsor Castle, the principle home of the Royal Family outside London. The castle houses St George's Chapel, a fine example of Gothic architecture and the Albert Memorial Chapel, commissioned by Queen Victoria after her husband's death. For the children Legoland has to be a must, combining wonderful Lego models with fun rides and activities.

The National Trust owns no less than 1,000 acres of Chiltern beech woodland and rolling farmland, as well as most of the lovely village of Bradenham. Aylesbury, the county town is a great centre for exploring Buckingham-shire, as well as being the main market centre for the fertile Vale of Aylesbury. To

Freeman's Marsh, Kennet Canal, Hungerford (STB)

the south is West Wycombe with its picturesque main street and West Wycombe Park, a fine eighteenth century Palladian mansion, once the home of the famous and flamboyant Sir Francis Dashwood, leader of the Hell-Fire Club. Hidden away in woodland near Kimble is Chequers, the official home of British Prime Ministers. Another spectacular stately home is Waddeson Manor, built in the French style for Baron de Rothschild, containing treasures which include a superb collection of Sevres porcelain. Many visitors will recognise the building as being featured in the TV series 'Howard's Way'.

Hertfordshire's magnificent cathedral of St Albans, which dominates the surrounding countryside, is where England's first recorded Christian martyr is buried. A fine museum houses one of the best Roman collections in the country. The Hertfordshire and Middlesex Wildlife Trust, based here in St Albans is responsible for sterling work in protecting land forms and natural habitats which is threatened by urban development. To the north of Hemel Hempstead the Ashridge Estate runs along the main ridge of the Chilterns and encloses some 4,000 acres of commons and woodlands. At the northern end of the estate the Ivinghoe Hills, an outstanding area of chalk downland are dominated by the Ivinghoe Beacon.

These counties may well cluster around the capital and seem to be increasingly urbanized. However, they stand alone in their variety of stately homes set in a remarkable amount of open space to enchant the visitor.

PLACES TO VISIT

This is a small selection of interesting places to visit. Many more are listed in our annual guide to Museums, Galleries, Historic Houses & Sites (see page 448)

Beale Park
Lower Basildon, Reading, Berksshire
Situated on the banks of the River Thames the park offers an extraordinary collection of rare birds and animals.

Bekonscot Model Village
Beaconsfield, Buckinghamshire
The oldest model village in the world displaying rural England in the 1930s. The attraction includes, in miniature, landscape gardens, houses, castles, churches and railway stations.

Knebworth House
Knebworth, Hertfordshire
Home of the Lytton family since 1490 and transformed into the Gothic masterpiece it is today in 1843, with a spectacular banquet hall. Its Victorian and Edwardian landscaped gardens also house a maze.

Windsor Castle
Windsor, Berkshire
The official residence of HM The Queen, situated on the River Thames. The State Apartments are furnished with some of the finest works of art in the country. Attractions within the Castle include Queen Mary's Doll House and St George's Chapel.

Woburn Abbey
Woburn, Bedfordshire
The Abbey became the Russell family home in 1619, within a 3,000 acre deer park. Collections of English silver, French and English furniture and art.

Bedfordshire, Berkshire, Buckinghamshire & Hertfordshire

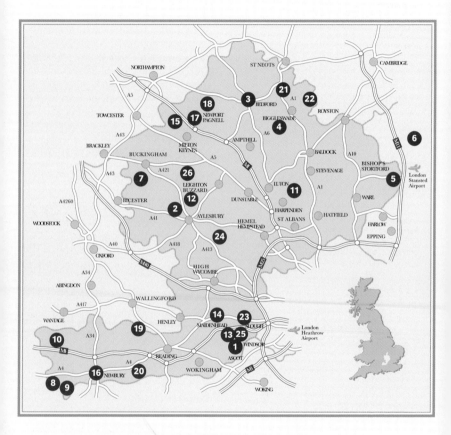

The Red Map References should be used to locate B & B properties on the pages that follow

ENNIS LODGE GUEST HOUSE Winkfield Road, Ascot, Berks SL5 7EX
John & Siegi Miles
Tel / Fax: 01344 621000

Map Ref: 1
A330, A329

Situated in central Ascot, Ennis Lodge offers top quality rooms with all facilities. It is close to M3, M4, Heathrow and main line station. Windsor and Legoland are only 10 minutes. German spoken.

B & B £25-£48pp, Rooms 1 single, 5 twin, all en-suite, No smoking, Children over 5, No dogs, Closed Xmas & New Year

---

LYNDRICK GUEST HOUSE The Avenue, Ascot, Berks SL5 7ND
Sue & Graham Chapman *Tel:* 01344 883520 *Fax:* 01344 891243
Email: mail@lyndrick.com *Web:* www.lyndrick.com

Map Ref: 1
M3, M4, M25, A30

Lyndrick Guest House offers quality accommodation only 25 minutes from Heathrow. Bedrooms have colour TV, tea/coffee, hair dryer and radio alarm. Delicious breakfasts are served in a pleasant conservatory. Special diets are happily catered for. London, Waterloo is 55 minutes by rail. The house is convenient for Wentworth and surrounding golf courses. The motorways and Bracknell and Windsor are nearby.

B & B from £30pp, C-Cards MC VS, Rooms 1 single, 2 double, 2 twin, most en-suite, Restricted smoking, No dogs, Open all year

---

WOODLANDS FARMHOUSE Doddershall, Quainton, Aylesbury, Bucks HP22 4DE
Mr & Mrs Creed
Tel: 01296 770225

Map Ref: 2
A41

Recently converted barns provide well equipped comfortable en-suite accommodation with tea/coffee facilites and colour televisions. A full English breakfast is provided in the main 18th century farmhouse. Milton Keynes and Oxford are only 30 minutes away.

B & B from £25pp, Rooms 1 double, 2 twin, 1 family, all en-suite, No smoking, Children welcome, No dogs, Open all year

---

KNIFE & CLEAVER INN The Grove, Houghton Conquest, Bedford, Beds MK45 3LA
Tel: 01234 740387 *Fax:* 01234 740900
Email: info@knifeandcleaver.com *Web:* www.knifeandcleaver.com

Map Ref: 3
A6

17th century inn with nine modern en-suite bedrooms in the quiet garden, three in an 18th century stable block. Air conditioned Victorian style conservatory restaurant overlooking the flowery terrace. Award winning menu specialising in fish but with an interesting choice for meat eaters and vegetarians with well balanced wine list, plus lighter meals in the 17th century oak panelled bar which features a log fire.

B & B from £32pp, C-Cards, Dinner from £20, Rooms 4 double, 4 twin, 1 family, all en-suite, Restricted smoking, Children welcome, No dogs, Closed after Xmas to New Year

---

OLD WARDEN GUESTHOUSE Shop & Post Office, Old Warden, Biggleswade, Beds SG18 9HQ

Tel: 01767 627201

Map Ref: 4
A1, B658

In one of Bedfordshire's most picturesque villages is this listed 19th century building, adjacent to the shop and post office. Situated between Biggleswade and Bedford and one mile from Shuttleworth Collection. Also near to the Swiss Gardens and the Falconry Centre. We offer a family atmosphere in the heart of the countryside.

B & B from £21pp, Rooms 2 double, 1 twin, all en-suite, Restricted smoking, Children welcome, No dogs, Closed Xmas & New Year

ANGLESEY HOUSE   16 Grailands, Bishops Stortford, Herts CM23 2RG   *Map Ref:* 5
Mrs Jean Windus   *Tel:* 01279 653614   M11, A120
Email: jeanwindus@aol.com   *Web:* www.angleseyhouse.com

Anglesey House is a spacious family home in a quiet area, yet 10 minutes walk from town with restaurants, cinema and station. All rooms have televisions, tea/coffee facilities, hairdryers and radio alarms. A lounge and garden are available. We hold a Welcome Host Charter and aim to make your stay enjoyable in a relaxed and friendly atmosphere. AA 4 Diamonds.

B & B £25-£30pp, C-Cards MC VS, Rooms 1 double, 2 twin, most en-suite, No smoking, Children over 8, No dogs, Closed Xmas & New Year

---

PLEASANT COTTAGE   Woodend Green, Henham, Bishops Stortford, Herts CM22 6AZ   *Map Ref:* 6
Julia & George Griffiths   A120, B1051
Tel / Fax: 01279 850792

Grade II listed thatched cottage situated in the corner of the village green with pretty duck ponds five minutes walk through the idyllic village of Henham. Rooms are beautifully furnished, have tea/coffee making facilities, colour television and garden views. A delicious breakfast is served in our cosy breakfast room. Cambridge and London are within reach by road and rail.

B & B £27.50-£31pp, Rooms 2 double en-suite, 1 twin en-suite shower, Restricted smoking, Children over 10, No dogs, Open all year

---

FIELD COTTAGE   Hillesden Hamlet, Bucks MK18 4BX   *Map Ref:* 7
Martin & Tessa Clarke   *Tel / Fax:* 01280 815360   *Mobile:* 07929 023904   A421
Email: martin.tessa@virgin.net

A seventeenth century thatched stone farmhouse set in four and a half acres with stunning views and nice walks. All rooms are centrally heated with colour television, tea making facilities and power showers. Private off-road parking. Convenient for Stowe Gardens, Claydon House, Waddesdon Manor, Oxford, the Cotswolds and Addington Equestrian Centre.

B & B £27.50-£35pp, Rooms 1 double en-suite, 1 twin pb, 1 single pb, Restricted smoking, Children & dogs welcome, Closed Xmas & New Year

---

MARSHGATE COTTAGE HOTEL   Marsh Lane, Hungerford, Berks RG17 0QX   *Map Ref:* 8
Carole Ticehurst   *Tel:* 01488 682307   *Fax:* 01488 685475   M4, A338
Email: reservations@marshgate.co.uk

Marshgate Cottage stands at the end of a country lane, close to Hungerford, four miles from the M4. Well equipped en-suite rooms are in a traditionally designed addition to the canalside 17th century thatched cottage. Lounge/bar. Car park. Hungerford has many antique and speciality shops, canal trips, pubs and restaurants. Ideal base for touring southern England. Superb walking.

B & B from £27.50pp, C-Cards MC VS, Rooms 1 single, 2 twin, 5 double, 2 family, No smoking, Children & dogs welcome, Closed Xmas

---

WILTON HOUSE   33 High Street, Hungerford, Berks RG17 0NF   *Map Ref:* 8
Mrs Deborah Welfare   *Tel:* 01488 684228   *Fax:* 01488 685037   M4, A4
Email: welfare@hotmail.com   *Web:* www.wiltonhouse.freeserve.co.uk

Wilton House is a classic English town house with a documented history that predates 1470. An early 18th century facade conceals medieval origins. The two en-suite large double bedrooms and dining room are in the elegant 18th century part of the house with wood panelling, open fireplaces and many other period features. The very highest standard is offered with delicious wholesome breakfasts.

B & B from £27pp, Rooms 1 double, 1 twin, both en-suite, No smoking, Children over 8, No dogs, Closed Xmas & New Year

TOTTERDOWN LODGE Inkpen, Hungerford, Berks RG17 9EA
Louisa Cosgrove *Tel:* 01488 668590
Email: louisa.cosgrove@btopenworld.com

Map Ref: 9
A4, A338

A delightful period property set in the beautiful Berkshire
countryside. This family run home offers all the luxury of a country
residence. The bedrooms share a private bathroom, there is a
guests sitting room, breakfast is served in the dining room in the
winter and the conservatory in the summer. Totterdown Lodge is ten
minutes from the M4 and 50 minutes from Heathrow Airport.

B & B from £30pp, Rooms 1 single, 1 twin, Smoking restrictions,
No children, Dogs by arrangement, Closed Xmas & New Year

FISHERS FARM Shefford Woodlands, Hungerford, Berks RG17 7AB
Mary Wilson *Tel:* 01488 648466 *Fax:* 01488 648706 *Mobile:* 07973 691901
Email: mail@fishersfarm.co.uk *Web:* www.fishersfarm.co.uk

Map Ref: 10
M4 J14

Fishers Farm is a historic farmhouse set in peaceful English
countryside on a working farm near Hungerford, West Berkshire. It
has spacious bedrooms with en-suite or private bathrooms, a large
garden and an indoor heated swimming pool. It is convenient for the
M4 motorway and an ideal base for visiting southern England. Fluent
Spanish, German and French spoken!

B & B £26-£28pp, Rooms 1 double en-suite, 1 double pb, 1 twin
en-suite, No smoking, Children welcome, No dogs, Open all year

---

PADDOCK LODGE Porters End, Kimpton, Herts SG4 8ER
Claire van Straubenzee *Tel:* 01438 832423 *Fax:* 01438 833527
Email: vanstraubenzee@btinternet.com

Map Ref: 11
M1, A1, B651

This is an oasis surrounded by cornfields, woods and lovely views,
yet only 30 minutes by train from Central London and 10 minutes
from Luton Airport. The house is large but cosy and the rooms are
bright and informal with comfortable beds, overlooking a spacious
garden. Claire's cooking is superb and she serves food in a pretty
dining room.

B & B from £27.50pp, Dinner from £20, Rooms 1 twin en-suite,
1 twin with private bathroom, Restricted smoking, Children over 2,
Dogs only in car, Closed Xmas & New Year

THE OLD FORGE BARN Ridings Way, Cublington, Leighton Buzzard, Beds LU7 0LW
Joan & Mike Waples *Tel / Fax:* 01296 681194
Email: waples@onlineuk.co.uk

Map Ref: 12
A413, A418

A converted barn in village location, close to Aylesbury, Leighton
Buzzard and Milton Keynes. Guests are provided with a private
bathroom, full English breakfast and off road parking. Convenient for
many well known attractions.

B & B from £25pp, Rooms 1 twin, No smoking, No children or
dogs, Open all year

BURCHETT'S PLACE COUNTRY HOUSE Burchett's Green, Maidenhead, Berks SL6 6QZ
The Hillier Family
Tel: 01628 825023 *Fax:* 01628 826672

Map Ref: 13
A4

Burchett's Place stands in private grounds in picturesque, unspoilt
countryside. The house offers country house elegance with a warm,
relaxed atmosphere. Ideal for exploring Berkshire countryside, close
to Marlow, Henley, Windsor, 20 mins from Heathrow and less than
an hour from London. Spacious bedrooms are furnished with
beautiful antiques. The drawing room has a magnificent open fire.
English breakfast is served.

B & B from £30pp, Rooms 1 single, 1 twin, 1 double, 1 family,
No smoking, Children over 12, Open all year

DUMBLEDORE Warren Row, Maidenhead, Berks RG10 8QS
Lavinia Rashleigh *Tel / Fax:* 01628 822723
Email: laviniarashleigh@faxvia.net

Map Ref: 14
A4, M4, M40

This delightful part 16th century Tudor country house stands in the pretty village of Warren Row. Close to Henley, Marlow and Maidenhead, it has easy access to M4 and M40, Heathrow and Gatwick. The charming bedrooms have television and tea/coffee facilities. Dumbledore is an ideal base for trips to London from Twyford station. A good choice of pubs and restaurants locally.

B & B £28-£30pp, Rooms 1 single, 1 twin, 1 double, all en-suite, No smoking, Children over 12, Open all year

---

WOODPECKER COTTAGE Warren Row, Maidenhead, Berks RG10 8QS
Michael & Joanna Power *Tel:* 01628 822772 *Fax:* 01628 822125
Email: power@woodpecker.co.uk *Web:* www.woodpeckercottage.com

Map Ref: 14
A4

A woodland retreat away from crowds, yet close to Heathrow, Windsor, Henley, Oxford. Set in a delightful garden surrounded by woods where deer abound. The ground floor bedrooms are well equipped and comfortable, the double room has its own entrance. A cosy sitting room has a wood stove in winter. An English breakfast includes homemade bread and jam. Local pubs and restaurants.

B & B £25-£27.50pp, Rooms 1 single, 1 double, both en-suite, 1 twin private bathroom, No smoking, Children over 8, No dogs, Closed Xmas & New Year

---

SPINNEY LODGE FARM Forest Road, Hanslope, Milton Keynes, Bucks MK19 7DE
Christina Payne
Tel: 01908 510267

Map Ref: 15
M1 J15, A508

An arable, beef and sheep farm, this lovely Victorian farmhouse with large gardens, has en-suite bedrooms with TV and tea/coffee facilities. Dinners are available. Many historic houses and gardens to explore, Woburn, Silverstone, Stowe and Althorp are an easy drive, also the towns of Northampton and Milton Keynes. Junction 15, M1 is a short drive. Ideally placed for business or holiday trips.

B & B £20-£25pp, Dinner from £10, Rooms 1 twin, 4 double, No smoking, Children over 12, No dogs, Closed Xmas

---

WHITE COTTAGE Newtown, Newbury, Berks RG20 9AP
Ellie Meiklejohn *Tel / Fax:* 01635 43097 *Mobile:* 07721 613224
Email: meiklejohn@onetel.net.uk

Map Ref: 16
A339

Delightful cottage in semi-rural position, just two miles south of Newbury. Comfortable and quiet accommodation. Ideally situated for easy access to Oxford, Winchester, Stonehenge, Bath, Portsmouth and Watership Down. Countryside suitable for walkers and biking. Dogs welcome.

B & B from £25pp, Rooms 1 single, 1 double, 1 twin, No smoking, Children welcome, Open all year

---

THE LIMES North Square, Newport Pagnell, Bucks MK16 8EP
Roy & Ruth Barton *Tel:* 01908 617041 *Fax:* 01908 217292 *Mobile:* 07860 908925
Email: royandruth@8thelimes.freeserve.co.uk

Map Ref: 17
M1 J14

Georgian town house with river frontage, off-road parking, private fishing and established gardens. Comfortable and beautifully furnished with antiques. All bedrooms have en-suite facilities and one has a four-poster bed. Good home cooking. Meeting/conference room available. Three miles from M1 junction 14. ETC 5 Diamonds, Silver Award, AA 5 Diamonds.

B & B from £35pp, C-Cards MC VS AE, Dinner available, Rooms 3 double, 1 twin, all en-suite, No smoking, Children over 10, No dogs, Open all year

CLIFTON PASTURES Clifton Reynes, Olney, Bucks MK46 5DW   *Map Ref:* 18
Andrew & Jane Finn-Kelcey *Tel:* 01234 711287 *Fax:* 01234 711233   M1 J14/A509
Email: finkel@kbnet.co.uk

Home to the Finn-Kelcey family for 3 generations, Clifton pastures
stands in its own grounds, the house enjoys wonderful views to the
Ouse valley. The atmosphere is relaxed in a country setting. Dinners
using vegetables from the kitchen garden with local produce, are
excellent. Althorp, Woburn Abbey and other places of interest are
nearby. Heathrow is 60 miles, Oxford and Cambridge 40.

B & B £39pp, C-Cards MC VS, Rooms 1 twin en suite, 1 twin
private bathroom, No smoking, Children over 12, No dogs, Closed
Xmas & New Year

PENNYFIELD BED & BREAKFAST The Coombe, Streatley, Reading, Berks RG8 9QT   *Map Ref:* 19
Mrs Maureen Vanstone *Tel / Fax:* 01491 872048 *Mobile:* 07774 946182   A329
Email: mandrvanstone@hotmail.com *Web:* http://web.onetel.net.uk/~mandrvanstone

Pennyfield is situated in a beautiful Thameside village near Goring
railway station and Thames and Ridgeway walks. Three en-suite
rooms, one with four poster. All rooms have fresh fruit, tea/coffee
facilities, fridge, television, iron and hairdryer. Local pubs serve good
traditional food within walking distance. Also use of hot covered spa
in a pretty terraced garden. ETC 4 Diamonds, Silver Award.

B & B from £27.50pp, Rooms 2 double, 1 twin, all en-suite,
No smoking, Children over 10, No dogs, Closed Xmas & New Year

---

THE OLD MANOR Whitehouse Green, Sulhamstead, Reading, Berks RG7 4EA   *Map Ref:* 20
Mrs Rosemary A G Sanders-Rose *Tel:* 0118 983 2423   M4 J12, A4
Email: rags-r@theoldmanor.fsbusiness.co.uk

A 17th century manor house with later additions, set in 10 acre
grounds and surrounded by farmland. Luxury bedrooms with en-
suite facilities and elegant furnishings, including one with four poster
bed and jacuzzi bath. The beautiful drawing room and gracious
dining room offer perfect relaxation and a country house party
atmosphere. A warm welcome awaits you. AA 5 Diamonds.

B & B from £35pp, Dinner from £12.50, Rooms 1 single, 2 double,
all en-suite, No smoking, Children over 12, No dogs, Closed Xmas
& New Year

HIGHFIELD FARM Great North Road, Sandy, Beds SG19 2AQ   *Map Ref:* 21
Margaret Codd *Tel:* 01767 682332 *Fax:* 01767 692503   A1, A421, A14
Email: margaret@highfield-farm.co.uk

Highfield Farm is a 300 acre arable farm in a peaceful location.
Beautifully relaxed and comfortable farmhouse, most of the
bedrooms are en-suite. There are three ground floor rooms which
are in converted stables. The gardens are large, and there is safe
parking. Cambridge, the Shuttleworth Collection, RSPB, Bedford
and London are all within easy reach. A warm welcome awaits you.

B & B £25-£45pp, C-Cards MC VS, Rooms 3 double, 4 twin,
1 family, all en-suite, No smoking, Children welcome, No dogs,
Open all year

ORCHARD COTTAGE 1 High Street, Wrestlingworth, Sandy, Beds SG19 2EW   *Map Ref:* 22
Mrs Joan M Strong   A1, B1040
Tel / Fax: 01767 631355

Orchard Cottage is a picturesque 16th century cottage, with modern
extension, formerly the village bakery. Standing in a large garden
situated in a quiet village on the B1042 with Bedford and Cambridge
within easy reach. Convenient for visiting the Shuttleworth collection,
RSPB and Wimpole Hall. Approximately five miles from the A1 and
ten miles from the M11.

B & B £21-£24pp, Rooms 2 single, 1 twin, 1 double, No smoking,
No dogs, Closed Xmas

RAMBLER GUEST HOUSE 1 Rambler Lane, London Road, Slough, Berks SL3 7RR   *Map Ref:* 23
M4 J6

Tel / Fax: 01753 517665

Rambler Guest House is a small family run quality guest house, close to town centre, bus and train station. Ideal for Windsor, Legoland, Heathrow and M4 junctions. All rooms have colour televisions and tea/coffee facilities. En-suites or family rooms are available. Serves full English breakfasts. Full Fire Certificate. Main road (A4) location. Own car park.

B & B from £35pp, C-Cards MC VS AE DC, Rooms 3 single, 5 twin, 2 double, 2 family, most en-suite, Restricted smoking, Children welcome, No dogs, Open all year

FIELD COTTAGE St Leonards, Tring, Herts HP23 6NS   *Map Ref:* 24
Mike & Sue Jepson   A41, A413, B4009
Tel: 01494 837602

A warm welcome awaits you at this Silver Award winning bed and breakfast. We are situated off a country lane, down a short bridlepath on the very edge of open fields, with easy access to the Ridgeway. The pretty cottage style bedrooms have televisions and tea/coffee facilities. Breakfast is served in our flower filled conservatory with panoramic views over adjoining fields. ETC 4 Diamonds.

B & B from £27.50pp, Rooms 1 single with pb, 1 double with en-suite, 1 twin with pb, No smoking, Children over 12, No dogs, Closed Xmas & New Year

ALMA LODGE 58 Alma Road, Windsor, Berks SL4 3HA   *Map Ref:* 25
Mr S Shipp   *Tel / Fax:* 01753 855620   M4 J6
Email: Almalodge@aol.com   *Web:* www.Almalodge.co.uk

Alma Lodge is a tastefully decorated Victorian house kept to a very high standard. It has been with the same family for over 60 years and offers very comfortable accommodation. All rooms are en-suite with colour televisions, radio and tea/coffee facilities. There is off road parking if required and it is situated close to the town centre, only a few minutes from M4 Junction 6.

B & B from £30pp, C-Cards MC VS AE, Rooms 1 single, 2 twin, 2 double, 1 family, all en-suite, No smoking, Children & dogs welcome, Open all year

BEAUMONT LODGE 1 Beaumont Road, Windsor, Berks SL4 1HY   *Map Ref:* 25
Brenda Hamshere   *Tel / Fax:* 01753 863436   *Mobile:* 07774 841273   M4 J6
Email: bhamshere@beaumontlodge.demon.co.uk

Built at the beginning of the 19th century, Beaumont Lodge, situated in a quiet residential area, has traditional solidity and character. All the rooms are equipped with en-suite bathrooms with bath and shower, the main double room also has a spa bath (wonderfully relaxing) and a television/video with a library of tapes. An ideal base from which to explore the numerous attractions of Windsor.

B & B £65-£75pp, C-Cards MC VS, Rooms 1 double, 2 twin, all en-suite, No smoking, Children welcome, No dogs, Open all year

THE CONGREGATIONAL CHURCH 15 Horn Street, Winslow, Bucks MK18 3AP   *Map Ref:* 26
Mrs Sarah Hood   M1, A41, A413
Tel / Fax: 01296 715717   *Mobile:* 07711 505031

A fascinating Victorian church turned into an enchanting home in the centre of Old Winslow. Each bedroom has its own stained glass window. The sitting room, with television, used to be the clergy room and the kitchen/breakfast room was the schoolroom. On one side of the aisle are the bedrooms and on the other side, the bathrooms. This house is certainly an original.

B & B from £22.50pp, Rooms 1 single, 1 double, 1 twin, Restricted smoking, Children over 12, No dogs, Open all year

Cambridgeshire & Northamptonshire

Cambridgeshire forms the western march of East Anglia and what this singularly flat county lacks in woodlands it more than makes up for in glorious rivers with the Great Ouse and the Nene. Within Cambridgeshire lies much of the Fen district, a vast area of highly fertile black farmland, once underwater but through many generations drained by cuts and sluices. The last undrained section of the Great Fens is Wicken Fen which now forms the oldest of the county's nature reserves, celebrating its centenary as a National Trust property in 1999. The William Thorpe Visitor Centre admirably explains the history of the Fen's evolution, 600 acres of wetland rich in plant life and displaying a remarkably extensive variety of habitats for birds.

Of course the jewel of the county must be Cambridge, the county town which lies in the chalk downland of the south by the River Cam, known to the Romans as Granta. The ancient college buildings, some founded as far back as the thirteenth century are a great attraction, but the city and university are dominated by the quite magnificent King's College Chapel renowned for its remarkable fan-vaulting and its Rubens painting, 'The Adoration of the Magi'. Beside the thirty or so colleges, the city is packed with interest for the visitor, such as the 'Bridge of Sighs' at St John's, built in 1831, copying its namesake in Venice and the intriguing Mathematical Bridge constructed in wood without using any bolts. Outside the city is

Wimpole Hall, a wonderful eighteenth century house set in an extensive wooded park, Anglesey Abbey, built on the site of an Augustine priory and dating from 1600, houses the famous Fairhaven collection of paintings and furniture and is set in 99 acres of superb landscaped gardens. The Duxford Air Museum, a part of London's Imperial War Museum, which holds probably Europe's largest collection of historic military aircraft, is also not to be missed.

Until 1965 Peterborough was administered as a separate county known as the Soke of Peterborough and boasts one of the finest Norman cathedrals in Britain, built between 1118 and 1258. The cathedral contains the tomb of Catherine of Aragon, Henry VIII's first wife. Mary Queen of Scots was buried here too but her body was removed to Westminster in 1612. Ely, taking its name from its one time major industry of eeling, is a city of great charm and can also claim a magnificent cathedral, founded in 673 by St Etheldreda. The octagonal tower dominates the flat land

Althorp House and Park

surrounding the city and, standing on an island protected by the treacherous fen, was originally a stronghold during the eleventh century for those resisting William the Conqueror. The city contains some fine medieval and Georgian buildings.

Northamptonshire has always been primarily a farming county, but is also an attractive holiday region. Northampton, the county town was largely destroyed by fire in 1675, and fortunately two of its most spectacular churches survived: the Norman church of St Peter and the remarkable round Holy Sepulchre. The town has at its centre, one of England's largest traditional open market squares. Northampton's museum contains the world's largest collection of boots and shoes, reflecting the town's importance in this industry. Its close neighbour Kettering, also a boot and shoe town,

has a wonderful museum housed in the manor house. To the south of Northampton, at Canons Ashby is the home of the Dryden family, the sixteenth century Canons Ashby House. This National Trust property, set in formal gardens and a seventy acre park, contains some fine Elizabethan wall paintings and Jacobean plasterwork. Lyveden New Bield, near Oundle, is also an excellent day out. This strange incomplete garden house of 1595, constructed in the shape of a cross is inscribed with religious quotations.

Within these two counties is a quite remarkable variation in scenery, ranging from the gently rolling chalk downs south of Cambridge to the bleak and windswept lonely fens. It continues from the great earthworks of Fleam Dyke, Devil's Dyke and Bran Ditch to the glorious churches and manor houses of Northamptonshire's 'spires and squires'.

PLACES TO VISIT

This is a small selection of interesting places to visit. Many more are listed in our annual guide to Museums, Galleries, Historic Houses & Sites (see page 448)

Althorp
Northampton
Home to the Spencer family for 500 years and the resting place of Diana, The Princess of Wales. An award-winning exhibition commemorates her life and work.

Ely Cathedral
Ely, Cambridgeshire
A fine Cathedral founded by St Etheldreda in 673 AD. The most outstanding feature being the Octagon built to replace the collapsed Norman tower. Also with a stained glass museum.

Kings College Chapel
Cambridge
The oldest Cambridge college, founded

in 1441 by Henry VI. Tours of the impressive architecture and spectacular perpendicular chapel.

Imperial War Museum
Duxford, Cambridgeshire
The centre for historic aviation where many rare aircraft, including Spitfire and Mustang, fly from. Visitors can also see aircraft restoration taking place.

Wimpole Hall
Arrington, Cambridgeshire
The most imposing mansion in Cambridgeshire. The servants quarters are impressive, as are the gardens, re-designed by Bridgeman, Brown and Repton.

Cambridgeshire &
Northamptonshire

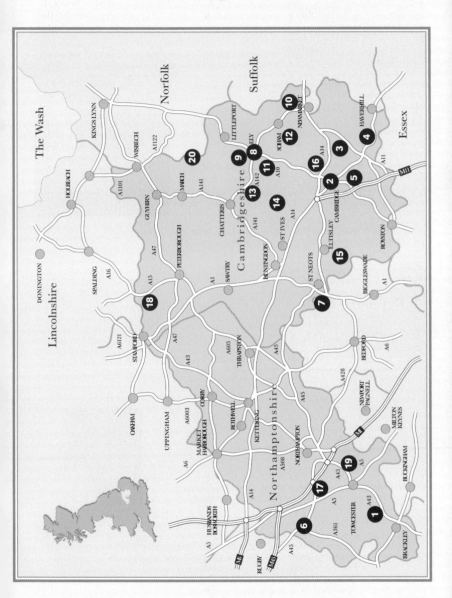

The Red Map References should be used to locate B & B properties on the pages that follow

ASTWELL MILL Helmdon, Brackley, Northants NN13 5QU   *Map Ref:* 1
Phyllis King   *Tel:* 01295 760507   *Fax:* 01295 768602   A43, B4525
Email: astwell01@aol.com

Astwell Mill is a converted water mill in open countryside, peacefully situated between two villages. There is an attractive garden with a large lake, stream and waterfalls. Superb views to be enjoyed from comfortably furnished bedrooms and a spacious lounge. Convenient for Silverstone, Stowe, Canons Ashby, Althorp and Sulgrave Manor. Astwell Mill is situated midway between the M1 and M40

B & B from £22.50pp, Rooms 2 double, 1 en-suite, No smoking, Children welcome, Kennel for dogs, Closed Xmas & New Year

CRISTINAS GUEST HOUSE 47 St Andrews Road, off Elizabeth Way, Cambridge, Cambs CB4 1DH
Cristina Celentano   *Tel:* 01223 365855/327700   *Fax:* 01223 365855   *Map Ref:* 2
Email: christinas.guesthouse@ntlworld.com   M11 J11

Guests are assured of a warm welcome at Cristinas Guest house. Ideally situated next to the city centre and the River Cam, close to the museums, galleries and the University Colleges. Most rooms feature colour tv, radio alarm, hairdryer and tea/coffee making facilities. In addition we have a residents lounge where guests can comfortably relax. Private, secure car park.

B & B £38-£57pp, Rooms 4 twin, 4 double, 1 family, some en-suite, Restricted smoking, Children welcome, No dogs, Open all year

HOME FROM HOME Bungalow rear of 78 Milton Road, Cambridge, Cambs CB4 1LA   *Map Ref:* 2
Tel: 01223 323555   *Fax:* 01223 563509   *Mobile:* 07740 594306   M11 J11
Email: homefromhome@tesco.net

A comfortable guest house with all rooms provided with their own facilities. It offers Home-from-Home hospitality and excellent breakfasts. Centrally located and easy access to M11 and A14. Parking available. Self-catering apartments also available.

B & B from £30pp, C-Cards MC VS, Rooms 1 double, 1 twin, No smoking, Children welcome, No dogs, Open all year

SYCAMORE HOUSE 56 High Street, Great Wilbraham, Cambridge, Cambs CB1 5JD   *Map Ref:* 3
Barry & Liz Canning   *Tel / Fax:* 01223 880751   *Mobile:* 07711 845300   M11, A1, A11, A14
Email: barry@thesycamorehouse.co.uk   *Web:* www.thesycamorehouse.co.uk

Pleasantly situated detached house in small village with shop, pub and good restaurants nearby. Five miles to Cambridge and Newmarket and excellent for racing, cycling, touring. All rooms have televisions and tea/coffee facilities. The large gardens extend to one acre. The breakfast in the conservatory overlooks the patio which guests are welcome to use. Off road parking for four cars.

B & B from £22.50pp, Rooms 1 single, 2 double, 1 public bathroom, No smoking, Children welcome, Dogs by arrangement, Closed Xmas & New Year

YARDLEYS Orchard Pightle, Hadstock, Cambridge, Cambs CB1 6PQ   *Map Ref:* 4
Gillian & John Ludgate   *Tel / Fax:* 01223 891822   M11/A11
Email: yardleys@waitrose.com   *Web:* www.users.waitrose.com/yardleys

Yardleys offers peace and quiet in a pretty village, Cambridge only 20 mins and Saffron Walden 10 mins. Warm welcome and excellent breakfasts in comfortable home with guests' television lounge, garden and conservatory. Well equipped bedrooms with tea/coffee facilities. Convenient for Stansted, Harwich, Duxford, Newmarket, Audley House and Anglesey Abbey. Evening meals by arrangement, or good local pubs and restaurants.

B & B from £24pp, C-Cards MC, Dinner from £11, Rooms 1 double, 2 twin, all en-suite, No smoking, Children welcome, No dogs, Closed Xmas and New Year

THE WATERMILL Linton Road, Hildersham, Cambridge, Cambs CB1 6BS
Mr & Mrs Hartland
Tel: 01223 891520

Map Ref: 4
A1307

A watermill is recorded here in the Domesday Book, although the present buildings are 18th/19th century. The house stands in six acres of land on the River Granta and has garden and water meadow views to the village beyond. Meals can be taken in the nearby Pear Tree. The Watermill is well located as Cambridge, Ely and Saffron Walden are not far.

B & B from £22pp, Rooms 1 double/family en-suite, No smoking, Children welcome, No dogs, Closed Xmas & New Year

SPRINGFIELD 16 Horn Lane, Linton, Cambridge, Cambs CB1 6HT
Mrs F B Rossiter
Tel: 01223 891383   *Fax:* 01223 890335

Map Ref: 4
M11, A1307

Springfield is an early Victorian family home furnished with antiques, centrally heated and strictly non-smoking. The reception rooms look across the lawn to the river and both bedrooms are en-suite with colour televisions and tea/coffee facilities. English breakfast is served in the conservatory or dining room and evening meals are available at a nearby pub.

B & B £20-£25pp, Rooms 2 double en-suite, No smoking, Children welcome, No dogs, Open all year

PURLINS 12 High Street, Little Shelford, Cambridge, Cambs CB2 5ES
David & Olga Hindley   *Tel / Fax:* 01223 842643
Email: dgallh@ndirect.co.uk

Map Ref: 5
M11, A10

An individually designed house set in two acres of fields and woodland in a pretty village on the Cam, four miles from Cambridge. An ideal centre for visiting colleges, cathedrals and country houses. The comfortable en-suite bedrooms (two ground floor) have colour television, radio and tea/coffee making facilities. Breakfasts will suit most tastes. Restaurants nearby. Parking for three cars.

B & B from £24pp, Rooms 2 double, 1 twin, all en-suite, No smoking, Children over 8, No dogs, Closed mid-Dec to Feb 1

THE OLD VICARAGE Moreton Pinkney, Daventry, Northants NN11 3SQ
Colonel & Mrs Eastwood   *Tel / Fax:* 01295 760057
Email: Tim@tandjeastwood.fsnet.co.uk   *Web:* www.tandjeastwood.fsnet.co.uk

Map Ref: 6
A43, A361

Two warm, comfortable bedrooms in a pretty, ironstone listed 18th century house. There is a twin room with bath and wc in a private wing and a double with a shower and wc. The house is attractively furnished with a lovely walled garden overlooking the church where you can sit, relax and have your meals in summer. Guests are made to feel very welcome.

B & B from £30pp, Dinner from £15, Rooms 1 double, 1 twin, No smoking, Children by arrangement, Dogs by arrangement, Closed Xmas & New Year

THE WHITE HORSE 103 Great North Road, Eaton Socon, Cambs PE19 8EL
Tel: 01480 474453   *Fax:* 01480 406650
Email: WHES@barclays.net

Map Ref: 7
A1

A comfortable 13th century Coaching Inn, with tea/coffee facilities and televisions in all rooms. The White Horse serves good food, wine and ales. Large car park. Convenient for all A1 destinations.

B & B from £27.50pp, C-Cards MC VS AE DC, Dinner from £5, Rooms 1 twin, 2 double, all en-suite, Children over 5, Dogs by arrangement, Closed Xmas & New Year

CATHEDRAL HOUSE 17 St Marys Street, Ely, Cambs CB7 4ER   Map Ref: 8
Jenny & Robin Farndale *Tel / Fax:* 01353 662124   A10
Email: farndale@cathedralhouse.co.uk *Web:* www.cathedralhouse.co.uk

Standing in the centre of Ely close to the cathedral known as 'the ship of the Fens'. A short walk to Cromwell's House, museums, shops and restaurants. A Grade II listed house which retains its original features. Bedrooms are well equipped, they overlook the tranquil walled garden. English or continental breakfast is served at a farmhouse table by an open fire.

B & B £25-£37.50pp, Rooms 1 twin, 1 double, 1 family, No smoking, Children by arrangement, No dogs, Closed Jan

NYTON HOTEL 7 Barton Road, Ely, Cambs CB7 4HZ   Map Ref: 8
Tel: 01353 662459 *Fax:* 01353 666217   A10
Email: nytonhotel@yahoo.co.uk

Nyton Hotel is situated in a quiet, residential area overlooking Fenland countryside and its adjoining golf-course. Close to city centre and Cathedral. Car parking.

B & B from £35pp, C-Cards MC VS AE DC, Dinner from £15, Rooms 2 single, 4 double, 2 twin, 2 family rooms, all en-suite, Children welcome, Dogs not in public rooms, Open all year

OLD EGREMONT HOUSE 31 Egremont Street, Ely, Cambs CB6 1AE   Map Ref: 8
Sheila & Jeremy Friend-Smith *Tel:* 01353 663118 *Fax:* 01353 614516   A10, A142
Email: sheilafriendsmith@hotmail.com

Delightful house dating from the 16th century with large south facing bedrooms overlooking an acre of walled garden. Both rooms have fine views of Ely Cathedral which is within five minutes walking distance. Locally baked bread, free-range eggs and homemade marmalade are enjoyed in our traditionally furnished dining room. Excellent restaurants and shops within easy walking distance.

B & B £24-£25pp, Rooms 1 double with private bathroom, 1 twin en-suite, No smoking, Children over 10, No dogs, Closed Xmas & New Year

HILL HOUSE FARM 9 Main Street, Coveney, Ely, Cambs CB6 2DJ   Map Ref: 9
Hilary Nix *Tel:* 01353 778369   A10, A142
Email: hill_house@madasafish.com

A warm welcome awaits at this Victorian farmhouse, in the village of Coveney, close to Ely. It enjoys open views to the countryside. Cambridge, Newmarket and Huntingdon are nearby, as are Norfolk, Suffolk, Wicken Fen and Welney Wildfowl Refuge. The warm and well equipped bedrooms are tastefully furnished, one ground floor bedroom. Guests are welcome to enjoy the lounge and garden.

B & B from £22pp, C-Cards MC VS, Rooms 1 twin, 2 double, all en-suite, No smoking, Children over 12, No dogs, Closed Xmas

QUEENSBERRY 196 Carter Street, Fordham, Ely, Cambs CB7 5JU   Map Ref: 10
Jan & Malcolm Roper   A14/A142
Tel: 01638 720916 *Fax:* 01638 720233

Welcome awaits here, a Georgian house set peacefully in large gardens on the edge of the village. 'Queensberry' is the ideal base from which to tour East Anglia, Cambridge city, historic cathedral city of Ely, the market town of Bury St Edmunds and Newmarket, the world's racing centre. Self-catering converted barn in the grounds and safe parking. Good restaurants within walking distance.

B & B £25-£30pp, Rooms 1 single, 1 twin, 1 double, 1 en-suite, self contained barn, No smoking, Children welcome, Dogs by Arrangement, Closed Xmas

SPRINGFIELDS Baileys at Springfields, Ely Road, Little Thetford, Ely, Cambs CB6 3HJ   *Map Ref:* 11
Mr & Mrs Derek L Bailey   *Tel:* 01353 663637   *Fax:* 01353 663130   A10
Email: springfields@tall?1.com

Award winning Springfields situated one mile from Ely Cathedral.
Nominated one of top 20 in country by 'Which?' Good B&B Guide
and has all the attributes you would expect to accompany this
prestigious award. Set in one acre landscape garden where a great
variety of birds can be seen. Spotless beautiful bedrooms. Secure
floodlit parking. Luxurious accommodation. Come and enjoy the
Springfield experience. ETC AA 5 Diamonds.

B & B £25-£35pp, Rooms 2 double en-suite, 1 twin private
shower, No smoking, Children over 12, No dogs, Closed Xmas &
New Year

SPINNEY ABBEY Stretham Road, Wicken, Ely, Cambs CB7 5XQ   *Map Ref:* 12
Mrs Valerie Fuller   *Tel:* 01353 720971   A1123
Email: spinney.abbey@tesco.net   *Web:* www.spinneyabbey.co.uk

This attractive Georgian Grade II listed farmhouse, surrounded by
pasture fields, stands next to our dairy farm which borders the NT
Nature Reserve Wicken Fen, on the southern edge of the Fens.
Guests are welcome to full use of spacious garden and all weather
tennis court. All rooms have private facilities.

B & B from £23pp, Rooms 1 double en-suite, 1 twin with pb,
1 triple en-suite, Children over 5, No dogs, Open all year

ROSENDALE LODGE 223 Main Street, Witchford, Ely, Cambs CB6 2HT   *Map Ref:* 13
                                                        A142
Tel: 01353 667700   *Fax:* 01353 667799

Elegant house with period furniture and secluded south facing
gardens. Spacious galleried dining/sitting room and individually
designed en-suite bedrooms. There is a choice of breakfasts and
also inns and restaurants nearby. Adjacent to Ely with its magnificent
Cathedral, museums and riverside amenities. Ideally situated for
Cambridge, Newmarket, or touring the villages of Cambridgeshire,
Norfolk and Suffolk.

B & B from £25pp, C-Cards MC VS, Rooms 2 double, 1 twin,
1 family room, all en-suite, No smoking, Children over 6, No dogs,
Open all year

HOLMEFIELDS 16 High Street, Bluntisham, Huntingdon, Cambs PE28 3LD   *Map Ref:* 14
Freda Carlyle   *Tel:* 01487 841435   M11, A14, A1123
Email: roy.carlyle@btinternet.com

A warm welcome awaits you at Holmefields a seventeenth century
Grade II listed thatched cottage set in a beautiful two acre garden.
The self-contained converted barn accommodation has its own
private entrance with double bedroom, lounge, fully-fitted kitchen
and bathroom. Breakfast served in the elegant dining room includes
organic free-range food, home-made bread and preserves. Ideal for
Cambridge, Ely, St Ives. Local pubs, restaurants. Cycle hire. Parking.
AA 5 Diamonds.

B & B from £30pp, Rooms 1 double en-suite, No smoking,
No children, Guide dogs only, Closed Xmas & New Year

MODEL FARM Longstowe Road, Little Gransden, Cambs SG19 3EA   *Map Ref:* 15
Mrs Sue Barlow   *Tel:* 01767 677361   *Fax:* 01767 677883   B1046
Email: bandb@modelfarm.org.uk   *Web:* modelfarm.org.uk

Model Farm was built in the 1870s of local bricks and retains many
of its original features. All guest rooms are en-suite with televisions
and tea/coffee making facilities. A variety of breakfasts are available
ranging from full English to a lighter continental version, plus our own
honey. Cambridge is a 20 minute drive and for an evening meal there
are several traditional country pubs.

B & B from £22.50pp, Rooms 3 double with en-suite, No smoking,
No children, Dogs by arrangement, Closed Xmas & New Year

AMBASSADOR LODGE 37 High Street, Milton, Cambs CB4 6DF   *Map Ref:* 16
                                                                                    A10
Tel: 01223 860168

Ambassador Lodge, converted farm cottages, family run in quiet location. 3 miles city centre. Within walking distance of River Cam and country park. Half a mile from renowned Cambridge Science Park. Easy access to A14, A1(M), M11. Usual facilities. Off road parking.

B & B from £24pp, Rooms 2 single, 1 twin, 1 double, 2 family, most en-suite, Restricted smoking, Children welcome, No dogs, Open all year

---

SWAN HOUSE Swan House, Dodford, Weedon, Northampton, Northants NN7 4SX   *Map Ref:* 17
Mrs Ali Chamberlain   M1, A5
Tel: 01327 341847   *Mobile:* 07765 502125

Separate annexe comprising two double rooms served by a shower and separate wc. Rooms have tea/coffee facilities and television. A former 17th century inn set in a quiet rural location surrounded by its own attractive gardens, off road parking. Good food available. One mile Althorp, five miles Silverstone, 15 miles M1, four miles attractive village with nice walks.

B & B from £22.50pp, Rooms 1 double, 1 twin, Children & dogs welcome, Open all year

---

ABBEY HOUSE West End Road, Maxey, Stamford, Cambs PE6 9EJ   *Map Ref:* 18
Tel: 01778 344642   *Fax:* 01778 342706   A15
Email: info@abbeyhouse.co.uk *Web:* www.abbeyhouse.co.uk

Abbey House, having all the appearance of a substantial Georgian House, hides a wealth of history and dates in part from 1190. The delightful gardens feature an 800 year old yew tree, the oldest in the county and there is a comfortable guest lounge with medieval features and log fires. It is within ten minutes drive of the centres of Stamford and Peterborough, and the A1M.

B & B £27-£32pp, C-Cards MC VS, Rooms 1 single, 5 double, 3 twin, 1 family, all en-suite, No smoking, Children welcome, No dogs, Closed Xmas & New Year

---

BEAM END Stoke Park, Stoke Bruerne, Towcester, Northants NN12 7RZ   *Map Ref:* 19
Pam Hart   *Tel:* 01604 864802   *Fax:* 01604 864637   A508
Email: beamend@bun.com

Converted Victorian stables offering idyllic situation with an acre of garden. It is a quiet location within easy reach of amenities with a mile of private road and safe parking. It is convenient for M1 junction 15, Northampton, Milton Keynes, Silverstone and Canals. Ideal for holidays and business stop-overs. ETC 4 Diamonds, Silver Award.

B & B from £28pp, Rooms 2 double, 1 twin, No smoking, Children over 2, No dogs, Closed Xmas & New Year

---

STOCKYARD FARM Wisbech Road, Welney, Wisbech, Cambs PE14 9RQ   *Map Ref:* 20
Mrs C Bennett   A1101
Tel: 01354 610433

Welcome to our former farmhouse, rurally situated between Ely and Wisbech. Both bedrooms have washbasins, hot drinks facilities, hairdryers and radios. There is a conservatory breakfast room and a guests' TV lounge. Free range produce is served and vegetarians are happily catered for. The Wildfowl and Wetlands Centre is nearby, and the Cathedral city of Ely is within easy reach.

B & B from £18pp, Rooms 1 double, 1 twin, No smoking, Children over 5, Dogs by arrangement, Open all year

---

Cheshire, Merseyside & Greater Manchester

Three great cities dominate this area and one could be excused for regarding the region as overwhelmingly industrial and certainly not a holiday venue. However, in contrast to this industrialism are some areas of quite remarkable beauty. Alderley Edge towers six hundred feet over the surrounding countryside, within easy reach of Manchester, giving glorious views across the Cheshire Plain. Bronze Age relics have been discovered here on this heavily wooded sandstone escarpment. Below Alderley Edge is Styal Country Park, an area of glorious woodlands and quiet riverside walks. Here also is the Quarry Bank Cotton Mill, a wonderfully restored Georgian mill where the costumed guides reveal the harrowing lives of the young mill workers of the past.

The Cheshire Plain is a rolling dairy farming region renowned for Cheshire cheese and the remarkable black and white half-timbered architecture. Scattered within this lovely area are some fascinating houses that the holiday maker simply must visit. Little Moreton Hall, regarded as the most perfect example of a timber-framed moated manor house in the country with musical evenings, suppers and special tours of the splendid wall paintings and knot garden. Tatton Park, the nineteenth century Wyatt house, set in over a thousand acres of deer park, is considered to be one of England's most complete historic estates open to visitors. The mansion is a treasure house of china, glass, paintings and furniture, the fifty acres of garden are an absolute joy. Lyme Park, the largest house in the county, was the home of the Legh family for 600 years and houses some magnificent Grinling Gibbons woodcarving as well as Mortlake tapestries and a significant collection of English clocks. This fine house incidentally was 'Pemberley' in the television adaptation of Jane Austen's 'Pride and Prejudice'. Just south of Altrincham is Dunham Massey, a wonderful Georgian house, once the home of the last Earl of Stamford. Set in over 250 acres of wooded deer park, the mansion houses excellent collections of eighteenth century furniture and Huguenot silver.

For the visitors to this region who like their interests centred in one place and who can resist the delights of touring the area, then Chester is undoubtedly the place to be; the city is steeped in history. The Romans built their fort, Deva, here in 79AD as a buttress against the hostile Welsh. When the Romans left in 383AD a prosperous trading centre had been established and continued to develop and prosper through the rule of successive Saxon and Norman overlords. The River Dee gave access to the sea and Chester developed as a port, importing

The River Dee (NWTB)

French wines, Irish linen and Spanish fruits and spices. The Benedictine Abbey, built in 1092 became in 1541 Chester Cathedral with beautiful woodcarvings in the choir stalls. There is much to see in the city, probably the most impressive sight being the Rows, two-tier shopping galleries which date from the Middle Ages. There are many fine buildings including the grand black and white facades. But Chester is by no means a city of the past, it can offer up to the minute entertainment and excellent shopping facilities.

Both Liverpool and Manchester have long histories as great industrial centres and ports. Much of the industrial and commercial life of the north west is centred on these two fine cities, but with the decline in heavy industry there has been a concerted effort to attract holiday visitors. However there is a marked contrast between the industrial buildings and the glorious civic buildings with magnificent museums and art galleries. Both cities can boast spectacular cathedrals, Liverpool has two modern cathedrals in quite distinct styles of ecclesiastical architecture and Manchester cathedral, built in the fifteenth century claims the widest nave in England. Liverpool's Albert Dock waterfront, with its massive warehouses has now become an impressive complex of shops, restaurants and television studios. Similarly Manchester's canal basin of Castlefield has been redeveloped as an urban heritage park and boasts the popular tourist attraction of Granada Studios. Both Manchester and Liverpool can offer theatres, cinemas and nightlife of the highest quality with shopping to match any city in the country. Whatever your holiday requirements, this is a region to suit the most discriminating tastes.

PLACES TO VISIT
This is a small selection of interesting places to visit. Many more are listed in our annual guide to Museums, Galleries, Historic Houses & Sites (see page 449)

Granada Studios
Manchester
A theme park based on Granada produced television programmes with Motion Master where seats move with the action and spectacular 3D effects. Coronation Street, Cracker and Sherlock Homes feature.

Liverpool Cathedral
Liverpool
The largest Anglican Cathedral in Britain with the highest Gothic arches, the largest organ and the heaviest ring of bells. The embroidery exhibition is a unique collection of Victorian and Edwardian embroidery on the triforium gallery.

Liverpool Museum
Liverpool
Important and diverse collections covering archaeology, ethnology and natural and physical sciences. Includes the award-winning Natural History Centre and planetarium.

Lyme Park
Disley, Cheshire
Transformed into an Italianate palace by the Venetian architect Leoni. The State Rooms boast Mortlake tapestries, Grinling Gibbons wood carvings and an important collection of English clocks. It is renowned for being Pemberley in the BBC adaptation of Pride and Prejudice.

Tatton Park
Knutsford, Cheshire
Historic mansion and estate with 2,000 acre deer park, medieval manor house, 50 acre garden and traditional working farm. Fine collections of furniture and paintings.

Cheshire, Merseyside &
Greater Manchester

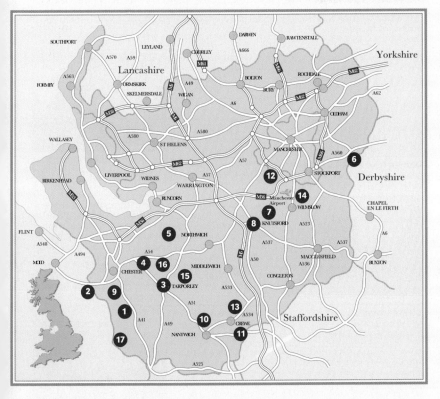

The Red Map References should be used to locate B & B properties on the pages that follow

GOLBORNE MANOR   Platts Lane, Hatton Heath, Chester, Cheshire CH3 9AN   *Map Ref:* 1
Ann Ikin   *Tel:* 01829 770310   *Fax:* 01829 770370   *Mobile:* 07774 695268   A41, M54
Web: www.golbornemanor.co.uk

An elegant 19th century country residence with glorious views. Beautifully renovated, it stands in 3 1/2 acres of grounds. Charming, spacious en-suite bedrooms with tea/coffee and TV, farmhouse breakfast. Lounge, croquet and table tennis. Large car park. Easy access to the motorway and North Wales coast. 5 1/2 miles south of Chester, turn right after D.P. Motors (on the left).

B & B from £30pp, Rooms 1 single, 1 double, 1 twin, 1 family, all en-suite, No smoking, Children welcome, No dogs, Open all year

---

THE MOUNT   Lesters Lane, Higher Kinnerton, Chester, Cheshire CH4 9BQ   *Map Ref:* 2
Jonathan & Rachel Major   *Tel / Fax:* 01244 660275   A55, A5104
Email: major@mountkinnerton.freeserve.co.uk

This Victorian country house with spacious rooms and lovely views stands in twelve acres with a tennis court. The Mount is well placed for exploring the North Wales coast and Cheshire. Just six miles from Chester and 45 minutes from Liverpool and Manchester, one hour from Anglesey. Bodnant Gardens, Port Sunlight and Chester. There is an excellent village pub.

B & B £25-£30pp, Rooms 2 twin, 1 double, all en-suite, No smoking, Children over 12, Dogs only in car, Closed Xmas

---

HIGHER HUXLEY HALL   Huxley, Chester, Cheshire CH3 9BZ   *Map Ref:* 3
Jeremy Marks & Pauline Marks   *Tel:* 01829 781484   *Fax:* 01829 781142   *Mobile:* 07970 229484   A51
Email: info@huxleyhall.co.uk   *Web:* www.huxleyhall.co.uk

Parts of this historic manor house date from before the 13th century; the land on which it stands is mentioned in the Domesday Book. The staircase is late Elizabethan and made of 'Armada' oak that was salvaged from ships broken up after the Spaniards were defeated. The house is furnished with antiques and is the essence of comfort and elegance. Also a large indoor swimming pool.

B & B £40-£45pp, C-Cards MC VS, Dinner from £23, Rooms 1 single, 1 double, 1 twin, 1 family, all en-suite, No smoking, Children welcome, No dogs, Open all year

---

GROVE HOUSE   Holme Street, Tarvin, Chester, Cheshire CH3 8EQ   *Map Ref:* 4
Mrs Helen Spiegelberg   *Tel:* 01829 740893   *Fax:* 01829 741769   M53, M56, A51, A54
Email: helen_s@btinternet.com

Grove House is a comfortable spacious Victorian home offering a warm welcome in a relaxing environment. There is an attractive garden and ample off-road parking. All rooms beautifully decorated with little extras for added comfort. Within easy reach for tourist attractions in North Wales, Liverpool, the Potteries and Manchester airport. NWTB awards and AA award winner 2001.

B & B £30-£40pp, Rooms 1 double en-suite, 1 twin en-suite, 1 single pb, Restricted smoking, Children over 12, No dogs, Closed Xmas & New Year

---

CHARNWOOD   Hollow Lane, Kingsley, Frodsham, Cheshire WA6 8EF   *Map Ref:* 5
Susan Klin   *Tel:* 01928 787097   *Fax:* 01928 788566   B5153
Email: susan.klin@talk21.com   *Web:* www.smoothhound.co.uk/hotels/charnwo2.html

Charnwood is set in landscape grounds in the delightful small village of Kingsley. A wide range of luxury accommodation is available including a private suite for sleeping up to five people. All rooms have televisions, tea/coffee facilities and hairdryers and the accommodation also has its own entrance. A full English breakfast is served in the dining room which overlooks the colourful garden.

B & B £18-£25pp, Rooms 2 single, 1 double, 1 twin, all en-suite, No smoking, Children welcome, No dogs, Open all year

NEEDHAMS FARM Uplands Road, Werneth Low, Gee Cross, Hyde, Cheshire SK14 3AG   *Map Ref:* 6
Mrs C Walsh   *Tel:* 0161 368 4610   *Fax:* 0161 367 9106   A560
Email: charlotte@needhamsfarm.co.uk   *Web:* www.needhamsfarm.co.uk

Needhams Farm is a 30 acre non-working farm which is a pleasant
drive from the Peak District. The 500 year old farmhouse has
exposed beams and an open fire in the bar/dining room, special
suppers are offered to children. The house enjoys excellent views
from all the rooms. It is well placed for Manchester city, the airport
and surrounding countryside. Residential licence.

B & B £20-£45pp, C-Cards MC VS, Dinner from £7, Rooms
1 single, 3 double, 1 twin, 1 family room, all en-suite, Children &
dogs welcome, Open all year

LONGVIEW HOTEL & RESTAURANT 51/55 Manchester Road, Knutsford, Cheshire WA16 0LX
Pauline & Stephen West   *Tel:* 01565 632119   *Fax:* 01565 652402   *Map Ref:* 7
Email: enquiries@longviewhotel.com   *Web:* www.longviewhotel.com   M6, A50

Longview Hotel stands in the market town of Knutsford, overlooking
the common. Antiques grace this lovely Victorian building, the
character has been retained, the comfort for visitors is also assured.
Decoration in the bedrooms reflects the importance of the warmth of
hospitality and relaxed atmosphere. This hotel is a perfect place to
stay whether for business or pleasure.

B & B £33.25-£65pp, C-Cards MC VS AE, Dinner from £12.50,
Rooms 6 single, 20 double, all en-suite, Restricted smoking,
Children & dogs welcome, Closed Xmas & New Year

THE HINTON Town Lane, Mobberley, Knutsford, Cheshire WA16 7HH   *Map Ref:* 7
Tel / Fax: 01565 873484   M6 J19, B5085
Web: www.hinton.co.uk

Award winning bed and breakfast for both business and private
guests. Beautifully appointed rooms with many extras and good
home cooking. Within easy reach of M6, M56, Manchester Airport
and Inter City rail network. Ideal touring base, on the B5085 between
Knutsford and Wilmslow. Within easy reach of motorway network.

B & B from £25pp, C-Cards MC VS AE DC, Dinner available,
Rooms 2 single, 1 double, 1 twin, 1 family room, all en-suite,
No smoking, Children welcome, No dogs, Open all year

THE OLD VICARAGE Moss Lane, Over Tabley, Knutsford, Cheshire WA16 0PL   *Map Ref:* 8
Alf & Norma Weston   M6 J19
Tel: 01565 652221   *Fax:* 01565 755918

Set in two acres of naturally wooded gardens, right in the heart of
rural Cheshire, yet only three minutes drive from M6 Junction 19
(Knutsford). In addition to traditional rural hospitality, the beautiful
restored and furnished 19th century vicarage offers an impressive
range of outstanding features designed for your comfort and
convenience.

B & B from £32.50pp, C-Cards MC VS, Dinner available, Rooms
2 double, 2 twin, 1 family, all en-suite, No smoking, Children over
10, No dogs, Closed Xmas & New Year

TILSTON LODGE Tilston, Malpas, Cheshire SY14 7DR   *Map Ref:* 9
Kathie & Neil Richie   A41
Tel / Fax: 01829 250223

A warm welcome awaits you at Tilston Lodge, a beautiful Victorian
Country House set in 16 acres of landscaped garden and pasture.
The house was originally built as a gentleman's hunting lodge and is
now a comfortable home, providing luxurious bed and breakfast for
a small number of guests. Peacefully situated on the fringe of a
delightful village.

B & B £34-£37pp, Rooms 2 double (four posters), 1 twin, all
en-suite, No smoking, Children welcome, No dogs, Closed Xmas

KILTEARN HOUSE 33 Hospital Street, Nantwich, Cheshire CW5 5RL
Terry & Jean Pearson *Tel:* 01270 628892 *Fax:* 01270 626646
Email: jpearson@crewe-nantwich.gov.uk

Map Ref: 10
M6 J16

Tudor house with Georgian front in quiet town centre next to 14th century church. Pretty walled garden and lock up car parking. Ten minutes from M6 junction 16. Excellent beds, freshly cooked organic food. Blue and white china and honeycomb for breakfast. Furnished antiques, fresh flowers. A warm welcome from friendly owners. Near Stapeley and Bridgmere Garden Centres.

B & B from £32.50pp, Rooms 1 single, 1 double, 1 twin, most en-suite, No smoking, Children welcome, Dogs by arrangement,

STOKE GRANGE FARM Chester Road, Nantwich, Cheshire CW5 6BT
Georgina West
Tel / Fax: 01270 625525

Map Ref: 10
M6, A51

An attractive farmhouse in a picturesque canalside location. Individually styled en-suite rooms with TV, a four poster bedroom has a balcony. Hearty breakfasts, vegetarians are catered for. Watch cruising canal boats, relax in the garden. Pets corner and peacocks. Excellent self catering accommodation available. Chetser and Crewe are minutes away. Near to Stapeley Water Gardens, Beeston and Chalmondeley castles and Tatton Park.

B & B from £30pp, Rooms 2 double, 1 twin, 1 family, Restricted smoking, Children welcome, No dogs, Open all year

OAKLAND HOUSE 252 Newcastle Road, Blakelow, Nantwich, Cheshire CW5 7ET
Sandra & Malcolm Groom
Tel: 01270 567134

Map Ref: 11
A500

Family owned and family run, five miles from M6 (J16), one and a half miles from Nantwich on the A500. Rural location. En-suite accommodation available in ground floor chalets as well as main house. Private car park. Full range of services available within the area. AA 5 Diamonds.

B & B from £22.50pp, C-Cards, Rooms 4 double, 3 twin, 1 family, 1 single, all en-suite, No smoking, Children welcome, Well behaved dogs, Open all year

LEA FARM Wrinehill Road, Wybunbury, Nantwich, Cheshire CW5 7NS
Jean Callwood
Tel / Fax: 01270 841429

Map Ref: 11
A500

Charming farmhouse in landscaped gardens where peacocks roam on a dairy farm. Spacious bedrooms and a luxury lounge for guests' relaxation, also a pool to enjoy and snooker, fishing may be arranged. From Nantwich take A51, left at Stapeley Water Gardens. End of road, right for village of Wybunbury, left down Wrinehill Road by church. Lea Farm is one mile from village.

B & B from £19pp, Rooms 1 double, 1 family, 1 twin, 2 en-suite, No smoking, Children & dogs welcome, Closed Xmas & New Year

BROOKLANDS LUXURY LODGE 208 Marsland Road, Sale M33 3NE
Mr L Bowker *Tel:* 0161 9733283
Web: www.SmoothHound.co.uk/hotels/brook.html

Map Ref: 12
M60 J7

Charming residence set in a beautiful garden. Free car park. Two minutes walk to Metro and five miles from the City and Airport. Shops, pubs, restaurants nearby on A6144. One mile from A56 and M60. Recommended by Which Good Bed and Breakfast Guide and AA 4 Diamonds. Convenient for the fabulous Trafford Shopping and Leisure Centre, Lowry Centre and Lancashire County Cricket Club.

B & B £23.50-£29.50pp, C-Cards MC VS AE DC, Dinner from £10, Rooms 4 single, 2 double, 1 twin, 2 family, most en-suite, No smoking, Children welcome, Only guide dogs, Open all year

GROVE HOUSE HOTEL & RESTAURANT Mill Lane, Wheelock, Sandbach, Cheshire CW11 4RD
Katherine & Richard Shaw   *Tel:* 01270 762582   *Fax:* 01270 759465   *Map Ref:* 13
Email: grovehousehotel@supanet.com   A504

A family run restaurant providing accommodation in a delightful Georgian house. There are just eight individually styled en-suite bedrooms with a welcoming and relaxed ambience. The restaurant is excellent and offers ambitious, modern cooking prepared by the chef/proprietor. In a quiet village on Trent and Mersey Canal, two miles from J17, M6. RAC Level Three, Dining Award.

B & B from £30pp, C-Cards MC VS AE, Dinner from £14, Rooms 1 single, 1 twin, 6 double, all en-suite, Restricted smoking, Children welcome, Dogs by arrangement, Closed Xmas & New Year

PEAR TREE COTTAGE COUNTRY GUEST HOUSE Church Lane, Woodford, Stockport, Cheshire
SK7 1PQ   Ann & David Oldham   *Tel / Fax:* 0161 439 5755   *Map Ref:* 14
Email: p-t-cottage@fsbdial.co.uk   *Web:* peartreecottage.gbr.cc   A34, A538

This pretty 16th century thatched cottage combines a peaceful countryside setting with luxury home comforts and a friendly welcome. All our guest rooms are tastefully furnished and beautifully decorated and enjoy delightful countryside views. Vacation parking and courtesy airport transport available if required. NWTB Best Bed & Breakfast Award winner for the last three years. ETB, AA 4 Diamonds.

B & B £30-£40pp, C-Cards MC VS AE, Dinner from £14.50, Rooms 1 single, 3 double, all en-suite, No smoking, Children over 12, No dogs, Closed Xmas & New Year

HILL HOUSE FARM Rushton, Tarporley, Cheshire CW6 9AU   *Map Ref:* 15
Catherine Rayner   *Tel:* 01829 732238   *Fax:* 01829 733929   *Mobile:* 07973 284863   A54, A49
Email: rayner@hillhousefarm.fsnet.co.uk

Hill House Farm is a Victorian former farmhouse situated in the middle of the beautiful Cheshire countryside. It offers spacious accommodation with comfortable bedrooms and a guests' sitting room with open log fire. The house is set in an acre of attractive gardens overlooking a further 12 acres of horse paddocks. Tea/coffee facilities. Aga cooked breakfast.

B & B from £25pp, Rooms 1 double, 1 twin, 1 family, No smoking, Children welcome, by arrangement, Closed Xmas and New Year

ROUGHLOW FARM Chapel Lane, Willington, Tarporley, Cheshire CW6 0PG   *Map Ref:* 16
Sally Sutcliffe   *Tel / Fax:* 01829 751199   M6, A54
Email: sutcliffe@roughlow.freeserve.co.uk   *Web:* roughlow.freeserve.co.uk

A delightful 18th century converted farmhouse in a quiet situation with wonderful views to Shropshire and Wales. Attractive garden with cobbled courtyard and tennis court. Elegantly furnished to a high standard with en-suite facilities one double bedroom has a private sitting room. Roughlow Farm is well situated for access to Manchester, Chester, Wales, Liverpool and M6.

B & B £25-£40pp, Rooms 2 double, 1 twin, all en-suite, No smoking, Children over 6, Dogs only in car, Open all year

WORTHENBURY MANOR Worthenbury, Wrexham, Cheshire LL13 0AW   *Map Ref:* 17
Ian & Elizabeth Taylor   A41, A525, B5069
Tel: 01948 770342   *Fax:* 01948 770711

A warm welcome awaits you at Worthenbury Manor; a rural retreat nestling between Wales, Cheshire and Shropshire. Relax in country house style and enjoy home cooked local produce and our own fresh bread. Then retire to a sumptuous four poster bed. Choose either the Georgian styled Captain Rayner's room or the Jacobean Oak Room. Both have televisions, hairdryers and bathrobes.

B & B £28-£38pp, Dinner from £18, Rooms 2 double, 1 en-suite and 1 with private bathroom, No smoking, Children over 10, No dogs, Closed Nov to Feb

Cornwall

Cornwall is a very special and separate part of Britain since it was isolated from the mainland by the River Tamar. Consequently it retains much of its Celtic character, in fact the name Cornwall comes from the Saxon Cornovii and Wealas meaning Welsh of the west. Historically this is a region of Iron and Bronze Age settlements and monuments, holy wells and ancient churches, a land criss-crossed by the paths of the early

Spectacular Coastline at Land's End (SWT)

saints. The intricate and decidedly rugged coastline of the county being vulnerable to invaders, it is a land of impressive castles. Tintagel Castle, perched on its headland, was claimed by Geoffrey of Monmouth in the twelfth century to be the birthplace of King Arthur and the twin castles of Pendennis and St Mawes were built by Henry VIII to protect the shipping in the River Fal. The wonderfully romantic St Michael's Mount on the rocky island dominating Mount's Bay was originally the site of a Benedictine chapel established by Edward the Confessor. The mount, joined at low tide to the mainland by a causeway gives magnificent views to Land's End and the Lizard.

The 300 miles of coastline is punctuated by the most enchanting array of quaint and picturesque fishing villages. Today Newlyn is the largest fish-landing station in England and Wales. Not that this county's seafaring activities were always strictly within the law, Cornwall is rich in stories of smuggling, wrecking and pirateering. For the visitor there is everything here to please with the Atlantic coast offering towering cliffs, mountainous seas and glorious sand dunes. In contrast the Cornish Riviera, altogether softer, gives wide golden beaches and mellow fishing villages. The shores of the Helford river, regarded by many as the most beautiful estuary in the country, is protected by the National Trust, as is much of the coastline, including Frenchman's Creek, the location of Daphne du Maurier's novel. The Cornwall Wildlife Trust, founded in 1962 by local people has established forty nature reserves covering over 3,000 acres.

The Cornish hinterland largely grew up around the mining and china clay industry. It is difficult to realise now that Cornwall once dominated the tin and copper markets of the world, but the remnants of the industry, the ruined mine engine houses, are scattered over the landscape. Bodmin Moor covers about a hundred square miles of eastern Cornwall, a bleak, windswept and lonely land of granite Tors and Brown Willy, at 1,377 feet, the county's highest point gives glorious views across the moor. On the edge of the moor, Bodmin, an ancient town established in the sixth century and from 1835 until 1989 the capital of Cornwall, runs steam trains to Bodmin Parkway, with stations for Cardinham Woods and Lanhydrock House, a lovely National Trust property overlooking the River Fowey. Truro, a medieval tin town and principal port for its export can claim the first Anglican cathedral to be built in England since London's St Paul's. The county town, dominated by the three-towered cathedral has a wealth of Regency and Georgian buildings. The centre of Cornwall certainly has a great deal to offer scenically but wherever you are in the county you are never more than twenty miles from the coast and it is the coastal resorts which act as a magnet to the vast majority of holiday makers. Looe, Fowey and Falmouth, the main seaside resorts on the Riviera coast, offer a dazzling array of seaside activities, enhanced by their glorious garden settings influenced by the warm Gulf Stream. No visitor should leave the county without seeing The Lost Gardens of Heligan, the magnificent gardens of the Tremayne family, wonderfully restored to their pre-First World War beauty, and now attracting over 300,000 visitors each year.

If the visitor to Cornwall should tire of the charms of the familiar resorts, then on the Isles of Scilly they will discover the nature reserve supreme. The five inhabited islands each have their own distinctive character with spectacular beaches, balmy climate and tranquil atmosphere. Tresco, of course is renowned for its sub-tropical Abbey Garden, a blaze of summer colour, but then Cornwall is truly a land for all seasons.

PLACES TO VISIT

This is a small selection of interesting places to visit. Many more are listed in our annual guide to Museums, Galleries, Historic Houses & Sites (see page 448)

The Eden Project
St Austell
The world's largest biodome construction which is home to a giant indoor rainforest and displaying plants found in tropical climates.

Flambards Victorian Village
Helston
A compelling life-size recreation of a lamplit village of bustling streets and alleyways with nearly 60 homes and shops, all authentically equipped and furnished with genuine artefacts.

Jamaica Inn Museum
Bolventor, Bodmin
Cornwall's legendary coaching house with a display of the life and works of Daphne du Maurier, a theatrical presentation of the history of the Inn and a fine collection of smugglers' relics.

Lost Gardens of Heligan
Pentewan, St Austell
The gardens, created in the nineteenth century were the finest in the country, but they were lost for many years. Now restored, they include 80 acres of pleasure grounds, a complex of walled gardens and a huge vegetable garden.

Tintagel Castle
Tintagel
Set on the North Cornwall Atlantic coastline stands the remains of this thirteenth century castle, supposedly King Arthur's Castle Fortress.

Cornwall

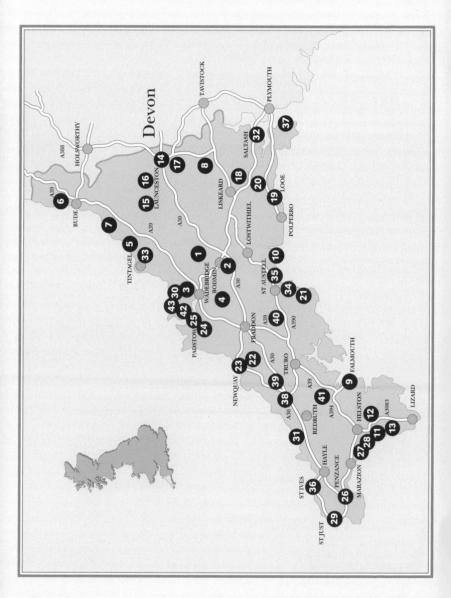

The Red Map References should be used to locate B & B properties on the pages that follow

LAVETHAN Blisland, Bodmin PL30 4QG
Christopher & Catherine Hartley *Tel:* 01208 850487 *Fax:* 01208 851387
Email: chrishartley@btconnect.com

Map Ref: 1
A30

A beautiful family home standing in 30 acres of fields and gardens which slope to the river. One of the prettiest Cornish villages in an area of oustanding beauty. Beautifully presented bedrooms, lovely old baths, and a drawing room with a piano and television. It's perfect here for golfers, riders and fishermen alike. There is a heated pool to enjoy.

B & B £35-£40pp, C-Cards MC VS, Dinner from £25, Rooms 2 double, 1 twin, all private bathrooms, No smoking in bedrooms, Children over 10, Dogs only by arrangement, Closed Xmas & New Year

---

BOKIDDICK FARM Lanivet, Bodmin PL30 5HP
Gill Hugo *Tel / Fax:* 01208 831481 *Mobile:* 07977 058194
Email: gillhugo@boddickfarm.co.uk *Web:* www.bokiddickfarm.co.uk

Map Ref: 2
A389

Lovely Georgian farmhouse, oak beams, wood panelling, in peaceful countryside with magnificent views. Only two miles from A30. The central location of our dairy farm is an ideal touring base for all Cornwall. Close to Eden Project and National Trust Lanhydrock House. On Saints Way Walk and Cornish Way Cycle Route. Pretty en-suite bedrooms. Delicious aga cooked breakfasts. A warm welcome.

B & B from £25pp, Rooms 4 double, 1 family, all en-suite, No smoking, Children over 5, No dogs, Closed Xmas & New Year

---

BOKELLY St Kew, Bodmin PL30 3DY
Lawrence & Maggie Gordon-Clark *Tel:* 01208 850325 *Fax:* 01208 850801
Email: bokelly@gordonclark.freeserve.co.uk

Map Ref: 3
A39

Bokelly is a 16th century manor farmhouse, close to Rock, Padstow and the beautiful beaches of Daymer Bay and Polzeath. There are stunning coastal walks and picturesque fishing villages. The house has a traditional sitting room with comfy sofas and open fireplace and also beautiful gardens and a tennis court. Several good restaurants, the Eden Project and Gaia Centre are nearby.

B & B from £30pp, Rooms 2 double, 1 twin, all en-suite, Restricted smoking, Children over 5, No dogs, Closed Xmas & New Year

---

TREGELLIST FARMHOUSE Tregellist, St Kew, Bodmin PL30 3HG
Mrs Jill Cleave *Tel:* 01208 880537 *Fax:* 01208 881017 *Mobile:* 07970 559637
Email: jillcleave@tregellist.fsbusiness.co.uk

Map Ref: 3
A30, A39

Tregellist Farmhouse is a 130 acre mixed farm set in pleasant countryside with lovely views. It is situated central for coast and moors. All bedrooms are beautifully furnished with beverage trays, colour televisions, radio alarms and hairdryers. The home cooked food is delicious and a warm welcome is given to all. Close to Camel Trail and 45 minutes drive from Eden Project.

B & B from £23pp, Dinner available, Rooms 3 double, 1 twin, 1 family, all en-suite, No smoking, Children welcome, No dogs, Closed Xmas & New Year

---

TREGAWNE Withiel, Bodmin PL30 5NR
David Jackson & Peta, Lady Linlithgow
Tel: 01208 831552 *Fax:* 01208 832122

Map Ref: 4
A30

A lovingly restored 18th century farmhouse, furnished with antiques. Spacious, elegant accommodation with Rutheirn valley views. Drawing room and heated pool. Ideal for the coasts and walking on the Saints Way and Camel Trail. Sandy beaches/surfing at Polzeath. Quality golf courses within ten miles. Sea fishing, sailing and riding. NT houses/gardens to visit. Padstow 1/2 hour. Eden Project 10 minutes.

B & B from £36pp, C-Cards MC VS, Dinner from £22.50, Rooms 2 double en-suite, 1 twin with bathroom, also 3 cottages, Children over 5, Dogs welcome, Open all year

OLD COACH HOUSE Tintagel Road, Boscastle PL35 0AS   *Map Ref:* 5
Tel: 01840 250398   *Fax:* 01840 250346   A39, B3263
Email: parsons@old-coach.co.uk   *Web:* www.old-coach.co.uk

A 350 year-old coach house which guarantees a warm and friendly welcome. The en-suite rooms are provided with tea/coffee facilities and there is a lounge for guests' use. It is situated in an area of outstanding beauty and makes for an ideal base for exploring Cornwall with local coastal and woodland walks. It is also close to the unspoilt National Trust harbour. Ample parking.

B & B from £19pp, C-Cards MC VS, Rooms 1 twin, 4 double, 3 family, all en-suite, Restricted smoking, Children welcome, Dogs by arrangement, Closed Xmas

TOLCARNE HOUSE HOTEL & RESTAURANT Tintagel Road, Boscastle PL35 0AS   *Map Ref:* 5
Margaret & Graham Crown   *Tel / Fax:* 01840 250654   A39, B3263
Email: crowntolhouse@eclipse.co.uk   *Web:* www.milford.co.uk/go/tolcarne

Tolcarne House is a charming Victorian house providing all modern comforts in a peaceful and friendly environment. There are spacious gardens and splendid views of unspoilt countryside, the National Trust owned coastline to the sea. Individual guest rooms are all en-suite. Ample car parking.

B & B £26-£34pp, C-Cards MC VS, Dinner available, Rooms 1 single, 2 twin, 4 double, 1 triple, all en-suite, Restricted smoking, Children over 10, Dogs by arrangement, Closed Dec to Jan

CLIFF HOTEL Maer Down, Bude EX23 8NG   *Map Ref:* 6
John Jeffs   *Tel / Fax:* 01288 353110   A39
Web: www.cliffhotel.co.uk

The Cliff Hotel is situated in Bude, a lovely part of Cornwall within five acres. It is in a prime position next to National Trust cliffs and only 200 yards from the beach. It boasts an indoor pool, mini gym, putting, tennis court and bowling green. Chef/proprietor.

B & B from £29.50pp, C-Cards MC VS, Dinner available, Rooms 1 double, 1 triple, 12 family, 1 luxury, all en-suite, Restricted smoking, Children welcome, No dogs in public areas, Closed Nov to Mar

ST GENNYS HOUSE St Gennys, Bude EX23 0NW   *Map Ref:* 7
Anthony & Jane Farquhar   *Tel:* 01840 230384   *Fax:* 01840 230537   A39
Email: ac.farquhar@talk21.com

The house is a Grade II listed former vicarage, part of which is 16th century and offers peace and tranquility in its own grounds. The accommodation includes a spacious drawing room and a dining room, both overlooking the sea and gardens. There are challenging walks from the house, and within easy reach are golf courses, sea-fishing, surfing and sandy beaches.

B & B £22-£30pp, Dinner from £12, Rooms 1 double, 1 twin, private bathrooms, 1 single, 1 twin, Restricted smoking, Children over 5, No dogs, Closed Xmas

GREEN PASTURES Longhill, Callington PL17 8AU   *Map Ref:* 8
Mrs J Chamberlain   *Tel:* 01579 382566   A390, A388
Email: greenpast@aol.com

A homely welcome in modern surroundings awaits you at Green Pastures. Set within our own grounds of 5 acres with extensive parking. We have panoramic views across the Tamar Valley towards Plymouth and Dartmoor. The city of Plymouth and towns of Tavistock, Launceston and Bodmin are all within a half hour drive. The north and south coasts are less than an hour by car.

B & B from £17.50pp, Rooms 1 double, 1 twin, 1 triple, all with private facilities, No smoking, Children welcome, No dogs, Open all year

DOLVEAN HOTEL 50 Melvill Road, Falmouth TR11 4DQ
Paul & Carol Crocker *Tel:* 01326 313658 *Fax:* 01326 313995
Email: reservations@dolvean.co.uk *Web:* www.dolvean.co.uk

Map Ref: 9
A39

Experience the elegance and comfort of our Victorian home, where
carefully chosen antiques, fine china and fascinating books create an
ambience where you can relax and feel at home. Each bedroom has
its own character, with pretty pictures and lots of ribbons and lace,
creating an atmosphere that makes every stay a special occasion.
AA, ETC 5 Diamonds, Silver Award.

B & B £30-£40pp, C-Cards, Rooms 3 single, 4 double, 2 twin,
2 king sized, all en-suite, No smoking, Children over 12, No dogs,
Closed Xmas

PROSPECT HOUSE 1 Church Road, Penryn, Falmouth TR10 8DA
Brendan & Sue Budd *Tel / Fax:* 01326 373198 *Email:* bbudd@freeuk.com
Web: www.cornwall-selectively.co.uk

Map Ref: 9
A39

Elegant listed Georgian townhouse beautifully furnished with large
comfortable beds in spacious rooms. Guest lounge. Peaceful
atmosphere with Cornish walled garden and Victorian conservatory.
Aga cooked breakfast and excellent pubs and restaurants nearby.
Convenient for Eden Project and National Maritime Museum,
Falmouth. Situated at the head of the Penryn river between Truro
and Falmouth. National Trust properties, walks and sailing nearby.
Convenient for the Eden Project.
B & B £27.50-£30pp, C-Cards MC VS, Rooms 1 single, 2 double,
1 twin, most en-suite, Smoking restricted, Children welcome, Dogs
by arrangement, Open all year

ROSEMULLION HOTEL Gyllyngvase Hill, Falmouth TR11 4DF
Gail Jones *Tel:* 01326 314690 *Fax:* 01326 210086 *Mobile:* 07974 770187
Email: gail@rosemullionhotel.demon.co.uk

Map Ref: 9
A39

Imposing tudor style building, offering quality accommodation in
smoke free atmosphere. En-suite rooms, sea views balcony. King
size beds. Large car park. Close to beaches and town centre. Eden
Project an hour away. Adults only. Sorry no pets. Four diamonds AA.
Ground floor rooms.

B & B £19.50-£24pp, Rooms 1 single, 9 double, 3 twin, all
en-suite, No smoking, No children or dogs, Closed Xmas

WICKHAM GUEST HOUSE 21 Gyllyngvase Terrace, Falmouth TR11 4DL
Steve & Jenny Lake *Tel:* 01326 311140
Email: enquiries@wickhamhotel.freeserve.co.uk *Web:* www.wickham-hotel.co.uk

Map Ref: 9
A39

A small guest house overlooking Falmouth Bay and close to the
railway station. It is only a convenient two minutes walk to the beach
or Princess Pavilion, with its attractive gardens and evening
entertainment and 10 minutes walk to the town centre. There are
televisions and tea/coffee facilities in all rooms with a guests' lounge.
Home cooking.

B & B from £19pp, C-Cards MC VS, Rooms 2 single, 1 twin,
2 double, 1 family, No smoking, Children welcome, No dogs,
Closed Xmas & New Year

CARNETHIC HOUSE Lambs Barn, Fowey PL23 1HQ
David & Trish Hogg *Tel:* 01726 833336 *Fax:* 01726 833296
Email: carnethic@btinternet.com *Web:* www.carnethic.co.uk

Map Ref: 10
A390, A3082

A Regency house in one and a half acres of mature gardens.
Carnethic House maintains an informal atmosphere and cooks all
food fresh with local fish being a speciality. Also a heated pool.

B & B from £30pp, Dinner available, Rooms 1 single, 4 double,
1 twin, 1 triple, 1 family, en-suite, No smoking, Children welcome,
Closed Dec to Jan

TREVANION 70 Lostwithiel Street, Fowey PL23 1BQ   *Map Ref:* 10
Jill & Bob Bullock   *Tel / Fax:* 01726 832602   A390, B3269
Email: trefoy@globalnet.co.uk   *Web:* www.users.globalnet.co.uk/~trefoy/fowey.htm

A warm welcome awaits you at this comfortable 16th century
Merchant's House situated in historic Fowey in the heart of Daphne
Du Maurier country. An ideal base from which to visit Eden Project,
Gardens of Heligan, NT houses/gardens or the beauty of the
Cornish Riviera. En-suite rooms are well furnished with tea/coffee
facilities and TV. Some parking for guests' cars.

B & B £22.50-£25pp, Rooms 1 double, 1 twin, 1 family, all en-
suite, No smoking, Children over 12, No dogs, Closed Nov to Mar

---

THE GARDENS Tresowes, Ashton, Helston TR13 9SY   *Map Ref:* 11
Moira & Goff Cattell   *Tel:* 01736 763299   A 394
Email: goff.and.moira@amserve.net

Perhaps this old cottage was home to Cornish miners, it was two
dwellings. It retains inglenooks, narrow staircases and low ceilings.
Bedrooms are crisp and comfortable, there is a sitting room with a
wood burner. Supper, using home grown vegetables is taken in the
conservatory. A pleasant drive from St.Michael's Mount, Penzance
and St.Ives, also The Lizard, good beaches, and the Helford River.

B & B £20-£25pp, Dinner from £13, Rooms 2 double (en-suite),
1 twin/double (with private bathroom), No smoking, No children or
dogs, Closed Xmas & New Year

THE OLD RECTORY Mawgan, Helston TR12 6AD   *Map Ref:* 12
Mrs Sue Leith   *Tel:* 01326 221261   *Fax:* 01326 221797   A394, A3083, B3293
Email: leith@euphony.net   *Web:* www.oldrectorymawgan.co.uk

This house is home to the Leith family, and stands in three acres of
valley garden, on the upper reaches of the mystical Helford River. All
the lovely south facing bedrooms are well propertioned, and light,
with private bathrooms. The Lizard peninsular has something unique
to offer everyone and we are only half an hour from Penzance,
Falmouth and Truro.

B & B from £35pp, Rooms 2 double, 2 twin, all with private
bathrooms, No smoking, Children over 12, Dogs by arrangement,
Closed Dec to Mar

MEAVER FARM Mullion, Helston TR12 7DN   *Map Ref:* 13
Jan & Russ Stanland   *Tel:* 01326 240128   *Fax:* 01326 240011   A394, A3083
Email: meaverfarm@eclipse.co.uk   *Web:* www.meaverfarm.co.uk

A 300 year old traditional Cornish farmhouse in a quiet valley.
Retains a cosy atmosphere with the log fires in the winter, the
exposed beams and the hot aga cooked food. There is a choice of
two four-poster double rooms and one twin room with en-suite
bathrooms. The house has a lovely garden orchard and acre fenced
field.

B & B from £24pp, Rooms 2 double, 1 twin, all en-suite,
No smoking, Children over 12, Dogs welcome, Open all year

HURDON FARM Launceston PL15 9LS   *Map Ref:* 14
Margaret Smith   A30
Tel: 01566 772955

Spacious 18th century farmhouse, quietly located on 400 acre
mixed working farm. Only five minutes from A30 and the ancient
capital of Cornwall, Launceston, this is an exceptional location for
exploring the rich variety of attractions of Devon and Cornwall.
Excellent use of local and home produce is used to create delicious
freshly home cooked four course dinners of imaginative flair.

B & B £20-£22pp, Dinner from £12.50, Rooms 1 single, 2 double,
2 twin, 1 family, all en-suite, No smoking, Children welcome, Guide
dogs only, Closed Nov to May

THE BARTON Laneast, near Launceston PL15 8PN
Gilly ffrench Blake *Tel:* 01566 880104 *Fax:* 01566 880103
Email: afb@totalise.co.uk

Map Ref: 15
A30, A395

The Barton is a Grade II listed Georgian Farmhouse with 30 acres and fishing on the Inny. The gardens and extensive grounds, including Holy Well, are peaceful with lovely views. Secure private parking. Simple dinner by arrangement.

B & B £25pp, Dinner available, Rooms 2 double en-suite, 1 twin with private bathroom, No smoking, Childen over 5, Kennel for dogs, Closed Xmas

---

STENHILL FARM North Petherwin, Launceston PL15 8NN
Mr & Mrs E Reddock *Tel / Fax:* 01566 785686
Email: e.reddock@btinternet.com *Web:* www.stenhill.com

Map Ref: 16
B3254

500 year old longhouse restored to preserve the charm of this Cornish home. Beams, exposed stone walls and granite fireplaces to appreciate. En-suite bedrooms, delightfully furnished and equipped. Dinners available. A former stable, now a self catering cottage with ground floor bedrooms, is available, wonderful views to the countryside and moors. Gardens of Heligan, Eden Project and NT properties are easily reached.

B & B £21.50-£31.25pp, Dinner from £12.50, Rooms 1 en-suite twin, No smoking, No children or dogs, Open all year

---

HORNACOTT South Petherwin, Launceston PL15 7LH
Jos & Mary Anne Otway-Ruthven *Tel / Fax:* 01566 782461
Email: otwayruthven@btinternet.com

Map Ref: 17
B3254

18th century house in a valley with gardens and a stream, in Cornwall's unspoilt countryside. A suite of twin bedroom with en-suite bathroom and sitting room with TV, CD player, bed and sitting rooms have garden facing French windows. Many places to visit within reach, Lanhydrock and Cotehele, Launceston, the ancient capital of Cornwall, Bodmin Moor and the coasts.

B & B from £30pp, Dinner from £18, Rooms 1 en-suite twin, No smoking, Children welcome, Dogs by arrangement, Closed Xmas & New Year

---

TREGONDALE FARM Menheniot, Liskeard PL14 3RG
Mrs Stephanie Rowe *Tel / Fax:* 01579 342407
Email: tregondale@connectfree.co.uk *Web:* www.tregondalefarm.co.uk

Map Ref: 18
A38

Come and join our family in the peace of the countryside, near the coast. Superior en-suite rooms and log fires for chilly evenings. Home produce is the speciality of the house, beautifully set in an original walled garden. Explore our farm trail through a wooded valley, a paradise for birds. Tennis, fishing and cycling available. Relax and unwind.

B & B £22.50-£25pp, C-Cards MC VS, Dinner from £12.50, Rooms 2 double, 1 twin, all en-suite, No smoking, Children welcome, No dogs, Open all year

---

FIELDHEAD HOTEL Portuan Road, Looe PL13 2DR
Gill & Barrie Pipkin *Tel:* 01503 262689 *Fax:* 01503 264114
Email: field.head@virgin.net *Web:* www.fieldheadhotel.co.uk

Map Ref: 19
A387

Large country house standing in beautiful gardens by the sea with spectacular views, patios and swimming pool. Rooms en-suite and well equipped, tastefully decorated, some have far-reaching sea views. The comfortable lounge and candlelit restaurant serving fresh local produce and seafood, enjoy views across Looe Bay. An easy waterside stroll to the town of Looe with its cobbled streets and pretty cottages. Parking.

B & B from £28pp, C-Cards MC VS, Dinner from £22, Rooms 1 single, 8 double, 3 twin, 3 family, Restricted smoking, Children welcome, Dogs by arrangement, Open all year

ST AUBYN'S Marine Drive, Hannafore, Looe PL13 2DH   *Map Ref:* 19
Peter & Di Bishop   *Tel:* 01503 264351   *Fax:* 01503 263670   A387
Email: welcome@staubyns.co.uk   *Web:* www.staubyns.co.uk

St.Aubyns is a an elegant Victorian home overlooking the sea at Hannafore. Guests are assured of friendly hospitality in spacious accommodation. The dining room and guests' lounge have spectacular views over Looe Bay. Some bedrooms also enjoy sea views. An extensive breakfast menu is offered, and for suppers, there is a variety of local restaurants, which specialise in fresh fish. AA 5 Diamonds.

B & B £23-£35pp, C-Cards MC VS, Rooms 2 single, 2 double, 4 double/twin, most en-suite, No smoking, Children over 5, No dogs, Closed Nov to Easter

---

COOMBE FARM Widegates, Looe PL13 1QN   *Map Ref:* 20
Martin & Sylvia Eades   *Tel:* 01503 240223   *Fax:* 01503 240895   B3253
Email: coombe_farm@hotmail.com   *Web:* www.coombefarmhotel.co.uk   *see Photo opposite*

Experience the magic of Cornwall. Enjoy warm, friendly hospitality, delicious food, log fires, a heated pool and luxurious surroundings. Coombe Farm stands in lovely grounds with superb views down a wooded valley to the sea. All the bedrooms are en-suite with satellite TV, tea/coffee facilities and direct dial telephone. Nearby golf, fishing, tennis and riding. ETC 4 Diamonds Highly Commended.

B & B £35-£38pp, C-Cards MC VS AE, Dinner from £17.50, Rooms 2 twin, 5 double, 3 family, all en-suite, No smoking, Children welcome, Dogs by arrangement, Closed Nov to end Feb

---

WOODLANDS GUEST HOUSE Trewollock, Gorran Haven, Mevagissey PL26 6NS   *Map Ref:* 21
Dianne Harrison   *Tel:* 01726 843821   B3273
Email: woodlands@gorranhaven.fsbusiness.co.uk   *Web:* www.woodlandsmevagissey.co.uk

Woodlands, standing in an acre of south facing gardens with two spring-fed ponds, has magnificent sea views across open fields and adjacent footpath links with the Cornish coastal path (half mile). This family run guest house offers mostly en-suite accommodation with tea/coffee facilities, TVs. Close to Lost Gardens of Heligan and the Eden Project. Ample parking is provided.

B & B £20-£30pp, Rooms 1 single, 1 twin, 3 double, 1 family, most en-suite, No smoking, Children welcome, No dogs, Closed Xmas & New Year

---

DEGEMBRIS FARMHOUSE St Newlyn East, Newquay TR8 5HY   *Map Ref:* 22
Kathy Woodley   *Tel:* 01872 510555   *Fax:* 01872 510230   A3058
Email: kathy@degembris.co.uk   *Web:* www.degembris.co.uk

The manor house built in the 16th century is now used as a barn. The present day house surrounded by gardens, was built two hundred years ago, many rooms have views over rolling countryside. Bedrooms are tastefully decorated and well equipped. Hearty breakfasts and traditional evening meals are served in the cosy dining room. Stroll along the farm trail through woodlands and cornfields.

B & B £22-£25pp, C-Cards MC VS, Dinner from £12.50, Rooms 1 single, 1 en-suite twin, 1 double, 2 en-suite family, No smoking, Children welcome, No dogs, Closed Xmas

---

THE WHITE HOUSE Watergate Bay, Newquay TR8 4AD   *Map Ref:* 23
Tel: 01637 860119   *Fax:* 01637 860449   A3059, B3276
Email: jenny.vallance@virgin.net

Quiet, elegant spacious country house with large gardens, overlooking Watergate Bay and the beach for sand castles and surfing. Beautifully appointed bed and breakfast suites and large, well equipped family apartments plus a converted chapel for romantic couples. Ideally situated between Padstow and Newquay for touring, walking and sports.

B & B from £25pp, Rooms 2 single, 2 double, Children over 10, Closed Nov to Apl

Coombe Farm, Widegates, near Looe

THE OLD MILL COUNTRY HOUSE Little Petherick, Padstow PL27 7QT *Map Ref:* 24
David & Debbie Walker *Tel:* 01841 540388 *Fax:* 0870 056 9360 A389
Email: dwalker@oldmillbandb.demon.co.uk

This is a 16th century Grade 11 listed cornmill complete with waterwheel. The house is furnished with antiques and interesting collections. The bedrooms are well presented, having either en-suite facilities, or a private bathroom. The Old Mill is set in its own streamside gardens at the head of Little Petherick Creek, two miles from Padstow. There are many fine pubs and restaurants in the area.

B & B £30-£32pp, C-Cards MC VS, Rooms 2 twin, 2 double, all en-suite, Restricted smoking, Children over 14, No dogs, Closed Nov to Mar

---

THE OLD CABBAGE PATCH Trevone Bay, Padstow PL28 8QX *Map Ref:* 25
Tel / Fax: 01841 520956 A389
Email: info@theoldcabbagepatch.co.uk *Web:* www.theoldcabbagepatch.co.uk

The Old Cabbage Patch is situated close to Trevone Beach with its beautiful, craggy surroundings where ever changing sun-sets can often be seen. Guest rooms are excellent with crisp cotton bedding and many useful facilities. Breakfast, served in our elegant dining room, is an absolute delight with a varied menu including vegetarian dishes. Special diets catered for with prior notice.

B & B from £27pp, C-Cards MC VS AE, Rooms 3 double, 1 twin, all en-suite, No smoking, No children or dogs, Closed Nov to Jan

---

CON AMORE 38 Morrab Road, Penzance TR18 4EX *Map Ref:* 26
Carol & Keith Richards *Tel / Fax:* 01736 363423 A30
Email: KRich30327@aol.com *Web:* www.con-amore.co.uk

Recommended and family run, Con Amore is ideally situated for relaxing or touring the Lands End Peninsula. Opposite sub-tropical gardens and 100 yards from the promenade and panoramic views over Mounts Bay and St Michael's Mount. Rooms have central heating, TV and tea/coffee facilities. They are tastefully and individually decorated. A varied menu catering for all tastes. Reduction for children sharing a room.

B & B from £13pp, C-Cards MC VS, Rooms 1 single, 2 twin, 3 double, 2 family most en-suite, Children & dogs welcome, Open all year

---

CORNERWAYS GUEST HOUSE 5 Leskinnick Street, Penzance TR18 2HA *Map Ref:* 26
John & Andrea Leggatt *Tel / Fax:* 01736 364645 A30
Email: enquiries@cornerways-penzance.co.uk *Web:* www.penzance.co.uk/cornerways

Cornerways Guest House is a listed town house close to bus and rail stations and makes for an ideal touring base. All rooms are en-suite with colour televisions and tea/coffee facilities. Dinner can be arranged and a vegetarian menu is also available.

B & B from £19pp, C-Cards MC VS, Dinner from £8.50, Rooms 1 single, 1 double, 1 twin, 1 triple, all en-suite, Restricted smoking, Dogs by arrangement, Closed mid-Jan to mid-Feb

---

WARWICK HOUSE 17 Regent Terrace, Penzance TR18 4DW *Map Ref:* 26
Julie Cavanagh A30
Tel / Fax: 01736 363881

A charming regency building, overlooking Mounts Bay. All of the rooms are en-suite and comfortable with beautiful sea views and flower filled patios face the sea for guests to relax on. The house is also in an ideal location for travellers, being near the station, sea port and heliport. Large car park. Non smoking.

B & B £23-£26pp, C-Cards MC VS, Rooms 1 single, 3 double, 1 twin, 1 triple, most en-suite, No smoking, Children over 4, Open all year

WOODSTOCK HOUSE 29 Morrab Road, Penzance TR18 4EZ
Cherry & John Hopkins *Tel / Fax:* 01736 369049
Email: WoodstocP@aol.com *Web:* www.innaccommodations.com/woodstock.html

Map Ref: 26
A00

Victorian guest house in Penzance near seafront and ideal for the Isles of Scilly ferry and heliport, railway and bus stations. Rooms have TV, radio, basins and tea/coffee makers, many rooms have en-suite shower/toilet. Special diets catered for. Drive into town past railway station, along seafront. Right into Morrab Road as you approach the Queen's Hotel, 'Woodstock' is 200m on right.

B & B from £15pp, Rooms 2 single, 3 double (one 4 poster), 3 twin, 1 family, Children welcome, Open all year

SOUTH COLENSO FARM Goldsithney, Penzance TR20 9JB
Rosalind Wyatt *Tel:* 01736 762290
Email: damian@dcwyatt.freeserve.co.uk

Map Ref: 27
A394

A spacious Georgian style farmhouse on an arable farm which is peaceful and secluded yet not isolated. A perfect location with sandy beaches and pretty coves nearby. Large en-suite bedrooms have lovely country views with colour television and tea/coffee facilities and a lounge with colour television for guests' use. A full English breakfast is served in our sunny dining room.

B & B from £19pp, Rooms 1 double, 1 twin, 1 family, all en-suite, No smoking, Children over 6, No dogs, Closed Nov to Mar

EDNOVEAN FARM Perranuthnoe, Penzance TR20 9LZ
Mrs Christine Taylor *Fax:* 01736 711883 *Tel:* 01736 710480
Email: info@ednoveanfarm.co.uk *Web:* www.ednoveanfarm.co.uk

Map Ref: 28
A394

A charming honeyed barn, set on a natural terrace, overlooking the sweep of Mounts Bay with St Michaels Mount. Surrounded by a series of mediterranean style courtyards with secluded seating areas. Choose from three elegant country style en-suite bedrooms, antique beds, patchwork quilts, fresh flowers and crisp linen. One bedroom with private terrace, another with four poster bed. Just relax.

B & B £27.50-£35pp, C-Cards MC VS AE, Rooms 3 double, all en-suite, No smoking, No children or dogs, Closed Xmas

EDNOVEAN HOUSE Perranuthnoe, Penzance TR20 9LZ
Clive & Jacqueline Whittington *Tel:* 01736 711071
Email: clive@ednoveanhouse.co.uk *Web:* www.ednoveanhouse.co.uk

Map Ref: 28
A394, A30

Ednovean House is a beautiful Victorian country house offering a warm welcome and comfortable rooms, most having en-suite facilities and panoramic sea views overlooking St Michaels Mount and Mounts Bay. Situated in one acre of lovely gardens and surrounded by farmland. TV lounge, small library, bar/dining room, ample parking. AA 4 Diamonds.

B & B £24-£27.50pp, C-Cards MC VS, Rooms 2 single, 4 double, 2 twin, most en-suite, Restricted smoking, Children over 7, Dogs by arrangement, Closed Xmas & New Year

QUILKYNS 1 St Pirans Way, Perranuthnoe, Penzance TR20 9NJ
Paul & Nuala Leeper *Tel:* 01736 719141
Email: paul@quilkyns.fsnet.co.uk *Web:* www.quilkyns.co.uk

Map Ref: 28
A394, A30

This family run bed and breakfast is in the heart of Perranuthnoe, a coastal village with a sandy beach. Well placed for St Michael's Mount. South facing rooms have wash basins, TV and tea/coffee facilities. The bath and shower rooms are close by with access to laundry room. Children welcome if family occupying both rooms. Village pub caters well for families.

B & B from £17pp, Rooms 1 twin, 1 double, No smoking, Children & dogs welcome, Closed Nov to Feb

THE BLACK WELL Botallack, St Just, Penzance TR19 7QH
Reg Blackwell
Tel / Fax: 01736 787461

Map Ref: 29
A30, A3071

The Black Well is situated on the scenic coast road between Lands End and St Ives. All bedrooms are en-suite with televisions and have either sea or country views. There are no parking problems. Guests enjoy walking the coastal footpath with its rugged coastline and magnificent views. Personal attention assured at all times.

B & B from £23pp, Rooms 1 double, 2 multiple, all en-suite, Restricted smoking, Children over 7, Dogs welcome, Open all year

---

BOSCEAN COUNTRY HOTEL Boswedden Road, St Just-in-Penwith, Penzance TR19 7QP
Dennis & Linda Wilson   *Tel / Fax:* 01736 788748
Email: Boscean@aol.com

Map Ref: 29
A3071

Standing in walled gardens, this beautiful house overlooks countryside and sea. Guests are assured of full central heating, log fires and home cooking, tea/coffee facilities in bedrooms. The lounge has a bar with a residents' licence. An ideal base from which to explore the west of Cornwall, St.Michael's Mount and St.Ives. Ideal for walking holidays, this is a family run hotel.

B & B from £23pp, Dinner from £13, Rooms 5 double, 5 twin, 2 family, all en-suite, Restricted smoking, Children welcome, Dogs by arrangement, Closed Xmas & New Year

---

LONG CROSS HOTEL & VICTORIAN GARDENS Trelights, Port Isaac PL29 3TF
Mr & Mrs Crawford   *Tel:* 01208 880243
Web: www.longcrosshotel.co.uk

Map Ref: 30
B3314

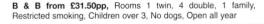

A Victorian country house with a unique garden and free house tavern. Bedrooms are en-suite with televisions and tea/coffee facilities. Some ground floor rooms, some have sea views. The hotel retains many of the Victorian features, the gardens are open to the public. The Tavern is a popular drinking and dining spot with an extensive menu and a famous beer garden.

B & B from £55 (min 3 nights)pp, Dinner available, Rooms 4 twin, 8 double, 3 family, Children & dogs welcome, Closed Xmas

---

AVIARY COURT Mary's Well, Illogan, Redruth TR16 4QZ
The Studley Family
Tel: 01209 842256   *Fax:* 01209 843744

Map Ref: 31
A30

A charming country house in two acres of gardens on the edge of Illogan Woods. Aviary Court is ideally located for visiting the coast, St Ives, Tate, the Lost Gardens of Heligan and the Eden project. Six well equipped individual bedrooms with tea/coffee making facilities, television and garden views. The family proprietors ensure a personal service offering good food using Cornish produce.

B & B from £31.50pp, Rooms 1 twin, 4 double, 1 family, Restricted smoking, Children over 3, No dogs, Open all year

BENSONS 1 The Hillside, Portreath, Redruth TR16 4LL　　　*Map Ref:* 31
Peter & Christine Smythe　　　　　　　　　　　　　　　　　　A00 B3300
Tel: 01209 842534　*Fax:* 01209 843578

Bensons is a modern guest house, overlooking the village, valley and
sea. All bedrooms are en-suite. A delicious breakfast is served in the
conservatory. There is a lovely sandy beach at Portreath with three
pubs and an excellent restaurant nearby. An ideal situation for
visiting Cornwall's gardens, The Eden Project and The Tate Gallery.

B & B from £20pp, Rooms 2 single, 2 double, all en-suite,
No smoking, Children over 12, No dogs, Closed Nov to Apr

LANTALLACK FARM Landrake, Saltash PL12 5AE　　　*Map Ref:* 32
Nicky Walker　*Tel / Fax:* 01752 851281　　　　　　　　　　A38
Email: lantallack@ukgateway.net　*Web:* www.lantallack.co.uk

This lovely Grade II Georgian farmhouse has breathtaking views over
undulating countryside, streams and wooded valleys. Delicious
breakfasts in the walled garden in summer and log fires in the winter
with a good collection of books and two grand pianos. Lantallack is
an inspiration for musicians, artists or anyone wanting to combine
fun with peace and tranquility. Also cottage with stunning views for
self-catering/art holidays.

B & B from £27.50pp, Rooms 1 double, 1 twin, both en-suite,
No smoking, Children by arrangement, No dogs, Closed Xmas &
New Year

ST MELLION HOTEL, GOLF & COUNTRY CLUB St Mellion, Saltash PL12 6SD　　　*Map Ref:* 32
Tel: 01579 351351　*Fax:* 01579 350537　　　　　　　　　　A388
Email: stmellion@americangolf.uk.com　*Web:* www.st-mellion.co.uk

St Mellion Hotel is at the compass pivot of Devon and Cornwall. The
visitor's perfect choice with world class golf, leisure facilities and
award winning food. Stay in either our comfortable hotel or luxury
fairway lodges and you will be guaranteed a break away to
remember.

B & B from £40pp, Dinner available, Rooms 16 twin, 8 double, all
en-suite, No smoking, Children welcome, No dogs, Open all year

PENKERRIS Penwinnick Road, St Agnes TR5 0PA　　　*Map Ref:* 33
Dorothy Gill-Carey　*Tel / Fax:* 01872 552262　　　　　　　　A39
Web: www.penkerris.co.uk

Penkerris is an enchanting Edwardian residence with its own
grounds in an unspoilt Cornish village. The rooms are beautiful and
Penkerris provides for the guests a piano, a television, log fires in the
winter and superb home cooking. There are dramatic cliff walks and
beaches nearby. RAC, AA, 2 Crowns. Les Routiers recommended.

B & B £15-£25pp, Dinner from £10, Rooms 2 single, 3 twin,
6 double, 3 family, some en-suite, Children & dogs welcome,
Open all year

ANCHORAGE HOUSE Nettles Corner, Tregrehan Mills, St Austell PL25 3RH　　　*Map Ref:* 34
Jane & Steve Epperson　*Tel:* 01726 814071　　　　　　　　A390
Email: stay@anchoragehouse.co.uk　*Web:* www.anchoragehouse.co.uk

Attention has been paid to the smallest detail in this impressive
house, accented with antiques, and featured in a national magazine.
Guests are treated to an outdoor heated pool, jacuzzi, satellite
television, large beds, conservatory and luxurious, sparklingly clean
en-suite rooms. Steven and Jane combine wonderful hospitality and
informality for a special stay. Perfect for visiting houses, gardens,
Heligan and Eden.

B & B £35-£39pp, C-Cards MC VS, Dinner £25, Rooms 3 double
en-suite, No smoking, No children or dogs, Closed Dec

NANSCAWEN MANOR HOUSE   Prideaux Road, Luxulyan Valley, St Blazey PL24 2SR   *Map Ref:* 35
Keith & Fiona Martin   *Tel:* 01726 814488   A390
Email: keith@nanscawen.com   *Web:* www.nanscawen.com

This Georgian manor house stands in a glorious setting. Guests are certain to be comfortable in beautiful bedrooms which offer either four poster, or six foot beds. Television, hairdryer, telephone and a tea/coffee tray is in each room. English breakfast or smoked salmon with scrambled eggs may be enjoyed. A good selection of pubs/restaurants locally. A swimmimng pool is available for guests' enjoyment.

B & B £40-£45pp, C-Cards MC VS, Rooms 2 double, 1 twin, all en-suite, No smoking, Children over 12, No dogs, Open all year

BLUE HAYES PRIVATE HOTEL   Trelyon Avenue, St Ives TR26 2AD   *Map Ref:* 36
Tel / Fax: 01736 797129   A30
Email: Malcolm@bluehayes.fsbusiness.co.uk   *Web:* www.bluehayes.co.uk

A country house by the sea at St Ives, set in its own grounds overlooking St Ives Bay and Harbour. Completely refurbished to a high standard. Own car park. Master Suite has balcony overlooking Bay and Harbour. Garden Suite has direct access to garden, Trelyon Suite has roof garden, balcony overlooking woodlands and with sea views. All rooms fully en-suite.

B & B from £45pp, No smoking, Children over 10, No dogs, Closed Nov to Feb

CHY-GARTH   Sea View Meadows, St Ives Road, Carbis Bay, St Ives TR26 2JX   *Map Ref:* 36
Mrs Ann Roberts   *Tel:* 01736 795677   *Mobile:* 07754 002649   A30, A3074
Email: ann@chy-garth.demon.co.uk   *Web:* www.stives-cornwall.co.uk/members/chy-garth.html

'Garden House by the sea' Chy-Garth is a detached guest house, standing in its own grounds with large lawned gardens to the front, leading to residents' patio area and private car park to the rear. St Ives Bay and Godrevy Lighthouse form a backdrop to this quiet residential area and most of the bedrooms have sea views over Carbis Bay which is just a short walk away. AA 4 Diamonds.

B & B £22-£32pp, C-Cards MC VS, Rooms 1 single, 4 double, 3 twin, 1 family, most en-suite, No smoking, Children over 8, No dogs, Open all year

THE GREY MULLET   2 Bunkers Hill, St Ives TR26 1LJ   *Map Ref:* 36
Ken Weston   *Tel:* 01736 796635   A3074
Email: greymulletguesthouse@lineone.net   *Web:* www.touristnetuk.com/sw/greymullet

An 18th century building in the old fishing and artists' quarter. Full of character with oak beams and granite walls hung with paintings and photographs. A warm welcome in homely surroundings. The en-suite bedrooms, some with four poster beds, have television and tea/coffee facilities, there is a sitting room with open fire. Ideal position for the harbour, beaches, restaurants and the Tate Gallery.

B & B £23-£26pp, C-Cards MC VS AE DC, Rooms 1 single, 1 twin, 5 double, most en-suite, No smoking, Children over 12, No dogs, Open all year

OLD VICARAGE HOTEL   Parc-an-Creet, St Ives TR26 2ES   *Map Ref:* 36
Mr Jack Sykes and Miss Dianne Sykes   *Tel:* 01736 796124   *Fax:* 01736 796343   B3306
Email: holidays@oldvicaragehotel.com   *Web:* www.oldvicaragehotel.com

The Old Vicarage, standing in wooded grounds in a quiet area, is a restored Victorian rectory retaining the period ambience, but with modern comforts. The lounge has a library, a television and a well stocked Victorian bar with piano. Large breakfast menu, including vegetarian. Eight bedrooms, mostly en-suite, all with TV and tea/coffee facilities. Large garden with putting green, badminton, swing and car park.

B & B from £26pp, C-Cards MC VS, Rooms 7 double/twin/family, all en-suite, Restricted smoking, Children & dogs welcome, Closed Oct to Easter

TREWINNARD 4 Parc Avenue, St Ives TR26 2DN   *Map Ref:* 36
Sam & Margaret Sears   *Tel:* 01736 794168   *Fax:* 01736 798161   *Mobile:* 07977 261856   A30
Email: trewinnard@cwcom.net   *Web:* www.trewinnard hotel stives.co.uk

A late Victorian residence in an elevated position with superb views over St Ives harbour, town and bay. All rooms are en-suite with television and hospitality tray and a four poster room is also available. For breakfast there is a choice of A la Carte, traditional, vegetarian and continental to suit all tastes. Coastal walks, golf courses, superb beaches and the Tate Gallery are all nearby.

B & B from £23pp, C-Cards MC VS, Rooms 2 single, 4 double, 1 family, all en-suite, No smoking, Children over 6, No dogs, Closed Nov to Mar

CLIFF HOUSE Kingsand, Torpoint PL10 1NJ   *Map Ref:* 37
Ann Heasman   *Tel:* 01752 823110   *Fax:* 01752 822595   A374, B3247
Email: chkingsand@aol.com   *Web:* www.cliffhse.abel.co.uk

Cliff House is a Grade II listed 17th century building, converted from two cottages into one house 150 years ago. There is a large first floor sitting room, with log fires in the winter and television, cd player and a 1908 refurbished Bluthner boudoir grand piano for guests to use. All food is freshly cooked with homemade soups, pates, mousses and freshly baked bread.

B & B £22-£27.50pp, Dinner from £10, Rooms 2 double, 1 twin, all en-suite, No smoking, Children by arrangement, No dogs, Open all year

THE OLD RECTORY St John-in-Cornwall, Torpoint PL11 3AW   *Map Ref:* 37
Clive & Button Poole   *Tel:* 01752 822275   *Fax:* 01752 823322   *Mobile:* 07870 509173   A374
Email: clive@oldrectory-stjohn.co.uk

Grade II listed house with subtropical garden and millpond located by tidal creek. Set in a quiet valley, guests can enjoy its understated elegance with its beautifully appointed bedrooms. A warm welcome, imaginative breakfasts and relaxing drawing room awaits. Coastal walks, beaches, moors, golf, sailing and National Trust properties are close by. NB: Water surrounds this property, therefore we cannot accept responsibility for the safety of children.

B & B from £32.50 (min 2 nights)pp, Rooms 1 twin, 2 double, private or en-suite, No smoking, Children by arrangement, Dogs by arrangement, Closed occasionally

ROCK COTTAGE Blackwater, Truro TR4 8EU   *Map Ref:* 38
Shirley Wakeling   *Tel / Fax:* 01872 560252   A30
Email: rockcottage@yahoo.com

18th century cottage, formerly the village schoolmaster's home, stands in a village 6 miles from Truro 3 miles from the ocean. Comfortable en-suite rooms with central heating, TV, radio and beverage tray. Charming stone walled lounge where guests are welcome to relax. Breakfast is served in our cosy dining room with an antique Cornish range. Ample parking and delightful gardens.

B & B from £22pp, C-Cards MC VS, Rooms 1 twin, 2 double, all en-suite, No smoking, No children or dogs, Closed Xmas & New Year

VENTONGIMPS MILL BARN Ventongimps, Callestick, Truro TR4 9LH   *Map Ref:* 39
Mr & Mrs Gibson   A3075
Tel: 01872 573275

A converted mill barn of slate and stone, in a hamlet in a sheltered valley. A stream runs through extensive gardens and lake on seven acres of fields and woods. Coastal paths, breathtaking views and the city of Truro is six miles. Suppers served in licensed bar, Portuguese cooking a speciality. Coastal village of Perranporth with miles of sandy beaches is two miles.

B & B from £18pp, Dinner from £10.50, Rooms 1 single, 1 twin, 2 double, 4 family, Restricted smoking, Children welcome, Dogs by arrangement, Open all year

PERRAN HOUSE Fore Street, Grampound, Truro TR2 4RS
John & Yvonne Diboll *Tel:* 01726 882066 *Fax:* 01726 882936
Email: perran-house@faxvia.net

Map Ref: 40
A390

Delightful 17th century cottage in the historic township of Grampound, within a beautiful conservation area in the centre of Cornwall. Ideally located for touring, walking and visiting the many nearby gardens which include the Lost gardens of Heligan and the newly constructed Eden Project. There are televisions and tea/coffee facilities in all of the rooms and off road parking is available.

B & B £16-£20pp, Rooms 2 single, 3 double, 1 twin, some en-suite, No smoking, Children welcome, No dogs, Open all year

---

APPLE TREE COTTAGE Laity Moor, Ponsanooth, Truro TR3 7HR
Ann Tremayne *Tel:* 01872 865047
Email: appletreecottage@talk21.com

Map Ref: 41
A39

A warm welcome is assured at Apple Tree Cottage, which is set amidst rolling countryside with delightful gardens and river. The cottage is furnished with country antiques, and the large lounge has a welcoming log fire. Traditional farmhouse breakfasts, cooked on the Aga, may be enjoyed in the sunlit dining room. There are several National Trust gardens just 15 minutes away.

B & B £23-£25pp, Rooms 2 double, No smoking, Children over 10, Dogs must be on lead, Closed mid-Dec to mid-Jan

---

SILVERMEAD GUEST HOUSE Rock, Wadebridge PL27 6LB
Barbara & Matthew Martin *Tel:* 01208 862425 *Fax:* 01208 862919
Web: www.silvermeadguesthouse.co.uk

Map Ref: 42
A39, B3314

Silvermead Guest House is a 10 bedroom family run licensed guest house overlooking the Camel Estuary. It adjoins St. Enodoc Golf courses with only two minutes walk to the beach and water sports centre. The accommodation is spacious and most of the rooms are en-suite.

B & B £20-£26pp, C-Cards VS AE, Dinner from £10, Rooms 2 single, 2 twin, 3 double, 3 family, Restricted smoking, Children welcome, Dogs by arrangement, Open all year

---

THE OLD VICARAGE St Minver, Wadebridge PL27 6QH
Sarah Tyson *Tel:* 01208 862951 *Fax:* 01208 863578
Email: g.tyson@virgin.net

Map Ref: 43
A39, B3314

Georgian vicarage on the edge of a delightful hamlet with views to the fields. 1 1/2 miles from Rock and other sailing and surfing beaches. Wonderful cliff walks. En-suite rooms, one has a four poster Napoleonic bed. Breakfasts include local honey, eggs, bacon and sausages. The Cornish houses of Pencarrow and Llanhydrock also the Eden Project, are easily found. Wadebridge is a few miles.

B & B £25-£30pp, Rooms 2 double (one 4 poster), 1 twin/childrens room, all en-suite, No smoking, Children welcome, Dogs by arrangement, Closed Xmas Day

---

PORTEATH BARN St Minver, Wadebridge PL27 6RA
Michael & Jo Bloor *Tel:* 01208 863605 *Fax:* 01208 863954
Email: mbloor@ukonline.co.uk

Map Ref: 43
B3314

This fine 19th century building stands in eight acres of a peaceful valley, the coast path and Epphaven cove a few minutes down a private track. Accommodation is in a separate wing. An excellent base from which to explore Cornwall and close to beaches, surfing, sailing, fishing, also the Camel Trail and golf courses at St Enodoc and Roserrow. Good eating places nearby.

B & B £22.50-£28pp, Rooms 1 double, 2 twin, Restricted smoking, Children over 12, Dogs by arrangement, Open all year

Cumbria

Consisting of the old counties of Cumberland, Westmorland and a substantial slice of Lancashire, the county of Cumbria is now the second largest of the English counties, containing within its boundaries the Lake District, a region of impressive grandeur. Cumbria attracts vast numbers of visitors at all times of the year to enjoy the climbing, scrambling, sailing, rambling and the joys of the open fells. Magnificent work is done in this area by the National Trust who are responsible for the conservation and management of around a quarter of the Lake District National Park which constitutes about a quarter of the Trust's total holdings in the British Isles.

One of the great delights of the Lake District, is that whatever the season it has its special attractions; spring with its fresh greenery, its snow-capped peaks and of course, Wordsworth's daffodils; summer with its sailing, rambling and lazy days by the lakes; autumn with its richly coloured foliage, its romantic misty scenery; and winter, when the mountains and lakes are seen in their most dramatic garb. The region is undoubtedly popular as a holiday venue but although some of the towns and villages may well be crowded at times, there is space for all who are prepared to take to the many bye-roads and footpaths. The lakes and mountains each have their own particular charm, and one of the great assets of the Lake District is that all this magnificent scenery is packed into a relatively small area

There are sixteen lakes ranging from Windermere, the largest at ten and a half miles in length, to little Brotherswater, only about half a mile long. Windermere is central to the popular holiday pursuits and is alive with activity, such as sailing, water skiing and pleasure boating. However, Ullswater, reached over the steep and winding Kirkstone Pass, is an altogether more peaceful and placid lake. Martindale, consisting of a cluster of valleys, by Ullswater, although only a short distance from the main road is wild and deserted with marvelous views and two interesting churches. By Gowbarrow Park is the lovely Aira Force waterfalls, a highlight of this valley.

The Lake District is undoubtedly Wordsworth country and there must be few corners that have not been lyrically described by the poet and his many writer friends who visited him here. Grasmere in the very centre of the region was his home for some years and Dove Cottage, where

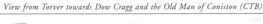

View from Torver towards Dow Cragg and the Old Man of Coniston (CTB)

he and his wife and sister Dorothy lived, is a magnet for William Wordsworth enthusiasts. The poet and members of his family are buried in the beautiful little churchyard in Grasmere, beside one of the most attractive churches in the district. Hawkshead, like Grasmere has close associations with Wordsworth. It was here that the poet attended the grammar school. Another well known resident of this area was Mrs Healis who lived at Near Sawrey. Better known as Beatrix Potter, her home Hill Top Farm attracts huge numbers of visitors each year.

Also nearby is Coniston Water, upon which in 1967 Donald Campbell was killed attempting a new world water speed record. Brantwood, on the eastern shore of the lake was the home of John Ruskin, whose grave in the local churchyard is marked with a fine green slate cross.

No visitor can fail to be enthralled by the history and sheer beauty of the Lake District, but Cumbria has much more to offer, Carlisle is a fine border town with excellent shopping facilities, the ruins of a Norman castle and an impressive cathedral; Kendal, the 'auld grey town' was the home of Henry VIII's sixth wife Catherine Parr and has many interesting museums; Appleby, once the county town of Westmorland is renowned for its June horse fair and gypsy gathering; while Cockermouth in the west was the birthplace of Wordsworth and luckily has not been spoilt by tourism. The far north of the county is rich in the history and folk lore of the border troubles with the south of the county leading conveniently into the glories of the Yorkshire Dales. The western coastline offers wonderful beaches.

PLACES TO VISIT

This is a small selection of interesting places to visit. Many more are listed in our annual guide to Museums, Galleries, Historic Houses & Sites (see page 448)

Carlisle Castle
Carlisle
A medieval fortress where visitors can explore fascinating ancient chambers, stairways, and dungeons and find the legendary 'licking stones'.

Dalemain Historic House & Garden
Penrith
Originally a twelfth century pele tower, the house was continually improved upon, with the Georgian facade added to the Elizabethan part of the house in the eighteenth century. There are three museums within the grounds.

Dove Cottage &
The Wordsworth Museum
Grasmere
The home of William Wordsworth from 1799 to 1808 where visitors are given a guided tour and can view the garden. Opposite is the museum with some of the greatest treasures of the age of Romanticism.

Hill Top
Sawrey, Ambleside
Beatrix Potter wrote many of her famous children's stories in this little seventeenth century stone house. When she died in 1943 she left Hill Top to the National Trust on the proviso that it was kept exactly how she left it, with her own furniture and china.

South Lakes Wild Animal Park
Crossgates, Dalton-in-Furness
The zoo is a world recognised centre for conservation, breeding and education with all of the animals gathered together by the continents they live on.

Cumbria

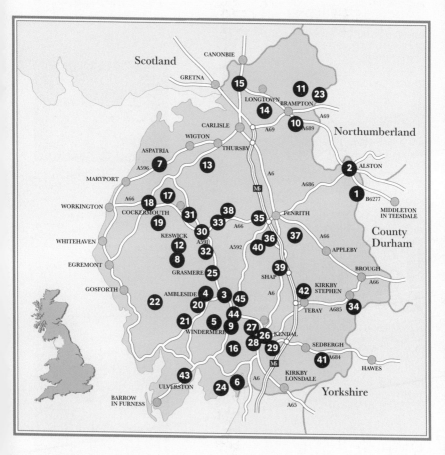

The Red Map References should be used to locate B & B properties on the pages that follow

25

IVY HOUSE Garrigill, Alston CA9 3DU
Mrs Laurie Humble *Tel:* 01434 382501 *Fax:* 01434 382660
Email: ivyhouse@garrigill.com *Web:* www.garrigill.com

Map Ref: 1
B6277

Ivy House is a 17th century farmhouse, recently converted into a very comfortable bed and breakfast. All bedrooms have en-suite facilities, televisions and tea/coffee facilities. Ivy House is situated in the picturesque village of Garrigill, on Alston Moor, amidst the breathtaking scenery of the North Pennines, a designated area of Outstanding Natural Beauty. Llama trekking attraction on-site.

C-Cards MC VS, Rooms 1 single, 2 double, all en-suite, No smoking, Children welcome, Dogs by arrangement, Open all year

BROWNSIDE HOUSE Leadgate, Alston CA9 3EL
Clare Le Marie *Tel:* 01434 382169/382100
Email: brownside_hse@hotmail.com

Map Ref: 2
A686

Alston in the unspoilt north Pennines is central for Lake District and Hadrians Wall. You can always expect a warm welcome at Brownside House which is set in this peaceful countryside with superb views. Relax over an evening meal in our lounge with log fire and television. All rooms have central heating and tea/coffee facilities. Weekly/short break terms.

B & B from £18pp, C-Cards MC VS, Dinner available, Rooms 1 double, 2 twin, No smoking, Children & dogs welcome, Open all year

BROADVIEW GUEST HOUSE Lake Road, Ambleside LA22 0DN
Alan & Sue Clarke *Tel:* 015394 32431
Email: enquiries@broadview-guesthouse.co.uk *Web:* www.broadview-guesthouse.co.uk

Map Ref: 3
M6 J36, A591

Broadview is a quality, friendly guest house situated in Ambleside, midway between the village and Lake Windermere at Waterhead. All rooms have televisions, tea/coffee facilities and alarm clock radios. The area provides excellent walks, some of which start from the door. Packed lunches, flask filling and drying facilities on request. Special breaks available all year.

B & B £18-£25pp, C-Cards MC VS AE, Rooms 3 double, 1 twin, 2 family, most en-suite, No smoking, Open all year

GLENSIDE Old Lake Road, Ambleside LA22 0DP
Tel: 015394 32635
Email: david-janice@glenside22.fsnet.co.uk

Map Ref: 3
M6 J36, A591

18th century farmhouse with old world charm and a offering high standard of accommodation. Ideally situated between the village and lake with walks from the door. Private parking, non-smoking.

B & B from £16pp, Rooms 2 double, 1 twin, No smoking, Children over 5, No dogs, Closed Dec to Jan

LATTENDALES GUEST HOUSE Compston Road, Ambleside LA22 9DJ
Tel: 015394 32368
Email: admin@latts.freeserve.co.uk *Web:* www.latts.freeserve.co.uk

Map Ref: 3
M6 J36, A591

A warm welcome awaits you at our small, friendly guest house. Lattendales is a traditional Victorian Lakeland home, situated close to the centre of Ambleside with views to the rear of Rothay Park and Loughrigg Fell beyond. We are central for walking or touring and offer comfortable en-suite accommodation with full English/vegetarian breakfast. Discounts for multiple nights.

B & B £20-£26pp, C-Cards MC VS, Dinner available, Rooms 2 single, 4 double, most en-suite, No smoking, Children over 10, No dogs, Open all year

2 SWISS VILLAS Vicarage Road, Ambleside LA22 9AE   *Map Ref:* 3
David Sowerbutts *Tel:* 015394 32691   A591
Email: sowerbutts@tinyworld.co.uk

A Victorian terrace house in the centre of Ambleside, near the
church, in an elevated position with access to the cinema, shops
and restaurants in town. Bedrooms have been recently refurbished
in traditional style they are well equipped. A choice of English or
vegetarian breakfast. You are sure of a friendly welcome and good
home cooking. A self catering house is available.

B & B from £21pp, Rooms 2 double, 1 twin, No smoking,
Children over 11, No dogs, Open all year

GREY FRIAR LODGE COUNTRY HOTEL Clappersgate, Ambleside LA22 9NE   *Map Ref:* 4
Pamela & David Veen *Tel / Fax:* 015394 33158   A593
Email: greyfriar@veen.freeserve.co.uk *Web:* www.cumbria-hotels.co.uk

A warm welcome awaits visitors to Pamela and David Veen's country
house. This delightful former vicarage enjoys magnificent views of
the Brathay River and Fells. The house is tastefully furnished with
antiques and bric a brac. Most en-suite bedrooms have antique or
four poster beds. Good traditional cooking is enjoyed by all.

B & B from £29pp, C-Cards MC VS, Dinner from £19.50, Rooms
2 twin, 6 double, all en-suite, No smoking, Children over 12,
No dogs, Closed mid-Dec to mid-Jan

BORWICK LODGE Outgate, Hawkshead, Ambleside LA22 0PU   *Map Ref:* 5
Rosemary & Colin Haskell *Tel / Fax:* 015394 36332   B5286
Email: borwicklodge@talk21.com *Web:* www.borwicklodge.com

Borwick Lodge has award winning accommodation of the highest
standards. A rather special 17th century country house with
magnificent panoramic views. Quietly secluded in the heart of the
Lakes, close to restaurants and inns. Beautiful bedrooms all en-suite
also two four poster king size rooms. Non-smoking. Residential
licence. ETC Silver Award.

B & B £25-£36pp, Rooms 4 double, 1 twin, 1 family, all en-suite,
No smoking, Children over 8, No dogs, Open all year

EES WYKE COUNTRY HOUSE Near Sawrey, Hawkshead, Ambleside LA22 0JZ   *Map Ref:* 5
Margaret & John Williams *Tel / Fax:* 015394 36393   A591, B5285, B5286
Email: eeswyke@aol.com

A fine Georgian country house, once a holiday home to Beatrix
Potter, where John and Margaret Williams create a friendly, relaxed
atmosphere. There are comfortable lounges and a spacious dining
room where delightful five course dinners are served. Most
bedrooms overlook the lake and have televisions, tea/coffee facilities
and hairdryers. Ample parking.

B & B £48-£50pp, Dinner from £15, Rooms 5 double, 3 twin, all
en-suite, Restricted smoking, Children over 8, Dogs not in public
rooms, Closed Jan to Mar

TOWER BANK ARMS Near Sawrey, Hawkshead, Ambleside LA22 0LF   *Map Ref:* 5
Philip James Broadley   B5285
Tel / Fax: 015394 36334

The Tower Bank Arms is known to generations of children as the
small country inn in the 'Tale of Jemima Puddleduck' by Beatrix
Potter our one time neighbour. All rooms are en-suite with colour
television, tea/coffee facilities and central heating. Pets by
arrangement. Bar meals available every day and night as well as
dinner. Ideally situated for walking, fishing and golf.

B & B from £26pp, C-Cards MC VS AE, Dinner from £7.50,
Rooms 1 twin, 2 double, all en-suite, Dogs by arrangement,
Closed Xmas

WEST VALE Far Sawrey, Hawkshead, Ambleside LA22 0LQ
Mrs D Pennington   *Tel:* 015394 42817   *Fax:* 015394 45302
Web: www.westvalecountryhouse.co.uk

Map Ref: 5
B5285

A warm welcome awaits you at this peaceful family-run guest house, with excellent cooking, log fire and fine views. Credit cards accepted.

B & B from £28pp, Dinner available, Rooms 3 double, 2 triple, 1 family, all en-suite, No smoking, Children over 7, No dogs, Open all year

BRACKEN FELL Outgate, Ambleside LA22 0NH
Peter & Anne Hart   *Tel:* 015394 36289
Email: hart.brackenfell@virgin.net   *Web:* www.brackenfell.com

Map Ref: 5
B5286

A delightful residence with 2 acres of gardens, situated in beautiful open countryside between Ambleside and Hawkshead. This comfortable home with its lovely accommodation, is ideally located for exploring the Lake District. Each bedroom has private facilities, TV, hairdryer, complimentary tea and coffee and super view. There is a comfortable lounge, dining room and ample private parking. Two inns within walking distance.

B & B £24-£27pp, Rooms 3 twin, 4 double, all en-suite, No smoking, Children over 9, No dogs, Open all year

WILLOWFIELD The Promenade, Arnside LA5 0AD
Janet & Ian Kerr   *Tel:* 01524 761354
Email: janet@willowfield.net1.co.uk   *Web:* www.willowfield.uk.com

Map Ref: 6
M6 J35a, A6

A relaxing, family-run, small private hotel for non-smokers. Quietly located with stunning estuary views towards the Lakeland hills, particularly from the conservatory dining room and lounge. Good traditional English food (table licence) including hearty breakfasts. Only seven miles from M6 junction 36.

B & B from £26.50pp, C-Cards MC VS, Dinner from £14, Rooms 2 single, 3 double, 3 twin, 2 family, most en-suite, No smoking, Children welcome, Dogs by arrangement, Open all year

AIGLE GILL FARM Aspatria CA7 2PL
Marjorie Bell   *Tel:* 016973 20260
Email: marjoriebell77@hotmail.com

Map Ref: 7
A596, M6

An attractive whitewashed Cumbrian farmhouse comfortable and spacious, visitors are assured of a warm welcome. The rooms are tastefully decorated. An excellent breakfast is served, a perfect start to a day exploring this beautiful part of England. We are situated within easy reach of the Northern lakes, Scottish Borders and the Solway coast. There is plenty of parking for guests' cars.

B & B from £18pp, Rooms 1 single, 1 double en-suite, No smoking, Children welcome, No dogs, Closed Nov to Jan

CASTLEMONT Aspatria CA7 2JU
David & Eleanor Lines   *Tel:* 016973 20205
Email: castlemont@tesco.net

Map Ref: 7
A596

A Victorian family residence set in 2 acres of garden with unrestricted views of the Northern Lakeland fells and Solway Firth. Built of Lazonby stone, Castlemont combines the best of gracious living with all modern facilities and an extensive breakfast menu. Eat well, sleep well and enjoy the Cumbrian experience that is Castlemont.

B & B from £18pp, C-Cards MC VS, Rooms 1 en-suite double, 1 twin, 1 family, No smoking, Children welcome, Open all year

GREENBANK Borrowdale CA12 5UY   *Map Ref:* 8
Jean Wood   *Tel:* 017687 77215   B5289
Email: jeanwwood@lineone.net   *Web:* www.greenbankcountryhousehotel.co.uk

Greenbank is in a quiet location which has superb views and 10 en-
suite bedrooms with tea/coffee facilities. The food, prepared by an
excellent chef, is only one of the comforts which Greenbank offers
including a residential licence, log fires and televison lounge. Highly
recommended as a centre for walking and exploring the Lakes. Car
parking. AA, RAC, ETC 4 Diamonds, Silver Award.

B & B from £30pp, C-Cards MC VS, Dinner from £15, Rooms
1 single, 7 double, 2 twin, 1 family, all en-suite, Restricted
smoking, Children over 2, No dogs, Closed Jan

HAZEL BANK COUNTRY HOUSE Rosthwaite, Borrowdale CA12 5XB   *Map Ref:* 8
Glen & Brenda Davies   *Tel:* 017687 77248   *Fax:* 017687 77373   M6, A66, B5289
Email: enquiries@hazelbankhotel.co.uk   *Web:* www.hazelbankhotel.co.uk

A Victorian residence renovated to create quality accommodation
with comfort to ensure a special stay. The house stands in four acres
in a lovely valley with Scafell Pike and Great Gable in walking
distance. All rooms are en-suite, boasting wonderful views of the
fells and the central Lakeland Peaks. Imaginatively presented
traditional dinners, using finest local ingredients. Gold Award and
Best in Cumbria 2001.

Dinner B & B from £50pp, C-Cards MC VS, Rooms 5 double,
3 twin, all en-suite, No smoking, No children or dogs, Open all year

BOWFELL COTTAGE Middle Entrance Drive, Storrs Park, Bowness-on-Windermere LA23 3JY
J & A Tomlinson   *Map Ref:* 9
Tel: 015394 44835   A5074

Traditional Lakeland cottage set in tranquil evergreen gardens, one
mile south of Bowness Bay. The long standing resident owners
specialise in good home cooking and a homely atmosphere with well
appointed accommodation. Conveniently situated for all local
activities and touring. Excellent secluded parking. An ideal position
for a restful holiday or quiet weekend in peaceful surroundings.

B & B from £20pp, Dinner available, Rooms 1 double en-suite,
1 twin, 1 triple, Restricted smoking, Children & dogs welcome,
Open all year

THE FAIRFIELD Brantfell Road, Bowness-on-Windermere LA23 3AE   *Map Ref:* 9
Ray & Barbara Hood   *Tel / Fax:* 015394 46565   A591
Email: Ray&barb@the-fairfield.co.uk   *Web:* www.the-fairfield.co.uk

A small, friendly 200 year old Lakeland hotel set in a peaceful garden
setting. The Fairfield is close to Bowness village and Lake
Windermere. The en-suite bedrooms are tastefully furnished, they
have colour TV, welcome trays and toiletries. There is a residents'
lounge with a bar. Breakfasts are a speciality. Leisure facilities are
available. On site parking.

B & B from £26pp, C-Cards MC VS, Rooms 1 single, 1 twin,
5 double, 2 family, all en-suite, No smoking, Children welcome,
No dogs, Closed Dec to Jan

LANGDALE VIEW GUEST HOUSE 114 Craig Walk, off Helm Road, Bowness-on-Windermere LA23
3AX   *Map Ref:* 9
Tel: 015394 44076   A591, A592

Langdale View is a quiet guest house with a friendly atmosphere. All
of the rooms are en-suite, some with lovely views. Very hospitable,
will collect guests from the station if need be and also provide
delicious home cooking. Non smoking.

B & B from £18pp, Dinner available, Rooms 1 single, 3 double,
1 twin, all en-suite, No smoking, Children over 5, No dogs, Open
all year

LAUREL COTTAGE St Martins Square, Kendal Road, Bowness-on-Windermere LA23 3EF   *Map Ref:* 9
John & Syma   *Tel / Fax:* 015394 45594   A591, A592
Email: enquiries@laurelcottage-bnb.co.uk   *Web:* www.laurelcottage-bnb.co.uk

Laurel Cottage is a charming 17th century cottage situated one minute from Lake Windermere. All rooms have colour televisions, central heating and tea/coffee facilities. There is a separate guests' dining room and television lounge with a car parking space for every room. Close to shops, pubs, restaurants and all local attractions nearby. Leisure club facilites.

B & B £20-£34pp, C-Cards MC VS, Rooms 2 single, 6 double, 2 four poster, 2 twin, 2 family, No smoking, Children welcome, No dogs, Open all year

---

LOWFELL COUNTRY HOUSE Ferney Green, Bowness-on-Windermere LA23 3ES   *Map Ref:* 9
Stephen & Louise Broughton   *Tel:* 015394 45612   *Fax:* 015394 48411   A591, A5074
Email: lowfell@talk21.com   *Web:* www.low-fell.co.uk

A 19th century gentleman's residence, this lovely Lakeland house five minutes from Windermere sits in an acre of wooded garden, offering a warm welcome, comfort and good food. Delicious breakfasts, either English, fish, omelettes or aga pancakes. On the second floor a 'hideaway' of two adjoining bedrooms has sloping ceilings and treetop views. Log fires and cosy sofas complement the comfort here.

B & B £26-£30pp, C-Cards MC, Rooms 1 twin/double, 1 family both en-suite, No smoking, Children welcome, No dogs, Closed Xmas & New Year

---

MELBOURNE GUEST HOUSE 2-3 Biskey Howe Road, Bowness-on-Windermere LA23 2JP
         Map Ref: 9
Tel: 015394 43475   A591, A592

Well positioned for walking or touring, a warm welcome awaits at our small friendly family run guest house close to the centre of Bowness-on-Windermere, lake and eating places.

B & B from £18.50pp, Rooms 1 single, 5 double, 1 triple, 1 family, most en-suite, No smoking, Children welcome, Open all year

---

STORRS GATE HOUSE Longtail Hill, Bowness-on-Windermere LA23 3JD   *Map Ref:* 9
Vince & Shirley Byrne   *Tel:* 015394 43272   A592, B5284
Email: enquiries@storrsgatehouse.co.uk   *Web:* www.storrsgatehouse.co.uk

Delightful, detached 19th century quality country guest house, in secluded gardens, only minutes from Lake Windermere. Fully en-suite rooms with colour televisions, clock/radio alarms and tea/coffee facilities, plus a king-size four poster. Excellent home cooking using local produce and hearty breakfasts feature homemade jams, marmalades, free range eggs and cumberland sausages. Log fires and ample parking. ETC 4 Diamonds.

B & B £21-£32pp, C-Cards MC VS, Dinner from £15, Rooms 2 double, 1 twin, 1 family, all en-suite/private facilities, No smoking, Children over 8, No dogs, Open all year

---

BLACKSMITHS ARMS Talkin Village, Brampton CA8 1LE   *Map Ref:* 10
         A66
Tel: 016977 3452   *Fax:* 016977 3396

Blacksmiths Arms is a country inn in scenic countryside half a mile from Talkin Tarn. Good walks, golf, sailing, wind surfing, fishing, Hadrian's Wall and Lake District are all within easy reach.

B & B from £22.50pp, Dinner available, Rooms 3 double, 2 twin, all en-suite, No smoking in bedrooms, Children welcome, No dogs, Open all year

COURTYARD COTTAGES Warren Bank, Station Road, Brampton CA8 1EX
Janet Hempstead *Tel:* 016977 41818 *Fax:* 016977 41398
Email: hempstead@warrenbank.demon.go.uk

Map Ref: 10
M0 A89

Perfect for a romantic weekend, a break or a stopover. Relax and be pampered. Accommodation is in one of two luxury en-suite bedrooms in a beautiful courtyard cottage of a Victorian mansion built in 1863 by the Earl of Carlisle and stands in three acres of grounds. Breakfast cooked on an Aga is served in your room providing total independence and privacy.

B & B £25-£35pp, Rooms 2 double en-suite, No smoking, No children or dogs, Closed Xmas & New Year

---

HULLERBANK Talkin, Brampton CA8 1LB
Mrs Sheila Stobbart *Tel / Fax:* 01697 746668
Email: info@hullerbank.freeserve.co.uk *Web:* www.smoothhound.co.uk/hotels/huller.html

Map Ref: 10
A66

Centrally situated for Hadrian's Wall, Scotland and Lake District. Hullerbank is an attractive pink washed farmhouse dated 1635-1751. Adjoining the house we have 14 acres of pasture on which we keep pedigree sheep. Our three bedrooms all have private facilities, colour televisions, tea/coffee facilities and electric underblankets. Nine miles from Carlisle J43 M6 and three miles from Brampton.

B & B £23.50-£24pp, C-Cards MC VS, Rooms 1 double with private bathroom, 2 twin en-suite, No smoking, Children over 12, No dogs, Closed Dec to Feb

---

CRACROP FARM Kirkcambeck, Brampton CA8 2BW
Marjorie Stobart *Tel:* 016977 48245 *Fax:* 016977 48333
Email: cracrop@aol.com

Map Ref: 11
M6, B6318

For a special holiday, Cracrop Farm is an excellent choice. A spacious farmhouse sits in a lovely garden on a working farm with breathtaking views. En-suite guest rooms well furnished with TV, central heating and hospitality trays. Delicious breakfasts. Guests can relax in sauna or spa bath or exercise in gym. Wonderful places to visit, Hadrian's Wall, Scottish Borders, Carlisle, Lake District.

B & B from £25pp, Rooms 1 single, 1 twin, 2 double, all en-suite, No smoking, Children over 12, No dogs, Closed Xmas

---

WOOD HOUSE Buttermere CA13 9XA
Michael & Judy McKenzie *Tel:* 017687 70208 *Fax:* 017687 70241
Web: www.wdhse.co.uk

Map Ref: 12
B5289

The view overlooking Wood House was chosen by JMW Turner RA for his famous painting of Buttermere in 1798. An inspector from a well-known publication recently wrote, 'the furnishings and decor are serene and beautiful though completely unpretentious. The bedrooms reach similarly high standards and enjoy lovely views.'

B & B from £35pp, Dinner from £19.50, Rooms 1 double, 2 twin, all en-suite, No smoking, Children over 16, No dogs, Closed Mid-Nov to mid-Feb

---

SWALEDALE WATCH Whelpo, Caldbeck CA7 8HQ
Arnold & Nan Savage *Tel / Fax:* 016974 78409
Email: nan.savage@talk21.com

Map Ref: 13
on B5299

Swaledale Watch is a 300 acre working farm. Enjoy great comfort, delicious food, beautiful surroundings and peaceful countryside. Central for touring, walking or discovering the rolling Northern fells. All rooms have private facilities, are tastefully decorated, have colour television, radio, tea-tray, clean fluffy towels daily and books for every interest. Walk into Caldbeck via the Howk, a wooded limestone gorge.

B & B £18-£21pp, Dinner available, Rooms 2 double, 2 triple, all en-suite, No smoking, Children welcome, No dogs, Closed over Xmas

NEW PALLYARDS Hethersgill, Carlisle CA6 6HZ   *Map Ref:* 14
John & Georgina Elwen   *Tel / Fax:* 01228 577308   A7
Email: info@newpallyards.freeserve.co.uk   *Web:* www.newpallyards.freeserve.co.uk

New Pallyards is a 65 acre mixed farm. Warmth and hospitality await you in this 18th century award winning modernised farmhouse. Dinners are available every evening by arrangement. Well placed for visiting Hadrian's Wall, also the Northern Lakes and Kielder water and forest. Country setting, easily accessible from M6, A7, M74. En-suite rooms, some ground floor rooms available.

B & B £22-£24pp, C-Cards MC VS, Dinner from £13, Rooms 2 twins, 3 double, 1 family, all en-suite, Restricted smoking, Children welcome, Dogs by arrangement, Open all year

BESSIESTOWN FARM COUNTRY GUEST HOUSE Catlowdy, Longtown, Carlisle CA6 5QP
Jack & Margaret Sisson   *Tel:* 01228 577219   *Fax:* 01228 577019   *Map Ref:* 15
Email: Bestbb2001@cs.com   *Web:* www.bessiestown.co.uk   A7, B6318

A lovely farm guest house offering a special comfort in a relaxed atmosphere. Delightfully decorated public rooms and pretty, en-suite bedrooms with TV, radio and hostess tray. Delicious home cooking using fresh produce. Residential licence. Stop off for England, Scotland and Northern Ireland. Indoor heated swimming pool open from May to September. Honeymoon suite. Family accommodation in comfortable courtyard cottages.

B & B from £26.50pp, Dinner from £13.50, Rooms 2 double, 1 family, 1 twin, also 3 Cottages, No smoking, Open all year

LIGHTWOOD FARMHOUSE COUNTRY GUEST HOUSE Cartmel Fell LA11 6NP   *Map Ref:* 16
Evelyn Cervetti   *Tel /* Fax: 015395 31454   A592
Email: enquiries@lightwoodguesthouse.co.uk   *Web:* www.lightwoodguesthouse.co.uk

This charming 17th century farmhouse retaining original oak beams and staircase, stands in 2 acres of gardens with unspoilt countryside views. 2 1/2 miles from the southern end of Lake Windermere. Excellent fell walking. All rooms are en-suite, tastefully decorated and furnished with central heating, tea/coffee making facilities, some with TV. Cosy lounge, log fire and TV. Good home cooking with home grown produce.

B & B from £24pp, C-Cards MC VS, Dinner from £14, Rooms 2 double, 2 twin, 2 family, all en-suite, Restricted smoking, Children welcome, No dogs, Closed Xmas

LAKESIDE Dubwath, Bassenthwaite Lake, Cockermouth CA13 9YD   *Map Ref:* 17
Steven Semple   A66
Tel: 017687 76358   *Fax:* 01768 776163

This elegant Edwardian double fronted house with oak floors and a panelled entrance hall, stands in its own garden overlooking Bassenthwaite Lake. All the bedrooms have en-suite facilities with tea/coffee making facilities and TV. The pleasant lounge overlooks the lake. There is a private car park and parking in the grounds. Keswick and Cumberland are a short drive away.

B & B £21-£23pp, Rooms 6 double, 2 twin, most en-suite, No smoking, Children welcome, No dogs, Open all year

LINK HOUSE Bassenthwaite Lake, Cockermouth CA13 9YD   *Map Ref:* 17
George & Isobel Kerr   *Tel:* 017687 76291   *Fax:* 017687 76670   A66
Email: linkhouse@lineone.net   *Web:* www.link-house.co.uk

A warm, friendly, family run, late Victorian country house set in a quieter part of the Lake District National Park at the northern end of Lake Bassenthwaite, with stunning views of the surrounding forests and Fells. All the attractive bedrooms have en-suite facilities, colour TV and tea/coffee making facilities. There is a conservatory bar, lounge and private car park exclusively for guests.

B & B £27-£29pp, C-Cards MC VS AE, Dinner from £15, Rooms 2 single, 3 double, 2 twin, 1 family, all en-suite, Restricted smoking, Children over 7, Dogs by arrangement, Open all year

LAMBFOOT HOUSE Embleton, Cockermouth CA13 9XL
Paul & Heather Taylor *Tel:* 017687 76424
Email: lambfoot@bushinternet.com

Map Ref: 17
A66

Rooms equipped to luxury hotel standard. All en-suite with romantic lighting, television and tea/coffee facilities with views over Fells. Separate dining room for guests with antique furniture. Garden and secure parking for guests. Friendly family establishment inside National Park and near a main road

B & B from £24pp, Rooms 1 single, 1 double, both en-suite, No smoking, Children welcome, No dogs, Open all year

SUNDAWN Carlisle Road, Bridekirk, Cockermouth CA13 0PA
Pauline & Bob Hodge *Tel:* 01900 822384 *Fax:* 01900 822885 *Mobile:* 07767 767122
Email: robert.hodge1@virgin.net *Web:* www.sundawn-guesthouse.co.uk

Map Ref: 18
A595

Sundawn is a large Victorian family home with tastefully decorated spacious rooms. Tourists and business travellers alike are welcome. The emphasis is on comfort and relaxation. From the conservatory, view the panorama of Lakeland Fells and the historic town of Cockermouth, birthplace of William Wordsworth. A scenic drive will take you into the heart of the Lake District.

B & B £17.50-£20pp, Rooms 1 double en-suite, 1 twin, 1 family en-suite, No smoking, Children welcome, No dogs, Closed mid-Dec to mid-Jan

NEW HOUSE FARM Buttermere Valley, Lorton, Cockermouth CA13 9UU
Hazel Thompson Tel / Fax: 01900 85404
Email: hazel@newhouse-farm.co.uk *Web:* www.newhouse-farm.co.uk

Map Ref: 19
B5289

This is the real Lake District without the crowds. With superb views from every window, New House Farm offers en-suite bedrooms, two lounges, a cosy dining room and original open fires. Delicious five course evening meals are served and hearty breakfasts enjoyed in the morning. Simply the best place to relax and unwind! WHICH? Cumbrian Hotel of the Year award winner.

B & B from £40pp, C-Cards MC VS AE, Dinner from £22, Rooms 2 twin, 3 double, all en-suite, No smoking, Children over 6, Dogs by arrangement, Open all year

TODDELL COTTAGE Brandlingill, Cockermouth CA13 0RB
Janet & Mike Wright Tel / Fax: 01900 828696 *Mobile:* 07787 856065
Email: toddell@waitrose.com *Web:* www.eden-bandb.co.uk

Map Ref: 19
A66

Toddell Cottage is a listed building of over 300 years and was originally a Cumbrian longhouse. Over the last 20 years it has been converted to modern standards without upsetting the balance of the delightfully beamed rooms. The breakfast table overflows with different ideas and has been nominated for an excellence award by the AA and dinner is a three course treat.

B & B £28-£30pp, Dinner from £16.50, Rooms 1 single, 1 double en-suite, 1 family en-suite, No smoking, Children over 5, No dogs, Closed Xmas & New Year

ARROWFIELD COUNTRY GUEST HOUSE Little Arrow, Coniston LA21 8AU
Stephanie & Malcolm Walton
Tel: 015394 41741

Map Ref: 20
A593

Elegant Victorian house with beautiful views of surrounding countryside, set in a peaceful location two miles from Coniston. Televisions, radios and tea/coffee facilities in all rooms with a spacious guest lounge. Delicious breakfast, served with homemade bread, preserves, honey and eggs from our free-range chickens. Immediate access to fells and various places nearby for eating in the evenings. Ample private parking.

B & B £23-£26pp, Rooms 1 single, 3 double, 1 twin, all en-suite, No smoking, Children welcome, No dogs, Closed Nov to Mar

WILSON ARMS Torver, Coniston LA21 8BB   *Map Ref:* 21
                                                                 A593

Tel: 015394 41237   *Fax:* 015394 41590

Wilson Arms is situated in the small village of Torver, three miles from Coniston. It is an ideal walking area in a good central location for touring the Lakes. The chef prepares meals with local fresh produce and keeps a well stocked bar and log fire on cooler days. Surrounded by beautiful fells.

B & B from £27pp, Dinner available, Rooms 4 double, 1 twin, 1 triple, 1 family, most en-suite, No smoking, Children welcome, No dogs, Open all year

THE BURNMOOR INN Boot, Eskdale CA19 1TG   *Map Ref:* 22
Harry & Paddington Berger *Tel:* 019467 23224 *Fax:* 019467 23337   A595
Email: stay@burnmoor.co.uk *Web:* www.burnmoor.co.uk

A warm 400 year old inn with en-suite comfort and good food in bar and restaurant (served all day). The resident proprietors Harry and Paddington Berger are also able to offer a two bedroom self catering cottage. Dogs are welcome in both the flat and cottage.

B & B from £27pp, Dinner available, Rooms 1 single, 3 double, 3 twin, 2 triple, all en-suite, No smoking, Children welcome, Open all year

BUSH NOOK Upper Denton, Gilsand CA8 7AF   *Map Ref:* 23
Paul & Judith Barton *Tel:* 016977 47194 *Fax:* 016977 47790   A69
Email: PaulAlBarton@bushnook.freeserve.co.uk *Web:* www.hadriansway.co.uk

Close to Hadrian's Wall, the North Pennines and Northumberland National Park, Bush Nook is ideally situated to explore this countryside. Visitors here can relax and enjoy traditional home cooking. English breakfast is served, and a four course dinner is available in our licensed dining room. TV, hairdryer and drink making facilities are provided. Warm hospitality awaits you at Bush Nook.

B & B from £18pp, Dinner from £10, Rooms 1 single, 1 twin, 2 double, most en-suite, No smoking, Children welcome, Dogs by arrangement, Open all year

GREENACRES COUNTRY GUEST HOUSE Lindale, Grange-over-Sands LA11 6LP   *Map Ref:* 24
Barbara & Ray Pettit   A590
Tel / Fax: 015395 34578

Greenacres is a 19th century cottage in the National Park village of Lindale, two miles from Grange over Sands and six miles from the shores of Lake Windermere. Greenacres provides luxury bedrooms, en-suite facilities and thoughtful extras including a lovely conservatory and cosy lounge with log fire. No smoking. Diets catered for. Golf courses nearby.

B & B from £25pp, Rooms 2 double, 1 twin, 1 family, all en-suite, No smoking, Children welcome, No dogs, Closed Xmas & New Year

MAYFIELDS 3 Mayfield Terrace, Kents Bank Road, Grange-over-Sands LA11 7DW   *Map Ref:* 24
Kate & Michael Thorburn   M6, A590
Tel: 015395 34730

Mayfields is externely well appointed, on the fringe of Grange-over-Sands, with a small forecourt garden and parking for three cars. The bedrooms have tea/coffee facilities, televisions, videos and hairdryers. Mayfields is highly recommended for excellent home cooking and there is a very pleasant lounge with a television and a fine piano. Sorry no smoking in the house, table licence.

B & B from £25pp, Dinner from £12, Rooms 1 single with pb, 1 double en-suite, 1 twin en-suite, No smoking, Children welcome, No dogs, Closed Xmas & New Year

RIVERSDALE Grasmere LA22 9RQ
Mariea & Chris Cook *Tel:* 015394 35619
Email: mariea.cook@tinyworld.co.uk *Web:* www.riversdalegrasmere.co.uk

Map Ref: 25
B5287 from A591

Quietly situated on the edge of the village, Riversdale is a typical Lakeland house, which was built in 1830, it overlooks the River Rothay, and enjoys lovely views. There is a lounge where guests may relax, and a delightful dining room where candlelit dinner is available. Grasmere is steeped in history and a favourite location for walkers and artists and explorers.

B & B £25-£30pp, Dinner £15, Rooms 2 double with en-suite shower, 1 twin with private bathroom, No smoking, No children or dogs, Open all year

RYELANDS Grasmere LA22 9SU
Lyn & John Kirkbride *Tel / Fax:* 015394 35076
Email: kirkbride.ryelands@virgin.net *Web:* www.ryelandsgrasmere.co.uk

Map Ref: 25
A591

A delightful Victorian house standing in peaceful gardens on the edge of a beautiful village. Your friendly hosts have restored their home to create elegant and comfortable rooms for guests, the perfect retreat from which to enjoy the Lake District. Walk from the house into the countryside, relax as you row round the Lake or make a pilgrimage to Wordsworth's Homes. Brochure available.

B & B £30-£35pp, Rooms 3 double, all en-suite, No smoking, Children over 10, No dogs, Closed Nov to mid-March

FAIRWAYS GUEST HOUSE 102 Windermere Road, Kendal LA9 5EZ
Eric & Mavis Paylor *Tel:* 01539 725564
Email: mp@fairwaysl.fsnet.co.uk

Map Ref: 26
M6 J37, A684

A Victorian guesthouse with a homely atmosphere and lovely views. All the rooms are en-suite and have tea/coffee facilities and a television, there is also one four poster bedroom. Within easy reach of the Lake District, Kendal town and the golf course.

B & B £18-£20pp, Rooms 3 double, 1 twin, 1 family, all en-suite, No smoking, Children welcome, No dogs, Open all year

GARNETT HOUSE FARM Burneside, Kendal LA9 5SF
Mrs Sylvia Beaty
Tel: 01539 724542

Map Ref: 27
A591

A 15th century farmhouse on a large dairy/sheep farm in lovely countryside off A591, only 10 minutes from Windermere. All bedrooms are en-suite, twin, double or family, they have TV, radio, tea/coffee facilities. Oak-panelled lounge, beams, an old spice cupboard and 4ft thick walls enhance the character here. Good parking. Lovely views and walks. 3 night breaks November to March.

B & B from £19pp, Rooms 5 double/family, 5 en-suite, No smoking, No dogs, Closed Xmas

CROOK HALL Crook, Kendal LA8 8LF
Pat Metcalfe
Tel / Fax: 01539 821352

Map Ref: 27
A684, M6

A warm welcome awaits guests here at this quietly situated Organic dairy sheep and water buffalo farm between Kendal and Windermere. This spacious historic farmhouse dates from the 15th century and was a favourite haunt of William Wordsworth. The rooms are elegantly furnished with ancient oak panelling in the lounge. Spectacular scenery abounds with good walking areas.

B & B from £18pp, Rooms 2 double, 1 family en-suite, No smoking, Children welcome, No dogs, Closed Dec to Apr

TARN HOUSE　18 Danes Road, Staveley, Kendal LA8 9PW
Mrs J Porter
Tel: 01539 821656　*Mobile:* 07771 516156

Map Ref: 27
A591

Tarn House is situated in a rural setting and within walking distance of the village amenities and local pubs which serve excellent bar meals. In the heart of the Lake District with all the major lakes within a short car journey. Each of our bedrooms are individually furnished and offer tea/coffee facilities, hairdryers and trouser presses. ETB 4 Diamonds.

B & B from £17pp, Rooms 3 double, 2 twin, 1 family, No smoking, Children over 10, No dogs, Closed December to February

CROSTHWAITE HOUSE　Crosthwaite, Kendal LA8 8BP
Robin & Marnie Dawson　*Tel / Fax:* 015395 68264
Email: robin@crosthwaitehouse.co.uk　*Web:* www.crosthwaitehouse.co.uk

Map Ref: 28
A5074

Mid 18th century building with unspoilt views of the Lyth and Winster valleys, only five miles from Bowness and Kendal. There is always a family atmosphere and good home cooking. Self-catering cottages are also available.

B & B from £22pp, Dinner available, Rooms 1 single, 3 double, 2 twin, all en-suite, No smoking, Children & dogs welcome, Closed Nov to Feb

TRANTHWAITE HALL　Underbarrow, Kendal LA8 8HG
Mrs D M Swindlehurst　*Tel:* 015395 68285
Email: tranthwaitehall@hotmail.com

Map Ref: 28
M6, A6

11th century magnificent farmhouse with beautiful beams, doors and a rare antique black iron range, is tastefully modernised with full central heating. Pretty, en-suite bedrooms are well equipped and have attractive fabrics and furnishings. This dairy/sheep farm is set in an unspoilt lane in a picturesque village between Kendal and Windermere, where flowers, deer and other wildlife can be seen. Good local pubs.

B & B from £23pp, Rooms 2 double, 1 twin, 1 family room, No smoking, Open all year

HIGHER HOUSE FARM　Oxenholme Lane, Natland, Kendal LA9 7QH
Valerie Sunter
Tel: 015395 61177　*Fax:* 015395 61520

Map Ref: 29
M6 J36, A6070

Higher House Farm is a 17th century beamed farmhouse situated in the tranquil village of Natland, one mile south of Kendal. Ideal for visiting the Lake District and Yorkshire Dales. Welcoming central heated guest house where all rooms are en-suite with colour televisions, tea/coffee facilities and delightful four poster. Delicious breakfasts. Top Twenty Landlady 1997/1999.

B & B £24.50-£29.50pp, Rooms 2 double, 1 twin, all en-suite, No smoking, Children over 12, Dogs by arrangement, Closed Xmas

CRAGG FARM　New Hutton, Kendal LA8 0BA
Olive Knowles　*Tel / Fax:* 01539 721760
Email: knowles.cragg@ukgateway.net　*Web:* www.cragg-farm.sagenet.co.uk

Map Ref: 29
A684

Cragg Farm is a charming 17th century farmhouse dated 1661, situated in a quiet picturesque corner of the Lake District, four miles from Kendal and three miles to M6 junction 37. Bedrooms have tea/coffee facilities and bathroom and there is a guest lounge with television. Ample parking. Full English breakfast. Ideal for touring the Lakes and Yorkshire Dales or a peaceful stop-over to/from Scotland.

B & B £17-£19pp, Rooms 1 single, 1 double, 1 family, Restricted smoking, Children welcome, Dogs by arrangement, Closed Dec to Feb

BLAVEN HOMESTAY Middleshaw, Old Hutton, Kendal LA8 0LZ   *Map Ref:* 29
Ms Janet Kaye   *Tel:* 01539 734894   *Fax:* 01539 727447   *Mobile:* 07801 796239   B6254
Email: jb@greenarrow.demon.co.uk   *Web:* www.blavenhomestay.co.uk

Award winning, 5 Diamond, Blaven is peacefully located beside a
pretty Lakeland trout stream in the medieval village of Old Hutton.
Convenient for the M6 and touring the Lakes and Dales. This lovely
Cumbrian house, in a recently converted barn, is seriously
comfortable and beautifully appointed with blazing log fires in winter
and streamside sun patio in the summer. Outstanding cooking (2
Dining Ribbons RAC).

B & B £28.50-£32.50pp, C-Cards MC VS, Dinner from £17.50,
Rooms 1 double, 1 family, all en-suite, No smoking, Children over
10, Dogs by arrangement, Open all year

THE ANCHORAGE 14 Ambleside Road, Keswick CA12 4DL   *Map Ref:* 30
James Brian and Iris Elener   *Tel:* 017687 72813   A66, A591
Email: anchorage.keswick@btopenworld.com

The Ancorage is a comfortable house, serving good home cooking,
with owners who make every effort to please. All of the rooms are
en-suite and car parking is available. Close to Lake and Parks, only
five minutes' walk to the town centre.

B & B from £21pp, Dinner available, Rooms 1 single, 3 double,
2 triple, Children over 5, No dogs, Closed Xmas

BERKELEY GUEST HOUSE The Heads, Keswick CA12 5ER   *Map Ref:* 30
Dennis & Barbara Crompton   *Tel:* 017687 74222   A66, A591
Email: berkeley@tesco.net   *Web:* www.berkeley-keswick.com

Berkeley Guest House is located on a quiet road overlooking
Borrowdale Valley to the front and Skiddaw Mountain to the rear.
Each comfortable room has splendid mountain views and good
facilities. Excellent breakfast choice. Close to the town centre and
lake. ETB 4 diamonds.'Which' B&B guide recommended.

B & B £18-£26pp, Rooms 1 single, 3 double, 1 triple, No smoking,
Children welcome, No dogs, Closed Xmas and Boxing day

CLAREMONT HOUSE Chestnut Hill, Keswick CA12 4LT   *Map Ref:* 30
Jackie & Peter Werfel   *Tel / Fax:* 017687 72089   A66, A591
Email: claremonthouse@btinternet.com   *Web:* www.claremonthousekeswick.co.uk

Claremont House was built about 150 years ago as a lodge house
to the Fieldside Estate. Jackie and Peter Werfel now offer you fine
bed and breakfast accommodation in pleasant surroundings.
Breakfast is served in an informal manner and all tastes are catered
for. It is an ideal base for exploring the Lake District which offers a
wide variety of leisure pursuits.

B & B £24-£27pp, Rooms 3 double, 1 twin, all en-suite,
No smoking, Children over 12, No dogs, Closed Jan to Easter

CRAGLANDS Penrith Road, Keswick CA12 4LJ   *Map Ref:* 30
Tel: 017687 74406   A66, A591
Email: keswick@craglands.freeserve.co.uk

Craglands is a charming Victorian house only 10 minutes from
Keswick town centre. All rooms are en-suite with views towards
Grisedale Pike and Latrigg. Ideally situated for walking and cycling
and close to historic stone circle. There is private parking and cycle
storage. Non-smoking. AA 4 Diamonds.

B & B £19-£25pp, Dinner available, Rooms 4 double, 1 twin,
all en-suite, No smoking, Children over 6, No dogs, Open all year

EDWARDENE HOTEL 26 Southey Street, Keswick CA12 4EF
Margaret & Derick Holman   *Tel:* 017687 73586   *Fax:* 017687 73824
Email: info@edwardenehotel.com   *Web:* www.edwardenehotel.com

Map Ref: 30
A66, A591

Close to the town centre of Keswick yet quietly situated, this 115 year old hotel is admired for its architecture. Stylishly decorated and full of character, there is a wonderfully restful lounge, overlooking Walla Crag, delightfully furnished en-suite rooms and other restaurants closeby. The Edwardene is a licensed hotel which caters happily for all dietary needs. Keswick is excellent for in and outdoor entertainment.

B & B from £28pp, C-Cards MC VS AE, Dinner from £13, Rooms 2 single, 6 double, 2 twin, 1 family, all en-suite, No smoking, No dogs, Open all year

---

GRANGE COUNTRY HOUSE Manor Brow, Keswick CA12 4BA
Duncan & Jane Miller   *Tel / Fax:* 017687 72500
Email: duncan.miller@btconnect.com

Map Ref: 30
A66, A591

A stroll from the Lake District town of Keswick, stands the elegant Grange Country House, which overlooks Keswick-on-Derwentwater and the Fells. Your hosts Duncan and Jane Miller take much care to ensure that visitors receive professional service, coupled with quality and style in a relaxed atmosphere. Breakfasts are full of variety, a perfect start to a day exploring the beauty of the Lake District.

B & B £28-£37.50pp, C-Cards MC VS, Rooms 7 double, 3 twin, all en-suite, No smoking, Children over 7, No dogs, Closed mid Nov to mid Feb

---

HONISTER HOUSE 1 Borrowdale Road, Keswick CA12 5DD
Sue & Phil Harrison   *Tel:* 017687 73181   *Fax:* 0870 120 2948
Email: philandsueh@aol.com   *Web:* www.honisterhouse.co.uk

Map Ref: 30
A66, A591

A warm welcome awaits you at our 18th century home. Four diamonds with sparkling and warm welcome awards. Centrally located close to all local amenities. Especially catering for walkers, cyclists and families. Televisions, tea/coffee making facilities with fresh coffee, hot chocolate and biscuits. Large Cumbrian or vegetarian breakfast. Car parking. Real fire. Discounts available. Send for brochure.

B & B £18-£30pp, Rooms 3 double, 2 twin, 2 family, all en-suite/private facilities, No smoking, Children welcome, No dogs, Open all year

---

RAVENSWORTH HOTEL 29 Station Street, Keswick CA12 5HH
Tony & Tina Russ   *Tel:* 017687 72476   *Fax:* 017687 75287
Email: info@ravensworth-hotel.co.uk   *Web:* www.ravensworth-hotel.co.uk

Map Ref: 30
A66, A591

The Ravensworth Hotel is ideally situated near the town centre and all its amenities. The lake and lower fells are a short walk away. Rooms are tastefully furnished they are well equipped with en-suite facilities, TV and beverage tray. The day starts with a wholesome breakfast, then enjoy the lakes by day, relax in our splendid lounge or Herdwick Bar in the evening.

B & B from £25pp, C-Cards MC VS AE, Rooms 5 double, 2 twin, 1 family, all en-suite, No smoking, Children welcome, No dogs, Closed Jan

---

SHEMARA GUEST HOUSE 27 Bank Street, Keswick CA12 5JZ
Richard & Jackie Atkinson
Tel: 017687 73936

Map Ref: 30
A66, A591

A friendly welcome awaits you at our quiet homely guest house, close to the town centre. All rooms are furnished to a high standard and have colour televisions, tea/coffee facilities, central heating, mountain views and those little extras. Excellent Cumberland or continental breakfasts. Some private parking. ETB & RAC 4 Diamonds.

B & B from £21pp, Rooms 2 twin, 6 double, 1 family, all en-suite, No smoking, Children over 2, Dogs by arrangement, Closed Xmas

THORNLEIGH 23 Bank Street, Keswick CA12 5JZ
Jill & Graham Green *Tel:* 017687 72863
Email: thornleigh@btinternet.com *Web:* www.btinternet.com/~thornleigh

Map Ref: 30
A66, A591

A traditional Lakeland house in the town of Keswick. Well equipped en-suite bedrooms are mainly situated at the rear of the building, free from most traffic sounds, wonderful views over mountains and fells. An idyllic base for walking or touring the Northern Lakes. Your hosts offer a warm welcome and advice on touring the area. A delicious English or Continental breakfast is offered.

B & B from £19pp, C-Cards, Rooms 5 double, 1 twin, all en-suite, Restricted smoking, Children over 5, No dogs, Open all year

---

WILLOW COTTAGE Bassenthwaite, Keswick CA12 4QP
Roy & Chris Beaty
Tel: 017687 76440

Map Ref: 31
A591

A warm welcome in a peaceful atmosphere awaits you at our tastefully converted lakeland barn. Relax by the wood burner or in our cottage garden with views towards Skiddaw Mountain. Breakfast on free-range eggs, homemade bread and preserves. Wild flower hedgerows, ducks by stream, 'country living.' Self catering also available. Come when you can and leave when you must.

B & B £22.50-£25pp, Rooms 1 double, 1 twin, both en-suite, No smoking, Children over 12, No dogs, Closed Dec

---

DALE HEAD HALL LAKESIDE HOTEL Lake Thirlmere, Keswick CA12 4TN
Alan & Shirley Lowe *Tel:* 017687 72478 *Fax:* 017687 71070
Email: onthelakeside@dale-head-hall.co.uk *Web:* www.dale-head-hall.co.uk

Map Ref: 32
A591

On the shores of Lake Thirlmere, in gardens and woodlands, stands this historic Elizabethan Hall. Lovingly restored into one of Lakeland's finest country house hotels, guests are offered a warm welcome, elegant accommodation (including a four poster) and award winning cuisine. North of Wordsworth's Grasmere, and the heart of the Lake District, this is an idyllic starting point for exploring this beautiful area.

B & B from £32.50pp, C-Cards MC VS AE, Dinner from £32.50, Rooms 11 double, 2 twin, 1 family, all en-suite, Restricted smoking, Children welcome, No dogs, Closed New Year

---

SCALES FARM COUNTRY GUEST HOUSE Scales, Threlkeld, Keswick CA12 4SY
Chris & Caroline Briggs *Tel / Fax:* 017687 79660
Email: scales@scalesfarm.com *Web:* www.scalesfarm.com

Map Ref: 33
A66

Chris and Caroline welcome you to their 17th century farmhouse which has been beautifully renovated. The farm is set on the slopes of Blencathra, 10 minutes from Keswick, with wonderful southerly views. Well equipped en-suite bedrooms, (three ground floor). The beamed sitting room has a woodburning stove, a full breakfast is served in the attractive dining room. Ample parking, pretty gardens.

B & B from £26pp, C-Cards MC VS, Rooms 2 twin, 3 double, 1 family/double, all en-suite, No smoking, Dogs by arrangement, Closed Xmas

---

AUGILL CASTLE Brough, Kirkby Stephen CA17 4DE
Wendy & Simon Bennett *Tel:* 017683 41937 *Fax:* 017683 41936
Email: augill@aol.com *Web:* www.augillcastle.co.uk

Map Ref: 34
A685/A66

Augill Castle stands in open country, the backdrop is the North Pennines with wonderful Dale and Fell views. Built in 1841 as a gentleman's residence, the castle has a fairytale aura. There is a music room and a Gothic blue dining room, where dinners of lamb, beef and pork may be enjoyed. Bedrooms are designed to compliment the history of this family home.

B & B £40-£50pp, C-Cards MC VS, Dinner from £22.50, Rooms 2 double, 1 king, 3 super king/twin (all en-suite 4 posters), No smoking, Children welcome, No dogs, Open all year

ING HILL LODGE near Outhgill, Mallerstang Dale, Kirkby Stephen CA17 4JT   *Map Ref:* 34
Tony Sawyer   *Tel:* 017683 71153   B6259
Email: IngHill@FSBDial.co.uk   *see Photo opposite*

Unwind in this small Georgian house in Mallerstang, on the fringe of the National Park. Superb views, quiet and peaceful for your relaxation. Excellent en-suite shower rooms, comfortable bedrooms mostly king size beds, TV and radio alarm. The Butler's Pantry is popular for making tea and coffee. You may choose your own breakfast. Lounge with books, maps and an open fire.

B & B £20-£25pp, Rooms 2 double, 1 twin, all en-suite, Restricted smoking, No children, Dogs welcome, Closed Jan to Feb

---

PARK HOUSE FARM Dalemain, Penrith CA11 0HB   *Map Ref:* 35
Mrs Mary Milburn   *Tel / Fax:* 01768 486212   M6 J40, A592
Email: park.house@faxvia.net   *Web:* www.eden-in-cumbria.co.uk/parkhouse

Wordsworth often visited this farm and the views he enjoyed are as glorious as ever. Country hospitality at its best in our traditional 18th century farmhouse with homemade baking, delicious preserves and freshly baked bread. A perfect place to relax, unwind and explore the area, whether walking or touring. A working sheepfarm within the LDNP set in a private valley near Ullswater.

B & B £19-£23pp, C-Cards MC VS, Rooms 1 double, 2 double/twin en-suite, Restricted smoking, Children welcome, Dogs not in house, Closed Dec to Feb

---

TYMPARON HALL Newbiggin, Stainton, Penrith CA11 0HS   *Map Ref:* 35
Margaret Taylor   *Tel / Fax:* 017684 83236   M6 J40, A66
Email: margaret@tymparon.freeserve.co.uk   *Web:* www.tymparon.freeserve.co.uk

Spacious and very comfortable 18th century manor house close to Lake Ullswater. En-suite bedrooms, tea/coffee facilities and a cosy lounge with a real fire on chilly evenings. Hearty breakfasts, delicious 3 course dinners with guests welcome to bring their own wine.

B & B from £25pp, Dinner from £12, Rooms 1 double, 1 twin, 1 family, all en-suite, No smoking, Children welcome, Dogs by arrangement, Open all year

---

BECKFOOT COUNTRY HOUSE Helton, Penrith CA10 2QB   *Map Ref:* 36
Lesley White   *Tel:* 01931 713241   *Fax:* 01931 713391   M6, A6
Email: bookings@beckfoot.co.uk   *Web:* www.beckfoot.co.uk

Nestling in the Lakeland Fells of the Lowther Valley near Haweswater Beckfoot Country House makes for an ideal walking base. It is set in three acres of gardens and boasts beautiful views of the Valley. Bedrooms are spacious and well appointed with one four poster bedroom. Packed lunches can be arranged. M6 exit 39 (south) and 40 (north). RSPB nearby.

B & B from £28pp, C-Cards MC VS AE, Dinner from £16, Rooms 1 single, 2 double, 1 triple, all en-suite, Restricted smoking, Children welcome, Dogs by arrangement, Closed Dec to Feb

---

MILL BECK COTTAGE Water Street, Morland, Penrith CA10 3AY   *Map Ref:* 37
Mrs Hardre Jackson   *Tel / Fax:* 01931 714567   M6, A6
Email: derekjackson@onetel.net.uk

A riverside character cottage overlooking fields in a quiet unspoilt village. On the border of National Park and the foot of Pennines. Easy drive to the M6 and the Lakes with the Yorkshire Dales only 45 minutes away. Comfortable attractive rooms with good reading lights, tea/coffee facilities and televisions. Morning sun sitting room and evening meals and packed lunches provided.

B & B from £21pp, Dinner available, Rooms 1 double, 1 twin, No smoking, Children over 12, Closed Xmas & New Year

Ing Hill Lodge, Mallerstang Dale, near Kirkby Stephen

NEAR HOWE FARM HOTEL Mungrisdale, Penrith CA11 0SH   *Map Ref:* 38
Christine Weightman   A66
Tel / Fax: 017687 79678

A family home in 300 acres of moorland. Many bedrooms have private facilities, all have tea/coffee facilities. Home cooking with every meal freshly prepared. TV lounge. Games room. Smaller lounge with bar and on cooler evenings a log fire. Local activities include golf, fishing, pony trekking, boating and walking. 3 Diamonds.

B & B £19-£24pp, Dinner from £11, Rooms 3 double, 1 twin, 3 family, also 7 bed cottage, Restricted smoking, Children & dogs welcome, Closed January

THE OLD VICARAGE Mungrisdale, Penrith CA11 0XR   *Map Ref:* 38
Gordon & Pauline Bambrough   *Tel:* 017687 79274   A66
Email: oldvic@mungo33.freeserve.co.uk

This is a spacious Victorian house of extreme charm and with full central heating. Situated in the unspoilt village of Mungrisdale which nestles at the foot of Souter Fell and Bowscale Fell. A pub and restaurant are near by, also walks to suit everyone, with wild flowers, birds and animals. Bedrooms are well equipped, there is a pleasant, relaxing lounge with television.

B & B from £22pp, Rooms 1 single, 1 twin, 1 double, 1 family, No smoking, Children welcome, No dogs, Closed Xmas

BROOKFIELD Shap, Penrith CA10 3PZ   *Map Ref:* 39
Les & Margaret Brunskill   M6, A6
Tel / Fax: 01931 716397

Brookfield offers excellent accommodation in Cumbria and is renowned for good food, comfort and attention to detail. All rooms are en-suite with tea/coffee facilities, hairdryers, radio/alarms and are centrally heated. Meals are served in the dining room where the home cooking is a speciality. There is also a well stocked bar and a residents' lounge. Ideal for touring Lakeland. AA 4 Diamonds.

B & B £19-£25pp, Dinner from £12.50, Rooms 1 single, 4 double, 4 twin, 1 family, most en-suite, No smoking, Children over 10, No dogs, Open all year

LAND ENDS COUNTRY LODGE Watermillock, Ullswater, Penrith CA11 0NB   *Map Ref:* 40
Tel: 017684 86438   *Fax:* 017684 86959   A592
Email: infolandends@btinternet.com   *Web:* www.landends.btinternet.co.uk

One mile from Ullswater, Land Ends is a haven of peace and quiet. Our traditional farmhouse has been tastefully restored providing 8 en-suite bedrooms, one with four poster, cosy lounge and bar. In 7 acre grounds with two lakes, red squirrels, owls, ducks and wonderful birdlife, this is the perfect place to relax. Light evening snacks available.

B & B from £26pp, Rooms 2 single, 3 double, 2 twin, 1 family, all en-suite, No smoking, Children welcome, No dogs, Closed Dec to Feb

SUN INN Main Street, Dent, Sedbergh LA10 5QL   *Map Ref:* 41
     A683, A684
Tel: 01539 625208

A 17th century inn with original beams in an outstanding conservation area. The Sun Inn has a reputation for good value bar meals and serves beer from the local Dent Brewery.

B & B from £20pp, Dinner available, Rooms 2 double, 1 twin, No smoking, Children welcome, No dogs, Open all year

CROSS KEYS INN Tebay CA10 3UY
Jaqueline & Peter Baister
Tel / Fax: 015396 24240

Map Ref: 42
M6 J38

A little gem of a pub just off junction 38 on M6. There are six bedrooms with three en-suite and three standard which are all nicely furnished with facilities. Food is served in the bar or in the Garden restaurant.

B & B from £18pp, Dinner from £4.25, Rooms 1 twin, 3 double, 2 family, Restricted smoking, Children welcome, No dogs, Open all year

PRIMROSE COTTAGE Orton Road, Tebay CA10 3TL
Helen Jones *Tel:* 015396 24791 *Mobile:* 07778 520930
Email: info@primrosecottagecumbria.co.uk *Web:* www.primrosecottagecumbria.co.uk

Map Ref: 42
M6

Primrose Cottage is situated near to the Lakes and Yorkshire Dales within one acre of garden and lawns and close to M6, junction 38. Therefore it is ideal for overnight stops and short breaks. It has excellent facilities with four-poster beds, a jacuzzi bath, fresh fruit and flowers with two pubs nearby for dinner. Also detached bungalow available with disabled facilities. ETC, RAC 4 Diamonds.

B & B from £20pp, Dinner from £11, Rooms 2 double, 1 twin, all en-suite, No children, Dogs welcome, Open all year

CHURCH WALK HOUSE Church Walk, Ulverston LA12 7EW
Martin Chadderton and John Clements *Tel:* 01229 582211
Email: churchwalk@mchadderton.freeserve.co.uk

Map Ref: 43
A590

A Grade II listed Georgian house with many period features located in town centre close to a wide choice of pubs and restaurants whilst being a 15 minute drive to the centre of the lakes. A guests' lounge and tea/coffee making facilities are provided. Car parking on quiet residential street nearby. Special attention given to meet all guests' needs including travel itineraries.

B & B £22.50-£25pp, Rooms 2 double, 1 en-suite and 1 private bathroom, 1 twin ensuite, No smoking, Children welcome, Dogs by arrangement, Open all year

THE ARCHWAY 13 College Road, Windermere LA23 1BU
Jonathan & Sarah Harris *Tel:* 015394 45613 *Fax:* 015394 45328
Email: archway@btinternet.com *Web:* www.communiken.com/archway

Map Ref: 44
A591

A comfortable Victorian guesthouse, enjoying superb mountain views. A warm welcome and good food are our priority, rooms are en-suite. A delicious breakfast offers homemade yoghurt, muesli and granola, dried and fresh fruits and a choice of cooked breakfast, pancakes or kippers. A three course dinner, or packed lunch, is available. Quietly situated, a short walk from the centre of Windermere.

B & B £20-£30pp, Dinner £15, Rooms 2 twin, 2 double, all en-suite, No smoking, Children over 10, No dogs, Open all year

THE BEAUMONT Holly Road, Windermere LA23 2AF
Jim & Barbara Casey *Tel:* 015394 47075 *Fax:* 015394 47075 *Mobile:* 07803 873205
Email: thebeaumonthotel@btinternet.com *Web:* www.lakesbeaumont.co.uk

Map Ref: 44
A591

The Beaumont is an elegant Victorian villa occupying an enviably tranquil location yet is only a few minutes walk to some of the finest restaurants in Windermere. The highest standards prevail and the lovely en-suite bedrooms, with three superb four poster rooms, are immaculate and provide all modern comforts. Superb breakfasts, genuine hospitality and excellent value. Private car park.

B & B £32-£50pp, C-Cards MC VS, Rooms 1 single, 7 double, 1 twin, 1 family, all en-suite, No smoking, Children over 10, No dogs, Closed Xmas

BEAUMONT Thornbarrow Road, Windermere LA23 2DG   *Map Ref:* 44
Bob & Maureen Theobald *Tel:* 015394 45521 *Fax:* 015394 46267   A591
Email: gbb@beaumont-holidays.co.uk *Web:* www.beaumont-holidays.co.uk

Bob and Maureen Theobald welcome you to Beaumont with a friendly atmosphere within a gracious Victorian house. Ideally located between Windermere and Bowness, in an elevated position in beautiful gardens with views of the fells. Five en-suite bedrooms (one with a four poster bed), all have TV, radio, tea/coffee facilities. One ground floor room. Guests have free use of private swimming pool/leisure club.

B & B £26-£38.50pp, C-Cards MC VS, Rooms 3 double, 1 twin, 1 family, all en-suite, No smoking, Children welcome, No dogs, Open all year

---

BECKSIDE Rayrigg Road, Windermere LA23 1EY   *Map Ref:* 44
Pauline Threfall   A591
Tel / Fax: 015394 43565 *Mobile:* 07702 111012

Beckside is perfectly situated near Windermere Lake in a superb garden setting and close to the famous 'Miller Howe'. Maps and guides are available for walks and tours. The bedrooms are fitted with televisions and tea/coffee facilities and English and vegetarian breakfasts are served. Private parking for cars.

B & B from £17.50pp, Rooms 2 double en-suite, 1 family, No smoking, Children over 3, Dogs by arrangement, Open all year

---

THE CHESTNUTS Prince's Road, Windermere LA23 2EF   *Map Ref:* 44
Peter & Chris Reed *Tel / Fax:* 015394 46999   A591
Email: peter@chesnuts-hotel.co.uk *Web:* www.chesnuts-hotel.co.uk

The Chestnuts offers delightful home from home comfort and service. The house is a century old, enjoying both lovely gardens and private parking. There are five elegantly furnished bedrooms with sumptuous king sized four posters and standard king sized beds, with either en-suite showers, baths or luxurious corner baths. All our guests have free use of nearby Parklands Leisure Club.

B & B from £25pp, C-Cards, Rooms 5 double, all en-suite, No smoking, Children & dogs welcome, Open all year

---

CORNER COTTAGE Old Hall Road, Windermere LA23 1HF   *Map Ref:* 44
Bob & Doris Read   A591
Tel / Fax: 015394 48226 *Mobile:* 07762 557600

A traditional 1913 Lakeland built house in two acres of secluded gardens. Use of guest lounge and gardens, where you can relax in after a long drive. Children can play in the garden without worrying. We also have cots and high chairs available for the tiny ones. Our dining room is spacious and extends through to the conservatory overlooking the garden.

B & B from £22.50pp, C-Cards MC VS, Dinner from £12, Rooms 2 double, 2 family, all en-suite, Children welcome, Only guide dogs, Open all year

---

FIR TREES Lake Road, Windermere LA23 2EQ   *Map Ref:* 44
Mark & Jill Drinkall *Tel:* 015394 42272 *Fax:* 015394 42512   A591
Email: firtreeshotel@msn.com *Web:* www.fir-trees.com

Fir Trees is our Windermere guest house of considerable character and charm. It was built in 1888 as a Victorian gentleman's residence and the beautiful pitch pine staircase and doors are both original features. Breakfasts are special at Fir Trees, traditionally English in style and cooked to perfection. We are within easy walking distance of the resort villages of Windermere and Bowness.

B & B from £22pp, C-Cards MC VS AE, Rooms 1 single, 6 double, 2 twin, 2 family, all en-suite, No smoking, Children welcome, No dogs, Closed Xmas & New Year

HAISTHORPE HOUSE   Holly Road, Windermere LA23 2AF
Angela & Michael Brown   *Tel:* 015394 43445   *Fax:* 015394 48875
Email: angela@haisthorpe-house.co.uk   *Web:* www.haisthorpe-house.co.uk

Map Ref: 44
M6 J36, A591

Award winning guest house set in a secluded but central location.
Superb breakfasts with local produce, homemade bread and
pastries. For those special occasions we have a four poster and a
jacuzzi room available. Free use of nearby private leisure club for
guests during their stay. Off street private parking.

B & B £19-£27pp, C-Cards MC VS, Rooms 1 single, 4 double,
1 twin, 1 family, all en-suite, No smoking, Children over 5,
No dogs, Closed Xmas

IVY BANK   Holly Road, Windermere LA23 2AF
Dick & Sue Clothier   *Tel:* 015394 42601
Email: ivybank@clara.co.uk   *Web:* www.ivybank.clara.co.uk

Map Ref: 44
A591

Pretty Victorian stone-built family home in quiet location close to
village centre and station. All bedrooms are en-suite, attractively
decorated and comfortably furnished. The atmosphere is informal
and there is a substantial choice for breakfast. The lake shore and
several beautiful view points are within 30 minutes' walk. Private car
park. Storage for cycles. Free use of local leisure club.

B & B £18-£25pp, C-Cards MC VS, Rooms 3 double, 1 twin,
1 triple, all en-suite, No smoking, Children welcome, Open all year

---

KIRKWOOD GUEST HOUSE   Prince's Road, Windermere LA23 2DD
Carol & Neil Cox   *Tel / Fax:* 015394 43907
Email: neil.cox@kirkwood51.freeserve.co.uk   *Web:* www.kirkwood51.co.uk

Map Ref: 44
A591

A large Victorian house situated on a quiet corner between
Windermere and Bowness ideal for exploring the Lake District.
Rooms are en-suite with TV, tea/coffee facilities and radio. Some
rooms have 4 poster beds, ideal for honeymoons or anniversaries. A
comfortable lounge for relaxing and an extensive breakfast menu
including vegetarian and special diets. Help with planning walks,
drives or mini bus tours.

B & B £24-£28pp, C-Cards, Rooms 3 twin, 3 double, 4 family,
all en-suite, No smoking, Children welcome, Dogs by
arrangement, Open all year

ORREST HEAD HOUSE   Kendal Road, Windermere LA23 1JG
Brenda Butterworth   *Tel / Fax:* 015394 44315
Email: bjb@orrest.co.uk   *Web:* www.orrest.co.uk

Map Ref: 44
A591

Orrest Head House is a charming country house dating back to the
16th century. All bedrooms are en-suite and have TV and tea/coffee
facilities. It is set in 3 acres of garden and woodland and has distant
views to mountains and lake. Close to the station and village with a
very homely atmosphere.

B & B from £22pp, Rooms 3 double, 2 twin, all en-suite,
No smoking, Children over 6, No dogs, Closed Xmas day

RAYRIGG VILLA GUEST HOUSE   Ellerthwaite Square, Windermere LA23 1DP
Linda & John Hayward   *Tel:* 015394 88342
Email: rayriggvilla@nascr.net   *Web:* www.rayriggvilla.co.uk

Map Ref: 44
A591

Lakeland-stone detached guest house built in 1873 as the home of
a prosperous corn merchant. Ideally situated on edge of
Windermere village, facing Library Gardens. All bedrooms have en-
suite or private facilities. Extensive full English breakfast with
alternatives. Private parking. Convenient for buses and trains. A
warm welcome assured from the owners, Linda and John Hayward.

B & B from £22.50pp, C-Cards MC VS, Rooms 4 double, 1 twin,
1 triple, 1 family, all en-suite, No smoking, Children welcome,
Guide dogs only, Closed Xmas

ROCKSIDE Ambleside Road, Windermere LA23 1QA   *Map Ref:* 44
Susan Coleman *Tel / Fax:* 015394 45343   A591
Email: suecoleman@aol.com *Web:* www.rockside-guesthouse.co.uk

This attractive stone house is just 150 yards from the village of Windermere, also near the train and bus station. Rockside offers superb accommodation, the bedrooms are well equipped with TV, tea/coffee facilities and hair dryer. Most rooms are en-suite. A good choice of hearty breakfasts to begin the day, then visitors are offered help with planning outings. Car park.

B & B from £19.50pp, C-Cards MC VS, Rooms 1 single, 2 twin, 4 double, 4 family, most en-suite, Restricted smoking, Children welcome, Small dogs by arrangement, Open all year

ST JOHNS Lake Road, Windermere LA23 2EQ   *Map Ref:* 44
Barry & Sue Watts *Tel:* 015394 43078   A591
Email: mail@st-johns-lodge.co.uk *Web:* www.st-johns-lodge.co.uk

St John's Lodge is a traditional Lakeland guesthouse well known for the quality of its food and comfortable, spotlessly clean en-suite rooms. Ideally situated only 10 minutes walk from Windermere village and the lake at Bowness Bay. Chef/proprietor cooks fabulous breakfasts/dinners using quality fresh local produce. Parking. Free use nearby luxury leisure facilities.

B & B from £19pp, C-Cards MC VS, Rooms 2 single, 8 double, 1 twin, 3 family, all en-suite, No smoking, Children over 4, Dogs by arrangement, Closed Xmas

UPPER OAKMERE 3 Upper Oak Street, Windermere LA23 2LB   *Map Ref:* 44
Tel: 015394 45649 *Mobile:* 07909 522691   A591
Email: rooneym@btconnect.com

Upper Oakmere is in an ideal situation, only 100 yards from the main high street. Friendly atmosphere and home cooking. Single people and party bookings catered for.

B & B from £16pp, Dinner available, Rooms 3 double, 1 twin, 1 triple, most en-suite, No smoking, Children welcome, Open all year

VILLA LODGE GUEST HOUSE Cross Street, Windermere LA23 1AE   *Map Ref:* 44
Mick & Fiona Rooney *Tel:* 015394 43318   A591
Email: rooneym@btconnect.com *Web:* www.villa-lodge.co.uk

Villa Lodge is a stylish guesthouse hidden away in Cross Street, high up overlooking Windermere village. It boasts magnificent views of the Fells and Lake Windermere. All bedrooms are tastefully decorated and very comfortable. The full menu breakfast is served in our spacious dining area with special diets catered for. There is a cosy lounge and sunny conservatory in which to relax.

B & B from £23pp, C-Cards MC VS, Dinner from £15, Rooms 2 single, 5 double, 1 twin, all en-suite, Restricted smoking, Children welcome, Dogs by arrangement, Open all year

MORTAL MAN HOTEL Troutbeck, Windermere LA23 1PL   *Map Ref:* 45
     A592
Tel: 015394 33193 *Fax:* 015394 32161

An ideal centre for walking, touring, golf and water sport holidays or just for a very quiet and restful holiday. Beautiful location with homely charm, set in the foothills of Wan fell Pike at the head of the Troutbeck Valley. We offer a relaxed, friendly, comfortable atmosphere in which to unwind. Boasting twelve en-suite rooms, two bars and a restaurant, all with spectacular views of the valley. Dogs and children always welcome.

B & B from £25pp, Dinner available, Rooms 6 double, 6 twin, all en-suite, Children over 5, Open all year

Derbyshire & Staffordshire

Derbyshire and Staffordshire between them contain a remarkable mix of pastoral and industrial scenery and the two counties share with Yorkshire and Cheshire the impressive Peak District. Kinder Scout, an exposed peat plateau, is the highest point of Derbyshire's Peak District, at the starting point of the Pennine Way National Trail, and gives glorious views across the county. Derbyshire's section of the Peak District covers no less than 555 square miles of the county and affords the visitor fine walking country. Castleton is an ideal holiday centre delightfully situated at the head of the Hope Valley, sheltering under the impressive ruins of Norman Peveril Castle, where the River Noe meets Peaks Hole Water. This is where the ancient craft of Well Dressing, the blessing of the water supply, takes place in June and July of each year. Nearby is the great limestone gorge of Winnats Pass, close to the Blue John mines of Treak Cliff cavern. Blue John is an amethyst-coloured stone, unique to these hills, and since the eighteenth century made into vases and ornaments. This is a region rich in caves with the impressive Speedwell Cavern approached by a mile long underground boat journey and Peak Cavern with its four hundred year old rope walk.

Buxton is an elegant spa town, greatly valued by the Romans who named it Aquae Arnemetiae, once visited by Mary Stuart on the instructions of Queen Elizabeth I. It was the aim of the fifth Duke of Devonshire to make Buxton a town to rival Bath. It never quite succeeded but in 1880 the largest unsupported dome in the world was built here. The town is a delight and houses an excellent museum featuring the Wonders of the Peak District exhibition. Matlock is another fine tourist center, bordering the Peak National Park, and from Matlock Bath, a former spa which occupies an extraordinary site within the deep Derwent Gorge, cable cars give access to the Heights of Abraham. Chatsworth House, home of the Duke and Duchess of Devonshire, is also well worth a visit and often referred to as a treasure house, with beautiful gardens landscaped by Capability Brown.

Derby is very much the product of the Industrial Revolution, although an ancient town established as a trading post at the foot of the Pennines. The eighteenth century growth of the town was largely due to its fine canal network and later it became a major rail centre. The silk, hosiery, cotton and lace industry also thrived here, its diverse skills led to its renown as a rail, aircraft and car manufacturer, notably the Rolls-Royce marque. However, today its fame rests on its high-grade porcelain. The city is an

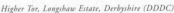

Higher Tor, Longshaw Estate, Derbyshire (DDDC)

important commercial and industrial centre boasting a superb City Museum and Art Gallery, housing paintings by the eighteenth century artist Joseph Wright of Derby.

Staffordshire, although losing much of the Black Country in 1974 to the West Midlands, nevertheless retained the Potteries, Arnold Bennett's 'Five Towns', immortalised in his novels, these five pottery towns became amalgamated to form Stoke-on-Trent in 1910. The presence of all the essential raw materials for pottery manufacture in the region encouraged the development of the industry, but it was the entrepreneurial skills of Wedgwood, Spode and Minton in the eighteenth century that made the potteries internationally famous. Stoke has opened up many of the old factories to visitors and has a wealth of fascinating museums. Just fifteen miles to the east is Alton Towers, Britain's most famous theme park,

built around the ruin of Pugin's Gothic home of the 15th Earl of Shrewsbury. Close by, the National Trust owns ten acres of Toothill Wood which includes Toothill Rock, a glorious viewpoint, and part of the Staffordshire Way, a long distance footpath. Within a short distance of Stoke-on-Trent is lovely Downs Banks, an area of rolling moorland presented to the National Trust in 1946 as a war memorial.

The visitor to this county must not miss Lichfield, a delightful mixture of medieval streets and mellow Regency houses. The cathedral is a fine triple-spired sandstone building dominating its seventeenth and nineteenth century close, separated from the city by the Stowe and Minster Pools and created from the ancient marshes. Despite its industrial history Staffordshire is still very much a farming county and contains a great deal of attractive countryside.

PLACES TO VISIT

This is a small selection of interesting places to visit. Many more are listed in our annual guide to Museums, Galleries, Historic Houses & Sites (see page 448)

Alton Towers
Alton, Staffordshire
Britain's biggest and best-known theme park, occupying a huge site, originally the estate of the Earls of Shrewsbury.

Chatsworth House
Bakewell, Derbyshire
The home of the Duke and Duchess of Devonshire is set in a 1000 acre park with sculptures and fountains. 26 rooms of the house are open to the public displaying magnificent paintings, silver and fine porcelain.

Derby Cathedral
Queen Street, Irongate, Derby
The second highest perpendicular tower in England built between 1510 and 1530. Nave designed by Robert Bakewell with a wrought iron screen so intricate it thatresembles lacework.

Heights of Abraham Cable Cars
Matlock Bath, Derbyshire
A cable car journey across the Derwent Valley to the summit of the hill top country park.

The Potteries Museum & Art Gallery
Hanley, Stoke-on-Trent
The world's finest collection of Staffordshire ceramics. Discover the story of Stoke-on-Trent's people, industry, products and landscapes and explore rich and diverse collections of paintings, drawings, prints, glass and costumes.

Shugborough Estate
Milford, Staffordshire
Eighteenth century mansion house with Grade 1 historic garden and park containing neo-classical monuments.

Derbyshire & Staffordshire

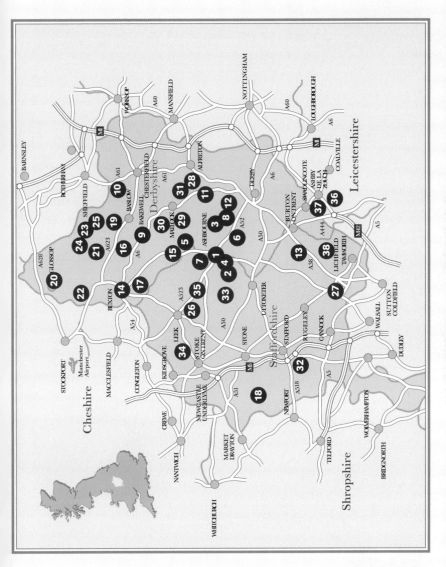

The Red Map References should be used to locate B & B properties on the pages that follow

OMNIA SOMNIA The Coach House, The Firs, Ashbourne, Derbys DE6 1HF　　*Map Ref:* 1
Alan & Paula Coker Mayes　*Tel:* 01335 300145　*Fax:* 01335 300958　*Mobile:* 07773 460795　　A52
Email: omnia.somnia@talk21.com　*Web:* www.ashbourne-town.com

This award winning, licensed establishment, nestling amongst trees in a quiet location close to town has achieved the highest grades from the ETC and AA inspection schemes. Formerly a Victorian coach house, now offering generous hospitality in luxurious surroundings, with every facility and some unexpected extras. Three very different rooms, each one special in its own way, await your discovery.

B & B £35-£40pp, C-Cards MC VS, Dinner from £21, Rooms 3 double en-suite, No smoking, No children, Dogs by arrangement, Open all year

CROSS FARM Main Road, Ellastone, Ashbourne, Derbys DE6 2GZ　　*Map Ref:* 2
　　　　　　　　　　　　　　　　　　　　　　　　　　　　　　B5032, B3033

Tel: 01335 324668　*Fax:* 01335 324039

19th century farmhouse in village with pleasant walks nearby and pub within walking distance. Ideal location for Alton Towers, Potteries, Uttoxeter racecourse and Peak District. Comfortable rooms with tea/coffee facilities and television with large family room available. Guest lounge and good parking. Traditional aga cooking and warm welcome await. Discount for children and special rates November to end of March.

B & B from £18pp, Rooms 2 double/twin, 1 family, all en-suite, No smoking, Children welcome, No dogs, Open all year

THE WHEELHOUSE Belper Road, Hulland Ward, Ashbourne, Derbys DE6 3EE　*Map Ref:* 3
Mrs H O'Gara　*Tel:* 01335 370953　*Mobile:* 07799 108122　　A517
Email: samax@supernet.com

This 18th century ex-public house is an ideal base for Chatsworth House, Dove Dale and Peak District. There are comfortable bedrooms with tea/coffee facilities and the guests' own lounge which has a television. Quality is our keynote with a high standard of cleanliness and renowned excellent breakfasts. The country pubs nearby serve meals. Ample parking. ETC 4 Diamonds.

B & B from £20pp, Rooms 1 double, 1 twin, both private bathroom, No smoking, Children over 3, Dogs by arrangement, Closed Nov to Feb

DOVE HOUSE Bridge Hill, Mayfield, Ashbourne, Derbys DE6 2HN　　*Map Ref:* 4
　　　　　　　　　　　　　　　　　　　　　　　　　　　　　　B5032

Tel: 01335 343329

Large detached Victorian house with conservatory, garden and a guest sitting room. One mile from Ashbourne and an ideal location for easy access to the Peak District, Chatsworth House, Alton Towers and the Potteries. National Cycle Network and Tissington Trail only one mile away.

B & B from £20pp, Dinner available, Rooms 1 en-suite double, Restricted smoking, No dogs, Closed Xmas & New Year

OLDFIELD HOUSE Snelston, Ashbourne, Derbys DE6 2EP　　*Map Ref:* 4
Edmund & Sue Jarvis　*Tel:* 01335 324510　*Fax:* 01335 324113　　A515
Email: suejarvis@beeb.net

A fine listed house set in a tranquil estate village in the glorious Dove valley, close to Ashbourne. Perfectly situated for exploring the Derbyshire Dales, visiting the great houses, or relaxing in a peaceful atmosphere. Upon arrival enjoy tea in the drawing room or in the garden with herbaceous borders, old roses, scrubs and trees. The bedrooms are well equipped and comfortable.

B & B from £32pp, Dinner from £20, Rooms 1 twin, 1 double en-suite or private facilities, Restricted smoking, No children or dogs, Closed Xmas & New Year

ROSE COTTAGE Snelston, Ashbourne, Derbys DE6 2DL
Cynthia Moore *Tel:* 01335 324230 *Fax:* 01335 324651
Email: pjmoore@beeb.net

Map Ref: 4
B5033, A515

A 19th century cottage standing in an acre of garden, with five acres of paddocks, a peaceful place to stay. A walk away from the pretty village of Snelston, it overlooks the beautiful valley of the River Dove. Good pubs locally, and restaurants in Ashbourne. The area offers wonderful walking and cycling, there are beautiful properties such as Chatsworth House and Sudbury Hall.

B & B £25-£27pp, Rooms 1 double en-suite, 1 twin, 1 single, private bath, No smoking, Children over 12, Dogs by arrangement, Closed Xmas

FLAXDALE HOUSE Parwich, Ashbourne, Derbys DE6 1QA
Michael & Gillian Radcliffe *Tel:* 01335 390252 *Fax:* 01335 390644 *Mobile:* 07740 626804
Email: mike@flaxdale.demon.co.uk *Web:* www.flaxdale.demon.co.uk

Map Ref: 5
A515

Delightful Georgian farmhouse in centre of attractive unspoilt village of Parwich. Ideally placed for Dovedale, Tissington, High Peak Trails, Carsington Water, the ancient sites of Arbor Low, Minninglow and Roystone Grange. There is also an abundance of public footpaths across open countryside. Off street parking, lounge, garden and radio, television and tea/coffee facilities in bedrooms.

B & B from £25pp, Rooms 1 double, 1 twin, both en-suite, No smoking, Children welcome, No dogs, Closed Xmas

SHIRLEY HALL Shirley, Ashbourne, Derbys DE6 3AS
Mrs Sylvia Foster *Tel / Fax:* 01335 360346
Email: sylviafoster@shirleyhallfarm.com *Web:* www.shirleyhallfarm.com

Map Ref: 6
A50, A52

Our tranquil old part-moated farmhouse is close to the ancient village of Shirley, tucked away amidst the fields. Our English breakfasts with homemade bread and preserves are renowned and the village pub, within walking distance, provides good evening meals. Excellent nearby walks and course fishing on our farm. ETB 4 Diamonds.

B & B £23-£26pp, Rooms 1 double, 1 twin, 1 family, all en-suite, No smoking, Children welcome, No dogs, Open all year

STANSHOPE HALL Stanshope, Ashbourne, Derbys DE6 2AD
Naomi Chambers & Nick Lourie *Tel:* 01335 310278 *Fax:* 01335 310470
Email: naomi@stanshope.demon.co.uk *Web:* www.stanshope.net

Map Ref: 7
A515

This 16th century hall dating from the 16th century, stands on the brow of a hill in the Peak District, it has been lovingly restored to retain its original features. Bedrooms are en-suite and well equipped. There is a drawing room with piano, record player and local information. Centrally heated throughout. Home cooked dinners with garden produce and an extensive breakfast menu. Brochure available.

B & B £25-£40pp, C-Cards MC VS, Dinner from £21, Rooms 1 twin, 2 double, all en-suite, Restricted smoking, Children welcome, no dogs, Closed Xmas

PARK VIEW FARM Weston Underwood, Ashbourne, Derbys DE6 4PA
Michael & Linda Adams *Tel / Fax:* 01335 360352 *Mobile:* 07771 573057
Email: enquiries@parkviewfarm.co.uk *Web:* www.parkviewfarm.co.uk

Map Ref: 8
A38

Standing in the Derbyshire countryside, this Victorian farmhouse overlooks the National Trusts's Kedleston Hall Estate, the views are wonderful. Guests are welcome to enjoy super country house hospitality. Bedrooms are double en-suite with romantic antique four poster beds and drinks facilities. Guests' own sitting room. Delicious breakfasts served. Pubs and restaurants locally. Derby City is a short drive, as is junction 25, M1.

B & B £30-£35pp, Rooms 3 double, all en-suite, No smoking, Children over 5, No dogs, Closed Xmas

EASTHORPE Buxton Road, Bakewell, Derbys DE45 1DA   *Map Ref:* 9
Marie Peters   A6
Tel: 01629 814929   *Mobile:* 07812714785

A warm welcome awaits you at this beautiful gothic style house. Excellent food, all diets catered for. All rooms are of a high standard of cleanliness with tea/coffee facilities, colour television and large family room with en-suite bathroom. Guests own lounge. A short stroll to town centre, close to Chatsworth and other attractions. Ideal for walkers and touring area.

B & B £20-£23pp, Rooms 1 double, 1 twin, 1 family, No smoking, Children over 5, No dogs, Open all year

---

MILLBROOK Furnace Lane, Monkwood, Barlow, Derbys S18 7SY   *Map Ref:* 10
Avril Turner   B6051
Tel: 0114 2890253   *Fax:* 0114 2891365   *Mobile:* 07831 398373

Millbrook is spacious and comfortable with en-suite facilities, drinks tray, TV, hairdryer, alarm radio, and guests' lounge, attention to detail ensures an enjoyable stay. Situated down a quiet lane surrounded by lovely countryside with many walks, yet within easy reach of Sheffield and Chesterfield and on the edge of the Peak District, with Chatsworth House and Haddon Hall close by. Good local pubs.

B & B from £25pp, Rooms 1 double, 1 twin, all en-suite, No smoking, Children welcome, No dogs, Closed Xmas & New Year

---

CHEVIN GREEN FARM Chevin Road, Belper, Derbys DE56 2UN   *Map Ref:* 11
Carl & Joan Postles   *Tel / Fax:* 01773 822328   A6, A517
Email: spostles@globalnet.co.uk   *Web:* www.chevingreenfarm.co.uk

Chevin Green Farm is a 38-acre mixed farm. This 200 year old beamed farmhouse has been extended and improved, with all the bedrooms offering en-suite facilities. Guests' own lounge and dining room with separate tables. Generous breakfasts using farms' free range eggs, sausages and bacon from local butcher. An ideal base for business people or holiday makers wishing to explore Derbyshire.

B & B £23-£26pp, C-Cards MC VS, Rooms 3 double, 2 twin, 1 family, all en-suite, No smoking, Children welcome, No dogs, Closed Xmas & New Year

---

DANNAH FARM COUNTRY HOUSE Bowmans Lane, Shottle, Belper, Derbys DE56 2DR   *Map Ref:* 12
Martin & Joan Slack   *Tel:* 01773 550273   *Fax:* 01773 550590   A517
Email: reservations@dannah.demon.co.uk   *Web:* www.dannah.co.uk

Close to Shottle Village, part of the Chatsworth estates, and originally a royal deer park, this working farm with 128 acres, has crops and beef cattle. The 18th century farmhouse is beautifully furnished, the bedrooms are very well equipped, and they look over fields and countryside. Special rooms with four posters, private sitting rooms and whirlpool baths. Excellent breakfasts, dinners by arrangement.

B & B £37.50-£55pp, C-Cards MC VS, Dinner from £19.50, Rooms 4 double, 2 twin, 1 single, 1 suite, all en-suite, Restricted smoking, Children welcome, No dogs, Closed Xmas

---

SHOTTLE HALL GUEST HOUSE White Lane, Shottle, Belper, Derbys DE56 2EB   *Map Ref:* 12
Philip Matthews   M1
Tel / Fax: 01773 550276

Best described as a home offering a warm welcome and good food. Part of the Chatsworth estate it dates from 1850 and has three acres of splendid gardens. It has a unique atmosphere with traditional freshly prepared food customised to guests requirements. Guests are free to relax in comfortable sofas or enjoy a stroll around the gardens. AA 4 diamonds.

B & B £27-£37pp, Dinner from £14.50, Rooms 1 single, 3 double, 3 twin, 2 family, most en-suite, Restricted smoking, Children & dogs welcome, Open all year

FAIRFIELD GUEST HOUSE 55 Main Street, Barton under Needwood, Burton upon Trent, Staffs
DE13 8AB   John & Valerie Frost   *Tel / Fax:* 01283 716396   *Map Ref:* 13
Email: hotel@fairield-uk.fsnet.co.uk   *Web:* www.fairfield.f2s.com/home.html   A38, B5016

A beautifully restored Victorian building, retaining many historical
features, tastefully furnished with full central heating and open fires.
Guests can enjoy the separate dining and sitting rooms with the
residential drinks licence. All bedrooms are en-suite with televisions,
tea/coffee facilities, hairdryers and sofas. Situated in the centre of
the village near the shops, five public houses and many country
walks.

B & B from £24pp, C-Cards, Dinner from £7, Rooms 1 double,
1 twin, 1 family, all en-suite, Restricted smoking, Children
welcome, No dogs, Open all year

BUXTONS VICTORIAN GUEST HOUSE 3A Broad Walk, Buxton, Derbys SK17 6JE   *Map Ref:* 14
Tel: 01298 78759   A6
Email: buxvic@x-stream.co.uk

Built in 1860 for the Duke of Devonshire, on a broad tree-lined
walkway overlooking the beautiful Pavilion Gardens and two minutes
walk to the Opera House. Somewhere very special. A delightful,
quiet home, tastefully furnished with en-suite bedrooms. Diets
catered for. Car park entrance from Hartington Road. Non-smoking.

B & B from £25pp, Rooms 4 double, 2 twin, 2 family, all en-suite,
No smoking, Children welcome, No dogs, Open all year

THE DEVONSHIRE ARMS Peak Forest, Buxton, Derbys SK17 8EJ   *Map Ref:* 14
Nick & Fiona Clough   *Tel:* 01298 23875   A6
Web: www.devarms.com

There is a warm welcome to all at The Devonshire Arms, a traditional
inn in the heart of The Peak District. The Inn is situated close to all
main attractions in this excellent walking country. All rooms are
refurbished to very high standard with en-suite facilities and they
serve excellent evening meals and fine traditional beers. Dogs and
children free.

B & B from £21pp, Dinner from £5.95, Rooms 3 double, 1 twin,
1 family, all en-suite, Children & dogs welcome, Closed Xmas

GRENDON GUEST HOUSE Bishops Lane, Buxton, Derbys SK17 6UN   *Map Ref:* 14
Tel: 01298 78831   *Fax:* 01298 79257   A6
Web: www.grendonguesthouse.co.uk

A beautiful Edwardian house in a peaceful location, set in lovely
gardens, where you can walk into the town or countryside from our
door. Remembered and revisited for our warm hospitality, luxurious
spacious rooms and exceptionally comfortable beds. You are spoilt
for choice at breakfast with homemade muesli, bread, fruit salad and
compotes adding to the special occasion. ETC 5 Diamonds, Gold
Award, Which? Hotel Guide recommended.

B & B from £24pp, C-Cards MC VS, Dinner available, Rooms
1 double, 1 twin, 1 four poster, all en-suite, No smoking, Children
over 9, No dogs, Open all year

GROSVENOR HOUSE HOTEL 1 Broad Walk, Buxton, Derbys SK17 6JE   *Map Ref:* 14
Graham & Anne Fairbairn   *Tel / Fax:* 01298 72439   A6
Web: www.cressbrook.co.uk/buxton

A privately run licensed Victorian hotel, enjoying splendid views of
the pavilion gardens and theatre. The atmosphere here is homely
and peaceful. Bedrooms, both standard and deluxe are tastefully
decorated and well equipped. Good home cooked traditional food.
Comfort and hospitality assured. Scenic countryside, Chatsworth
and Haddon Hall nearby. AA, ETC 4 Diamonds. Which?
Recommended.

B & B from £25pp, Rooms 5 double, 1 twin, 2 family, all en-suite,
Smoking in lounge only, Children over 8, Guide dogs only, Open
all year

HAREFIELD 15 Marlborough Road, Buxton, Derbys SK17 6RD
George & Ruth Hardie *Tel / Fax:* 01298 24029
Email: hardie@harefieldl.freeserve.co.uk *Web:* www.harefieldl.freeserve.co.uk

Map Ref: 14
A6

Elegant Victorian property set in its own grounds overlooking Buxton. Quiet location just a few minutes' walk from the historic town centre and an ideal base for exploring the beautiful Peak District. Spacious and comfortable accommodation with en-suite bedrooms and one four poster. A friendly atmosphere is assured with delicious food and lovely gardens to enjoy.

B & B from £23pp, Dinner available, Rooms 1 single, 2 double (1 four poster), 2 twin, all en-suite, No smoking, No children or dogs, Open all year

BIGGIN HALL Biggin-by-Hartington, Buxton, Derbys SK17 0DH
James Moffett *Tel:* 01298 84451 *Fax:* 01298 84681
Email: bigginhall@compuserve.com *Web:* www.bigginhall.co.uk

Map Ref: 15
A515

Biggin Hall is a 17th century old hall Grade II* listed building, 1000ft up in tranquil countryside in the Peak District National Park. Superbly renovated with log fires and antiques. Centrally heated, all rooms with bathroom en-suite. Comfortable and quiet. Wonderful home cooking. Uncrowded footpaths from the grounds through some of England's finest scenery. Close to Chatsworth, Haddon Hall and Kedleston Hall.

B & B from £30pp, C-Cards MC VS AE, Dinner from £12, Rooms 9 double, 10 twin, all en-suite, Restricted smoking, Children over 11, No dogs in main house, Open all year

THE MANIFOLD INN Hulme End, Hartington, Buxton, Derbys SK17 0EX
Mr & Mrs F Lipp *Tel:* 01298 84537
Web: www.themanifoldinn.co.uk

Map Ref: 15
A515, B5054

The Manifold Inn is a 200 year old coaching inn offering warm hospitality and good pub food at sensible prices. Accommodation is in the Old Blacksmith's shop in a secluded rear courtyard. All rooms have en-suite shower rooms, colour televisions, tea/coffee facilities and telephone. Well lit car park in courtyard. ETB 3 Crown Commended.

B & B £20-£35pp, Dinner from £6, Rooms 4 double, 1 twin, all en-suite, Children welcome, Dogs in outside kennel, Closed Xmas

CRESSBROOK HALL & COTTAGES Cressbrook, near Bakewell, Buxton, Derbys SK17 8SY
Len & Bobby Hull-Bailey *Tel:* 01298 871289 *Fax:* 01298 871845
Email: stay@cressbrookhall.co.uk *Web:* www.cressbrookhall.co.uk

Map Ref: 16
A6, A623

Accommodation with a difference. Enjoy this magnificent family home built in 1835, is set in 23 acres, with spectacular views around the compass. This is exceptional countryside for walking, with excellent pubs and restaurants very closeby. The bedrooms are elegant and well equipped with television and tea/coffee making facilities. Chatsworth House and Haddon Hall are 10 minutes.

B & B from £32.50pp, C-Cards MC VS DC, Dinner from £18.50, Rooms 2 double, 1 twin, 1 family, all en-suite, No smoking, Children welcome, No dogs, Closed mid-Dec to New Year

STADEN GRANGE COUNTRY HOUSE Staden Lane, Staden, Buxton, Derbys SK17 9RZ
Mrs MacKenzie
Tel: 01298 24965 *Fax:* 01298 72067

Map Ref: 17
A515

Staden Grange is a 250-acre beef farm on the outskirts of Buxton. It is a spacious residence and stands in a magnificent scenic area. The house has been carefully extended, and now enjoys uninterrupted views over open farmland. Some ground floor rooms are available, which are ideal for the elderly or guests with pets. A four poster room or suite is available.

B & B from £25pp, Rooms 6 double, 4 twin, 1 family, all en-suite, Children & dogs welcome, Closed Xmas & New Year

SLINDON HOUSE FARM Slindon, Eccleshall, Staffs ST21 6LX
Mrs Helen Bonsall *Tel:* 01782 791237
Email: bonsallslindonhouse@supanet.com

Map Ref: 18
A519

Slindon House Farm offers comfortable and spacious accommodation. Between junctions 14 and 15 of the M6 on the A519, it is ideally located for an overnight break or a longer stay to visit local attractions. Nearby are the Potteries, Ironbridge, Shugborough, Bridgemere and the County Showground. There is also a good selection of eating places nearby. ETC 4 Diamonds.

B & B £20-£23pp, Rooms 1 double with private bathroom, 1 twin en-suite, No smoking, Children welcome, No dogs, Open all year

DELF VIEW HOUSE Church Street, Eyam, Derbys S32 5QH
David & Meirlys Lewis *Tel:* 01433 631533 *Fax:* 01433 631972
Email: lewis@delfview.co.uk *Web:* www.lewis@delfview.co.uk

Map Ref: 19
A623

An elegant, peaceful Georgian country House in historic Eyam, located in the Peak National Park. Antiques, paintings and books provide a wonderful ambience in the spacious bedrooms and the drawing room where complimentary tea is served on arrival. Superb breakfasts in the 17th century beamed dining room are a splendid start for walking or for visiting Chatsworth, Haddon, Hardwick and Eyam Hall. Parking.

B & B from £25pp, Rooms 1 twin, 2 double, 1 en-suite, No smoking, Children over 12, Open all year

BRENTWOOD 120 Glossop Road, Charlesworth, Glossop, Derbys SK13 5HB
Dr & Mrs E A Ehlinger
Tel: 01457 869001

Map Ref: 20
A626

A pretty bungalow with large landscaped gardens in a village location on the A626. All rooms have tea/coffee facilities and central heating, plus guests are provided with their own lounge. There are places to eat nearby and local pubs. It is in a good walking area, only half an hour from Manchester Airport, with ample parking.

B & B from £20pp, Rooms 2 double, 1 twin, all en-suite, No smoking, Children & dogs welcome, Closed Xmas & New Year

ROCK FARM Monks Road, Glossop, Derbys SK13 6JZ
Margaret Child *Tel / Fax:* 01457 861086
Email: pfc@rockfarm99.freeserve.co.uk *Web:* www.rockfarm99.freeserve.co.uk

Map Ref: 20
M67, A624

Character farmhouse in picturesque Peak District location with panoramic views and good walking. Extremely comfortable accommodation together with very friendly attentive service. Beamed bedrooms with hospitality tray and television and an inglenook fireplace in dining room with separate guest lounge available all day. Top twenty finalist in both the 2000/1 and 2001/2 AA Landlady of the Year Awards. AA 4 Diamonds.

B & B from £19pp, Rooms 1 double, 1 twin, No smoking, Children & dogs welcome, Closed Xmas & New Year

HOLLY HOUSE Windmill, Great Hucklow, Derbys SK17 8RE
Sheila Acland Martin *Tel:* 01298 871568
Email: holly.house@which.net

Map Ref: 21
A623, B6049

Peak Park, quiet hamlet, 1800's stone farmhouse, wonderful views. Walking distance to local hostelries. Easy access Castleton, Edale, Bakewell, Eyam Hall and Monsale Dale. Tastefully furnished bedrooms, tea/coffee facilities, wheelchair access and sauna. Highly regarded breakfasts, organic cereals, fresh orange juice and homemade bread/cake. Refreshments on arrival. ETC 4 Diamonds.

B & B £19-£25pp, Rooms 1 double, 1 twin, No smoking, Children by arrangement, No dogs, Closed Xmas & New Year

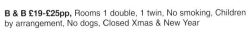

COTE BANK FARM Buxworth, High Peak, Derbys SK23 7NP   *Map Ref:* 22
Pamela & Nick Broadhurst *Tel / Fax:* 01663 750566   A6, B6062
Email: cotebank@btinternet.com

Wake to bird song and views, feast on a breakfast of freshly baked bread and homemade preserves, then enjoy a walk across our peaceful sheep farm and the Peak District hills. Relax in our pretty garden, curl up by the log fire or explore the markets and the stately homes of Derbyshire. En-suite bedrooms, tea making facilities and TV. Safe parking.

B & B from £25pp, Rooms 1 twin, 2 double, all en-suite, No smoking, Children over 10, No dogs, Closed Nov to Mar

---

THE OUTPOST Shatton, Bamford, Hope Valley, Derbys S33 0BG   *Map Ref:* 23
Janet Elliott *Tel:* 01433 651400 *Mobile:* 07909 921268   A625
Email: theoutpost@connectfree.co.uk *Web:* www.talk.to/outpost

The Outpost is a quietly situated house, furnished with quality hand made furniture. The homely atmosphere is evident throughout. The bedrooms are well equipped, the breakfasts include home baked bread and preserves. Dinner and breakfast are served either at the family table or in the conservatory, which gives views over the well kept gardens. Chatsworth, Castleton, Derwent Reservoirs closeby.

B & B £20-£30pp, Rooms 1 single, 1 double en-suite, 1 twin en-suite, No smoking, Children welcome, No dogs, Closed Xmas & New Year

---

BARGATE COTTAGE Market Place, Castleton, Hope Valley, Derbys S33 8WQ   *Map Ref:* 24
Fiona Saxon *Tel:* 01433 620201   A6187
Email: fionasaxon@bargatecottage78.freeserve.co.uk *Web:* www.peakland.com/bargate

A warm welcome awaits you at our 17th century cottage, quietly situated below Peveril Cottage, just overlooking the village green, in this beautiful historic village. The delightful rooms are all en-suite with televisions, tea/coffee facilities, radio alarms and central heating. We are in the heart of the Peak District and ideal for walking, touring or relaxing.

B & B £21.50-£23.50pp, Rooms 2 double, 1 twin, all en-suite, No smoking, Children over 12, No dogs, Closed Xmas

---

RAMBLERS REST Mill Bridge, Castleton, Hope Valley, Derbys S33 8WR   *Map Ref:* 24
Mary Gillott   A623
Tel: 01433 620125

The Ramblers Rest is a quietly situated 17th century guest house in the picturesque village of Castleton. Close to the castle and caverns. We have five double rooms, all have television and tea making facilities. A warm welcome awaits you.

B & B from £17.50pp, Rooms 2 single, 5 double, 2 twin, 1 family, some en-suit, Children & dogs welcome, Closed Xmas

---

UNDERLEIGH HOUSE off Edale Road, Hope, Hope Valley, Derbys S33 6RF   *Map Ref:* 24
Philip & Vivienne Taylor *Tel:* 01433 621372 *Fax:* 01433 621324   A6187 (formally A625)
Email: underleigh.house@btinternet.com *Web:* www.underleighhouse.co.uk

In an idyllic location, this extended cottage and barn conversion (dating from 1873) is the perfect base for exploring the Peak District. Underleigh is in the heart of magnificent walking country. Each bedroom is well furnished with many thoughtful extras. Delicious breakfasts are served in the flagstoned dining hall. The beamed lounge with a log fire, is the perfect place to relax.

B & B from £33pp, C-Cards MC VS, Rooms 3 double, 2 twin, 1 suite, all en-suite, No smoking, Children over 12, Dogs by arrangement, Closed Xmas & New Year

HIGHLOW HALL Hathersage, Hope Valley, Derbys S32 1AX
Mr & Mrs M B Walker
Tel / Fax: 01433 650393

Map Ref: 25
A6187

Highlow Hall is the most haunted house in Derbyshire, a 16th century manor house with incredible views of the Derbyshire Moors. Famous for its connection with the Bronte family, due to Charlotte Bronte having written 'Jane Eyre' here. Perfect base for walkers. Fully licensed.

B & B from £30pp, Rooms 2 double, 1 twin, all en-suite, No smoking, Children over 12, No dogs, Closed Xmas & New Year

POLLY'S B & B Moorview Cottage, Cannonfields, Hathersage, Hope Valley, Derbys S32 1AG
Polly Fisher   *Map Ref:* 25
Tel: 01433 650110   *Mobile:* 07765 774968   A6187

The cottage nestles in a quiet location with stunning views of surrounding countryside and as Stanage Edge is close by, it is ideally situated for climbers and walkers. A warm welcome awaits you at Moorview, where an imaginative breakfast menu is offered with our famous mumbled eggs. Here you will find everything you need for a relaxing break.

B & B from £23pp, Rooms 2 double, 1 twin, 1 family, all en-suite, No smoking, Children over 5, No dogs, Open all year

CHOIR COTTAGE & CHOIR HOUSE Ostlers Lane, Cheddleton, Leek, Staffs ST13 7HS   *Map Ref:* 26
William & Elaine Sutcliffe   *Tel:* 01538 360561   A520
Email: enquiries@choircottage.co.uk   *Web:* www.choircottage.co.uk

Beautifully appointed en-suite four poster bedrooms in 17th century stone cottage, once a resting place for ostlers. The cottage is adjacent to owners home and offers excellent standard of accommodation. Cheddleton and the surrounding areas are well served with over 600 miles of footpaths. 20 minutes from Alton Towers. Potteries and Peak District nearby. Recommended in Which? Hotel Guide, AA and ETC Gold Award 5 Diamonds.

B & B £25-£30pp, Rooms 1 double, 1 family, both en-suite, No smoking, Children welcome, No dogs, Closed Xmas day & Boxing day

PROSPECT HOUSE 334 Cheadle Road, Cheddleton, Leek, Staffs ST13 7BW
Rolf & Jackie Griffiths   *Tel:* 01782 550639
Email: prospect@talk21.com   *Web:* www.touristnetuk.com/WM/prospect/index

Map Ref: 26
A520

Charming 19th century converted coach house. Beamed en-suite rooms in courtyard setting offer cosy comfort, charm and freedom of access. Delightful country and canalside walks. Close to Peak District, Alton Towers, potteries and Steam Railway. ETC 4 Diamonds.

B & B £21-£22.50pp, C-Cards MC VS, Dinner from £12.50, Rooms 1 single, 1 double, 1 twin, 2 family, all en-suite, No smoking, Children welcome, Dogs by arrangement, Open all year

ALTAIR HOUSE 21 Shakespeare Avenue, Lichfield, Staffs WS14 9BE
Tel: 01543 252900   *Mobile:* 07968 265843

Map Ref: 27
A38

Altair House is situated in a quiet cul-de-sac on the south side of Lichfield within walking distance of the rail and bus stations. Useful for people wishing to visit the NEC and only three miles to Whittington Barracks. Motorway link M6, A38.

B & B from £18pp, Rooms 1 single, 2 twin, Children welcome, No dogs, Closed Xmas

MOUNT TABOR HOUSE Bowns Hill, Crich, Matlock, Derbys DE4 5DG   *Map Ref:* 28
Fay & Steve Whitehead   *Tel / Fax:* 01773 857008   *Mobile:* 07977 078266   B5035, A6, A38, M1 J26/28
Email: mountabor@email.msn.com

Once a chapel, Mount Tabor House enjoys stunning views over the Amber Valley. En-suite bedrooms are well furnished, one king size/twin bed with a corner bath, both are well equipped and have garden views. Meals, including vegetarian, may be enjoyed al fresco, overlooking garden and countryside. Crich is home to the National Tramway Museum, Crich Pottery and Peak Practice.

B & B £25-£27.50pp, C-Cards MC VS, Dinner from £17.50, Rooms 1 double/twin/family, 1 twin/double, 1 family, all en-suite, No smoking, Children welcome, No dogs, Closed Xmas & New Year

---

HAWTHORN COTTAGE Well Street, Elton, Matlock, Derbys DE4 2BY   *Map Ref:* 29
Mrs J Wright   B5057
Tel: 01629 650372   *Mobile:* 07980 202173

Tucked away in a picturesque corner of conservation village this cosy 17th century cottage offers luxurious self-contained ground floor accommodation. Double en-suite with own lounge/dining room, fridge, television, video, hairdryer and tea/coffee making facilities. Secluded sunny patio, glorious views over miles of open countryside. Hearty breakfasts. Warm welcome. Ideally situated for Peak District/Derbyshire Dales. ETC 4 Diamonds, Silver Award.

B & B £22-£24pp, Rooms double en-suite, No smoking, No children or dogs, Open all year

---

MANOR HOUSE Main Road, Wensley, Matlock, Derbys DE4 2LL   *Map Ref:* 29
Paul & Margaret Elliott   B5057
Tel / Fax: 01629 734360   *Mobile:* 07831 583300

A warm welcome awaits visitors at this small semi-detached 18th century farm cottage with beautiful views well hidden from the hustle and bustle of the busy world. A large garden is available to guests and for the energetic a network of walks waiting to be explored after their full English breakfast. Near to Chatsworth House, Haddon Hall and White Peaks.

B & B £24-£27.50pp, Rooms 1 double, 1 twin, No smoking, Children over 15, No dogs, Open all year

---

ROBERTSWOOD Farley Hill, Matlock, Derbys DE4 3LL   *Map Ref:* 30
Brenda & John Andrew   *Tel / Fax:* 01629 55642   A6
Email: robertswood@supanet.com   *Web:* www.robertswood.com

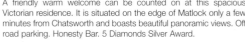

A friendly warm welcome can be counted on at this spacious Victorian residence. It is situated on the edge of Matlock only a few minutes from Chatsworth and boasts beautiful panoramic views. Off road parking. Honesty Bar. 5 Diamonds Silver Award.

B & B £25-£30pp, C-Cards MC VS, Dinner available, Rooms 6 double, 2 twin, all en-suite, No smoking, Children over 10, No dogs, Open all year

---

HEARTHSTONE FARM Riber, Matlock, Derbys DE4 5JW   *Map Ref:* 31
Joyce & Ian Gilman   *Tel:* 01629 534304   *Fax:* 01629 534372   A6, A615
Email: bed_and_breakfast@hearthstonefarm.fs.business.co.uk

Hearthstone Farm is situated high on the hill above Matlock, on the edge of the small village of Riber. This 150 acre family run farm dates back to the 16th century and offers a warm and comfortable environment from which to explore the beautiful Derbyshire Dales. All rooms have tea/coffee making facilities and colour television. Meals are prepared using home grown produce wherever possible.

B & B from £25pp, Dinner from £12.50, Rooms 1 double with pb, 1 double en-suite, 1 twin en-suite, No smoking, Children welcome, Well behaved dogs, Closed Xmas & New Year

LITTLEMOOR WOOD FARM Littlemoor Lane, Riber, Matlock, Derbys DE4 5JS   *Map Ref:* 31
Gilly Groom   *Tel:* 01629 534302   *Fax:* 01629 534008   A6, A615
Email: gillygroom@ntlworld.com   *Web:* www.aplaceinthecountry.co.uk

A peaceful farmhouse at the edge of the Derbyshire Dales and the
Peak Park, in 20 acres with wonderful views is the perfect place to
unwind. Rooms are attractive, comfortable and well equipped.
Hearty breakfasts including home produced bacon and sausages,
vegetarian/special diets catered for. Stately homes including
Chatsworth House and others are nearby. Ashbourne, Bakewell and
M1 Junction 28 within 20 minutes.

B & B from £25pp, C-Cards MC VS, Dinner from £12.50, Rooms
1 double, 1 double/twin, both private facilities, No smoking,
Children over 8, No dogs, Closed Xmas & New Year

CHARTLEY MANOR FARM Chartley, Stafford, Staffs ST18 0LN   *Map Ref:* 32
Jeremy & Sarah Allen   A518
Tel / Fax: 01889 270891   *Mobile:* 07958 304836

Set in parkland, opposite Chartley Castle, prison of Mary Queen of
Scots, this half timbered manor house has oak panelled bedrooms,
four poster beds, log fires and exquisite furniture. Large gardens with
ee lined walks. Bedrooms, one with a hidden priest's hole door, are
flower filled and comfortable. English breakfast including black
pudding and Staffordshire oat cakes. Award winning local pub.

B & B £25-£35pp, C-Cards MC VS, Dinner available, Rooms
2 double, 1 twin, all en-suite, Restricted smoking, Children over
12, Dogs by arrangement, Closed Xmas day

SLAB BRIDGE COTTAGE Little Onn, Church Eaton, Stafford, Staffs ST20 0AY   *Map Ref:* 32
Diana and David Walkerdine   M6, A5
Tel: 01785 840220

This 19th century cottage is situated in a quiet idyllic setting beside
the Shropshire Union Canal. Rooms have tea/coffee
making facilities. Close to the M6 Junction 12, it is convenient to the
potteries, Peak District, Alton Towers and North Wales. Canal boat
trips with dinner on board are available, subject to prior
arrangement.

B & B from £23pp, Dinner from £15, Rooms 2 double with private
facilities, No smoking, Children welcome, Dogs by arrangement,
Closed Xmas & New Year

FARRIERS COTTAGE & MEWS Woodhouse Farm, Nabb Lane, Croxden, near Alton, Stoke-on-Trent,
Staffs ST14 5JB   Diana Ball   *Tel:* 01889 507507   *Fax:* 01889 507282   *Map Ref:* 33
Mobile: 07803 530655   *Email:* ddeb@lineone.net   *Web:* www.alton-towers.glo.cc   B5030

Enchanting picturebook cottage with window boxes full of fragrant
flowers, standing on a quiet country lane. A peaceful haven offering
a relaxed atmosphere, hearty breakfast, de-luxe en-suite
accommodation and stunning views. Close to Alton Towers, the
Potteries and many other visitor attractions. CCTV protected car
park. Special breaks available. AA ETC 4 Diamonds, Silver Award.

B & B from £19pp, C-Cards MC VS, Rooms 3 double, 1 twin,
1 family, all en-suite, No smoking, Children over 5, No dogs,
Open all year

THE HOLLIES Clay Lake, Endon, Stoke-on-Trent, Staffs ST9 9DD   *Map Ref:* 34
Anne Hodgson   B5051, A53
Tel / Fax: 01782 503252

A lovely Victorian home in a quiet location, with comfortable well
appointed en-suite bedrooms with televisions and tea/coffee
facilities. There is also a pleasant dining room overlooking a large
garden. Good base for the Potteries, Alton Towers, Peak District and
National Trust Properties. Private car park. Restaurant nearby. A
warm welcome assured.

B & B from £20pp, Rooms 2 double, 2 twin, 1 family, all en-suite,
No smoking, Children welcome, Dogs by arrangement, Open all
year

BEEHIVE GUEST HOUSE Churnet View Road, Oakamoor, Stoke-on-Trent, Staffs ST10 3AE
Colin & Ruth Franks   *Tel / Fax:* 01538 702420   *Map Ref:* 33
Email: thebeehiveoakamoor@btinternet.com   *Web:* www.thebeehiveguesthouse.co.uk   A52, A521, B5417

The Beehive is a family run, non smoking guest house situated in the peaceful village of Oakamoor overlooking the River Churnet. All rooms en-suite, some with four-poster beds, central heating, colour televisions and tea/coffee facilities. Private Parking. Ideal for visiting the world famous Potteries and the Peak District. The thrills of Alton Towers are only one mile away.

B & B from £22pp, C-Cards MC VS, Rooms 3 double, 2 family, all en-suite, No smoking, Children welcome, No dogs, Open all year

LEEHOUSE FARM Leek Road, Waterstones, Stoke-on-Trent, Staffs ST10 3HW   *Map Ref:* 35
Josie & Jim Little   A523
Tel: 01538 308439

Josie and Jim welcome you to their lovely farmhouse. It is ideally situated for the Derbyshire Dales, Staffordshire moorlands, the famous potteries and Alton Towers. Our spacious en-suite bedrooms are centrally heated with TV and tea/coffee making facilities. Ample parking, and secure parking for bicycles. ETC 4 Diamonds, Silver Award.

B & B from £20pp, Rooms 1 twin, 2 double, all en-suite, Restricted smoking, Children over 8, Dogs by arrangement, Closed Xmas

MEASHAM HOUSE FARM Gallows Lane, Measham, Swadlincote, Derbys DE12 7HD   *Map Ref:* 36
                                                                    M42 J11, A42, B4116
Tel / Fax: 01530 270465

Measham House is a 500 acre mixed farm with accommodation available in the 200 year old Grade II listed Georgian farmhouse. Situated two miles from M42 junction 12, and eight miles from M1 junction 22

B & B from £22pp, Rooms 2 twin, 1 triple, all en-suite, No smoking, Children welcome, Open all year

THE OLD HALL Netherseal, Swadlincote, Derbys DE12 8DF   *Map Ref:* 37
Clemency Wilkins   *Tel:* 01283 760258   *Fax:* 01283 762991   A444/M42 J11
Email: clemencywilkins@hotmail.com

The Old Hall, a Grade II listed house dating from 1640, is situated in 18 acres of lakeside gardens, woodland and fields. Originally a monastery, the house retains its character and features but with modern conveniences. Bedrooms are quiet, comfortable, spacious, attractively furnished and well equipped.Ideally situated for visiting Calke Abbey, Chatsworth, Kedleston and Shugborough. 25 mins from NEC and Castle Donington.

B & B from £26pp, Dinner from £16, Rooms 1 twin, 2 double en-suite/private bathroom, No smoking, No children or dogs, Closed Xmas & New Year

THE OLD RECTORY Elford, Tamworth, Staffs B79 9DA   *Map Ref:* 38
Mrs Lawrie Ward   A513
Tel: 01827 383233   *Fax:* 01827 383630

An idyllic and peaceful setting with two acres of gardens running down to the River Tame and views of the countryside. A well charted history includes the reported sighting of a friendly ghost. There are traditional furnishings and dinner is served either in the formal dining room or the Aga warmed kitchen. The cooking is a blend of traditional with imaginative ideas.

B & B from £32.50pp, Dinner from £19.50, Rooms 1 double en-suite, 1 twin en-suite, Restricted smoking, Children over 5, No dogs, Closed Xmas & New Year

Devon

Devon is a superb holiday region and few counties in England can match its variety of scenery with two contrasting coastlines and some quite spectacular countryside. The northern coast, Devon's longest unspoilt coastline, is an impressive array of high cliffs along the Bristol Channel and a series of great headlands protecting fine broad sandy beaches from the wild Atlantic gales. Here are small resorts of a very special charm including Lynton, an ideal holiday center, adjoining the

Haytor on Dartmoor (SWT)

lovely Valley of the Rocks Visitor Centre. Five hundred feet below is Lynmouth, joined to Lynton by a zig-zag path and a hundred year old cliff railway. It is a romantic and picturesque fishing village, backed by glorious wooded cliffs and the home of the Exmoor National Park. The largest seaside resort of North Devon is Ilfracombe, which until the arrival of the railway at the end of the nineteenth century was only a small fishing town. However its dramatic rocky headlands and quaint sheltered

bays attracted large numbers of holiday makers. The town still retains much of its old character. Further west, the little town of Clovelly needs no introduction being one of the most photographed villages in the country, its steep cobbled single street, picturesque cottages and little harbour has made it a tourist attraction for well over a century. Bideford, a highly successful port on the River Torridge from the seventeenth century, is also a fine holiday center and was in fact the basis for Charles Kingsley's famous novel Westward Ho! It was the great Elizabethan seafarer, Sir Richard Grenville who secured Bideford's first town charter.

Devon's south coast, like its north coast, can claim massive cliffs, but the climate is altogether softer and balmier. This region includes the English Riviera, a wonderful stretch of golden beaches, palm trees and vivid blue seas. Torquay is the largest and most impressive of Devon's resorts and its singularly mild climate ensured its development during the late eighteenth century as a holiday centre. There is much to enjoy here, with its yachting and fishing harbour, fine gardens, sandy beaches and its exotic pavilion. Sidmouth is an elegant resort which, like Torquay, developed from a small fishing village during the eighteenth century and grew in popularity following the visit of the young Princess Victoria in 1819. Now the highlight of the summer season is its folk festival in late July to early August which offers music, dance, street theatre and family shows.

Plymouth, where Drake played his infamous game of bowls, is the largest city in the southwest. Flanked by the estuaries of the Rivers Tamar and Plym, the Hoe, overlooking Plymouth Sound, gives magnificent views across the sea and headlands. Drake's Island, used as a fort from 1860, is in the centre with the mile long breakwater beyond. The centre of Plymouth was largely destroyed during the Second World War, however, there is much to see of historic significance centred around the Barbican, the site of the original town, including a fish market and Tudor and Jacobean buildings. Round the coast is Dartmouth, another ancient port, sheltering in the mouth of the Dart estuary and built up a steep hillside. Dartmouth Castle built in the late fifteenth century stands on rocks at the entrance to the river.

Attractive as the Devon coasts are, the centre of the county holds its own fascination. Exeter, like Plymouth, was severely damaged during the Second World War but still retains a great deal of its character. The magnificent cathedral with its two massive Norman towers thankfully survived the destruction and contains the priceless Exeter Book of Anglo-Saxon poetry. The remarkable thirteenth century underground water system can be explored by guided tours and the Maritime Museum is also a fine visitor attraction, housing over a hundred historic vessels.

The large number of cairns, hut circles and Bronze Age remains suggest that Dartmoor was far from deserted in the distant past, but climatic change ensured that this large area of Devon was to become the largest expanse of wilderness in southern Britain. Massive granite peaks rise over 2,000 feet out of this bleak gorse and heather upland. The Dartmoor National Park covers over 365 square miles and the Exmoor National Park, once a great hunting region, is now an area of glorious scenery, open walking country and the haunt of red deer and wild ponies.

PLACES TO VISIT

This is a small selection of interesting places to visit. Many more are listed in our annual guide to Museums, Galleries, Historic Houses & Sites (see page 448)

Buckland Abbey
Yelverton
A Cistercian monastery that became the home of Sir Francis Drake. Craft workshops, herb garden and estate walks.

Exeter Cathedral
Exeter
A Norman Cathedral built in the twelfth century with impressive vaulted ceiling, medieval stained glass and carved tombs.

National Marine Aquarium
Coxside, Plymouth
State of the art aquarium and as near as you will get to being submerged without getting wet with a shark theatre, a live coral reef and a wave tank.

Plymouth Dome
The Hoe, Plymouth
Takes the visitor through the centuries in Plymouth from the sights and sounds of Elizabethan times to the Blitz. Audiovisual presentations and reconstructions.

Underground Passages
Exeter
City passages built in medieval times to carry water into the city, the only one of its kind in Britain open to the public.

Devon

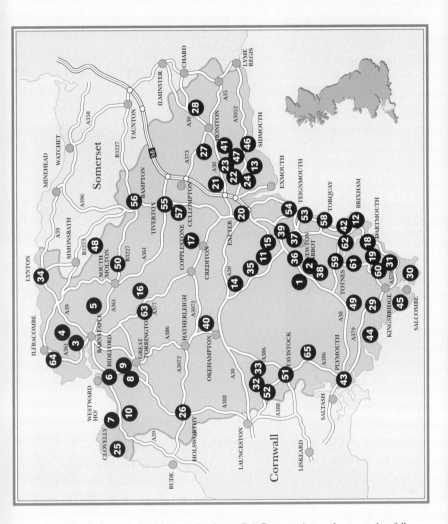

The Red Map References should be used to locate B & B properties on the pages that follow

WELLPRITTON FARM Holne, Ashburton TQ13 7RX
David & Susan Grey *Tel:* 01364 631273
Email: info@wellprittonfarm.com *Web:* www.wellprittonfarm.com

Map Ref: 1
A38

A lovely Dartmoor farmhouse with wonderful views, in the heart of the countryside, 3 miles A38 Express way, 1/2 an hour to Exeter/Plymouth/Torbay. Excellent food, cream teas as featured in the West country Good Food Guide 1999. Some en-suite rooms all are well equipped. An original residents' lounge, an outdoor swimming pool, and pets to enjoy. Most country pursuits nearby.

B & B from £20pp, C-Cards MC VS, Dinner from £10, Rooms 2 twin, 2 double, most en-suite, Restricted smoking, Children over 5, Dogs welcome, Closed Xmas & New Year

---

RIVERSMEAD Newbridge, Ashburton TQ13 7NT
Mrs Joy Hasler
Tel: 01364 631224

Map Ref: 2
A38

Riversmead, set in one acre of garden with stream in the picturesque River Dart Valley, offers quality en-suite accommodation with stunning views from all aspects. Guests sitting room with colour television, tea/coffee making facilities, comfortable dining room and ample parking.

B & B from £22pp, Rooms 2 double, 1 twin, all en-suite, Restricted smoking, Children over 8, Dogs by arrangement, Open all year

---

BRADIFORD COTTAGE Halls Mill Lane, Bradiford, Barnstaple EX31 4DP
Jane & Tony Hare *Tel / Fax:* 01271 345039
Web: www.humesfarm.co.uk

Map Ref: 3
A361

A family run 17th century cottage set in the countryside, just one mile form Barnstable. Ideally situated for exploring the stunning Atlantic coastline and the scenic beauty of Exmoor. Lovely, comfortable rooms, attractive garden and use of heated swimming pool. Excellent pub food within easy walking distance.

B & B from £15pp, Rooms 1 single, 2 double, 1 twin, No smoking, Children over 8, No dogs, Open all year

---

HOME PARK Lower Blakewell, Muddiford, Barnstaple EX31 4ET
Mari Lethaby
Tel / Fax: 01271 342955

Map Ref: 4
A39, B3230

Set on a Deer Valley hillside with a half-acre garden that slopes away to a vista of natural scenic beauty, Home Park, combines tranquility with a high standard of modern comfort. The warmth and comfort of the en-suite rooms of Home Park are enhanced by the genuine farmhouse cuisine where pastry is a speciality. Every room has tea trays, hairdryers and televisions. AA 4 Diamonds.

B & B £20-£25pp, Dinner from £10, Rooms 1 double, 1 family en-suite, No smoking, Children welcome, No dogs, Closed Xmas & New Year

---

HUXTABLE FARM West Buckland, Barnstaple EX32 0SR
Antony & Jackie Payne *Tel / Fax:* 01598 760254
Email: gbbenquiries@huxtablefarm.co.uk *Web:* www.huxtablefarm.co.uk

Map Ref: 5
A361

Enjoy a candelit dinner with complimentary homemade wine in this mediaeval longhouse (dating back to 1520). Huxtable Farm has oak panelling, beams and bread ovens. Secluded sheep farm with wildlife and panoramic views, ideally situated on the Tarka Trail. Explore Exmoor National Park and North Devon's coastline. A tennis court, sauna, fitness and games room are for guests' pleasure. Log fires in winter.

B & B £25-£26pp, C-Cards MC VS, Dinner from £16, Rooms 1 twin, 3 double, 2 family, all en-suite/private, Restricted smoking, Children welcome, No dogs, Closed Dec to Jan

Lower Waytown, Horns Cross, near Clovelly

THE MOUNT Northdown Road, Bideford EX39 3LP
Heather & Andrew Laugharne *Tel:* 01237 473748 *Fax:* 01271 373813
Email: andrew@themountbideford.fsnet.co.uk *Web:* www.themount1.cjb.net

Map Ref: 6
A39

A charming Georgian licensed guest house, only a five minute walk from the town centre. Well furnished and decorated within a partly walled garden. Convenient for Exmoor, Dartmoor and North Devon coast. Car parking available.

B & B from £25pp, C-Cards MC VS AE, Rooms 2 single, 2 double, 2 twin, 1 family, all en-suite, No smoking, Children welcome, No dogs, Closed Xmas

---

LOWER WAYTOWN Horns Cross, near Clovelly, Bideford EX39 5DN
Annette & Colin Penny
Tel: 01237 451787 *Fax:* 01237 451817

Map Ref: 7
A39
see Photo on page 105

This beautifully converted barn and roundhouse has been transformed into a delightful, spacious home, tastefully furnished with antiques. The unique round beamed guests' sitting room adjoins the dining room where delicious breakfasts are served. Bedrooms are en-suite and very comfortable. Relax in extensive grounds with ponds, waterfowl and black swans. Lower Waytown is situated in unspoilt countryside with spectacular scenery, pretty coves and coastal footpaths.

B & B from £26pp, Rooms 1 twin, 2 double, all en-suite, No smoking, Children over 12, No dogs, Closed Xmas & New Year

---

BEARA FARMHOUSE Buckland Brewer, Bideford EX39 5EH
Ann & Richard Dorsett
Tel: 01237 451666

Map Ref: 8
A388

This traditional Devon farmhouse with stone floors, beams and inglenooks, stands down a track overlooking fields and woods in a peaceful location, guests are invited to relax here. Vegetarians may enjoy the free range eggs. Excellent pub in Buckland Brewer. Beara Farmhouse is well placed for visits to Clovelly, Rosemoor Gardens, Torrington, the Tarka Trail and the South West coastal path.

B & B from £25pp, Dinner from £12, Rooms 1 double, 1 twin, both en-suite, No smoking, No children or dogs, Closed Mid Dec to 6th Jan

---

RIVERSDALE Weare Gifford, Riversdale, Bideford EX39 4QR
Maggie & Eddie Ellison *Tel:* 01237 423676
Email: Riversdale@connectfree.co.uk

Map Ref: 9
A386

A 200 year old country house beside the River Torridge. Bedrooms are en-suite with television, refreshment tray, flowers and toiletries. The beamed sitting room with stone fireplace, leads to an elegant dining room where breakfast is served (including porridge, smoked haddock.). Ideal walking, golfing, watersports, the Tarka Trail and fishing our private beat. RHS Rosemoor, Dartington Crystal, Clovelly, Westward Ho! and Arlington Court.

B & B from £24pp, Rooms 1 twin, 2 double, all en-suite, No smoking, Children welcome, No dogs, Closed Oct to Mar

---

STROXWORTHY FARM Woolfadisworthy, Bideford EX39 5QB
Mrs Beck
Tel: 01237 431333 *Fax:* 01237 470987

Map Ref: 10
A39

Delightfully positioned on a working dairy farm only four and a half miles from picturesque Clovelly. Ideally situated for touring north Devon and Cornwall, but also within easy reach of Exmoor and Dartmoor. All bedrooms are en-suite with tea/coffee making facilities and televisions. Guests are welcome to relax in the comfortable lounge and there is also ample off road parking.

B & B from £20pp, Rooms 2 double, 1 twin, 1 family, all en-suite, Restricted smoking, Children over 5, No dogs, Closed Nov to Mar

BROOKFIELD HOUSE   Challabrook Lane, Bovey Tracey TQ13 9DF   *Map Ref:* 11
Frances & Laurence Pearce   *Tel:* 01626 836181   *Fax:* 01626 836182   A382
Email: brookfieldh@tinyworld.co.uk   *Web:* www.hotellink.co.uk/bovey/brookfield

Spacious early Edwardian residence on the edge of Bovey Tracey and Dartmoor, set in two acres of park-like gardens. Secluded tranquility within walking distance of town and moor. The bedrooms are decorated in individual styles, each with pleasant seating areas. Breakfasts are an experience to savour with full Devonshire to house specialities. Secure parking. ETC 4 Diamonds, Silver Award.

B & B £25-£30pp, C-Cards MC VS AE, Rooms 2 double with en-suite, 1 twin with pb, No smoking, Children over 12, Only guide dogs, Closed December to January

WHITSTONE FARM   Bovey Tracey TQ13 9NA   *Map Ref:* 11
Katie Bunn   *Tel:* 01626 832258   *Fax:* 01626 836494   A382, A38
Email: katie@reynolds2000.co.uk

A warm welcome awaits where luxury accommodation is offered. The farmhouse stands in three acres, which is home to over 250 specimen trees. The guests' lounge enjoys views to Dartmoor. This is a perfectly peaceful location, however, Bovey Tracey is just five minutes away. Ideally situated for exploring South Devon. National Trust properties, gardens, steam railways, coastal and moorland walking are nearby. Secure parking.

B & B from £27.50pp, Dinner from £18, Rooms 1 twin, 2 double, all en-suite, No smoking, Children over 15, No dogs, Closed Xmas & New Year

ANCHORAGE GUEST HOUSE   170 New Road, Brixham TQ5 8DA   *Map Ref:* 12
   A380, A3022

Tel / Fax: 01803 852960

The chalet style bungalow, set in award winning gardens, offers very comfortable, mostly en-suite, accommodation. The Anchorage provides good home cooking, a friendly atmosphere and ample parking. A good base for exploring Dartmoor and the South Devon Coast. 'Brixham's best kept secret', Daily Telegraph, June 1999.

B & B from £16pp, C-Cards MC VS AE, Dinner available, Rooms 2 single, 3 double, 1 twin, 1 triple, Restricted smoking, Children welcome, No dogs, Closed occasionally

LUFFLANDS   Yettington, Budleigh Salterton EX9 7BP   *Map Ref:* 13
Brenda & Colin Goode   *Tel:* 01395 568422   *Fax:* 01395 568810   B3178
Email: lufflands@compuserve.com   *Web:* www.lufflands.co.uk

This is 17th century welcoming, comfortable farmhouse may be found in the hamlet of Yettington, 3 miles from the sea at Budleigh Salterton. It is ideal for walking, touring or relaxing. All rooms are well equipped, breakfast is freshly cooked to order and served in the original farmhouse kitchen. Children welcome. Country views, large garden and ample parking. Close to beaches.

B & B £19-£22pp, C-Cards MC VS, Rooms 1 single, 1 double, 1 family, all en-suite/private, No smoking, Children welcome, Dogs by arrangement, Open all year

GLENDARAH HOUSE   Lower Street, Chagford TQ13 8BZ   *Map Ref:* 14
John & Sylvia Croxen   *Tel:* 01647 433270   *Fax:* 01647 433483   *Mobile:* 07720 845920   A382
Email: enquiries@glendarah-house.co.uk   *Web:* www.glendarah-house.co.uk

A comfortable Victorian house with beautiful views in a peaceful location, only a short walk from the village centre. Glendarah House provides friendly service and en-suite rooms with all facilities. Good base for walking and cycling with excellent pubs and restaurants nearby.

B & B from £25pp, C-Cards MC VS, Rooms 1 single, 3 twin, 3 double, all en-suite, No smoking, Children over 10, Dogs in Coach House only, Closed Xmas & New Year

PARFORD WELL Sandy Park, Chagford TQ13 8JW   *Map Ref:* 14
T Daniel   A382
Tel: 01647 433353

Parford Well is a comfortable and stylishly furnished house in a walled garden within the Dartmoor National Park, standing below Castle Drogo. Attractive bedrooms are well equipped and comfortable. Wonderful walks on the doorstep, in the valley of the River Teign and on the Moor. The ideal place for a few days' break to get away from everything. Quality breakfasts, using local produce.

B & B from £25pp, Rooms 1 twin, 1 double, both en-suite, 1 private double, No smoking, Children over 8, No dogs, Closed Xmas & New Year

---

FARMBOROUGH HOUSE Old Exeter Road, Chudleigh TQ13 0DR   *Map Ref:* 15
Deirdre & Bernard Aldridge   *Tel / Fax:* 01626 853258   A38
Email: holidays@farmborough-house.com   *Web:* www.farmborough-house.com

Comfortable Edwardian house hidden away from the road in a secluded rural setting. Situated between Haldon Forest and Dartmoor with easy access from the A38. Farmborough is the ideal base for exploring South Devon with golfing, fishing or walking nearby. A hearty traditional breakfast comes from the aga with tea and cakes on arrival. AA 4 Diamonds, ETC 4 Diamonds, Silver Award.

B & B £22.50-£26pp, Dinner from £10, Rooms 2 double, 1 twin, all en-suite, No smoking, Children over 14, No dogs, Closed Xmas & New Year

---

THE OLD BAKEHOUSE South Molton Street, Chulmleigh EX18 7BW   *Map Ref:* 16
Colin & Holly Burls   *Tel / Fax:* 01769 580074   A377
Email: theoldbakehouse@talk21.com   *Web:* www.theaa.co.uk/region13/79183.html

Historic thatched house in beautiful hilltop village with immaculately presented bedrooms around a peaceful courtyard garden. Every luxury is provided including full central heating, log fires and a guests sitting room with books and games. The licensed reataurant serves excellent home cooked dishes, including local specialities and special diets are taken into consideration. Children are welcome, but sorry, no pets.

B & B from £25.50pp, C-Cards MC VS, Dinner from £11.50, Rooms 2 double, 2 twin, all en-suite, No smoking, Children over 5, No dogs, Closed Feb

---

JELLICOE'S Higher Holn, Upham, Cheriton Fitzpaine, Crediton EX17 4HN   *Map Ref:* 17
Michael Jellicoe   *Tel / Fax:* 01363 866165   A3270
Email: bodkings@jellicoes.co.uk   *Web:* www.jellicoes.co.uk

Come and share our peaceful house and garden in beautiful countryside with distant views of Dartmoor. The cosy sitting room has space for all our guests, a wood burning stove supplements the central heating. Meals are served in our mediterranean kitchen/dining room with blue and white decor and tiled floor. We use as much local produce as we can and often have themed nights.

B & B from £22pp, Dinner from £12, Rooms 2 double, 1 twin, 1 family, all en-suite, No smoking, Children welcome, No dogs, Closed Xmas & New Year

---

CAMPBELLS 5 Mount Boone, Dartmouth TQ6 9PB   *Map Ref:* 18
Angela Campbell   *Tel / Fax:* 01803 833438   A3122
Web: www.webmachine.co.uk/campbells

Voted best B&B in the South Hams in 1999 and 2001. Friendly and comfortable with many added extras. Quiet location only a few minutes walk from the town centre. Both bedrooms have stunning panoramic views; beautifully furnished with comfortable double beds and colour TV. Flexible breakfasts with West Country food and home-baking. Off road parking.

B & B from £30pp, Dinner from £25, Rooms 2 double with en-suite, Restricted smoking, Children welcome, No dogs, Closed Oct to Apr

HEDLEY HOUSE 37 Newcomen Road, Dartmouth TQ6 9BN   Map Ref: 18
Anthony & Diana Burden   A3122
Tel: 01803 832885   *Mobile:* 07713 024648

Attractive Grade II listed Georgian house overlooking the River Dart.
The bedrooms have stunning views of the river and on to the sea.
Breakfast is served in the lovely dining room whilst the furnished
guests' lounge leads on to a pretty courtyard. Only a few minutes
walk to town centre, shops and restaurants.

B & B £32.50-£35pp, Rooms 2 double, 1 twin, all en-suite,
No smoking, Children over 16, No dogs, Closed Xmas

WOODSIDE COTTAGE BED & BREAKFAST Blackawton, Dartmouth TQ9 7BL   Map Ref: 19
Tim & Sally Adams   *Tel:* 01803 712375   A3122
Email: woodside-cottage@lineone.net   *Web:* www.woodside-cottage-devon.co.uk

Experience the peace and quiet of country life in this fine 18th
century house, formerly a gamekeeper's cottage with stunning views
set in a beautiful South Hams valleys, only 4 miles from Dartmouth.
The house is extremely comfortable with attractive gardens with
magnificent views. Guests are offered homemade tea and cakes on
arrival. The en-suite bedrooms enjoy wonderful views across the
Devon countryside.

B & B from £25pp, Rooms 2 double, 1 twin, all en-suite,
No smoking, Children over 12, No dogs, Closed Nov to Feb

BROOME COURT Broomhill, Dartmouth TQ6 0LD   Map Ref: 19
Tom Boughton & Jan Bird   A3122
Tel: 01803 834275   *Fax:* 01803 833260

Tucked into a south facing hill, overlooking 3 copses and surrounded
by green, undulating Devon countryside rich in wildlife, the old farm
buildings encircle a courtyard with flowers and shrubs. In the
farmhouse kitchen your hosts will provide the sort of breakfast that
dreams are made of. No noise or smell of traffic at Broomhill, but
peace and tranquillity of the Devon countryside.

B & B from £35pp, Rooms 1 twin, 2 double, all en-suite, also
family unit, Restricted smoking, Children over 12, Dogs by
arrangement, Open all year

RAFFLES 11 Blackall Road, Exeter EX4 4HD   Map Ref: 20
Sue & Richard Hyde   *Tel / Fax:* 01392 270200   Exeter Central
Email: raffleshtl@btinternet.com   *Web:* www.raffles-exeter.co.uk

A large Victorian house with antiques, providing comfort and style,
retaining Victorian quality. A delightful walled garden, yet Raffles is
minutes from the city centre. Richard and Sue provide high quality
accommodation with friendly service. Rooms are en-suite and well
equipped, with central heating. Lock up garages are available by
request. An excellent base from which to explore Devon.

B & B from £25pp, C-Cards MC VS AE, Dinner from £16, Rooms
2 single, 1 twin, 2 double, 2 family, all en-suite, Restricted
smoking, Children welcome, Dogs by arrangement, Open all year

HOLBROOK FARM Clyst Honiton, Exeter EX5 2HR   Map Ref: 21
Mrs H Glanvill   *Tel / Fax:* 01392 367000   A30
Email: heatherglanvill@holbrookfarm.co.uk   *Web:* www.holbrookfarm.co.uk

We hope to make your stay at Holbrook Farm special. We have
delightful en-suite rooms with beautiful views. Treat yourself to a
tasty breakfast using fresh local produce at separate tables. We are
in a peaceful location and ideally situated for Exeter, the coast,
National Trust and the Moors. Sample the excellent local pubs or try
our delicious suppers. Safe parking.

B & B from £21pp, Dinner from £9, Rooms 1 double, 1 twin,
1 family, all en-suite, No smoking, Children welcome, No dogs,
Closed Xmas & New Year

WOOD BARTON Farringdon, Exeter EX5 2HY   *Map Ref:* 22
Jackie Bolt *Tel:* 01395 233407 *Fax:* 01395 227226   A3052
Email: jackie_bolt@hotmail.com

A 17th century farmhouse in quiet countryside, yet only 3 miles from junction 30, M5. An excellent traditional English breakfast which is cooked on the Aga. Bedrooms are spacious and well equipped, each one has an en-suite bathroom, they have central heating. The city of Exeter is a short drive also sandy beaches, National Trust houses and golf courses. Good local eating places.

B & B from £21pp, Rooms 1 twin, 1 double, 1 family, all en-suite, No smoking, Children welcome, No dogs, Closed Xmas & New Year

---

DANSON HOUSE Marsh Green, Exeter EX5 2ES   *Map Ref:* 23
Dennis & Jenny Hobbs *Tel:* 01404 823260 *Fax:* 01404 823898   A30
Email: dh2789@eclipse.co.uk *Web:* www.eclipse.co.uk/danson

Large country house set in mature gardens, affording total peace and quiet. Ideal base for exploring the coast, moors and the beautiful cathedral city of Exeter. Excellent award-winning en-suite accommodation in spacious, highly appointed rooms. Breakfast served in oak-furnished dining room amongst a friendly family atmosphere. No smoking in house.

B & B from £22pp, Dinner available, Rooms 1 double, 2 triple, all en-suite, No smoking, Children welcome, No dogs, Open all year

---

LOWER MARSH FARM Marsh Green, Exeter EX5 2EX   *Map Ref:* 23
Sian Wroe *Tel:* 01404 822432 *Fax:* 01404 823330   A30/B3180
Email: lowermarshfarm@talk21.com

A beautiful 17th century listed farmhouse set in grounds of lawns, orchards, ponds, streams, stables and paddocks on the outskirts of Marsh Green in the rolling countryside. The accommodation is gracious and comfortable, the three bedrooms being generously equipped. There is a charming sitting room which has a log fire in winter. Breakfasts are traditional, vegetarians are catered for. An excellent pub locally.

B & B £23-£26pp, Rooms 2 double, 1 twin, all en-suite, No smoking, Children welcome, Dogs by arrangement, Open all year

---

THE GRANGE Stoke Hill, Exeter EX4 7JH   *Map Ref:* 23
Tel: 01392 259723   A30
Email: dudleythegrange@aol.com

The Grange is a country house on a hillside set in three acres of Woodland overlooking Exeter and the surrounding countryside and yet only two miles from Exeter City Centre. All bedrooms are en-suite with colour televisions and tea/coffee facilities. Ideally situated for exploring Exeter, Dartmoor and coastal areas.

B & B from £18pp, Rooms 3 double, 1 twin, all en-suite, No smoking, Children over 12, No dogs, Open all year

---

RYDON FARM Woodbury, Exeter EX5 1LB   *Map Ref:* 24
Mrs Sally Glanvill *Tel / Fax:* 01395 232341   B3179
Email: sallyglanvill@hotmail.com

A 16th century Devon longhouse on a working dairy farm which has been farmed by my husband's family for many generations. Guests return time after time to enjoy our hospitality with exposed beams, an inglenook fireplace and a romantic four poster. Delicious farmhouse breakfasts using fresh local produce and several local pubs and restaurants are nearby. AA, ETC 4 Diamonds.

B & B £24-£28pp, Rooms 1 double, 1 twin, 1 family, all en-suite, Restricted smoking, Children & dogs welcome, Open all year

DOCTON MILL Lymebridge, Hartland EX39 6EA

Map Ref: 25

Mr & Mrs J Borrett *Tel / Fax:* 01237 441369

A39

Email: john@doctonmill.freeserve.co.uk *Web:* www.doctonmill.co.uk

Docton Mill nestles in one of Devon's magical valleys with its renowned gardens and beautiful mill, listed in the Domesday book. The en-suite rooms all boast beautiful views over the valley, river and gardens and breakfast is served in the lounge overlooking the millwheel. The gardens abound with an array of shrubbery and was featured in BBC's 'Through the Garden Gate' and ITV's 'Discovering Gardens'.

B & B from £37.50pp, C-Cards MC VS, Dinner from £25.50, Rooms 1 double, 1 twin, both en-suite, No smoking, Children welcome, No dogs, Closed Xmas & New Year

---

ELM PARK FARM Elm Park, Bridgerule, Holsworthy EX22 7EL

Map Ref: 26

Sylvia Lucas

A3072, B3254

Tel / Fax: 01288 381231

Elm Park Farm is 10 minutes from Bude beaches and ideal for touring both Devon and Cornwall. We have spacious en-suite family rooms with colour televisions and tea/coffee facilities. Children especially welcomed with pony rides and games room. However there is also an antique furnished lounge for the adults to relax in. Wholesome home cooking using local produce.

B & B £18-£20pp, Dinner available, Rooms 3 family, all en-suite, Restricted smoking, Children welcome, Dogs by arrangement, Closed Dec to Feb

---

LEWORTHY FARMHOUSE Lower Leworthy, near Pyworthy, Holsworthy EX22 6SJ

Map Ref: 26

Pat Jennings

A388, A3072

Tel: 01409 259469

This is a peaceful place of flower filled lanes, buzzards soaring and wild deer roaming. Relax in our gardens, with coffee, wine, or cream tea. Swallows swoop, nuthatches and woodpeckers visit. Stroll the orchard, meadow and lake. Beautiful, en-suite rooms, fresh milk, flowers, quality teas, pretty china, books, and pristine bed linen, charming lounge. Delicious breakfasts and evening meals. Good pub grub.

B & B £20-£22pp, Dinner from £15, Rooms 1 twin, 2 double, 1 family, all en-suite or private bathroom, No smoking, Children welcome, No dogs, Open all year

---

WESSINGTON FARM Awliscombe, Honiton EX14 3NU

Map Ref: 27

Mrs Roz Summers *Tel:* 01404 42280 *Fax:* 01404 45271 *Mobile:* 07989 300392

A30, A373

Email: bandb@eastdevon.com *Web:* www.eastdevon.com/bedandbreakfast

Elegant Victorian stone farmhouse situated in an area of outstanding beauty, with wonderful panoramic views over open countryside. English Tourism Council inspected 4 Diamonds plus prestigious Silver Award. High standard rooms, warm friendly atmosphere and traditional aga cooked breakfasts. On A373, two miles from Honiton and picturesque coastline only 20 minutes. Rooms with en-suite, televisions and tea/coffee facilities

B & B £21-£30pp, Rooms 1 double en-suite, 2 twin en-suite/private bathroom, No smoking, Children welcome, No dogs, Open all year

---

WOODHAYES Honiton EX14 4TP

Map Ref: 27

Mr & Mrs Noel Page-Turner *Tel / Fax:* 01404 42011 *Mobile:* 07941 444560

A30

Email: cmpt@inweb.co.uk

A classical listed Georgian house which is surrounded by 150 acres of wood and pasture land and an acre of carefully tended garden. Christy produces excellent meals using produce from their farm and vegetable garden and guests dine by candlelight in the 18th century dining room hung with ancestral portraits. The market town of Honiton is just one mile away.

B & B from £37pp, C-Cards MC VS, Dinner from £24, Rooms 1 single, 1 double, 1 twin, all en-suite, Restricted smoking, Children welcome, Dogs by arrangement, Closed Feb

---

COURTMOOR FARM Upottery, Honiton EX14 9QA　　　　　*Map Ref:* 28
Rosalind & Bob Buxton　*Tel:* 01404 861565　　　　　　　　　A30
Email: courtmoor.farm@btinternet.com　*Web:* www.btinternet.com/~courtmoor.farm

Courtmoor Farm is set back a quarter of a mile from the A30 in 17 acres of grounds. Rosalind and Bob Buxton offer a warm welcome in peaceful surroundings. Each well equipped room has fine views, there are several private sitting areas. Evening meals are available, the premises are licensed. The farmhouse is ideally situated for both North and South coasts, also moorland.

B & B from £20pp, C-Cards MC VS, Dinner from £12, Rooms 1 twin, 1 double, 1 family, all en-suite, No smoking, Children welcome, No dogs, Closed Xmas & New Year

---

HELLIERS FARM Ashford, Aveton Gifford, Kingsbridge TQ7 4ND　　*Map Ref:* 29
Mrs C Lancaster　*Tel / Fax:* 01548 550689　*Mobile:* 07929 382670　　A379
Email: helliersfarm@ukonline.co.uk　*Web:* www.helliers.co.uk

Helliers Farm is a small working sheep farm on a hillside, overlooking a lovely valley, set in the heart of Devon's unspoilt countryside. It is within easy reach of beaches, moors, golf courses, National Trust houses and walks. The charming bedrooms all have tea/coffee trays, family, double and twin are en-suite and 1 single bedroom. ETC 4 Diamonds.

B & B from £23pp, Rooms 1 single, 1 double, 1 twin, 1 family, most en-suite, No smoking, Children welcome, Closed Xmas & New Year

---

HIGHWELL HOUSE Churchstow, Kingsbridge TQ7 3QP　　　　*Map Ref:* 29
Anthea Pope　*Tel:* 01548 852131　　　　　　　　　　　　A379, A381
Web: www.highwellhouse.co.uk

Idyllic secluded country house set in beautiful and peaceful two acres of mature gardens between spectacular coast and Kingsbridge. Ideal location for exploring South Hams. Luxury double and twin bedded en-suite rooms with remote televisions, tea/coffee facilities and hairdryers. Delicious breakfast with fruits from the garden, served in the conservatory. Non smoking. Private parking. AA 4 Diamonds.

B & B £21-£25pp, Rooms 2 double, 1 twin, all en-suite, No smoking, Children over 3, No dogs, Closed Dec to Jan

---

SOUTH ALLINGTON HOUSE Chivelstone, Kingsbridge TQ7 2NB　　*Map Ref:* 30
Barbara & Edward Baker　*Tel:* 01548 511272　*Fax:* 01548 511421　　A379
Email: barbara@sthallingtonbnb.demon.co.uk　*Web:* www.sthallingtonbnb.demon.co.uk

South Allington House is a working farm set in beautiful grounds in a quiet hamlet between Start Point and Prawle Point in the South Hams. If you want peace and quiet this is just the place for you. Two four poster beds available. Guests are free to use the grounds during the day, and we can provide tennis court, croquet and course fishing for your entertainment.

B & B £23.50-£33.25pp, Rooms 1 single, 5 double, 2 twin, 1 family, most en-suite, No smoking, Children over 4, No dogs, Closed Xmas

---

LITTLE PITTAFORD Slapton, Kingsbridge TQ7 2QG　　　　*Map Ref:* 31
David & Penny Cadogan　*Tel:* 01548 580418　*Fax:* 01548 580406　　A379
Email: littlepittaford@compuserve.com　*Web:* www.littlepittaford.co.uk

South facing and tucked away in a beautiful and tranquil setting. Close to Slapton and the sea. Light and airy rooms with televisions, flowers, crisp cotton sheets and supremely comfortable beds. Warm welcoming guest sitting room with a log fire. Superb food and a dining room looking out over the lovely garden and stream to the surrounding countryside.

B & B £33-£35pp, C-Cards MC VS, Dinner from £18, Rooms 2 double, 1 family, all en-suite, No smoking, Children welcome, No dogs, Closed Xmas

---

STOWFORD HOUSE Stowford, Lewdown EX20 4BZ
Alison Pardoe *Tel:* 01566 783415 *Fax:* 01566 783109
Email: alison@stowfordhouse.com *Web:* www.stowfordhouse.com

Map Ref: 32
M5, A30

Stowford House is a delightful Georgian country house set in the beautiful countryside of West Devon. Many of its original features have been retained, creating a special charm and ambience. The house, its garden and the surrounding area offer a tranquil escape from the pressures of modern life. Evening meals are available by prior arrangement. Ideal for exploring Devon and Cornwall.

B & B £23-£30pp, Dinner £14, Rooms 2 double, 2 twin, most en-suite, No smoking, Children over 14, No dogs, Closed Xmas

TOR COTTAGE Chillaton, Lifton PL16 0JE
Mrs Maureen Rowlatt *Tel:* 01822 860248 *Fax:* 01822 860126
Email: info@torcottage.co.uk *Web:* www.torcottage.co.uk

Map Ref: 32
M5, A30

Enjoy the ambience of this special place. Complete peace and privacy in beautiful en-suite bedsitting rooms, each with logfire, private garden and terraces. At the streamside there is a hidden valley and in the summer guests have use of our heated pool. Close to Eden Project, Dartmoor, coasts and gardens. Special rates, 3 nights for 2 Autumn/Spring. All England Award Winner ETC, AA, plus Gold Excellence Oscar. AA Guest of the Year for England 2002.

B & B from £57.50pp, C-Cards MC VS, Rooms 3 double, 1 twin, all en-suite, No smoking, Children over 14, No dogs, Closed Xmas & New Year

MOOR VIEW HOUSE Vale Down, Lydford EX20 4BB
The Sharples Family
Tel / Fax: 01822 820220

Map Ref: 33
A386

A family run country house hotel on the edge of Dartmoor, peacefully set in two acres of gardens. Moor View House can arrange dinner for their guests and always serve fine food and sound wine. After dinner guests are free to relax with log fires blazing in the winter. Walking, fishing, riding, shooting and golf are many of the leisure pursuits available during the day. AA, RAC 5 Diamonds.

B & B from £30pp, Dinner available, Rooms 3 double, 1 twin, all en-suite, No smoking, Children over 12, Open all year

GLENVILLE HOUSE 2 Tors Road, Lynmouth EX35 6ET
Tel: 01598 752202
Email: tricia@glenvillelynmouth.co.uk *Web:* www.glenvillelynmouth.co.uk

Map Ref: 34
A39

This delightful riverside Victorian house is a haven of peace and tranquility. Tastefully decorated bedrooms and attractive en-suites. All rooms with clock/radios, hairdryers and tea/coffee facilities. Elegant lounge overlooking river. The idyllic setting in wooded valley with picturesque harbour, village and unique water-powered cliff railway offers the guest spectacular scenery and beautiful walks. AA 4 Diamonds.

B & B from £23pp, Rooms 1 single, 4 double, 1 twin, most en-suite, No smoking, Children over 12, No dogs, Closed Dec to Feb

ALFORD HOUSE HOTEL Alford Terrace, Lynton EX35 6AT
Mark & Christine Channing *Tel / Fax:* 01598 752359
Email: enquiries@alfordhouse.co.uk *Web:* www.alfordhouse.co.uk

Map Ref: 34
A39

Alford House is an elegant Georgian style hotel with spectacular views over Lynton and Exmoor coastline. Delightful en-suite rooms with some four poster beds. Relaxing and peaceful atmosphere, warm hospitality and outstanding food and fine wine. Bargain breaks available.

B & B £22-£25pp, C-Cards MC VS, Dinner available, Rooms 6 double, 1 twin, all en-suite, No smoking, Children over 12, Dogs by arrangement, Closed Nov to Jan, open Xmas

CROFT HOUSE HOTEL Lydiate Lane, Lynton EX35 6HE
Jane & Terry Woolnough *Tel / Fax:* 01598 752391
Email: jane.woolnough@lineone.net

Map Ref: 34
A39

Croft House Hotel nestling in the old village, is our lovely Grade II Regency hotel built in 1828 for a sea captain and provides old world hospitality with modern day facilities. Special breaks with romantic four poster bedrooms and dinner served by candlelight. Fully licensed bar and attractive walled patio garden. Within easy walking distance of Valley of the Rocks. ETC 4 Diamonds.

B & B from £19pp, C-Cards MC VS, Rooms 5 double, 2 twin, most en-suite, No smoking, No children or dogs, Closed Nov to Feb

INGLESIDE HOTEL Lynton EX35 6HW
Tel: 01598 752223
Email: Johnpauldevon@aol.com

Map Ref: 34
A39

Small, family run hotel in premier position overlooking village. High standards of accommodation is assured with all rooms having en-suites, colour televisions and beverage facilities. Lynton is the perfect centre to enjoy the magnificent beauty of Exmoor's coast, cliff, rivers and countryside, whether walking or motoring. Safe car park for guests of hotel only.

B & B from £20pp, Dinner available, Rooms 5 double, 2 family, all en-suite, No smoking, Small dogs, Open all year

BLACKALLER HOTEL & RESTAURANT North Bovey, Moretonhampstead TQ13 8QY
Peter Hunt & Hazel Phillips *Tel:* 01647 440322 *Fax:* 01647 441131
Email: peter@blackaller.fsbusiness.co.uk *Web:* www.blackaller.co.uk

Map Ref: 35
A382, B3212

A 17th Century woollen mill in a peaceful riverside location on the eastern side of Dartmoor. Hosts keep bees and Jacob sheep. Home produced lamb and honey served. All rooms en-suite. The daily changing dinner menu is created with flair and features in major food guides. Licensed, wonderful place to unwind from the pressures of life.

B & B from £35pp, Dinner from £24, Rooms 3 double en-suite, No smoking, Children over 13, Dogs welcome, Closed Jan & Feb

GREAT DOCCOMBE FARM Doccombe, Moretonhampstead TQ13 8SS
David & Gill Oakey *Tel:* 01647 440694
Email: david.oakey3@btopenworld.com

Map Ref: 35
A382, B3212

This 300 year old farmhouse is situated in a pretty Dartmoor hamlet within Dartmoor National Park. The rooms are en-suite and guests can enjoy the delicious farmhouse cooking. Ideal for exploring Dartmoor's delights.

B & B from £40pp, Rooms 1 double, 1 triple, No smoking, Children welcome, No dogs, Open all year

GREAT SLONCOMBE FARM Moretonhampstead TQ13 8QF
Trudie Merchant *Tel / Fax:* 01647 440595
Email: hmerchant@sloncombe.freeserve.co.uk *Web:* www.greatsloncombefarm.co.uk

Map Ref: 35
A382, B3212

Share the magic of Dartmoor whilst staying in our lovely 13th century farmhouse full of interesting historical features. Set amongst meadows and woodland full of flowers and wildlife, this is a welcoming place to relax and explore the moors and Devon countryside. Comfortable en-suite rooms with every facility. Delicious Devonshire suppers and breakfasts.

B & B from £23pp, Dinner from £13, Rooms 2 double, 1 twin, No smoking, Children over 8, Dogs by arrangement, Open all year

GREAT WOOSTON FARM Moretonhampstead TQ13 8QA
Mary Cuming
Tel / Fax: 01647 440367   *Mobile:* 07798 670590

Map Ref: 35
A382, B3212

Great Wooston is a 280 acre mixed farm, situated within Dartmoor National Park high above the Teign Valley. There are wonderful views across open moorland and plenty of walks. The house is surrounded by well tended gardens, there is a barbecue and picnic area. Of the three comfortable rooms, two are en-suite, one has a four poster bed.

B & B £20-£24pp, C-Cards MC VS, Rooms 2 double (1 four poster), both en-suite, 1 twin with pb, No smoking, Children over 8, No dogs, Open all year

MOORCOTE COUNTRY GUEST HOUSE Chagford Cross, Moretonhampstead TQ13 8LS *Map Ref:* 35
Pat & Paul Lambert   *Tel:* 01647 440966
Email: moorcote@smartone.co.uk

A382

Situated in the Dartmoor National Park this Victorian house is set well back from the road in attractive mature gardens. The house is tastefully furnished, with most bedrooms benefitting from stunning views of Dartmoor countryside. Walking distance from the town. Ample parking in the grounds. Eating places nearby. ETC, AA 4 Diamonds.

B & B £19-£21pp, Rooms 2 double, 1 twin, 2 family, all en-suite, No smoking, Children over 5, No dogs, Closed Nov to Feb

CHIPLEY FARM Bickington, Newton Abbot TQ12 6JW
Louisa Westcott   *Tel:* 01626 821486/947   *Fax:* 01626 821486
Email: Louisa@chipleyfarmholidays.co.uk   *Web:* www.chipleyfarmholidays.co.uk

Map Ref: 36
A38, A383

Louisa, an artist, and Fred, a farmer, welcome you to their working dairy farm. Near rugged moor, sandy beaches, historic towns, pretty villages, and numerous tourist attractions, their delightful modern farmhouse nestles into the southern slope of a beautiful Devon valley. The AA have presented Louisa and Fred with a major hospitality award for their unique, relaxed family atmosphere, delicious breakfasts and farmhouse suppers.

B & B from £20pp, Dinner from £12.50, Rooms 1 double, 1 twin, 1 single, 1 family en-suite, No smoking, Children welcome, No dogs, Open all year

PENPARK Bickington, Newton Abbot TQ12 6LH
Madeleine Gregson   *Tel:* 01626 821314   *Fax:* 01626 821101
Email: gregson.penpark@ukgateway.net   *Web:* www.penpark.co.uk

Map Ref: 36
A38, A383

Penpark is a beautiful country house within the Dartmoor National Park. Designed by Clough Williams Ellis (of Portmeirion fame), it has superb hilltop views and five acres of secluded gardens and woodland. Light spacious rooms elegantly furnished with one garden room and also a tennis court. Perfect location for exploring Moor, beaches and Devon.

B & B £25-£28pp, Rooms 2 double, 1 twin, all private facilities, No smoking, Children welcome, No dogs, Open all year

THE THATCHED COTTAGE 9 Crossley Moor Road, Kingsteignton, Newton Abbot TQ12 3LE
Janice & Klaus Wiemeyer   *Tel:* 01626 365650
Email: thatched@globalnet.co.uk

Map Ref: 37
A380

The Thatched Cottage is a grade II listed 16th century Devon longhouse of great character. The restaurant is licensed and features a large open fireplace, home cooked food of the finest standard is served. Rooms have colour TV and tea/coffee facilities. Pretty garden and private car park. Easy access to Dartmoor, sandy beaches and the coastline.

B & B from £25pp, C-Cards MC VS, Dinner from £14.50, Rooms 1 single, 2 king size/twin, No smoking, No dogs, Open all year

SLADESDOWN FARM Landscove, near Ashburton, Newton Abbot TQ13 7ND　　*Map Ref:* 38
Sue & John Haddy *Tel / Fax:* 01364 653973 *Mobile:* 07803 712347　　　　　　　A38
Email: sue@sladesdownfarm.co.uk *Web:* www.sladesdownfarm.co.uk

A warm welcome awaits you at Sladesdown Farm, set in the Hem Valley, with peaceful walks. Both of the en-suite rooms are double with a sitting area, television and hot drinks. There is also a family unit of two rooms with private bathroom. Close to the Moors and coast yet only two miles off the A38. ETC 4 Diamonds, Silver Award.

B & B from £22.50pp, Rooms 2 double en-suite, 1 family with private bathroom, No smoking, Children welcome, No dogs, Closed Xmas

---

SAMPSONS THATCH HOTEL RESTAURANT Preston, Newton Abbot TQ12 3PP　　*Map Ref:* 39
Nigel Bell *Tel / Fax:* 01626 354913　　　　　　　　　　　A38, A380, B3195, B3193
Email: nigel@sampsonsfarm.com *Web:* www.sampsonsfarm.com

Although only five minutes from the A38 and A380, Sampsons Thatch is set in its own grounds in a tiny village. Our own renowned restaurant serving delicious Devon country produce and our own hens provide your eggs for breakfast. Pretty, en-suite rooms around a courtyard, special disabled en-suite. Dartmoor views and river walks. Secure parking. Category 1 Access Scheme. AA 4 Diamonds Rosette.

B & B £25-£50pp, C-Cards MC VS, Dinner from £12.50, Rooms 8 double en-suite, luxury apartment, Restricted smoking, Children welcome, Dogs by arrangement, Open all year

---

HIGHER CADHAM FARM Jacobstowe, Okehampton EX20 3RB　　　　*Map Ref:* 40
Jenny King *Tel:* 01837 851647 *Fax:* 01837 857410　　　　　　　　M5, A30
Web: www.highercadham.co.uk

This lovely family farm is situated in the centre of Devon making it ideal for touring. The rooms are well equipped and the hearty farmhouse fare using local produce is extremely popular with regular guests. Lots of extras are available: bike hire, packed lunches, licenced bar and cream teas with lashings of local clotted cream. An oasis in the Devon countryside.

B & B £20-£25pp, C-Cards MC VS DC, Dinner from £12.50, Rooms 1 single, 2 double, 3 twin, 3 family, most en-suite, Restricted smoking, Children over 1, Dogs by arrangement, Closed Xmas & New Year

---

NORMANDY HOUSE 5 Cornhill, Ottery St Mary EX11 1DW　　　　*Map Ref:* 41
Michael & Emma-Louise Rice *Tel:* 01404 811088 *Fax:* 01404 811023　　A30
Email: peterg.field@dial.pipex.com

A charming Grade II Georgian townhouse opposite the beautiful 14th century St Mary's church, offering individually decorated en-suite bedrooms with full facilities and warm hospitality. Licensed candlelit bistro offers freshly prepared food including selected home-grown produce. Terraced patio garden. AA/ETC 4 Diamond Silver Award. 'Which' recommended.

B & B from £24.75pp, C-Cards MC VS, Dinner from £12.95, Rooms 1 single, 3 double, 1 twin, all en-suite, Restricted smoking, Children over 6, No dogs, Closed Xmas & New Year

---

ELBERRY FARM Broadsands, Paignton TQ4 6HJ　　　　　　*Map Ref:* 42
Mandy Tooze *Tel / Fax:* 01803 842939　　　　　　　　　　A379
Web: www.elberryfarm.co.uk

A beef, poultry and arable farm, between two beaches within a two minute walk. Broadsands, a safe beach, was awarded the European Blue Flag 1994. A pitch and putt golf course is opposite, the zoo, town centre and National park are a short drive. Well equipped, comfortable bedrooms, guests are welcome to relax in the lounge and enjoy the garden. Baby sitting available.

B & B from £15pp, Dinner from £7, Rooms 1 twin, 2 double/family, 1 en-suite double, No smoking, Children welcome, Dogs by arrangement, Closed Dec

BERKELEYS OF ST JAMES 4 St James Place East, The Hoe, Plymouth PL1 3AS
Tel / Fax: 01752 221654   *Mobile:* 0467425199
Web: www.SmoothHound.co.uk/hotels/berkely2.html

Map Ref: 43
A38, A379, A386

Berkeley's of St.James is an elegant non smoking Victorian townhouse, tucked away from the main thoroughfare in quiet, pleasant and relaxing surroundings. Ideally situated on Plymouth Hoe, within walking distance to the sea front, historic Barbican, ferry port, theatre, pavilions, city centre and university. Excellent breakfast menu, serving free range organic produce where possible. Private and secure parking available.

B & B from £22.50pp, C-Cards MC VS, Rooms 1 single, 3 double, 1 twin/family, all en-suite, No smoking, Children welcome, No dogs, Closed Xmas & New Year

---

DUDLEY HOTEL 42 Sutherland Road, Mutley, Plymouth PL4 6BN
Tel: 01752 668322   *Fax:* 01752 673763
Email: butler@dudleyhotel.fsnet.co.uk

Map Ref: 43
A38, A379

A charming Victorian Hotel with an enviable reputation for comfort and cleanliness. Situated in the heart of historic Plymouth, we are within easy walking distance of the city centre, university and railway station. All rooms have recently been refurbished and are well equipped with colour televisions. etc. An ideal choice for business or pleasure.

B & B from £20pp, C-Cards MC VS, Dinner from £12, Rooms 1 single, 1 double, 2 twin, 2 family, No smoking in bedrooms, Children welcome, Dogs by arrangement, Open all year

---

BUGLE ROCKS Battisborough, Holbeton, Plymouth PL8 1JX
Jan Stockman   *Tel:* 01752 830422   *Fax:* 01752 830558
Email: buglerocks@hotmail.com

Map Ref: 44
A379

Bugle Rocks is a converted coach house nestling in a tranquil, secluded valley overlooking the sea. Close to the spectacular coastal footpath, only five minutes from the famous Mothecombe beach. In an area of outstanding natural beauty, but only 25 minutes from Plymouth and 90 minutes from the Eden Project with Dartmoor on the doorstep.

B & B from £25pp, Rooms 1 single, 3 double, all en-suite, Children welcome, Dogs by arrangement, Closed Xmas & New Year

---

BARNICOTT Bridgend Hill, Newton Ferrers, Plymouth PL8 1BA
Pat & John Urry
Tel: 01752 872843

Map Ref: 44
A379, B3186

Barnicott is a 16th century thatched cottage in an area of outstanding natural beauty on a river valley. Short drives to beaches and Dartmoor National Park. There are three inns nearby with one bistro serving evening meals. Bedrooms have wash basins, heating, colour televisions, hospitality trays and rural views. Private parking.

B & B from £16pp, Rooms 1 twin, 2 double, Restricted smoking, Children welcome, No dogs, Closed Dec to Jan

---

CROWN YEALM Newton Ferrers, Plymouth PL8 1AW
Mrs Jill Johnson
Tel / Fax: 01752 872365

Map Ref: 44
A379, B3186

South facing between Dartmoor and the South Devon coast, sharing River Yealm estuary with twin waterside villages, Newton Ferrars and Noss Mayo. Our guest rooms overlook garden and sun deck to waters edge, have central heating, private showers or family bathroom and comfortable beds. Good breakfasts and excellent dining choice within short stroll. Beautiful coastal footpath one mile. Safe off road parking.

B & B £20-£23pp, Rooms 1 double, 1 twin with private shower, 1 family with pb, Restricted smoking, Children welcome, Dogs by arrangement, Closed end Sep to mid-Oct

THE YEOMAN'S COUNTRY HOUSE Collaton, Salcombe TQ7 3DJ   *Map Ref:* 45
Greg Dicker   *Tel:* 01548 560085   *Fax:* 01548 562070   A381
Email: yeomanshouse@easicom.com   *Web:* www.yeomanshouse.co.uk

Fine listed thatched 16th century longhouse in 20 acre hidden valley with wonderful walking and beaches nearby. Luxurious en-suite bedrooms with antiques, refreshment trays, televisions and lavender scented linens and a four poster room. Beamed sitting room for guests with log fires in the winter. Extensive English breakfasts with organic produce and home baked bread. House party weekends with candlelit dinner parties for eight people.

B & B £37.50-£60pp, Dinner from £30, Rooms 3 double, 1 twin, all en-suite, No smoking, No children or dogs, Closed Xmas & New Year

---

CHERITON GUEST HOUSE Vicarage Road, Sidmouth EX10 8UQ   *Map Ref:* 46
Diana & John Lee   A3052
Tel / Fax: 01395 513810

Cheriton Guest House is a large town house which backs on to the River Sid, with the 'Byes' parkland beyond. There is a comfortable lounge with TV, and all the en-suite bedrooms have central heating, TV and tea/coffee making facilities. The garden is beautiful and secluded. Individual winners of Sidmouth in Bloom. There is some private parking.

B & B from £20pp, Dinner from £10, Rooms 3 single, 5 double/twin, 2 family, all en-suite, No smoking, Children welcome, Dogs by arrangement, Open all year

PEEKS HOUSE Harpford, Sidmouth EX10 0NH   *Map Ref:* 47
Fiona & Brian Rees   A3052
Tel / Fax: 01395 567664

Beautiful Regency house in the Hamlet of Harpford on the banks of the River Otter. 3 miles from Sidmouth and the medieval town of Ottery St Mary. 20 minutes from the M5, it is a peaceful area. Well equipped comfortable rooms are en-suite. Sumptuous English breakfasts, evening meals are available. A perfect location for visiting the attractions in Devon and the West Country.

B & B from £28pp, Dinner from £20, Rooms 2 twin, 2 double, all en-suite, No smoking, Children over 16, No dogs, Closed Nov to Feb

---

BARKHAM Sandyway, Simonsbath EX36 3LU   *Map Ref:* 48
John & Penny Adie   *Tel / Fax:* 01643 831370   A361
Email: adie.exmoor@btinternet.com   *Web:* www.exmoor-vacations.co.uk

In a hidden valley in the Exmoor National Park you can relax and enjoy our lovely old farmhouse. There is a beautiful oak panelled dining room, where you can enjoy delicious candlelit dinners, in winter, log fires are lit in the drawing room. The bedrooms are pleasant and comfortable. Barkham enjoys wonderful valley views with its woods, streams and waterfalls.

B & B £28-£35pp, Dinner from £18, Rooms 1 double en-suite, 1 private single, 1 double en-suite, No smoking, Children over 12, No dogs, Closed Xmas

THE GRANARY Harbourneford, South Brent TQ10 9DT   *Map Ref:* 49
Brenda & Alan Willey   *Tel / Fax:* 01364 73930   A38
Email: granary@ic24.net   *Web:* www.granary.ic24.net

The Granary, a light and spacious converted barn, is ideal for exploring Dartmoor, the south coast, National Trust Properties and Dartington. Brenda and Alan recently returned from South Africa and have created a unique comfortable retreat. The elegant en-suite rooms have all amenities plus little luxuries that make a stay memorable. Golf, fishing and horse riding nearby.

B & B £30-£35pp, Dinner from £22, Rooms 2 double, 1 twin, all en-suite, No smoking, Children over 14, Dogs by arrangement, Closed Jan

KERSCOTT FARM Exmoor, South Molton EX36 4QG
Theresa Sampson *Tel:* 01769 550262 *Fax:* 01769 550910
Email: kerscott.farm@virgin.net *Web:* www.devon-bandb-kerscott.co.uk

Map Ref: 50
B3227/A361

Enjoy a restful break at our Exmoor working farm mentioned
Domesday Book (1086) in a tranquil location. Olde worlde 16th
century farmhouse has a fascinating interior with antiques, pictures
and china. Superb elevated position with beautiful views overlooking
Exmoor and surrounding countryside. Pretty, tastefully furnished en-
suite bedrooms with TV. Highly acclaimed, varied home baked food,
tested pure spring water. Award winning farmhouse.

B & B £22-£23pp, Dinner from £10, Rooms 1 twin, 2 double,
all en-suite, No smoking, No children or dogs, Closed Xmas

ACORN COTTAGE Heathfield, Tavistock PL19 0LQ
Viv & Bob Powell-Thomas *Tel:* 01822 810038
Email: viv@acorncot.fsnet.co.uk *Web:* www.geocities.com/acorncottage

Map Ref: 51
A386

Acorn Cottage is a 17th century Grade II listed former farmhouse
with many original features. There is a private Guests' Lounge and
guests have their own key to come and go as they please. Situated
on the edge of Dartmoor National Park, with lovely views over the
surrounding countryside, it is a perfect location for visiting the many
beaches and coastal towns of Devon/Cornwall.

B & B from £18pp, C-Cards MC VS AE, Rooms 1 double, 2 twin,
all en-suite, No smoking, Children over 6, Dogs by arrangement,
Open all year

APRIL COTTAGE 12 Mount Tavy Road, Tavistock PL19 9JB
Sandra Callaghan
Tel: 01822 613280

Map Ref: 51
A386

Victorian character cottage situated on the banks of the River Tavy
in a pretty garden setting only five minutes level walk to town centre.
The bedrooms have been carefully furnished with attention to detail.
Enjoy a delicious full English breakfast in the conservatory
overlooking the river. There is also a comfortable television lounge
with seasonal log fires.

B & B from £20pp, Dinner from £7.50, Rooms 1 double, 1 twin,
1 family, all en-suite, No smoking, Children over 5, No dogs, Open
all year

BEERA FARMHOUSE Milton Abbot, Tavistock PL19 8PL
Hilary Tucker *Tel / Fax:* 01822 870216
Email: robert.tucker@farming.co.uk *Web:* www.beerafarmbedandbreakfast.com

Map Ref: 52
A30, B3362

Come and relax on our beautiful, peaceful working farm on the
Devon/Cornwall border. Ideal base for touring the West Country, the
coasts, National Trust properties, Eden Project and Dartmoor are all
within easy reach. All rooms have tea/coffee facilities and TV.
Excellent evening meals by prior arrangement. Lounge, piano, log
fire. Brochure available. Wonderful hospitality.

B & B from £20pp, C-Cards MC VS, Dinner from £13, Rooms 2
double, 1 twin, all en-suite, No smoking, Children welcome,
No dogs, Open all year

FONTHILL Torquay Road, Shaldon, Teignmouth TQ14 0AX
Jennifer Graeme *Tel / Fax:* 01626 872344
Email: swanphoto2@aol.com

Map Ref: 53
A379

Fonthill stands in beautiful grounds of 25 acres, close to the village
of Shaldon. Three delightful bedrooms have garden and river views.
Easy walk from village pubs. A hard tennis court for guests' use, the
coastal path to Torquay is nearby. Dartmoor National Park is easily
reached, as are Plymouth, Exeter and several fine National Trust
properties. Fonthill is a Highly Commended establishment.

B & B from £28pp, Rooms 3 twin with private or en-suite
bathroom, No smoking, No dogs, Closed Nov to Mar

RINGMORE HOUSE Brook Lane, Shaldon, Teignmouth TQ14 0AJ   *Map Ref:* 53
Robert & Helen Scull   *Tel:* 01626 873323   *Fax:* 01626 873353   A379
Email: hscull@aol.com   *Web:* www.ringmorehouse.co.uk

Grade II listed house within 12 metres of the Estuary, in lovely gardens. Easy walk to village and beaches. Guests are brought tea in bed, and are offered homemade bread and jams, within a huge breakfast menu. Meals available. A 4 poster bed is available, all rooms beautifully furnished and have TV. Self catering cottage adjacent to the house, has views over the gardens.

B & B from £25pp, Rooms 1 twin, 3 double, some en-suite, No smoking, Children over 8, No dogs, Closed Xmas

---

VIRGINIA COTTAGE Brook Lane, Shaldon, Teignmouth TQ14 0HL   *Map Ref:* 53
Jennifer & Michael Britton   B3199
Tel / Fax: 01626 872634

Virginia Cottage is a grade II listed 17th century house set in a one acre, partly walled garden. The pretty bedrooms offer either en-suite or private facilities and tea/coffee makers, they have garden views. An attractive sitting room has a large inglenook fireplace. This is a perfect location for exploring the interest of Dartmoor and Devon. Car parking in grounds.

B & B from £25pp, Rooms 2 double en-suite, 1 double with private bathroom, No smoking, Children over 12, No dogs, Closed Dec to Mar

---

WYTCHWOOD West Buckeridge, Teignmouth TQ14 8NF   *Map Ref:* 54
Jennifer Richardson Brown   *Tel:* 01626 773482   *Mobile:* 07971 783454   B3192
Email: wytchwood@yahoo.com   *Web:* www.messages.to/wytchwood

Award Winning Wytchwood has an outstanding reputation for lavish hospitality and traditional home cooking. Panoramic views, beautiful garden, parking, stylish interior design and the prettiest en-suite bedrooms. Homemade bread and rolls, jams, preserves, orchard honey and fresh garden produce. Delicious Devonshire cream teas, sponges and cakes. Many culinary awards. Historic sites and beautiful beaches nearby. Superb golf courses and good traditional pubs.

B & B from £25pp, C-Cards MC VS, Rooms 1 twin, 2 double, en-suite/private, No smoking, No dogs, Open all year

---

LOWER COLLIPRIEST FARM Tiverton EX16 4PT   *Map Ref:* 55
Mrs Olive   *Tel:* 01884 252321   A361
Email: linda@lowercollipriest.co.uk   *Web:* www.lowercollipriest.co.uk

Lower Collipriest is a 221 acre dairy and livestock farm with accommodation within a thatched farmhouse built around a courtyard garden. The food served is delicious as local produce is used in the super fresh home cooking. Guests are welcome to enjoy the scenic walks on the farm by the pond and the river. AA 4 Diamonds, ETC 4 Diamonds and Silver Award.

B & B from £25pp, C-Cards MC VS, Dinner available, Rooms 2 single, 3 twin, all en-suite, No smoking, No children or dogs, Closed Nov to Jan

---

BAMPTON GALLERY 2/4 Brook Street, Bampton, Tiverton EX16 9LY   *Map Ref:* 56
Gerald & Pauline Chidwick   *Tel:* 01398 331354   *Fax:* 01398 331119   A396
Email: bampgall@aol.com   *Web:* www.bampton.org.uk

Intriguing stone-built house and antique shop, central to a conservation town which was 'Britain in Bloom' national large village section winners 1998 and 2000. The rooms are charming and peaceful overlooking pretty gardens. Close to Knightshayes and Exmoor. Excellent local facilities and walks.

B & B from £24pp, Rooms 1 double, 2 twin, all en-suite, No smoking, No dogs, Open all year

THE BARK HOUSE Oakford Bridge, Bampton, Tiverton EX16 9HZ
Alastair Kameen & Justine Hill   *Tel:* 01398 351236
Web: www.barkhouse.co.uk

Map Ref: 56
A396

Be pampered at this charming hotel, situated in the beautiful Exe valley between Devon and Exmoor, and standing in woodland and gardens. Emphasis is placed on West Country produce in the elegant restaurant. The lounge has a log fire in all but the hottest weather. Bedrooms are well furnished, some luxuriously. All have TV and phone. AA 5 Diamonds, Breakfast and Dinner Awards.

B & B from £39.50pp, Dinner £25, Rooms 3 double, 2 twin, all en-suite/private, Restricted smoking, Closed most Mon/Tue

---

MANOR MILL HOUSE Bampton, Tiverton EX16 9LP
Chris & Kathy Ayres   *Tel:* 01398 332211   *Fax:* 01398 332009
Email: stay@manormill.demon.co.uk   *Web:* www.manormill.demon.co.uk

Map Ref: 56
A396

A relaxing 17th century miller's house with beams, inglenooks, four-posters and delicious breakfasts using local produce. All rooms are en-suite with televisions, tea/coffee facilities and 24-hour access. Parking is available on site and evening meals are available locally. Manor Mill House is an ideal location for exploring Exmoor, the coasts, National Trust properties and walking.

B & B from £22pp, C-Cards MC VS, Rooms 2 twin/double, 1 double, all en-suite, No smoking, Children over 12, No dogs, Open all year

---

NEWHOUSE FARM Oakford, Tiverton EX16 9JE
Anne Boldry   *Tel / Fax:* 01398 351347
Email: anne.boldry@btclick.com   *Web:* www.smoothhound.co.uk/hotels/newhs

Map Ref: 56
A396

Enjoy a real taste of country living at our 17th century farmhouse set in its own valley. Start the day with a farmhouse breakfast with homemade bread and preserves. Discover historic houses and gardens, antique shops, village pubs and farmers' markets. Return to the peace and quiet of our comfortable home, all bedrooms en-suite and individually furnished.

B & B £21-£23pp, Dinner from £13, Rooms 2 double, 1 twin, all en-suite, No smoking, No children or dogs, Closed New Year

---

OLD RECTORY Oakford, Tiverton EX16 9EW
Mr & Mrs Rostron   *Tel / Fax:* 01398 351486
Email: prot@oakford57.fsnet.co.uk   *Web:* www.oakforddevon.co.uk

Map Ref: 56
A396

Situated on the edge of the village this charming Victorian property is set in several acres of gardens and vineyards. The spacious rooms are decorated and furnished with elegance. Enjoyable home cooking and a delightful location together with the unobtrusive friendliness of the owners ensure a pleasurable stay. AA 4 Diamonds.

B & B £18.50-£22.50pp, Dinner from £12.50, Rooms 1 double en-suite, 1 twin, No smoking, No children or dogs, Closed Xmas & New Year

---

BICKLEIGH COTTAGE HOTEL Bickleigh, Tiverton EX16 8RJ
R S H & P M Cochrane
Tel: 01884 855230

Map Ref: 57
A396

Situated by the River Exe near Bickleigh Bridge, Bickleigh Cottage Hotel has been owned by the Cochrane family since 1933, the original cottage was built circa 1640. All the bedrooms are en-suite with tea/coffee facilities. This is a perfect centre for touring Devon. Exeter, Tiverton Castle, Knighthayes Court and Killerton House are all nearby.

B & B from £23.50pp, C-Cards MC VS, Rooms 1 single, 2 twin, 2 double, all en-suite, Restricted smoking, Children over 14, No dogs, Closed Oct to Apr

BLUE HAZE HOTEL Seaway Lane, Torquay TQ2 6PS   *Map Ref:* 58
Doug Newton & Hazel Newton *Tel / Fax:* 01803 607186   A379
Email: mail@bluehazehotel.co.uk *Web:* www.bluehazehotel.co.uk

A tranquil setting with lovely grounds in a quiet country lane, leading down to the sea situates Blue Haze Hotel in one of the best locations in Torquay. Nine comfortable quality rooms, each with a bathroom and all sparkling clean, quiet and well appointed. Splendid West country breakfasts with fresh eggs from Dartmoor, local speciality sausages, Somerset cheeses, Devon honey and homemade muffins.

B & B from £28pp, C-Cards MC VS AE DC, Rooms 4 double, 2 twin, 3 family, all en-suite, No smoking, Children welcome, No dogs, Closed Oct to March

CLOVELLY GUEST HOUSE 91 Avenue Road, Chelston, Torquay TQ2 5LH   *Map Ref:* 58
Kevin & Diane Francis *Tel / Fax:* 01803 292286   A380
Email: clovellytorquay@ntlworld.com *Web:* http://homepage.ntlworld.com/clovelly.guesthouse

Clovelly Guest House provides excellent accommodation with a friendly relaxed atmosphere. En-suite rooms are available plus a large family room. The food is excellent and special rates are available for families. Level walk to beach with a courtesy pick up from coach and train stations.

B & B from £12pp, Rooms 2 single, 2 double, 2 family, Restricted smoking, Children welcome, Dogs by arrangement, Open all year

COLINDALE HOTEL 20 Rathmore Road, Chelston, Torquay TQ2 6NY   *Map Ref:* 58
Barry Greenwood-Smith   A380
Tel: 01803 293947 *Mobile:* 077860 83275

Colindale is a charming Victorian town house just 400 yards from the seafront overlooking open parkland with an abundance of trees and greenery. All rooms are individually decorated all with high standards of comfort and cleanliness. Breakfast buffet with choice of yogurts, cereals, porridge, fresh fruit and fish, to set you up for the day's outings. Televisions in all rooms.

B & B £22-£25pp, C-Cards MC VS, Dinner from £15, Rooms 1 single, 4 double, 1 twin, 1 family, all en-suite, Restricted smoking, Children over 6, No dogs, Open all year

FAIRMOUNT HOUSE HOTEL Herbert Road, Chelston, Torquay TQ2 6RW   *Map Ref:* 58
Shaun & Carole Burke *Tel / Fax:* 01803 605446   A380
Email: Fairmounthouse@aol.com

Somewhere special, unhurried English breakfast, quiet undisturbed nights. Feel completely at home at our small family run hotel in a peaceful setting away from the busy sea front and near Cocking village and country park. There are miles of beaches and coves, and within walking distance, an excellent range of attractions. Fairmount offers quality, comfort and genuine friendly service.

B & B £28-£33pp, C-Cards MC VS, Dinner from £12, Rooms 1 single, 4 double, 2 family, 1 twin, all en-suite, No smoking, Children & dogs welcome, Closed Xmas & New Year

HEATHCLIFF HOUSE HOTEL 16 Newton Road, Torquay TQ2 5BZ   *Map Ref:* 58
Jill & Steve Sanders *Tel / Fax:* 01803 211580   A380
Email: hhhtorquay@btclick.com

Formerly a Vicarage, Heathcliff House is now a friendly family run hotel that retains its Victorian charm. All rooms are en-suite with televisions and tea/coffee facilities. Meals are served in the licensed bar. Perfect for a main holiday or touring Devon's picturesque coast and countryside. Large car park. Featured in Agatha Christie Guide.

B & B £17.50-£25pp, C-Cards MC VS, Rooms 8 double, 2 family, all en-suite, Restricted smoking, Children over 3, No dogs, Closed Xmas & New Year

KINGSTON HOUSE 75 Avenue Road, Torquay TQ2 5LL
Teresa & Giovanni Butto *Tel:* 01803 212760
Email: Butto@Kingstonhousehotel.co.uk *Web:* www.Kingstonehousehotel.co.uk

Map Ref: 58
A380

Kingston House combines Victorian elegance with modern day comforts, guests here are welcomed to warm hospitality in a relaxed and informal atmosphere. There is a comfortable lounge for relaxation, and a sunny terrace to enjoy. The hotel is conveniently situated for the sea front, harbour and town, also Torre Abbey and its beautiful gardens. Private car park. Favourable weekly terms available.

B & B £19-£26.50pp, Rooms 2 single, 2 twin, 2 double, No smoking, Children over 8, No dogs, Closed mid-Nov to Mar

MULBERRY HOUSE 1 Scarborough Road, Torquay TQ2 5UJ
Lesley Cooper
Tel: 01803 213639 *Mobile:* 07712 984579

Map Ref: 58
A38

Mulberry House is a Victorian, National-Heritage-Listed, corner terraced property in Torquay Devon, with a small restaurant. A short level walk from the seafront and town, it is popular with tourists and local residents alike, and is listed in many leading food and hotel food guides. The rooms are spacious, light and charming with antique pine furniture, Egyptian cotton bed linen and goose down duvets.

B & B from £25pp, Dinner from £17.50, Rooms 2 double, 1 twin, all en-suite, No smoking, Children welcome, No dogs, Open all year

OLD FOLLATON Plymouth Road, Totnes TQ9 5NA
Tel: 01803 865441 *Fax:* 01803 863597
Email: bondb@oldfollaton.co.uk *Web:* www.oldfollaton.co.uk

Map Ref: 59
A38, A384

A delightful Georgian country house, offering accommodation of the highest standard in a friendly and informal atmosphere. It is the ideal location surrounded by a wealth of places to visit, superb coastal and countryside walks and the splendour of Dartmoor.

B & B from £25pp, Rooms 3, all en-suite, No smoking, Children over 5, No dogs, Open all year

THE OLD FORGE AT TOTNES Seymour Place, Totnes TQ9 5AY
David Miller and Christine Hillier
Tel: 01803 862174 *Fax:* 01803 865385

Map Ref: 59
A38, A384

A warm welcome in this historic 600 year old stone building with cobbled drive and coach arch leading into the walled garden, a rural haven, minutes from Totnes centre. Luxurious, cosy cottage style well equipped en-suite rooms. Licensed. Own Parking. Huge breakfast menu, (traditional, vegetarian, and special diets). Conservatory leisure lounge with spa. Speciality golf breaks. Blacksmith's forge as featured on the Holiday programme.

B & B £27-£48pp, C-Cards MC VS, Rooms 1 single, 2 twin, 2 double, 5 family, all en-suite, No smoking, Children welcome, Guide dogs only, Open all year

HIGHER TORR FARM East Allington, Totnes TQ9 7QH
Mrs Helen Baker *Tel / Fax:* 01548 521248
Email: Helen@hrtorr.freeserve.co.uk

Map Ref: 60
A381

Relax in our spacious, comfortable farmhouse, in the South Devon hills, with panoramic views of Dartmoor. Richard and Helen welcome you to their home. Guests are encouraged to explore the farm and walkways. En-suite bedrooms have tea/coffee making facilities, clock radio and colour television. A full English breakfast is served. Parking for cars and boats. Central to Dartmoor/Salcombe, beaches and Kingsbridge town.

B & B £20-£25pp, Rooms 1 twin, 1 double, both en-suite, Children welcome, No dogs, Closed Xmas

ORCHARD HOUSE Horner, Halwell, Totnes TQ9 7LB *Map Ref:* 61
Helen Worth *Tel:* 01548 821448 A381
Web: www.orchard-house-halwell.co.uk

In a hamlet of the South Hams, between Totnes and Kingsbridge, Orchard House lies beneath an old cider orchard, a fifteen minute drive from the coast and Dartmoor. Superb accommodation, spacious, well equipped, en-suite bedrooms with beautiful furnishings. Guests' own sitting room with a log fire in winter. Breakfasts are generous and varied using local produce. A large mature garden, and parking.

B & B £20-£23pp, Rooms 2 double, 1 twin/family, all en-suite, No smoking, Children over 3, No dogs, Closed Nov to Feb

THE RED SLIPPER Stoke Gabriel, Totnes TQ9 6RU *Map Ref:* 62
Clive & Pam Wigfall A385
Tel / Fax: 01803 782315

A small, friendly, licensed establishment appointed to a high standard, located in the centre of a picturesque village on the River Dart. The attractive, en-suite, bedrooms (mainly on the ground floor) are generously equipped. A courtyard garden is available all day. Dinner available on request. From Thursday to Saturday an A' la Carte menu is served, also traditional Sunday. lunches. Parking Available.

B & B from £24.50pp, Dinner from £12.50, Rooms 3 twin, 1 double, 1 family, all en-suite, Restricted smoking, Children & dogs welcome, Open all year

SPRINGFIELD GARDEN Atherington, Umberleigh EX37 9JA *Map Ref:* 63
Mr & Mrs Swann *Tel / Fax:* 01769 560034 A377
Email: broadgdn@eurobell.co.uk *Web:* www.broadgdn.eurobell.co.uk

Traditional English house in a countryside setting with panoramic views and a cottage garden. We offer something special in our en-suite rooms which are furnished with care with power showers, tea/coffee facilities, televisions, fridges and fresh milk. Plus we provide a lounge for relaxation in the evenings. Perfect North Devon base, trips to the Eden Project, Lynmouth, Exmoor, Barnstaple, Clovelly and RHS Rosemoor. AA 5 Diamond.

B & B £18-£25pp, C-Cards MC VS, Dinner £15, Rooms 1 single, 1 double, 1 twin, all en-suite, No smoking, Children over 13, Dogs by arrangement, Open all year

SUNNYCLIFFE HOTEL Chapel Hill, Mortehoe, Woolacombe EX34 7EB *Map Ref:* 64
John & Jan Woodward *Tel:* 01271 870597 A361
Email: jj@sunnycliffe.freeserve.co.uk

A small, award winning quality hotel set above a picturesque Devon Cove on the Heritage coast. The well equipped bedrooms are en-suite and they have magnificent sea views. A five course dinner with a varied menu is offered. Plenty of lovely walks through hidden valleys, coastal paths where the countryside greets the sea in scenic beauty. Regret no children or pets. Brochure available.

B & B from £25pp, C-Cards MC VS, Dinner £15, Rooms 6 double, 2 twin, Restricted smoking, No children or dogs, Closed Nov to Feb

TORRFIELDS Sheepstor, Yelverton PL20 6PF *Map Ref:* 65
Mrs Seabrook *Tel:* 01822 852161 A386
Email: torrfields@beeb.net *Web:* www.users.eggconnect.net/seabrook.torrfields.htm

A warm welcome is guaranteed at Torrfields, a modern house in its own grounds. There is direct access on to the Moorland, ideal for walkers and motoring to north and south Devon coasts and Cornwall. Home cooked food from own grown or locally grown produce with homemade bread.

B & B from £20pp, Dinner available, Rooms 2 double, No smoking, Children welcome, No dogs, Closed Dec

Dorset

Dorset is largely Hardy's Wessex. There is hardly a part of the county that does not appear, although under a pseudonym, in one of Thomas Hardy's books. In the north of the county a region of sandy heathland stretches from the border with Hampshire to the centre of Dorset, while a range of chalk downs rolls to the east towards Salisbury Plain. In the south, the coast consists of a narrow broken ridge of chalky cliffs, the most easterly known as the Purbeck Hills.

Weymouth to the east lying behind a curving bay, is an elegant resort made famous by George III, who popularized the seaside as a leisure pursuit. The Isle of Portland, not strictly speaking an island, is attached to the mainland of Weymouth by a shingle bank created by the deposition of millions of pebbles through the process of long-shore drift. The bank encloses a lagoon known as the Fleet, a glorious haven for birds and a magnet for anglers. The view from the lighthouse, Portland Bill, is just spectacular, on the very edge of treacherous jagged cliffs.

The Dorset coast is renowned for its fossils, particularly around Lyme Regis, a lovely late Georgian seaside town favoured by the novelist Jane Austen, and the Cobb, the historic harbour wall was also the setting for John Fowles' The French Lieutenant's Woman. Further to the east is West Lulworth famous for Lulworth Cove, a truly enchanting circular bay, virtually surrounded by high cliffs. The whole area around West Lulworth, a picturesque village of thatched cottages, is wonderful walking country. Swanage is a medieval fishing village that developed into a fine seaside holiday resort with the coming of the railway. Its setting is superb against the Purbeck Hills, with the wide sweep of the bay in front. The Purbeck Ridge offers a spectacular panorama of Poole harbour. Poole is set on Britain's largest natural harbour, once the base for smugglers and buccaneers, now the home port of hosts of pleasure craft, particularly yachting. Brownsea Island within Poole harbour is a five hundred acre island of heath and woodland with glorious views of the Dorset coast. The island includes a two hundred acre nature reserve leased to the Dorset Wildlife Trust, a haven for a wide variety of wildlife including the red squirrel. Bournemouth, with a long sandy beach is a fine shopping centre, attracting visitors from a wide area. The public gardens, stretching from the sea into the centre of the town are splendid. Bournemouth is also gaining a reputation among the youth for its varied nightlife, almost to

Dorset's Heritage Coast (STB)

Dorset

rival Brighton's. Nearby Christchurch is an alternative base from which to explore the area and its beautiful priory with both Norman and Tudor architecture is definitely a site of interest.

The National Trust cares for much of coastal Dorset. The heathland behind Studland beach is a National Nature Reserve, particularly interesting in winter because of its large variety of over-wintering birds. The Studland peninsular is part of the large Corfe Castle estate. The Castle itself is one of the most impressive ruins in the country, strategically placed in the only gap in the chalk ridge which cuts Purbeck off. This important royal castle was besieiged twice during the civil war, but seized and destroyed in the second attempt in 1646 by the Parliamentary forces.

The county town of Dorchester is built on the site of a Roman town, with the nearby ancient Neolithic henge, the Maumbury Rings, being used in Roman times as an amphitheatre. The town boasts some fine Georgian buildings and the High Street has a particularly impressive variety of town houses. The Shire Hall preserves the old county court as a memorial to the Tolpuddle Martyrs who were tried here in 1834. Thomas Hardy lived and worked in Dorchester and his novel, The Mayor of Casterbridge, so brilliantly describes life in the town during the nineteenth century. To the north is Cerne Abbas, overlooked by the extraordinary prehistoric hill-carving of the Cerne Giant, a naked man carrying a club, and believed to be associated with pagan fertility rites, although there is still much dispute as to his true origins.

PLACES TO VISIT

This is a small selection of interesting places to visit. Many more are listed in our annual guide to Museums, Galleries, Historic Houses & Sites (see page 448)

Athelhampton House and Gardens
Athelhampton, Dorchester
Thomas Hardy was a frequent visitor here, one of the finest fifteenth century houses in Britain with magnificently furnished rooms and Grade I gardens including the world famous topiary pyramids.

Brewers Quay and Timewalk Journey
Weymouth
Travel back 600 years and discover Weymouth's history with Spanish Galleon and Georgian ballroom with a speciality shopping village and craft centre and Courtyard Restaurant.

Compton Acres Gardens
Poole
Ten seperate world gardens overlooking

Poole Harbour, including a Spanish Water Garden, Egyptian Court Garden and now a Sensory Sculpture Garden.

Corfe Castle
Wareham
The castle was built in the eleventh century on a steep hill. Many fine Norman and early English feautures have survived to this day. Visitors can see the remains of the eleventh century enclosure and hall and an early twelfth century great tower.

Dorset County Museum
Dorchester
Winner of Best Museum of Social History Award 1998, displays Dorset's history from the earliest times with wildlife, geography and famous figures.

Dorset

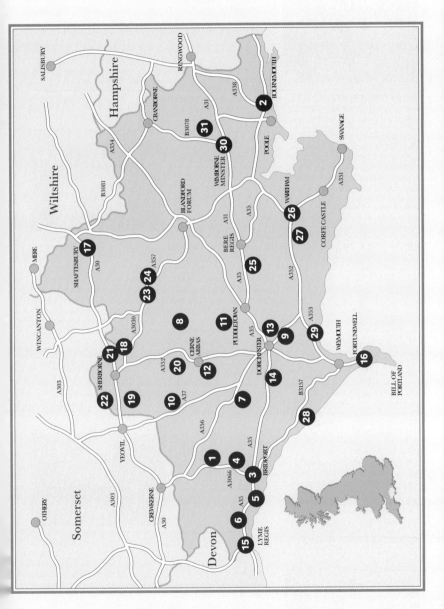

The Red Map References should be used to locate B & B properties on the pages that follow

BEAM COTTAGE 16 North Street, Beaminster DT8 3DZ   *Map Ref:* 1
Tel: 01308 863639   A3066
Email: margie@Beam-Cottage.fsnet.co.uk

An attractive Grade II listed cottage in the centre of Beaminster with a secluded and pretty garden. All rooms are en-suite with private sitting rooms and evening meals are available on request. Also available is a pretty twin bedded cottage in the garden.

B & B from £25pp, Rooms 1 double, 1 twin, 1 family, all en-suite, Restricted smoking, Children welcome, Open all year

---

AMITIE GUEST HOUSE 1247 Christchurch Rd, Bournemouth BH7 6BP   *Map Ref:* 2
Jenny & Paul Stevenson *Tel:* 01202 427255 *Fax:* 01202 461488   A338
Email: b&b@amitie.co.uk *Web:* www.amitie.co.uk

Easy to find on the A35, near the town centre and award winning beaches. All rooms are en-suite with televisions, tea/coffee facilities, radio alarm clocks, hairdryers, shaving points, individually controlled central heating and a daily chamber service. Own keys are provided, a healthy breakfast is included and parking an added bonus. Special occasions catered for.

B & B from £27pp, Rooms 1 single, 3 double, 2 twin, 1 family, all en-suite, Restricted smoking, Children over 12, Guide dogs only, Open all year

---

CHASE LODGE Herbert Road, Alum Chine, Bournemouth BH4 8HD   *Map Ref:* 2
Mr & Mrs W Webb *Tel:* 01202 768515 *Fax:* 01202 757847   A338
Email: chaselodge@hotmail.com *Web:* www.tuckedup.com/chaselodge.html

A charming Edwardian family run hotel in a quiet location with comfy residents' lounge and daily paper. Only a short walk to sandy beaches, or shops and restaurants in Westbourne. Tea/coffee and colour televisions in all rooms. Breakfast and mouth-watering picnics are available packed into cool bags. Excellent centre for exploring Dorset/New Forest/Purbecks/Hardy country. Special music courses Autumn/Spring. Car park.

B & B from £21pp, Rooms 1 twin, 3 double, 2 family, all en-suite/private, No smoking, Children welcome, No dogs, Closed Xmas & New Year

---

THE COTTAGE PRIVATE HOTEL 12 Southern Road, Southbourne, Bournemouth BH6 3SR
Valarie & Ronald Halliwell *Tel:* 01202 422764 *Fax:* 01202 381442   *Map Ref:* 2
Email: ron+val@rjvhalliwell.force9.co.uk *Web:* www.smoothhound.co.uk/hotels/cottage3   A338

A charming family run licensed private hotel in restful location near Blue Flag beach yet convenient for the New Forest and Dorset countryside. Noted for home prepared fresh cooking, cleanliness and tastefully furnished accommodation. Totally non-smoking. Minimum age for children is twelve years. Acclaimed for award winning floral displays. Ample parking.

B & B from £25pp, Dinner available, Rooms 2 double, 2 twin, 2 triple, all en-suite/private facilities, No smoking, Children over 12, No dogs, Closed Oct to Apr

---

GERVIS COURT HOTEL 38 Gervis Road, Bournemouth BH1 3DH   *Map Ref:* 2
Alan & Jackie Edwards *Tel:* 01202 556871 *Fax:* 01202 467066   A338
Email: enquiries@gerviscourthotel.co.uk *Web:* www.gerviscourthotel.co.uk

A charming, Victorian villa, standing in grounds amongst pine trees. Bedrooms are comfortably furnished and well equipped, there are some on the ground floor. A short walk to the beach, shops, theatres, clubs and conference centre. Excellent choice of restaurants, pubs and clubs nearby. Gervis Court is ideally located for exploring Bournemouth, Poole, the New Forest and the Dorset Coast.

B & B £20-£30pp, C-Cards MC VS, Rooms 1 single, 2 family, 2 twin, 8 double, No smoking, Children welcome, No dogs, Open all year

ROSEMOUNT 32 Bryanstone Road, Talbot Woods, Bournemouth BH3 7JF   *Map Ref:* 2
Mary Barrett *Tel:* 01202 462729   A347
Email: rosemount@dandenong32.freeserve.co.uk   *Web:* www.dandenong32.freeserve.co.uk

Stay in this lovely Edwardian house and enjoy the warm atmosphere, good food, and the beautiful Dorset sights. The seafront and the New Forest National Park are a short drive away and Bournemouth University is within walking distance. We provide a very high standard of cleanliness, decor and modern comfortable furnishings. The bedrooms are fully en-suite and well equipped.

B & B from £17.50pp, Rooms 3 single (one en-suite), 1 twin en-suite, 1 double en-suite, No smoking, Children over 10, No dogs, Closed Xmas day

SHADY NOOK GUEST HOUSE 3 Upper Terrace Road, Bournemouth BH2 5NW   *Map Ref:* 2
Paul & Avril Holdaway *Tel:* 01202 551557   A338
Email: shady.nook@btinternet.com

A centrally located, charming Victorian residence close to shops, gardens, beaches, entertainment and conference centre. Bright, comfortable rooms, most en-suite with tea/coffee facilities, Sky television and full central heating. Special diets are catered for and there are also reduced rates for children. Parking by arrangement. Cheerful atmosphere.

B & B £18-£28pp, Dinner available, Rooms 3 double, 2 twin, 2 family, most en-suite, Restricted smoking, Children welcome, Dogs by arrangement, Closed Xmas & New Year

WYCHCOTE HOTEL 2 Somerville Road, West Cliff, Bournemouth BH2 5LH   *Map Ref:* 2
Tel: 01202 557898   A338
Email: info@wychcote.co.uk   *Web:* www.wychcote.co.uk

Small well appointed Victorian house hotel peacefully situated in its own tree-lined grounds. Short walk to town centre, beach and entertainments. Two lounges overlooking the garden. Standard, deluxe and superior rooms available including four poster beds. All rooms en-suite, all have colour television, hospitality tray and radio alarm. Four course breakfast with good choice of cereal, fresh fruit and juices.

B & B £27-£42pp, C-Cards MC VS, Rooms 1 single, 8 double, 3 twin, all en-suite, No smoking, No children or dogs, Closed Jan to Feb

BRITMEAD HOUSE 154 West Bay Road, Bridport DT6 4EG   *Map Ref:* 3
Alan & Louisa Hardy *Tel:* 01308 422941 *Fax:* 01308 422516   A35
Email: britmead@talk21.com *Web:* www.britmeadhouse.co.uk

This is an elegant, spacious and tastefully decorated house, situated a short walk from West Bay harbour and coastal path. The bedrooms are individually presented and they are well equipped. The lounge and dining room overlook the garden. Britmead House is renowned for hospitality and comfort. There is also swimming, golf, fossil hunting, sea fishing and walking in the area. Private parking.

B & B £22-£32pp, C-Cards MC VS, Rooms 3 double, 2 twin, 2 family, all en-suite, Restricted smoking, Children welcome, Dogs by arrangement, Open all year

SPRAY COPSE FARM Lee Lane, Bradpole, Bridport DT6 4AP   *Map Ref:* 4
Stuart & Ginnie Stacey *Tel:* 01308 458510 *Fax:* 01308 421015 *Mobile:* 07850 300044   A35
Email: spraycopse@lineone.net *Web:* www.spraycopsefarm.com

A peaceful farmhouse in 3 acres of garden with a lake, Bridport is 1 mile, West Bay is also 1 mile, where the BBC series Harbour Lights was filmed. The farmhouse is built from local stone, it has beamed ceilings, log fires and large, well equipped bedrooms. Breakfast and evening meals are served in the spacious farmhouse kitchen. Excellent pubs. Ideal for walking.

B & B £25-£30pp, Dinner from £18, Rooms 1 single, 1 double, 1 twin, 1 family, all en-suite/private, No smoking, Children over 4, Dogs not in bedrooms, Closed Nov to Mar

CHAMP'S LAND Brighthay Lane, North Chideock, Bridport DT6 6JZ   *Map Ref:* 5
Mrs Miranda Tennant   A35
Tel: 01297 489314

Luxury accommodation in a golden stone 17th century former farmhouse. Filled with antique furniture and beautifully decorated with log fires and guests' own sitting room. The house is situated peacefully in a no-through lane with the sea only one mile away where there are wonderful walks. There are several pubs and restaurants nearby and also many historic houses and gardens to visit.

B & B £30-£35pp, Rooms 1 double, 1 twin, both with private bathroom, No smoking, Children over 14, Dogs welcome, Closed Xmas & New Year

---

CANDIDA HOUSE Whitchurch Canonicorum, Bridport DT6 6RQ   *Map Ref:* 6
Mrs C Bain   *Tel / Fax:* 01297 489629   A35
Email: candida@globalnet.co.uk   *Web:* holidayaccom.com/candida-house

This former Georgian rectory in a tranquil Dorset village, two miles from the sea, has been our family home for over 20 years. Our guests are offered centrally heated, comfortably furnished double or twin bedded rooms with en-suite bathrooms, televisions and tea/coffee facilities. The peaceful ambience and warmth of hospitality should make you feel at home. Delicious breakfasts.

B & B £25-£30pp, C-Cards, Rooms 1 double, 2 twin, all en-suite, No smoking, No children or dogs, Closed Nov to Mar

---

GRAYS FARMHOUSE Clift Lane, Toller Porcorum, Dorchester DT2 0EJ   *Map Ref:* 7
Rosie & Roger Britton   *Tel:* 01308 485574   *Mobile:* 07971 235115   A35, A356
Email: rosie@farmhousebnb.co.uk   *Web:* www.farmhousebnb.co.uk

Stand on the grassy ramparts of Eggardon Hillfort and gaze across a valley to this romantically secluded farmhouse, set amongst ancient wildflower meadows and medieval woodland. Follow the sleepy lanes to the former shooting lodge with its enormous flagstones, studded doors, chunky beams, vibrant paintings and tranquil bedrooms. Relish being welcomed like old friends into this magical corner of West Dorset.

B & B from £23pp, Rooms 1 double, 1 family, both en-suite, No smoking, Children welcome, Dogs by arrangement, Closed Xmas & New Year

---

HOLYLEAS HOUSE Buckland Newton, Dorchester DT2 7DP   *Map Ref:* 8
Tia Bunkall   *Tel:* 01300 345214   *Fax:* 01305 264488   *Mobile:* 07968 341887   A352
Email: tiabunkall@holyleas.fsnet.co.uk

The family labrador greets visitors to this friendly country house standing in walled gardens. Buckland Newton is a peaceful village between Sherborne and Dorchester surrounded by rolling hills. Superb for walking, visiting houses, gardens and the coastline. Beautiful rooms with fine views. Guests' sitting room has a log fire where you can relax. Breakfast includes free range eggs, home made marmalade. Good pubs nearby.

B & B from £22.50pp, Rooms 1 single, 1 twin, 1 double, all en-suite/private, No smoking, Children & dogs welcome, Closed Xmas & New Year

---

REW COTTAGE Buckland Newton, Dorchester DT2 7DN   *Map Ref:* 8
Annette & Rupert McCarthy   A35, A352
Tel / Fax: 01300 345467

Visitors are assured of a warm welcome. Located in Thomas Hardy country, the cottage is surrounded by farmland with lovely views. Ideal for walking or touring, it is within easy reach of Sherborne, Dorchester and the sea. Bedrooms are comfortably furnished and well equipped. Breakfast offers a good choice to include traditional, with homemade marmalades and preserves. Attractive pubs and restaurants locally.

B & B £22.50-£26pp, Rooms 1 twin, 1 double, Restricted smoking, Children by arrangement, Dogs by arrangement, Closed mid-Dec to mid-Jan

Brambles, near Dorchester

HIGHER CAME FARM HOUSE Higher Came, Dorchester DT2 8NR   *Map Ref:* 9
Lisa Bowden *Tel / Fax:* 01305 268908   A354
Email: highercame@eurolink.ltd.net

A beautiful 17th century farmhouse peacefully nestling in the heart of Dorset's Hardy country, within easy reach of Dorchester, Weymouth and Bridport. Walking here is superb, as is fishing, sailing and sight seeing. This traditional farmhouse has spacious attractively furnished bedrooms, all have television tea/coffee facilities and hairdryers. Home cooked breakfast using local produce. Relaxing, comfortable residents' lounge and a large garden.

B & B £25-£32pp, C-Cards MC VS, Rooms 1 double/twin en-suite, 1 double/twin, 1 double, both pb, Restricted smoking, Children welcome, Dogs by arrangement, Open all year

BRAMBLES Woolcombe, Melbury Bubb, Dorchester DT2 0NJ   *Map Ref:* 10
Anita & Andre Millorit   A37
Tel: 01935 83672   *Fax:* 01935 83003   *see Photo on page 131*

Delightful thatched cottage in peaceful countryside near to Dorchester and Sherborne, and a short drive to the coast. Beautifully appointed and well equipped, it offers every comfort, and a friendly welcome. Pretty bedrooms always have fresh flowers. A wide choice of breakfast, including traditional, continental, vegetarian or fruit platter. Many places of interest and walks to explore. Parking within the grounds.

B & B £20-£25pp, Dinner available, Rooms 2 single, 1 twin en-suite, 1 double en-suite, No smoking, Children welcome, No dogs, Closed Xmas & New Year

MUSTON MANOR Piddlehinton, Dorchester DT2 7SY   *Map Ref:* 11
Mr & Mrs O B N Paine   B3143
Tel: 01305 848242

Built in 1609 by the Churchill family, Muston Manor remained in their ownership until bought by the Paine family in 1975. Standing in five acres, surrounded by farmland in the peaceful valley of Piddle, bedrooms are large, warm and comfortable, and well furnished. There is a heated swimming pool in Summer. An excellent local network of footpaths. Super local pubs.

B & B from £22pp, Rooms 2 double, 1 en-suite, No smoking, Children over 10, Dogs by arrangement, Closed Nov to Feb

LAMPERTS COTTAGE Sydling St Nicholas, Cerne Abbas, Dorchester DT2 9NU   *Map Ref:* 12
Nicky Willis *Tel:* 01300 341659   *Fax:* 01300 341699   A37
Email: nickywillis@teso.net

A 16th century thatched listed cottage with a stream running in front. Bedrooms are prettily decorated, they are centrally heated and have tea/coffee makers. Breakfast is served in the dining room with an inglenook fireplace, bread oven and beams. The countryside is excellent for walking with footpaths over chalk hills and through hidden valleys. Guidebooks/maps available to borrow. AA 3 Diamonds.

B & B from £21pp, C-Cards, Rooms 1 twin, 1 double, 1 family, Restricted smoking, Children over 8, Dogs by arrangement, Open all year

LOWER LEWELL FARMHOUSE West Stafford, Dorchester DT2 8AP   *Map Ref:* 13
Marian Tomblin   A35, A352
Tel: 01305 267169

A 17th century farmhouse situated among a patchwork of fields in rolling countryside, reputed to be Talbothays Dairy from Thomas Hardy's 'Tess of the D'Urbervilles'. Built in Portland stone this is a homely farmhouse with beams, log fires and space. Hearty breakfasts from the farmhouse kitchen are served in the dining room with an inglenook. Good local pubs offering snacks and meals.

B & B from £20pp, Rooms 1 twin, 1 double, 1 family, Open all year

YELLOWHAM FARMHOUSE Yellowham Wood, Dorchester DT2 8RW
Tel: 01305 262892   *Fax:* 01305 257707
Email: b&b@yellowham.freeserve.co.uk   *Web:* www.yellowham.freeserve.co.uk

Map Ref: 13
A35

Situated in the very heart of Hardy country on the edge of the idyllic Yellowham Wood in 120 acres of farmland and 130 acres of woodland. The farm contains an abundance of flora and fauna which has been encouraged over the years. The accommodation is on the ground floor. Located one and a half miles east of Dorchester, off A35.

B & B £25-£28pp, C-Cards MC VS AE, Dinner available, Rooms 4 double, 1 twin, all en-suite, No smoking, Children over 6, Dogs by arrangement, Open all year

CHURCHVIEW GUEST HOUSE Winterbourne Abbas, Dorchester DT2 9LS
Michael & Jane Deller   *Tel / Fax:* 01305 889296
Email: stay@churchview.co.uk   *Web:* www.churchview.co.uk

Map Ref: 14
A35

A beautiful 17th century guest house set in a small village near Dorchester, offers a warm welcome and delicious home cooked meals. Character bedrooms with hospitality trays, TV and radio. Meals taken in our period dining room feature local produce, cream and cheese. Two comfortable lounges and licensed bar. Your hosts will give every assistance with information to ensure a memorable stay.

B & B £24-£31pp, C-Cards MC VS, Dinner from £14, Rooms 1 single, 3 twin, 4 double, 1 family, all en-suite/private, No smoking, Children over 5, Dogs welcome, Closed Xmas & New Year

THE OLD RECTORY Winterbourne Steepleton, Dorchester DT2 9LG
Capt & Mrs M Tree   *Tel:* 01305 889468   *Fax:* 01305 889737   *Mobile:* 07818 037183
Email: trees@eurobell.co.uk   *Web:* www.trees.eurobell.co.uk

Map Ref: 14
A35

Built in 1850 on one acre of land in a quiet hamlet with beautiful surroundings. Close to Weymouth beaches and historic Dorchester and their varied restaurants with pubs nearby. However private dining is available on request with minimum of six persons. We specialise in giving a good nights sleep and a copious breakfast with many homemade produces. French spoken. No credit card facilities.

B & B £25-£55pp, Dinner available, Rooms 4 double, twin or family, all en-suite, No smoking, Children welcome, No dogs, Closed Xmas & New Year

OLD LYME GUEST HOUSE 29 Coombe Street, Lyme Regis DT7 3PP
Paul Rhodes and Valerie Ayling   *Tel:* 01297 442929
Email: oldlyme.guesthouse@virgin.net   *Web:* www.oldlymeguesthouse.co.uk

Map Ref: 15
A35, A3052

English Tourism's Top Gold Award winning guest house. Historic 18th century building refurbished to a very high standard. Comfortable en-suite rooms all with television and tea/coffee facilities. Guest lounge. Ideal location in a quiet street in the heart of the picturesque old town. Three minutes level walk to the sea, shops and restaurants. Free parking nearby for our guests.

B & B £21-£27pp, Rooms 4 double, 1 family, all en-suite, No smoking, Children over 5, No dogs, Closed Xmas

RASHWOOD LODGE Clappentail Lane, Lyme Regis DT7 3LZ
Mrs Diana Lake
Tel: 01297 445700

Map Ref: 15
A35, A3052

Rashwood Lodge is an unusual octagonal house located on the Western hillside with views over Lyme Bay. Just a short walk away is the coastal footpath and Ware Cliff famed for its part in 'The French Lieutenant's Woman'. The rooms have televisions and tea/coffee making facilities, benefitting from their south facing aspect which overlooks a large and colourful garden set in peaceful surroundings.

B & B £23-£27pp, Rooms 2 double, 1 twin, 1 en-suite, 2 private bathrooms, No smoking, Children over 4, Dogs by arrangement, Closed Nov to Feb

THE RED HOUSE Sidmouth Road, Lyme Regis DT7 3ES *Map Ref:* 15
Tony & Vicky Norman *Tel / Fax:* 01297 442055 A35, A3052, B3165
Email: red.house@virgin.net *Web:* www.SmoothHound.co.uk/hotels.redhous2.html

At 450 feet above sea level in historic Lyme Regis The Red House, built for a famous maritime inventor in 1928, commands stunning views along the Dorset Coast over Golden Cap. Bedrooms have televisions, tea/coffee making facilities, a fridge and fresh flowers. Breakfast is served on the terrace in fine weather. There are many fine restaurants, cafes and pubs within short distance.

B & B £20-£27pp, C-Cards MC VS, Rooms 1 double, 2 twin, all en-suite, No smoking, Children over 8, No dogs, Closed November to March

QUEEN ANNE HOUSE 2-4 Fortuneswell, Portland DT5 1LP *Map Ref:* 16
Margaret Dunlop *Tel:* 01305 820028 *Fax:* 01305 824389 *Mobile:* 07712 765482 A354
Web: www.queenannehouse.com

Queen Anne House is a beautifully renovated Grade II listed building circa 1720. It has survived virtually unspoiled compared to most of the townhouses of this period. We have 3 luxury double bedrooms with tester beds, ensuite bathrooms, televisions and tea/coffee facilities. Suitable for romantic weekends. Close to Portland Bill, Weymouth and the famous Chesil Beach.

B & B from £27.50pp, Rooms 3 double, all en-suite, No smoking, Children welcome, Only guide dogs, Open all year

THE KNOLL Bleke Street, Shaftesbury SP7 8AH *Map Ref:* 17
Bryan & Kate Pickard *Tel:* 01747 855243 A30, A350
Email: pickshaftesbury@compuserve.com *Web:* www.pick-art.org.uk

Spacious Victorian family house in large gardens. Easy walk to town centre, shops, restaurants and famous Gold Hill. With panoramic views over three counties at the home of an artist and quilter, this is a special place to stay.

B & B £50-£52pp, Rooms 1 double en-suite, No smoking, No children or dogs, Closed Nov to Feb

CLIFF HOUSE Breach Lane, Shaftesbury SP7 8LF *Map Ref:* 17
Diana & David Pow *Tel / Fax:* 01747 852548 *Mobile:* 07990 574849 A30, A350
Email: dianaepow@aol.com *Web:* cliff-house.co.uk

Traditional Regency Grade II listed property in acre of walled mature garden. Varied choice of delicious English breakfasts and homemade jams using fruit from garden. One bedroom looks towards church and hills beyond. Both are quiet with large en-suite bathrooms, televisions and tea/coffee making facilities. Town centre within walking distance with magnificent views, Gold Hill, pubs and restaurants. Ideal for short breaks to explore Dorset.

B & B £27.50-£30pp, Rooms 2 twin, all en-suite, No smoking, Children over 5, No dogs, Closed Xmas

MUNDEN HOUSE Mundens Lane, Alweston, Sherborne DT9 5HU *Map Ref:* 18
Sylvia & Joe Benjamin *Tel:* 01963 23150 *Fax:* 01963 23153 *Mobile:* 07971 846246 A3030
Email: sylvia@mundenhouse.demon.co.uk *Web:* www.mundenhouse.demon.co.uk

A warm welcome awaits you at Munden House. Tastefully furnished and decorated, all bedrooms are en-suite with hospitality trays, trouser press and hairdryer. Located in the Blackmore Vale on the outskirts of the historic town of Sherborne with its castles, Abbey and antique shops. There are excellent restaurants and pubs to suit all tastes, a golf course and two tennis courts nearby.

B & B £32.50-£45pp, C-Cards MC VS, Rooms 4 double, 2 twin, 1 family, all en-suite, No smoking, Children welcome, No dogs, Open all year

HEARTSEASE COTTAGE North Street, Bradford Abbas, Sherborne DT9 6SA
Robin & Wendy Dann   *Tel / Fax:* 01935 475480   *Mobile:* 07929 717019
Email: heartsease@talk21.com

Map Ref: 19
A30

'Heartsease' describes our cottage better than any brochure.
Delightful old honey coloured stone cottage, huge conservatory
looking on to idyllic garden, beautiful Dorset village lane. Themed
bedrooms, guests' sitting room. Large choice of breakfasts and
dinners, that you would love to have at home - but never have time.
Discounts over 1 night. ETC 5 Diamonds and Silver Award.

B & B from £22pp, Dinner from £13, Rooms 1 double, 2 twin,
en-suite or private bathroom, Restricted smoking, Children over 8,
No dogs, Open all year

ALMSHOUSE FARM Hermitage, Holnest, Sherborne DT9 6HA
Mrs Jenny Mayo
Tel / Fax: 01963 210296

Map Ref: 20
A352

Spoil yourself and stay on our traditional working dairy farm situated
in a totally unspoiled part of Dorset. Listed farmhouse retains its age
and beauty whilst boasting every modern convenience. All rooms
have TV and tea/coffee making facilities. Wander the charming
garden, surrounding fields or lanes and build an appetite for a real
breakfast. Golf, fishing and riding nearby. AA ETC 4 Diamonds, Silver
Award.

B & B from £23pp, Rooms 2 double, 1 twin, all en-suite,
Restricted smoking, Children over 10, No dogs, Closed Dec & Jan

---

THE OLD VICARAGE Sherborne Road, Milborne Port, Sherborne DT9 5AT
Jorgen Kunath and Anthony Ma   *Tel:* 01963 251117   *Fax:* 01963 251515
Email: theoldvicarage@milborneport.freeserve.co.uk   *Web:* www.milborneport.freeserve.co.uk

Map Ref: 21
A30

The Old Vivarage is a listed Victorian Gothic building elegantly
furnished with antiques, it is set in 3.5 acres of beautiful grounds.
The spacious lounge and dining room afford magnificent views of
open country. On Fridays and Saturdays one of the partners, a highly
acclaimed chef, prepares dinner. On other nights food can be
provided by a pub restaurant 200 yards away.

B & B from £29pp, C-Cards MC VS, Dinner from £22, Rooms
1 single, 3 double, 2 twin, 1 family, all en-suite, Restricted
smoking, Children over 5, Dogs in coach house, Closed Jan

THE ALDERS Sandford Orcas, Sherborne DT9 4SB
John & Sue Ferdinando   *Tel:* 01963 220666
Email: jonsue@thealdersbb.com   *Web:* www.thealdersbb.com

Map Ref: 22
A30

Secluded stone house set in old walled garden, in picturesque
conservation village near Sherborne. House is tastefully furnished
with original watercolour paintings and hand-built pottery. There is a
wood burning fire in lounge with inglenook fireplace. Good
breakfasts served around large farmhouse table. Excellent food
available in traditional friendly village pub.

B & B £22.50-£25pp, Rooms 1 double, 1 twin, 1 family, all
en-suites, No smoking, Children welcome, No dogs, Closed Xmas

---

STOURCASTLE LODGE Goughs Close, Sturminster Newton DT10 1BU
Jill & Ken Hookham-Bassett   *Tel:* 01258 472320   *Fax:* 01258 473381
Email: enquiries@stourcastle-lodge.co.uk   *Web:* www.stourcastle-lodge.co.uk

Map Ref: 23
B3092

This residence offers high standards and quality, the bedrooms have
Victorian bedsteads, antiques, and modern, well equipped
bathrooms some with whirlpool baths. Oak beams, log fires and
views of the garden from every room. Jill is a gold medalist chef,
baked poussin with creamy curry sauce followed by boozy bread
and butter pudding makes this is an excellent place to both stay and
eat.

B & B £32-£39pp, C-Cards MC VS, Dinner from £19.50, Rooms
1 twin, 4 doubles, all en-suite, Restricted smoking, No children or
dogs, Open all year

FIDDLEFORD MILLHOUSE Fiddleford, Sturminster Newton DT10 2BX
Jennifer & Anthony Ingleton
Tel: 01258 472786

Map Ref: 24
A357

A magical Grade I listed farm/manor house of great architectural interest with a lovely garden running down to the river. Beautifully furnished and decorated, there are 3 large bedrooms for guests, 1 with a half tester bed and 16th century moulded plaster ceiling, 1 large bedroom with a king size 4 poster and 1 pretty double bedroom. Nearby is a good pub. Excellent walking.

B & B from £20pp, Rooms 3 double, 1 en-suite, No smoking, Children over 12, Dogs by arrangement, Open all year

LAWRENCES FARM Southover, Tolpuddle DT2 7HF
Mr & Mrs R Slocock *Tel:* 01305 848460 *Fax:* 01305 849060
Email: sally.slocock@virgin.net *Web:* www.goflyfishing.co.uk

Map Ref: 25
A35

Lawrences Farm, set in 59 acres of wood and water meadows, nestles in Dorset's famous Hardy country. Fly fishing is available on our own lakes and rivers and guests are welcome to use our large heated swimming pool and grounds. The coast, pubs and restaurants are within easy reach. Accommodation includes two guests' lounges and en-suite rooms have colour televisions and tea/coffee facilities.

B & B £22pp, Rooms 2 single, 1 twin, 1 family, most en-suite, No smoking in bedrooms, Children over 8, Dogs by arrangement, Closed Xmas & New Year

BRADLE FARMHOUSE Bradle Farm, Church Knowle, Wareham BH20 5NU
Mrs Gillian Hole *Tel:* 01929 780712 *Fax:* 01929 481144
Email: bradlefarmhouse@farmersweekly.net *Web:* www.smoothhound.co.uk/hotels/bradle.html

Map Ref: 26
A351

Relax and unwind in our period farmhouse in the heart of Purbeck on 550 acre farm. Our accommodation is very spacious with all facilities to ensure comfort provided and breakfast is served in our traditionally furnished dining room where there is a choice of breakfasts. A warm friendly family atmosphere is assured with us here at Bradle, come and sample what we have to offer.

B & B £23-£25pp, Rooms 2 double, 1 twin, all en-suite, No smoking, Children over 8, No dogs, Closed Xmas day & Boxing day

WEST COOMBE FARMHOUSE Coombe Keynes, Wareham BH20 5PS
Rachel & Peter Brachi *Tel:* 01929 462889 *Fax:* 01929 405863
Email: west.coombe.farmhouse@barclays.net *Web:* www.westcoombefarmhouse.co.uk

Map Ref: 27
B3071

Discover a peaceful way of life when you stay at this restored Georgian farmhouse in the delightful village of Coombe Keynes, close to Lulworth Cove. Explore the beautiful coastline, historic houses and gardens Dorset has to offer, or borrow our mountain bikes. Excellent choice of country pubs and restaurants close by. Your hosts pride themselves on offering a relaxing holiday.

B & B £20-£27.50pp, Rooms 1 single, 1 twin, 1 double, all en-suite, No smoking, Children over 12, No dogs, Closed Xmas

LONG COPPICE Bindon Lane, East Stoke, Wareham BH20 6AS
Sarah Lowman *Tel:* 01929 463123
Email: Sarah@long-coppice.freeserve.co.uk

Map Ref: 27
A352

In a peaceful country lane close to the village of Wool, ideally situated for relaxing in rural surroundings, we are near to local attractions, beaches, coastal path and cycle routes. 8 acres of garden, woodlands/meadows, a haven for wildlife, many birds visit us. Rooms are spacious and comfortable, the family room has direct access to the garden. Good pubs nearby.

B & B from £20pp, Rooms 1 twin, 1 family, both en-suite, No smoking, Children welcome, Dogs by arrangement, Closed Xmas

CORFE GATE HOUSE Coryates, Abbotsbury, Weymouth DT3 4HW
Maureen Adams *Tel:* 01305 871483
Email: maureenadams@corfegatehouse.co.uk

Map Ref: 28
B3157

Victorian house of character, quietly situated in the countryside, but with easy access to Dorchester and Weymouth. Our galleried dining hall, sitting room for our guests, and bedrooms (equipped with hospitality trays and colour TV) are all tastefully decorated and furnished to a high standard. Parking and nearby eating establishments. ETB 5 Diamonds, Silver Award.

B & B from £22.50pp, Rooms 1 double, 1 twin, 1 family, all en-suite, No smoking, Children welcome, No dogs, Closed Oct to Easter

---

DINGLE DELL Church Lane, Osmington, Weymouth DT3 6EW
Joyce & Bill Norman *Tel / Fax:* 01305 832378
Email: Norman.dingledell@btinternet.com

Map Ref: 29
A353

Dingle Dell sits at the edge of this charming village, a mile from the coast. Set back among old apple trees in its own lovely garden, it provides a peaceful spot to relax, and a pleasant base from which to explore the area. Large, attractively presented, comfortable rooms overlook gardens and countryside. Generous English breakfasts, special diets by request. A warm welcome guaranteed.

B & B from £21pp, Rooms 1 twin, 1 double en-suite, No smoking, No children or dogs, Closed Nov to Feb

---

ASHTON LODGE 10 Oakley Hill, Wimborne Minster BH21 1QH
Brian & Anne Gooch *Tel:* 01202 883423 *Fax:* 01202 886180
Email: ashtonlodge@ukgateway.net *Web:* www.ashtonlodge.ukgateway.net

Map Ref: 30
A31

Spacious detached house with off road parking, centrally located to explore the area. All bedrooms are tastefully decorated and furnished to a high standard of comfort. A full breakfast is served in the dining room overlooking the attractive garden, which is a feature of the house that guests can relax in. Whether on holiday or business we plan for you to have an enjoyable stay.

B & B from £24pp, Rooms 2 single, 1 twin, 2 double/family with en-suite, No smoking, Children welcome, No dogs, Open all year

---

PEACEHAVEN B&B 282 Sopwith Crescent, Merley, Wimborne Minster BH21 1XL

Map Ref: 30
A31

Tel: 01202 880281

We will always give you a warm and friendly welcome to our comfortable homely accommodation in a modern bungalow. All rooms are on the ground floor with hot/cold water and colour television. Buses stop outside for Poole, Wimborne and Bournemouth. In easy reach of beaches, New Forest and many more attractions.

B & B £20-£25pp, Rooms 2 double, Open all year

THORNHILL Holt, Wimborne Minster BH21 7DJ
John & Sara Turnbull *Tel:* 01202 889434
Email: sct@gardener.com

Map Ref: 31
A31

Thornhill is an attractive thatched home set in peaceful surroundings, you will receive a warm welcome here. The garden is large, and there is a hard tennis court. The house is situated 3 1/2 miles from Wimborne, and it lies away from the road, the location is ideal for exploring the coast, New Forest and Salisbury area. Local pubs offering good food.

B & B from £22pp, Rooms 1 single, 1 twin, 1 double, No smoking, Children over 14, No dogs, Open all year

Essex

To experience the real Essex, the visitor has to get away from the main roads. The southwest of the county has been, and is still being, slowly but surely swallowed up by London, and much of the county not yet consumed is nevertheless heavily influenced by the capital. The north bank of the Thames and the southern border of Essex from Tilbury to Southend-on-Sea is a complex array of container ports, oil and gas installations and industry of all descriptions, and yet six thousand acres of Epping Forest survives, all that is left of a sixty thousand acre royal hunting ground. At Hatfield Fot, near Bishop's Stortford, lies over a thousand acres of ancient woodland, remains of more of Essex's royal forests. This historic landscape has been designated a Site of Special Scientific Interest. There is a wealth of pollarded hornbeams and oaks supporting a wide variety of wildlife, wonderful walking country and coarse fishing on two lakes.

Colchester is a great centre for the holiday visitor and claims to be Britain's oldest town, and certainly it was there before the Romans established their legionary base and capital in 43AD. The Normans built a castle here in 1076, with Europe's largest Norman keep, which now houses an excellent museum. The town in fact possesses a number of first class museums including the intriguing Hollytrees Museum of toys and curios. For lovers of zoos, the Colchester Zoo covers over forty acres and houses many endangered species. At Halstead to the west is a magnificent eighteenth century weatherboarded watermill. Further west is Saffron Walden, a wonderful old market town with a wealth of historical and architectural interest, with many fascinating houses clustering round the largest parish church in Essex, the church of St Mary the Virgin, which was beautifully rebuilt in the 1500s. From medieval times until the eighteenth century this was the centre for growing the saffron crocus, hence the town's name. English Heritage cares for the magnificent Jacobean mansion at Audley End, just a mile from Saffron Walden. The house, completed in

Colchester Castle Museum seen from the park

1616, stands in glorious parkland landscaped by Capability Brown and includes an Adam bridge and temple. To the south is Great Dunmow, a pleasant old town with the strange tradition of awarding each leap year the Dunmow Flitch of bacon to idyllically married couples.

The county town of Chelmsford is based upon a town planned by the Bishop of London in 1199, although there was a much earlier settlement here, established on the Roman road between Colchester and London. With the development of the railway in 1843 the town swiftly grew as an industrial centre. The county can also boast two highly popular seaside resorts; Clacton-on-Sea has a seven mile stretch of sandy beach and a large number of holiday attractions, including the Living Ocean Aquarium with its sharks, rays and sealions, the Magic City indoor play centre for children and a pier. Southend-on-Sea, at the southern end of the coast, began life as a humble seaside village, only to blossom into an important resort with the arrival of the railway. The bracing sea air and comparatively low rainfall attracted hosts of daytrippers from London and there is much to do with parks, museums, all-the-fun-of-the-fair, restaurants, theatres and night clubs, plus excellent shopping.

However, the Essex coast is far from being just a bucket and spade region; Maldon, renowned for its barges grew prosperous on its barge traffic to London and now stages barge races. Goggeshal is a lovely old cloth and lace town and can claim in Paycocke's House probably the finest half-timbered house in England. Danbury, Essex's second highest spot gives spectacular views across the emotive Blackwater Estuary and Northey Island, a bird reserve and site for saltmarsh plants within the Estuary.

Essex is a bustling county of high activity, but there is much to attract the holiday maker. There is a wide choice of things to see and do and for the less active there are some lovely areas of quiet calm.

PLACES TO VISIT

This is a small selection of interesting places to visit. Many more are listed in our annual guide to Museums, Galleries, Historic Houses & Sites (see page 448)

Audley End House and Gardens
Audley End, Saffron Walden,
Built by the first Earl of Suffolk this Jacobean house has gardens designed by Capability Brown and a magnificent Great Hall with seventeenth century plaster ceilings, and furniture by Robert Adam.

Colchester Castle Museum
Colchester
The largest Norman Castle Keep in Europe with fascinating archaeological collections and an illustration of Colchester's early history.

Hedingham Castle
Halstead
A majestic Norman Castle built in 1140, home of the de Veres and visited by many famous monarchs of the past. A splendid banqueting hall and minstrels gallery.

Sir Alfred Munnings Art Museum
Dedham, Colchester
The home, studios and grounds where Sir Alfred Munnings KCVO lived and painted for 40 years. A large collection representing his life's work.

Essex

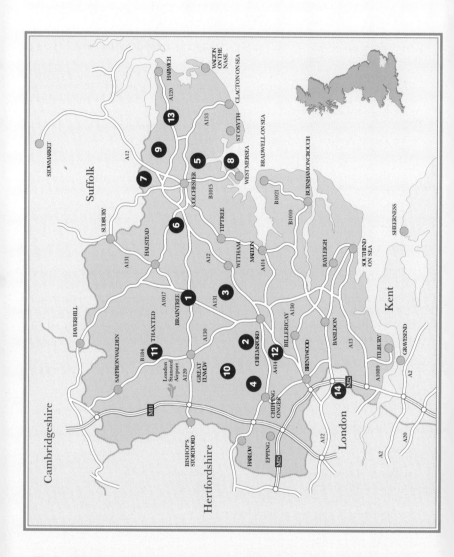

The Red Map References should be used to locate B & B properties on the pages that follow

SPICERS FARM Rotten End, Wethersfield, Braintree CM7 4AL
Delia Douse   *Tel / Fax:* 01371 851021
Email: info@spicers-farm.co.uk   *Web:* www.spicers-farm.co.uk

Map Ref: 1
B1053

Attractive farmhouse with large garden in tranquil setting. Well appointed bedrooms are all en-suite with colour television, tea/coffee making facilities, clock radios and all have lovely views. Plenty of safe parking. Enjoy a Continental or traditional English breakfast in our conservatory overlooking the beautiful valley. Convenient for Stansted, Harwich, Cambridge and Constable country.

B & B £19-£21pp, Rooms 1 double, 2 twin, all en-suite, No smoking, Children welcome, No dogs, Closed Xmas & New Year

---

FITZJOHNS FARMHOUSE Mashbury Road, Great Waltham, Chelmsford CM3 1EJ
Roslyn Renwick *Tel:* 01245 360204/361224 *Fax:* 01245 361724 *Mobile:* 07808 078834
Email: rosrenwick@aol.com

Map Ref: 2
A130

This 13th century farmhouse surrounded by countryside, is only 20 minutes from Stansted airport. A timber framed home, this is a charming, old Essex hall. Breakfast is served in the warmth of the kitchen, homemade bread and free range eggs are on offer. A tennis court and a lovely garden are for guests to enjoy. Suppers, and lifts to the airport are offered.

B & B £28-£35pp, Dinner from £12.50, Rooms 1 twin, 1 double, private bathroom, No smoking, Children welcome, No dogs, Open all year

---

OLD BAKERY Waltham Road, Terling, Chelmsford CM3 2QR
Mrs T F Lewis
Tel: 01245 233363

Map Ref: 3
A12

A warm welcome awaits you at this converted bakery in the small village of Terling, four miles from the A12, overlooking open farmland and on the Essex Way.

B & B from £22.50pp, Rooms 1 double, 1 twin, all en-suite, No smoking, Children over 10, No dogs, Open all year

---

DIGGINS FARM Fyfield, Chipping Ongar CM5 0PP
Margaret Frost
Tel: 01277 899303   *Fax:* 01277 899015

Map Ref: 4
M11, B184

16th century oak beamed Grade II listed family run farmhouse set in 440 acres of arable farmland in tranquil position. Bedrooms are spacious and tastefully decorated. Conveniently situated for Stansted Airport, mainline train and underground transport links. Two pubs, fishing lakes and two golf courses nearby. Visitors can be sure of a warm welcome.

B & B from £25pp, Rooms 1 double, 1 twin, 1 family, most en-suite, No smoking, Children over 12, No dogs, Closed Xmas & New Year

---

LIVE & LET LIVE 2 Alma Street, Wivenhoe, Colchester CO7 9DL
Mrs Linda Tritton *Tel:* 01206 823100 *Mobile:* 07976 246082
Email: lindatritton@hotmail.com

Map Ref: 5
A133, A12

This early Victorian house is set in the heart of a conservation area and within yards of the quayside and a beautiful river walk. Large breakfast menu and delicious home made meals on request. There are excellent pubs nearby. Rooms have tea/coffee making facilities and TV and there is a sitting room overlooking the river. The local car park is nearby. Beth Chattos Gardens and historic town of Colchester close by.

B & B from £23pp, Dinner from £12.50, Rooms 1 single, 1 twin, Restricted smoking, Children over 10, No dogs, Closed Xmas & New Year

OLD HOUSE Fordstreet, Aldham, Colchester CO6 3PH
Mrs Patricia Mitchell
Tel / Fax: 01206 240456

Map Ref: 6
A12, A1124

Historic 14th century 'Old Hall' house with friendly atmosphere, oak beams, log fires, a large garden and ample parking. All rooms have tea/coffee facilities, electric blankets and televisions. Only five miles west of Colchester, an ideal situation for exploring East Anglian mediaeval villages and churches and half an hour from Harwich Ferry. Three pubs within 150 yards on A1124.

B & B from £22.50pp, C-Cards MC VS, Rooms 1 single, 1 twin, 1 family, 1 en-suite, 2 private bathroom, Restricted smoking, Children welcome, No dogs, Open all year

---

ROUND HILL HOUSE Parsonage Hill, Boxted, Colchester CO4 5ST
Jeremy & Mary Carter *Tel / Fax:* 01206 272392 *Mobile:* 07904 292127
Email: jermar@appleonline.net

Map Ref: 7
A134

Drive into the stableyard where friendly lurchers greet you. The garden stretches away to the Ha-Ha beyond which cattle graze. Indoors, antique furniture, persian rugs and flowers blend with every modern convenience for guests' comfort. Play the baby grand piano in the drawing room, breakfast in the beautiful garden or elegant dining room. No wonder guests return year after year.

B & B £25-£30pp, Dinner from £22.50, Rooms 1 twin, 1 family, both en-suite, Restricted smoking, Children welcome, Dogs by arrangement, Open all year

---

BROMANS FARM East Mersea, Colchester CO5 8UE
Ruth Dence
Tel / Fax: 01206 383235

Map Ref: 8
B1025

This 14th century farmhouse near to the sea, is a sunny house with a conservatory, here guests may relax, though in winter, the sitting room with its log fire is the perfect place to rest. Home baked bread is served at breakfast, after which perhaps a wonderful day of walking and watching the Brent geese. Restaurant and pub locally.

B & B from £25pp, Rooms 1 double, 1 twin, both with private bathroom, Restricted smoking, Children welcome, Dogs by arrangement, Open all year

---

MAY'S BARN FARM May's Lane, off Long Road West, Dedham CO7 6EW
Mrs Jean Freeman *Tel:* 01206 323191
Email: maysbarn@talk21.com *Web:* www.mays.barn.btinternet.co.uk

Map Ref: 9
B1029

Looking for absolute quiet and seclusion? Then May's Barn Farm is for you, situated a quarter mile off-road down a secluded private drive, with delightful views over Dedham Vale, immortalised by the artist John Constable. The rooms are large, comfortable and traditionally furnished and, if the weather is cold, we will light a log fire for you in the guests' cosy sitting room.

B & B £21-£22.50pp, Rooms 1 double, 1 twin, 1 en-suite, 1 private, Restricted smoking, Children over 10, No dogs, Open all year

---

www.stayinstyle.com

All homes listed feature on our Website and those that have their own E-mail address or Website address can be accessed direct

GARNISH HALL Margaret Roding, Dunmow CM6 1QL
Anna Pitt *Tel:* 01245 231209 *Fax:* 01245 231224 *Mobile:* 07773 024415
Email: anna@garnishhallfsnet.co.uk

Map Ref: 10
A1060

Garnish Hall was once a moated country house, parts of which were built in the 13th century. It is on the A1060 and ideal for the Reid Rooms and Punch Bowl. Stands in seven acres adjoining a Norman church with perhaps the best porchway in Essex. Lovely views and spacious rooms. Come as visitors, leave as friends and come again.

B & B from £27.50pp, Dinner from £15, Rooms 2 double, 1 family, all en-suite, No smoking, Children & dogs welcome, Closed Xmas

CROSSWAYS GUEST HOUSE 32 Town Street, Thaxted, Dunmow CM6 2LA
Michael Millett & Jose Dominguez Soult
Tel: 01371 830348

Map Ref: 11
B1051

Elegant sixteenth century house in the centre of historic Thaxted facing the 600 year old Guildhall. Large comfortable bedrooms with tea/coffee making facilities, colour television, radio/alarm. Good local restaurants and pubs in walking distance. ETC AA 4 Diamond, Silver Award.

B & B £28-£40pp, Rooms 1 double, 1 twin, both en-suite, No smoking, Children over 12, No dogs, Open all year

YEW TREE HOUSE Mill Green Road, Fryerning, Ingatestone CM4 0HS
Elizabeth & Tony Dickinson
Tel: 01277 352580

Map Ref: 12
M25, A12, B1002

Although this quiet secluded house nestles behind high yew hedges in peaceful countryside, it is only 30 minutes by train from Ingatestone station to London. Guests have their own lounge, with television, looking out to the walled garden. Elizabeth is a trained cook and provides dinner if ordered in advance. Ample car parking.

B & B from £35pp, Dinner from £15, Rooms 2 double en-suite/private bathroom, Restricted smoking, Children over 12, No dogs, Closed Xmas & New Year

DAIRY HOUSE FARM Bradfield Road, Wix, Manningtree CO11 2SR
Bridget & Alan Whitworth *Tel:* 01255 870322 *Fax:* 01255 870186
Email: bridgetwhitworth@hotmail.com

Map Ref: 13
A120

Spacious Victorian farmhouse on 700 acre family farm. En-suite rooms have open countryside views. There is a cosy guests' lounge for tea and homemade cakes. The atmosphere is relaxed and friendly - a real home from home. Ideal for Harwich ferries, sandy beaches, Beth Chatto's Garden, Constable country, historic Colchester and pretty Suffolk villages. ETC AA 5 Diamonds.

B & B from £22pp, Rooms 1 double, 1 twin, both en-suite, Restricted smoking, Children over 12, Guide dogs only, Open all year

CORNER FARM Fen Lane, North Ockendon, Upminster RM14 3RB
Tel: 01708 851310 *Fax:* 01708 852025
Email: corner.farm@virgin.net

Map Ref: 14
A12, M25

Accommodation is in a detached bungalow situated in rural surroundings with no public transport. Breakfast is served in the conservatory of the farmhouse. Upminster station is four miles away and London 25 minutes on train. To find us from the M25 Junction 29, take A127 Southend. Immediately take slip road B186 Brentwood. Turn right, go to mini roundabout, turn left. First left is Fen Lane.

B & B from £25pp, C-Cards MC VS, Rooms 2 single, 2 twin, No smoking, Children over 10, No dogs, Open all year

Gloucestershire

Few counties can compete with Gloucestershire in scenic beauty and entrancing small towns and villages, but then few counties can claim such attributes as the Cotswold Hills, the Forest of Dean and the Vales of Severn and Berkeley. The rolling grasslands of the Cotswolds, ideal for sheep farming, covers the glorious golden limestone which has been extensively quarried for centuries, providing the building material that has made the landscape so attractive. Dover's Hill, to the north of Chipping Campden, forms a natural amphitheatre on a spur of the Cotswolds, where the 'Cotswold Olympic Games' are held each June. The games established in 1612 by Robert Dover were revived in 1951. Chipping Campden itself is a fine town of impressive stone buildings, probably the grandest being the fourteenth century home of William Grevel, a prosperous wool merchant. Cirencester has arguably the finest 'wool' church in the Cotswolds, its ideal setting at the crossing of the Fosse Way and Ermin Way ensured its prominence and prosperity from Roman times.

Bibury in the Cotswolds (STB)

To the west lies the Forest of Dean, probably the wildest part of Gloucestershire and an area exploited for iron and coal since Roman times, the whole region being a fine expanse of open heath and woodland criss-crossed with paths. The Dean Heritage Centre is well worth a visit with the Clearwell Caves, a network of miners tunnels, open to visitors. The world's largest collection of wildfowl covering over one hundred and fifty different species can be seen at Slimbridge Wildfowl and Wetlands Trust, which was founded by artist and naturalist Peter Scott in 1946. On the eastern bank of the River Severn lies the Vale of Berkeley, thousands of acres of low-lying land, a region of lovely lanes and hump-backed bridges overlooked by Berkeley Castle where Edward II was murdered in 1327.

Of course two great towns dominate the county: Gloucester and Cheltenham. Gloucester is a city of contrasts, from its fascinating medieval centre to its revitalised nineteenth century docks. The docks, once linked to the sea by the Gloucester-Sharpness Canal, now form an attractive business and leisure complex which includes the National Waterways Museum. It also boasts a magnificent Gothic Cathedral, built in 1089. Based upon a Norman abbey, its massive piers contrast with the delicate fourteenth century vaulting of the choir, which houses the largest stained glass window in England. This fine city has interest for everyone, and is one of the locations of the Three Choirs Festival, the oldest music festival in Europe. Gloucester's neighbour, Cheltenham, is an elegant Regency spa and was transformed from a small spa village into a fashionable centre through the patronage of George III. The mineral spring was discovered here in 1715 by, according to legend, a flock of pigeons, on the site which is now Ladies College. Visitors are still able to taste the healing waters, now housed by the Pittville Pump Room. The Promenade and Montpellier Street are excellent shopping centres and the town can claim superb open spaces and gardens including Pittville Park, the Imperial Gardens and Montpellier Gardens. Nearby is Prestbury, the most haunted village in Britain, and also the location of Cheltenham Race Course. To the north is Tewksbury, a handsome medieval town with an abbey church, one of England's finest examples of Norman ecclesiastical architecture. The town is rich in lovely timber-framed buildings with a long and fascinating history and was the site of a decisive battle during the War of the Roses. Therefore the impressive town museum in Barton Street with details of all of the history is well worth a visit.

This is also a county of never to be forgotten gardens, including Rosemary Verey's Barnsley House, with its knot and herb gardens and world famous potager, an inspiration all year round. Hidcote Manor Garden near Chipping Campden must be one of the most delightful gardens in England, an 'Arts and Crafts' masterpiece created by the horticulturist Major Lawrence Johnston. Of a quite different character is Chedworth Roman Villa which was excavated in 1864 and is set in a glorious wooded combe. Alternatively is Westbury Court Garden, a formal water garden, the earliest of its kind in the country.

PLACES TO VISIT

This is a small selection of interesting places to visit. Many more are listed in our annual guide to Museums, Galleries, Historic Houses & Sites (see page 448)

Berkeley Castle
Berkeley
Home of the Berkeley family for 850 years and particularly famous for the dungeon where Edward II was gruesomely murdered in 1327.

Clearwell Caves Ancient Iron Mines
Royal Forest of Dean, Coleford
Iron ore has been mined here for over 3,000 years to form an incredible system of underground tunnels and chambers. Eight caverns are now open to the public with geological and mining displays.

Gloucester Cathedral
Gloucester
This Gothic Cathedral is the focus of the city with its perpendicular style and a Great Cloister with the oldest fan vaulting in the country.

National Waterways Museum
Gloucestershire Docks, Gloucester
A fascinating museum based within Gloucester Docks with a passenger boat taking visitors for both short and long trips down the canal.

Slimbridge Wildfowl and Wetlands Trust
Slimbridge

Set in 800 acres of varied wetland habitat where wildfowl can be observed in their natural environment with over 2,300 birds from 200 species.

Gloucestershire

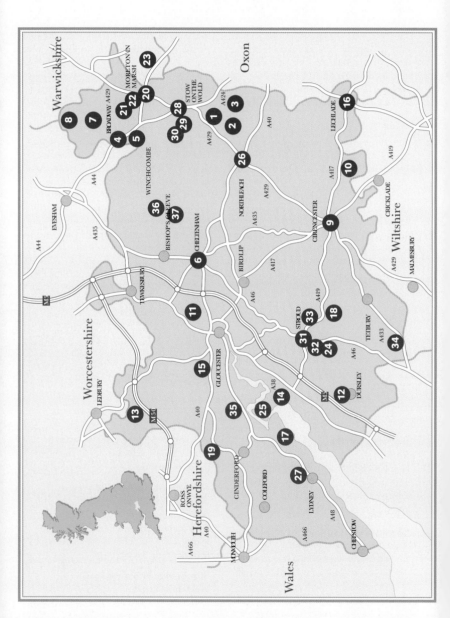

The Red Map References should be used to locate B & B properties on the pages that follow

APPLE PIE HOUSE HOTEL Whiteshoots Hill, Bourton-on-the-Water GL54 2LE
Tel: 01451 820387   *Fax:* 01451 812821
Email: hotel@bourton.com   *Web:* www.bourton.com

Map Ref: 1
A429, A424

A family-run hotel with friendly atmosphere and traditional home cooking. Panoramic views of the surrounding countryside can be enjoyed from most bedrooms. Bourton-on-the-Water is close by and the hotel is within easy driving distance of Cirencester, Cheltenham and Stratford.

B & B from £30pp, C-Cards MC VS AE, Dinner available, Rooms 7 double, 1 twin, 1 triple, 1 family, all en-suite, Restricted smoking, Children & dogs welcome, Open all year

COOMBE HOUSE Rissington Road, Bourton-on-the-Water GL54 2DT
Richard & Pat Stagg   *Tel:* 01451 821966   *Fax:* 01451 810477
Email: coombe.house@virgin.net   *Web:* www.smoothhound.co.uk/hotels/coombeho

Map Ref: 1
A40, A429

Coombe House is a quiet non-smoking haven. Ideal for guests who appreciate high levels of comfort and cleanliness in a relaxed atmosphere. Six pretty en-suite bedrooms. Private patio overlooks the lovely garden. A charming drawing room for guests. The perfect central base from which to explore the whole of the Cotswolds.

B & B from £30pp, C-Cards MC VS, Rooms 4 double, 2 twin, en-suite, No smoking, No children or dogs, Closed Jan to Feb

LANSDOWNE HOUSE ater GL54 2AT
Paul & Linda Garwood   *Tel:* 01451 820812   *Fax:* 01451 822484
Email: directory@lansdownehouse.co.uk   *Web:* www.lansdownehouse.co.uk

Map Ref: 1
A40, A429

Large period stone family house. Tastefully furnished, en-suite accommodation with a combination of old and antique furniture. All rooms have tea/coffee making facilities and colour television. There is parking and a garden for guests' use and a good selection of guide books to help you explore the area.

B & B £20-£23pp, Rooms 2 double, 1 triple, all en-suite, Restricted smoking, Children welcome, No dogs, Closed Xmas & New Year

CHURCH HOUSE Clapton-on-the-Hill, Bourton-on-the-Water GL54 2LG
Mrs Caroline Nesbitt
Tel: 01451 822532   *Fax:* 01451 822472

Map Ref: 2
A40, A429

A restored 17th century Cotswold family home in the hamlet of Clapton-on-the-Hill, offering seclusion and privacy, whilst commanding wonderful views across the Windrush Valley and to the tiny 12th century church. Beamed bedrooms with sloping ceilings, guests have a private drawing room, and a dining room, open to the eaves. Good local pubs. Church House is well located for visiting the Cotswolds.

B & B £30-£35pp, Rooms 1 double, 1 twin, both en-suite, Restricted smoking, Children welcome, Dogs by arrangement, Closed Xmas

FARNCOMBE Clapton-on-the-Hill, Bourton-on-the-Water GL54 2LG
Julia Wright   *Tel / Fax:* 01451 820120   *Mobile:* 07714 703142
Email: jwrightbb@aol.com   *Web:* www.farncombecotswolds.com

Map Ref: 2
A40, A429

Come and share our peace and tranquility. Superb views are to be enjoyed whilst making Farncombe your base to tour or walk the Cotswolds. We are two miles south of Bourton-on-the-Water and offer two attractive doubles with showers and one twin en-suite. Our full and varied breakfast menu includes homemade bread, preserves and our own free-range eggs. We await your call.

B & B £21-£23pp, Rooms 2 double with showers, 1 twin with en-suite, No smoking, Children over 10, No dogs, Closed Xmas & New Year

UPPER FARM Clapton-on-the-Hill, Bourton-on-the-Water GL54 2LG   *Map Ref:* 2
Helen Adams   A429
Tel: 01451 820453   *Fax:* 01451 810185

A working friendly family farm of 140 acres in a peaceful Cotswold village 2 miles from Bourton-on-the-Water. The listed 17th century restored farmhouse, offers exceptional accommodation and farmhouse fayre. The heated bedrooms are of individual character some are en-suite, one is on the ground floor. From its hill position, Upper Farm enjoys panoramic views, it makes an ideal base for touring. Brochure available.

B & B from £20pp, Rooms 3 double, 1 family, 1 twin, some en-suite, No smoking, Children over 5, Closed Dec to Feb

---

STEPPING STONE Rectory Lane, Great Rissington, Bourton-on-the-Water GL54 2LL   *Map Ref:* 3
Roger & Sandra Freeman   *Tel:* 01451 821385   *Fax:* 01451 821008   A424
Email: ststbandb@aol.com

In a large garden on the edge of the picturesque village of Great Rissington, Stepping Stone provides quiet and comfortable accommodation for over night and longer stays. Two doubles, self contained, with a sitting area. The house has country views and there are some lovely walks. Located 3 miles from Bourton-on-the-Water and 200 metres from the Lamb restaurant and bar. Open all year.

B & B from £27.50pp, C-Cards MC VS, Rooms 1 single, 1 twin, 3 double en-suite, No smoking, Children over 12, Dogs by arrangement, Closed Xmas

---

MILL HAY HOUSE Snowshill Road, Broadway WR12 7JS   *Map Ref:* 4
Annette Gorton   *Tel:* 01386 852498   *Fax:* 01386 858038   *Mobile:* 07979 860734   A44
Email: millhayhouse@aol.com   *Web:* www.broadway-cotswolds.co.uk/milhay

When you stay at Mill Hay, the first thing you will feel is the tranquility and calm of a real country house. Every modern comfort has been installed whilst retaining charm and character. All rooms have views of the gardens and surrounding rolling countryside and afternoon tea and light suppers are available on request. Above all you will enjoy complete privacy.

B & B from £45pp, C-Cards MC VS, Rooms 2 double, 1 twin, all en-suite, No smoking, No children or dogs, Open all year

---

WHITEACRES GUEST HOUSE Station Road, Broadway WR12 7DE   *Map Ref:* 4
Stan & Jenny Buchan   *Tel:* 01386 852320   A44
Email: whiteacres@btinternet.com   *Web:* www.broadway-cotswolds.co.uk

This Victorian country house standing in well-tended gardens offers guests five en-suite bedrooms, two with four-poster beds. There is a residents' lounge and off-road parking. Only four minutes walk from the village centre. Reductions for four or more nights.

B & B from £25pp, Rooms 4 double, 1 twin, all en-suite, No smoking, No dogs, Open all year

---

WINDRUSH HOUSE Station Road, Broadway WR12 7DE   *Map Ref:* 4
Susan & Richard Pinder   *Tel:* 01386 853577   *Fax:* 01386 853790   *Mobile:* 07909 691545   A44, B4632
Email: richard@broadway-windrush.co.uk   *Web:* www.broadway-windrush.co.uk

Elegant and spacious detached Edwardian house offering superb accommodation, only three minutes walk from the heart of Broadway village. Beautiful garden and lounge for guests' use. All the usual comforts provided and more including soaps, handcreams, hairdryers, sewing kits, mineral water, internet access and clothes washed and dried. AA RAC ETC 4 Diamonds, Silver Award and Warm Welcome Awards.

B & B £25-£32.50pp, C-Cards MC VS, Dinner from £12.50, Rooms 1 single, 4 double, 2 twin, 1 family, all en-suite, No smoking, Children & dogs welcome, Open all year

BURHILL FARM Buckland, Broadway WR12 7LY　　　　*Map Ref:* 5
Pam Hutcheon　*Tel / Fax:* 01386 858171　　　　　　　　　B4632
Email: burhillfarm@yahoo.co.uk　*Web:* www.burhillfarm.co.uk

A warm welcome awaits guests at our mainly grass farm lying in the folds of the Cotswolds, just 2 miles south of Broadway. Both of the guest rooms are en-suite and have TV and tea/coffee facilities. The Cotswold Way runs through the middle of the farm providing lovely walks. There are many pretty, well known villages to visit nearby.

B & B from £22.50pp, Rooms 2 double, both en-suite, No smoking, Children welcome, No dogs, Closed Xmas

ASHWOOD HOUSE Snowshill, Broadway WR12 7JU　　*Map Ref:* 5
Jon & Sue Collett　　　　　　　　　　　　　　　　　　A44
Tel: 01386 853678

Enjoying spectacular views Ashwood House stands at the head of the Snowshill valley. Jon and Sue Collett welcome guests to this beautiful setting on the outskirts of the Cotswold village of Snowshill. The spacious double en-suite room is comfortably furnished and well equipped. A separate staircase allows complete freedom. Restaurants abound in Broadway, or the Snowshill Arms offers good bar meals and ales.

B & B from £25pp, Rooms 1 double en-suite, No smoking, Children welcome, No dogs, Closed Xmas

GEORGIAN HOUSE 77 Montpellier Terrace, Cheltenham GL50 1XA　　*Map Ref:* 6
Penny & Alex Gamez　*Tel:* 01242 515577　*Fax:* 01242 545929　　A40
Email: georgian_house@yahoo.com　*Web:* georgianhouse.net

Take three beautiful bedrooms in an elegant Georgian home, set them among the charming terraces of Montpellier, add a warm welcome from your hosts, Penny and Alex, and there you have Georgian House. Each en-suite room has satellite television, phone with a modem socket, ironing facilities, trouser press and fridge. Our delicious English breakfasts include fresh fruit - the perfect combination! Parking available.

B & B £30-£40pp, C-Cards MC VS AE DC, Rooms 3 double en-suite, No smoking, No children or dogs, Closed Xmas & New Year

PARKVIEW 4 Pittville Crescent, Cheltenham GL52 2QZ　　*Map Ref:* 6
John & Sandra Sparrey　*Tel:* 01242 575567　　　　　　　A40
Email: jospa@tr250.freeserve.co.uk

Parkview is a fine regency house standing in Cheltenham's nicest area, looking onto Pittville Park. It still has many of the features from that period and there are many old documents on the walls. The bedrooms are beautiful and have tea/coffee facilities and televisions. The centre of Cheltenham is 10 minutes walk away and the Cotswold villages are easy to visit in the nearby hills.

B & B £20-£25pp, Rooms 1 single, 1 twin, 1 family, Restricted smoking, Children & dogs welcome, Open all year

CATBROOK HOUSE Catbrook, Chipping Campden GL55 6DE　　*Map Ref:* 7
Anne & Matthias Klein　*Tel:* 01386 841499　*Fax:* 01386 849248　A44, B4081
Email: m.klein@virgin.net

Welcome to our traditional Cotswolds stone building only five minutes from town centre. Enjoy the tranquility, wonderful views and individually designed cosy bedrooms with most comfortable beds. Hairdryer, radio/clock, tea/coffee facilities are provided and a tasty English breakfast is served in the Edwardian style dining room. Centrally located for touring the Cotswolds and Shakespeare country. AA 4 Diamonds.

B & B from £22.50pp, Rooms 2 double with private shower, 1 twin en-suite, No smoking, Children over 9, No dogs, Closed Xmas

HOLLY HOUSE Ebrington, Chipping Campden GL55 6NL   *Map Ref:* 7
Mr & Mrs Jeffrey Hutsby *Tel:* 01386 593213 *Fax:* 01386 593181 *Mobile:* 07790 516311   A44, A429
Email: hutsby@talk21.com *Web:* www.stratford-upon-avon.co.uk/hollyhouse.htm

Holly House is a lovely property, situated in the centre of the picturesque Cotswold village of Ebrington. All rooms are beautifully appointed with en-suite facilities, televisions, tea/coffee facilities and hairdryers. There is a garden room for guests' use and ample private parking. Ideally situated for touring the Cotswolds and Shakespeare country. AA 4 Diamonds.

B & B £23-£24pp, Rooms 1 double, 1 twin, 1 family, all en-suite, No smoking, Children welcome, No dogs, Open all year

---

M'DINA COURTYARD Park Road, Chipping Campden GL55 6EA   *Map Ref:* 7
Tel: 01386 841752 *Fax:* 01386 840942   A44, A429
Email: barbara@mdina-bandb.co.uk *Web:* www.mdina-bandb.co.uk

Award winning M'Dina Courtyard is a character Cotswold-stone house, apartment and 250-year-old cottage, in idyllic courtyard setting. Located at the quieter end of Chipping Campden's historic High Street with its excellent choice of eating establishments and variety of interesting shops. All rooms are en-suite with colour televisions, tea/coffee facilities and much more. Off-road parking. ETC 4 Diamonds, Silver Award.

B & B from £27.50pp, Rooms 2 double, 1 triple, all en-suite, No smoking, Children welcome, Open all year

---

WYLDLANDS Broad Campden, Chipping Campden GL55 6UR   *Map Ref:* 7
Mrs June Wadey   A44
Tel: 01386 840478 *Fax:* 01386 849031

Highly recommended non-smoking accommodation situated in the quiet conservation village of Broad Campden. Overlooking beautiful countryside and a television featured garden, Wyldlands is an ideal base to explore the Cotswolds and Shakespeare country. A choice of breakfast menu is offered and we have private parking. There is also a traditional inn close by.

B & B from £24pp, Rooms 1 single, 1 double, 1 twin, all en-suite/private, No smoking, Children welcome, No dogs, Closed Xmas

---

NINEVEH FARM Campden Road, Mickleton, Chipping Campden GL55 6PS   *Map Ref:* 8
Alison & Michael Yardley *Tel:* 01386 438923   B4081
Email: stay@ninevehfarm.co.uk *Web:* www.ninevehfarm.co.uk

A warm welcome is guaranteed at this 18th century farmhouse with oak beams and flagstone floors. Gardens of one and a half acres in open countryside just a half mile from village pubs. Ideal for exploring Cotswolds, Stratford-upon-Avon and Warwick. Free loan of bicycles. Non-smoking. All major payment cards accepted.

B & B from £25pp, C-Cards MC VS AE DC, Rooms 3 double, 2 twin, 1 family, all en-suite, No smoking, Children over 5, No dogs, Open all year

---

OLD COURT Coxwell Street, Cirencester GL7 2BQ   *Map Ref:* 9
Stephen & Anna Langton *Tel:* 01285 653164 *Fax:* 01285 642803   A419, A417, A429
Email: langton@cripps.f9.co.uk *Web:* www.old-court.com

A 17th century wool stapler's house standing near the Church in Cirencester's quietest street. Beautifully restored, the house displays interesting features including a Bath stone fireplace in the panelled dining room. Visitors enjoy a delicious breakfast, in the garden on sunny mornings. Bedrooms are special, with generous curtains, fine furniture and every comfort. Close to Cirencester Park, for walking and watching polo.

B & B from £32.50pp, C-Cards MC VS AE, Rooms 2 twin, 2 double (1 fourposter), all en-suite shower or bath, No smoking, Children & dogs welcome, Closed Xmas & New Year

THE MASONS ARMS Meysey Hampton, Cirencester GL7 5JT
Andrew & Jane O'Dell   *Tel / Fax:* 01285 850164
Email: Jane@themasonsarms.freeserve.co.uk

Map Ref: 10
A417

Dating from the 17th century, The Masons Arms is situated on the southern fringe of the Cotswolds. It is peaceful and very comfortable with beams, open fires, and the well equipped bedrooms have en-suite facilities. The heart of the Masons is the bar, where local guests and visitors enjoy a convivial atmosphere. Excellent home cooked food with a varied menu.

B & B from £30pp, Dinner from £8.95, Rooms 9 singles, 3 twin, 6 double, 2 family, all en-suite, Children welcome, Dogs by arrangement, Open all year

---

FROGFURLONG COTTAGE Frogfurlong Lane, Down Hatherley GL2 9QE
Clive & Anna Rooke
Tel / Fax: 01452 730430

Map Ref: 11
A38

Frogfurlong Cottage has two self-contained suites offering tranquility and a truly 'get away from it all' break. A double en-suite with jacuzzi and direct access to the 30ft indoor heated swimming pool, and a twin/kingsize en-suite with shower. Both are well equipped. The 18th century cottage, surrounded by fields, is situated in the green-belt area. Local attractions include Cotswolds, Malverns and Forest of Dean.

B & B from £22pp, Dinner from £14.50, Rooms 2 double en-suite, No smoking, No children or dogs, Closed Xmas

---

DRAKESTONE HOUSE Stinchcombe, Dursley GL11 6AS
Hugh & Crystal St John-Mildmay
Tel / Fax: 01453 542140

Map Ref: 12
M5, A38, B4060

Drakestone is in a beautiful and protected area of the Cotswolds. The house is a fine example of an arts and crafts building and the gardens, which are slowly being restored, were laid out at the same time. The atmosphere is informal and Hugh and Crystal offer you a warm welcome and an enjoyable stay. Plenty of walks and places nearby to see.

B & B from £31.50pp, Dinner from £17.50, Rooms 1 double with pb, 2 twin with 1 pb, No smoking, Children welcome, Dogs not in house, Closed Dec to Feb

---

THE OLD WINERY Welsh House Lane, Dymock GL18 1LR
Michael & Jo Kingham
Tel / Fax: 01531 890824

Map Ref: 13
M50 J2

Relax on the terrace or beside the wood burner in this beautiful spot where Gloucestershire, Herefordshire and Worcestershire meet. A high standard of comfort and a warm welcome await you at this former winery. In a peaceful setting, overlooking vineyards, this is an ideal area for walking. Plenty of interesting places to visit nearby. Brochure available.

B & B £30-£32pp, Dinner from £18, Rooms 1 twin en-suite, No smoking, Children welcome, No dogs, Closed Xmas & New Year

---

ARCHWAY HOUSE The Green, Frampton-on-Severn GL2 7DY
Mike & Sheila Brown   *Tel:* 01452 740752   *Fax:* 01452 741629
Email: mike.brown@archwayhouse.fsnet.co.uk

Map Ref: 14
M5 J13

200-year-old Georgian house in a secluded Gloucestershire village, standing at the end of Rosamunds Green, the longest village green in England. Near to the River Severn with the Severn Way and cycle route 41 both running through the village. Slimbridge Wildfowl and Wetlands Trust is four miles south and two miles from Junction 13 of M5.

B & B £22.50-£30pp, Dinner from £10, Rooms 1 single, 1 double, 3 twin, some en-suite, No smoking, Children welcome, Dogs by arrangement, Closed Xmas & New Year

THE OLD SCHOOL HOUSE Whittles Lane, Frampton-on-Severn GL2 7EB   *Map Ref:* 14
Mrs Carol Alexander   *Tel:* 01452 740457   *Fax:* 01452 741721   M5 J13
Email: theoldies@f-o-s.freeserve.co.uk

We are situated down a quiet lane off the village green which is the longest in England. The house is over 250 years old with a wealth of beams. There are many attractions in the locality including Slimbridge, Berkleley Castle, Gloucester Docks, Cheltenham, Bath and Bristol. Several eating places nearby. Come and relax in a home from home where a warm welcome awaits.

B & B from £26.50pp, Rooms 1 double, 1 twin, both en-suite, Restricted smoking, Children over 10, Dogs by arrangement, Closed Xmas & New Year

EDGEWOOD HOUSE Churcham, Gloucester GL2 8AA   *Map Ref:* 15
Mr & Mrs P Stevens   A40
Tel: 01452 750232

Edgewood House is a large country house set in two acres of lovely gardens. Spacious, comfortable bedrooms with colour televisions and tea/coffee facilities. Guests own lounge. Generous breakfasts, excellent eating places nearby. Ample parking in grounds. Ideal for visiting Wye Valley, Malverns and Cotswolds. Near view-point for Severn Bore tidal wave. ETC, AA 4 Diamonds.

B & B from £23pp, Rooms 1 double, 1 twin, family, all en-suite/private, No smoking, Children over 10, No dogs, Closed Xmas & New Year

CAMBRAI LODGE Oak Street, Lechlade-on-Thames GL7 3AY   *Map Ref:* 16
J Titchener   A417
Tel: 01367 253173   *Mobile:* 07860 150467

Family run, Cambrai Lodge is located in an attractive village on the River Thames. The double bedroom includes a four poster. It is five miles to Burford A361, and Swindon is 12 miles. An ideal base for touring the Cotswolds; nearby is Kemscott Manor with its William Morris furnishing and the 18th century Buscot House. Ample off road parking.

B & B from £23.50pp, Rooms 2 single, 1 twin, 1 double, 1 family, some en-suite, No smoking, Children welcome, Dogs by arrangement, Open all year

VINEY HILL COUNTRY GUEST HOUSE Lower Viney Farm, Blakeney, Lydney GL15 4LT *Map Ref:* 17
Stephen & Lynda Parsons   *Tel:* 01594 516000   *Fax:* 01594 516018   A48
Email: bookings@vineyhill.com   *Web:* www.vineyhill.com

Viney Hill is a delightful period house built in 1741 and recently tastefully renovated and extended. The house has half an acre of lawns and gardens, set in the beautiful Gloucestershire countryside adjacent to the magnificent Royal Forest of Dean and Wye Valley. All rooms are en-suite with remote control television, hospitality tray, hairdryer and central heating. Off road parking.

B & B from £28pp, C-Cards MC VS, Dinner from £17, Rooms 3 double, 1 twin, all en-suite, No smoking, No children or dogs, Closed Xmas & New Year

www.stayinstyle.com

All homes listed feature on our Website and those that have their own E-mail address or Website address can be accessed direct

HUNTERS LODGE Dr Browns Road, Minchinhampton GL6 9BT
Margaret & Peter Helm
Tel: 01453 883588 *Fax:* 01453 731449

A beautifully furnished Cotswold Stone house situated 650ft up in South Cotswolds on the edge of National Trust land, Minchinhampton Common. The well equipped, spacious bedrooms have en-suite or private bathrooms. There is a lounge for guests, which leads into a delightful conservatory and garden. An ideal centre for walking and touring the Cotswold towns. Information on menus, maps and brochures is available.

B & B £23-£25pp, Rooms 1 twin, 2 double/twin, all en-suite/private, No smoking, Children over 10, No dogs, Closed Xmas

---

GUNN MILL HOUSE Lower Spout Lane, Mitcheldean GL17 0EA
David & Caroline Anderson *Tel / Fax:* 01594 827577
Email: info@gunnmillhouse.co.uk *Web:* www.gunnmillhouse.co.uk

The Forest of Dean offers endless opportunities for walking, driving, pony trekking, trail cycling or canoeing. All this to occupy your days, between restful nights in the relaxing environment of our home. The furniture is elegant, the beds comfortable, the decor eclectic, reflecting our many trips abroad. The refurbished en-suite bathrooms are large, most with old fashioned baths and showers.

B & B from £25pp, C-Cards MC VS, Dinner from £24.50, Rooms 5 double, 2 twin, 1 family, all en-suite, No smoking, Children welcome, Dogs by arrangement, Open all year

---

THE BELL INN High Street, Moreton-in-Marsh GL56 0AF
Keith & Pam Pendry *Tel:* 01608 651688 *Fax:* 01608 652195
Email: keith.pendry@virgin.net *Web:* www.bellinncotswold.com

The Bell Inn, has five en-suite rooms which include televisions and drinks facilities. It is furnished to a high standard which is complemented by the Les Routiers 2000 Housekeeping Award and other merits. This traditional coaching inn is open all day, our bar and non-smoking area serving from an extensive food and drink menu.

B & B from £25pp, C-Cards MC VS AE, Dinner available, Rooms 1 double/single, twin/single, 3 family, all en-suite, Children welcome, Dogs by arrangement, Open all year

---

TREETOPS GUEST HOUSE London Road, Moreton-in-Marsh GL56 0HE
Elizabeth & Brian Dean *Tel / Fax:* 01608 651036
Email: treetops1@talk21

A beautiful family home offering traditional bed and breakfast. Six attractive bedrooms with en-suite facilities, two are on the ground floor, therefore suitable for disabled persons or wheelchair users. Rooms are well equipped and comfortably furnished. There is a sun lounge and a delightful secluded garden. Cots/high chair available. Ideally situated for exploring the Cotswolds. A warm and homely atmosphere awaits you here.

B & B £22.50-£25pp, C-Cards MC VS, Rooms 4 double, 2 twin, all en-suite, No smoking, Children & dogs welcome, Closed Xmas

---

THE MALINS 21 Station Road, Blockley, Moreton-in-Marsh GL56 9ED
Jill & John Malin *Tel / Fax:* 01386 700402
Email: johnmalin@talk21.com *Web:* www.chippingcampden.co.uk/themalins.htm

A delightful Cotswold stone house on edge of beautiful, peaceful and historic village. All rooms are en-suite and are tastefully decorated and colour co-ordinated. Facilities include colour television, tea and coffee, clock/radio, hairdryer and magazines. Local hotels and pub are within a few minutes walk. Ideal base for touring Cotswolds and Shakespeare country. Local knowledge a speciality.

B & B from £21pp, Rooms 1 double, 2 twin, all en-suite, No smoking, Children welcome, Dogs by arrangement, Open all year

NEW FARM Dorn, Moreton-in-Marsh GL56 9NS
Catherine Righton *Tel:* 01608 650782 *Fax:* 01608 652704 *Mobile:* 07712 919849
Email: cath.righton@amserve.net

Map Ref: 22
A429

Old Cotswold farmhouse in small hamlet. Guests can enjoy, at very competitive prices, well appointed, spacious bedrooms with private facilities, colour TV, coffee/tea tray. Beautiful double four-poster bedroom and very attractive twin room. All rooms furnished with antiques. Dining room has large impressive fireplace. Breakfast menu - hot crispy bread served.

B & B from £20pp, Rooms 2 double, 1 twin, 1 family, all en-suite, No smoking, Children over 8, No dogs, Open all year

RIGSIDE Little Compton, Moreton-in-Marsh GL56 0RR
David & Susan Cox *Tel / Fax:* 01608 674128
Email: rigside@lineone.net

Map Ref: 23
A44, A429

Set in one acre of landscaped gardens and surrounded by open countryside, we are half a mile from village of Little Compton. Well appointed bedrooms; two en-suite, with radio alarm, television and tea/coffee facilities. Guest television lounge and bathroom. Excellent eateries within easy reach and off road parking. Ideal base for walking, exploring the Cotswolds, Oxford and Stratford. AA 4 Diamonds.

B & B £22-£24pp, Rooms 1 single, 2 double with ensuite, 1 twin, Restricted smoking, Children over 12, No dogs, Closed Xmas & New Year

JUBILEE COTTAGE Avening Road, Nailsworth GL6 0BS
John & Jeanette Hensser *Tel:* 01453 833947
Email: jhensser@tiscali.co.uk *Web:* www.Jubilee-Cottage.co.uk

Map Ref: 24
A46

Traditional Cotswold family house offering comfortable, peaceful accommodation and generous breakfasts. Close to the town and its shops and restaurants. Jubilee Cottage has off street parking and relaxing gardens. Nearby are Gatcombe, Tetbury, Badminton and Cheltenham with Bath and Bristol in easy reach. All rooms have televisions, tea/coffee facilities and access to bathroom or shower facilities. A warm welcome assured.

B & B £20-£26pp, Rooms 2 double with private facilities, No smoking, Children by arrangement, Dogs by arrangement, Open all year

THE LAURELS Inchbrook, Nailsworth GL5 5HA
Lesley Williams-Allen *Tel / Fax:* 01453 834021
Email: laurels@inchrook.fsnet.co.uk

Map Ref: 24
A46

A rambling old house with a warm atmosphere, you can relax beside a fire in the study, play snooker or board games in the beamed lounge, or enjoy the licensed dining room with excellent meals. Enjoy the wildlife which come to feed by the stream. En-suite bedrooms are well equipped. There is an outdoor heated pool for guests' enjoyment. Self catering cottage available.

B & B from £20pp, Dinner from £12, Rooms 2 double, 2 twin, 3 family, all en-suite, No smoking, Children & dogs welcome, Open all year

GROVE FARM Bullo Pill, Newnham-on-Severn GL14 1DZ
Penny & David Hill *Tel / Fax:* 01594 516304
Email: Hilldavidag@cs.com

Map Ref: 25
A48

Traditional farmhouse on an organic dairy farm with panoramic views over the River Severn to the Cotswold Hills. Meander through the woods or relax by the log fire in the drawing room. A perfect base for exploring the Forest of Dean and Wye Valley. Surrounded by fields and woods the peace is only occasionally broken by the resident guinea fowl.

B & B £20-£25pp, Rooms 1 double, 1 twin, private bath and/or shower, Children welcome, Dogs by arrangement, Open all year

SWAN HOUSE COUNTRY GUESTHOUSE High Street, Newnham-on-Severn GL14 1BY
Elaine & Philip Sheldrake *Tel:* 01594 516504 *Fax:* 01594 516177
Email: prsheldrake@cs.com

Map Ref: 25
A48, A38

All of our beautiful individually designed bedrooms have colour televisions, tea/coffee facilities and home made biscuits on each tray. We have a peaceful guest lounge and are licensed to serve alcohol. Delicious dinners are also available. Car park. Pets are very welcome.

B & B from £25pp, Dinner available, Rooms 5 double, 1 twin, 1 family, all en-suite, Children & dogs welcome, Open all year

---

COTTESWOLD HOUSE Market Place, Northleach GL54 3EG
Pauline & Frank Powell *Tel / Fax:* 01451 860493
Email: cotteswoldhouse@talk21.com *Web:* www.cotteswoldhouse.com

Map Ref: 26
A40, A429

Cotteswold House is a 400 year old wool merchant's home with beams, original panelling and a Tudor archway. There is a luxury private suite and double and twin rooms with private bathrooms. The rooms are spacious, elegant and well equipped. Enjoy traditional English food and a friendly welcome. The house stands in the centre of Northleach in the heart of the Cotswolds.

B & B £25-£37.50pp, C-Cards MC VS, Rooms 1 luxury double suite, 1 double, 1 twin, all with pb, No smoking, No children or dogs, Closed Xmas & New Year

---

NORTHFIELD Cirencester Road, Northleach GL54 3JL
Pauline Loving *Tel / Fax:* 01451 860427
Email: nrthfieldO@aol.com

Map Ref: 26
A429, A40

This detached family house stands close to all services in the small market town of Northleach. The bedrooms offer en-suite facilities and they are well equipped and warm. Guests are welcome to enjoy the large well tended gardens, and also to enjoy delicious evening meals. A log fire warms the lounge. A brochure is available on request.

B & B from £25pp, C-Cards MC VS, Dinner available, Rooms 2 double, 1 twin/family, all en-suite, No smoking, Children welcome, No dogs, Closed Xmas & New Year

---

EDALE HOUSE Folly Road, Parkend, near Lydney, Royal Forest of Dean GL15 4JF
Christine & Alan Parkes *Tel:* 01594 562835 *Fax:* 01594 564488
Email: edale@lineone.net *Web:* www.edalehouse.co.uk

Map Ref: 27
A48, B4234

Fine Georgian residence facing the cricket green in the village of Parkend at the heart of the Royal Forest of Dean. Once the home of Bill Tandy, author of 'A Doctor in the Forest', the house has been restored to provide comfortable accommodation. Delicious, imaginative cuisine served in the attractive dining room. Within easy reach of Wye Valley. Riding, cycling, canoeing, walking, are closeby.

B & B £23-£28.50pp, C-Cards MC VS, Dinner from £13.50, Rooms 1 twin, 4 double, all en-suite, Restricted smoking, Children by arrangement, Dogs by arrangement, Closed New Year

---

CORSHAM FIELD FARMHOUSE Bledington Road, Stow-on-the-Wold GL54 1JH

Map Ref: 28
A424, A429

Tel: 01451 831750

Homely farmhouse with breathtaking views in a 100 acre farm. Ideally situated for exploring the Cotswolds. En-suite and standard rooms are fitted with televisions and tea/coffee facilities plus a guest lounge. Good food is available at a pub just five minutes walk away.

B & B from £20pp, Rooms 2 double, 2 twin, 3 family, most en-suite, Open all year

THE LIMES Evesham Road, Stow-on-the-Wold GL54 1EJ   *Map Ref:* 28
Helen & Graham Keyte   A424
Tel / Fax: 01451 830034/831056

A large Victorian family house, well established offering bed and breakfast for 30 years. Pleasantly situated, with views over the fields and the garden with an ornamental pool. Lovely bedrooms, spacious and well equipped. A few minutes walk to the town centre. Car parking available. A choice of breakfast, vegetarian diets are catered for. Many guests from home and abroad, return each year.

B & B from £21.50pp, Rooms 3 double, 1 family, 1 twin, 4 en-suite, 1 private, Children welcome, Dogs by arrangement, Closed Xmas

---

RECTORY FARMHOUSE Lower Swell, near Stow-on-the-Wold GL54 1LH   *Map Ref:* 29
Sybil Gisby *Tel:* 01451 832351   A429
Email: rectory.farmhouse@cw-warwick.co.uk

Rectory Farmhouse is an historic 17th century traditional Cotswold farmhouse located in the quiet hamlet of Lower Swell. Superb double bedrooms enjoy stunning views over open countryside to Stow-on-the-Wold. All bedrooms are centrally heated and have luxurious en-suite bathrooms. Cheltenham, Oxford and Stratford-upon-Avon are easily accessible. Whether in Summer or Winter, Rectory farmhouse is an ideal base for exploring the Cotswolds.

B & B from £32.50pp, Rooms 3 double en-suite, No smoking, Children over 16, No dogs, Closed Xmas & New Year

---

SOUTH HILL LODGE Fosseway, Stow-on-the-Wold GL54 1JU   *Map Ref:* 28
Linda & Barry Digby *Tel:* 01451 831083 *Mobile:* 07890 111808   A429
Email: digby@southilllodge.freeserve.co.uk *Web:* www.SmoothHound.co.uk/hotels/southhill

The quintessential country house, overlooking the Cotswold hills and villages. All rooms decorated and furnished to the highest standards. Delightful gardens. A warm welcome all year round. Stow is an ideal base for touring the Cotswolds and the town itself is well known for its antiques and art galleries, plus many restaurants. Secure private parking.

B & B from £25pp, Rooms 2 double, 1 twin, 1 en-suite, No smoking, Children over 14, No dogs, Open all year

---

WINDY RIDGE Longborough, Stow-on-the-Wold GL56 0QY   *Map Ref:* 30
Cecil J Williams *Tel:* 01451 832328/830465 *Fax:* 01451 831489   A424
Email: nick@windy-ridge.co.uk *Web:* www.windy-ridge.co.uk

A small country estate, situated in the Cotswold hills, overlooking the Evenlode Valley. Beautiful family home displaying wonderful features, mullioned windows, gables and Norfolk reed thatched roofs. Generously furnished bedrooms and a pine-panelled sitting room. The house is set in a prize winning garden. An outdoor heated swimming pool, tennis court, billiard/snooker room and a 10 acre arboretum. A super pub two minutes away.

B & B from £40pp, Rooms 2 double, both en-suite, 1 double, with private bathroom, No smoking in bedrooms, Children over 15, No dogs, Open all year

---

HYDE CREST Cirencester Road, Stroud GL6 8PE   *Map Ref:* 31
Tel: 01453 731631   A419
Email: hydecrest@compuserve.com *Web:* www.hydecrest.co.uk

A lovely comfortably furnished country house with all rooms in ground floor annexe and patios into the garden. Good pub/restaurant opposite. Excellent walking, horse riding, gliding and golf locally. Beautiful countryside convenient for Bath, Bristol, Cheltenham and rest of Cotswolds. Main line train/bus to London.

B & B from £22.50pp, Rooms 2 double, 1 twin, all en-suite, No smoking, Children over 7, Dogs welcome, Closed Xmas

LAMFIELD Rodborough Common, Stroud GL5 5DA
Caroline Garrett
Tel: 01453 873452

Map Ref: 31
A46, A419

Lamfield dates back to 1757 and is situated 500ft above sea level, bordering National Trust common land, two miles south east of Stroud with beautiful views across the valleys. Washbasins are provided in both bedrooms and the bathroom is shared. There is a television lounge and ample parking within the grounds. A warm welcome is assured here.

B & B from £19pp, Rooms 1 twin, 1 double, No children or dogs, Closed Xmas & New Year

HOPE COTTAGE Box, Stroud GL6 9HD
Sheila & Garth Brunsdon   *Tel:* 01453 832076
Email: garth.brunsdon@virgin.net

Map Ref: 32
A46, A419

For peace, this charming village of Box ten miles from Cirencester is unrivalled. Hope Cottage is in an area of outstanding natural beauty. Enjoy the charm of this delightful house, set in three acres with gardens and an outdoor heated pool for guests'enjoyment. Very comfortable en-suite rooms all with king-size bed, settee, TV and hospitality tray. English breakfasts. Excellent local restaurants and pubs.

B & B from £25pp, Rooms 2 double, 1 twin, all en-suite, No smoking, Children welcome, No dogs, Closed Dec

INSCHDENE Atcombe Road, South Woodchester, Stroud GL5 5EW
Mrs Wendy Swait   *Tel / Fax:* 01453 873254
Email: malcolm.swait@repp.co.uk   *Web:* www.inschdene.co.uk

Map Ref: 32
A46, A419

Inschdene is a comfortable family house set in an acre of garden near the centre of a quiet village. Large double room with en-suite bathroom, adjoining two twin rooms, one with washbasin. All rooms have televisions and tea/coffee facilities. Excellent food at the village pubs.

B & B from £17.50pp, Rooms 1 double, 2 twin, No smoking, Children welcome, Dogs in car only, Open all year

PRETORIA VILLA Wells Road, Eastcombe, Stroud GL6 7EE
Mrs Glynis Solomon
Tel / Fax: 01452 770435

Map Ref: 33
A419

Enjoy luxurious bed and breakfast in a relaxed family country house, set in peaceful secluded gardens. The spacious bedrooms have hospitality trays and hairdryers and guests have their own comfortable lounge with delicious breakfasts served in the dining room. Evening meals by prior arrangement, although many good eating places nearby. Personal service and comfort guaranteed. ETC 4 Diamonds.

B & B from £22pp, Dinner from £14, Rooms 1 single, 1 double, 1 twin en-suite, No smoking, Children welcome, No dogs, Closed Xmas & New Year

HYDE WOOD HOUSE Cirencester Road, Minchinhampton, Stroud GL6 8PE
Elizabeth Hayward   *Tel / Fax:* 01453 885504
Email: info@hydewoodhouse.co.uk   *Web:* www.hydewoodhouse.co.uk

Map Ref: 18
A419

Hyde Wood House is a comfortable and welcoming family home, originally built as a working farmhouse. It is located approximately one mile from Minchinhampton village centre. The house is tastefully furnished and there is a log fire to be found in the comfortable lounge on cold winter evenings. All bedrooms have en-suite bathrooms, with remote control television and radio. Choice of breakfasts available.

B & B from £25pp, Rooms 1 double, 1 twin, en-suite, No smoking, No children or dogs, Closed Xmas & New Year

TAVERN HOUSE Willesley, Tetbury GL8 8QU
Mrs V Kingston *Tel:* 01666 880444 *Fax:* 01666 880254
Email: tavernhousehotel@ukbusiness.com

Map Ref: 34
A433
see Photo opposite

A delightfully situated 17th century former Cotswold coaching Inn. 1 mile from Westonbirt Arboretum. All rooms are en-suite with direct-dial phone, colour TV, tea maker, hair dryer and trouser press. Guests' lounge. Charming secluded walled garden. Ample parking. Convenient for visiting Bath, Bourton-on-the-Water, Stow, Bristol and Cheltenham. ETB Silver Award winner 1993.

B & B from £32.50pp, Rooms 1 twin, 3 double, all en-suite, Restricted smoking, Children over 10, No dogs, Open all year

---

BOXBUSH BARN Rodley, Westbury-on-Severn GL14 1QZ
Mrs Pat White *Tel / Fax:* 01452 760949
Email: bed&breakfast@boxbushbarn.fsnet.co.uk

Map Ref: 35
A48

Pat and Alun offer a warm welcome to their timber framed barn set in unspoilt countryside. Guest rooms feature beams and have televisions and tea/coffee facilities. Full English breakfast includes local free-range eggs, bacon and sausages from a local prize winning butcher. Visit the Forest of Dean, Wye Valley and the Cotswolds. ETC 5 Diamonds, Gold Award.

B & B £22.50-£27.50pp, Rooms 1 double, 1 twin, 1 en-suite, 1 private, No smoking, Children over 10, No dogs, Closed Nov to Feb

---

GOWER HOUSE 16 North Street, Winchcombe GL54 5LH
Sally & Mick Simmonds
Tel: 01242 602616 *Mobile:* 07811 387495

Map Ref: 36
B4632

A 17th century town house conveniently situated close to the centre of Winchcombe, a small country town on the 'Cotswold Way'. An ideal base for exploring the Cotswolds. Ramblers, cyclists and motorists receive a warm welcome. The three well equipped, comfortable bedrooms have full central heating. A lounge area with television and a secluded garden for guests' use. Off street parking includes two garages.

B & B from £22.50pp, Rooms 2 twin/double en-suite, 1 double private bathroom, Restricted smoking, No dogs, Closed Xmas & New Years Eve

---

SUDELEY HILL FARM Winchcombe GL54 5JB
Mrs B Scudamore
Tel / Fax: 01242 602344

Map Ref: 37
A46

A friendly welcome awaits you to our 15th century listed farmhouse on a family run mixed farm of 800 acres, situated above Sudeley Castle with panoramic views over the valley. Comfortable en-suite rooms with many extras, a sitting room with log fires and a separate dining room overlooking the large garden. One mile out of Winchcombe where there is excellent pub food.

B & B from £30pp, Rooms 1 double, 2 triple, all en-suite, Restricted smoking, Children welcome, No dogs, Closed Xmas

---

WESLEY HOUSE High Street, Winchcombe GL54 5LJ
Matthew Brown
Tel: 01242 602366 *Fax:* 01242 609046

Map Ref: 36
A46

A charming, half timbered house built around 1435, once a merchant's residence now provides every comfort for guests, it retains the character of this medieval building. Cosy bedrooms, individually designed. The log fire in the lounge offers a welcome after dinner in our renowned restaurant. The food is exciting with an emphasis on freshness of produce. Ideal location for exploring the Cotswolds.

B & B £35-£40pp, Dinner from £15.50, Rooms 1 single, 2 twin, 4 double, all en-suite, No smoking, Children welcome, No dogs, Open all year

Tavern House, Willesley, near Tetbury

Hampshire & The Isle of Wight

Hampshire is a county of remarkable scenic variations. The best is arguably in the east around Selborne and the far west in the New Forest region. The water meadows with its rivers providing some of the finest fly fishing in Britain and between the rolling chalk downs in the north and the gloriously scenic South Downs lies rich and fertile farm land. The coast is of course dominated by the two great ports, Southampton and Portsmouth. Southampton has a busy container and passenger port and its unique tidal system made it the premier port for the great 'Queens' liners. The Romans had a military port here, and in 1620 the Pilgrim Fathers set sail for the New World from Southampton, before putting in at Plymouth. Despite considerable bombing damage, much of the charming medieval town remains. The city is a thriving shopping centre and possesses some extremely good aviation and maritime museums. Portsmouth, a few miles along the coast, is a fascinating naval town which grew enormously during the eighteenth century. The Point, at the narrow entrance to the harbour is singularly picturesque and is a fine place to view the ships. Nelson's flagship 'Victory' is in dry dock at the entrance to the Royal Dockyard. The dockyard also contains the excellent Royal Navy Museum as well as the 'Mary Rose', Henry VIII's warship, raised from the seabed in 1982, the Mary Rose Museum, and the restored HMS Warrior, the first iron-clad warship, built in 1860.

The New Forest, the largest of William the Conqueror's hunting forests to survive, is a mixture of woodland, heath and open grazing. In the fifteenth century much of the timber from the forest was used in the building of ships for the navy. The National Trust controls 1,400 acres of Bramshaw Commons and Manorial Wastes, together with land at Hale Purliew and Hightown Common, all grazed by commoner's stock. This is splendid territory for walking, camping and picnics as there are no major hills with wild ponies and red deer having the right of way as they graze. The Ornamental Drive at Bolderwood is a perfect place to enjoy the woodland and see the deer from observation platforms. The New Forest Museum at Lyndhurst is well worth a visit with the town still retaining its ancient Verder's Court dealing with forest rights.

Selbourne, in the east of Hampshire, is a lovely holiday location for exploring the glorious hills and valleys and Selbourne Common, covering 240 acres and is an area of outstanding natural beauty. At the centre of Hampshire is Winchester, the capital of Wessex from the time of Alfred the Great, and

New Forest Ponies (STB)

the capital of England from the tenth century up until the Norman Conquest. Winchester became the main religious and commercial centre in medieval times, and the cathedral, the longest Gothic cathedral in Europe, has an outstanding Norman crypt and contains the finest set of medieval chantry chapels in the country, plus the grave of Jane Austen. The city is crammed with buildings of style and interest, many built with Georgian brick, the Royal Hampshire Regiment Museum being one of the most attractive. The thirteenth century great hall is the only surviving part of the castle and displays King Arthur's round table, an early medieval fake. To travel the length of the River Test, one of England's finest trout rivers is a joy. The Test valley contains a wealth of picturesque villages including the

three Wallops, Over, Middle and Nether, renowned for their thatched cottages and lovely churches.

The Isle of Wight, reached by ferry either from Southampton, Portsmouth or Lymington is designed to appeal to the holiday visitor. There is much to see, the green whaleback hills on the south coast offer superb views, and at the western end of Tennyson Down are the spectacular chalk pinnacles known as The Needles. Yarmouth is a pretty port of whitewashed cottages, once an important medieval port and one of the numerous Solent Forts built by Henry VIII. Cowes, Shanklin, Sandown and Bembridge are all resorts with an individual character. The island has a distinctive Victorian atmosphere, and of course no visitor should leave without seeing Osborne House, Queen Victoria's retreat.

PLACES TO VISIT

This is a small selection of interesting places to visit. Many more are listed in our annual guide to Museums, Galleries, Historic Houses & Sites (see page 448)

Beaulieu Motor Museum
Beaulieu, Brockenhurst
Over 250 exhibits showing the history of motoring from 1896 within 75 acres of grounds, plus abbey ruins and a display of monastic life.

Breamore House
Breamore, Fordingbridge
Elizabethan manor house with fine collections, also Breamore Countryside Museum depicting the days when the village was self-sufficient.

Flagship Portsmouth
Portsmouth
This is home to some of the country's greatest flagships, such as King Henry VIII's Mary Rose, Lord Nelson's HMS Victory and mighty HMS Warrior.

Highclere Castle and Gardens
Highclere
A Victorian mansion, home to the Carnarvons, designed by Sir Charles Barry, set in parkland by 'Capability' Brown.

Jane Austen's House
Chawton
The house where Jane Austen wrote most of her work is now a museum dedicated to her life and works.

Winchester Cathedral
Winchester
A Norman Cathedral largely redesigned in the fourteenth century with the longest nave in Europe and superbly carved choir stalls. Also the burial place of many Saxon Kings.

Hampshire & The Isle of Wight

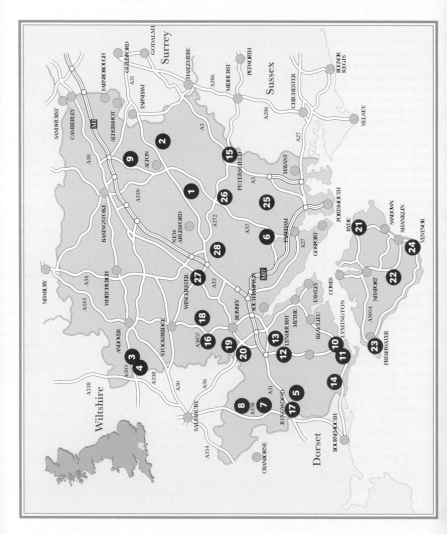

The Red Map References should be used to locate B & B properties on the pages that follow

THICKETS Swelling Hill, Ropley, Alresford SO24 0DA
David & Sue Lloyd-Evans
Tel: 01962 772467

Map Ref: 1
A31

A spacious country house in a two acre garden with fine views across the Hampshire countryside. 2 comfortable, twin bedded rooms with private bath or shower room. Guests' own sitting room with television. English breakfast is served. A few minutes drive to Jane Austen's House, Winchester is twenty minutes away. Salisbury, Chichester and The New Forest all within reach. Heathrow Airport 1 hour.

B & B from £22.50pp, Rooms 2 twin, both with private facilities, Restricted smoking, Children over 10, No dogs, Closed Xmas & New Year

---

THE VICARAGE East Worldham, Alton GU34 3AS
Wendy Bradford *Tel:* 01420 82392 *Fax:* 01420 82367 *Mobile:* 07778 800804
Email: wenrose@bigfoot.com *Web:* www.altonbedandbreakfast.co.uk

Map Ref: 2
A31, A325, B3004

Warm friendly peaceful country vicarage with a lovely mature garden in beautiful Hampshire countryside. Two miles from Alton station, off the B3004 and three miles from Jane Austen's village of Chawton and Gilbert Whites, Selborne. Twenty minutes to Basingstoke and Farnham and a half hour from Winchester and Portsmouth, one hour to New Forest. Ample parking and good food in pub within walking distance.

B & B £20-£23pp, Rooms 1 single/twin, 1 double/twin, 1 double, No smoking, Children over 7, Dogs by arrangement, Closed Xmas & New Year

---

BROADWATER Amport, Andover SP11 8AY
Carolyn Mallam *Tel / Fax:* 01264 772240
Email: carolyn@dmac.co.uk *Web:* www.dmac.co.uk/carolyn

Map Ref: 3
A303

This is a listed thatched cottage in a delightful secluded garden, providing a relaxed and cosy atmosphere in a peaceful village setting. The bedrooms are large, with en-suite facilities. The sitting room has an open log fire in winter. Excellent stopover for West Country and airport travellers (A303 half a mile). Stonehenge only 15 minutes' drive, Salisbury and Winchester 30 minutes.

B & B £25-£30pp, C-Cards MC VS, Rooms 2 twin en-suite, No smoking in bedrooms, Children over 8, No dogs, Open all year

---

MAY COTTAGE Thruxton, Andover SP11 8LZ
Tom & Fiona Biddolph
Tel: 01264 771241 *Fax:* 01264 771770 *Mobile:* 07768 242166

Map Ref: 3
A303

Dating to 1740, the cottage is situated in a picturesque village with a post office and an Inn. A comfortably furnished home, the bedrooms offer en-suite/private bathrooms, they are well equipped, one is on the ground floor. Guests' own sitting and dining rooms. An ideal base for visiting ancient cities, stately homes and gardens, within easy reach of ports and airports. Parking.

B & B from £27.50pp, Rooms 1 single, 2 twin, 1 double, most en-suite, No smoking, Children over 6, No dogs, Closed Xmas

---

LAINS COTTAGE Quarley, Andover SP11 8PX
Tel: 01264 889697 *Fax:* 01264 889227
Email: lains-cott-hols@dial.pipex.com

Map Ref: 4
A303

Lains Cottage is a charming thatched house set in an acre of cottage garden. The house has been carefully restored to combine modern comforts with traditional cottage style. The A303 is half a mile away giving easy access to London, the West Country, Stonehenge, Salisbury and Winchester.

B & B from £30pp, Rooms 1 double, 2 twin, all en-suite, No smoking, Children over 8, No dogs, Open all year

HOLMANS Bisterne Close, Burley BH24 4AZ   *Map Ref:* 5
Robin & Mary Ford   A31, A35
Tel / Fax: 01425 402307

A charming house in the heart of the New Forest in four acres of land, it has stabling for guests' horses. A warm welcome is assured, the bedrooms are en-suite, tastefully furnished and well equipped. There is a colour television in the lounge which has an adjoining orangery. Cosy log fires in winter. Superb walking, horse riding and carriage driving. Golf nearby.

B & B from £27.50pp, Rooms 1 twin, 2 double, all en-suite, No smoking, Children welcome, No dogs in bedrooms, Closed Xmas

---

CHIPHALL ACRE Droxford Road (A32), Wickham, Fareham PO17 5AY   *Map Ref:* 6
Mr & Mrs Stevens   *Tel / Fax:* 01329 833188   M27, M3
Email: mavis.stevens@zoom.co.uk   *Web:* www.chiphallacre.co.uk

Chiphall Acre is a beautifully situated house standing in a secluded garden full of interesting plants. The bedrooms are on the ground floor overlooking the garden. They are well presented, warm and well equipped. A wide choice of home made and free range produce is offered. The house is conveniently situated for the M27, M3, Winchester Cathedral and the Channel Ports.

B & B from £26pp, Rooms 1 twin, 1 double, 1 family en-suite, No smoking, Children welcome, No dogs, Open all year

---

ALDERHOLT MILL Sandleheath Road, Fordingbridge SP6 1PU   *Map Ref:* 7
Sandra & Richard Harte   *Tel:* 01425 653130   *Fax:* 01425 652868   A338
Email: alderholt-mill@zetnet.co.uk   *Web:* www.alderholtmill.co.uk

A picturesque working water mill in a delightful and tranquil corner of rural England. The speciality of the house is bread made with our own freshly milled flour. The bedrooms are en-suite with tea/coffee facilities and televisions, plus there is a television lounge and lovely riverside gardens with private fishing. Situated close to the New Forest for walking, riding and cycling. Self catering flat for 2 also available.

B & B £21-£25pp, C-Cards, Dinner from £13, Rooms 1 single, 3 double, 1 twin, most en-suite, No smoking, Children over 8, Dogs by arrangement, Closed Xmas & New Year

---

GREEN PATCH Furzehill, Fordingbridge SP6 2PS   *Map Ref:* 7
Meg Mulcahy   A338
Tel: 01425 652387   *Fax:* 01425 656594

An elegant house offering a warm welcome standing in a beautiful setting of eight acres. Wonderful views and direct access onto the New Forest. Rooms are spacious and well equipped. A wide choice of breakfasts is served in the oak panelled dining room or on the terrace. Huge conservatory and garden. Easy reach of Bournemouth, Southampton, Salisbury, Winchester, Portsmouth. Good eating places nearby.

B & B £22-£27.50pp, Rooms 1 twin, 1 double, 1 family, 1 en-suite, 2 private, No smoking, Children over 5, No dogs, Open all year

---

SANDY CORNER Ogdens North, Fordingbridge SP6 2QD   *Map Ref:* 7
Sue Browne   A338
Tel: 01425 657295

Sandy Corner is a small holding in a quiet rural location in the New Forest. Accommodation includes a downstairs bedroom and guests' sitting room with television. Evening meals, by prior arrangement, with home-grown produce when available. Several local pubs, one within walking distance, and restaurants nearby.

B & B £24-£28pp, Dinner available, Rooms 2 double en-suite, No smoking, No children, Dogs on lead, Closed Xmas

COTTAGE CREST Castle Hill, Woodgreen, Fordingbridge SP6 2AX
Mrs G Cadman
Tel: 01725 512009

Map Ref: 8
A338

Situated on the edge of the New Forest in 4 acres of garden surrounded by forest with superb views of the River Avon. Spacious bedrooms are decorated to a high standard. A short walk to the village with a pub serving excellent meals. Within easy reach of the coast and Isle of Wight. Ideal for relaxing and well placed for visiting the area.

B & B £23-£24pp, Rooms 1 twin, 2 double, all en-suite, Children over 10, No dogs, Closed Xmas

---

STREET FARMHOUSE Alton Road, South Warnborough, Hook RG29 1RS
Colin & Wendy Turner
Tel / Fax: 01256 862225

Map Ref: 9
M3 J5, B3349

16th century farmhouse on the edge of old Hampshire village. Restored with beams, a large inglenook and other features. Pretty, light and warm bedrooms. Superb breakfasts in an elegant dining room. Large garden with outdoor heated pool. Chawton village (home of Jane Austen) 6 miles. Excellent pubs nearby. An ideal base to explore Southern England. London, 1 hour. M3 (junction 5) 4 miles.

B & B from £17pp, C-Cards MC VS, Dinner from £16, Rooms 2 twin, 1 en-suite, Restricted smoking, Children welcome, No dogs, Open all year

---

AUPLANDS 22 Southampton Road, Lymington SO41 9GG
Sue Broomfield　*Tel / Fax:* 01590 675944
Email: s.broomfield@btinternet.com　*Web:* www.btinternet.com/~Auplands

Map Ref: 10
A337

A delightful period house ideally situated adjacent to the main High Street with its quaint shops and places to eat and drink to suit all tastes. A stroll takes you onto the Quay and Marinas, with a short drive to the forest, beach and ferry terminal. All rooms are en-suite, with colour television, tea/coffee facilities and traditionally furnished. Ample off road parking.

B & B from £20pp, Rooms 2 double, 1 twin, all en-suite, No smoking, Children & dogs welcome, Open all year

---

JEVINGTON 47 Waterford Lane, Lymington SO41 3PT
Ian & Jane Carruthers　*Tel / Fax:* 01590 672148
Email: jevingtonbb@lineone.net　*Web:* www.caruthers.co.uk

Map Ref: 10
A337

A comfortable home, situated in a quiet lane midway between the High street and the Marina. An ideal base for the New Forest, Solent walks and 10 minutes drive to Isle of Wight ferry. Tea/coffee facilities and TV in all rooms. Off street parking. Children welcome. Convenient for Bournemouth, Southampton and Winchester. Bike hire, sailing and walks can all be arranged.

B & B from £23pp, Rooms 1 twin, 1 double, 1 family, all en-suite, No smoking, Children & dogs welcome, Open all year

---

WEST LODGE 40 Southampton Road, Lymington SO41 9GG
Josephine & David Jeffcock　*Tel:* 01590 672237　*Fax:* 01590 673592
Email: Jeffcock@amserve.net.

Map Ref: 10
A337, B3054

A town house on the main road, but surprisingly quiet. The Jeffcocks are impeccably mannered and care about their guests. Edwardian house some lovely furniture. Deep red dining room, family portraits. Bedrooms traditionally furnished with TVs and tea/coffee. Parking behind the house. Garden. Numerous cafes, restaurants and inns a stroll away. Within easy reach of sea, Mariners IOW, New Forest, interesting towns, gardens and houses.

B & B £25-£30pp, Rooms 1 single, 1 double, 1 twin, all en-suite, No smoking, Children over 8, No dogs, Closed Xmas & New Year

OUR BENCH 9 Lodge Road, Pennington, Lymington SO41 8HH   *Map Ref:* 11
Roger & Mary Lewis   *Tel:* 01590 673141   A337
Email: enquiries@ourbench.co.uk   *Web:* www.ourbench.co.uk

Award winning guest house between the New Forest and the coast. With optional evening meals and a four course breakfast. All rooms are en-suite, and have televisions and tea/coffee facilities. An indoor heated pool, jacuzzi, and sauna is available for your private enjoyment. Sorry we cannot cater for smokers or children. Self catering cottages also available. ETC 4 Diamonds, England for Excellence Silver Award.

B & B from £24pp, C-Cards MC VS, Rooms 1 single, 1 double, 1 twin, all en-suite, No smoking, No children or dogs, Open all year

THE PENNY FARTHING HOTEL Romsey Road, Lyndhurst SO43 7AA   *Map Ref:* 12
Mike and Joan   *Tel:* 023 8028 4422   *Fax:* 023 8028 4488   A337
Email: stay@pennyfarthinghotel.co.uk   *Web:* www.pennyfarthinghotel.co.uk

The Penny Farthing Hotel is a cheerful, small hotel situated in Lyndhurst village centre in the New Forest. The bedrooms offer en-suite facilities with colour TV, a tea/coffee tray, telephone and comfortable furnishings. The hotel has a bar, a car park and a cycle store. We also have some neighbouring cottages available for B&B or self-catering.

B & B £29.50-£45pp, C-Cards MC VS AE, Rooms 1 single, 2 twin, 6 double, 2 family, Restricted smoking, Children welcome, No dogs, Closed Xmas

FOREST GATE LODGE 161 Lyndhurst Road, Ashurst, Lyndhurst SO40 7AW   *Map Ref:* 13
     A35
Tel / Fax: 023 8029 3026

Large Victorian house with direct access to the New Forest and its attractions, including walking, riding and cycling. Pubs and restaurants nearby and Lyndhurst, capital of the New Forest, is only five minutes drive. Full English breakfast or a vegetarian option is available by prior arrangement. Special rates are available from October to March: Three nights for the price of two.

B & B from £20pp, Rooms 3 double, 1 twin, 1 family, all en-suite, No smoking, No dogs, Open all year

YEW TREE FARM Bashley Common Road, New Milton BH25 5SH   *Map Ref:* 14
Mrs Daphne Matthews   A35
Tel / Fax: 01425 611041

A small holding with nine acres of grassland, guests are assured of total relaxation in two lovely bed sitting rooms marvellously comfortable, with double or twin beds with own bathrooms, in a traditional, cosy, thatched farm house on the edge of the New Forest. Breakfasts may be enjoyed in the bedroom, dinners are by arrangement. Private entrance and ample parking. Easily located.

B & B £35-£45pp, Dinner available, Rooms 1 twin private bathroom, 1 double en-suite, No smoking, No children or dogs, Closed occasionally

1 THE SPAIN Sheep Street, Petersfield GU32 3JZ   *Map Ref:* 15
Jennifer Tarver   *Tel:* 01730 263261   *Fax:* 01730 261084   A3, A272
Email: allantarver@cwcom.net

A delightful 18th century house with a walled garden in the old part of Petersfield. Every room has a television and tea/coffee facilities. Convenient for the railway station and close to numerous good eating places with Uppark, Chawton and Old Portsmouth within easy reach. Wonderful walking.

B & B from £21pp, Rooms 2 twin, 1 double en-suite, No smoking, Children welcome, dogs by arrangement., Open all year

FORTITUDE COTTAGE 51 Broad Street, Portsmouth PO1 2JD
Maggie & Mike Hall   *Tel / Fax:* 023 9282 3748
Email: fortcott@aol.com   *Web:* www.fortitudecottage.co.uk

Map Ref: 16
at Southern End of A3

A charming town house overlooking the quayside in Old Portsmouth, built on the site of a 16th century cottage, and named after an 18th century warship. Immaculately maintained bedrooms and bathrooms needlepoint pictures and flowers abound. Breakfast is served in a beamed room with views over the water. Britain in Bloom awards for window boxes and hanging baskets, and Heartbeat for healthy food choices.

B & B from £25pp, C-Cards MC VS AE, Rooms 1 double en-suite, 2 twin en-suite/private bathroom, No smoking, Children over 10, No dogs, Closed Xmas

---

HAMILTON HOUSE 95 Victoria Road North, Southsea, Portsmouth PO5 1PS
Tel / Fax: 023 9282 3502
Email: sandra@hamiltonhouse.co.uk   *Web:* www.hamiltonhouse.co.uk

Map Ref: 16
M3, A3

Delightful, family run establishment centrally located with five minutes' drive from continental and Isle of Wight ferry ports, city centres, stations, university and historic ships museums. Bright, modern rooms with colour televisions and tea/coffee facilities. Ideal touring base. English breakfast served from 6.15am. Nightly and weekly stays welcome all year. Proprietors Graham and Sandra Tubb.

B & B £21-£25pp, C-Cards MC VS, Rooms 1 single, 2 double, 3 twin, 1 triple, 2 family, No smoking, Children welcome, No dogs, Open all year

---

AMBERWOOD 3/5 Top Lane, Ringwood BH24 1LF
Graham & Anne Maynard   *Tel / Fax:* 01425 476615   *Mobile:* 07715 561588
Email: maynsing@aol.com   *Web:* amberwoodbandb.co.uk

Map Ref: 17
A31

Amberwood is a delightful Victorian home in a quiet lane close to Ringwood town centre with its excellent choice of restaurants and pubs. Our rooms have televisions and tea/coffee facilities and are attractively decorated and comfortable. Breakfast is served in a lovely conservatory overlooking a beautiful garden. Off road parking is available.

B & B £22-£24pp, Rooms 1 single, 1 double, 1 twin, all en-suite, Restricted smoking, Children over 12, No dogs, Closed Xmas & New Year

---

THE OLD COTTAGE Cowpitts Lane, North Poulner, Ringwood BH24 3JX
Sue & Tony Theobald   *Tel / Fax:* 01425 477956   *Mobile:* 07860 453038
Email: forestgatewines@btinternet.com

Map Ref: 17
A31

This seventeenth century thatched and beamed cottage is a haven of peace, set in an acre of gardens with excellent views over the New Forest. An ideal centre for touring with riding, cycling, walking, bird and animal watching all close. The charming en-suite bedrooms are comfortable with television, radio and tea/coffee making facilities.

B & B £22-£28pp, Rooms 2 double/family, 1 twin, all en-suite, No smoking, Children over 8, No dogs, Closed Dec

---

OLD STACKS 154 Hightown Road, Ringwood BH24 1NP
Joan Peck   *Tel / Fax:* 01425 473840
Email: oldstacksbandb@aol.com

Map Ref: 17
A31

A warm welcome and home from home hospitality awaits in this delightful, spacious bungalow and lovely garden. The twin en-suite room has its own garden entrance and the double room has a large adjoining bathroom. Both rooms have television and beverage facilities. Enjoy an excellent breakfast, then explore the beautiful New Forest and the South Coast. A country inn is nearby. ETC AA 4 Diamonds.

B & B from £20pp, Rooms 1 double with private bathroom, 1 twin en-suite, No smoking, Children over 12, No dogs, Closed Xmas & New Year

---

CRANFORD FARM Rudd Lane, Braishfield, Romsey SO51 0PU   *Map Ref:* 18
Brian John Charles Brooks   A27
Tel / Fax: 01794 368216

Cranford Farm is a large secluded farmhouse set in three acres of farmland, located in the beautiful Test valley. All rooms are comfortably furnished with televisions, tea/coffee facilities and en-suite bathrooms. Good traditional English breakfasts and a warm welcome await you. Just off the A3057, between Braishfield and Michelmersh.

B & B £22.50-£32.50pp, Rooms 2 double, 1 twin, both en-suite, No smoking, Children over 6, No dogs, Closed Xmas & New Year

---

KINTAIL Salisbury Road, Shootash, Romsey SO51 6GA   *Map Ref:* 19
Jill Mansbridge   A27
Tel / Fax: 01794 513849

A small friendly home on the edge of New Forest, situated on the A27 Salisbury road. The bedrooms are quiet and offer tea/coffee facilities with residents also having access to their own lounge. Within easy reach of Winchester, Salisbury, Stonehenge and Hillier's arboretum. Local pubs serve good food at reasonable prices. Non smoking. Ample parking.

B & B from £20pp, Rooms 1 double en-suite, 1 twin with private bathroom, No smoking, No children or dogs, Closed Nov to Apr

---

RANVILLES FARM HOUSE Romsey SO51 6AA   *Map Ref:* 20
Bill & Anthea Hughes   M27, A3090
Tel / Fax: 02380 814481

Dating from the 15th century, this Grade Two Star listed house provides a peaceful setting surrounded by five acres of gardens and paddock. En-suite rooms are attractively decorated and furnished with antiques. The dining room overlooks the barnyard. Ranvilles Farm House is three miles from the New Forest and about a mile from Romsey, a small town close to Winchester and Salisbury.

B & B from £25pp, Rooms 1 single, 1 twin, 2 double, 1 family, all en-suite, No smoking, Children & dogs welcome, Closed Xmas & New Year

---

SILLWOOD ACRE Church Road, Binstead, Ryde, Isle of Wight PO33 3TB   *Map Ref:* 21
Mrs Deborah Hart   *Tel:* 01983 563553   A3054
Email: sillwood.acre@virgin.net

Large Victorian house set in one acre of informal gardens with occasional sightings of red squirrels. Relaxed and friendly with a quiet atmosphere. Spacious bedrooms, all en-suite with colour television, radio, tea/coffee facilities and hairdryer. Ample off road parking. Five minutes drive to Ryde shops and to mainland ferries. Ideally situated for touring the whole island. ETC 4 Diamonds.

B & B from £20pp, Rooms 2 double, 1 twin, all en-suite, No smoking, Children over 5, No dogs, Open all year

---

NORTH COURT Shorwell, Isle of Wight PO30 3JG   *Map Ref:* 22
Mrs Christine Harrison   *Tel:* 01983 740415   *Fax:* 01983 740409   B3323, B3399
Email: john@north-court.demon.co.uk   *Web:* www.wightfarmholidays.co.uk/northcourt

North Court is situated amongst the Downs in a small village and was built in 1615. It is best suited for those wanting a relaxing stay in a historical house situated in magnificent gardens of 15 acres. These are made up of a walled garden, stream and mediterranean terraces which lead you to the Crown Inn for evening meals. Sea and Osbourne nearby.

B & B £24-£30pp, Rooms 1 single, 3 double, 3 twin, all en-suite, No smoking, Children welcome, Dogs by arrangement, Closed Xmas & New Year

STRANG HALL Uplands, Totland Bay, Isle of Wight PO39 0DZ   *Map Ref:* 23
Vera F McMullan   B3322
Tel / Fax: 01983 753189

An Edwardian family home in the hills above Totland Bay, enjoying
views over the Downs and the Solent. Built in the Arts and Craft
style, it offers comfortable accommodation. The beaches of Totland
Bay and Colwell Bay are within walking distance, as is the Totland
Church and village post office. Freshwater is one mile, here is a
library, medical centre and an indoor pool.

B & B from £25pp, Dinner from £20, Rooms 1 single, 1 twin,
1 double, 1 family, some en-suite, Restricted smoking, Children
welcome, No dogs, Closed Xmas & New Year

CORNERWAYS 39 Madeira Road, Ventnor, Isle of Wight PO38 1QS   *Map Ref:* 24
Doreen & Ian Malcolm   *Tel:* 01983 852323   A3055
Web: www.cornerwaysventnor.co.uk

We would like to have the opportunity of welcoming you to
Cornerways, a small family run hotel in a quiet location with
magnificent views over sea and downs. Cornerways has been
described by our guests as a comfortable and friendly place with an
informal atmosphere, 'a home from home.' We love it here and we
hope you will too.

B & B from £20pp, C-Cards MC VS AE, Rooms 3 double, 1 twin,
2 family, all en-suite, Restricted smoking, Children welcome,
No dogs, Closed Nov to Feb

UNDER ROCK COUNTRY HOUSE B & B Shore Road, Bonchurch, Ventnor, Isle of Wight PO38 1RF
James Pritchett *Tel:* 01983 855274   *Map Ref:* 24
Web: www.under-rock.co.uk   A3055

Under Rock is an unusual house set in large sub-tropical gardens
close to Horsehoe Bay. Rooms have en-suite or private facilities.
Guests have use of an octagonal sitting room, terrace and gardens.
Bonchurch is a picturesque coastal village with duck pond and
literary associations with Dickens and Tennyson. There are good
eating places in the village, or at nearby Ventnor and Shanklin.

B & B £23-£27pp, Rooms 2 double, 1 twin, all en-suite/private
facilities, No smoking, No children or dogs, Closed Nov to Feb

CAMS Hambledon, Waterlooville PO7 4SP   *Map Ref:* 25
Julian & Valerie Fawcett   B2150, A3
Tel: 023 9263 2865   *Fax:* 023 9263 2691

This is a beautiful Grade 11 Listed house with Jacobean origins.
Bedrooms are comfortably equipped. Breakfast is served in a 17th
century pine panelled dining room with French windows onto the
lawn. There is a large garden with fine trees, tennis court and ample
parking. Cams is well placed for Winchester, Chichester and
Portsmouth. A good pub serving excellent food within walking
distance.

B & B from £24pp, Rooms 2 double, 2 twin, some en-suite,
No smoking, Children welcome, Dogs by arrangement, Closed
Xmas & New Year

HOME PADDOCKS West Meon GU32 1NA   *Map Ref:* 26
Raye & Simon Ward *Tel:* 01730 829241 *Fax:* 01730 829577   A32, A272
Email: homepaddocks@compuserve.com

This family home is situated on the outskirts of West Meon, it stands
in a large garden with tennis court and croquet lawn. Dating to the
1560s, there is a Victorian conservatory. Comfortable bedrooms with
garden views, have private facilities. Ideal for Winchester,
Southampton, the New Forest and the South Coast. A good
selection of pubs, restaurants, golf courses and gardens to visit.

B & B from £22.50pp, Dinner from £15, Rooms 2 en-suite twin,
Restricted smoking, Children by arrangement, Dogs by
arrangement, Closed Xmas

ACACIA 44 Kilham Lane, Winchester SO22 5PT
Shirley Buchanan   *Tel / Fax:* 01962 852259
Email: shirley.buchanan@btclick.com   *Web:* www.btinternet.com/~eric.buchanan

Map Ref: 27
M27, M3

Our friendly home is set in beautiful gardens, five minutes' drive from the city centre, offering you a peaceful stay. Double and twin bedrooms with en-suite bathrooms and tea/coffee facilities and good choice of food for breakfast, plus guests' sitting room. Excellent and easy access for road and rail communications for many tourist areas, all within one hour, including London, Portsmouth, New Forest and Stonehenge.

B & B £25-£27pp, Rooms 2 double, 1 twin, all en-suite, No smoking, Children over 10, No dogs, Closed Dec to Mar

---

4 ALEXANDRA TERRACE Winchester SO23 9SP
Mrs Gill Dowson   *Tel:* 01962 863356   *Fax:* 01962 868826
Email: gill.dowson@virgin.net

Map Ref: 27
M27, M3

There is a warm and distinctive feel to this beautifully renovated 1860s mews house which is centrally situated in a conservation area with free parking. The comfortable and welcoming bedrooms include televisions and tea/coffee facilities. Buffet breakfast is served with freshly squeezed orange juice, fresh fruit salad, compote, organic yoghurt, homemade bread and also full English.

B & B £32.50pp, C-Cards MC VS, Rooms 1 double, 1 twin, both en-suite, No smoking, Children over 12, No dogs, Closed Xmas & New Year

---

BRYMER HOUSE 29-30 St Faith's Road, St Cross, Winchester SO23 9QD
Fizzy & Guy Warren   *Tel:* 01962 867428   *Fax:* 01962 868624
Email: brymerhouse@aol.com

Map Ref: 27
M27, M3

Brymer House offers quiet and comfortable accommodation in your own half of a beautifully furnished town house, a short walk to Cathedral city centre and water meadows. The en-suite bedrooms with tea/coffee facilities and televisions are small and cosy. There is an 'honesty box' in the dining room for drinks, open fire in the sitting room, delicious breakfasts and easy parking.

B & B £25-£30pp, Rooms 1 double, 1 twin, both en-suite, Restricted smoking, Children over 7, No dogs, Closed Xmas

---

GREAT HUNTS PLACE Owslebury, Winchester SO21 1JL
Tim & Sue Torrington   *Tel:* 01962 777234   *Fax:* 01962 777242
Email: tt@byngs.freeserve.co.uk   *Web:* www.byngs.freeserve.co.uk

Map Ref: 28
M3, A34, A272

Originally two Edwardian cottages, Great Hunts Place was converted and 'Georgianised' in the 1970s. The house sits in 15 acres of its own land, and enjoys views over the surrounding countryside. This traditionally furnished house may be found on the Pilgrim's way, so it makes it an ideal location for those who enjoy walking. The historic town of Winchester is only six miles away.

B & B £25-£30pp, Rooms 1 twin en suite, 1 twin with private bathroom, Children over 10, No dogs, Closed Xmas & New Year

---

LANG HOUSE 27 Chilbolton Avenue, Winchester SO22 5HE
Sheila Hooper   *Tel / Fax:* 01962 860620
Email: sheila@langhouse0.demon.co.uk

Map Ref: 27
M27, M3

Lang House is an elegant detached family home overlooking Royal Winchester golf course. All rooms are en-suite or with private bathrooms. Excellent breakfasts and warm and welcoming service. Ample off road parking and easy access to city centre. Tea/coffee making facilities and televisions in all rooms. A no smoking house.

B & B from £27pp, Rooms 3 double, 1 twin, all en-suite or private bathroom, No smoking, Children over 7, No dogs, Closed Xmas & New Year

Herefordshire & Worcestershire

These two counties, joined in 1974, share the dramatic Malvern Hills which lie along the Severn Plain, separating the low plains of Herefordshire from the glorious Vale of Evesham. This jagged ridge was exploited as a defensive site by Iron Age man, who built their ancient forts at Worcestershire Beacon and Herefordshire Beacon from which there are wonderful views to the hills of the Welsh Marches and to the Cotswold escarpment. Great Malvern, at the centre of this lovely area, is an ideal base for the holidaymaker. The town developed as a spa during the nineteenth century and is renowned for its crystal clear water, its Victorian character and the fine fifteenth century priory tower which dominates the district. Sir Edward Elgar, whose 'Pomp and Circumstance' marches were inspired by the Malverns, was born at Lower Broadheath in 1857 and his works are annually performed as part of the Malvern and Worcester Music Festivals. Worcester, famous for its manufacture of porcelain since 1862, was made a diocese in 680AD and its present cathedral, begun in the eleventh century has an impressive Norman crypt. The city possesses some quite remarkable examples of domestic architecture including The Commandery, once a hospice for travellers in the eleventh century and the headquarters of Charles II during the Battle of Worcester, now is a museum of local history. The battles of the Civil War are recalled in nearby Ledbury where Ledbury Park, which dates from 1600, was the Royalist headquarters during the local skirmishes. The town is an ancient market town with its seventeenth century market hall still retaining its original wooden pillars. The church of St Michael and All Angels has a fine detached bell tower with a slender spire. To the west at Brockhampton, the National Trust owns almost 1,700 acres of wonderful woodlands and parkland open to the public with waymarked footpaths to follow and superb views. Lower Brockhampton boasts the interesting ruins of a twelfth century chapel and a splendid late fourteenth century moated manor house with an unusual half-timbered gatehouse.

Hereford, the ancient capital of West Mercia, stands in a commanding position over the River Wye. It was founded in the seventh century as an outpost on the border with Celtic Wales. The glorious cathedral contains the Mappa Mundi, a circular map of

Severn Valley Railway crossing the River Severn (WCC)

171

the world painted on vellum and showing Jerusalem at the centre of the world, believed to have been completed in 1290. The cathedral also contains a remarkable library of 1,500 chained books. The area benefits from the cider industry and Hereford is the home of the largest Cider Maker in the world with the Cider Museum and King Offa Distillery celebrating this important trade.

The River Wye meanders in wide loops through the county on its course from Plynlimon to Chepstow. It is really spectacular at many locations, but few quite as superb as at Symond's Yat where the Wye passes through a deep gorge protected by massive cliffs giving spectacular panoramic views. Ross-on-Wye is a charming market town standing on a sandstone bluff overlooking the Wye. It is a town with lovely public gardens, and some fine half-timbered and Georgian houses. Leominster in the north, wonderfully located at the junction of Pinsley

Brook and the River Lugg amongst cider-apple orchards and hopfields, is yet another town full of fascinating buildings, with an excellent folk museum. Its priory is a gem, but the timber-framed Grange, once the market hall, is Herefordshire's most elaborately carved building and a very rare surviving example of the work of John Abel, the king's carpenter.

The Vale of Evesham is a picture in the spring when the fruit trees are in blossom. The town of Evesham, at the centre of the fruit growing area, developed around the now ruined Benedictine abbey whose bell tower of 1539 dominates the delightful riverside gardens. The interesting obelisk on Green Hill is a memorial to Simon de Montfort, the father of the House of Commons, who died in battle in 1265. No visitor should leave this part of the county without visiting Broadway, one of the prettiest small towns in the region and the gateway to the Cotswolds.

PLACES TO VISIT

This is a small selection of interesting places to visit. Many more are listed in our annual guide to Museums, Galleries, Historic Houses & Sites (see page 448)

Hanbury Hall
Hanbury, Droitwich, Worcestershire
A William & Mary style house with fine collections of porcelain and Dutch flower paintings, as well as recreated eighteenth century formal gardens.

Eastnor Castle
Eastnor, Ledbury, Herefordshire
A magnificent Georgian castle, home to the Hervey-Bathurst family and set in a large deer park. There are many outdoor activities and within the house, tapestries, fine art and armour.

Severn Valley Railway
Bewdley, Worcestershire
Preserved standard gauge steam railway, services operating through 16 scenic miles along the River Severn. One of the largest collections of locomotives and rolling stock in the country.

Worcester Cathedral
College Green, Worcester
This Norman Cathedral was founded in 679 AD with an impressive bell-tower, completed in 1374. It houses King John's tomb and Prince Arthur's Chantry.

Herefordshire & Worcestershire

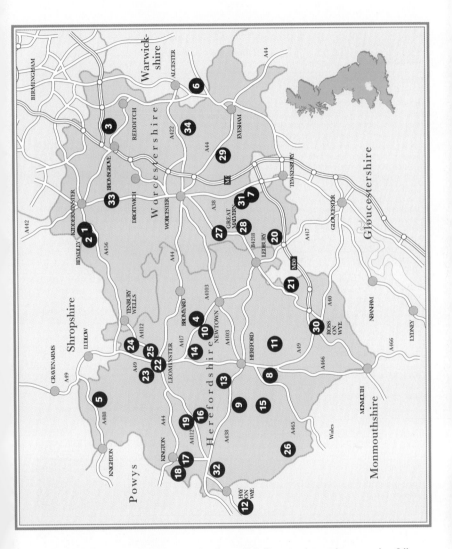

The Red Map References should be used to locate B & B properties on the pages that follow

BANK HOUSE 14 Lower Park, Bewdley, Worcs DY12 2DP   *Map Ref:* 1
Fleur Nightingale *Tel / Fax:* 01299 402652 *Mobile:* 07890 001339   A456
Email: fleur.nightingale@virgin.net

Bank House is a Victorian home, situated close to the town centre. We offer spacious bedrooms, colour televisions, tea/coffee making facilities, generous breakfasts and a warm, homely atmosphere. There is enough space for parking two cars off road. Close to the Severn Valley Railway and the Wyre Forest. We are just a few minutes from the Worcestershire Way.

B & B from £20pp, Rooms 1 single, 1 twin, 1 family, No smoking, Children welcome, No dogs, Closed Xmas & New Year

---

TARN Long Bank, Bewdley, Worcs DY12 2QT   *Map Ref:* 2
Topsy Beves   A456
Tel: 01299 402243

Attractive country house with a library in 17 acres of gardens and fields with spectacular views. Excellent breakfasts with home baked rolls are served. Conveniently situated for Worcestershire Way Walk (guests can be collected), Wyre Forest, River Severn (fishing), Midland Safari Park, Severn Valley Steam Railway, gardens, stately homes, golf. Two miles west of Georgian Bewdley on A456. There is ample parking.

B & B from £18pp, Rooms 2 single, 2 twin, No smoking, Children welcome, No dogs, Closed Nov to Feb

---

ROSA LODGE 38 Station Road, Blackwell, Worcs B60 1PZ   *Map Ref:* 3
Sandra Shakespeare *Tel / Fax:* 0121 445 5440   M5, M40, M42
Email: sandra@rosalodge.co.uk *Web:* www.rosalodge.co.uk

Rose Lodge is a 5 Diamond premier selected establishment offering high quality luxury en-suite rooms. Within easy reach of Birmingham, Stratford, Warwick and NEC. One and a half miles from motorway complex M5, M42, M40. Superb food is served in our Edwardian style dining room. Free parking. Most bedrooms look out over the beautifully laid out garden with access through the conservatory.

B & B from £30pp, Dinner available, Rooms 2 double, 1 twin, 1 single, all en-suite, Restricted smoking, Children over 14, Guide dogs only, Open all year

---

DOVECOTE BARN Stoke Lacy, Bromyard, Herefs HR7 4HJ   *Map Ref:* 4
Roger & Judy Young *Tel:* 01432 820968 *Fax:* 01432 820969 *Mobile:* 07775 916372   A465
Email: dovecotebarn@mail.com

A 17th century Grade II listed barn, sympathetically converted to the highest standards of comfort. Traditional English breakfasts or smoked salmon with scrambled eggs are complemented with fresh fruits and homemade bread. For dinner we are willing to taxi you at no cost to a pub or restaurant or enjoy our homecooked delights. Near to the Forest of Dean and the Brecon Beacons.

B & B from £22.25pp, Dinner £17.50, Rooms 1 double en-suite, 1 double private bathroom, 1 single, No smoking, Children welcome, No dogs, Open all year

---

UPPER BUCKTON FARM Leintwardine, Craven Arms, Herefs SY7 0JU   *Map Ref:* 5
Hayden & Yvonne Lloyd   A49
Tel / Fax: 01547 540634 *Mobile:* 07974 116149

This elegant Georgian farmhouse looks south over the River Teme towards the Wigmore Rolls, surrounded by a beautiful garden with millstream and 12th century motte. Every comfort, excellent dinners and log fires complete this oasis of peace and beauty. Being in the Welsh Marches guests have many interesting castles, gardens, National Trust properties and the Black and White villages of Herefordshire to visit.

B & B from £30pp, Dinner from £20, Rooms 3 double, 2 twin, all en-suite, No smoking, Children welcome, No dogs in house, Open all year

BREDON VIEW GUEST HOUSE Village Street, Harvington, Evesham, Worcs WR11 8NQ   *Map Ref:* 6
Sue & Ian Roberts   *Tel / Fax:* 01386 871484   *Mobile:* 07799 850490   A46
Email: b.v.circa1898@bushinternet.com   *Web:* www.brendonview.heartuk.net

A warm welcome awaits you at our beautifully decorated home with en-suite bedrooms, including one four poster, combi televisions, tea/coffee facilities, hairdryers and ironing facilities. Guest are welcome to use the guest lounge and snooker table in the dining room. We have off road parking and are ideally situated for exploring Stratford and the Cotswolds. ETC 4 Diamonds, Silver Award.

B & B £20-£25pp, Rooms 2 double, 1 twin, all en-suite, No smoking, Children over 10, No dogs, Open all year

---

OLD PARSONAGE FARM Hanley Castle, Worcs WR8 0BU   *Map Ref:* 7
Ann Addison   *Tel / Fax:* 01684 310124   M5 & M50, B4209
Email: OPWines@aol.com

eBuilt in 1777, the farm sits on the edge of the village of Hanley Castle. Wonderful views over the Malvern Hills from the delightful garden. Surrounded by farmland, it has access to footpaths. Original features include a vaulted ceiling, an inglenook and a bread oven. The Addisons specialise in food and wine, guests may enjoy 4 courses with wine from an extensive wine list.

B & B £22.50-£28.50pp, Dinner £16.90, Rooms 2 double, 1 double/twin/family, 2 en-suite, Restricted smoking, Children over 12, Dogs by arrangement, Closed Mid-Dec to Mid-Jan

---

HOLLY HOUSE FARM Allensmore, Hereford, Herefs HR2 9BH   *Map Ref:* 8
Diana Sinclair   *Tel:* 01432 277294   *Fax:* 01432 261285   *Mobile:* 07889 830223   A465
Email: hollyhousefarm@aol.com

Holly House Farm is a delightful family country farmhouse stabling horses, situated in beautiful and peaceful open countryside. Bedrooms en-suite or with private bathroom, central heating, television and tea/coffee making facilities. Ideal base for Hereford, Black Mountains, Brecon and Malvern Hills, Wye Valley, Welsh borders and market towns. Ample car parking.

B & B £20-£25pp, Rooms 2 twin, 2 double, 1 single, all en-suite/private bathroom, Restricted smoking, Children & dogs welcome, Closed Xmas

---

THE OLD RECTORY Byford, Hereford, Herefs HR4 7LD   *Map Ref:* 9
Charles & Audrey Mayson   *Tel:* 01981 590218   *Fax:* 01981 590499   A438
Email: info@cm-Ltd.com

Byford is a hamlet in beautiful Herefordshire close to the River Wye on the Wye Valley walk. A Georgian home, with elegant and spacious rooms, the dining room has ceiling to floor windows with panelled pine shutters and doors. A magnificent cedar tree dominates the garden. Large en-suite bedrooms with parkland views, have sofas, books and television. Villages, churches, mountains and gardens to visit.

B & B from £21.50pp, Dinner from £12.50, Rooms 1 twin, 2 double, all en-suite, No smoking, Children welcome, No dogs in house, Closed Nov to Feb

---

FELTON HOUSE Felton, Hereford, Herefs HR1 3PH   *Map Ref:* 10
Marjorie & Brian Roby   *Tel / Fax:* 01432 820366   A417
Email: bandb@ereal.net   *Web:* www.Smoothhound.co.uk/hotels/felton.html

On arrival relax with complimentary refreshments in a country house of character set in four acres of tranquil gardens. Sleep soundly in a comfortable antique or four poster bed and awake refreshed to enjoy the best and purest Herefordshire food in a superb Victorian dining room. Excellent evening meals at fine local inns. ETC Gold Award. AA Top Breakfast Award.

B & B £25pp, Rooms 1 single, 2 double, 1 twin, 1 family, all en-suite, No smoking, Children & dogs welcome, Closed Xmas & New Year

THE BOWENS COUNTRY HOUSE Fownhope, Hereford, Herefs HR1 4PS   *Map Ref:* 11
Carol Hart *Tel / Fax:* 01432 860430   B4224
Email: Thebowenshotel@aol.com *Web:* www.thebowenshotel.co.uk

Peacefully situated on the edge of the village on the B4224 in the Wye Valley AONB, midway between Hereford and Ross-on-Wye. Ideal for touring, walking, and exploring the Welsh Borders, Malverns, Cotswolds, Brecon Beacons and the countryside of Herefordshire. Restored 17th century house set in two acres of gardens. Comfortable, en-suite bedrooms. Oak beamed lounge with inglenook. Superb home cooked meals, using local/home produce.

B & B £25-£32.50pp, C-Cards MC VS, Dinner from £15, Rooms 2 single, 6 double/twin, 2 family, all en-suite, Restricted smoking, Children welcome, Dogs by arrangement, Open all year

---

THE HARP INN Hay Road, Glasbury-on-Wye, Hereford, Herefs HR3 5NR   *Map Ref:* 12
David & Lynda White *Tel:* 01497 847 373   A438
Email: harpinn@talk21.com

A Welsh village pub four miles from Hay-on-Wye, the town of books. Ideal for touring the Black Mountains and Brecon Beacons. All rooms are equipped with central heating, televisions and tea/coffee facilities. Canoeing, pony trekking, golf, walking available locally, also popular area with artists and bird watchers. Home cooked food including vegetarian or children's option if required and served with real ale.

B & B from £19pp, C-Cards MC VS, Dinner from £8, Rooms 2 double, 2 twin, all en-suite, Restricted smoking, Children welcome, No dogs, Open all year

---

APPLETREE COTTAGE Mansell Lacy, Hereford, Herefs HR4 7HH   *Map Ref:* 13
Monica Barker *Tel:* 01981 590688   A480
Email: monica.barker@tesco.net

Once a cider house, eventually two converted farm cottages, one was built in 1450, Appletree Cottage is warm and comfortable with full central heating. The open plan sitting room has a wood burning stove which ensures warmth throughout the house. English breakfasts are served. We are surrounded by many places of interest, and Hereford and the village of Weobley are a short drive.

B & B £17-£22pp, Rooms 2 twin (1 en-suite), No smoking, No children or dogs, Open all year

---

THE VAULD FARM The Vauld, Marden, Hereford, Herefs HR1 3HA   *Map Ref:* 14
Jean Bengry   A49
Tel: 01568 797898

Perfect for relaxing and discovering Herefordshire. A 16th century manor with spacious en-suite bedrooms including a four poster. Lounge areas with television and tea/coffee facilities, overlooking the duck pond and countryside. Breakfast and evening meals are served in the dining room with a large open fire, massive beams overhead and flagstone floor. Guests may bring their own wine. Quiet location with parking. Hereford 8 miles.

B & B from £25pp, Dinner from £20, Rooms 1 twin, 2 double, 1 family, all en-suite, Restricted smoking, Children over 12, No dogs, Open all year

---

UPPER GILVACH FARM St Margarets, Vowchurch, Hereford, Herefs HR2 0QY   *Map Ref:* 15
Alan & Ruth Watkins *Tel / Fax:* 01981 510618   B4348
Email: ruth@uppergilvach.freeserve.co.uk *Web:* www.golden-valley.co.uk/gilvach

Family run farm between Golden Valley and Black Mountains. The 300 year old farmhouse in the family since early last century offers three attractively furnished bedrooms, all en-suite, colour television and hospitality trays. Peace and comfort in a relaxing atmosphere. Licensed. Delicious evening meals and hearty breakfasts using local and home grown produce. ETB 4 Diamonds, Silver Award. Holiday caravan available.

B & B £25-£30pp, C-Cards MC VS, Dinner from £14, Rooms 1 single/twin, 1 double, 1 family, all en-suite, No smoking, Children welcome, No dogs, Open all year

GARNSTONE HOUSE Weobley, Hereford, Herefs HR4 8QP
Mrs Dawn MacLeod
Tel: 01544 318943   *Fax:* 01544 318197

Map Ref: 16
A4112

Comfortable and friendly accommodation in peaceful setting, one mile from Weobley. Lovely garden with many unusual herbaceous plants, clematis a speciality. Dinner by arrangement with good home cooking. Television and tea/coffee facilities with hand basins in both rooms. Easy reach of numerous gardens and places of interest. Good walks and excellent local restaurants.

B & B from £25pp, Dinner available, Rooms 1 double, 1 twin, Restricted smoking, Children welcome, Dogs by arrangement, Closed Xmas

---

MILL ORCHARD Kingstone, Herefs HR2 9ES
Jackie & Harry Cleveland   *Tel:* 01981 250326   *Fax:* 01981 250520
Email: cleveland@millorchard.co.uk   *Web:* www.millorchard.co.uk

Map Ref: 15
A465

A country house set in one acre of south facing gardens overlooking lovely countryside on the edge of the Golden Valley, only six miles from Hereford. Bedrooms have colour televisions, refreshment trays and hairdryers. Delicious breakfasts using local and homemade produce. Visitors can relax in the guest lounge and there are good pubs and restaurants nearby. 4 Diamonds, Gold award.

B & B from £26pp, Rooms 2 double, 1 twin, all en-suite, No smoking, Children over 12, Dogs by arrangement, Closed Dec & Jan

---

BOLLINGHAM HOUSE Eardisley, Kington, Herefs HR5 3LE
John & Stephanie Grant   *Tel:* 01544 327326   *Fax:* 01544 327880
Email: bollhouse@bigfoot.com

Map Ref: 17
A4111

Quite breathtaking. This residence overlooks one of the finest views in England. Gracious rooms with log fires, spacious bedrooms, fresh flowers and an English garden to enjoy. The gardens include terracing, ponds and a walled garden. Outside the dining room window is a Victorian chapel. Bollingham House is conveniently situated for the Welsh Marches, Offa's Dyke, Hay-on-Wye and golf at Kington Golf Club.

B & B from £25pp, Dinner from £14.50, Rooms 1 twin, 2 double, all private bathrooms, Restricted smoking, Children welcome, Dogs by arrangement, Closed Xmas & New Year

---

HALL'S MILL HOUSE Huntington, Kington, Herefs HR5 3QA
Grace Watson
Tel: 01497 831409

Map Ref: 18
A438, A44

Recently modernised, Mill House, is tucked away in an unspoilt peaceful valley. Rooms are cosy with exposed beams and slate window sills and guests have run of the house, but the lovely kitchen tends to be the gravitational centre of this home. Easy access to Offa's Dyke, Welsh border country, churches, castles, Hay-on-Wye and the Black Mountains.

B & B £18-£22pp, Dinner from £12, Rooms 1 double, 1 double en-suite, 1 twin, No smoking, Children over 5, No dogs, Closed Xmas & New Year

---

UPPER NEWTON FARMHOUSE Kinnersley, Herefs HR3 6QB
Jon & Pearl Taylor   *Tel / Fax:* 01544 327727
Email: jtaylor@click.kc3.co.uk   *Web:* www.uppernewton.herefordshire.com

Map Ref: 19
A4112, A438

AA Landlady of the year 2000, we pay attention to detail and provide delicious local, seasonal food. The Stable accommodation offers a suite of rooms for guests to relax in. Beautifully decorated, totally equipped with luxurious extras. Information about local walks, farm diary, local attractions, long distance paths are provided. Pearl delights in helping guests to enjoy their stay. Lovely gardens and stunning views.

B & B from £25pp, Rooms 1 twin, 2 double, all en-suite, No smoking, No children or dogs, Open all year

GROVE HOUSE Bromsberrow Heath, Ledbury, Herefs HR8 1PE   *Map Ref:* 20
Michael & Ellen Ross   *Tel:* 01531 650584   *Mobile:* 07960 166903   M50, A417
Email: rossgrovehouse@amserve.net

Michael and Ellen Ross's 15th century Grade II listed home stands in 13 acres of fields and garden within easy reach of the Cotswolds. The beams, panelling and open fires provide a sympathetic setting for the gleaming antiques and fresh flowers. Spacious bedrooms, two with four poster beds, have bowls of fruit, homemade biscuits and televisions. A tennis court is also available, use of a neighbour's swimming pool.

B & B from £36.50pp, Dinner from £23.50, Rooms 2 double, 1 twin, 1 family, all en-suite, Restricted smoking, Children welcome, Dogs not in bedrooms, Closed Xmas & New Year

---

BODENHAM FARM Much Marcle, Ledbury, Herefs HR8 2NJ   *Map Ref:* 21
Lynda Morgan   *Tel:* 01531 660222   *Mobile:* 07754 415604   A449
Email: bodenhamfarm@lineone.net

18th century listed farmhouse set in five acres of wooded grounds. The property was refurbished but retains many original features including oak beams and polished elm floors. Two four-poster bedrooms plus one twin room and drawing and dining rooms for sole use of guests. Set on lower slopes of Marcle Ridge between market towns of Ross-on-Wye and Ledbury.

B & B £22.50-£25pp, Rooms 2 double, 1 twin, all en-suite, No smoking, No children or dogs, Closed Xmas & New Year

---

HALLEND Kynaston, Much Marcle, Ledbury, Herefs HR8 2PD   *Map Ref:* 21
Mrs Angela Jefferson   *Tel:* 01531 670225   *Fax:* 01531 670747   *Mobile:* 07774 269910   A449, A4172
Email: khjefferson@hallend91.freeserve.co.uk

Hospitality is warm and welcoming at Hallend. Bring your own wine for dinner in the dining room with its collection of modern marine paintings. Summer breakfasts are set in the geranium filled conservatory by the outdoor heated pool. 400 acres surround this Georgian listed home full of light and colour with stunning views and superb walks.

B & B from £37.50pp, C-Cards VS, Dinner from £22.50, Rooms 2 double, 1 twin, all en-suite, No smoking, Children over 12, No dogs, Closed Xmas & New Year

---

HEATH HOUSE Stoke Prior, Leominster, Herefs HR6 0NF   *Map Ref:* 22
Karen Cholerton   *Tel / Fax:* 01568 760385   *Mobile:* 07720 887391   A44
Email: heathhouse@onetel.net.uk

Heath House is a lovely stone farmhouse situated in quiet countryside, near Leominster. Ideal as a centre for Ludlow, Hay and the Malverns, also the unspoilt Wye Valley and the Marches. The bedrooms are en-suite with televisions and tea/coffee facilities and breakfasts are served in the farmhouse kitchen. A brochure is available.

B & B from £25pp, Rooms 2 twin en-suite, No smoking, Children over 7, Dogs by arrangement, Closed Xmas & New Year

---

HIGHFIELD Newtown, Ivington Road, Leominster, Herefs HR6 8QD
Catherine & Marguerite Fothergill *Tel:* 01568 613216
Email: info@stay-at-highfield.co.uk *Web:* www.stay-at-highfield.co.uk

Map Ref: 22
A44, A49

Highfield stands in a large garden with unspoilt views of farmland
and distant mountains. The house was built in Edwardian times and
accommodation is elegant, comfortable, friendly and attractively
decorated. Meals are carefully prepared from fresh ingredients, and
are served in the charming dining room. All diets are catered for and
wine is available. Groups are welcome.

B & B from £20pp, Dinner from £13.50, Rooms 1 double, 2 twin
en-suite/private, Restricted smoking, No children or dogs, Closed
Nov to Feb

EYTON OLD HALL Eyton, Leominster, Herefs HR6 0AQ
James & Henrietta Varley *Tel:* 01568 612551 *Fax:* 01568 616100
Email: varleyeoh@hotmail.com *Web:* eytonoldhall.fsnet.co.uk

Map Ref: 23
A44, A49

A quiet, comfortable house with fine views over the Welsh hills,
midway between Hereford and Ludlow. There are interesting
gardens to visit and excellent local food nearby. Guests have their
own dining room and sitting room to relax in. The bedrooms are
charmingly furnished, with luxury linen and towels. Televisions can
be provided on request.

B & B £25pp, Dinner from £17.50, Rooms 2 double, 2 twin, all
en-suite, Restricted smoking, Children over 5, Well behaved dogs,
Closed Xmas & New Year

THE HILLS FARM Leysters, Leominster, Herefs HR6 0HP
Peter & Jane Conolly *Tel:* 01568 750205 *Fax:* 01568 750306
Email: conolly@bigwig.net

Map Ref: 24
A4112

The Hill Farm dates to the 16th century, and Jane, the AA Landlady
of the Year 1999, and Peter provide exceptionally comfortable
accommodation. Three bedrooms in individual barn conversions,
and two in the main house. Rooms are en-suite with panoramic
views. The guests' sitting room has local maps, books and
magazines. A scrumptious dinner, when prebooked, is served at
7pm, please bring your own drinks.

B & B from £28pp, C-Cards MC VS, Dinner from £19, Rooms
2 twin, 3 double, all en-suite, No smoking, No children or dogs,
Closed Nov to Mar

LOWER BACHE HOUSE Kimbolton, Leominster, Herefs HR6 0ER
Rose & Leslie Wiles *Tel:* 01568 750304
Email: leslie.wiles@care4free.net

Map Ref: 25
A4112

This award winning seventeenth century house, is set in fourteen
acres of private nature reserve in a tiny valley. It provides four self-
contained suites, each with a sitting room. There are water colours,
original prints, plants, books and ornaments which create a
comfortable atmosphere. A renowned cuisine, using local organic
produce, complete the hallmarks of peace, privacy and fine food.

B & B from £29.50pp, Dinner from £15.50, Rooms 2 twin,
2 double, all en-suite, No smoking, Children over 8, No dogs,
Open all year

MIDDLE TREWERN Longtown, Herefs HR2 0LN
Antony Egremont-Lee
Tel: 01873 860670

Map Ref: 26
A465

A place of peace and tranquility on the edge of the Black Mountains
with magnificent views. The early 17th century longhouse is full of
history with open fires, panelled walls and huge oak beams, as is the
local border country with its castles and beautiful scenery. There are
televisions in the bedrooms and excellent local pubs for meals.

B & B from £25pp, Rooms 1 twin, 2 family, Restricted smoking,
Children & dogs welcome, Open all year

WYCHE KEEP 22 Wyche Road, Malvern, Worcs WR14 4EG   *Map Ref:* 27
Judith & Jon Williams   *Tel:* 01684 567018   *Fax:* 01684 892304   B4218
Email: wychekeep@aol.com   *Web:* www.jks.org/wychekeep

An arts and crafts castle style house, perched high on the Malvern Hills, built by the family of Sir Stanley Baldwin, to enjoy the spectacular 60 mile views. Three luxury double suites, including four poster. English cooking is a speciality, guests can enjoy four course candlelit dinners, served in a 'house party' atmosphere, in front of a log fire. Fully licensed. Magical setting. Private parking.

B & B £30-£35pp, Dinner from £20, Rooms 2 twin, 1 double, all en-suite, No smoking, No children or dogs, Open all year

---

THE DELL HOUSE Green Lane, Malvern Wells, Malvern, Worcs WR14 4HU   *Map Ref:* 28
Mrs Diana Knight   *Tel:* 01684 564448   *Fax:* 01684 893974   *Mobile:* 07974 701123   A449
Email: diana@dellhouse.co.uk   *Web:* www.dellhouse.co.uk

There are stunning views at this country house in its own two acres of gardens on the slopes of the Malvern Hills. Enjoy full English or continental breakfast in the elegant morning room. Spacious bedrooms offer en-suite bathroom facilities, televisions, radio alarms and hospitality trays. Direct access to the hill paths. Easy walking distance to the Showground. AA 4 Diamonds.

B & B £25-£30pp, Rooms 1 single, 2 double, 1 twin, all en-suite, No smoking, Children over 10, No dogs, Open all year

---

ARBOUR HOUSE Main Road, Wyre Piddle, Pershore, Worcs WR10 2HU   *Map Ref:* 29
Rob & Liz Brownsdon   *Tel / Fax:* 01386 555833   *Mobile:* 07879 423250   M5, A44, A38, A46, A40
Email: arbourhouse@faxvia.net

Originally a labourer's cottage in the 1550's, Arbour House became the prosperous George Inn and in 1651, it is said that Cromwell's soldiers took ale here and slept in nearby fields. Wyre Piddle is in the vale of Evesham, famous for its Spring Blossom Trail and local produce, also an ideal base for visiting the Cotswolds, Worcester, Malvern and Stratford.

B & B £24-£26pp, Rooms 1 double, 2 twin, all en-suite, No smoking, Children over 10, No dogs, Open all year

---

BRYNHEULOG Howle Hill, Ross-on-Wye, Herefs HR9 5SP   *Map Ref:* 30
Mrs H Smith   A49, A40
Tel / Fax: 01989 562051

High quality accommodation in picturesque village with beautiful views over rolling countryside. Four poster beds and jacuzzi available and superb meals are served with homemade breads and preserves. Central for touring Cotswolds, Malvern Hills, Shakespeare's country and Tintern Abbey. For the adventurous, cycling in Royal Forest of Dean, golf, canoeing, quad biking, hovercrafts, clay pigeon shooting, archery and orienteering.

B & B from £20pp, Dinner available, Rooms 1 double, 1 twin, both en-suite, 1 four poster, 1 family, Smoking restricted, Children welcome, Dogs by arrangement, Open all year

---

TILTRIDGE FARM & VINEYARD Upper Hook Road, Upton-upon-Severn, Worcs WR8 0SA
Sandy Barker   *Tel:* 01684 592906   *Fax:* 01684 594142   *Map Ref:* 31
Email: elgarwine@aol.com   M5, M50

Welcoming Georgian farmhouse set in vineyards between the attractive riverside town of Upton-on-Severn and the Malvern Hills. Lots of exposed beams and an inglenook fireplace with tea/coffee facilities and televisions in the rooms. Bumper breakfast using local produce such as homemade jams, jellies and eggs from our own chickens. You are also welcome to a free wine tasting.

B & B £22-£24pp, Rooms 2 double, 1 twin, all en-suite, No smoking, Children welcome, Dogs by arrangement, Closed Xmas & New Year

WELLAND COURT Upton-upon-Severn, Worcs WR8 0ST   *Map Ref:* 31
Philip & Elizabeth Archer *Tel / Fax:* 01684 594426 *Mobile:* 07767 796364   A1
Email: archer@wellandcourt.freeserve.co.uk *Web:* www.wellandcourt.co.uk

This small manor house with 26 acres is situated at the foot of the majestic Malvern Hills with a 2 acre lake for trout fishing. It welcomes horse owning guests and can provide stabling and grazing. Furnished with period antiques it is an ideal venue for functions where up to 40 people can be catered for.

B & B from £35pp, Rooms 1 double, 2 twin, all en-suite, Restricted smoking, Children over 6, Dogs not in house, Closed Xmas day

---

WINFORTON COURT Winforton, Herefs HR3 6EA   *Map Ref:* 32
Mrs Jackie Kingdon   A438
Tel / Fax: 01544 328498

A romantic historic manor circa 1500 in the beautiful Wye Valley, close to Hay-on-Wye and local restaurants with golf and canoe hire. Spacious en-suite rooms with luxury touches. Free wine for special occasions, king-size four posters, beams, log fires, library and elegant drawing room. Hearty traditional or vegetarian breakfasts. Winforton Court awaits you with a warm welcome.

B & B £27-£36pp, Rooms 3 double en-suite, No smoking, No children, Dogs welcome, Closed Xmas

---

GARDEN COTTAGES Crossway Green, Hartlebury, Worcester, Worcs DY13 9SL   *Map Ref:* 33
Pauline Terry *Tel / Fax:* 01299 250626   A449
Email: accommodation@mamod.co.uk *Web:* www.gardencottages.co.uk

In a rural position close to the main A440 Worcester/Kidderminster road, Birmingham and the M5, the cottage is half an hour from Stratford-upon-Avon and the Cotswolds. It has attractive grounds, oak beams and parking. The bedrooms are well equipped. Guests can enjoy the sitting room and sun lounge. An evening meal is available, good pubs and restaurants locally, some within walking distance.

B & B from £25pp, Rooms 1 single, 1 double, 1 twin, 1 family, Restricted smoking, Children welcome, No dogs, Closed Xmas

---

YEW TREE HOUSE Norchard, Crossway Green, Worcester, Worcs DY13 9SN   *Map Ref:* 33
Lynne & Paul Knight *Tel:* 01299 250921 *Fax:* 01299 253472 *Mobile:* 07971 112621   A449
Email: paul@knightp.swinternet.co.uk *Web:* www.yewtreeworcester.co.uk

Elegant Georgian farmhouse and 'Cider House' cottage, both with a wealth of beams and shrouded in history. Built in 1754, stepping over the threshold of Yew Tree House is a fascinating mix of elegance and atmosphere. Peacefully tucked away but convenient to all motorway systems and sightseeing. Beautifully appointed en-suite rooms with TV and hospitality tray. Splended breakfasts are provided.

B & B £25-£27.50pp, Rooms 2 double, 2 twin, 1 family, all en-suite, No smoking, Children welcome, Dogs by arrangement, Open all year

---

BOOT INN Radford Road, Flyford Flavell, Worcester, Worcs WR7 4BS   *Map Ref:* 34
Norman & Sue Hughes *Tel:* 01386 462658 *Fax:* 01386 462547   A422
Email: owortley@hotmail.com *Web:* www.thebootinn.com

Part 13th century, this family run, traditional award winning country inn is situated in the heart of rural Worcestershire. It is ideally located for touring the Cotswolds and Stratford-upon-Avon. Wonderful location, beautiful scenery. Special week-end breaks.

B & B £27.50-£37.50pp, C-Cards MC VS AE, Dinner available, Rooms 4 double, 1 twin, all en-suite, No smoking, Children by arrangement, No dogs, Open all year

Kent

Kent is without doubt the 'Garden of England', the soil is remarkably fertile and the county is crowded with orchards, market gardens, fields of vegetables and some hop fields, although not so many as there used to be. Being the closest part of England to mainland Europe, Kent has been the main route between London and the Continent since Julius Caesar landed here in 55BC, to be followed by St Augustine and his missionaries from Rome in 597AD, and the Saxons four centuries later. This is a county of great activity and greatly contrasting scenery with the North Downs cutting through the whole of Kent and culminating in the spectacular White Cliffs of Dover. The Romney Marshes, once renowned for smuggling, are a low lying and windswept region where the sea has receded, leaving the drained marshes grazed by Romney sheep. Here the Royal Military Canal, built as a defence during the Napoleonic Wars, runs through Hythe, one of the Cinque Ports and terminus of the Romney, Hythe and Dymchurch Railway.

Folkstone has probably seen more upheaval than most towns, not least during the Second World War. However, the old town still thankfully retains much of its charm, including the fine Victorian section and The Leas, a wonderful cliff-top Promenade. Folkstone's major change in recent years has been the on-going devel-opment around the landfall point of the Channel Tunnel. Its near neighbour, Dover, an important cross-Channel port since Roman times, despite much destruction during World War Two, still offers the visitor some interesting architecture and of course the castle, one of Europe's most impressive medieval fortresses. The White Cliffs Experience is an interactive view of Dover's history, a fascinating tunnel system which is open to the public. Margate, Ramsgate, and Broadstairs, on the north eastern tip of Kent, each with their own particular character, present a delightful seaside holiday region. Margate, one of England's earliest coastal resorts, has over nine miles of sandy beach with safe swimming and a pier built in 1810 and Ramsgate, a busy cross-Channel terminal has its attractive Royal Esplanade, amusement parks and Pavilion with a splendid 500 berth marina. Broadstairs, very much a family resort still retains its village atmosphere and was popular with Charles Dickens who had several holiday homes here. Its Annual Folk Festival Week in August is one of the leading folk festivals in southern England.

Maidstone, the county town which stands on the rivers Medway and Len, is a perfect centre for visitors exploring the delights of the valley of the Medway. There are glorious river walks, gardens, boating and excellent fishing. Positioned close to Cranbrook

Penshurst Place Gardens (SEETB)

is Sissinghurst Castle Garden, the magnificent five and a half acre connoisseur's garden created by Vita Sackville-West and her husband. Just four miles from Maidstone is the wonderfully romantic Leeds Castle, built in the eleventh century on two islands in a lake, upon which black swans swim. Canterbury, on the River Stour, like so many of the cities in this part of England suffered greatly in the bombings of the Second World War, but miraculously the lovely cathedral was spared. Built in Caen limestone, along with Bell Harry, its great central tower, the cathedral includes an outstanding collection of twelfth and thirteenth century stained glass. Here the shrine of Thomas a Becket, murdered on the steps of the cathedral in 1170, became an important place of pilgrimage in the Middle Ages. This prompted Geoffrey Chaucer to write his colourful catalogue of pilgrims in his "Canterbury Tales", now dramatized in a disused church on St Margaret's Street.

Kent is renowned for its spectacular stately homes. Knowle at Sevenoaks in a magnificent deer park is the largest private house in England, dating from 1456, it was enlarged by the 1st Earl of Dorset, to whom it was granted by Elizabeth I. It was the history of this house upon which Virginia Woolf, a frequent visitor, based her novel Orlando. Penshurst Place is an outstanding example of fourteenth century domestic architecture, while nearby Hever Castle, a fine moated Tudor house was the birthplace of Anne Boleyn. Another attraction to this lovely county is Chartwell near Westerham, the home of Sir Winston Churchill from 1924 until his death in 1965. The house is filled with mementoes of the great man.

PLACES TO VISIT

This is a small selection of interesting places to visit. Many more are listed in our annual guide to Museums, Galleries, Historic Houses & Sites (see page 448)

Canterbury Cathedral
Canterbury
Dominating the skyline at 557 feet the Cathedral has held pilgrimage status since 1170 when Thomas Becket was martyred. The earliest part of the Cathedral is the Romanesque crypt circa 1100.

Dover Castle
Dover
Magnificent medieval fortress with Anglo-Saxon church and Roman lighthouse. Discover the top secret World War II wartime tunnels, deep in the White Cliffs of Dover.

Leeds Castle
Maidstone, Kent
Shrouded in mist, mystery and legend, Leeds Castle, dubbed the loveliest Castle in the world, rises from its own lake. Built in 857 AD the Castle has been home to six medieval queens of England.

Penshurst Place and Gardens
Penshurst, Tonbridge
One of England's greatest family owned stately homes. A medieval manor home with fine collections of paintings, tapestries and furniture. Tudor gardens and an adventure playground.

Kent

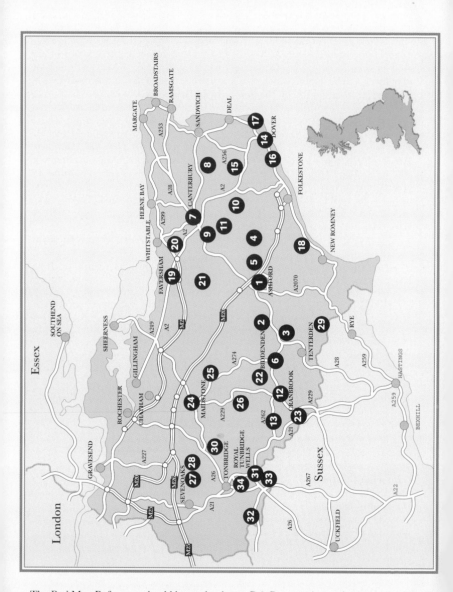

The Red Map References should be used to locate B & B properties on the pages that follow

TERRY HOUSE Warehorne, Ashford TN26 2LS   *Map Ref:* 1
The Sherston Family   *Tel:* 01233 732443   *Fax:* 01233 732466   *Mobile:* 07850 910227   M20
Email: jsherston@uk.online.co.uk

Attractive 18th century house, beautifully modernised and situated on Romney Marsh in peaceful lovely surroundings. Wonderful stable converted to a bedroom, bathroom, sitting room and private terrace with garden furniture. Ideal accommodation, suitable for several nights with all rooms providing televisions and tea/coffee facilities. Excellent village pub nearby, also close to Rye, Sissinghurst and Channel Tunnel.

B & B £22-£30pp, Rooms 1 double en-suite, 2 twin, 1 with private bathroom, No smoking, Children over 10, Dogs by arrangement, Open all year

---

THE COACH HOUSE Oakmead Farm, Bethersden, Ashford TN26 3DU   *Map Ref:* 2
Bernard & Else Broad   A28
Tel / Fax: 01233 820583

The Coach House is one mile from Bethersden village, it stands in 5 acres of gardens and paddocks. The bedrooms are equipped with TV and tea/coffee making facilities. There is a choice of breakfast from local produce. Dutch is spoken. Guests are warmly welcomed to an informal atmosphere. The house is within easy reach of the Euro tunnel, Leeds Castle and Canterbury.

B & B from £20pp, Rooms 1 twin, 1 double, 1 family, all en-suite/private, Restricted smoking, Children welcome, No dogs, Closed Oct to Mar

---

LITTLE HODGEHAM Smarden Road, Bethersden, Ashford TN26 3HE   *Map Ref:* 2
Anne & Mark Bradbury   *Tel:* 01233 850323   *Fax:* 01233 850006   M20/A28
Email: little.hodgeham@virgin.net   *Web:* www.littlehodgeham.co.uk

16th century cottage in mature gardens, minutes from M20 and Ashford International Station. Charming, restored cottage, it provides stylishly decorated accommodation, en-suite facilities in a peaceful location. A king size four poster, a galleried ceiling and beams, bedrooms enjoy delightful garden and farm views. A large sitting room, a cosy dining room, perfect setting for dinner parties, and English breakfasts. Wonderful garden, 24 foot pool.

B & B £30-£32.50pp, Dinner from £18, Rooms 1 twin, 1 suite with King size 4 poster, both en-suite, No smoking, Children welcome, Open all year

---

LION HOUSE Church Hill, High Halden, Ashford TN26 3LS   *Map Ref:* 3
Gerald & Caroline Mullins   *Tel / Fax:* 01233 850446   A28
Email: lionhouse@tinyworld.co.uk   *Web:* www.lionhouse.org.uk

On the village green with pub, village shop, historic church, Lion House is a listed Queen Anne farmhouse in a large garden. Guests receive a friendly welcome and comfortable, centrally heated en-suite accommodation, a private dining room and patio garden. Within easy reach Sissinghurst and Leeds castles, Canterbury, channel tunnel and ports. Early departures and late arrivals catered for. Suppers by arrangement.

B & B from £20pp, Dinner from £15, Rooms 1 single, 1 twin, 1 family, all en-suite, Restricted smoking, Children welcome, No dogs, Closed Xmas

---

BOLDENS WOOD Fiddling Lane, Stowting, Ashford TN25 6AP   *Map Ref:* 4
Duncan & Alison Taylor   *Tel / Fax:* 01303 812011   A28, M20
Email: Duncan@MulberryMarine.com

Boldens Wood is modern accommodation situated in unspoilt countryside with televisions and tea/coffee facilities in each room. There is a guest lounge, easy parking and full English breakfasts with a country pub nearby. Children love our friendly chickens, ducks, sheep and cows and wildlife walks can be enjoyed in private woodland. Easy access Channel Tunnel and ferry ports. Early start breakfast (before 6.30am) if required.

B & B from £18.50pp, Rooms 1 single, 1 double/twin, No smoking, Children welcome, No dogs, Closed Xmas & New Year

BULLTOWN FARMHOUSE Bulltown Lane, West Brabourne, Ashford TN25 5NB   *Map Ref:* 4
Lilly Wilton *Tel:* 01233 813505 *Fax:* 01227 709544   M20
Email: wiltons@bulltown.fsnet.co.uk

An attractively restored 15th century, timber framed Kentish farmhouse on the south west side of the North Downs and Pilgrim's Way. The countryside is unspoiled, wonderful walking. In one acre of cottage gardens, it is surrounded by farmland. Channel Tunnel 10 minutes. Canterbury and the Channel port 10 and 15 miles respectively. Excellent inns nearby. Rooms are large, period furnished and have unspoilt outlooks.

B & B from £22.50pp, Rooms 1 double, 1 twin, 1 family, all en-suite, No smoking, Children welcome, No dogs, Open all year

---

WARREN COTTAGE HOTEL & RESTAURANT 136 The Street, Willesborough, Ashford TN24 0NB
Tel: 01233 621905 *Fax:* 01233 623400   *Map Ref:* 5
Email: general@warrencottage.co.uk *Web:* www.warencottage.co.uk   A28, M20

Warren Cottage is a 17th century hotel and restaurant, set in two and a half acres, where a cosy atmosphere awaits. All rooms have en-suite facilities with colour televisions. Large car park. Only minutes from M20 junction 10, Ashford International Station, Channel Tunnel, Dover and Folkestone.

B & B from £34.95pp, C-Cards MC VS, Dinner available, Rooms 1 single, 3 double, 1 twin, 1 family, all en-suite, No smoking, Children & dogs welcome, Open all year

---

BISHOPSDALE OAST Cranbrook Road, Biddenden TN27 8DR   *Map Ref:* 6
Iain & Jane Drysdale *Tel:* 01580 291027 *Fax:* 01580 292321   A28
Email: drysdale@bishopsdaleoast.co.uk *Web:* www.bishopsdaleoast.co.uk

In a quiet secluded area in the heart of the Weald of Kent, Bishopsdale Oast, resting in four acres of wild and cultivated gardens, offers a relaxed friendly atmosphere with lovely walks and views. Guests can enjoy meals in the dining room or on the terrace and then relax in front of a log fire, stroll around the gardens or play a game of croquet.

B & B £27.50-£30pp, C-Cards MC VS, Dinner from £22, Rooms 2 double, 2 twin, 1 family, all en-suite, Restricted smoking, Children over 12, No dogs, Closed Xmas

---

ABBERLEY HOUSE 115 Whitstable Road, Canterbury CT2 8EF   *Map Ref:* 7
Mr & Mrs Allcorn   A2, A28
Tel: 01227 450265 *Fax:* 01227 478626

Abberley House is a comfortable family run guest house in a residential area and within easy walking to the centre and University. Tea/coffee making facilities are available in the rooms with one double en-suite and traditional or continental breakfast is served. Parking for three cars. A self catering cottage is also available.

B & B from £21pp, Rooms 2 double, 1 twin, No smoking, No dogs, Open all year

---

CHAUCER LODGE 62 New Dover Road, Canterbury CT1 3DT   *Map Ref:* 7
Maria & Alistair Wilson *Tel / Fax:* 01227 459141   A2, A28
Email: wchaucerldg@aol.com *Web:* www.thechaucerlodge.co.uk

Maria and Alistair Wilson extend a warm, friendly welcome to their comfortable family run guest house. Chaucer Lodge has a high standard of cleanliness with well appointed bedrooms which have colour televisions, hairdryers, clock radios, fridges and tea/coffee facilities. Close to town centre, Canterbury Cathedral, theatre and to bus, coach and railway stations. Private and secure parking.

B & B from £22pp, C-Cards MC VS, Dinner available, Rooms 1 single, 2 double, 2 twin, 1 triple, 1 family, all en-suite, No smoking, Children welcome, No dogs, Open all year

CLARE ELLEN GUEST HOUSE　9 Victoria Road, Canterbury CT1 3SG　　　*Map Ref:* 7
Loraine Williams　*Tel:* 01227 760205　*Fax:* 01227 784482　　　　　　　　　A28
Email: loraine.williams@clareellenguesthouse.co.uk　*Web:* www.clareellenguesthouse.co.uk

Clare Ellen Guest House offers a warm welcome and bed and breakfast in style. The bedrooms are large, elegant and well equipped. An English breakfast is served, and by request, special diets are catered for. Numerous restaurants and pubs nearby. The house is ideally situated for walking to the city centre and cathedral, Marlow theatre and Canterbury bus station. Private car park.

B & B £24.50-£27pp, C-Cards MC VS, Rooms 1 single, 2 double, 2 twin, 1 family, all en-suite, Restricted smoking, Children welcome, No dogs, Open all year

---

MAYNARD COTTAGE　106 Wincheap, Canterbury CT1 3RS　　　　　*Map Ref:* 7
Fiona Ely　*Tel:* 07951 496836　　　　　　　　　　　　　　　　　　　　A28
Email: fionaely@onetel.net.uk　*Web:* www.SmoothHound.co.uk/hotels/maynard.html

A 17th century cottage dating back to 1695. One bedroom, decorated to a high standard with furnishings to match and en-suite facilities. A hairdryer and toiletries, tea/coffee facilities with biscuits and home made cakes are offered. There are easy chairs TV and radio alarm. Hearty breakfasts and evening meals from Monday to Thursday. 6 minutes walk to the centre, station is three minutes.

B & B £22.50-£30pp, C-Cards MC VS AE, Dinner from £16, Rooms 1 twin/family/double en-suite, No smoking, Children welcome, No dogs, Open all year

---

ORIEL LODGE　3 Queens Avenue, Canterbury CT2 8AY　　　　　　*Map Ref:* 7
Keith & Anthea Rishworth　*Tel / Fax:* 01227 462845　　　　　　　　A2, A28
Email: info@oriel-lodge.co.uk　*Web:* www.oriel-lodge.co.uk

Situated in a tree-lined residential avenue, very near the city centre and restaurants, is an attractive Edwardian house with six well-furnished bedrooms and clean, up-to-date facilities. Afternoon tea is served in the garden or the lounge with a log fire. Private parking. ETC 4 Diamonds, Silver Award. AA and Which? Recommended.

B & B from £23pp, C-Cards MC VS DC, Rooms 1 single, 3 double, 1 twin, 1 family, some en-suite, Restricted smoking, Children over 6, No dogs, Open all year

---

SYLVAN COTTAGE　Nackington Road, Canterbury CT4 7AY　　　　*Map Ref:* 7
Chris & Jac Bray　*Tel:* 01227 765307　*Fax:* 01227 478411　　　　A2, B2068
Email: jac@sylvan5.fsnet.co.uk　*Web:* www.sylvancottage.co.uk

17th century cottage with beams and inglenooks. Great location for walkers, cyclists, channel-hoppers, and families. Twenty minute walk to the city, close to the County Cricket ground. Cotton bed-linen, modern bathrooms, comfortable sitting room opening into a garden surrounded by fields. Parking, or we can collect from the stations. Walk across the fields to the pub, or join us for supper, bring your wine.

B & B from £20pp, Dinner £10, Rooms 1 twin, 1 double, 1 double/family, all en-suite, No smoking, Children welcome, No dogs, Closed occasionally

---

THANINGTON HOTEL　140 Wincheap, Canterbury CT1 3RY　　　　*Map Ref:* 7
Jill & David Jenkins　*Tel:* 01227 453227　*Fax:* 01227 453225　　　　A28
Email: thanington@lineone.net　*Web:* www.thanington-hotel.co.uk

Enjoy the comfort and facilities of this special Georgian bed and breakfast hotel, just a short stroll from the city centre. Beautiful bedrooms, king size beds and four posters for added luxury. Indoor heated swimming pool. Walled garden. Secure car park. Convenient for Channel Tunnel, ports and historic castles and gardens of Kent.

B & B from £34pp, C-Cards MC VS AE DC, Rooms 10 double 3 twin 2 family, Restricted smoking, Small dogs welcome, Open all year

ZAN STEL LODGE 140 Old Dover Road, Canterbury CT1 3NX
Zandra & Ron Stedman
Tel: 01227 453654

Map Ref: 7
B2068, A2
see Photo opposite

A gracious Edwardian house offering value for money accommodation, and individually styled bedrooms with little niceties that usually meet with guests' approval. The elegant dining room overlooks a pretty cottage garden including fishponds which help to enhance the ambience for a relaxing stay. Enjoy your stay in a very homely atmosphere. ETB 4 Diamonds, Silver Award.

B & B from £23pp, Rooms 2 double, 1 twin, 1 family, 2 en-suite, No smoking, Open all year

GREAT WEDDINGTON Ash, Canterbury CT3 2AR
Kate & Neil Gunn *Tel:* 01304 813407 *Fax:* 01304 812531 *Mobile:* 07710 287889
Email: traveltale@aol.com *Web:* www.greatweddington.co.uk

Map Ref: 8
A257

This fine Regency Country House is set in four acres of lovely gardens and paddocks, surrounded by farmland. The house has an elegant drawing room, which leads off an imposing hallway, and a garden door that opens onto a pretty terrace. There is also a hard tennis court which guests can use. Within easy reach of Canterbury, Dover and the Channel Tunnel at Folkestone.

B & B from £37.50pp, C-Cards, Dinner from £25, Rooms 3 twin en-suite, No smoking, Children over 8, Dogs by arrangement, Closed Xmas & New Year

CROCKSHARD FARMHOUSE Wingham, Canterbury CT3 1NY
Nicola Ellen *Tel:* 01227 720464 *Fax:* 01227 721929
Email: crockshard_bnb@yahoo.com

Map Ref: 8
A2, A256

An exceptionally attractive period farmhouse in beautiful gardens and countryside. Breakfast is served with homemade bread, jam and eggs. Tea/coffee facilities available in the three comfortable family bedrooms and the drawing room is equipped with a television. Ideal for Canterbury, channel ports and Kent. Golf, horse riding and many places to eat are nearby.

B & B from £20pp, Rooms 1 double, 3 quad, most en-suite, Restricted smoking, Children welcome, Dogs by arrangement, Open all year

STOUR FARM Riverside, Chartham, Canterbury CT4 7NX
Jane & Jeremy Wilson *Tel / Fax:* 01227 731977
Email: info@stourfarm.co.uk *Web:* www.stourfarm.co.uk

Map Ref: 9
A28

An attractive barn conversion overlooking the River Stour, only three miles from Canterbury Cathedral. Superb accommodation in a choice of two en-suite guest rooms. A further studio style twin room is available and this can be let on a self-catering basis. A full cooked breakfast is served in the guests' dining room or, weather permitting, on the sun terrace.

B & B from £25pp, C-Cards MC VS, Rooms 2 double, 1 twin, all en-suite, No smoking, Children over 12, No dogs, Open all year

HOMEWOOD FARM Agester Lane, Denton, Canterbury CT4 6NR
Linda Warburton
Tel / Fax: 01227 832611 *Mobile:* 07703 627947

Map Ref: 10
A2

Mark and Linda welcome you to a quiet countryside farm. Rooms include televisions, videos, tea/coffee facilities and snacks and there is an extensive choice of fresh cooked food. Good base for walking and cycling, Canterbury City, channel crossings and touring. Easy access to the many attractions Kent has to offer with guests being able to view lambs and ewes in the springtime.

B & B £20-£23pp, Rooms 1 double, 1 twin, private bathroom, No smoking, Children welcome, Dogs by arrangement, Open all year

Zan Stel Lodge, Canterbury

BOWER FARM HOUSE Stelling Minnis, Canterbury CT4 6BB   *Map Ref:* 10
Anne & Nick Hunt   *Tel:* 01227 709430   M20, B2068
Email: book@bowerbb.freeserve.co.uk   *Web:* www.kentac.co.uk/bowerfm

This charming, heavily beamed 17th century Kentish farmhouse is set in the middle of a mediaeval common. Breakfast is enjoyed in front of a large inglenook with new laid eggs and fresh bread. Guests' lounge has a television and piano and both of the delightful bedrooms have tea/coffee facilities. Car parking. Easy access to Channel Tunnel.

B & B from £22pp, Rooms 1 twin, 1 double, both en-suite, No smoking, Children welcome, Dogs by arrangement, Closed Xmas & New Year

GREAT FIELD FARM Misling Lane, Stelling Minnis, Canterbury CT4 6DE   *Map Ref:* 10
Mrs Lewana Castle   *Tel / Fax:* 01227 709223   M20, B2068
Email: greatfieldfarm@aol.com

Comfortable spacious farmhouse sitting amidst pleasant gardens and paddocks with friendly ponies. Three en-suite rooms with televisions and one family room with jacuzzi-style air bath. Two bedrooms have their own lounges, one with a kitchen. Hearty breakfasts and homegrown fruits. An ideal location for exploring Kent, convenient for Canterbury, Chunnel and ferries. ETC 4 Diamond, Silver Award.

B & B £20-£25pp, C-Cards MC VS, Rooms 2 double, 1 twin, all en-suite, No smoking, Children welcome, No dogs, Open all year

UPPER ANSDORE Duckpit Lane, Petham, Canterbury CT4 5QB   *Map Ref:* 11
Roger & Susan Linch   *Tel:* 01227 700672   *Fax:* 01227 700840   B2068, A2
Email: upperansdore@hotels-activebooking.com   *Web:* www.smoothhound.co.uk/hotels/upperans.html

A medieval farmhouse in a quiet secluded valley, with beautiful views. Once the home of the Lord Mayor of London, it overlooks a nature reserve, sample over 600 years of history. Breakfast is served in the oak beamed dining room with Tudor inglenook fireplace and furnished with antiques. Canterbury is just 15 minutes and Dover 30 minutes. SAE please for a colour brochure.

B & B £21-£22.50pp, C-Cards MC VS, Rooms 1 twin, 3 double, 1 family, all en-suite, No smoking, Children over 5, Dogs welcome, Closed Xmas

HALLWOOD FARM OAST Hallwood Farm, Hawkhurst Road, Cranbrook TN17 2SP   *Map Ref:* 12
Mrs Sarah Wickham   *Tel:* 01580 712416   A229
Email: email@hallwoodfarm.co.uk   *Web:* www.hallwoodfarm.co.uk

A traditional old oasthouse now converted into a spacious and comfortable home for the Wickham family who still farm the 250 acres of Hallwood. Quietly situated down a private lane the oast overlooks the farmyard. Two beamed en-suite bedrooms offer every comfort and a hearty breakfast is served in the sunny dining room. Central for both Kent and Sussex.

B & B £22.50-£27.50pp, Rooms 1 double, 1 twin, all en-suite, No smoking, No children or dogs, Closed Dec to Jan

MOUNT HOUSE Ranters Lane, Goudhurst, Cranbrook TN17 1HN   *Map Ref:* 13
David Sargent   *Tel:* 01580 211230   *Fax:* 01580 212373   A262
Email: davidmargaretsargent@compuserve.com

An 18th century Grade II listed country house full of character and set in a beautiful two acre garden. Particularly caters for visitors to the many well known gardens in the area, including Sissinghurst, Great Dixter, Pashley Manor and Scotney Castle. ETB 4 Diamonds.

B & B £25-£27.50pp, Rooms 1 double, 1 twin en-suite, No smoking, Children over 12, No dogs, Closed Oct to Mar

CASTLE HOUSE 10 Castle Hill Road, Dover CT16 1QW　　　　*Map Ref:* 14
Rodney & Elizabeth Dimech　*Tel:* 01304 201656　*Fax:* 01304 210197　　A2/M2 and A20/M20
Email: Dimechr@aol.com　*Web:* www.castle-guesthouse.co.uk

Castle House is ideally situated being just below Dover Castle and
close to the town centre, ferries, hoverport, cruise liner terminal and
just 10 minutes from the channel tunnel. The food is good, the
accommodation comfortable, and guests are welcomed to genuine
hospitality by Rodney and Elizabeth. The bedrooms are well
equipped, and to start the day, a hearty breakfast is served.

B & B £20-£25pp, C-Cards MC VS AE, Rooms 4 double, 1 twin,
1 single., No smoking, Open all year

NUMBER ONE GUEST HOUSE 1 Castle Street, Dover CT16 1QH　　*Map Ref:* 14
Margaret and Adeline Reidy　*Tel:* 01304 202007　*Fax:* 01304 214078　　A20, A2
Email: res@number1guesthouse.co.uk　*Web:* www.number1guesthouse.co.uk

This Georgian house offers cosy en-suite rooms with televisions and
breakfast in bed. Old fashioned hospitality makes for a snug
atmosphere and those little extra touches ensure a comfortable stay.
Walled garden, lock up garages and early departures are taken into
consideration. Convenient for the Port, Channel Tunnel, bus, trains
and town centre.

B & B £20-£26pp, Rooms 3 double, 1 twin, 1 family, all en-suite,
Children welcome, No dogs, Open all year

COLRET HOUSE The Green, Coldred, Dover CT15 5AP　　　　*Map Ref:* 15
Jacquelyn White　*Tel / Fax:* 01304 830388　　　　　　　　　　　　A2
Email: jackie.colret@evnet.co.uk

Colret House is an early Edwardian property within large maintained
gardens and is situated beside the village green in a conservation
area. The purpose built en-suite garden rooms have televisions,
tea/coffee facilities, radio and hairdryers. Ample secure parking.
Ideal for overnight stop for ferries and tunnel. Close to Canterbury,
Sandwich and White Cliffs area.

B & B from £25pp, Rooms 1 twin, 1 double, both en-suite,
Restricted smoking, Children & dogs welcome, Open all year

THE OLD VICARAGE Chilverton Elms, Hougham, Dover CT15 7AS　*Map Ref:* 16
Judy Evison　*Tel:* 01304 210668　*Fax:* 01304 225118　　　　　　　A20
Email: vicarage@csi.com

This award winning country guest house enjoys an outstanding
position set in wooded gardens with open views over the Elms Vale.
The Old Vicarage is only 2 miles from the bustle of the port of Dover.
Many visitors return frequently for short breaks, to enjoy the
elegance, peace and quiet. There are good local pubs and
restaurants.

B & B £35-£40pp, C-Cards MC VS, Rooms 1 double en-suite,
1 double private, 1 family private, Not in bedrooms, Children
welcome, No dogs, Closed Xmas & New Year

WALLETT'S COURT COUNTRY HOUSE HOTEL West Cliffe, St Margaret's, Dover CT15 6EW
The Oakley Family　*Tel:* 01304 852424　*Fax:* 01304 853430　　*Map Ref:* 17
Email: stay@wallettscourt.com　*Web:* www.wallettscourt.com　　　A258, A2
A Norman house, restored in 1627, discovered derelict in 1975,
rescued with passion, commitment and care since. Sea air, cliffs,
gulls, mists. Rooms are full of character simple elegance prevails.
The restaurant is popular locally for Chris Oakley's sophisticated
modern British cooking prepared with real professional care. A
recent barn conversion provides a haven of relaxation with indoor
pools, sauna, steam room and spa.

B & B from £45pp, C-Cards MC VS AE, Dinner from £20, Rooms
2 twin, 10 double, 4 four poster/suite, all en-suite, Restricted
smoking, Children welcome, No dogs, Open all year

WATERSIDE GUEST HOUSE 15 Hythe Road, Dymchurch TN29 0LN   *Map Ref:* 18
Mrs Sharon Tinklin   *Tel / Fax:* 01303 872253   A259
Email: info@watersideguesthouse.co.uk   *Web:* www.watersideguesthouse.co.uk

We are renowned at Waterside for our warm welcome where every guest becomes part of the family. All meals at Waterside are served in our cottage style dining room, or weather permitting, on our waterside terraces, both of which enjoy picturesque views. We offer traditional and creative cuisine using local produce and we also provide afternoon tea. Ideal for exploring Kent.

B & B £20-£22.50pp, C-Cards MC VS, Dinner from £4, Rooms 2 double, 2 twin, 1 family, all en-suite, Restricted smoking, Children welcome, No dogs, Open all year

---

PRESTON LEA Canterbury Road, Faversham ME13 8XA   *Map Ref:* 19
Alan & Catherine Turner   *Tel:* 01795 535266   *Fax:* 01795 533388   A2
Email: preston.lea@which.net   *Web:* http://homepages.which.net/~alan.turner10

A unique and elegant Victorian house standing in a large secluded garden on the edge of Faversham. Spacious, sunny bedrooms have garden views and antique furniture. There is a beautiful drawing room and a panelled dining room. Delicious breakfasts are served, some good restaurants nearby. 15 minutes from Canterbury, 35 minutes to the Eurotunnel, and 70 minutes by train to London.

B & B £28-£30pp, C-Cards MC VS, Rooms 2 double, 1 twin, all en-suite, No smoking, Children welcome, No dogs, Open all year

---

TENTERDEN HOUSE 209 The Street, Boughton, Faversham ME13 9BL   *Map Ref:* 20
Prudence Latham   M2, A2
Tel: 01227 751593

Renovated gardener's cottage provides two en-suite bedrooms which can be used separately or together for families or friends. Situated in the village, close to Canterbury, the ferry ports and Euro Tunnel, ideally placed for day trips to France and for touring Kent. Off-road parking is provided. Full English breakfast served in the main house, excellent pubs and restaurants locally.

B & B from £20pp, Rooms 1 twin, 1 double, both en-suite, Children welcome, No dogs, Closed Xmas

---

LEAVELAND COURT Leaveland, Faversham ME13 0NP   *Map Ref:* 21
Corrine Scutt   *Tel:* 01233 740596   *Fax:* 01233 740015   A251, M2
Email: leaveland@mail.com

A 15th Century timber framed farmhouse with adjoining granary and stables. In a quiet setting the house nestles between 13th century Leaveland Church and woodlands it is the heart of the 500 acre working farm. Offering a high standard of accommodation and cuisine, a warm welcome is assured. Bedrooms are en-suite. Guests are invited to use the heated outdoor pool set in secluded gardens.

B & B from £25pp, Rooms 1 twin, 2 double, all en-suite, No smoking, Children welcome, Dogs by arrangement, Closed Nov to Feb

---

MAPLEHURST MILL Mill Lane, Frittenden TN17 2DT   *Map Ref:* 22
Kenneth & Heather Parker   *Tel:* 01580 852203   *Fax:* 01580 852117   A229
Email: maplehurst@clara.net   *Web:* www.home.clara.net/maplehurst

A romantic watermill near Sissinghurst, guests enjoy the comforts of tasteful, en-suite bedrooms, a cosy drawing room which stables the millstream, and delicious breakfasts and candlelit dinners using home produce supplemented by a good wine list. Wildlife and flowers abound in 11 acres of water meadows and landscaped gardens, there is a heated pool. The mill has featured in many national magazine articles.

B & B from £38pp, C-Cards MC VS, Dinner from £24, Rooms 2 twin, 3 double, all en-suite, No smoking, Children over 12, No dogs, Closed Xmas & New Year

SOUTHGATE-LITTLE FOWLERS Rye Road, Hawkhurst TN18 5DA
Tel / Fax: 01580 752526
Email: Susan.Woodard@southgate.uk.net *Web:* www.southgate.uk.net/

Map Ref: 23
A21, A229

A 17th century house with antique furnishings and beautiful bedrooms, views and gardens. A superb breakfast is served in an original Victorian flower conservatory. Warm hospitality and only a few minutes walk for evening meals. Close to Rye, Dixter, Sissinghurst, Hever and many National Trust attractions. Car parking. Please view our comprehensive website. RAC 5 Diamonds.

B & B £25-£30pp, Rooms 1 double, 1 twin, 1 family, 1 four poster, all en-suite, No smoking, Children over 7, No dogs, Closed Dec to Jan

THE WREN'S NEST Hastings Road, Hawkhurst TN18 4RT
Mrs Lynne Rodger
Tel / Fax: 01580 754919

Map Ref: 23
A21, A229

Built in traditional Kentish style, with oak beamed vaulted ceilings, the Wrens Nest's suites have been designed specifically for the comfort and pleasure of our guests. The suites are entered via their own front door, allowing absolute privacy and freedom. Start the day with a nutritious hearty English breakfast, made only of the best quality produce, served in the cottage dining room.

B & B £27.50-£30pp, Rooms 3 double en-suite, No smoking, Children over 10, No dogs, Closed Dec to Mar

WILLINGTON COURT 1 Willington Street, Bearstead, Maidstone ME15 8JW
Sylvette Cabrisseau
Tel: 01622 738885 *Fax:* 01622 631790

Map Ref: 24
A229, A274

A charming Grade II listed Waldean/Tudor building offering elegant accommodation with four-poster beds. All rooms have televisions, hospitality trays, hairdryers and direct dial telephones, plus extras for a touch of luxury. Adjacent to Mote Park and near Leeds Castle with easy access to London, Dover and the Channel Tunnel. ETB, AA and RAC 4 Diamonds.

B & B from £27.50pp, Rooms 2 single, 6 double, 1 twin, all private facilities, Restricted smoking, No dogs, Open all year

LANGLEY OAST Langley Park, Langley, Maidstone ME17 3NQ
Mrs M Clifford *Tel / Fax:* 01622 863523
Email: margaret@langleyoast.freeserve.co.uk

Map Ref: 25
M20, A274

A warm and friendly welcome awaits you at this authentic Kentish oasthouse which has been lovingly converted by its present owners and offers a luxurious break in a quiet and secluded location. The two rooms are round and one has a jacuzzi en-suite. Close to Leeds Castle, this is an ideal touring base to visit the many Kentish attractions or perhaps as a stop over to or from the continent.

B & B £22.50-£35pp, Rooms 1 single, 2 double, 2 twin, 1 family, most en-suite, No smoking, Children welcome, No dogs, Closed Xmas & New Year

MERZIE MEADOWS Hunton Road, Marden TN12 9SL
Pamela & Rodney Mumford *Tel / Fax:* 01622 820500 *Mobile:* 07762 713077
Web: www.smoothound.co.uk/hotels/merzie.html

Map Ref: 26
A229, B2079

A country home with water fowl and horse paddocks. Tranquil surroundings and central for historical interest including Leeds, Sissinghurst Castle and London. The gardens are beautiful, they display year round interest. Traditional elegance combines with modern comforts, spacious rooms are decorated to a high standard, a guest wing has a sitting room, study and terrace. Rooms overlook landscaped gardens with a swimming pool.

B & B £25-£30pp, Rooms 2 double, guest wing triple, all en-suite, Restricted smoking, Children over 14, No dogs, Closed mid-Dec to mid-Feb

TANNER HOUSE Tanner Farm, Goudhurst Road, Marden TN12 9ND
Mrs Lesley Mannington *Tel:* 01622 831214 *Fax:* 01622 832472
Email: tannerhouse@cs.com *Web:* www.tannerfarmpark.co.uk

Map Ref: 26
B2079

A Tudor Farmhouse on 150 acre family farm in Kent Weald. Ideal base for wealth of local attractions. All rooms en-suite with shower, colour television, refreshments and genuine four poster double. Also a guest lounge and inglenook dining room. Quality cuisine using local produce plus own jams and preserves. Ideal for a stopover, weekend or holiday. Caravan park also available.

B & B £22.50-£25pp, C-Cards MC VS, Rooms 1 double, 2 twin, all en-suite, No smoking, Children over 12, No dogs, Closed Xmas

---

ROSEWOOD Ismays Road, Ivy Hatch, Sevenoaks TN15 0PA
Mr & Mrs Turner-Radford *Tel / Fax:* 01732 810496
Email: rosewood@covenantblessings.co.uk

Map Ref: 27
A227

Family home built in 1750 in a peaceful country setting. An easy walk to local Ightham Mote and local pubs, also close to M20, M25 and M26. Sevenoaks station is nearby and from there London is only 30 minutes by train. ETB 4 Diamonds.

B & B from £45pp, Rooms 1 double, 1 twin, 1 family, 2 en-suite and 1 private, No smoking, Children welcome, Dogs by arrangement, Closed Xmas

JORDANS Sheet Hill, Plaxtol, Sevenoaks TN15 0PU
Mrs Jo Lindsay
Tel / Fax: 01732 810379

Map Ref: 28
A227

An exquisite 15th century Tudor house in the picturesque village of Plaxtol Jordans, awarded a historic building of Kent plaque, has an enchanting cottage garden. There are oak beams, inglenook leaded windows, it is furnished with antiques and paintings many by Mrs Lindsay, who is a Blue Badge Guide and can help plan your tour. Jordans is close to many places of historic interest.

B & B from £33pp, Rooms 2 double/single, 2 en-suite, No smoking, Children over 12, No dogs, Closed mid-Dec to mid-Jan

---

OXNEY FARM Moons Green, Wittersham, Tenterden TN30 7PS
Eve Burnett *Tel:* 01797 270558 *Fax:* 01797 270958
Email: oxneyf@globalnet.co.uk *Web:* www.users.globalnet.co.uk/~oxneyf

Map Ref: 29
B2082

A warm welcome from Kent Hospitality Award winner awaits. Convenient for the Channel Tunnel/ferry ports. Spacious, comfortable farmhouse, with a luxurious indoor pool, in rural surroundings. Area steeped in history, scenery and culture. Miniature ponies add charm to the friendly atmosphere. Directions: from Tenterden or Rye, B2082 to Wittersham, at Swan Inn, into Swan Street, Oxney Farm is 1.3 miles on the left.

B & B £25-£30pp, C-Cards MC VS, Rooms 1 twin, 2 double, all en-suite, No smoking, No children or dogs, Open all year

---

LEAVERS OAST Stanford Lane, Hadlow, Tonbridge TN11 0JN
Anne & Denis Turner *Tel / Fax:* 01732 850924 *Mobile:* 07771 663250
Email: denis@leavers-oast.freeserve.co.uk

Map Ref: 30
A26

A warm welcome awaits, an excellent base for touring historic sites, including Leeds and Hever Castles, Chartwell and Sissinghurst. Built circa 1880, the accommodation is modernised, and an attractive garden has been created. The bedrooms are comfortable and spacious, two are in roundels, the other in the barn. There are are many good places to eat or by prior arrangement, excellent evening meals are available.

B & B from £27.50pp, Dinner from £22, Rooms 1 twin, 2 double, 1 en-suite, No smoking, Children from 12, No dogs, Open all year

ASH TREE COTTAGE 7 Eden Road, Tunbridge Wells TN1 1TS
Richard & Sue Rogers   *Tel:* 01892 541317   *Fax:* 01892 616770
Mobile: 07780 708854   *Email:* rogersashtree@excite.co.uk

Map Ref: 31
M25, A21, A26

An attractive house in a very quiet area of Royal Tunbridge Wells. Close to High Street, Pantiles and station. The comfortable bedrooms have en-suite bathrooms, radios, televisions, tea/coffee facilities and plenty of tourist information. An excellent choice of restaurants and country pubs nearby, many places of interest are within easy reach. London is only 50 minutes by train. Private parking.

B & B from £25pp, Rooms 1 double, 1 twin, both en-suite, No smoking, Children over 8, No dogs, Closed Xmas & New Year

---

40 YORK ROAD Tunbridge Wells TN1 1JY
Patricia Lobo
Tel / Fax: 01892 531342

Map Ref: 31
M25, A21, A26

Regency house in the centre of Tunbridge Wells. Delightful enclosed courtyard garden. Hostess Patricia Lobo, a professional cook, caters for vegetarians. Bedroom one offers a balconied bay window, bedrooom two enjoys a lovely view to the garden. A good variety of shops and restaurants. Much to see, Hever, Scotney, Leeds Castles. Walking distance of mainline station for London. Gatwick and Channel Ports easily reached.

B & B from £27pp, Dinner from £18, Rooms 2 double/twin en-suite, No smoking in bedrooms, Children over 12, No dogs, Closed Xmas & New Year

---

MANOR COURT FARM Ashurst, Tunbridge Wells TN3 9TB
Tel: 01892 740279   *Fax:* 01892 740919
Email: jsoyke@jsoyke.freeserve.co.uk   *Web:* manorcourtfarm.co.uk

Map Ref: 32
A264

A Georgian farmhouse with friendly atmosphere, spacious rooms and lovely views on a 350 acre sheep and arable farm. Fishing, tennis and swimming are available by arrangement and the large garden also has a secluded campsite. Good base for walking, cycling and touring South East England. Chartwell, Leeds Castle, Sissinghurst and Hever are all within easy reach. London 45 minutes by train from Tonbridge.

B & B from £22pp, Rooms 1 double, 2 twin, Restricted smoking, Children welcome, Open all year

---

THE OLD PARSONAGE Church Lane, Frant, Tunbridge Wells TN3 9DX
Mary & Tony Dakin   *Tel / Fax:* 01892 750773
Email: oldparson@aol.com   *Web:* www.theoldparsonagehotel.co.uk

Map Ref: 33
A267

This award winning country house offers top quality accommodation in an idyllic location, next to the church in pretty Frant village. All rooms are luxuriously appointed and include every modern convenience, plus an extensive information pack for sightseeing in Kent and Sussex. The Old Parsonage stands in its own secluded gardens with two village pubs just a few minutes walk away.

B & B £36-£46pp, C-Cards MC VS, Rooms 2 double, 2 twin, all en-suite, No smoking, Children over 7, Dogs by arrangement, Closed Xmas

---

NUMBER TEN Modest Corner, Southborough, Tunbridge Wells TN4 0LS
Anneke Leemhuis   *Tel / Fax:* 01892 522450   *Mobile:* 07966 190102
Email: modestanneke@lineone.net

Map Ref: 34
A26, A21

In a hamlet with beautiful views and lovely walks, Number Ten is a stone's throw away from Royal Tunbridge Wells and Tonbridge railway station, Well equipped bedrooms and excellent showers in the bathrooms. A unique welcoming and homely atmosphere, only the birds wake you in the morning. English breakfast is served in the garden, weather permitting. Dutch, German and a little French spoken.

B & B £22.50-£25pp, Dinner from £15, Rooms 2 twin, 1 double en-suite, Restricted smoking, Children & dogs welcome, Closed Xmas & New Year

Lancashire

To many, Lancashire is L.S. Lowry country, a county of vast clattering mills, long lines of millworkers' terraced houses, dirt, smoke and noise. Certainly this was once the case, after all it was the coal, iron-ore, damp climate and swiftly flowing water that firmly established the Industrial Revolution in this rich region. Towns expanded, and with the growing cotton industry fortunes were made and great municipal buildings and private houses were constructed, reflecting the personal and public pride in the new prosperity. Therefore with the ever expanding towns there was a great need for close resorts to cater for the all too short breaks from toil. The result was that Lancashire is now blessed with some of the finest seaside resorts in the country. Blackpool with its 518 feet high imitation of the Eiffel Tower must be the Queen of English holiday resorts. Once the destination for a Victorian day-out for the millworkers of the cotton towns, the resort is now famed internationally, the season having been considerably lengthened by the spectacular Illuminations. This wonderful blaze of colour stretches for miles along the seafront and lasts from August until November. There is everything here that the holiday maker could wish for; amusement arcades line the pavements of the Golden Mile and the Pleasure Beach claims the world's highest and fastest rollercoaster. But behind the brash face of Blackpool is a resort of fine gardens, parks and lovely surrounding countryside.

In the north of the county, Morecambe, once known as Bradford-by-the-Sea for obvious reasons, swiftly developed when the railway brought hoards of day trippers to the resort. Never as popular as its sister Blackpool, the town can nevertheless offer many attractions, which include the tasty Morecambe Bay shrimps. Preston at the head of the Ribble estuary, is now the administrative centre of Lancashire, and was the home of Sir Richard Arkwright who invented the spinning frame that revolutionised the textile industry. The town also has some excellent architecture reflecting Preston's prosperity during the Industrial Revolution, of which The Harris Museum and Art Gallery, built in the Classical style, is a fine example. Lancaster, dominated by its medieval castle of John of Gaunt, Duke of Lancaster, is an ancient city with a formidable history. The House of Lancaster provided kings of England for 62 years until Henry VI was deposed during the War of the Roses.

Within a very short distance of the great cities of this region is some glorious countryside. The Trough of Bowland, the largest area of unspoiled and remote countryside in the county, gives exhilarating views across the Fylde and the Wyre valley. North of Bury is the Stubbins Estate, 436 acres of woodland and fields

The Ribble Valley (NWTB)

owned by the National Trust, giving access from Rossendale Valley to Holcombe Moor, a bleak area of rough grassland and heath, notable especially for its numerous bird species. The Martin Mere Wildlife and Wetlands Trust acquired in 1972 is 363 acres of marshland and internationally renowned as a wildfowl centre. It was originally one of England's largest lakes until drained in the eighteenth century. The area was allowed to revert to wetland and now attracts up to a tenth of the world's population of pink-footed geese in the winter. Parbold Beacon is the highest point in the south of the county and gives wonderful views across the Lancashire Plain.

The east of the county contains some fine cotton towns with Clitheroe, an ancient town with a Norman keep, one of the earliest stone buildings in the county. Just four miles away is mysterious Pendle Hill, a superb view point but most famous for the Witches of Pendle, who in the early seventeenth century lived in villages along the lower slopes of the hill until their execution at Lancaster Castle in 1612. It was at Burnley where the textile industry in this region really began, with the invention of the fulling mill and the Leeds and Liverpool Canal, which runs through the town, brought prosperity to Burnley during the Industrial Revolution. Burnley Mechanics Arts and Entertainments Centre is well known nationally as a jazz and blues venue. Chorley in the west has a unique 'Flat Iron' market and nearby Duxbury Park is a haunt of red squirrel, foxes and herons.

PLACES TO VISIT

This is a small selection of interesting places to visit. Many more are listed in our annual guide to Museums, Galleries, Historic Houses & Sites (see page 449)

PLACES TO VISIT

This is a small selection of interesting places to visit. Many more are listed in our annual guide to Museums, Galleries, Historic Houses & Sites (see page 448)

Astley Hall Museum and Art Gallery
Astley Park, Chorley
The Hall dates back to Elizabethan times with the Art Gallery playing host to temporary exhibitions. The collections range from 18th century creamware to the first Rugby League Cup.

Blackpool Tower
The Promenade, Blackpool
Proud Victorian landmark, over 100 years old, offering a variety of family attractions from the children's Jungle Jim to tea dances in the famous Tower Ballroom.

Lancaster Castle
Lancaster
King John has said to have held court at this Castle where many trials and executions have taken place. There is a large display of miniature coats of arms in the Shire Hall.

Rufford Old Hall
Rufford, Ormskirk
One of the finest sixteenth century buildings in Lancashire where Shakespeare is said to have performed for the owner. It houses a magnificent hall with an intricately carved moveable wooden screen.

Lancashire

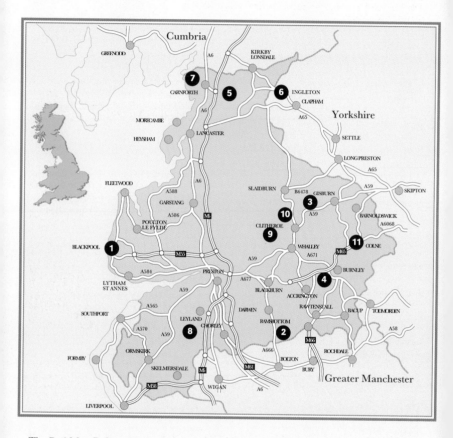

The Red Map References should be used to locate B & B properties on the pages that follow

ASH LODGE HOTEL 131 Hornby Road, Blackpool FY1 4JG
Margaret & Mary Harrison   *Tel:* 01253 627637/ 0800 0685221
Email: admin@ashlodgehotel.co.uk   *Web:* www.ashlodgehotel.co.uk

Map Ref: 1
M55

The hotel offers quiet, clean and comfortable accommodation with a television lounge and well stocked bar. All bedrooms are en-suite and offer tea/coffee facilities. Own car park. Within easy reach of Blackpool Tower, Winter Gardens, Golden Mile and Central Pier. For further information check on our website.

B & B from £19pp, C-Cards MC VS, Dinner from £6, Rooms 4 double, 1 twin, 5 family, all en-suite, Children welcome, No dogs, Closed Xmas & New Year

---

CAMELOT HOUSE 24 Crystal Road, South Shore, Blackpool FY1 6BS
Noreen Westhead
Tel: 01253 345636

Map Ref: 1
M55

Camelot House is family run and provides highly maintained comfortable accommodation and good home cooking with a choice of menu. All bedrooms have central heating, tea/coffee facilities, personal keys, televisions and en-suites are available. Adjoining promenade midway between central and south piers. Convenient for all amenities. Parties welcome.

B & B £12-£20pp, Dinner from £15, Rooms 4 double, 5 family, some en-suite, Restricted smoking, Children welcome, Small dogs by arrangement, Closed Nov to Mar

---

RAFFLES HOTEL 73/75 Hornby Road, Blackpool FY1 4QJ
Tel: 01253 294713   *Fax:* 01253 294240
Email: enq@raffleshotelblackpool.co.uk   *Web:* www.raffleshotelblackpool.co.uk

Map Ref: 1
M55

An excellent location for theatres, promenade, shops, restaurants, tourist spots and conference venues. Family-run private hotel with character, as featured on BBC Summer Holiday 2001. The proprietor is also the chef. Entered in Good Hotel Guide 2000-2002.

B & B from £21pp, C-Cards MC VS, Dinner from £12, Rooms 1 single, 11 double, 3 twin, 2 family, all en-suite, Restricted smoking, Children & dogs welcome, Open all year

---

SUNRAY 42 Knowle Avenue, Off Queens Promenade, Blackpool FY2 9TQ
Jean & John Dodgson   *Tel:* 01253 351937   *Fax:* 01253 593307
Email: sun.ray@cwcom.net

Map Ref: 1
M55

Same owners for 31 years. Very comfortable semi-detached house in quiet residential northern part of town 300 yards off Queens Promenade. From Blackpool Tower drive north along Promenade for two miles and at Uncle Tom's Cabin turn right. Sunray is about 300 yards down on the left. Particularly good terms for senior citizens and discount for weekly booking.

B & B £25-£30pp, C-Cards MC VS AE, Dinner from £13, Rooms 3 single, 2 double, 2 twin, 2 family, all en-suite, Restricted smoking, Children welcome, Dogs by arrangement, Closed Nov to Mar

---

PELTON HALL FARM Bury Road, Turton, Bolton BL7 0BS

Map Ref: 2
M60, M61

Tel: 01204 852207   *Mobile:* 07712 336618

A 17th century farmhouse in a conservation area with panoramic views overlooking a fishing lake and open countryside. A warm welcome awaits with excellent en-suite accommodation. The farmhouse is five minutes' walk from two village pubs and restaurants and is convenient for the motorway network. ETC 4 Diamonds.

B & B from £35pp, Rooms 1 double, 1 twin, 1 family, No smoking, No dogs, Open all year

MIDDLE FLASS LODGE Settle Road, Bolton-by-Bowland BB7 4NY
Joan M Simpson and Nigel E Quayle *Tel:* 01200 447259 *Fax:* 01200 447300
Email: info@middleflasslodge.fsnet.co.uk *Web:* www.mflodge.freeservers.com

Map Ref: 3
A59

Tasteful barn conversion offering unrivalled views across the Forest of Bowland. Peaceful location in open countryside. Ideal base for dales and lakes, walking and touring. Neat and cosy rooms with full facilities. Always personal and professional attention. Chef prepared cuisine by proprietor served in our restaurant lounge with stove to relax in. Table licensed, ample parking and gardens.

B & B £23-£30pp, C-Cards MC VS, Dinner from £18, Rooms 2 double, 2 twin, 1 family, all en-suite, No smoking, Children welcome, Dogs not in house,

EAVES BARN FARM Hapton, Burnley BB12 7LP
Mrs M Butler *Tel / Fax:* 01282 771591 *Mobile:* 07798 836005
Web: www.eavesbarnfarm.co.uk

Map Ref: 4
A679, M65

A working farm with a cottage attached to the house offering luxurious facilities. The guests' lounge has a log fire and antique furniture. Well equipped bedrooms with en-suite facilities. English breakfast is served in the Victorian style conservatory. 'Best Bed & Breakfast' in Lancashire 1992. The Ribble Valley, Fylde Coast, Lake District, Yorkshire Dales and the Lancashire hills are within easy reach.

B & B £25-£30pp, Dinner from £14, Rooms 1 single, 1 double, 1 twin, all en-suite, Restricted smoking, Children over 12, No dogs, Closed Xmas & New Year

CAPERNWRAY HOUSE Capernwray, Carnforth LA6 1AE
Roy & Melanie Smith *Tel / Fax:* 01524 732363 *Mobile:* 07740 972220
Email: thesmiths@capernwrayhouse.com *Web:* www.capernwrayhouse.com

Map Ref: 5
M6 J35

A warm welcome is assured from the Smith family who are pleased to offer comfortable centrally heated accommodation in delightful surroundings. All rooms have colour television, clock/radio, range of toiletries, hairdryer, tea/coffee making facilities and beautiful views of the countryside. Breakfast consists of locally grown produce, freshly cured bacon and free range eggs, with home made bread and preserves. ETC 4 Diamonds, Silver Award.

B & B £22-£30pp, C-Cards MC VS, Dinner from £12.50, Rooms 2 double en-suite, 1 twin en-suite, 1 single pb, No smoking, Children over 5, No dogs, Closed Xmas & New Year

NEW CAPERNWRAY FARM Capernwray, Carnforth LA6 1AD
Peter & Sally Townend *Tel / Fax:* 01524 734284
Email: newcapfarm@aol.com *Web:* www.newcapfarm.co.uk

Map Ref: 5
M6 J35

A welcoming friendly atmosphere and superb accommodation at this 17th century former farmhouse, full of character with beautiful countryside. Luxuriously equipped with king-sized and queen-sized beds and renowned for excellent candle-lit dinners (bring own wines). Detailed help with routes, an ideal stop for London to Scotland and for Lake District and Yorkshire Dales. AA, ETC 5 Diamonds.

B & B £33-£39pp, C-Cards MC VS, Dinner from £19.50, Rooms 1 double, 1 twin, both en-suite, 1 double private showerroom, No smoking, Children over 10, Dogs by arrangement, Closed Nov to Apr

INGLEBOROUGH VIEW GUEST HOUSE Main Street, Ingleton, Carnforth LA6 3HH
Mrs Anne Brown *Tel:* 015242 41523
Email: anne@ingleboroughview.co.uk *Web:* www.ingleboroughview.co.uk

Map Ref: 6
A65

Ingleborough View, an attractive Victorian stone built house has splendid views of Ingleborough mountain and surrounding countryside. A recent extension has formed a spacious first floor dining room with separate tables and the rear of the property is enhanced by an attractive elevated patio overlooking the River Greta. Only five minutes walk to village centre, shops, inns and cafes.

B & B £19-£22pp, Rooms 3 double, 2 twin, 1 family, all en-suite, Children welcome, No dogs, Open all year

THE BOWER Yealand Conyers, Carnforth LA5 9SF
Michael & Sally-Ann Rothwell *Tel:* 01524 734585 *Fax:* 01524 730710
Email: info@thebower.co.uk *Web:* www.thebower.co.uk

Map Ref: 7
M6, A6

The Bower is a tranquil Georgian house set in an area of outstanding natural beauty just south of the Lake District. The Rothwells are keen bridge players and love classical music. In the spacious hall is a harpsicord which Michael plays with skill and pleasure. Guests are provided with every comfort in this beautifully furnished home. Convivial candle-lit kitchen suppers by prior arrangement.

B & B £28.50-£33.50pp, C-Cards MC VS, Dinner from £13, Rooms 1 double/twin en-suite, 1 double private bathroom, No smoking, Children over 12, No dogs, Open all year

PARR HALL FARM Parr Lane, Eccleston, Chorley PR7 5SL
Mrs & Mrs Motley *Tel:* 01257 451917 *Fax:* 01257 453749
Email: parrhall@talk21.com

Map Ref: 8
M6, A49, B5250

18th century farmhouse set in extensive mature gardens. Quiet village location within walking distance of good pubs and restaurants. Local attractions include Martin Mere, Rufford Old Hall. Lancashire coast and West Pennine Moors. Good area for walking, cycling, golf, fishing and horse riding. M6 (J27) North on B5250 for 5 miles, Parr Lane is on right. Safe off road parking.

B & B from £25pp, C-Cards MC VS, Rooms 1 single, 2 double, 1 twin, 1 family, most en-suite, No smoking, Children welcome, No dogs, Open all year

ALDEN COTTAGE Kemple End, Birdy Brow, Stonyhurst, Clitheroe BB7 9QY
Brenda Carpenter *Tel / Fax:* 01254 826468
Email: carpenter@aldencottage.f9.co.uk

Map Ref: 9
M6 J31, A59

Luxury accommodation in an idyllic 17th century country cottage situated in area of outstanding natural beauty overlooking the Ribble and Hodder Valleys. Charmingly furnished rooms with all modern comforts, fresh flowers, chocolates and private facilities with jacuzzi bath and shower. Perfect for a peaceful and relaxing stay. ETC 4 Diamonds, Gold Award. Ribble Valley Civic Design and Conservation Award.

B & B from £24.50pp, Rooms 2 double, 1 twin, all en-suite or private bathroom, No smoking, Children welcome, No dogs, Open all year

PETER BARN COUNTRY HOUSE Cross Lane, Waddington, Clitheroe BB7 3JH
Jean & Gordon Smith *Tel:* 01200 428585 *Mobile:* 07970 826370
Email: jean@peterbarn.fsnet.co.uk

Map Ref: 10
A59, B6478

Jean and Gordon invite you into their charming old stone tithe barn surrounded by large gardens with stream and ponds. Relax in the first floor sitting room with its beams, log fires and sumptuous sofas. There are three delightful bedrooms and delicious breakfasts with local produce, homemade jams and marmalade. Winner of Best Village Award. ETC 4 Diamonds.

B & B £25-£26pp, Rooms 2 double, 1 twin, all en-suite, No smoking, Children over 8, No dogs, Closed Xmas & New Year

HIGHER WANLESS FARM Red Lane, Colne BB8 7JP
Mrs Carole Mitson *Tel:* 01282 865301 *Fax:* 01282 865823
Email: wanlessfarm@bun.com *Web:* www.stayinlancs.co.uk

Map Ref: 11
M65 J13

Situated in a beautiful tranquil location alongside the Leeds/Liverpool Canal, Higher Wanless is ideal for a relaxing break, a convenient centre for touring the pretty area of Pendle. Enjoy a hearty Lancashire breakfast to start your day off in the best possible way, then come and meet our friendly Shire horses, or take a leisurely stroll along the canal.

B & B from £23pp, Rooms 1 single with en-suite shower, 1 twin, 1 family en-suite, Restricted smoking, Children over 10, No dogs, Closed mid-Dec to mid-Jan

Leicestershire, Nottinghamshire & Rutland

Leicestershire, a county at the very heart of England, is endowed with some of the country's largest and most impressive estates. A largely agricultural county on the eastern side with the industrial East Midlands on the western side. The City of Leicester, situated on the River Soar, is the county town and a major commercial and industrial centre. It has a magnificent museum overlooking the site of the Roman baths and the half-timbered medieval Guildhall in Castle Park, the scene of a great banquet celebrating the defeat of the Spanish Armada. The de Montfort Hall recalls Simon de Montfort, the first Earl of Leicester, a great benefactor of the city, who led the revolt against his brother-in-law, Henry III, and set the pattern for future parliamentary government. Leicester is an excellent centre for touring the region, displayed by the statue outside the railway station, of travel pioneer Thomas Cook, who organised his first tour from here in 1841. To the north of the city is Loughborough where Cook brought that first excursion to a temperance meeting. The town is an important educational centre and a fine holiday base, being surrounded by Charnwood Forest. A wonderful area of high undulating countryside punctuated by rocky granite outcrops and scattered with lovely grey-stone villages. It was right here at Bradgate House, surrounded by glorious parkland and open heath that the tragic queen-for-nine-days, Lady Jane Grey lived. To the east is Melton Mowbray, famous for its cheese and pork pies, with

its wolds presenting wonderful walking country. Much of the countryside here is planted with small coverts for the breeding of foxes, the land being hunted by the Quorn, Cottesmore and Belvoir Hunts. The kennels of the Belvoir Hunt are housed at Belvoir Castle, a fairytale castle, seat of the Dukes of Rutland since the days of Henry VIII. However the present handsome building is a Gothic revival structure built in 1816 by Wyatt, with lovely gardens, overlooking the beautiful Vale of Belvoir. In the west is Ashby-de-la-Zouch, a former spa with some fine Georgian buildings. Its fifteenth century manor of Lord Hastings was reputedly the setting for Sir Walter Scott's 'Ivanhoe' and the Staunton Harold church here is one of the very few churches to be built during the Commonwealth.

Rutland became a part of Leicestershire with the 1974 reorganisation, and not without considerable opposition. A mere fifteen miles in length and eleven in width, it was England's smallest county, and with a history going back to before the twelfth century. A large

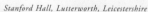
Stanford Hall, Lutterworth, Leicestershire

part of the county now lies beneath Rutland Water, one of the largest man-made lakes in Europe, providing major recreational facilities, including fishing, sailing and pleasure cruises, as well as drinking water for the East Midlands.

Nottinghamshire, lying on the low ground of the Trent basin is renowned as the county of Robin Hood, the outlaw who roamed this region and lived in Sherwood Forest, a royal hunting forest which once covered over 160 square miles. Sherwood Forest County Park contains the ancient Major Oak, reputedly the home of Robin, while Edwinstowe Church is claimed to be the scene of his marriage to Maid Marion. The historic city of Nottingham is a fine shopping centre, its old market square was the location of the ancient Goose Fair, now moved to the Forest area. The seventeenth century castle became a museum in 1878 but below the castle is the intriguing Trip To Jerusalem Inn, said to have been established in the days of the Crusades. Clumber Park, the former estate of the Dukes of Newcastle is a glorious 3,800 acres of parkland, farmland, lake and woodlands and includes the largest double lime avenue in Europe as well as an 80 acre lake. Clumber's walled garden includes a Victorian Apiary and Vineries and Tools exhibition. Southwell, to the north of Nottingham can claim one of the most delightful cathedrals in the country. Its Chapter House, begun in 1292, contains some remarkable stone carving depicting the oak, maple, vine and ivy leaves of Sherwood Forest. Eastwood is the birthplace of D.H.Lawrence, the author of 'Sons and Lovers', and celebrates his life with his miner's terraced house having since been converted into a museum.

PLACES TO VISIT

This is a small selection of interesting places to visit. Many more are listed in our annual guide to Museums, Galleries, Historic Houses & Sites (see page 448)

Belvoir Castle
near Grantham
Home of the Duke and Duchess of Rutland, the castle has a notable collection of art treasures and also houses the Queen's Royal Lancers' Museum.

Newstead Abbey
Ravenshead, Nottinghamshire
The birthplace of Lord Byron where you can see his own apartments as well as the elegant Salon and the Baronial Great Hall. Set in I gardens with waterfalls, lakes, themed gardens and ponds..

Bosworth Battlefield Visitor Centre
Market Bosworth, Leicestershire
An interpretation of the Battle of Bosworth 1485 through a film theatre, exhibitions and models.

Southwell Minster
Southwell, Nottinghamshire
Originally a monastery founded in the 10th century or earlier, the church begun in 1108, was raised to cathedral status in the late 19th century. Famous for its carved foliage decoration.

Stanford Hall
Lutterworth, Leicestershire
Built in the 1690s for Sir Roger Cave, home to his descendants with exquisite architecture, a library with over 5,000 books and a motorcycle museum.

Leicestershire,
Nottinghamshire & Rutland

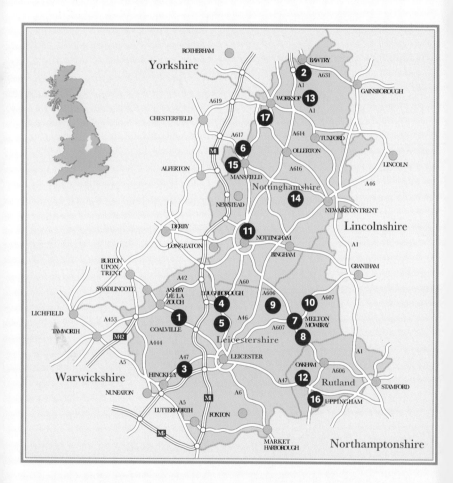

The Red Map References should be used to locate B & B properties on the pages that follow

ABBOTS OAK COUNTRY HOUSE Warren Hills Road, Greenhill, Coalville, Leics LE67 4UY
Mrs Carolyn Voce   *Map Ref:* 1
Tel / Fax: 01530 832328   M1 J22, A511

A beautiful Grade II listed home boasting a wealth of carved oak panelling including a three storey staircase reputedly from Nell Gwynn's townhouse. Whether visiting for business or pleasure, relax in nature gardens and woodland. Play tennis and dine by candlelight prior to returning to your spacious comfortable bedroom.

B & B £30-£45pp, Dinner from £20, Rooms 3 double, 1 twin, all en-suite, Restricted smoking, Children & dogs welcome, Open all year

CHURCH LANE FARM HOUSE Ravenstone, Coalville, Leics LE67 2AE   *Map Ref:* 1
Ann Thorne   *Tel:* 01530 810536   *Fax:* 01530 811299   *Mobile:* 07973 772341   A571
Email: annthorne@ravenstone-guesthouse.co.uk   *Web:* www.ravenstone-guesthouse.co.uk

Charming Queen Anne Leicestershire farmhouse in a doomsday village and National Forest. An artist's and designer's home. Quiet rural location but close to motorway hub so ideally placed for tourism or business. Enjoy traditional Leicestershire dishes supplemented with a hint of the unusual in our beamed dining room. Full residents license. Small house parties. Airport parking. Access Donnington and Mallory circuits. AA ETC 4 Diamonds.

B & B £27.50-£31.50pp, C-Cards MC VS, Dinner from £20, Rooms 2 double, 2 twin, all en-suite, No smoking, No children, Dogs by arrangement, Closed Xmas & New Year

THE OLD GEORGE DRAGON Scrooby, near Bawtry, Doncaster, Notts DN10 6AU   *Map Ref:* 2
John & Georgina Smithers   A638, A1M
Tel: 01302 711840

An attractive 18th century cottage, in the picturesque village of Scrooby, internationally known for its links with the Pilgrim Fathers and Robin Hood country. The accommodation is tastefully furnished, it retains its original features. The bedrooms have en-suite or private facilities, TV and a tea and coffee tray. The Old George Dragon is two miles from the A1 M, it is not a pub.

B & B from £20pp, Rooms 1 twin, 2 double, all en-suite, Open all year

BADGERS MOUNT 6 Station Road, Elmesthorpe, Hinckley, Leics LE9 7SG   *Map Ref:* 3
Jill Hirons and Ivor Poxon   *Tel / Fax:* 01455 848161   M69, A47
Email: info@badgersmount.com   *Web:* www.badgersmount.com

Badgers Mount is set in countryside surroundings between M1 and M69 for easy travel to Leicester, Coventry, Birmingham and many Midlands tourist attractions. The atmosphere is relaxed and informal. It has a residential licence with bar room overlooking large patio, spacious gardens and outdoor swimming pool heated for summer use.

B & B from £22.50pp, C-Cards MC VS, Dinner from £8.50, Rooms 1 single, 7 double, 1 twin, 3 family, all en-suite, Restricted smoking, Children welcome, No dogs, Closed Xmas & New Year

CHARNWOOD LODGE 136 Leicester Road, Loughborough, Leics LE11 2AQ   *Map Ref:* 4
Elizabeth & Klaus Charwat   *Tel:* 01509 211120   *Fax:* 01509 211121   M1
Email: charnwoodlodge@charwat.freeserve.co.uk   *Web:* www.charnwoodlodge.com

Charnwood Lodge is a spacious Victorian guest house, completely refurbished and approached by a tree-lined driveway off the main road. It stands in quiet surroundings but it is within five minutes of the town centre and nearby Charnwood Forest. All rooms have en-suite facilities with one room having a four poster bed. There is a conservatory for guests' use. Licensed.

B & B from £30pp, Dinner available, Rooms 1 single, 3 double, 2 family, 1 twin, 1 four poster, Open all year

BARLEYLOFT GUEST HOUSE 33A Hawcliffe Road, Mountsorrel, Loughborough, Leics LE12 7AQ
Mrs M A Pegg   *Map Ref:* 5
Tel: 01509 413514   M1, A6

A spacious bungalow set in a quiet, rural location with riverside walking, yet only 10 minutes to the M1. A comfortable base for working away from home with a guests' fridge, microwave, toaster and 24-hour use of dining room facilities. Televisions and tea/coffee facilities in all rooms and a hearty English breakfast from 7.00am. Good nearby takeaways, supermarkets, local pubs and excellent restaurants. Extensive parking. Good standards of service.

B & B from £19pp, Rooms 1 single, 2 double/single, 1 twin/single, 2 family, Children & dogs welcome, Open all year

---

TITCHFIELD GUEST HOUSE 300/302 Chesterfield Road North, Pleasley, Mansfield, Notts NG19 7QU
Betty Hinchley   *Map Ref:* 6
Tel: 01623 810921/810356   *Fax:* 01623 810356   M1, A617

This is a family run guest house with an adjoining garage for parking facilities. There is a TV lounge, and a TV in all bedrooms. A kitchen is available for making hot drinks etc. Guests are welcome to use the garden. Sherwood Forest and Peak District are within easy reach. A warm and friendly welcome is assured here.

B & B from £18pp, C-Cards MC VS, Rooms 4 single, 2 twin, 1 double, 1 family, Restricted smoking, Children welcome, Dogs by arrangement, Closed Xmas

---

QUORN LODGE HOTEL 46 Asfordby, Melton Mowbray, Leics LE13 0HR   *Map Ref:* 7
Julie Sturt   *Tel:* 01664 566660   *Fax:* 01664 480660   A46, A606
Email: QuornLodge@aol.com   *Web:* QuornLodge.co.uk

An original Hunting Lodge, the hotel is a short walk from the busy market town renowned for Pork Pies and Stilton cheese. Excellent food and wine served in our delightful restaurant overlooking the garden. Luxury at affordable prices in our 19 individually designed en-suite bedrooms. Special weekend breaks available.

B & B from £32.50pp, C-Cards, Dinner available, Rooms 6 single, 8 double, 3 twin, 1 triple, all en-suite, Restricted smoking, Children welcome, No dogs, Closed Dec 26/27 & New Years day

---

SULNEY FIELDS Colonel's Lane, Melton Mowbray, Notts LE14 3BD   *Map Ref:* 7
Hilary Collinson   *Tel:* 01664 822204   *Fax:* 01664 823976   A46, A606
Email: hillyc@talk21.com

Sulney Fields is a large family house situated in a quiet position with stunning views. Most rooms have private bathrooms, tea/coffee facilities and televisions. There are many good local pubs, one within walking distance and a sitting room available for guests' use.

B & B £20-£22.50pp, Rooms 1 single, 2 double with 1 pb, 2 twin with 1 pb, No smoking, Children & dogs welcome, Closed Xmas & New Year

---

THE GRANGE New Road, Burton Lazars, Melton Mowbray, Leics LE14 2UU   *Map Ref:* 8
Pam & Ralph Holden   A606
Tel / Fax: 01664 560775

This beautiful country house surrounds you with elegance comfort and friendly care, outstanding views and a lovely formal garden of two and a half acres. Each bedroom is en-suite with telephone, TV and tea/coffee facilities. The drawing room is furnished with antiques and has open log fire. One and a half miles to Melton Mowbray. 7 miles to Oakham.

B & B from £22.25pp, C-Cards MC VS, Rooms 1 single, 1 twin, 1 double, 1 family, all en-suite, Restricted smoking, Children welcome, No dogs, Open all year

HILLSIDE HOUSE 27 Melton Road, Burton Lazars, Melton Mowbray, Leics LE14 2UR   *Map Ref:* 8
Sue & Peter Goodwin *Tel:* 01664 566312 *Fax:* 01664 501819   A606
Email: sue&peter@hillside-house.co.uk *Web:* www.hillside-house.co.uk

Hillside House is a charmingly converted old farm building
overlooking rolling countryside. Comfortable accommodation is
offered in 3 bedrooms with en-suite or private bathrooms. All rooms
have TV, hospitality trays, central heating, radio/alarm and hair
dryers. Close to Melton Mowbray, Rutland and centrally located for
many interesting places. Guests are welcome to use the garden.

B & B £19-£22pp, Rooms 1 double en-suite, 1 twin en-suite,
1 twin private bathroom, Restricted smoking, Children over 10, No
dogs, Closed Xmas & New Year

GORSE HOUSE 33 Main Street, Grimston, Melton Mowbray, Leics LE14 3BZ   *Map Ref:* 9
Lyn & Richard Cowdell *Tel / Fax:* 01664 813537 *Mobile:* 07768 341848   M1/A46
Email: cowdell@gorsehouse.co.uk *Web:* www.gorsehouse.co.uk

Convenient for both Nottingham and Leicester, 2 miles from the A46,
this extended 17th century cottage is situated in the pretty village of
Grimston which is peaceful and unhurried. The garden is attractive,
the bedrooms are light and airy, the house offers comfort and
relaxation. Beautiful countryside for walking, riding and touring.
Stables available. Ragdale Hall Hydro nearby, good food 100 yards
away.

B & B £20-£25pp, Rooms 2 double/twin en-suite, No smoking,
Children over 12, No dogs, Open all year

BRYN BARN 38 High Street, Waltham-on-the-Wolds, Melton Mowbray, Leics LE14 4AH   *Map Ref:* 10
Andrew & Glena Rowlands   A607
Tel: 01664 464783 *Fax:* 01664 464138

Bryn Barn is a charming barn and stable conversion, set in secluded
cottage gardens within a picturesque conservation village in the
beautiful Belvoir Vale. The high standard accommodation includes a
comfortable guest lounge. Within walking distance are two village
pubs providing a choice of good quality evening meals. An ideal
location for visiting Rutland Water, Melton Mowbray and Belvoir
Castle. AA 4 Diamonds.

B & B from £20pp, Rooms 2 double, 1 twin, 1 family, en-suite or
private bathroom, No smoking, Children welcome, Dogs by
arrangement, Closed Xmas & New Year

GREENWOOD LODGE CITY GUEST HOUSE Third Avenue, Sherwood Rise, Nottingham, Notts
NG7 6JH Michael & Sheila Spratt *Tel / Fax:* 0115 9621206   *Map Ref:* 11
Email: coolspratt@aol.com   A60 Mansfield Rd

Warm and welcoming Victorian house, Greenwood Lodge is less
than 1 mile from the city centre. All the rooms are en-suite with
tea/coffee facilities, trouser press, TV and telephone. Magnificent
conservatory dining room in elegant gardens. Within a short distance
of Newstead Abbey, Chatsworth House, Sherwood Forest and
Belvoir Castle.

B & B from £28pp, Rooms 1 single, 1 twin, 2 double, 2 four-
poster, all en-suite, No smoking, Children welcome, Dogs by
arrangement, Open all year

THE OLD RECTORY Belton in Rutland, Oakham LE15 9LE   *Map Ref:* 12
Richard & Vanessa Peach *Tel:* 01572 717279 *Fax:* 01572 717343   A47
Email: bb@iepuk.com *Web:* www.rutnet.co.uk/orb

A Victorian country house with guest annexe in charming
conservation village overlooking Eyebrook valley and rolling Rutland
countryside. Comfortable and varied selection of rooms, mostly en-
suite, with direct outside access. Small farm environment with
excellent farmhouse breakfasts and a pub within 100 yards. Lots to
see and do: Rutland Water, castles, stately home, country parks,
forestry and Barnsdal gardens.

B & B £17-£28pp, C-Cards MC VS, Rooms 1 single, 2 double,
4 twin, some en-suite, No smoking, Children welcome, Dogs by
arrangement, Open all year

BARNS COUNTRY GUEST HOUSE Morton Farm, Babworth, Retford, Notts DN22 8HA   *Map Ref:* 13
Harry & Mary Kay   *Tel:* 01777 706336   *Fax:* 01777 709773   A1, B6420
Email: harry@Thebarns.co.uk   *Web:* www.Thebarns.co.uk

Oak beams and log fires await the discerning traveller in this charming eighteenth century former farm. Enjoy an Aga cooked breakfast. Situated in open countryside on B6420 convenient for the A1, Clumber Park and The Mayflower Trail.

B & B £22-£35pp, C-Cards MC VS, Rooms 5 double, 1 twin, all en-suite, No smoking, Children over 8, No dogs, Closed Xmas & New Year

---

THE OLD FORGE 2 Burgage Lane, Southwell, Notts NG25 0ER   *Map Ref:* 14
Hilary Marston   *Tel:* 01636 812809   *Fax:* 01636 816302   *Mobile:* 07980 277510   A612
Web: www.southwellonline.co.uk/localpages/theoldforge

We are situated in a quiet but central location. Our atmosphere is friendly and informal, our decor pretty and our furniture mainly antique. You will see that we are avid acquisitors of all things old! There are books to browse over and, weather permitting, a secluded patio to relax on, complete with fish pond and waterfall.

B & B £32-£34pp, C-Cards MC VS, Rooms 2 double, 1 twin, 1 family, all en-suite, No smoking, Children & dogs welcome, Closed Xmas & New Year

---

DALESTORTH HOUSE Skegby Lane, Skegby, Sutton-in-Ashfield, Notts NG17 3DH   *Map Ref:* 15
Mr & Mrs Jordan   A617, M1
Tel: 01623 551110   *Fax:* 01623 442241

An 18th century Georgian ancestral house modernised to hotel standard. Clean, comfortable and family run with colour televisions and tea/coffee facilities. Ideal for visiting relations, friends and business acquaintances in the Mansfield or Sutton area. Car parking. Five miles from junction 28, M1.

B & B from £15pp, Rooms 5 single, 3 double, 3 twin, 2 family, Restricted smoking, Children welcome, No dogs, Open all year

---

GARDEN HOTEL High Street West, Uppingham LE15 9QD   *Map Ref:* 16
Tel: 01572 822352   *Fax:* 01572 821156   A47
Email: gardenhotel@btinternet.com

A historic hotel with friendly repution and homely reputation. Garden Hotel offers en-suite rooms with colour televisions, telephones, radios and tea/coffee facilities. There is also a comfortable lounge bar and walled garden for guests to relax in. Traditional British home cooking is served with a good wine list. The best kept secret in Rutland.

B & B from £35pp, C-Cards, Dinner from £20, Rooms 4 single, 4 double, 1 twin, 1 family, all en-suite, No smoking, Children & dogs welcome, Open all year

---

BROWNS The Old Orchard Cottage, Holbeck, Worksop, Notts S80 3NF   *Map Ref:* 17
Mrs Joan Brown   *Tel / Fax:* 01909 720659   A60, A616
Email: browns@holbeck.fsnet.co.uk   *Web:* www.smoothhound.co.uk/hotels/browns

A 1730 country cottage in one acre of gardens in a peaceful hamlet. There are three separate en-suite garden lodges, one with king-size four poster bed, with garden terraces to each lodge. Cross over the driveway over the shallow ford and stay somewhere special. One of only two 1998 national 'England for Excellence' Silver Award winners and 'Heart of England Bed and Breakfast 1998' winner.

B & B £23-£30pp, Rooms 2 double, 1 twin, all en-suite, No smoking, Children over 8, No dogs, Closed Xmas & New Year

Lincolnshire

Lincolnshire may well be flat, but dull it certainly is not. The county radiates from the flat shores of the North Sea, north to Yorkshire and west to the Midlands. The land is particularly flat where it joins the Wash and the Fens in the south but cutting through the centre is the Lincolnshire Edge, a ridge of chalk, upon which stands Lincoln, its triple towered cathedral gloriously dominating all the surrounding countryside. Lincoln cathedral is exceptional indeed, one of England's finest, largely rebuilt during the thirteenth and fourteenth centuries following an earthquake in 1185. The cathedral is renowned for its decagonal chapter house with its magnificent intricately carved Angel Choir, and the famous Lincolnshire Imp, a stone carving with the story that the imp was caught flirting with the angels and so was turned to stone. The historic city of Lincoln has much to attract the visitor with the Norman castle walls walk, the Jew's House, St Mary's Guild Hall, the Usher Gallery and the fine Georgian and medieval houses in Minster Yard. The statue of Lord Tennyson the poet, who was a great lover of this county, stands outside the cathedral. His poem, 'Maud', of 'come into the garden' fame is said to be linked to the lovely gardens of Harrington Hall in the Lincolnshire Wolds. These uplands, though only about 500 feet, are designated as an Area of Outstanding Natural Beauty and stretch from Dorset to Yorkshire containing the prehistoric ridge top routes and give fine views across the county.

The Holland region in the southwest is in effect a continuation of the Cambridgeshire fen country, drained in the seventeenth century and renowned for its flower bulb industry. Spalding is the hub of this area and holds a Flower Parade every May, surely the greatest free pageant of colour in the country, when over three million tulips are used to decorate floats, and accompanied by bands parade the streets. On the southern rim of Lincolnshire, within the flood plain of the River Welland, are the Deepings, Market Deeping and Deeping St James, with its lovely church and rare Georgian tower. Nearby, Stamford, designated England's first conservation area in 1967, contains a remarkable number of excellent buildings in the lovely local stone. The Church of St Martin houses the alabaster monument to Lord Burghley, whose palatial mansion, Burghley House, stands on the outskirts of the town in its Capability Brown landscaped park. Built for William Cecil, chief minister to Elizabeth I, the house contains some remarkable Italian plaster work.

Lincoln Castle from Cathedral (LCC)

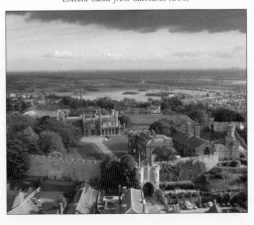

To the north is Boston, once England's second most important port. The historic market town is dominated by the magnificent Church of St Botolph, England's largest parish church, known as the Boston Stump, where from its tower a third of Lincolnshire can be seen. It was, incidentally, from Boston that the main group of the 'Pilgrim Fathers' embarked in the 'Mayflower'.

For the visitor interested in the rich history of this region there is more than enough to satisfy the most inquiring mind, but for the visitor intent upon the pleasures of the seaside there is Skegness with its wide sandy beaches. From the early nineteenth century the little fishing village was attracting holiday visitors, but with the arrival of the railway and with the innovative planning of the Earl of Scarborough, the main landowner, the town swiftly developed into what it is today, a first class holiday resort. To the north, its sister resort Mablethorpe, has miles of golden sands as well as an animal and bird garden with a seal sanctuary.

Of course the Plain of Lincolnshire was renowned during the Second World War for its RAF airfields. Scampton was the home base of 617 Squadron, the 'Dambusters', and at Coningsby the Battle of Britain's Memorial Flight has its home with its display of Spitfires, a Hurricane and a Lancaster. Horncastle, north of Coningsby, standing between the Wolds and the Fens, was a Roman settlement and an important medieval trading center. Today the town is a fascinating mixture of styles. Further north, Louth, another Area of Outstanding Natural Beauty, is ideal for exploring the Lincolnshire Wolds and the exceptionally attractive Hubbards Hills valley.

PLACES TO VISIT

This is a small selection of interesting places to visit. Many more are listed in our annual guide to Museums, Galleries, Historic Houses & Sites (see page 448)

Belton House, Park and Gardens
Belton, Grantham
Built in 1685 for Sir John Brownlow, with alterations by James Wyatt in the 1770s. Fine collections and gardens with an orangery.

Burghley House
Stamford
The largest and grandest house of the first Elizabethan Age, completed by William Cecil, Lord Burghley, in 1587. 18 state rooms are open with fine art, furniture and paintings and grounds designed by 'Capability' Brown.

Lincoln Castle
Lincoln
A medieval castle with grassy lawns inside the walls, a Magna Carta exhibition and old Victorian Prison. Reconstructed Westgate and popular events throughout the summer.

Lincoln Cathedral
Lincoln
One of the largest churches in England and inside the visitor can find two famous stained glass windows, the Dean's Eye and the Bishop's Eye, as well as the famous Lincoln Imp.

Lincolnshire

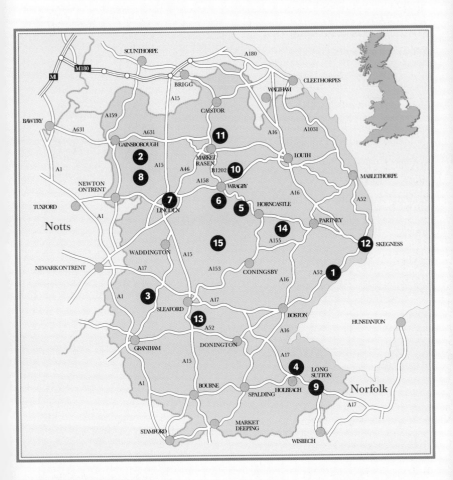

The Red Map References should be used to locate B & B properties on the pages that follow

THE OLD VICARAGE Church Lane, Wrangle, Boston PE22 9EP *Map Ref:* 1
Michael & Julia Brotherton   *Tel:* 01205 870688   *Fax:* 01205 871857   *Mobile:* 07867 893665   A52
Email: jb141@aol.com

Built with local handmade bricks which have mellowed gloriously, this impressive, listed Queen Anne vicarage is in a dream-like village setting. The sitting room is panelled throughout and the typical square Lincolnshire hall with stone flags leads to a red pine staircase with more panelling. Michael, ex-navy and ex-MP, and Julia both love cooking and have a huge fruit and vegetable garden.

B & B from £27.50pp, Dinner from £24.50, Rooms 1 double, 1 twin, No smoking, Children welcome, No dogs, Closed Xmas & New Year

---

THE BLACK SWAN GUEST HOUSE 21 High Street, Marton Village, Gainsborough DN21 5AH
Alan & Valerie Ball   *Tel / Fax:* 01427 718878   *Map Ref:* 2
Email: info@blackswan-marton.co.uk   *Web:* www.blackswan-marton.co.uk   A15, A156, A1500

Originally an 18th century coaching inn, with an existing cellar believed to have been slept in by Oliver Cromwell during the Battle of Gainsborough. We provide businessmen with personal care to suit their appointments and needs and also we provide tourists with an excellent base for many sites of ancient and modern historical significance. Four poster beds, guest lounge and comfortable dining room.

B & B from £30pp, C-Cards MC VS, Rooms 2 single, 4 double, 1 twin, 1 family, all en-suite, No smoking, Children welcome, No dogs, Open all year

---

CHURCHFIELD HOUSE Hough Lane, Carlton Scroop, Grantham NG32 3BA *Map Ref:* 3
Mrs Bridget Hankinson   A607
Tel: 01400 250387   *Fax:* 01400 250241   *Mobile:* 07909 921866

An attractive family single storey house with more character than many period homes, set in lovely gardens in a quiet village near the A1 between Grantham, Newark and Lincoln. Chintz curtains with matching padded headboards in the bedrooms make for a comfortable stay with tea/coffee facilities. Bathroom for own private use. Always a warm welcome, including a full English breakfast.

B & B from £19.75pp, Dinner from £16, Rooms 1 double, 1 twin with private bathroom, Restricted smoking, No children or dogs, Closed New Year

---

CACKLE HILL HOUSE Cackle Hill Lane, Holbeach PE12 8BS *Map Ref:* 4
Maureen Biggadike   *Tel:* 01406 426721   *Fax:* 01406 424659   A17
Email: cacklehill2@netscapeonline.co.uk

A warm welcome awaits at our comfortable home set in a rural position. The rooms are tastefully furnished, have en-suite/private facilities and hospitality trays. There is a guests' lounge with TV. The house is ideally situated for exploring the area, there are many attractions, from museums and monuments to miles of golden sands. The counties of Norfolk and Cambridgshire are within a pleasant drive.

B & B from £20pp, Rooms 1 double en-suite, 1 twin en-suite, 1 twin pb, No smoking, Children over 10, Dogs by arrangement, Closed Xmas & New Year

---

PIPWELL MANOR Washway Road, Saracen's Head, Holbeach PE12 8AL *Map Ref:* 4
Lesley Honnor   *Tel / Fax:* 01406 423119   A17
Email: honnor@pipwellmanor.freeserve.co.uk

Georgian house built around 1740, a Grade II listed building. Tastefully restored in the appropriate style it retains its original features. All bedrooms are attractive and well furnished. Parking is available, guests are welcomed with home made cakes and tea. Pipwell Manor stands amid gardens in a small village off the A17 in the Lincolnshire Fens. A lovely place to stay. 'Country Living'.

B & B from £23pp, Rooms 2 double, 1 twin, all en-suite/private, No smoking, No children or dogs, Closed Xmas & New Year

BAUMBER PARK Baumber, Horncastle LN9 5NE
Mrs C Harrison
Tel: 01507 578235   *Fax:* 01507 578417   *Mobile:* 07977 722776

Map Ref: 5
A158

A period farmhouse in a quiet parkland setting on mixed farm. Large gardens, wildlife pond, grass tennis court, bedrooms with lovely views. Antique furniture, guest lounge, log fires, books and parking. Close to Lincolnshire Wolds. Excellent walking, cycling, golfing and riding. Stabling available. Historic Lincoln, market towns and antiques shops. ETB 4 Diamonds.

B & B from £22.50pp, Dinner from £10, Rooms 1 double, 1 twin, all en-suite/private, Restricted smoking, Children welcome, Dogs by arrangement, Closed Xmas & New Year

GREENFIELD FARM Mill Lane/Cow Lane, Minting, Horncastle LN9 5PJ
Judy & Hugh Bankes Price   *Tel / Fax:* 01507 578457   *Mobile:* 07768 368829
Email: greenfieldfarm@farming.co.uk

Map Ref: 6
A158

A lovely home, surrounded by grounds dominated by a wildlife pond. Centrally placed, Lincoln Cathedral is 15 minutes, the Lincolnshire Wolds five minutes. Close to the aviation trails, antique centres and Cadwell Park. Bedrooms have modern en-suite shower rooms with heated towel rails, tea/coffee making and wonderful views. Farmhouse breakfast is served, try the Lincolnshire sausages and homemade marmalade. Parking, pub one mile.

B & B from £22pp, Rooms 2 double, 1 twin, all en-suite/private, No smoking, Children over 10, No dogs, Closed mid-Dec to mid-Jan

CARLINE GUEST HOUSE 1-3 Carline Road, Lincoln LN1 1HL
Barry & Jackie Woods
Tel / Fax: 01522 530422

Map Ref: 7
A15, A46, A158

The Carline is a charming double fronted Edwardian house. We offer attractive well appointed rooms with many extra facilities. Warm friendly hospitality, totally non-smoking for your comfort and safety, private off-street and garaged parking. We are a short stroll from The Lawns Visitor Centre, castle and cathedral area. AA 4 Diamonds.

B & B from £22pp, Rooms 6 double, 2 twin, all en-suite, No smoking, Children over 2, No dogs, Closed Xmas & New Year

MINSTER LODGE HOTEL 3 Church Lane, Lincoln LN2 1QJ
John & Margaret Baumber   *Tel / Fax:* 01522 513220
Email: info@minsterlodge.co.uk   *Web:* www.minsterlodge.co.uk

Map Ref: 7
A15, A46, A158

This family owned Victorian residence, refurbished to a high standard, is your personal 'Home away from Home'. In a premier situation, within walking distance to the Cathedral, castle, museum, university, Usher Gallery and Lawn Exhibition Centre. An excellent selection of restaurants and tourist shops.' A lovely place with extra-ordinary hospitality,' Philip Lader, US Ambassador, London.' A superb experience in every way!' International organist.

B & B from £35pp, C-Cards MC VS AE, Rooms 6 single, 3 twin, 6 double, 2 family, all en-suite, No smoking, Children welcome, No dogs, Open all year

ORCHARD HOUSE 119 Yarborough Road, Lincoln LN1 1HR
June Williams   *Tel:* 01522 528795   *Mobile:* 07939 548742
Email: orchardhouse50@hotmail.com   *Web:* orchardhouselincoln.com

Map Ref: 7
A15, A57, A158

Orchard House is a small friendly guesthouse set in one third of an acre with ample private parking. Ideally situated in the centre of Lincoln. All our rooms are centrally heated with en-suites, colour televisions, tea/coffee making facilities, clock radios, hairdryers and shaver points. The full English breakfast is our speciality with eggs from our own hens.

B & B from £20pp, Rooms 1 double, 1 twin, 1 family, all en-suite, Restricted smoking, Children over 5, No dogs, Open all year

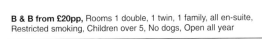

ST CLEMENTS LODGE 21 Langworth Gate, Lincoln LN2 4AD   *Map Ref:* 7
Janet & Bill Turner   A15, A57, A158
Tel / Fax: 01522 521532

Only three minutes walk from the magnificent Cathedral and Castle and other tourist attractions of Lincoln, St Clements Lodge. Janet's breakfasts, cooked to order, are renowned and are enjoyed again and again by guests who regularly return and she was a finalist in the AA Landlady of the Year competition 2001. The winner of the Lincoln City Tourism Accommodation Establishment of the Year award.

B & B from £25pp, Rooms 1 double, 2 twin, 1 family, all en-suite, No smoking, Children welcome, No dogs, Closed Xmas & New Year

---

GALLOWDALE FARM Tillbridge Lane, Stow Park, Sturton-by-Stow, Lincoln LN1 2AH   *Map Ref:* 8
Marijke & Kevin Chamberlain   *Tel:* 01427 787964   A15
Email: gallowdalefarm@hotmail.com

Gallowdale is a Grade II listed building set in 32 acres of land and surrounded by countryside. All rooms are bright, clean and airy with televisions and tea/coffee facilities, en-suites also available. Full English breakfast is provided and stabling and grazing are available. Four miles from Lincolnshire Show Ground and seven miles for the Historic City of Lincoln.

B & B from £20pp, Rooms 1 single, 4 double, 1 twin, all en-suite, No smoking, Children welcome, Dogs by arrangement, Open all year

---

DELAMORE HOUSE Park Road, Long Sutton PE12 9DJ   *Map Ref:* 9
Sue & John Foley   A17
Tel: 01406 365540

An historic Georgian house offering high standards of accommodation, is ideally placed for touring, cycling, golf and wildlife. The north Norfolk coast, Sandringham and cathedral cities are within easy reach. Rooms are equipped with a television and hospitality tray. Other facilities include a guests' lounge, open fires, private parking, gardens and a heated indoor swimming pool in summer.

B & B from £20pp, Rooms 2 double, 1 twin, 2 en-suite, No smoking, Children welcome, Dogs by arrangement, Closed Xmas & New Year

---

BODKIN LODGE Grange Farm, Torrington Lane, East Barkwith, Market Rasen LN8 5RY   *Map Ref:* 10
Anne & Richard Stamp   A157
Tel / Fax: 01673 858249   *Mobile:* 07951 079475

Expect speciality food like toasted plum bread by a real fire, Lincolnshire sausages, home baked organic bread at breakfast. Quiet ground floor bedrooms have tea trays, television, even teddies, French windows, sweeping farmland views, en-suite bathrooms with both bath and shower. There's an award winning farm trail, trout fishing, a village pub nearby. ETC Bed and Breakfast of the Year 2000.

B & B £25-£30pp, Dinner from £12, Rooms 1 double, 1 twin, both en-suite, No smoking, Children over 10, No dogs, Closed Xmas & New Year

---

THE GRANGE Torrington Lane, East Barkwith, Market Rasen LN8 5RY   *Map Ref:* 10
Sarah Stamp   *Tel:* 01673 858670   B1202, A158
Email: jonathanstamp@farmersweekly.net   *Web:* www.the-grange.f2s.com

The Stamp family give you a warm welcome to their beautiful Georgian farmhouse, nestled peacefully in quiet countryside with views of Lincoln to the West and the Wolds to the East. En-suite double rooms tastefully decorated with every facility for comfort and care. Delicious meals using fresh local produce. Guests' sitting room with log fires. An immaculate farm with award winning farm trail for guests' use, lawn tennis and trout lake.

B & B from £22.50pp, Dinner available, Rooms 2 double en-suite, 1 family, No smoking, Children welcome, No dogs, Closed Xmas & New Year

BLAVEN Walesby Hill, Walesby, Market Rasen LN8 3UW
Mrs Jacqy Braithwaite *Tel:* 01673 838352
Email: blaven@amserve.net

Map Ref: 11
A46

Nestling at the foot of The Wolds in an Area of Outstanding Natural Beauty, on The Viking Way and Hull to Harwich cycle route, we offer peace, tranquility and a warm welcome. Being equal distance from Lincoln, Louth, Grimsby and Brigg, Blaven is ideal for exploring the historic city of Lincoln, The Wolds or coast. Off-road parking available. AA 4 Diamonds.

B & B from £19.50pp, Rooms 1 double, 1 twin, No smoking, Children welcome, No dogs, Closed Xmas & New Year

WILLOW FARM Thorpe Fendykes, Skegness PE24 4QH
Tim & Sue Evans *Tel:* 01754 830316
Email: willowfarmhols@aol.com *Web:* www.willowfarmholidays.fsnet.co.uk

Map Ref: 12
A52

Friendly hosts welcome guests all year round to Willow Farm, a working farm with ponies, goats and free range hens in a quiet hamlet. The comfortable en-suite rooms are fitted with televisions and other luxuries. Only 10 minutes by car from the seaside resort of Skegness. Wheelchair accessible. Riding available. Brochure.

B & B from £15pp, Dinner available, Rooms 1 double, 1 twin, 1 family, all en-suite, Restricted smoking, Children welcome, Dogs by arrangement, Open all year

THE TALLY HO INN Aswarby, Sleaford NG34 8SA
Chris Shepherdson
Tel: 01529 455205

Map Ref: 13
A15, A17, A52

A traditional, friendly 17th century listed country inn with en-suite rooms located in carefully converted stables. A welcoming atmosphere and plenty of character with an a la carte restaurant and bar meals.

B & B from £35pp, C-Cards VS, Dinner available, Rooms 2 double, 4 twin, all en-suite, Children & dogs welcome, Closed Boxing day

WHITE OAK GRANGE Hagworthingham, Spilsby PE23 4LX
Mrs Jan Morris-Holmes *Tel:* 01507 588376 *Fax:* 01507 588377
Web: www.whiteoakgrange.com

Map Ref: 14
A158

Fine country house luxuriously furnished and set in six acres of beautiful gardens enjoying spectacular views over the Lincolnshire Wolds. Open log fires echo the warmth of our welcome and hospitality. Our cooking is our speciality, using vegetables from the garden and local produce. Private trout fishing and wonderful walks in this Tennyson country. Licensed. ETC 4 Diamonds, Silver Award.

B & B from £25pp, Dinner from £15, Rooms 2 double, 1 twin, 3 en-suite, No smoking, Children over 10, No dogs, Closed Xmas & New Year

CLAREMONT GUEST HOUSE 9/11 Witham Road, Woodhall Spa LN10 6RW
Claire Brennan
Tel: 01526 352000

Map Ref: 15
A153

A homely traditional unspoilt Victorian house in Lincolnshire's unique resort. Televisions and tea/coffee facilities are available in all rooms. Off-street parking and a peaceful garden is available for guests with good food nearby. Ideal for exploring Lincolnshire or enjoying Woodhall Spa's many attractions.

B & B from £15pp, Rooms 2 single, 2 double, 1 twin, 5 family, some en-suite, Restricted smoking, No children, Dogs by arrangement, Open all year

London

Two thousand years of history has seen a Roman settlement by the River Thames develop into a capital city of over seven million people. The strategic position of London was recognised by William the Conqueror who built his White Tower here, the hub of the Tower of London. However, the crowded unhygienic housing was a breeding ground of disease and as a consequence London suffered badly from the Black Death in 1348 and the Plague of 1665. The Great Fire of the following year cleansed the city of the pestilence and in consuming four fifths of the dreadful medieval slums made way for the spacious and considered planning of a new city. This noble city remained largely in this form until the bombing of the Second World War led to another period of rebuilding. For the holiday visitor there is everything here one could wish for and there is no doubt that by far the best way to enjoy the sights of London is from the top of a grand old London double-decker bus.

A large proportion of the city's attractions are to be found in the West End, with Trafalgar Square the ed centre. Over- looked by Nelson's Column, the visitor can easily spend the day within a very short distance of this landmark. The National Gallery and the Church of St. Martin-in-the-Fields take up two sides of the Square with the impressive Admiralty Arch taking up the third and leading to The Mall, at the end of which stands Buckingham Palace, the Queen's main residence. On one side of

The Mall is the royal St James' Park, beyond which is Birdcage Walk leading back to the very hub of Westminster, Parliament Square. Here stands the Houses of Parliament with the famous clock tower housing the great bell, Big Ben with each minute hand on the clock faces measuring fourteen feet in length! Across the Square is Westminster Abbey, Britain's most important church, begun by Edward the Confessor in the eleventh century. Almost all monarchs of England have been crowned here since William the Conqueror. The Abbey contains memorials to some of the most famous figures in English history.

The City, a square mile of the ancient city of London is the financial centre of the capital and retains much of its medieval street plan. Here stands the other great London church and landmark, St Paul's Cathedral, the baroque masterpiece of Sir Christopher Wren and the burial place of Wren, Lord Nelson and the Duke of Wellington. Nearby is one of the

The Tower of London

capital's most popular tourist attractions; the Tower of London, built by William the Conqueror after 1066, home of the Crown Jewels and regalia, the headsman's axe and the Tower's famous ravens. London is also a city of remarkable pageantry and ceremony where the Changing of the Guard at Buckingham Palace, the Mounting the Guard at Horse Guards in Whitehall and the Ceremony of the Keys at the Tower of London draw a number of visitors everyday. And then of course there are numerous annual and casual events which include the impressive Lord Mayor's Show and the various colourful carnivals. If the history, pageant and tradition of the city becomes too rich a fare then there is the London of world famous shops, Oxford Street and Regent Street cannot fail to fascinate even the window shoppers. For the specialist

shoppers there is St James' Street, for the bookworms there is Charing Cross Road, and for the visitor who merely wants a 'bargain' there is a multitude of street markets, Camden Lock, Portobello Road and Brick Lane. There are restaurants, nightclubs and theatres to suit every taste, Soho and Covent Garden constitute the heart of London's nightlife. The National Film Theatre on the South Bank is the leading repertory cinema, and London theatres offer everything from musicals to Shakespeare. However, London also houses some of the world's finest museums and galleries, both traditional and modern, The National Gallery, The National Portrait Gallery, The British Museum, The Victoria and Albert Museum, The Tate Gallery, The Imperial War Museum and The Museum of the Moving Image with its hi-tech displays and hands-on exhibits.

PLACES TO VISIT

This is a small selection of interesting places to visit. Many more are listed in our annual guide to Museums, Galleries, Historic Houses & Sites (see page 448)

Buckingham Palace
London SW1
The State Rooms are open from August to September (by ticket only). The Queen's Gallery reopens in Spring 2002, and the Royal Mews is open all year.

Kew Gardens
Kew, Richmond
The royal Botanic Gardens at Kew cover 300 acres with living collections of over 40,000 varieties of plants. There are also two art galleries.

London Eye
South Bank, London SE1
At 440 feet high, the world's highest

observation wheel, providing a 30 minute slow moving hover over London.

Tate Modern
London SE1
The Tate Gallery of modern Art with displays of 20th century art ranging from Andy Warhol paintings to Henry Moore bronzes.

The Tower of London
South Bank, London EC3
Over the past 900 years the Tower has served as a royal fortress, a prison, a place of execution, an armoury, a mint - now and for the past 600 years it houses the Crown Jewels.

London Underground System

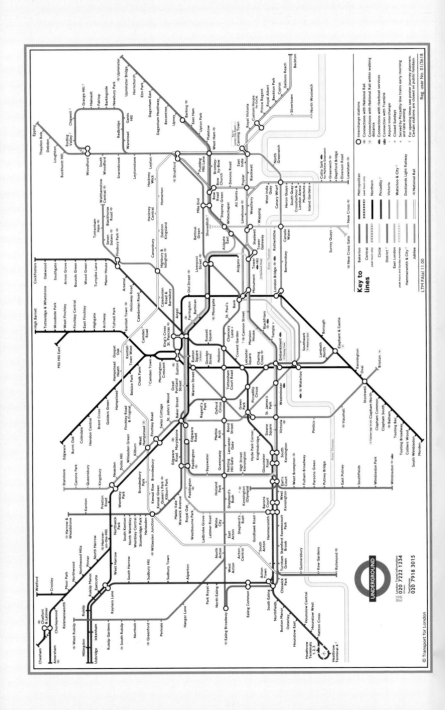

London

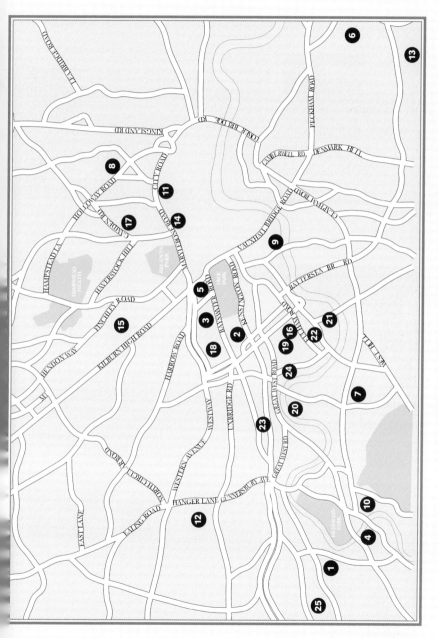

The Red Map References should be used to locate B & B properties on the pages that follow

ASHDOWNE HOUSE 9 Pownall Gardens, Hounslow TW3 1YW *Map Ref:* 1
Peter Horne *Tel:* 020 8572 0008 *Fax:* 020 8570 1939 *Tube:* Hounslow Central
Email: mail@ashdownehouse.com *Web:* www.ashdownehouse.com

A Victorian property which has been completely refurbished. The house, which retains many of its original features, has large elegant rooms which are fully heated and very comfortable. There are televisions, radios and tea/coffee facilities in all rooms. The house is within walking distance of Hounslow High Street with its excellent shopping facilities, pubs and places to eat. Convenient for Heathrow. ETC 4 Diamonds, Silver Award.

B & B from £39.50pp, C-Cards MC VS, Rooms 2 single, 3 double, 2 twin, all en-suite, No smoking, Children over 15, No dogs, Closed Xmas & New Year

101 ABBOTSBURY ROAD London W14 8EP *Map Ref:* 2
Sunny Murray *Tel:* 020 7602 0179 *Fax:* 020 7602 1036 *Mobile:* 07768 362562 *Tube:* Holland Park
Email: al.sunny@101abb.freeserve.co.uk

Abbotsbury Road is situated opposite beautiful Holland Park with shops, restaurants and the tube within five minutes walk, close to Notting Hill. One light double bedroom with bath/shower next door and fridge and kettle on landing outside. Both bedrooms are prettily decorated with English chintz and have televisions. Continental breakfasts from eight o'clock downstairs.

B & B £40-£45pp, Rooms 1 single, 1 double, No smoking, Children over 10, No dogs, Open all year

ALBRO HOUSE HOTEL 155 Sussex Gardens, London W2 2RY *Map Ref:* 3
Tel: 020 7724 2931 *Fax:* 020 7262 2278 *Tube:* Paddington
Email: joe@albrohotel.freeserve.co.uk *Web:* www.hotels-england.co.uk/hotel/albro

Albro House Hotel is ideally located in a safe pleasant area near public transport. The en-suite rooms are nicely decorated and we serve a full English breakfast. We speak several languages and promise a friendly welcome. Some parking available.

B & B from £40pp, Rooms 2 single, 6 double, 6 twin, 1 triple, 3 family, Children welcome, No dogs, Open all year

AVALON COTTAGE 50 Moor Mead Road, St Margarets, Twickenham TW1 1JS *Map Ref:* 4
Barbara & Terry Thompson *Tel:* 020 8744 2178 *Fax:* 020 8891 2444 *Rail:* St Margarets
Email: avalon@mead99.freeserve.co.uk

Avalon Cottage is a private Edwardian house in St Margarets, overlooking a park and tennis courts. We are ideally situated for business and tourist visits to the Richmond/Twickenham areas. A train journey to central London (Waterloo) is only 20 minutes but we are also convenient for M3/M4/M25. Heathrow/Gatwick accessible. Free, on street parking.

B & B from £30pp, Rooms 1 single, 1 double en-suite, No smoking, Children welcome, No dogs, Open all year

BOSTON COURT HOTEL 26 Upper Berkeley Street, Marble Arch, London W1H 7QL *Map Ref:* 5
Tel: 020 7723 1445 *Fax:* 020 7262 8823 *Tube:* Marble Arch
Email: info@bostoncourthotel.co.uk *Web:* bostoncourthotel.co.uk

A small comfortable and friendly Victorian style bed and breakfast in central London. Only two minutes walk from Marble Arch, Oxford St shops and Hyde Park. Continental breakfast included. Modern private bath, shower and toilet, direct dial telephone, satellite colour television, refrigerator, fans, tea/coffee facilities and hair dryer available in all rooms. Access at all times.

B & B £32.50-£39.50pp, C-Cards MC VS, Rooms 2 single, 1 twin, 1 double, 1 triple, 1 family, with showers, Children welcome, No dogs, Open all year

57 BREAKSPEARS ROAD London SE4 1XR
Biddy Bunzl *Tel / Fax:* 020 8469 3162
Email: bunzl@btinternet.com

Map Ref: 6
Rail: Brockley

A warm and relaxed environment awaits you. This stunning Victorian residence is set in a quiet tree-lined avenue and features one of London's most unusual sub-tropical gardens. Decorated in strong colours and exhibiting many original works of art, each room has an individual style. Only 10 minutes via train to the West End and close to a cultural panorama of historic locations.

B & B from £30pp, Rooms 1 double, 1 twin, both en-suite, No smoking, Children over 8, No dogs, Closed Xmas & New Year

---

3 BRIAR WALK Putney, London SW15 6UD
Tremayne & Phyllis Rennell *Tel:* 020 8785 2338   *Fax:* 020 8785 7338
Email: tremrod@aol.com   *Web:* www.briarwalkbnb.com

Map Ref: 7
Rail: Barnes

Edwardian house in quiet road in Putney. Cosy rooms with laid back homely atmosphere, en-suite twin room having tea/coffee making facilities. Apartment comprises twin beds, sitting area, en-suite bathroom, fully fitted kitchen. All rooms have television. We are a sporting family; Tremayne is a top-class sportsman who has played rugby at international level and is a keen exponent of golf, bridge, backgammon and chess.

B & B from £35pp, Rooms 1 single, 1 twin en-suite, apartment - twin en-suite, No smoking, Children welcome, Dogs by arrangement, Closed Xmas

---

562 CALEDONIAN ROAD Holloway, London N7 9SD
Betty & Frank Merchant
Tel: 020 7607 0930

Map Ref: 8
Tube: Islington

Small private house only four miles from Piccadilly with the underground nearby where you can go direct to Heathrow. St Pancras, Euston and Kings Cross Stations are within a short distance and it is only two minutes to A1. In a perfect position for many bus routes, including direct to Trafalgar Square. All tourist attractions can easily be reached. Unrestricted street parking.

B & B from £20pp, Rooms 1 single, 1 double, 1 family, No smoking, Children over 10, No dogs, Closed Xmas

---

CARLTON HOTEL 90 Belgrave Road, Victoria, London SW1V 2BJ
Tel: 020 7976 6634/932 0913   *Fax:* 020 7821 8020
Email: info@cityhotelcarlton.co.uk   *Web:* www.cityhotelcarlton.co.uk

Map Ref: 9
Tube: Victoria

A small, friendly bed and breakfast near Victoria station and within walking distance of famous landmarks such as Buckingham Palace, Trafalgar Square and Piccadilly Circus.

B & B from £45pp, Rooms 4 single, 5 double, 2 twin, 6 triple, most en-suite, Children welcome, No dogs, Open all year

---

CHALON HOUSE 8 Spring Terrace, Paradise Road, Richmond TW9 1LW
Mrs Ann Zaina *Tel:* 020 8332 1121   *Fax:* 020 8332 1131   *Mobile:* 07802 295437
Email: virgilioz@aol.com

Map Ref: 10
Tube: Richmond

Listed Georgian townhouse. Quality en-suite bedrooms with big comfortable beds and breakfast tailored to your taste. Five minutes' walk to Richmond station and seven miles to central London. Picnic in Kew Gardens or relax at one of the many traditional pubs along the Thames. ETC 5 Diamonds, Gold Award.

B & B £37.50-£40pp, Dinner available, Rooms 1 double, 2 twin, all en-suite, No smoking, No children or dogs, Closed mid Dec to mid Jan

CLIFTON HOTEL 7 St Chad Street, Kings Cross, London WC1H 8BD   *Map Ref:* 11
Ann Lawrence & Enzo Danelon   *Tube:* Kings Cross
Tel / Fax: 020 7837 4452

A small and friendly, family run B&B hotel. Five minutes walk from King's Cross and St Pancras Stations and 10 minutes' walk from Euston Station. It is only 15 minutes by underground to Oxford Street, the West End and the city. All rooms have a colour television.

B & B from £18pp, Rooms 2 single, 8 double (4 en suite), 1 family, Children welcome, No dogs, Closed Xmas & New Year

DEL A RUE HOUSE Ealing, London W5 3XP   *Map Ref:* 12
Anne & Richard   *Tel / Fax:* 020 8566 7976   *Tube:* South Ealing
Email: stay@londonhometohome.com   *Web:* www.londonhometohome.com

In a pretty 1930's Tudor style home, a spacious self-contained studio, comprising a king-size double bed, en-suite shower bathroom, a kitchenette and a living/dining area with television. A bed can be added for a third guest. Situated in a quiet backwater, 12 minutes walk from South Ealing underground station (Piccadilly line). Linen is provided, also breakfast foods. A pet cat.

B & B from £31pp, Rooms 1 double/triple, en-suite

FLORENCE STREET Florence Street, Islington, London N1 2FW   *Map Ref:* 8
Valerie Rossmore   *Tel / Fax:* 020 7359 5293   *Mobile:* 07890845198   *Tube:* Islington
Email: valerie.rossmore@onmail.co.uk

This friendly vibrant house is set in the heart of Islington with excellent theatres, fine restaurants, cafes and a famous antique market close by. The house is beautifully decorated throughout with an artistic and theatrical feel. There is a stunning conservatory with a Moroccan theme where guests can relax, with a pretty garden beyond. Occasional share of spacious 'shaker' bathroom.

B & B from £42.50pp, Rooms 1 single, 1 double, No smoking, Children over 14, No dogs, Open all year

24 FOX HILL Crystal Palace, London SE19 2XE   *Map Ref:* 13
Sue & Tim Haigh   *Tel:* 020 8768 0059   *Fax:* 020 8768 0063   *Rail:* Cryslal Palace
Email: suehaigh@foxhill-bandb.co.uk   *Web:* www.foxhill-bandb.co.uk

Built towards the end of the 19th century this large family house is situated in Crystal Palace, the highest spot in London. The garden has been redesigned to include a large pond to attract and house wildlife and a patio where meals can be taken. Sue used to work as a tourist guide and will help you get the most out of your time in London.

B & B from £40pp, Dinner from £20, Rooms 1 single, 1 double en-suite, 1 twin with pb, No smoking, Children over 5, No dogs, Open all year

GARTH HOTEL 69 Gower Street, London WC1E 6HU   *Map Ref:* 14
Tel: 020 7636 5761   *Fax:* 020 7637 4854   *Tube:* Euston Square
Email: garth.hotel@virgin.net   *Web:* www.garthhotel-london.com

A centrally situated family run bed and breakfast accommodation, recently refurbished. Convenient for shops, theatres and travel. Televisions, direct dial telephone and tea/coffee facilities in all bedrooms some of which are en-suite.

B & B from £32pp, C-Cards MC VS AE DC, Rooms 3 single, 4 double, 5 twin, 3 triple, 2 family, Children & dogs welcome, Open all year

79 GREENCROFT GARDENS London NW6 3LJ
Penelope Lyndon-Stanford   *Tel / Fax:* 020 7624 7849
Email: penny@lyndon-stanford.freeserve.co.uk

Map Ref: 15
Tube: Swiss Cottage

Situated in a quiet road this Edwardian semi-detached spacious family house, with some off-street parking, is twenty minutes walk from Lords Cricket Ground, seven minutes walk from underground stations - West End twenty minutes by tube. The drawing room has French windows on to a walled garden. An ideal base from which to explore London, yet also quiet and secluded.

B & B from £45pp, Dinner from £32, Rooms 2 double en-suite, 1 single private bathroom, No smoking, Children welcome, Dogs by arrangement, Open all year

---

5 HARTISMERE ROAD London SW6 7TS
Mrs Joan Lee
Tel / Fax: 020 7385 0337   *Mobile:* 07812 698058

Map Ref: 16
Tube: Fulham Broadway

Cosy Victorian house in quiet mews near busy Fulham Road, five minutes from Fulham Broadway underground and excellent bus service. Many local restaurants, comfortable rooms with television. Antique furniture but new beds, robes, mineral water in rooms. Continental breakfast with home made preserves. Sunny flower filled patio.

B & B from £35pp, Rooms 1 double, 1 single shared bathroom, No smoking, Children over 12, No dogs, Closed occasionally

---

THE HOUSE ON THE CRESCENT Ealing, London W5 2RN
Anita & David   *Tel / Fax:* 020 8566 7976
Email: stay@londonhometohome.com *Web:* www.londnhometohome.com

Map Ref: 12
Tube: Ealing Broadway

In their spacious Victorian home, Anita and David offer two attractively decorated rooms with twin or king-size beds, each with washbasin and sharing a guest bathroom. Television and hot drinks tray. Ealing Broadway Centre's shops, restaurants and underground station (District and Central lines) are a five minute walk. They have a pet cat and dog.

B & B from £26pp, Rooms 2 double/twin with guest bathroom, No smoking,

---

THE JAPANESE HOUSE Camden, London NW1 9XD
Sue & Rodger   *Tel / Fax:* 020 8566 7976
Email: stay@londonhometohome.com *Web:* www.londonhometohome.com

Map Ref: 17
Tube: Camden Town

Two immaculate rooms available in this modern home, designed by the architect owner. A suite of a double room with a low platform bed, a single room and a guest bathroom. The open-plan dining room overlooks a courtyard garden. The family pet is Peckham the macaw. Camden Market and Camden underground station are a ten minute walk.

B & B from £41pp, Rooms 1 single, 1 double, private bathroom, No smoking,

---

9 KENSINGTON PARK ROAD London W11 3BY
Bev & Ben Turnbull   *Tel:* 020 7229 0231   *Fax:* 020 7792 1266
Mobile: 07973 239203   *Email:* bevturnbull@hotmail.com

Map Ref: 18
Tube: Notting Hill Gate

Take in the village atmosphere of Portobello Market and Notting Hill. This mid-Victorian townhouse is situated ideally for Central London's theatres, shops and restaurants with the tube only two minutes away. The Turnbulls are flexible hosts and you can borrow the key to nearby Ladbroke Square Gardens. The elegant sitting room contrasts with the minimalist state of the art kitchen.

B & B from £45pp, Rooms 1 double, 1 twin, both en-suite, No smoking, Children over 12, No dogs, Open all year

LILY HOUSE Fulham, London SW6 7UH
Dulce & Manuel *Tel / Fax:* 020 8566 7976
Email: stay@londonhometohome.com *Web:* www.londonhometohome.com
Map Ref: 19
Tube: Fulham Broadway

Two double rooms with en-suite bathrooms are available in a charmingly updated Victorian home. Situated just a five-minute walk from Fulham Broadway, with its underground station (District line), designer shops and restaurants. Bus services to Harrods, Chelsea and Kensington. Manuel, who is a chef, serves an English or Portuguese breakfast.

B & B from £35pp, Rooms 2 double, en-suite, No smoking,

LINCOLN HOUSE HOTEL 33 Gloucester Place, London W1U 8HY
Joseph Sheriff *Tel:* 020 7486 7630 *Fax:* 020 7486 0166
Email: reservations@lincoln-house-hotel.co.uk *Web:* www.lincoln-house-hotel.co.uk
Map Ref: 5
Tube: Marble Arch

Built in the days of King George III, our bed and breakfast hotel offers Georgian charms and character. En-suite rooms with modern comforts and competitively priced. Located in the heart of London's West End, next to Oxford Street, the famous shopping attractions and close to theatreland. Ideal for business and leisure. Commended by many distinguished guide books.

B & B from £39pp, C-Cards MC VS AE DC, Rooms 6 single, 8 double, 4 twin, 3 triple, 2 family, all en-suite, Children welcome, No dogs, Open all year

---

29 LONSDALE ROAD London SW13 9JP
Jillie Morris
Tel: 020 8748 2111 *Fax:* 020 8846 8003
Map Ref: 20
Tube: Hammersmith

A beautiful double fronted spacious family run home, with off street parking. Close to the River Thames. Offering two double bedrooms with en-suite beathrooms, televison, coffee/tea making facilities. One single room. The breakfast room overlooks a lovely one-third acre mature walled garden. Easy access to Heathrow, 15 minutes central London. Nearest underground Hammersmith five minutes walk. Also self contained coach house available.

B & B from £35pp, Rooms 1 single, 2 double en-suite, No smoking, Children over 12, Dogs by arrangement, Closed Xmas & New Year

---

NELSON HOUSE Parsons Green, London SW6 3AH
Dolores & Bert *Tel / Fax:* 020 8566 7976
Email: stay@londonhometohome.com *Web:* www.londonhometohome.com
Map Ref: 21
Tube: Parsons Green

Comfortable accommodation for two or three guests in a spacious room with a queen-sized bed, plus a sofa bed, and en-suite shower and washbasin. Expect a friendly and informal atmosphere. Some of London's trendiest restaurants are nearby, at Chelsea Harbour. Parsons Green underground station (District line) is a ten minute walk. Pet dog and cat.

B & B from £32pp, Rooms 1 double/triple en-suite, No smoking,

---

NUMBER NINETY-SIX 96 Tachbrook Street, London SW1V 2NB
Mrs Helen Douglas *Tel:* 020 7932 0969 *Fax:* 020 7821 5454
Email: helen@numberninety-six.co.uk *Web:* www.numberninety-six.co.uk
Map Ref: 9
Tube: Pimlico

Number Ninety-Six offers a high standard of accommodation in the heart of Pimlico. There is a magnificent king size four poster bedroom with en-suite bathroom. Continental breakfast with newspaper, freshly squeezed orange juice and home made jams. Television, radio, laundry service and telephone are provided. Ideal for guests who want hotel facilities without paying their prices. Pimlico tube station is at the bottom of the street.

B & B from £55pp, Rooms 1 double with four poster en-suite, No smoking, Children over 8, No dogs, Open all year

8 PARTHENIA ROAD Fulham, London SW6 4BD   *Map Ref:* 22
Caroline Docker *Tel:* 020 7384 1165 *Fax:* 020 7371 8819   *Tube:* Parsons Green
Mobile: 07767 436487 *Email:* carolinedocker@angelwings.co.uk

The house is in a quiet conservation area close to restaurants and antique shops in the Kings Road. The bedroom is comfortable and well decorated, television and tea/coffee making facilities are provided. Breakfast is served in a dining room filled with antiques and overlooking the flower garden. Taxi, underground and bus services are all within minutes' walk.

B & B £40-£45pp (min 2 nights), Rooms 1 double/twin en-suite shower, No smoking, Children over 12, No dogs, Open all year

11 QUEEN ANNE'S GROVE Bedford Park, London W4 1HW   *Map Ref:* 23
Elisabeth Whittaker *Tel:* 020 8995 9255   *Tube:* Turnham Green
Email: elisabeth.whittaker@virgin.net

Queen Anne's Grove is a very quiet street in the heart of Bedford Park, Chiswick, the world's first garden suburb. Visitors have sole use of a small, fully equipped kitchen stocked with initial breakfast requirements including homemade bread and marmalade. Chiswick is situated in West London and is convenient for Heathrow Airport and motorways. Turnham Green tube is only a four minute walk away.

B & B from £30pp, Rooms 1 twin en-suite, Restricted smoking, Children over 16, Dogs by arrangement, Open all year

131 QUEEN'S ROAD Richmond TW10 6HF   *Map Ref:* 10
Ian & Margaret Andrew   *Tube:* Richmond
Tel / Fax: 020 8948 6893

This is the spare bedroom of a 1930's family house close to Richmond Park and with good public transport to Central London by bus or underground. There is a train to Waterloo and guests can also be met at Heathrow. Close to Hampton Court, Richmond Theatre and the Orange Tree Theatres. Free parking in the drive or across the road.

B & B from £30pp, Dinner from £30, Rooms 1 twin with private bathroom, No smoking, Children over 4, No dogs, Closed Xmas & New Year

67 RANNOCH ROAD Hammersmith, London W6 9SS   *Map Ref:* 24
Sohel & Anne Armanios   *Tube:* Hammersmith
Tel: 020 7385 4904 *Fax:* 020 7610 3235

A comfortable, central, quiet family home close to the river, pubs and restaurants. Excellent transport facilities with direct lines to all attractions, Heathrow, Gatwick, Eurostar and Stansted. An ideal base for sight seeing, courses, concerts and business events since it is near to Earls Court/Olympia Exhibitions and Albert Hall. Central heating, television and continental breakfast. Reduction for children. Single occupancy £34.

B & B £24pp, Rooms double/twin/triple, Restricted smoking, Children welcome, No dogs, Open all year

SKYLARK BED & BREAKFAST 297 Bath Road, Hounslow West TW3 3DB   *Map Ref:* 25
Mr Parmar   *Tube:* Hounslow West
Tel: 020 8577 8455 *Fax:* 020 8577 8741

Skylark is the perfect location for travellers, with Heathrow only three miles away. It is situated at the second underground station from the Airport and Central London is only 30 minutes away. All rooms are en-suite with televisions and tea/coffee facilities. There are many shops and restaurants nearby and ample parking

B & B from £30pp, Rooms 18 en-suite, Restricted smoking, Children welcome, No dogs, Open all year

Norfolk

The fact that the National Trust owns so much of Norfolk indicates just what an attractive county this is. Of course, the Norwich School of English Landscape Painters appreciated the wide panoramic skies, the wonderful cloud formations and the glorious seascapes many years before the Trust took an interest. However, one of the great advantages of this fine county is that there are still parts relatively unexplored. The north Norfolk coast has so much to offer the holiday visitor, the naturalist in particular, holding the largest saltmarshes in Europe. Blakeney Point, the three and a half mile long sand and shingle spit is the summer home for over eleven species of seabird, and winter home for large flocks of brent geese. Common seals also breed off the point of the spit.

To the south, King's Lynn, known as Bishop's Lynn until confiscated by Henry VIII, was a powerful and prosperous member of the Hanseatic League, the North European Merchants Group. The town is a delightful cluster of medieval lanes around the waterfront and the fifteenth century St George's Guildhall of 1420 is thought to be the oldest guildhall in England. Just outside King's Lynn is situated the country retreat of the Queen and the Duke of Edinburgh, Sandringham. It houses a grand collection of guns and armour brought back from the far east in 1876 plus a fascinating museum in the old coach and stable block.

This region is an ideal holiday centre with so much to see, including 2,000 acres of beach and four miles of tidal foreshore with sand dunes and saltmarshes, which include the site of the Roman fort of Branodunum. Visitors can also visit the National Nature Reserve on Scolt Head Island, an important breeding site for tern. Nobody could leave this northern coast without sampling the delights of Cromer and its crabs and Little Walsingham, a centre of pilgrimage for nine hundred years. Nearby is Wells-next-the-Sea which is not only famous for its whelks but is also home to Holkham Hall a majestic stately home in 3000 acre deer park with the interesting Bygones Museum.

Burnham Mill (EETB)

Great Yarmouth, with one of the most attractive waterfronts in England, protected from the rages of the North Sea behind its spit of land, has for over a thousand years been an important port but then during the nineteenth century was 'discovered' by the Victorians. Now five miles of promenade, golden beaches and a spectacular pleasure beach make Great Yarmouth one of the country's major seaside resorts. The visitor must not miss South Quay, a sixteenth century building with a nineteenth century facade, now a fascinating museum of domestic life.

The Norfolk Broads is a triangular area of the county which stretches from Stalham in the north to Norwich in the west and Lowestoft in the southeast, attracting thousands of visitors each year with its lakes and waterways offering glorious leisurely sailing. The Rivers Ant, Chet, Thurne, Bure, Yare and Waveney link the Broads and are jam-packed with pleasure craft. If you want to avoid the crowds there are still many streams and rivulets giving peace and tranquillity. Without doubt, to fully appreciate this wonderful region it must be enjoyed from a boat, and Wroxham and Hoveton are at the very heart of the Broads scene with boatyards and river craft of every description.

Norwich is the queen of this lovely county and the perfect base to explore the whole area. A university city with antique and speciality shops galore, also offering some fine buildings, Elm Hill, Colegate and Bridewell Alley. The city can boast thirty-three medieval churches, but without doubt the gem is the eleventh century cathedral. It displays some of the best Gothic architecture in Britain with its spire being second in height to Salisbury. Whatever you wish to learn about the lovely county of Norfolk is contained within the quite splendid museums of Norwich, including the Bridewell Museum in Bridewell Alley, which explains the trades, industries and daily life of Norwich over the last two hundred years. The Castle Museum is also not to be missed, with its celebrated paintings by the Norwich School, so aptly encapsulating the very spirit of the county.

PLACES TO VISIT

This is a small selection of interesting places to visit. Many more are listed in our annual guide to Museums, Galleries, Historic Houses & Sites (see page 448)

Blickling Hall
Blickling, Norwich
One of England's great Jacobean houses with fine collections of pictures, furniture and tapestries. The grounds include an extensive formal garden, a crescent shaped lake, and an orangery and temple built by the Ivorys

Holkham Hall
Wells-next-the-Sea, Norfolk
An eighteenth century Palladian-style mansion set in a great agricultural estate and a living treasure house of artistic and architectural history.

Norfolk Lavender
Heacham, King's Lynn
A family enterprise and the oldest established lavender farm in England. Lavender is distilled from the flowers and the oil made into a wide range of gifts.

Norwich Cathedral
The Close, Norwich
The Norman Cathedral was begun in 1096, made of Caen stone with a 315 foot high spire. The stone vaulting roof replaced the existing wooden one in the 14th century and tells the story of the Bible.

Sandringham House and Museum
Sandringham, King's Lynn
The country retreat of HM Queen Elizabeth was built in 1870 by the Prince and Princess of Wales and stands in 60 acres of grounds and lakes, with important royal collections on display.

Thursford Collection
Thursford, Fakenham
A splendid collection of old road engines and mechanical organs, all richly decorated and engraved with regular musical evenings.

Norfolk

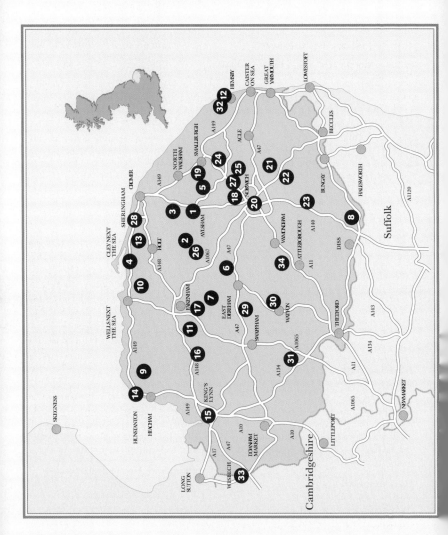

The Red Map References should be used to locate B & B properties on the pages that follow

228

THE OLD PUMP HOUSE Holman Road, Aylsham NR11 6BY
Tony & Lynda Richardson
Tel / Fax: 01263 733789

Map Ref: 1
A140

A lovely old Georgian farmhouse with a warm atmosphere and much character, near the edge of town, a step away from the church and market place. Attractive, nicely furnished, well equipped rooms, all with television, tea and coffee making facilities. Breakfast is served in the Red Room overlooking the garden. Parking. The Broads are nearby, also numerous stately homes and gardens and the coast.

B & B from £24pp, C-Cards MC VS, Rooms 1 single, 2 double, 2 twin, 1 family, most en-suite, No smoking, Well behaved children, No dogs, Closed Xmas & New Year

THE BUCKINGHAMSHIRE ARMS Blickling, Aylsham NR11 6AT
Robert Dawson-Smith
Tel: 01263 732133

Map Ref: 2
A140

e 70001240saraThe Buckinghamshire Arms, one of North Norfolk's most beautiful inns, at the gates to Blickling Hall. It boasts four poster accommodation, delicious food and real ales. During the warmer months you can also enjoy eating al fresco in our glorious garden. A perfect choice if you want to get away from it all.

B & B £25-£30pp, C-Cards MC VS, Dinner from £16.50, Rooms 3 double, 1 en-suite, Restricted smoking, Children over 6, Dogs by arrangement, Closed Xmas

THE SARACENS HEAD Wolterton, near Erpingham, Aylsham NR11 7LX
Robert Dawson-Smith *Tel:* 01263 768909 *Fax:* 01263 768993
Web: www.saracenshead-norfolk.co.uk

Map Ref: 3
A140

Escape the rat race at The Saracens Head where the emphasis is on food, local ales and a comprehensive wine list. Our rooms have all creature comforts including televisions. Near Blickling, Mannington, Wolterton Halls and the beautiful Norfolk countryside and coastline, but away from usual touristy routes too!

B & B from £30pp, Rooms 3 double, 1 twin, 1 family, all en-suite, Restricted smoking, Children welcome, Well behaved dogs, Open all year

OLD TOWN HALL HOUSE Coast Road, Cley next the Sea NR25 7RZ
Fraser & Louise Wibberley *Tel / Fax:* 01263 740284
Web: www.oldtownhallhouse.co.uk

Map Ref: 4
A149

Double fronted Victorian house situated in the heart of beautiful Cley village. Offers three good sized rooms with one double, two twin or super king size. All have private facilites, two being en-suite. Backing on to the salt marshes and River Glaven, and a short walk from Cley Beach makes this the perfect place for a relaxing break. Holiday cottage also available.

B & B from £25pp, Rooms 1 double, 2 twin/superking, all en-suite, No smoking, Children over 12, No dogs, Open all year

THE HEDGES Tunstead Road, Coltishall NR12 7AL
David and Verity *Tel:* 01603 738361 *Fax:* 01603 738983 *Mobile:* 0776 5826234
Email: thehedges@msn.com *Web:* www.hedgesbandb.co.uk

Map Ref: 5
A149

Hear evening owlsong and the dawn chorus at this friendly family run guesthouse. Set in one and a half acres of peaceful gardens surrounded by open countryside, yet convenient for local amenities. Ideal base for exploring the Norfolk Broads, Norwich and the coast. Families welcome. Spacious guest lounge with log fires, licensed, plenty of parking.

B & B from £22pp, C-Cards MC VS, Dinner available, Rooms 1 double, 2 twin, 2 family, all en-suite, No smoking, Children welcome, No dogs, Closed Xmas

---

BARTLES LODGE Church Street, Elsing, Dereham NR20 3EA
David & Annie Bartlett
Tel: 01362 637177

Map Ref: 6
A47, A1067

If you would like a peaceful stay in the heart of Norfolk's beautiful country yet close to some fine beaches, then Bartles Lodge will suit. It overlooks 12 acres of meadows and fishing lakes. En-suite rooms are decorated in country style. The Lodge is fully licensed, the local pub is nearby. Telephone us so that we can tell you about our lovely home.

B & B from £23pp, Rooms 4 double, 3 twin, Open all year

PEACOCK HOUSE Peacock Lane, Old Beetley, Dereham NR20 4DG
Peter & Jenny Bell *Tel:* 01362 860371 *Mobile:* 07979 013258
Email: PeakH@aol.com *Web:* www.smoothhound.co.uk/hotels.peacockh.html

Map Ref: 7
B1110
see Photo opposite

Beautiful old farmhouse, peacefully situated in lovely garden and grounds, offering excellent accommodation with all facilities, guests' lounge with open fires, beamed dining room, home cooking and a warm welcome. Centrally situated with Norwich, Sandringham, NT houses and the coast all within easy reach, and golf, fishing and swimming all close by. ETC 4 Diamonds, Gold Award.

B & B from £22.50pp, Rooms 1 twin, 1 double, 1 family, all en-suite, No smoking, Children welcome, Dogs by arrangement, Open all year

---

SHILLINGSTONE Church Road, Old Beetley, Dereham NR20 4AB
Jeanne Partridge *Tel:* 01362 861099 *Fax:* 01362 869153 *Mobile:* 07721 306190
Email: jeannepartridge@UKgateway.net *Web:* www.norfolkshillingstone.co.uk

Map Ref: 7
A1067, B1146

A modern country house in the quiet and peaceful village of Beetley. All accommodation is en-suite with colour televisions and hostess tray. Guests have their own lounge to relax in and full English breakfasts to enjoy. An ideal base for touring Norfolk coast, Broads, Norwich, Sandringham, Gressinghall Museum and National Trust properties. Fishing, golf, swimming and pubs nearby.

B & B from £20pp, C-Cards, Rooms 2 twin, 1 double, all en-suite, No smoking, Children & dogs welcome, Open all year

---

GROVE THORPE Grove Road, Brockdish, Diss IP21 4JR
Angela & John Morrish *Tel / Fax:* 01379 668305
Email: b-b@grovethorpe.freeserve.co.uk *Web:* www.grovethorpe.co.uk

Map Ref: 8
A143

A 17th century Grade II listed house in nine acres of secluded grounds, with private fishing lake, duck pond and horses. Beautifully renovated with inglenook fireplaces and beams, full of warmth and character. Generously equipped en-suite bedrooms with colour television. Dinner served by arrangement, some evenings. Local inns nearby. Central for Norwich, Norfolk Broads, Bressingham Gardens, Heritage coast, Diss town is five miles.

B & B £26-£35pp, Rooms 3 double/twin, all en-suite, 1 ground floor, No smoking, Children over 12, No dogs, Closed Xmas & New Year

---

NORTH FARMHOUSE Station Road, Docking PE31 8LS
Helen & Roger Roberts *Tel:* 01485 518493
Email: northfarmhouse@aol.com

Map Ref: 9
A149

This is an attractive typical Norfolk Flint and brick building standing in an acre, it is at least 300 years old. We are excellently situated for anyone wishing to visit the North West Norfolk area and Sandringham. We are fairly central for Kings Lynn, Wells, Fakenham and Hunstanton. The area is superb for walking, bird watching, cycling, golf and beaches.

B & B £18-£25pp, Rooms 1 double, 1 twin, both with pb, 1 family en-suite, No smoking, Children & dogs welcome, Closed Xmas & New Year

Peacock House, Old Beetley, near Dereham

STAFFORDSHIRE HOUSE Docking PE31 8LS   *Map Ref:* 9
Vaughan & Susan Williams **Tel:** 01485 518709 **Mobile:** 07774 609357   A149
Email: enquiries@staffordshirehouse **Web:** www.staffordshirehouse.com

Informal country style bed and breakfast, four miles from the glorious North Norfolk Coast and Burnham Market. The bedrooms are simply stylish, all have televisions and tea/coffee facilities. Guests can relax in the residents' Drawing Room around a roaring fire in winter, or enjoy the garden in summer, as well as spending a fortune in our stunning Interiors Shop!

B & B from £22.50pp, C-Cards MC VS, Rooms 1 single, 2 double, Restricted smoking, Children welcome, No dogs,

ABBOTT FARM Walsingham Road, Binham, Fakenham NR21 0AW   *Map Ref:* 10
Tel / Fax: 01328 830519 **Mobile:** 0780 884 7582   A149
Email: abbotfarm@btinternet.com

A modern brick built farm bungalow within a 126 acre arable farm. Its features include a loft conversion, an airy conservatory and rural views of north Norfolk including the historic Binham Priory.

B & B from £18pp, Rooms 1 double, 1 twin, both en-suite, No smoking, Children welcome, Open all year

MANOR FARM BARN Tatterford, Fakenham NR21 7AZ   *Map Ref:* 11
Michael & Jane Davidson-Houston   A148
Tel: 01485 528393

A beautiful barn conversion, with delightful views over farmland. A most delightful and peaceful setting. The barn is attractively decorated and very comfortable. Dinner will include home grown produce. Manor Farm Barn is located very near to the coast. Holkham, Wells and Walsingham are within short driving distance.

B & B from £22pp, Dinner from £14, Rooms 1 double/twin pb, 1 double/twin with private shower, Closed Xmas

TOWER COTTAGE Black Street, Winterton-on-Sea, Great Yarmouth NR29 4AP   *Map Ref:* 12
Alan & Muriel Webster   Black Street
Tel: 01493 394053

A charming flint cottage standing in a pretty village opposite the 12th century church. Attractive bedrooms are well equipped, one double en-suite with its own sitting room, is in a converted barn. Generous breakfasts served amongst the grapevines in the conservatory. A beautiful, sandy beach and village pub serving good food, a few minutes walk. Norfolk broads two miles, Norwich 19 miles.

B & B £19-£21pp, Rooms 1 twin own bathroom, 1 double shower/wc, 1 double en-suite, Restricted smoking, Children over 8, No dogs, Open all year

ROSEDALE FARM GUESTHOUSE Holt Road, Weybourne, Holt NR25 7ST   *Map Ref:* 13
Charles & Pauline Lacoste **Tel:** 01263 588778   A149 Coast Road
Email: rosedale.lacoste@tinyworld.co.uk

A traditional flint and brick farmhouse situated within walled gardens on the Norfolk coastline, equi-distant from Cley-next-the-Sea and Cromer. Sheringham Park and Kelling Heath are on the doorstep, the Shire Horse Centre, Felbrigg, Blickling Holkham Hall and Thursford Museum are nearby. Excellent cuisine awaits you, residents' sitting room and large comfortable bedrooms. Licensed. Cycle hire available. Heated pool. Self catering cottage available.

B & B from £27.50pp, Dinner from £16, Rooms 1 twin, 2 double, 1 family, all en-suite, Restricted smoking, Children welcome, Dogs small extra charge, Closed Xmas

FIELDSEND 26 Homefields Road, Hunstanton PE36 5HL
Sheila & John Tweedy Smith
Tel / Fax: 01485 532593

Map Ref: 14
A149

Stay at Fieldsend and enjoy the comfort of a large Edwardian house, which is close to the town centre and the sea with panoramic views over the Wash. Bedrooms are individually decorated by the owner who specialises in rag rolling and making curtains. One bedroom has a four poster. Delicious breakfasts are served by a Cordon Bleu cook. Parking in the grounds.

B & B from £22.50pp, Rooms 1 twin, 2 double, all en-suite /private, Children welcome, No dogs, Open all year

THE GABLES 28 Austin Street, Hunstanton PE36 6AW
Mrs Barbara Bamfield *Tel:* 01485 532514
Email: bbatthegables@aol.com *Web:* www.the gableshunstanton.co.uk

Map Ref: 14
A149

A lovely Edwardian house totally refurbished with glorious sea views, superb breakfasts, delicious evening meals and all en-suite facilities. Ideal location for all local amenities. Children very welcome. AA 4 Diamonds.

B & B £20-£25pp, C-Cards, Dinner from £12.99, Rooms 1 double, 1 twin, 3 family, all en-suite, No smoking, Children welcome, No dogs, Open all year

FAIRLIGHT LODGE 79 Goodwins Road, King's Lynn PE30 5PE
Steve & Joella Nash *Tel:* 01553 762234 *Fax:* 01553 770280
Email: joella@nash42.freeserve.co.uk *Web:* www.fairlightlodge.co.uk

Map Ref: 15
A10, A47

Lovely owner-run Victorian house with friendly atmosphere and well appointed rooms. Ground floor en-suite rooms available, comprehensive breakfast menu and private parking. Easy walking distance from town centre, bus and railway stations.

B & B from £18pp, Rooms 2 single, 2 double, 3 twin, most en-suite, No smoking, Children welcome, Closed Xmas

LOWER FARM Harpley, King's Lynn PE31 6TU
Amanda Case
Tel: 01485 520240 *Fax:* 01845 520240

Map Ref: 16
A148

A large, comfortable family home in delightful countryside, off the beaten track. There are family dogs and horses, and stabling for visitors' use. Spacious bedrooms offer some welcome extras. There are lovely garden views. The house is south east of Sandringham, one and a half miles from Pedders Way, 20 minutes from the coast. There is an excellent village pub. Parking available.

B & B £20-£25pp, Rooms 1 twin private bathroom, 2 double en-suite, No smoking, Children over 12, Dogs in stables, Open all year

MANOR HOUSE FARM Wellingham, King's Lynn PE32 2TH
Elisabeth Ellis
Tel: 01328 838227 *Fax:* 01328 838348

Map Ref: 17
A1065

In the heart of Norfolk surrounded by lovely gardens next to tiny 13th century church, stands this conservation, award winning Farm. Beautifully converted stables. Spacious sitting room, small kitchen. Charming and comfortable, antiques, rugs and cushions complete the restful ambience. Delicious breakfast, using home produce is served in the main house. 20 minutes coast, close to Sandringham, and many interesting places. Wheelchair friendly.

B & B from £25pp, Rooms 1 twin, 1 double, both en-suite, Restricted smoking, Children over 10, Dogs by arrangement, Open all year

FOREST EDGE Mill Road, Edingthorpe, North Walsham NR28 9SJ   *Map Ref:* 18
George & Carol Robertson-Burnett *Tel:* 01692 500350 *Fax:* 01692 406128   B1150
Mobile: 07941 927327 *Email:* grb4ghots@aol.com *Web:* www.ghlinns.co.uk

Delightful accommodation in a beautiful country setting. Perfect for exploring the Norfolk Coast and Broads, yet still within easy reach of town and city. Superior rooms and a friendly environment combined with eight acres of grounds make Forest Edge the ideal choice. Conference facilities, tennis, gymnasium, sauna and stabling also available by adding only small additional charges.

B & B from £22.50pp, Rooms 2 double, 1 twin, all en-suite, No smoking, Children over 11, No dogs, Closed Xmas & New Year

WHITE HOUSE FARM Knapton, North Walsham NR28 0RX   *Map Ref:* 18
Colin & Fiona Goodhead *Tel:* 01263 721344   A149
Email: goodhead@whfarm.swinternet.co.uk *Web:* www.geocities.com/whitehousefarmnorfolk

Relax in our Grade II listed farmhouse and enjoy the acre of tranquil gardens overlooking farmland. Comfortable accommodation with four-poster bed, en-suite bedrooms and log fires. Excellent food (evening meals available) with the emphasis on home-grown and local produce. Ample parking. AA 4 Diamonds.

B & B £20-£24pp, C-Cards MC VS, Rooms 1 double, 1 twin, 1 family, all en-suite, No smoking, Children welcome, No dogs, Open all year

HOLLY GROVE Worstead, North Walsham NR28 9RQ   *Map Ref:* 19
Michael & Bibby Horwood *Tel:* 01692 535546 *Mobile:* 07770 963055   A149
Email: michaelhorwood@freenetname.co.uk *Web:* Broadland.com/Hollygrove

This is a peaceful place, built in 1810, the house displays Georgian charm and modern comforts, there is a heated pool to enjoy. The comfortable bedrooms are furnished in country house style. Home made bread is offered at breakfast, Bibby is a cordon Bleu cook. The local pub serves suppers. The beauty of North Norfolk is on the doorstep of this lovely home.

B & B £23-£25pp, Rooms 1 double/family en-suite, 1 twin with private shower, No smoking, Children welcome, No dogs, Closed Xmas & New Year & Crufts

BEAUFORT LODGE 62 Earlham Road, Norwich NR2 3DF   *Map Ref:* 20
Tel: 01603 627928 *Fax:* 01603 440712   A140
Email: beaufort-lodge@faxvia.net *Web:* www.accomodata.co.uk/beaufort.htm

Julia and Chris Dobbins invite you to their spacious Victorian home, where you can be sure of a warm and friendly welcome. Completely refurbished and tastefully decorated to the highest standard. We offer en-suite facilities, colour television, hospitality trays, full central heating and a completely non-smoking environment to ensure your comfort. We have ample parking and are within easy walking distance of the city centre. Brochure on request.

B & B from £25pp, Rooms 2 single, 2 double, all en-suite, No smoking, No children or dogs, Closed New Year

OLD THORN BARN Wymondham Road, Hethel, Norwich NR14 8EU   *Map Ref:* 20
Mrs Gina Pickwell *Tel:* 01953 607785 *Fax:* 08452 814216 *Mobile:* 07754 052420   A11
Email: gina@oldthornbarn.co.uk *Web:* www.oldthornbarn.co.uk

The barn is surrounded by beautiful Norfolk countryside and is central to many places of interest. The bedrooms are cosily furnished and are all en-suite. Breakfast is served in the Longbarn where a woodburner in the dining area and lounge area creates a relaxed atmosphere. ETC 4 Diamonds, Silver Award and Top Spot Gold Award.

B & B from £24pp, C-Cards MC VS, Rooms 5 single, 3 double, 2 twin, all en-suite, No smoking, Children welcome, No dogs, Open all year

THE WHITE HOUSE Bramerton, Norwich NR14 7DW
Mrs Elizabeth Perowne
Tel: 01508 538673

Map Ref: 21
A146

Self contained flat within charming 17th century Broadland village house, 10 minutes from Norwich and 15 minutes from the University. There is a large comfortable sitting room overlooking the garden where guests are most welcome to play croquet, table tennis or simply relax in the gazebo. The rooms are available for bed and breakfast or self catering.

B & B from £25pp, Dinner from £12, Rooms 1 double en-suite, 2 twin with private bathrooms, No smoking, Children welcome, Dogs by arrangement, Open all year

---

THE OLD RECTORY Hall Road, Framingham Earl, Norwich NR14 7SB
Bruce & Sue Wellings *Tel:* 01508 493590 *Fax:* 01508 495110
Email: brucewellings@drivedevice.freeserve.co.uk

Map Ref: 22
A146

A beautifully restored and extended 17th century house set in two acres of garden adjacent to the Norman church of St. Andrew. Convenient for Broads and Norfolk / Suffolk coasts and situated four and a half miles south of the historic city of Norwich. A visitor's lounge is provided with a woodburner and a wealth of beams. Ample parking. Local pubs/restaurants serve excellent food.

B & B from £22pp, Rooms 1 twin, 1 double, No smoking, Children welcome, No dogs, Closed Xmas & New Year

---

FOXHOLE FARM Foxhole, Saxlingham Thorpe, Norwich NR15 1UG
John & Pauline Spear *Tel / Fax:* 01508 499226
Email: foxholefarm@hotmail.com

Map Ref: 23
A140

A friendly welcome, comfortable bedrooms with en-suite facilities, plus generous English breakfasts, ensure a thoroughly enjoyable stay at this spacious farmhouse. We are eight miles south of Norwich, just off the A140, and well situated for restaurants and pubs serving food. ETC AA 4 Diamonds.

B & B £19-£25pp, Rooms 1 double, 1 twin, both en-suite, No smoking, Children over 14, No dogs, Closed Xmas & New Year

---

GREENACRES FARMHOUSE Woodgreen, Long Stratton, Norwich NR15 2RR
Joanna Douglas *Tel / Fax:* 01508 530261
Email: greenacresfarm@tinyworld.co.uk

Map Ref: 23
A140

17th century farmhouse on a common, wildlife abounds, ten miles from Norwich. Well equipped bedrooms, tastefully furnished to compliment the oak beams and antiques. There is a relaxing beamed sitting room and a sunny dining room to enjoy. Snooker table and all weather tennis court. Jo is trained in therapeutic massage, aromatherapy and reflexology, she gladly offers this service to guests.

B & B from £22.50pp, Rooms 1 twin, 2 double, all private /en-suite, No smoking, No children or dogs, Open all year

---

REGENCY GUEST HOUSE The Street, Neatishead, Norwich NR12 8AD
Alan & Sue Wrigley *Tel / Fax:* 01692 630233
Email: wrigleyregency@talk21.com *Web:* www.norfolkbroads.com/regency

Map Ref: 24
A1151

A 17th century property in picturesque Broads village. Laura Ashley decorated rooms with TV and tea/coffee facilities. Well renowned name for generous English breakfasts served in oak panelled breakfast room. Accent on personal service. Ideal for rambles, cycling, bird watching and boating. Six miles to the coast and 10 miles to Norwich. Suppers available or two lovely eating places within walking distance.

B & B from £22pp, Rooms 2 double, 2 twin, 1 family, some en-suite, Restricted smoking, Children & dogs welcome, Open all year

CARR HOUSE Low Road, Strumpshaw, Norwich NR13 4HT   *Map Ref:* 25
Margot Dunham   *Tel:* 01603 713041   *Mobile:* 07759 349641   A47
Email: margotdunham@supanet.com

Carr House is situated overlooking Strumpshaw Fen RSPB Reserve with a large garden and fishing lake. All rooms in our peaceful home are comfortably furnished with hospitality trays and televisions. Locally there is boating, horse riding, fishing and birdwatching. We also have good reasonable pub food within walking distance and a restaurant. Norwich is only seven miles away. Good public transport and Park/Ride (3 miles).

B & B £40-£50pp, Rooms 2 double, 1 twin, all en-suite, No smoking, Children over 5, Dogs kept in kennel, Open all year

---

WESTWOOD BARN Crabgate Lane South, Wood Dalling, Norwich NR11 6SW   *Map Ref:* 26
Mrs Sentinella   B1149
Tel: 01263 584108

Westwood Barn offers outstanding en-suite accommodation on ground floor level. Magnificent rooms, original beams, beautiful four poster room. An idyllic rural location for discovering the charms of north Norfolk. The picturesque village of Heydon which has been the location of many films, is two miles away. National Trust properties, the historic city of Norwich, the coast and Broads within a twelve mile radius.

B & B from £23pp, Rooms 1 twin, 2 double, all en-suite, 1 four poster, Children welcome, No dogs, Open all year

---

WROXHAM PARK LODGE GUEST HOUSE 142 Norwich Road, Wroxham, Norwich NR12 8SA
    Map Ref: 27
Tel: 01603 782991   A11

A warm welcome is always given on arrival at this comfortable Victorian house where all the rooms are en-suite. Garden and private parking. Situated in Broads capital of Wroxham and central for touring all Broads amenities. North Norfolk Coast, Norwich and Bure Valley Railway are nearby.

B & B from £20pp, Rooms 2 double, 1 twin, all en-suite, Children welcome, Open all year

---

FAIRLAWNS 26 Hooks Hill Road, Sheringham NR26 8NL   *Map Ref:* 28
Mrs Barbara Rowe   A149
Tel: 01263 824717   *Fax:* 01263 824115

Lovely Victorian house set in tranquil landscaped gardens, half a mile from sea, golf course and town centre. Offers five double bedrooms, each with en-suite bathrooms, colour televisions and beverage trays. Breakfasts are substantial and an imaginative dinner menu is available as well as bar service.

B & B £25-£37pp, Dinner from £12.50, Rooms 2 double, 2 twin, 1 family, all en-suite, Restricted smoking, Children welcome, No dogs, Closed Xmas & New Year

---

WATERSIDE COTTAGE Ivy Todd, Necton, Swaffham PE37 8JB   *Map Ref:* 29
Mrs Debbie Chapman   A47, A1065
Tel: 01760 441460   *Fax:* 01760 441637

Eighteenth century stream-side cottage in rural hamlet, yet only one and a half miles from A47. Beamed double bedroom and bathroom with views over open fields, reached by private staircase. Television and hospitality tray. Afternoon teas and evening meals are available by arrangement. Quiet lanes ideal for walking and cycling. Norwich, Sandringham, coast and several National Trust properties easily reached by car.

B & B from £20pp, Dinner from £12.50, Rooms 1 double, en-suite, No smoking, Dogs by arrangement, Closed Xmas & New Year

WHITE HALL Carbrooke, near Watton, Thetford IP25 6SG
Mrs S Carr *Tel:* 01953 885950 *Fax:* 01953 884420
Email: shirleycarr@whitehall.uk.net

Map Ref: 30
B1108

Elegant listed Georgian house standing in delightful grounds with a large pond, surrounded by fields. Spacious, centrally heated, log fires, early morning tea and evening drinks ensure an enjoyable stay. Situated on the edge of Carbrooke village and in the centre of the interesting area of Breckland, we are ideally situated for the attractions in Norfolk and north Suffolk. Good local eating places.

B & B from £21pp, Rooms 1 double en-suite, 1 twin, 1 double, Restricted smoking, Children welcome, Dogs by arrangement, Open all year

OLD BOTTLE HOUSE Cranwich, Mundford, Thetford IP26 5JL
Marion Ford
Tel: 01842 878012

Map Ref: 31
A134

A warm welcome is assured at this 275 year old former coaching inn, which has a lovely garden and rural views, it is wonderfully positioned on the edge of Thetford Forest. Spacious, well equipped bedrooms. Delicious meals are served in the dining room which has an inglenook fireplace. There is a pleasant seating area on a galleried landing, guests may relax here.

B & B from £22.50pp, Dinner from £14, Rooms 2 twin, 1 double/family, No smoking, Children over 5, No dogs, Closed Xmas & New Year

WHITE HOUSE FARM The Street, West Somerton NR29 4EA
George & Prue Dobinson *Tel:* 01493 393991
Email: WhiteHouseFarm@connectfree.co.uk

Map Ref: 32
A149

A welcoming, old farmhouse providing good food, space and quiet for a relaxing hoiday with comfortable bedrooms, guest sitting-room, conservatory and sunny walled gardens. Near the Broads', a wonderful beach and nature reserves. One guest said 'Peaceful, warm and welcoming'.

B & B from £20pp, Rooms 2 en-suite double, 1 twin, No smoking, Children welcome, No dogs, Closed Xmas & New Year

SOMERVILLE HOUSE Church Road, Terrington St John, Wisbech PE14 7RY
Colin & Mibette Sussams *Tel / Fax:* 01945 880952
Email: somervillemc@hotmail.com *Web:* www.somervillehouse.co.uk

Map Ref: 33
A47, A17

Country house dating back 300 years, set in two acres of mature garden with many trees and a crinkle crankle wall. Spacious en-suite bedrooms with tea/coffee making facilities, comfortable lounges and fine dining restaurant with residential licence. Ideal location for exploring the Fens and North Norfolk. ETC 4 Diamonds.

B & B from £25pp, C-Cards MC VS, Dinner from £13.50, Rooms 1 single, 1 double, 1 twin, 2 en-suite, Restricted smoking, Children welcome, No dogs, Closed Xmas

HOME FARM Morley, Wymondham NR18 9SU
Mrs M Morter
Tel / Fax: 01953 602581

Map Ref: 34
A11

A warm welcome awaits you in our comfortable accommodation set in four acres in a quiet location with a secluded garden. Half a mile from A11 with Attleborough and Wymondham both three miles away. Norwich is only 20 minutes and Norfolk Broads, 45 minutes. Televisions, tea/coffee facilities and central heating in all rooms. Snetterton race track 15 minutes.

B & B from £18pp, Rooms 2 double, 1 twin, No smoking, Children over 5, No dogs, Closed Xmas

Northumbria

The most northerly of the English counties can indeed justifiably claim to have everything that the holiday maker could desire, and certainly no brief visit could possibly give anything but the smallest indication of what is on offer. The coastline is magnificent with its mile upon mile of wide sandy beaches, links and dunes, nature reserves, picturesque rocky offshore islands and sturdy squat spectacular castles. Bamburgh, once the Saxon capital of the region, has a superb castle, built in the twelfth century. The castle looks out over the Farne Islands, twenty-eight dolerite rock islands, famous as a bird sanctuary and the breeding ground for grey seal. The lighthouse on Longstone was manned by Grace Darling and her father. Grace Darling was a local heroine who rowed out to rescue the crew of a ship which had struck the rocks and the Grace Darling Museum at Bamburgh records her life and heroism, her tomb is in the churchyard. Then to the north, Lindisfarne Castle stands on Holy Island, accessible by a narrow causeway. The castle, built in 1550, dominates the little island where St Cuthbert lived and died. Nearby is Newton Pool, a fresh water lake behind the dunes, a nature reserve, home to breeding birds including blackheaded gulls, mute swans and reed bunting. Whitley Bay and Tynmouth boast award winning beaches while Saltburn-by-the-Sea, a little Victorian seaside resort has a fascinating Smugglers Heritage Centre. The Lifeboat Museum at Redcar, another seaside resort, contains the 'Zetland', the world's oldest surviving lifeboat.

The visitor to this region could be excused for never leaving the coast, such is the wealth of interest, but this would be a mistake as inland there are just as many delights. The City of Durham is an attraction not to be resisted, the cradle of Christianity in England and the historic capital of the northeast. The history and tradition of the region is centred on the magnificent Norman cathedral and its adjacent castle. The cathedral contains the shrine of St Cuthbert and that of the Venerable Bede. However, even though the castle is now used as university accommodation, visitors are still invited to explore it, developed from a Nortte and bailey.

Because of its remoteness the Northumberland National Park is one of the least visited parks. The vast Kielder Forest spreads over a large section of western Northumberland, the home of red squirrels and deer. Kielder Water is the largest man-made reservoir in

Hadrian's Wall, Northumberland (NTB)

Europe and offers water sports and activities of every description. The southern part of the national park holds the largest Roman monument in Great Britain, Hadrian's Wall. Stretching from Newcastle on the northeast coast to the Solway Firth on the coast of Cumbria, this great fortification at the northern most point of the Roman empire was planned in 122AD by the Roman Emperor Hadrian to separate the Britons from the Picts. To walk the wall is a wonderful experience, and the views from the Great Whin Sill, the hard rock base of so much of the wall, are spectacular. To obtain a potted history of the whole of this remarkable region the holiday visitor must call at the North of England Open Air Museum at Beamish. Here the award-winning museum tells the social history of the North of England. A northern industrial village of the early 1900s is evocatively re-created, complete with colliers' cottages and even trams.

There is so much impressive scenery and architecture to see that it is all too easy to miss the smaller gems, such as the lovely gardens of Howick Hall built in 1782, the home of the second Earl Grey after whom the tea was named and the Cragside House and gardens near Morpeth, the first house in the world to be lit by hydro-electric power. Gibside, near Burnopfield, has a beautiful park designed by Capability Brown and the Palladian-style chapel within the grounds was the Bowes family mausoleum. No visitor should leave this region without visiting the Bowes Museum by the small market town of Barnard Castle on the banks of the River Tees. The museum contains a fine collection of furniture, ceramics and paintings and the famous mechanical Silver Swan by John Cox.

PLACES TO VISIT

This is a small selection of interesting places to visit. Many more are listed in our annual guide to Museums, Galleries, Historic Houses & Sites (see page 448)

Alnwick Castle
Alnwick, Northumberland
The seat of Duke of Northumberland whose family, the Percys, have lived here since 1309. A treasure trove of fine furniture and paintings.

Auckland Castle
Bishop Auckland, County Durham
Home of the Bishops of Durham for over 800 years, set in delightful rural countryside. Attractions are the Magnificent Chapel, Throne Room and Long Dining Room.

Captain Cook Birthplace Museum
Middlesbrough
Near the site of the cottage where Captain James Cook was born in 1728. Displays depict his life from his time in Great Ayton to his employment at Staines and Whitby.

Durham Cathedral
Durham
The Cathedral building, dating back 900 years, is widely regarded as one of the most complete and perfect examples of Romanesque architecture in existence. It is the final resting place of St Cuthbert, the greatest of the early English saints.

North of England Open Air Museum
Beamish, County Durham
Living, working experience of life as it was in the Great North in the early 1800s and 1900s, set in 300 acres of beautiful countryside and winner of British Museum of the Year.

Northumbria

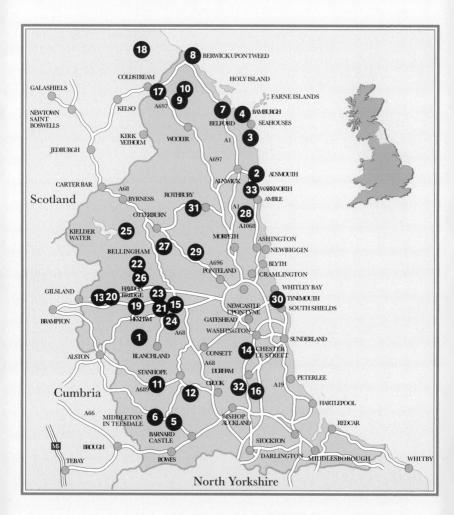

GALASHIELS

COLDSTREAM

BERWICK UPON TWEED

HOLY ISLAND

FARNE ISLANDS

NEWTOWN
SAINT
BOSWELLS

KELSO

A697

BAMBURGH

BELFORD

SEAHOUSES

KIRK
YETHOLM

WOOLER

A1

JEDBURGH

A697

CARTER BAR

A68

ALNWICK

ALNMOUTH

Scotland

BYRNESS

ROTHBURY

WARKWORTH

AMBLE

OTTERBURN

A1

A1068

KIELDER
WATER

MORPETH

ASHINGTON

BELLINGHAM

NEWBIGGIN

A696

BLYTH

PONTELAND

CRAMLINGTON

GILSLAND

HAYDON
BRIDGE

WHITLEY BAY

TYNEMOUTH

SOUTH SHIELDS

BRAMPTON

HEXHAM

NEWCASTLE
UPON TYNE

GATESHEAD

WASHINGTON

A68

SUNDERLAND

CONSETT

CHESTER
LE STREET

ALSTON

BLANCHLAND

A68

DURHAM

PETERLEE

STANHOPE

CROOK

A19

Cumbria

A689

HARTLEPOOL

A66

MIDDLETON
IN TEESDALE

BISHOP
AUCKLAND

M6

BROUGH

BARNARD
CASTLE

STOCKTON

REDCAR

TEBAY

BOWES

DARLINGTON

MIDDLESBOROUGH

WHITBY

North Yorkshire

The Red Map References should be used to locate B & B properties on the pages that follow

THORNLEY HOUSE Allendale NE47 9NH   *Map Ref:* 1
E Finn   *Tel:* 01434 683255   B6303
Email: e.finn@ukonline.co.uk *Web:* www.ukonline.co.uk/e.finn

Beautiful country house in spacious grounds surrounded by fields and woodland. One mile from Allendale. Relaxed comfortable accommodation, well equipped, roomy light bedrooms. Two lounges, one with television, one with a Steinway grand piano, books, games, maps, good home baking. Bring your own wine. Marvellous, sometimes guided walks, and bird watching. Hadrian's Wall, Kielder Forest nearby. Vegetarian meals and packed lunches.

B & B from £20.50pp, Dinner from £13, Rooms 1 twin, 2 double, all en-suite, No smoking, Children over 10, Dogs by arrangement, Open all year

---

MARINE HOUSE PRIVATE HOTEL Alnmouth NE66 2RW   *Map Ref:* 2
John & Christina Tanney   *Tel:* 01665 830349   A1
Email: tanney@marinehouse.freeserve.co.uk

Relax in the friendly atmosphere of this 200 year old charming listed building on the edge of the village golf links, enjoying wondeful sea views. Individually appointed en-suite bedrooms are well equipped. Four course gourmet candlelit dinners by our resident chef. Cocktail bar, spacious seafront lounge. Visit the Farne Islands or Alnwick Gardens. Discover the Roman Wall. Impressive border fortresses, ruins and stately homes.

B & B from £28pp, Dinner from £14, Rooms 6 double, 2 twin, 2 family all en-suite, Restricted smoking, Children over 7, Dogs welcome, Open all year

---

NORTH CHARLTON FARM Chathill, Alnwick NE67 5HP   *Map Ref:* 3
Mrs Sylvia Armstrong   *Tel:* 01665 579443   *Fax:* 01665 579407   A1
Email: ncharlton@agric.snowgoose

Come and visit us and have tea in our homely, yet luxurious and spacious, farmhouse. Furnished to a very high standard with tea/coffee facilities and televisions in our large bedrooms with fantastic views to the sea. We offer home cooking and a warm welcome when you arrive.

B & B from £30pp, Rooms 2 double en-suite, 1 twin with private bathroom, Restricted smoking, Children over 10, No dogs, Closed Xmas & New Year

---

BROOME 22 Ingram Road, Bamburgh NE69 7BT   *Map Ref:* 4
Mary Dixon   *Tel:* 01668 214287   *Mobile:* 07971 248230   B6341 from A1
Email: MDixon4394@aol.com

Broome is situated in a quiet location overlooking open fields. Accommodation is offered in a self contained wing, where visitors can enjoy the benefit of their own sitting area, and sun patio for relaxing days. Breakfast includes delicious locally cured bacon, kippers and 'Bamburgh Bangers' (sausages). The area is one of outstanding natural beauty, with long stretches of beaches overlooked by castles.

B & B £25-£27.50pp, Dinner from £18.50, Rooms 1 double, 1 twin, No smoking, Children over 12, No dogs, Closed Xmas

---

CLOUD HIGH Eggleston, Barnard Castle DL12 0AU   *Map Ref:* 5
Frank & Eileen Bell   *Tel / Fax:* 01833 650644   B6278
Email: cloudhigh@btinternet.com *Web:* www.cloudhigh-teesdale.co.uk

Idyllically situated at 1000ft in peaceful countryside. Cloud High commands magnificent unrivalled views of Teesdale and surrounding dales. Here the emphasis is on comfort, quality and relaxation with every amenity in the lovely en-suite bedrooms and private lounge. Breakfasts are our speciality with a choice of traditional or interesting alternatives.

B & B £23-£26pp, Rooms 1 twin, 2 double, all en-suite, No smoking, Children over 12, No dogs, Closed Xmas & New Year

BRUNSWICK HOUSE 55 Market Place, Middleton-in-Teesdale, Barnard Castle DL12 0QH   *Map Ref:* 6
Andrew and Sheila Milnes   *Tel:* 01833 640393   B6277
Email: enquiries@brunswickhouse.net   *Web:* www.brunswickhouse.net

Charming stone built house dating from 1760, with beamed ceilings and original fireplaces, thoughtfully combined with all modern comforts. The perfect centre from which to enjoy the delights of Teesdale's unspoilt countryside, quiet roads and flower-filled meadows. Outstanding home cooking using wherever possible only fresh and local produce.

B & B £20-£24pp, C-Cards MC VS AE, Dinner from £17, Rooms 3 double, 2 twin, all en-suite, No smoking, Children welcome, No dogs, Closed Xmas

---

MARKET CROSS GUEST HOUSE 1 Church Street, Belford NE70 7LS   *Map Ref:* 7
Jill & John Hodge   *Tel:* 01668 213013   A1
Email: details@marketcross.net   *Web:* www.marketcross.net

This 200 year old guesthouse offers quality en-suite accommodation and hospitality that is renowned. Situated in the centre of Belford village, close to friendly pubs and restaurants. Market Cross provides the perfect base to explore the castles and coastline of North Northumberland. Our stylishly decorated rooms include all expected comforts and many extras. Our breakfast menu is second to none.

B & B £22.50-£30pp, C-Cards MC VS, Rooms 2 double, 2 twin, 1 family, all en-suite, No smoking, Children welcome, Dogs by arrangement, Closed Xmas & New Year

---

OAKWOOD HOUSE 3 Cragside Avenue, Belford NE70 7NA   *Map Ref:* 7
Mrs Maureen Allan   *Tel:* 01668 213303   *Mobile:* 07759856746   A1
Email: maureenatoakwood@talk21.com

Stone floors, hand embroidered pictures and little treasures from around the world, are all to be found in our country style home. Set in a quiet woodland area of the village with panoramic views, we are a small friendly establishment noted for our high standards and good home cooking. A tourist board gold award winning property.

B & B £21-£23pp, Rooms 1 double, 1 twin, both en-suite, No smoking, No children or dogs, Closed Nov to Feb

---

DERVAIG GUEST HOUSE 1 North Road, Berwick-upon-Tweed TD15 1PW   *Map Ref:* 8
Anne Tait   *Tel:* 01289 307378   *Fax:* 01289 332321   *Mobile:* 07813 632208   A1
Email: dervaig@talk21.com   *Web:* www.dervaig-guesthouse.co.uk

Dervaig Guest House is a superb Victorian house set in beautiful gardens in a quiet part of town, only four minutes walk from the centre. Guest rooms are tastefully furnished to give that special touch and all have televisions and tea/coffee facilities. Guests are welcome to enjoy the lovely walled garden and fish pond. Close to all local attractions.

B & B £20-£27pp, C-Cards MC VS DC, Rooms 3 double, 3 twin, 2 family, all en-suite, Restricted smoking, Children welcome, Dogs by arrangement, Open all year

---

OLD VICARAGE 24 Church Road, Tweedmouth, Berwick-upon-Tweed TD15 2AN   *Map Ref:* 8
Tina Richardson   *Tel:* 01289 306909   *Fax:* 01289 309052   A1
Email: stay@oldvicarageberwick.co.uk   *Web:* www.oldvicarageberwick.co.uk

Old Vicarage is set in a peaceful location only 10 minutes' walk from the town centre and beautiful beaches. Spacious bedrooms are tastefully decorated with many thoughtful extras. An outstanding breakfast served in our elegant dining room will ensure a perfect start to your day. We look forward to welcoming you. ETC AA 4 Diamonds.

B & B from £18pp, Rooms 1 single, 4 double, 1 twin, 1 triple, most en-suite, Restricted smoking, Children welcome, No dogs, Closed Xmas & New Year

THE OLD POST OFFICE 2 Old Post Office Cottages, Ford, Berwick-upon-Tweed TD15 2QA
Joan Wait *Tel:* 01890 820286 *Mobile:* 07803819452　　　　*Map Ref:* 9
Email: jwait309139627@aol.com　　　　　　　　　　　　　　　　A697

Once a Victorian farmhouse and former post office, now a family run bed and breakfast. Joan and Eddie offer you spacious, comfortable accommodation in the tranquil and historic village of Ford where a warm welcome always awaits you. Within easy reach of Holy Island and Scottish Borders. Local riding and fishing, golf courses within 12 miles. Sorry no credit cards.

B & B £20-£22pp, Rooms 1 double, 1 twin, 1 triple, all en-suite, Children welcome, Dogs by arrangement, Closed Xmas & New Year

HIGH STEADS Lowick, Berwick-Upon-Tweed TD15 2QE　　　　　*Map Ref:* 10
Mr & Mrs S Newington-Bridges *Tel / Fax:* 01289 388689 *Mobile:* 07850 108305　　A1
Email: Highstead@AOL.Com

High Steads is an 18th century Grade II listed farmhouse with magnificent views of the Cheviots. We have a double en-suite and twin en-suite with guests' drawing room providing television, video and extensive video library. AA 4 Diamonds. Also the AA have awarded us their coveted Eggcup Award for 'The Very Best Breakfast', North Northumberland Local Food Awards 'Bronze Award 2001'.

B & B £22.50-£25pp, Rooms 1 double, 1 twin, both en-suite, Restricted smoking, Children over 8, Dogs only in Summer house, Open all year

THE OLD MANSE 5 Cheviot View, Lowick, Berwick-upon-Tweed TD15 2TY　　*Map Ref:* 10
Mrs Barbara Huddart *Tel:* 01289 388264 *Mobile:* 07980 850394　　　　A1
Email: glenc99@aol.com

This Georgian Grade II church manse was built in 1823 and is beautifully furnished with antiques retaining much of its original charm. Barbara Huddart, born locally, has excellent knowledge of the region and will assist you when planning your day's itinerary, and if you ask, you may be given a rendition of the Northumbrian Small Pipes.

B & B £25-£27.50pp, Rooms 1 double, 1 twin, both en-suite, No smoking, Children welcome, No dogs, Closed Xmas & New Year

LOW CORNRIGGS Low Cornriggs Farm, Cowshill, Bishop Auckland DL13 1AQ　　*Map Ref:* 11
Mrs Janet Elliott *Tel:* 01388 537600 *Fax:* 01388 537777　　　　A689
Email: enquiries@lowcornriggsfarm.fsnet.co.uk *Web:* www.britnett.com/lowcornriggsfarm

In the heart of the North Pennines, Low Cornriggs is something special with wonderful views. Two hundred year old farmhouse renovated to a high standard. Breakfast served in the conservatory, evening meals in licensed dining room. All bedrooms are en-suite with tea trays. Warm and cosy. Excellent location, on-site riding school that offers treks and lessons. A warm welcome awaits.

B & B £22-£23pp, Dinner from £13, Rooms 1 double, 1 twin, 1 family, all en-suite, No smoking, Children welcome, Small well behaved dogs, Open all year

LANDS FARM Westgate-in-Weardale, Bishop Auckland DL13 1SN　　*Map Ref:* 11
Mrs B Reed　　　　　　　　　　　　　　　　　　　　　　　A689
Tel / Fax: 01388 517210 *Mobile:* 07803 054819

An old stone-built farmhouse within walking distance of Westgate village. Relax in the conservatory over looking the large garden and listen to the gentle trickle of Swinhope burn. Accommodation is in centrally heated rooms with luxury en-suite facilities, television and tea/coffee making. English or continental breakfast is served. Ideal base for walkers and for touring Durham, Hadrian's Wall and Beamish Museum.

B & B from £23pp, Rooms 1 double, 1 family, both en-suite, Children welcome, No dogs, Open all year

COVES HOUSE FARM Wolsingham, Bishop Auckland DL13 3BG   *Map Ref:* 12
Anthony & Marguerite Todd   A689
Tel: 01388 527375   *Fax:* 01388 526157

Grade II* early seventeenth century higgledy piggledy farmhouse lovingly restored by present owners. Secluded situation amongst 400 acres of dramatic hill farmland. Extremely comfortable twin bedded room with private bathroom and sitting room in own wing. Home cooked food using local produce. 12 miles from Durham and its magnificent cathedral.

B & B from £32pp, Dinner from £24, Rooms 1 twin with private bathroom, Restricted smoking, Children over 12, Dogs by arrangement, Closed occasionally

---

HOLMHEAD GUEST HOUSE on Thirlwall Castle Farm, Hadrians Wall, Greenhead, Brampton CA8 7HY
Brian & Pauline Staff   *Tel / Fax:* 016977 47402   *Map Ref:* 13
Email: Holmhead@hadrianswall.freeserve.co.uk   *Web:* www.bandbhadrianswall.com   M6 J43, A69, B6318

Lovely farmhouse built with Hadrian's wall stones, near the most spectacular remains. Quality cooking using fresh produce, guests dine at candlelit table in dinner party style. Speciality list of organically produced wines featuring world award winners. Cocktail bar, television, books, maps and guides in the lounge. Your host is a former Northumbria Tour Guide and an expert on Hadrian's Wall.

B & B from £28pp, C-Cards MC VS, Dinner from £19.50, Rooms 2 twin, 1 double, 1 family, all en-suite, No smoking, Children welcome, No dogs, Closed Xmas & New Year

---

WALDRIDGE FELL GUEST HOUSE Old Waldridge Village, Chester-le-Street DH2 3RY   *Map Ref:* 14
Mr & Mrs Sharratt   *Tel:* 0191 389 1908   A167
Email: bbchesterlestreet@btinternet.com   *Web:* www.smoothhound.co.uk/hotels/waldridgefell.html

Former stone built village chapel situated on the edge of a country park, surrounded by panoramic views and country walks, yet only one and a half miles from the market town of Chester-Le-Street. Comfortable bedrooms with televisions, tea/coffee facilities, radio alarms and hairdryers. Central for Beamish, Durham, Newcastle, Gateshead and Washington. Private parking. ETC, AA 4 Diamonds.

B & B from £24pp, Rooms 1 single, 2 double, 3 family, all en-suite, No smoking, Children welcome, No dogs, Closed Xmas & New Year

---

CLIVE HOUSE Appletree Lane, Corbridge NE45 5DN   *Map Ref:* 15
Ann Hodgson   *Tel:* 01434 632617   *Mobile:* 07949 766143   A68, A69
Email: atclive@supanet.com

Built in 1840 as part of Corbridge village school, Clive House has been converted to provide lovely bedrooms, one has a four-poster. En-suite rooms are well equipped. The village centre with speciality shops and eating places is a few minutes walk. At the centre of Hadrian's Wall country, Corbridge is an ideal base for exploring Northumberland, a convenient break between York and Edinburgh.

B & B from £28pp, Rooms 3 double, 1 single, all en-suite, No smoking, No children or dogs, Closed Xmas

---

LOW FOTHERLEY FARMHOUSE BED & BREAKFAST Low Fotherley Farm, Riding Mill, Corbridge
NE44 6BB   Mrs Lesley Adamson   *Tel / Fax:* 01434 682277   *Mobile:* 07752 375175   *Map Ref:* 15
Email: hugh@lowfotherley.fsnet.co.uk   *Web:* www.westfarm.freeserve.co.uk   A695

Low Fotherley is an impressive Victorian farmhouse built around 1895. It is situated on the A68 in the beautiful Northumbrian countryside, close to the market towns of Hexham and Corbridge. The bedrooms are comfortable and spacious with televisions, tea/coffee facilities and hairdryers. Enjoy your farmhouse breakfast cooked on the aga with homemade jams and marmalade. ETB 4 Diamonds.

B & B from £20pp, Rooms 1 double, 1 family, 1 en-suite, 1 private, No smoking, Children welcome, Dogs by arrangement, Closed Xmas & New Year

Holmhead Guest House, Greenhead, near Brampton

ASH HOUSE 24 The Green, Cornforth DL17 9JH   *Map Ref:* 16
Delia Slack *Tel:* 01740 654654 *Mobile:* 07711 133547   A1M, A167, A688
Email: delden@btopenworld.com

Ash House is a charming Victorian home situated on a quiet conservation village green. The elegant rooms are individually presented with antiques and beautiful fabrics, they have lovely open views. The house is ideally placed being between York and Edinburgh. It is adjacent to the A1 (M) motorway, junction 61, and 8 minutes from Durham city. Private parking. A warm welcome assured. Excellent value.

B & B from £20pp, Rooms 1 twin, 1 double, 1 family, Restricted smoking, Children over 8, Dogs welcome, Closed Xmas & New Year

---

IVY COTTAGE 1 Croft Gardens, Crookham, Cornhill-on-Tweed TD12 4SY   *Map Ref:* 17
Doreen Johnson *Tel / Fax:* 01890 820667 *Mobile:* 07974 759898   A697
Email: ajoh540455@aol.com

Situated in the heart of Crookham Village, Ivy Cottage is perfect for exploring the Northumberland countryside. Rooms have well appointed private bathrooms, huge terry towels and bathrobes, hairdryers, colour television, tea/coffee making facilities, crisp embroidered bed linen and fresh flowers. Breakfast is served in the large farmhouse style kitchen or the formal dining room, feasting on local produce. AA 5 Diamonds.

B & B £27.50-£30pp, Dinner from £22, Rooms 1 double, 1 twin, both with private bathroom, No smoking, Children over 8, Dogs welcome, Open all year

---

EWART HOUSE Whitsome, by Duns TD11 3NB   *Map Ref:* 18
Mrs L Inness *Tel:* 01890 870271 *Mobile:* 07957 873450   B6461
Email: charles.inness@virgin.net

The Inness's welcome you to their converted 18th century coaching inn, within easy reach of many historic border towns. All facilities available. The best of local produce cooked by Louise, a cordon bleu cook. Information on local eateries, events, sporting facilities and transport available in advance.

B & B £22-£25pp, Dinner from £15, Rooms 1 single, 1 double, 1 twin en-suite, No smoking, Children over 6, Dogs by arrangement, Closed New Year

---

HADRIAN LODGE North Road, Above Haydon Bridge, Hadrians Wall NE47 6NF   *Map Ref:* 19
Lynne Murray *Tel:* 01434 688688   A69
Email: hadrianlodge@hadrianswall.co.uk

Hadrian Lodge is in a tranquil rural location set in beautiful open pasture bordered by pine forests overlooking the lakes. Fishing is available and situated two miles from Hadrian's Wall it provides the ideal base to explore the Northumberland National Park. Tearoom, licensed bar and delicious food. Brochure available.

B & B from £22.50pp, Dinner from £5, Rooms 1 single, 2 twin, 3 double, 3 family, most en-suite, Children welcome, No dogs, Open all year

---

BROOMSHAW HILL FARM Willia Road, Haltwhistle NE49 9NP   *Map Ref:* 20
Mrs Jean Brown *Tel / Fax:* 01434 320866 *Mobile:* 07714 385828   A69
Email: broomshaw@msn.com *Web:* www.broomshaw.co.uk

Original 18th century farmhouse, enlarged and modernised to high standards, whilst retaining its old world charm. Quietly situated on the conjunction of a bridleway and footpath in a wooded valley beside Haltwhistle Burn. Hadrian's Wall and major Roman sites are only a short distance away. 5 Diamonds, Gold Award.

B & B £23-£24pp, Rooms 2 double, 1 twin, all en-suite, No smoking, No children or dogs, Closed Nov to Feb

CARRSGATE EAST Bardon Mill, Hexham NE47 7EX   Map Ref: 21
Mrs Lesley Armstrong *Tel:* 01434 344376 *Fax:* 01434 344011 *Mobile:* 07710 981533   A69
Email: lesley@carrsgate-east.com *Web:* www.carrsgate-east.com

Comfortable 17th century home in relaxed surroundings with great
views. A retreat from the hustle and bustle of everyday life. We have
two double en-suite room with televisions and tea/coffee facilities.
Only two miles from Hadrians Wall and settlements, an ideal base for
exploring Northumberland. Walks, beautiful countryside, Newcastle,
Carlisle, the Lake District and many historic attractions within one
hours drive.

B & B from £25pp, Rooms 2 double en-suite, No smoking,
No children or dogs, Closed Nov to Feb

WESTFIELD GUEST HOUSE Bellingham, Hexham NE48 2DP   Map Ref: 22
Barbara Lockhart *Tel:* 01434 220340 *Fax:* 01434 220356   B6320
Email: barbaralockhart@hotmail.com *Web:* www.westfield-house.net

This truly hospitable home was built as a cosy Victorian residence,
with nearly an acre of gardens. Five bedrooms which include four
en-suite, one with a four poster, are totally comfortable, with more
than a touch of luxury. Superb breakfasts and dinners, traditional
cooking at its best. Lounge available. Wonderful countryside,
Roman wall, castles and National Trust properties. Safe parking.
Licensed.

B & B from £28pp, C-Cards MC VS, Dinner from £16, Rooms
1 twin, 1 four poster, 1 family, all en-suite., No smoking, Children
welcome, No dogs, Closed Xmas & New Year

DENE HOUSE Juniper, Hexham NE46 1SJ   Map Ref: 21
Mrs Margaret Massey *Tel / Fax:* 01434 673413   A68
Email: margaret@denehouse-hexham.co.uk *Web:* www.denehouse-hexham.co.uk

Stone farmhouse with beamed ceilings and log fires in quiet rural
setting, four miles south of Hexham. Guests are welcomed with
refreshments while they relax in The Sun Room. Aga cooked
breakfasts with homemade bread and preserves. Hadrians Wall,
Beamish Museam and National Trust properties within easy reach.
Former winners of Best Bed and Breakfast in Northumbria. ETC 4
Diamonds.

B & B from £22.50pp, C-Cards MC VS AE, Rooms 1 single,
1 double en-suite, 1 twin en-suite, No smoking, Children & dogs
welcome, Open all year

ALLERWASH FARM HOUSE Newbrough, Hexham NE47 5AB   Map Ref: 23
Ian & Angela Clyde   A69, B6319
Tel / Fax: 01434 674574

A detached, late Georgian, stonebuilt farmhouse, providing
accommodation in style and elegance with good food. Open fires in
the two drawing rooms add to the warmth of the house, elegant
furnishings plus antiques and paintings make this a real house of
distinction. West facing secluded gardens are surrounded by
delightful rolling countryside. An ideal base for touring, with the Lake
District, Northumberland Coast and Newcastle only an hour's drive.

B & B £32.50-£35pp, Dinner from £22.50, Rooms 1 double,
1 twin, both en-suite, No smoking, Children over 8, Dogs by
arrangement, Open all year

RYE HILL FARM Slaley, Hexham NE47 0AH   Map Ref: 24
Elizabeth Courage *Tel / Fax:* 01434 673259   A68, A69, B6306
Email: enquiries@consult-courage.co.uk *Web:* www.ryehillfarm.co.uk

Rye Hill Farm invites you to enjoy Northumberland whilst living in the
family atmosphere of a cosy farmhouse. En-suite, centrally heated
bedrooms, large bath towels. English breakfast, three course
evening meal served in the dining room with a log fire and table
licence. Pay phone and tourist information in the reception lounge.
There is a games room, guests may look around the farm.

B & B £22.50-£28pp, C-Cards MC VS, Dinner from £14, Rooms
3 double, 1 twin, 2 family, Restricted smoking, Children & dogs
welcome, Open all year

THE PHEASANT INN by Kielder Water, Stannersburn, Falstone, Hexham NE48 1DD   *Map Ref:* 25
Tel / Fax: 01434 240382   A68
Web: www.the pheasantinn.com

An historic inn with beamed ceilings, open fires and home cooking. Fishing, riding and water sports are nearby. Close to Kielder Water, Hadrian's Wall and the Scottish border.

B & B from £25pp, C-Cards MC VS, Dinner available, Rooms 4 double, 3 twin, 1 family, all en-suite, Restricted smoking, Children welcome, Pets by arrangement, Closed Xmas day and Boxing day

---

THE HERMITAGE Swinburne, Hexham NE48 4DG   *Map Ref:* 26
Simon & Kate Stewart   A6079
Tel: 01434 681248   *Fax:* 01434 681110

An elegant, comfortable house furnished with antiques and family pictures. Rooms are spacious and beautifully decorated. The large, well kept garden has a terrace to enjoy in the evenings, and a tennis court. The drawing room has an open fire and a television, there is total peace and quiet. The house is convenient for the Roman Wall and Northumberland castles and mansions. Parking.

B & B from £30pp, Rooms 1 single, 2 twin, 1 double, all en-suite/private, Restricted smoking, Children over 10, Dogs by arrangement, Closed Oct to Mar

---

PLEVNA HOUSE West Woodburn, Hexham NE48 2RA   *Map Ref:* 27
Dorothy and John Pickford   *Tel:* 01434 270369   *Fax:* 01434 270179   *Mobile:* 07703 778323   A68
Email: plevnaho@aol.com   *Web:* www.plevnahouse.ntb.org.uk

Plevna is a traditional stone-built country house with beautiful gardens and views. Central for Scottish Borders, Hadrian's Wall, Kielder, the coast and the National Trust's Wallington and Cragside. We have two double bedrooms, both en-suite with televisions and hospitality trays. The dining room and residents' lounge have log fires in the winter. Comfort, relaxation and a warm welcome are assured. ETC 4 Diamond, Silver Award.

B & B £18-£20pp, Dinner from £12, Rooms 2 double en-suite, No smoking, Children welcome, No dogs, Closed Xmas & New Year

---

ESHOTT HALL Morpeth NE65 9EP   *Map Ref:* 28
Margaret Sanderson   *Tel:* 01670 787777   *Fax:* 01670 787999   A1
Email: thehall@eshott.com   *Web:* www.eshott.com

Sitting peacefully amongst towering cedars of Lebanon in thirty acres of grounds, Eshott is adjacent to the Heritage Coastline and close to the Cheviot Foothills. Enjoy style, grace and comfort with fine dining in this beautiful Georgian mansion, only about one mile east of the A1 and 20 minutes north of Newcastle.

B & B from £38pp, C-Cards, Dinner from £25, Rooms 2 double, 2 twin, 2 single, all en-suite, Restricted smoking, Babies/Children over 12, Dogs by arrangement, Closed Xmas & New Year

---

SHIELDHALL Wallington by Kirkharle, Morpeth NE61 4AQ   *Map Ref:* 29
Stephen & Celia Gay   *Tel:* 01830 540387   *Fax:* 01830 540490   B6342, A696
Email: Robinson.Gay@btinternet.com

17th century restored former home of Capability Brown, set in the heart of the Northumbrian Borders in rolling landscape overlooking the National Trust's estate of Wallington. Every bedroom is furnished individually, and has its own entrance into the central courtyard. Pre-ordered dinners are served in a candlelit dining room. Many heritage sites such as Hadrian's Wall, within easy driving distance of Shieldhall.

B & B £22.50-£28.50pp, C-Cards MC VS, Dinner available, Rooms 2 double, 1 twin, No smoking, No children, Dogs by arrangement, Closed Nov-Mar

MARTINEAU GUEST HOUSE 57 Front Street, Tynemouth, North Shields NE30 4BX   *Map Ref:* 30
Christine & Roger Ponton   *Tel:* 0191 296 0746   *Mobile:* 07946 501863   A19
Email: martineau.house@ukgateway.net   *Web:* www.martineau-house.co.uk

Martineau House is named after Harriet Martineau, acclaimed
novelist, political economist and England's first female journalist who
convalesced here between 1840 and 1845. Recently restored it
offers luxury accommodation with panoramic views of Tynemouth
Priory and the River Tyne. Traditional Northumbrian dishes - North
Shields kippers, homemade fish cakes, potato cakes, tipsy porridge
or a 'Big Geordie' breakfast. ETC 4 Diamonds, Silver Award.

B & B from £25pp, Rooms 2 double, 1 twin, all en-suite, No
smoking, Children over 12, No dogs, Closed first 2 weeks in Jan

---

ORCHARD GUEST HOUSE High Street, Rothbury NE65 7TL   *Map Ref:* 31
Mrs Jean Pickard   *Tel:* 01669 620684   B6341
Email: jpickard@orchardguesthouse.co.uk   *Web:* www.orchardguesthouse.co.uk

A charming Georgian guesthouse in the centre of a lovely village. We
offer a warm welcome, quality accommodation and excellent freshly
cooked breakfasts. Rothbury is the ideal location for exploring the
coast, castles and beautiful countryside of Northumberland. Evening
meals available within easy walking distance. Comfortable guest
lounge with books and information.

B & B from £23pp, Rooms 2 double, 4 twin, some en-suite, No
smoking, Children welcome, No dogs, Closed Xmas & New Year

THROPTON DEMESNE FARMHOUSE Thropton, Rothbury NE65 7LT   *Map Ref:* 31
Kris Rogerson   B6341
Tel: 01669 620196

This old stone farmhouse surveys the Coquet River and Cheviot hills.
Well equipped bedrooms have their own bathrooms. Guests' sitting
room has log fires, outside is a pretty garden. Kris provides light
suppers on request, also packed lunches. The Northumberland
National Park is closeby, Rothbury with its National Park Information
Centre and National Trust and English Heritage houses and gardens
are within easy reach.

B & B from £23pp, Dinner from £8.50, Rooms 1 twin, 2 double,
all en-suite, No smoking, Children by arrangement, No dogs,
Open all year

IDSLEY HOUSE 4 Green Lane, Spennymoor DL16 6HD   *Map Ref:* 32
Joan, David Dartnall   A167, A688
Tel: 01388 814237

Idsley House is a large long established guest house in a quiet area
just off the A167/A688 8 minutes from Durham city. All rooms are
spacious and furnished to a high standard. Breakfast is served in a
pleasant conservatory. Double, twin and family rooms are en-suite
and have TV and welcome trays. Ample safe parking in walled
garden. Evening meals by arrangement.

B & B from £24pp, C-Cards MC VS AE, Rooms 1 single,
1 double, 2 twin, 1 family, all en-suite, Restricted smoking,
Children & dogs welcome, Closed Xmas & New Year

NORTH COTTAGE Birling, Warkworth NE65 0EX   *Map Ref:* 33
John & Edith Howliston   *Tel:* 01665 711263   A1068
Email: edithandjohn@another.com   *Web:* www.accta.co.uk/north

North Cottage dates back to the 17th century and it has a homely
atmosphere. Substantial full English breakfasts are offered, and
afternoon tea is served free on arrival. The bedrooms are on the
ground floor, and they have tea/coffee facilities, electric blanket,
clock radio and colour TV. The double and twin rooms are en-suite
and the single room has a wash basin.

B & B £22-£24pp, Rooms 2 double, 1 twin, 1 single, most
en-suite, No smoking, Children welcome, No dogs, Closed Xmas
& New Year

Oxfordshire

Lying midway between the Thames estuary and the River Severn, with the glorious Cotswolds to the north, the chalk hills of the Chilterns in the south and with the basins of the Thames and Cherwell forming the central plain, Oxfordshire must be one of England's most attractive counties. The Oxfordshire Chilterns is a wonderful area of beechwoods and chalk, here the Ridgeway, a pre-Roman track follows the western escarpment and runs to the Vale of the White Horse with its spectacular Iron Age hill figure known as the White Horse of Uffington. Here the Buscot and Coleshill estates, some 7,500 acres of farmland and woodland which includes Badbury Hill, belong to the National Trust. The Iron-Age hill-fort gives spectacular views over the upper Thames Valley and south to the Berkshire Downs. To the southeast of Watlington with its Elizabethan cottages and fine Georgian inn, the 'Hare and Hounds', on an escarpment of the Chilterns, Watlington Hill, at 700 feet, gives splendid views over much of the county. The hill is skirted by the Upper Icknield Way, a superb region for walkers and for the naturalist the area is a fascinating district of lovely yew forests, whitebeam, dogwood and hawthorn.

The Oxfordshire Cotswolds are a delight, offering the visitor excellent walking, through a countryside of honey-coloured limestone villages, cottage gardens and rich russet-coloured fields hemmed with their drystone walls. Chipping Norton, a wonderful old wool town with its fine fifteenth century church and handsome stone buildings is a great centre from which to explore the area. Burford is also an excellent holiday centre, rich in fine buildings indicating its prosperity as a wool town, it boasts a magnificent church and a picturesque medieval bridge across the Windrush. Further south is the Cotswold Wildlife Park, 120 acres of gardens surrounding a Gothic style manor house with a variety of animals and wildlife in spacious enclosures, including white rhinos and tigers. Nearby is Minster Lovell, one of this county's prettiest villages, a long cottage lined street with Minster Lovell Hall, a quite fascinating medieval fortified manor house, a ruin steeped in legend. Banbury, in the north of the county, is an interesting centre renowned for its cross, which was destroyed by Puritans in 1602, later to be replaced by the Victorians. The town is famous also for its mouth-watering Banbury cakes, made to a 350 year old recipe. To the south is the town of Bicester, an ancient town of Roman origin and a noted hunting centre, with some extremely attractive buildings in Market End and Sheep Street. To the west at Woodstock is Blenheim Palace, a vast and sumptuous treasure

Blenheim Palace from the East (STB)

house, built to the design of John Vanbrugh for John Churchill the first Duke of Malborough, as a gift from Queen Anne in recognition of his victory at Blenheim in 1704. The palace was the birthplace in 1874 of Winston Churchill, the great war leader and stands in a great park laid out by Henry Wise and modified later by 'Capability' Brown.

At the centre of this glorious county lies Oxford with its stunning heritage of historic buildings. Delightfully situated on the Thames or Isis, with large swathes of greenery it is easy to forget that Oxford is an important industrial, commercial and residential city. Oxford can offer all that one would expect of a modern city, fine shops, excellent cinemas and theatres. There are sightseeing buses touring the city at regular intervals and boating on the Thames and Cherwell. From the twelfth century the city has been an important centre of learning. The most famous of its colleges, Christ Church, known as 'The House', was founded by Cardinal Wolsey. Each of the colleges, set in cloistered seclusion behind high walls has its own distinctive charm and treasures. Christ Church has in its picture gallery, works by Durer and Michelangelo and New College has in its chapel a statue of Lazarus by Jacob Epstein. Alongside these Oxford colleges have developed some remarkable public buildings, the Sheldonian Theatre built in 1664, the Radcliffe Camera, the Bodleian Library with over five and a half million volumes and the Ashmolean Museum, a treasure house of art and antiquities including a ninth century brooch made for King Alfred.

PLACES TO VISIT
This is a small selection of interesting places to visit. Many more are listed in our annual guide to Museums, Galleries, Historic Houses & Sites (see page 448)

Blenheim Palace
Woodstock
The home of the 11th Duke of Marlborough and birthplace of Winston Churchill. The park consists of over 2,000 acres, landscaped by 'Capability' Brown, a lake, Vanbrugh's Grand Bridge and Column of Victory.

Cotswold Wildlife Park
Burford, Oxford
This 200 acre landscaped parkland surrounds a Gothic-style manor house and has a varied collection of animals from all over the world.

Didcot Railway Centre
Didcot
A unique collection of Great Western Railway steam engines, coaches, wagons, buildings and artefacts.

The Oxford Story
6 Broad Street, Oxford
An excellent introduction to Oxford with 900 years of University history told in one hour. From scientists to poets, astronomers to comedians.

River and Rowing Museum
Mill Meadows, Henley-on-Thames
A spectacular journey through over 250,000 years of life on the river with three main galleries dedicated to the River Thames, the international sport of rowing and the town of Henley.

Stonor
Henley-on-Thames
Home of Lord and Lady Camoys and the Stonor family for over 800 years. Contains a fine collection of items from Britain, Europe and America. Extensive gardens and park

Oxfordshire

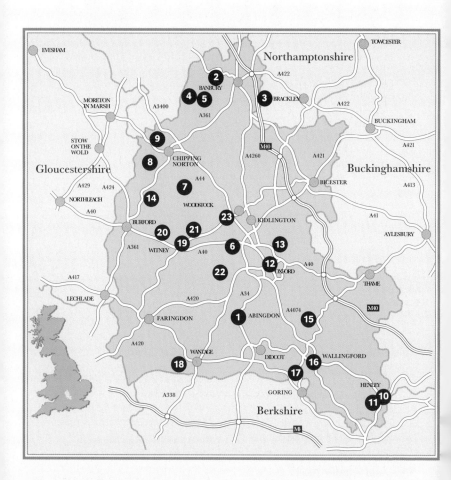

EVESHAM

TOWCESTER

Northamptonshire

A422

MORETON
IN MARSH

A3400

2

BANBURY

4 **5**

A361

3 BRACKLEY

A422

BUCKINGHAM

A421

STOW
ON THE
WOLD

9

M40

A4260

A421

Buckinghamshire

Gloucestershire

8

CHIPPING
NORTON

BICESTER

A413

A429 A424

7

A44

NORTHLEACH

14

WOODSTOCK

A41

A40

BURFORD

23

KIDLINGTON

AYLESBURY

20 **21**

19

6

13

A361

WITNEY

A40

12 OXFORD

A40

THAME

A417

22

M40

LECHLADE

A34

A420

FARINGDON

1 ABINGDON

A4074

15

A420

WANTAGE

DIDCOT

16 WALLINGFORD

18

17

HENLEY

A338

GORING

11 **10**

Berkshire

M1

The Red Map References should be used to locate B & B properties on the pages that follow

252

22 EAST ST HELEN STREET Abingdon OX14 5EB   *Map Ref:* 1
Mrs Howard *Tel:* 01235 550979 *Fax:* 01235 533278   A34, A415
Email: srhoward@talk21.com

Attractive 18th century house situated in a charming street in the centre of town close to the river. Organic breakfasts, served in the flag stoned dining room, include fresh and stewed fruit, home made muesli, marmalade and wholemeal bread. A speciality is scrambled eggs with ham or smoked salmon and mushrooms. Overflow guests stay in a nearby house where William III stayed during the Revolution.

B & B £26-£32pp, Rooms 3 single, 1 twin, 2 double, 1 en-suite, No smoking, Children welcome, Guide Dogs only, Closed Xmas, New Year & Easter

---

SWALLOWS BARN Shutford Road, Balscote, Banbury OX15 6JJ   *Map Ref:* 2
Stephen & Marypen Wills *Tel:* 01295 738325 *Fax:* 01295 738314   A422
Email: s.wills@swallowsbarn.freeserve.co.uk

Spacious honey stone house blends into the rural scene, the old stone wall a backdrop to the waterfall and charming garden. The guest room is large, sunny and comfortable with country antiques, sofa, tea and television. We can accommodate extra family. Breakfast is taken at the Georgian table, or on the terrace. Walks abound and Oxford, Stratford-upon-Avon and Warwick are an easy drive.

B & B from £25pp, Rooms 1 double/twin or family en-suite, Restricted smoking, Children welcome, Dogs by arrangement, Closed Mid-Dec to Mid-Jan

---

HOME FARMHOUSE Charlton, Banbury OX17 3DR   *Map Ref:* 3
Col & Mrs Grove-White *Tel / Fax:* 01295 811683   M40
Email: grovewhite@lineone.net *Web:* www.homefarmhouse.co.uk

Over 400 years old, this is a charming, welcoming house with exposed beams, winding staircases and inglenook fireplaces. The house is furnished in harmony with its age, but with the emphasis on comfort. One hour from Heathrow, it is an ideal base for visiting Oxford, Stratford-upon-Avon, Warwick Castle, the Cotswolds, Blenheim, Woburn, Waddesdon, Hidcote, Kiftsgate and Sezincote. Also close to Bicester Village.

B & B from £31pp, C-Cards MC VS, Dinner from £25, Rooms 2 twin/double, 1 double, all en-suite/private, No smoking, Children over 12, Dogs by arrangement, Closed Xmas

---

COLLEGE FARMHOUSE Kings Sutton, Banbury OX17 3PS   *Map Ref:* 3
Stephen & Sara Allday *Tel:* 01295 811473 *Fax:* 01295 812505 *Mobile:* 07803 600064   A4260
Email: SEAllday@cs.com *Web:* www.banburytown.co.uk/accom/collegefarm

Set in own secluded grounds with lovely views, overlooking own lake. Guests free to wander round at their leisure. Older parts of the house date back to 18th century and has been decorated to a high standard. Guests are able to relax in the Drawing Room or watch television in front of a log fire in the large inglenook fireplace.

B & B from £30pp, C-Cards MC VS, Dinner from £18, Rooms 1 double, 2 twin, all en-suite, No smoking, Children welcome, No dogs, Closed Xmas & New Year

---

MINE HILL HOUSE Lower Brailes, Banbury OX15 5BJ   *Map Ref:* 4
Hester & Edward Sale   B4035
Tel: 01608 685594

Built in 1733, on top of a hill with stunning views over unspoilt countryside this Cotswold farmhouse is full of paintings, flagstone floors and log fires. Hester is a highly trained cook, she is delighted to cook dinner. Superb location to explore the Cotswolds, Stratford, Oxford, Blenheim Palace the gardens of Hidcote and Kiftsgate, are within a 20 mile radius. Golf course nearby.

B & B from £25pp, Dinner from £20, Rooms 1 twin, 1 double, both en-suite/private, Restricted smoking, Children welcome, Dogs by arrangement, Closed Xmas

GOWER'S CLOSE Main Street, Sibford Gower, Banbury OX15 5RW
Judith Hitching
Tel: 01295 780348

Map Ref: 5
B4035

Gower's Close is an intriguing seventeenth century village house, thatched and beamed, and set in a sleepy Cotswold village. Expect to enjoy good food, music, books, conversation, laughter and log fires in this informal house, with an idyllic cottage garden. Oxford, Blenheim Palace, Stratford-upon-Avon and Hidcote Gardens are all within 30 minutes drive.

B & B from £35pp, Rooms 1 double, 1 twin, both en-suite, No smoking, Children over 10, No dogs, Closed Xmas & New Year

---

BURLEIGH FARM Bladon Road, Cassington OX29 4EA
Jane Cook *Tel:* 01865 881352
Email: jcook@farmline.com

Map Ref: 6
A40, A4095

A listed stone farmhouse in a quiet position, a working farm on the Duke of Marlborough's Estate. Comfortable bedrooms all have television and coffee/tea making facilities. There is a relaxing garden for guests' use. The farmhouse is convenient for visits to the beautiful Blenheim Palace, the University City of Oxford and the Cotswolds. Burford, Bibury and Chipping Norton are an easy drive.

B & B from £22.50pp, Rooms 1 twin, 1 family/double, both en-suite, No smoking, Open all year

---

BANBURY HILL FARM Enstone Road, Charlbury OX7 3JH
Mr & Mrs G Widdows *Tel:* 0800 0853474 *Fax:* 01608 811891
Email: angelawiddows@gfwiddows.f9.co.uk *Web:* www.charlburyoxfordaccom.co.uk

Map Ref: 7
A44, A361

A Stone farmhouse, commanding spectacular views overlooks the small township of Charlbury and the ancient Wychwood Forest. Banbury Hill Farm offers en-suite rooms, central heating, colour televisions, hospitality trays, comfortable beds and scrumptious full English breakfasts. Ideal for touring Oxford, Stratford, Burford, Cotswold and Woodstock.

B & B from £18pp, Rooms 1 single, 2 double, 3 twin, 7 family, most en-suite, No smoking, Children welcome, No dogs, Closed Dec to early Jan

---

THE FORGE Church Road, Churchill, Chipping Norton OX7 6NJ
Jon & Lin Price *Tel:* 01608 658173 *Fax:* 01608 659262 *Mobile:* 07799 076538
Email: jon@theforge.co.uk *Web:* www.theforge.co.uk

Map Ref: 8
A44, A361, B4450

The Forge is almost 200 years old and was once the village blacksmiths. Today it is a comfortable home, retaining many of the original features. All rooms have colour television and tea/coffee making facilities. Off street parking. Hearty breakfast including a selection of fruits, cereals, juice and traditional cooked full English breakfast. Several good pubs and restaurants in the area. Ideal for exploring the Cotswolds and surrounding area.

B & B from £27.50pp, C-Cards MC VS, Rooms 5 double, 1 twin, all en-suite, No smoking, Children over 12, No dogs, Closed Xmas & New Year

---

RECTORY FARM Salford, Chipping Norton OX7 5YZ
Nigel & Elizabeth Colston *Tel / Fax:* 01608 643209 *Mobile:* 07866 834208
Email: colston@rectoryfarm75.freeserve.co.uk

Map Ref: 9
A44

Rectory Farm is a 200 hundred year old working Cotswold farm, standing in 450 acres of beautiful North Cotswold country. A mature garden leads down to two trout lakes, where fishing is available for guests. This traditionally furnished family home with large, light filled rooms is in an ideal situation to explore the Cotswolds as many of the historic towns are all within a pleasant drive.

B & B from £34pp, Dinner from £14, Rooms 1 double en-suite, 1 double, 1 twin both private bathroom, Restricted smoking, Children welcome, Dogs by arrangement, Closed Dec & Jan

ALFTRUDIS 8 Norman Avenue, Henley-on-Thames RG9 1SG
Sue Lambert *Tel:* 01491 573099 *Fax:* 01491 411747 *Mobile:* 07802 408643
Email: sue@alftrudis.fsnet.co.uk *Web:* alftrudis.co.uk

Map Ref: 10
A4130, A4155

Alftrudis is a handsome Victorian Grade II listed home situated in a
quiet secluded tree lined cul-de-sac, only a minutes walk from the
town centre, station and river. All rooms have television and
tea/coffee making facilities. Alftrumis has a ETC 4 Diamond grading
and is recommended in the Which? Best B&B Guide. Parking is
easy, either in the driveway or avenue.

B & B from £27.50pp, Rooms 1 double, 1 twin, both en-suite,
No smoking, Children over 8, No dogs, Closed Xmas & New Year

HERNES Henley-on-Thames RG9 4NT
Mr & Mrs Richard Ovey *Tel:* 01491 573245 *Fax:* 01491 574645
Email: oveyhernes@aol.com *Web:* smoothhound.co.uk/hotels/hernes

Map Ref: 10
A4130

Hernes is situated in the heart of the Thames Valley and Chilterns. It
is surrounded by spacious gardens and lawns which overlook its
own farm and parkland. The family has lived here for five generations
and you will experience a gentle, relaxed atmosphere with a warm
welcome from Richard and Gillian. Ideal base for touring the home
counties.

B & B £37.50-£45pp, Rooms 2 double, 1 twin, most en-suite,
No smoking, Children over 13, No dogs, Closed Dec to Feb

SLATER'S FARM Peppard Common, Henley-on-Thames RG9 5JL
Mrs Penny Howden
Tel / Fax: 01491 628675

Map Ref: 11
B481

Slater's Farm is a quiet and welcoming Georgian country house set
in an acre of lovely garden with a hard tennis court, which guests are
welcome to use. There are some wonderful walks through unspoiled
countryside. It is only a short walk to good traditional pubs. The
Chilterns, Windsor, Oxford, Cotswolds are all within easy driving
distance. French and German spoken.

B & B from £24pp, Dinner from £16, Rooms 2 twin, 1 double,
2 private, Restricted smoking, Children welcome, No dogs, Closed
Xmas & New Year

COTSWOLD HOUSE 363 Banbury Road, Oxford OX2 7PL
Derek & Hilary Walker *Tel / Fax:* 01865 310558
Email: d.r.walker@talk21.com *Web:* www.house363.freeserve.co.uk

Map Ref: 12
M40, A40, A43

Cotswold House is situated in the leafy suburb of North Oxford,
almost two miles from the City Centre. This Cotswold stone house
has been built and furnished to a standard rarely found today. While
at Cotswold House you can enjoy one of our special breakfasts with
a vegetarian option. This area has many fine restaurants and pubs
offering an excellent variety of food.

B & B £34-£37pp, C-Cards MC VS, Rooms 2 single, 2 double,
1 twin, 2 family, all en-suite, No smoking, Children over 6,
No dogs, Open all year

GREEN GABLES 326 Abingdon Road, Oxford OX1 4TE
Parvesh & Narinder Bhella *Tel:* 01865 725870 *Fax:* 01865 723115
Email: green.gables@virgin.net

Map Ref: 12
A4144

Built in 1914 for a local toy merchant, this Edwardian house displays
much character. It is well placed as the house stands one mile from
the city centre, on a frequent bus route. A pleasant riverside walk
beside the Thames also takes you to the centre. The bedrooms are
light, bright and spacious one ground floor room, suitable for
disabled guests. Private parking.

B & B from £27pp, Rooms 1 single, 2 twin, 4 double, 2 family,
all en-suite, No smoking, No dogs, Closed Xmas & New Year

HIGHFIELD WEST GUEST HOUSE 188 Cumnor Hill, Oxford OX2 9PJ   *Map Ref:* 12
Diana & Richard Mitchell   *Tel:* 01865 863007   A34, A40
Email: highfieldwest@email.msn.com   *Web:* www.oxfordcity.co.uk/accom/highfield-west/

Comfortable home in a residential location with a large outdoor heated pool in the summer season. Good access to city centre and ring road. The Cotswolds and Blenheim Palace nearby. London, Bath and Stratford-upon-Avon are within daily travelling distance. Diana and Richard are always pleased to provide local information and help you enjoy your visit.

B & B from £25pp, Rooms 2 single, 1 double, 1 twin, 1 family, most en-suite, No smoking, Children welcome, Dogs by arrangement, Closed Xmas & New Year

PICKWICK'S GUEST HOUSE 15/17 London Road, Headington, Oxford OX3 7SP   *Map Ref:* 12
Tel: 01865 750487   *Fax:* 01865 742208   A34, A40
Email: pickwicks@fiscali.co.uk   *Web:* www.pickwicks.oxfree.com

Comfortable, friendly, family run guest house within five minutes' drive of Oxford ring road and M40 motorway. Nearby coach stop for 24-house service to central London, Heathrow and Gatwick airports. Close to Oxford city centre, Oxford Brookes University, John Radcliffe, Nuffield and Churchill hospitals. Free parking, lounge, bar and garden.

B & B £28-£32.50pp, C-Cards MC VS AE DC, Rooms 4 single, 5 double, 2 twin, 4 triple, most en-suite, Restricted smoking, Children welcome, Dogs by arrangement, Closed Xmas week

PINE CASTLE HOTEL 290/292 Iffley Road, Oxford OX4 4AE   *Map Ref:* 12
Mrs S Pavlovic   A4158
Tel: 01865 241497   *Fax:* 01865 727230

Pine Castle is a home from home for guests. The comfortable rooms are well furnished, generously equipped and have a selection of reading material. Smokers are welcome to use the lounge where there is also a small bar. Well situated midway between the Ring Road and the city centre and served by an excellent local bus service. River walk close by.

B & B from £32.50pp, Rooms 2 twin, 5 double, 1 family, all en-suite, Restricted smoking, Children welcome, No dogs, Closed Xmas & New Year

THE BUNGALOW Cherwell Farm, Mill Lane, Old Marston, Oxford OX3 0QF   *Map Ref:* 13
Mr R A Burden *Tel:* 01865 557171   *Mobile:* 07703 162125   A40
Email: anthonyhenry@anthonyhenry.freeserve.co.uk

A modern bungalow set in five acres in a quiet location surrounded by open countryside. Only four miles from city centre but no bus route. Televisions and tea/ coffee facilities are in all rooms. Non-smoking. Private parking.

B & B from £23pp, Rooms 2 double, 2 twin, some en-suite, No smoking, Children over 8, No dogs, Closed Nov to Feb

SHIPTON GRANGE HOUSE Shipton-under-Wychwood OX7 6DG   *Map Ref:* 14
Veronica Hill   A361
Tel: 01993 831298   *Fax:* 01993 832082   *Mobile:* 07971 426843

A unique conversion of a Georgian Coach House and stabling, situated in the former grounds of Shipton Court, in a walled garden and approached by a gated archway. Three well equipped, elegantly furnished guest bedrooms. Shipton Grange House is delightful, it is ideal for visiting Blenheim Palace, Oxford, Stratford, Warwick and many beautiful gardens. There are some excellent restaurants nearby.

B & B from £29pp, Rooms 1 twin, 2 double, all en-suite/private, No smoking, Children over 12, No dogs, Closed Xmas

THE MANOR Stadhampton OX44 7UL　　　　　　　　　　*Map Ref:* 15
Anthea & Stephen Savage *Tel:* 01865 891999 *Fax:* 01865 891640 *Mobile:* 07771 822911　　A329
Email: action@timebeam.com

Set back on the Village Green this 17th century stone house is only
eight miles from Oxford. The guest bedrooms have views of the
garden and there is a large drawing room, where log fires blaze in
winter, available for guests' use. There is an excellent restaurant
within walking distance and many others a short drive away.

B & B from £40pp, Rooms 1 double private bathroom, 1 double,
1 twin, both en-suite, No smoking, Children welcome, No dogs,
Closed Xmas & New Year

LITTLE GABLES 166 Crowmarsh Hill, Wallingford OX10 8BG　　　*Map Ref:* 16
Jill & Tony Reeves *Tel:* 01491 837834 *Fax:* 01491 834426 *Mobile:* 07860 148882　　A4130
Email: jill@stayingaway.com *Web:* www.stayingaway.com

A detached house offering a warm welcome, rooms are well
furnished with television, fridge and tea/coffee facilities. There is a
garden seating area for guests and English or continental breakfasts
to choose from. Easy access to M4 and M40 with a local bus service
to Reading, Oxford and Henley. Close to Ridgeway Path and the
Thames Path with packed lunches available on request.

B & B from £27.50pp, Rooms 1 single, 2 double, 2 twin, 2 family,
most en-suite, No smoking, Children welcome, No dogs, Closed
Xmas

THE WELL COTTAGE Caps Lane, Cholsey, Wallingford OX10 9HQ　　　*Map Ref:* 17
Joanna Alexander *Tel:* 01491 651959 *Fax:* 01491 651675 *Mobile:* 07887 958920　　A329
Email: thewellcottage@talk21.com

A delightful cottage in beautiful surroundings close to River Thames
and the historic town of Wallingford. The secluded garden flat has
two twin bedrooms with en-suite bathrooms and each has its own
private entrance. Further accommodation is available in the house.

B & B £15-£25pp, Rooms 1 double, 2 twin, most en-suite,
Children & dogs welcome, Closed Xmas & New Year

RIDGEWAY HOUSE West Street, Childrey, Wantage OX12 9UL　　　*Map Ref:* 18
Maxine Roberts　　　　　　　　　　　　　　　　　　　　　　　　B4507
Tel: 01235 751538

Set in the beautiful village of Childrey, which is close to the market
town of Wantage, this is an ideal base for exploring Oxford, the
Cotswolds, White Horse Hill, and for walking the Ridgeway. The
rooms have fresh fruit, flowers, en-suite facilities and beautiful views.
There is a delicious breakfast choice, to include homemade bread
and jams. Private car park.

B & B from £22.50pp, Rooms 2 single, 2 twin, 2 double, 2 family,
all en-suite, No smoking, Children welcome, Dogs by
arrangement, Open all year

FIELD VIEW Wood Green, Witney OX28 1DE　　　　　　　*Map Ref:* 19
Liz & John Simpson *Tel:* 01993 705485 *Mobile:* 07768 614347　　A40, A4095
Email: jsimpson@netcomuk.co.uk *Web:* www.netcomuk.co.uk/~kearse/index.html

An attractive Cotswold stone house set in two acres situated on
picturesque Wood Green, midway between between Oxford
University and the Cotswolds. The setting is peaceful and guests are
welcomed to a warm and friendly atmosphere. An ideal centre for
touring, yet the lively market town of Witney is eight minutes walk
from the house. There are three well equipped, comfortable en-suite
rooms.

B & B from £24pp, Rooms 2 twin, 1 double, all en-suite,
No smoking, No children or dogs, Closed Xmas & New Year

THE OLD VICARAGE Minster Lovell, Witney OX8 5RR
Bridget Geddes *Tel:* 01993 775630 *Fax:* 01993 772534
Email: ageddes@lix.compulink.co.uk

Map Ref: 20
A40

Built in the 19th century, the River Windrush trickles through the garden. The church and ruins of Minster Lovell Hall stand closeby. The Garden House is ideal for a self-catering arrangement. A four poster bedroom is in the main house. The village pub is within walking distance. An easy drive from Stratford, Burford, Cirencester and Oxford. A wonderful location for Cotswold exploring.

B & B from £37.50pp, Rooms 2 double, with private bath, No smoking in bedrooms, Children over 6, No dogs, Closed Xmas & Easter

GORSELANDS HALL Boddington Lane, North Leigh, Witney OX29 6PU
Mr & Mrs N Hamilton *Tel:* 01993 882292 *Fax:* 01993 883629
Email: hamilton@gorselandshall.com *Web:* www.gorselandshall.com

Map Ref: 21
A4095/A40

A lovely old Cotswold stone country house with oak beams and flagstone floors in a delightful rural setting. Large secluded garden with a grass tennis court. Ideal for Blenheim Palace, the Cotswolds and Oxford. Roman villa close by. Good walking country. Comfortable attractively furnished bedrooms with views of the garden or the surrounding countryside. All rooms are en-suite.

B & B £22.50-£25pp, C-Cards MC VS AE, Rooms 1 twin, 4 double, 1 family, all en-suite, No smoking, Children welcome, Dogs by arrangement, Open all year

RECTORY FARM Northmoor, Witney OX8 1SX
Mary Anne Florey *Tel:* 01865 300207 *Fax:* 01865 300559 *Mobile:* 07974 102198
Email: pj.florey@farmline.com

Map Ref: 22
A415

Come and enjoy the happy buzz in our family home with a relaxed informal atmosphere. A 16th century farmhouse, 10 miles west of Oxford, where a warm welcome awaits you, along with tea and homemade shortbread to refresh you after your journey. Both en-suite rooms are light and airy with stone arched, mullioned windows, tudor fireplaces and timbered and exposed walls.

B & B £25-£27pp, Rooms 1 double, 1 twin, both en-suite, No smoking, No children or dogs, Closed Mid-Dec to mid-Jan

WYNFORD HOUSE 79 Main Road, Long Hanborough, Woodstock OX29 8JX
Mrs Carol Ellis
Tel: 01993 881402 *Fax:* 01993 883661

Map Ref: 23
A4095, A44

A warm welcome awaits you in our comfortable home which is situated in the village of Long Hanborough, 1 mile from Bladon, 3 miles from Woodstock and Blenheim Palace. There is colour TV and tea/coffee facilities in all rooms. Good local pubs are within walking distance. Wynford House is conveniently situated for Oxford, Woodstock and the Cotswolds. Many good walks locally.

B & B from £22pp, Rooms 1 family, 1 twin, 1 double, 1 en-suite, No smoking, Children welcome, Dogs by arrangement, Closed Xmas & New Year

MANOR FARMHOUSE Manor Road, Bladon, Woodstock OX20 1RU
Helen Stevenson *Tel / Fax:* 01993 812168
Email: helstevenson@hotmail.com *Web:* www.oxlink.co.uk/woodstock/manor-farmhouse/

Map Ref: 23
A4095

Listed Cotswold stone house (1720) in quiet conservation area of Bladon village, within walking distance of pubs, one mile from Blenheim Palace. Ideal for exploring Oxford and the Cotswolds. Double room featured in a Laura Ashley catalogue. Small twin room has a spiral staircase, so is not for the unsprightly. They share a shower room, so are ideal for 4 people travelling together.

B & B from £24pp, Rooms 1 twin, 1 double, No smoking, Children welcome, Dogs by arrangement, Closed Xmas & New Year

Shropshire

Strangely enough, this rich agricultural county was the cradle of the Industrial Revolution, but then Shropshire is a county of intriguing contrasts. Only fifty miles in length and forty miles wide the county is virtually cut in two by the River Severn which flows across the county from the Welsh border in the west to Shrewsbury. The Shropshire Plain, which stretches from Whitchurch in the north to Church Stretton in the southwest is dominated by the Wrekin, a long, domed hill of volcanic rock, the oldest in England, heavily wooded and with a steep promontory overlooking the Severn Valley. In the southwest of the county are the rugged Stiperstones, and in the south the Clee Hills. Between the Clee Hills and Wenlock Edge lies the glorious valley of the Corve, leading to Ludlow, one of England's best preserved medieval and Georgian towns. Broad Street is the most celebrated of the town's thoroughfares, a wonderful mixture of timber-framed Tudor buildings and seventeenth to nineteenth century brick facades. The cathedral-like Church of St Lawrence is renowned for its wonderful fifteenth century carved misericords. The poet AE Housman, whose poetry, and in particular his 'A Shropshire Lad' effectively depicts this wonderful rural county, is buried in the churchyard. Ludlow Castle, built in 1085 by Roger Montgomery, Earl of Shrewsbury, holds in its inner bailey, outdoor performances of Shakespeare plays during the Ludlow Festival in June and July. The town is ideal for exploring the Welsh Marches and the South Shropshire Hills. In the southwest lies The Long Mynd, an area of high and lonely moorland and splendid walking country. The National Trust owns almost six thousand acres of this heather covered upland. To enjoy this region a good starting point is the Carding Mill Valley from which radiate paths leading to a number of prehistoric remains, hill forts and burial grounds and to the ancient Port Way track which traverses the hill. The Trust owns some 550 acres of Wenlock Edge, the thick wooded limestone escarpment running from Craven Arms to Ironbridge is internationally famous for its coral reef exposures.

In the north of the county are the lovely Shropshire meres with Ellesmere being the attractive capital of the region. A former canal town, Ellesmere has a wealth of charming timber-framed and Georgian houses bordering The Mere, a haven for water fowl and the largest of the town's nine lakes. Ellesmere is a fine holiday centre and a magnet for lovers of small boats. Oswestry, to the west and very Welsh in character, can claim some

Iron Bridge near Telford (ST)

fine nineteenth century buildings, witness to the town's prosperity when in 1860 it became the headquarters of the Cambrian Railway. The town is also the birthplace of the composer, Walford Davies.

Shrewsbury, the county town and a perfect base to explore the county, is wonderfully situated within a tight loop of the meandering Severn. The town became strategically important soon after the Norman Conquest when William the Conqueror entrusted Roger de Montgomery to build his castle. The castle was converted to a house during the eighteenth century and the church of the abbey founded here by the same Roger de Montgomery was made famous by Ellis Peters in The Brother Cadfael novels. The town prospered during the Tudor period and possesses some remarkably fine timber-framed houses. Its prosperity continued, thanks to the rich trade in wool, resulting in Owen's

Mansion and Ireland's Mansion. Shrewsbury's later popularity among fashionable society produced a magnificent selection of Georgian houses. The town's museums are well worth a visit, Rowley House Museum displays an excellent interpretation of the early history of Shrewsbury.

Attractive and seductive as rural Shropshire is, no visitor should leave the county without visiting the Ironbridge Gorge. Here the Industrial Revolution was born and England established as the first industrial nation. Here also we saw the precursor of change to the whole country, particularly the Midlands and northern England. The Iron Bridge itself is merely the centre of a complex of fascinating sites. The outstanding Ironbridge Gorge Museum skilfully brings to life the story of this region, while at Blists Hill Open Air Museum a working Victorian town is recreated in forty-two acres of woodland.

PLACES TO VISIT

This is a small selection of interesting places to visit. Many more are listed in our annual guide to Museums, Galleries, Historic Houses & Sites (see page 448)

Ironbridge Gorge Museums
Ironbridge, Telford
The history of the world's first cast-iron bridge. It is home to nine superb attractions.

Hawkstone Park
Weston-under-Redcastle, Shrewsbury
Created in the eighteenth century by the Hill family, this Grade I listed park offers visitors a magical world of caves, cliffs, hidden pathways, grottos and nearly 100 acres of hilly terrain.

Ludlow Castle
Castle Square, Ludlow
Built between 1086 to 1094 to maintain the English Kingdom of William the

Conqueror and was later enlarged as a palace. Once home to the princes in the tower and Prince Arthur and his bride, Catherine of Aragon.

The Shrewsbury Quest
Abbey Foregate, Shrewsbury
A twelfth century visitor attraction where you can solve mysteries, create illuminated manuscripts, play medieval games and relax in the beautiful herb garden.

Wroxeter Roman City Museum
Wroxeter, Shrewsbury
Once the forth largest city in Roman Britain, the city depicts life as it was, using excavations of Roman relics, paintings and drawings

Shropshire

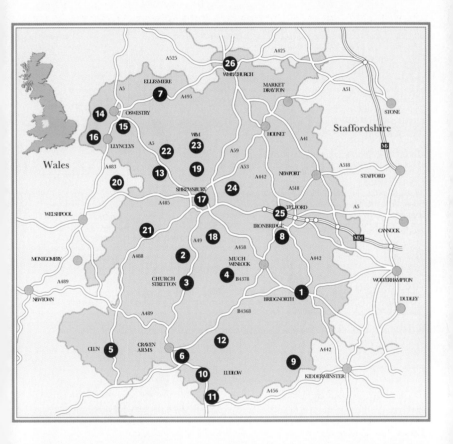

The Red Map References should be used to locate B & B properties on the pages that follow

OLDFIELD COTTAGE Oldfield, Bridgnorth WV16 6AQ   *Map Ref:* 1
Eileen Reynolds *Tel / Fax:* 01746 789257   B4364
Email: oldfield.cottage@talk21.com *Web:* www.oldfield.bridgnorthshropshire.com

Set in a traditional rural area Oldfield Cottage is only four miles from the ancient market town of Bridgnorth. The two en-suite rooms are in a tastefully converted stable building and each room has two twin beds, tea/coffee facilities, televisions, comfortable chairs and glorious views.

B & B from £22.50pp, Rooms 2 twin en-suite, No smoking, Children over 12, Dogs by arrangement, Closed Xmas & New Year

---

JINLYE Castle Hill, All Stretton, Church Stretton SY6 6JP   *Map Ref:* 2
Janet Tory *Tel / Fax:* 01694 723243   A49, B4370
Email: info@jinlye.co.uk

Award winning guest house in 15 acres amidst the Shropshire Highlands where a stroll from the house provides some stunning views. Once a crofter's cottage now provides luxurious and peaceful accommodation, there are Inglenook fireplaces, beamed ceilings and spacious lounges. The conservatory overlooks the garden, full of rare plants. The spacious en-suite bedrooms have magnificent views and ground floor rooms are available.

B & B £27-£35pp, Rooms 4 twin, 4 double, all en-suite, Restricted smoking, Children over 12, Dogs welcome, Open all year

---

LAWLEY HOUSE Smethcott, Church Stretton SY6 6NX   *Map Ref:* 3
Jackie Scarratt *Tel:* 01694 751236 *Fax:* 01694 751396   A49
Email: lawleyhouse@easicom.com *Web:* lawleyhouse.co.uk

With original Victorian features and a stunning conservatory, Lawley House is set in three acres of delightful gardens and grounds with spectacular views. Spacious bedrooms are supremely comfortable with every luxury from colour televisions to tea trays with fresh milk in cool box. Lavish traditional breakfasts, excellent local pubs and restaurants. A glowing visitor's book shows guests return again and again.

B & B £22-£30pp, Rooms 1 double, 1 twin, both en-suite, No smoking, Children over 12, Dogs by arrangement, Closed Xmas & New Year

---

GILBERRIES HALL FARM Gilberries Lane, Wall-upon-Heywood, Church Stretton SY6 7HZ
Mrs C J Hotchkiss   *Map Ref:* 4
Tel: 01694 771253   A49, B4371

Guests can enjoy panoramic views from comfortable en-suite rooms, one on the ground floor, together with indoor heated swimming pool and traditional farmhouse hospitality. AA 4 Diamonds.

B & B £24-£26pp, Rooms 1 single, 1 double, 1 twin, all en-suite, No smoking, Children over 10, No dogs, Closed Nov to Jan

---

THE BIRCHES MILL Clun SY7 8NL   *Map Ref:* 5
Gill Della Casa & Andrew Farmer *Tel / Fax:* 01588 640409   A488
Email: gill@birchesmill.fsnet.co.uk *Web:* www.virtual-shropshire.co.uk/birchesmill

Set in a beautiful secluded valley on the banks of the River Unk, surrounded by excellent walks and abundant wildlife, our 17th century country house is a haven of peace and quiet with friendly and informal hospitality. Three miles from the picturesque village of Clun and a short drive from historic Ludlow.

B & B £26-£32pp, Dinner from £19, Rooms 2 double, 1 twin, all en-suite, No smoking, Children over 8, No dogs, Closed Nov to Mar

NEW HOUSE FARM Clun SY7 8NJ
Miriam Ellison *Tel:* 01588 638314

Map Ref: 5
A488, A489

Email: sarah@bishopscastle.co.uk *Web:* www.new-house-clun.co.uk

Retreat to the remote 18th Century farm house set high in Clun Hills near Welsh Border. Unspoilt countryside, quiet roads, walks from the doorstep. The farm also includes its own Iron Age Hill Fort. Alternatively, sit and relax with a good book in a large country garden. Two very spacious bedrooms with outstanding views, period furnished - all facilties provided. Ring for brochure. ETC 5 Diamonds, Gold Award.

B & B £25-£27.50pp, Rooms 1 family, 1 twin, both en-suite/private, No smoking, Children over 10, Dogs by arrangement, Closed Nov to Mar

---

THE FIRS Norton, Craven Arms SY7 9LS
Tel / Fax: 01588 672511 *Mobile:* 07977 697903

Map Ref: 6
A49, B4368

Email: thefirs@go2.co.uk *Web:* www.go2.co.uk/firs

An elegant Victorian stone house, 125 years old, standing in two acres of garden. Large en-suite rooms overlook the Corve Dale with views reaching to the Malvern Hills. Just a good walk to Stokesay Castle - 'not to be missed' - and a quick drive to Powis Castle, Ironbridge and Ludlow with its award-winning restaurants. Plus self-catering garden annexe. ETC 4 Diamonds.

B & B from £22.50pp, Rooms 2 double, 1 twin, most en-suite, No smoking, Children welcome, Dogs in annexe only, Open all year

---

GREENBANKS Coptiviney, Ellesmere SY12 0ND
Christopher & Tanda Wilson-Clarke *Tel / Fax* 01691 623420

Map Ref: 7
M54, M56, A5, A528

Mobile: 07967 605124 *Email:* wilson.clarke@ukonline.co.uk *Web:* www.wolseylodges.co.uk

Greenbanks is an attractive Victorian house within view of the magnificent Welsh hills, peacefully situated in the tranquility of this unspoilt rural area. Here you will find a warm welcome and a friendly relaxed atmosphere. The extensive garden includes a lovely woodland walk, wildlife pond and synthetic grass tennis court. The historic centres of Shrewsbury, Wrexham and Chester are nearby.

B & B from £35pp, Dinner from £20, Rooms 1 double, 1 twin, both en-suite, No smoking, Children over 12, Dogs only outside, Closed Xmas & New Year

---

THE LIBRARY HOUSE 11 Severn Bank, Ironbridge TF8 7AN
Chris & George Maddocks *Tel:* 01952 432299 *Fax:* 01952 433967 *Mobile:* 07713850063

Map Ref: 8
A442

Email: info@libraryhouse.com *Web:* www.libraryhouse.com

A well restored Grade II listed building situated in the world heritage site of the Ironbridge Gorge, about 60 metres from Ironbridge itself. Central for the museums and Telford's many business parks. A warm welcome awaits in en-suite rooms, all have a television and video plus tea/coffee facilities. We are a totally no smoking house.

B & B £27.50-£30pp, Rooms 4 single, 3 double, 1 twin, 1 family, all en-suite, No smoking, Children over 10, Dogs by arrangement, Closed Dec to Feb

---

THE SEVERN TROW Church Road, Jackfield, Ironbridge TF8 7ND
Pauline Hanningan *Tel:* 01952 883551

Map Ref: 8
M54, A442

Email: paulineseverntrow@lineone.net *Web:* www.theseverntrow.fsnet.co.uk

For centuries, travellers have enjoyed the hospitality of The Severn Trow, a former ale house, lodgings and brothel, catering for boatmen of the river. Today guests can enjoy four poster beds in well equipped rooms. English breakfast is served, vegetarian or special diets on request. Some accommodation is suitable for guests of limited mobility. A lounge is available. Parking.

B & B £23-£28pp, Rooms 3 double en-suite, No smoking, Children by arrangement, Dogs by arrangement, Closed Nov to Dec

THE OLD BAKE HOUSE 46/47 High Street, Cleobury Mortimer, Kidderminster DY14 8DQ   *Map Ref:* 9
Robert & Joan Neil   *Tel:* 01299 270193   A4117
Email: old-bake-house@amserve.net   *Web:* smoothhound.co.uk/hotels/oldbakehouse

This Grade II listed building, situated in the main street, was originally two houses built in the late 18th century, and contains oak beams, dormer and bay windows. It is fully heated with radios and tea/coffee facilities in the bedrooms, a residents' lounge with television and a separate dining room. Evening meals by arrangement with coeliacs and vegetarians catered for.

B & B from £27.50pp, Dinner from £8, Rooms 1 double, 2 twin, all en-suite, Restricted smoking, Children by arrangement, Dogs by arrangement, Closed Xmas & New Year

---

NUMBER TWENTY EIGHT 28 Lower Broad Street, Ludlow SY8 1PQ   *Map Ref:* 10
Patricia & Philip Ross   *Tel:* 01584 876996   *Fax:* 01584 876860   A49, B4361
Email: ross@no28.co.uk   *Web:* www.no28.co.uk

A warm welcome awaits in these six period town houses, each with 21st century comforts! All rooms are en-suite and individually furnished to the highest standards. Ludlow boasts more Michelin restaurants within walking distance of Number Twenty Eight than you can shake a knife and fork at. Come, therefore to Number Twenty Eight to live like a lord and to Ludlow to eat like one! Reservations 0800 081 5000.

B & B £37.50-£50pp, C-Cards MC VS, Rooms 5 double, 1 twin, 3 family suite, all en-suite, No smoking, Children & dogs welcome,

---

THE MARCLE Brimfield, Ludlow SY8 4NE   *Map Ref:* 11
Patricia Jones   *Tel / Fax:* 01584 711459   *Mobile:* 07968 491458   A456, A49
Email: marcle@supanet.com   *Web:* www.marcle.com

Delightful 16th century house stands in the centre of this pretty village. Extensively renovated, exposed beams, timbered walls and other features abound. The elegantly furnished lounge and other areas are impeccably decorated. Three bedrooms, decorated with pretty wallpapers and equipped with modern facilities. Well tended lawns and gardens, and hospitality from the family is welcoming. AA 4 Diamonds, Selected. ETB 2 Crowns Highly Commended.

B & B from £27pp, Dinner from £15, Rooms 1 twin, 2 double, all en-suite, No smoking, Children over 12, No dogs, Closed Jan to Mar

---

RAVENSCOURT MANOR Wooferton, Ludlow SY8 4AL   *Map Ref:* 11
Michael & Elizabeth Purnell   A49, A456
Tel: 01584 711905   *Fax:* 01587 711905   *Mobile:* 07855 797845

Ravenscourt is a superb Tudor manor set in lovely grounds, restored to an extremely high standard with every modern facility. Only two and a half miles from Ludlow and convenient for walking, golfing and an excellent centre for touring. Your comfort and welcome are assured with full central heating and en-suite rooms with tea/coffee facilities. Also two self catering cottages. 4 Diamonds, Gold Award.

B & B from £27.50pp, Rooms 2 double, 1 twin, all en-suite, Restricted smoking, Children welcome, Dogs not in house, Closed Nov & Jan

---

SHORTGROVE Brimfield Common, Ludlow SY8 4NZ   *Map Ref:* 11
Beryl Maxwell   A49
Tel: 01584 711418

Grade two listed Elizabethan timber framed house with gardens and grounds of three and a half acres in peace and quiet. The house is exceptional with every comfort to make a stay memorable. Food is excellent, Beryl is a cookery tutor. Nearby are castles, NT houses, antiques shops, Hereford, Ludlow, black and white villages, Hay on Wye, Mortimer Forest for walking and riding.

B & B from £28pp, Dinner from £22, Rooms 1 en-suite twin, 1 private double, No smoking, No children or dogs, Closed Oct to Easter

CLEETON COURT Cleeton St Mary, near Ludlow DY14 0QZ
Mrs Ros Woodward   *Tel / Fax:* 01584 823379   *Mobile:* 07778 903136
Email: jk.stranghan@talk21.com   *Web:* www.cleetoncourt.co.uk

Map Ref: 12
A4117

A part 14th century farmhouse, completely renovated in 1997, Cleeton Court is an attractive and comfortable family home. Breakfast is served in a sunny oak beamed dining room and a beautiful drawing room is available for guests. Good local pubs and Ludlow with its Michelin starred restaurants is only eight miles away.

B & B £27.50-£32.50pp, Rooms 1 double, 1 twin, both en-suite, Restricted smoking, Children over 5, No dogs, Closed Xmas & New Year

---

TOP FARMHOUSE Knockin, Oswestry SY10 8HN
Pam Morrissey   *Tel:* 01691 682582   *Fax:* 01691 682070
Email: p.a.m@knockin.freeserve.co.uk   *Web:* www.topfarmknockin.co.uk

Map Ref: 13
A5

Black and white 16th century house in Knockin village, offering old fashioned hospitality and modern comforts. Spacious well equipped bedrooms. Hearty breakfasts served in an elegant dining room overlooking the garden, there is a guests' drawing room with a grand piano. Within walking distance of good pub food. Convenient for Wales, Chester, Shrewsbury, Oswestry. Chirk and Powis Castle close by.

B & B from £23pp, C-Cards, Rooms 1 twin, 1 double, 1 family, all en-suite, No smoking in dining room, Children over 12, Dogs welcome, Open all year

---

THE OLD VICARAGE Llansilin, Oswestry SY10 7PX
Pam Johnson   *Tel:* 01691 791345
Email: pam@vicarage-guests.co.uk   *Web:* www.vicarage-guests.co.uk

Map Ref: 14
B4580

Come and relax in our secluded and tranquil Georgian home and mature gardens enjoying views of unspoilt countryside on the Shropshire Welsh border. After a peaceful night's sleep in a spacious en-suite bedroom linger over a hearty breakfast with truly free-range eggs and homemade preserves before enjoying all that this area has to offer.

B & B £22-£24pp, Rooms 2 double en-suite, 1 twin with private shower, No smoking, Children over 12, No dogs, Closed Xmas & New Year

---

ASHFIELD FARMHOUSE Maesbury, Oswestry SY10 8JH
Mrs Margaret Jones   *Tel / Fax:* 01691 653589   *Mobile:* 07989 477414
Email: marg@ashfieldfarmhouse.co.uk   *Web:* www.ashfieldfarmhouse.co.uk

Map Ref: 15
A5, A483

Roses ramble around this 16th century coach house and Georgian farmhouse. One mile from Oswestry, A5, A483. Scented gardens, lovely views, excellent hospitality. Exceptionally pretty, en-suite rooms, cottagey and spacious. Flowers and olde worlde charm fill the rooms. Parking. Short walk canalside Inn and boathire. Chester, Llangollen, Shrewsbury and Ironbridge closeby. Castles, lakes and valleys of North Wales. Business people welcome.

B & B from £20pp, C-Cards MC VS AE, Rooms 3 double/single/ twin/family, 2 family, 2 en-suite, 1 private, Restricted smoking, Children & dogs welcome, Open all year

---

FOUR GABLES Nantmawr, Oswestry SY10 9HH
June & Bill Braddick
Tel: 01691 828708

Map Ref: 16
A5

A warm welcome and home cooked food is assured at this country home, set in a hamlet on the Welsh borders. The lounge overlooks five acres of gardens, abundant with wildlife, excellent for bird watchers. The garden and coarse fishing pools were featured on BBC television. The countryside is unspoilt and near to riding and Offa's Dyke footpaths. Licensed to sell alcohol to guests.

B & B from £25pp, Dinner from £10, Rooms 1 twin, 2 double, all en-suite, Children welcome, No dogs, Closed Xmas & New Year

---

FIELDSIDE 38 London Road, Shrewsbury SY2 6NX   *Map Ref:* 17
Rosemary Brookes *Tel:* 01743 353143 *Fax:* 01743 354687   A5, A49
Email: robrookes@btinternet.com *Web:* www.fieldsideguesthouse.co.uk

Fieldside is a lovely Victorian house built in 1835 and set in peaceful, attractive gardens. The tastefully decorated, centrally heated bedrooms have en-suite facilities, welcome tray, television and hairdryer. Fieldside is a non-smoking establishment and has off-road parking for all guests. It is situated one mile from the town centre and is within easy reach of main access routes to Shrewsbury.

B & B £22.50-£27.50pp, Rooms 2 single, 4 double, 2 twin, most en-suite, No smoking, Open all year

---

ACTON PIGOT Acton Burnell, Shrewsbury SY5 7PH   *Map Ref:* 18
Hildegard Owen *Tel:* 01694 731209 *Fax:* 01694 731399   A458
Email: acton@farmline.com *Web:* www.actonpigot.co.uk

Set in two acres of established gardens, this 17th century farmhouse holds a warm welcome for all. The bedrooms have en-suite bathrooms, tea/coffee facilities, televisions and enjoy wonderful views of Shropshire countryside. Please do look at our web site to view the bedrooms and gardens.

B & B from £27.50pp, Dinner from £15, Rooms 1 double, 1 twin, 1 family, all en-suite, No smoking, Children welcome, Dogs by arrangement, Open all year

---

THE OLD STATION Leaton, Bomere Heath, Shrewsbury SY4 3AP   *Map Ref:* 19
Colin & Margaret Langley *Tel:* 01939 290905 *Mobile:* 07885 526307   B5067
Web: www.leisurelinxuk.com

Situated amongst farmland and by a village cricket ground stands this former country railway station set in two acres of grounds. It has been extensively enlarged and renovated to the highest standards with antique furniture and differing colour schemes. Shower rooms are in highly decorated Victorian-style with power showers. Only four miles from the historic town of Shrewsbury.

B & B £20-£27.50pp, Dinner from £10, Rooms 4 double, 2 family, all en-suite or private bathroom, No smoking, Children over 10, Dogs by arrangement, Open all year

---

BRIMFORD HOUSE Brimford House, Criggion, Shrewsbury SY5 9AU   *Map Ref:* 20
Elizabeth Dawson *Tel / Fax:* 01938 570235   B4393
Email: info@brimford.co.uk *Web:* www.brimford.co.uk

Elegant Georgian farmhouse between Shrewsbury and Welshpool. Tranquil scenic countryside on the Shropshire Welsh border, wonderful for walks and wildlife. Enjoy log fires and romantic weekends in our stylish spacious bedrooms, all en-suite. A hearty farmhouse breakfast is served with homemade preserves, free-range eggs and venison sausages. Country pub only three minutes walk. Private fishing. Mid week discounts available.

B & B from £22.50pp, Rooms 2 double, 1 twin, all en-suite, No smoking, Children welcome, Dogs by arrangement, Open all year

---

CRICKLEWOOD COTTAGE Ploxgreen, Minsterley, Shrewsbury SY5 0HT   *Map Ref:* 21
Paul Costello *Tel:* 01743 791229   A488
Email: paul.crickcott@bushinternet.com *Web:* www.SmoothHound.co.uk/hotels/crickle

Delightful 18th century cottage at the foot of Stiperstones Hills, retaining its original character with exposed beams, inglenook fireplace and traditional furnishings. Beautiful countryside views from bedrooms and sun room where breakfast is served. Inviting cottage garden and trout stream. Excellent restaurants and inns nearby. Ideal for Shrewsbury and Ironbridge. Brochure available.

B & B from £23.50pp, Rooms 2 double, 1 twin, all en-suite, No smoking, Children over 8, No dogs, Open all year

---

BROWNHILL HOUSE Ruyton XI Towns, Shrewsbury SY4 1LR
Yoland & Roger Brown *Tel:* 01939 261121 *Fax:* 01939 260626
Email: brownhill@eleventowns.co.uk *Web:* www.eleventowns.co.uk

Map Ref: 22
A5, B4397

Olde Worlde standards, modern facilities and a relaxed atmosphere. The unique two acre garden has beautiful views. Easy access to the historic attractions of Shropshire and North Wales, Ironbridge, Snowdonia, Chester to Ludlow. Pubs within walking distance. An extensive breakfast menu is offered and dinners are available using local produce, bring your own wine. Good restaurants nearby. Tea and coffee is always available.

B & B £17.50-£24pp, C-Cards MC VS, Dinner from £14, Rooms 1 single, 1 twin, 1 double, all en-suite, Restricted smoking, Children welcome, No dogs, Open all year

LOWE HALL FARM Wem, Shrewsbury SY4 5UE
Mrs Ann Jones *Tel / Fax:* 01939 232236
Email: bandb@lowehallfarm.demon.co.uk *Web:* www.lowehallfarm.demon.co.uk

Map Ref: 23
B5476

Historically famous 16th century listed farmhouse with extensive gardens and newly renovated moat, a haven of peace and tranquility. Inside is a splendid Jacobean staircase, Charles II fireplace, antique furnishings and fine paintings. Tastefully decorated and centrally heated with en-suite bedrooms which have televisions, bathrobes, hairdryers and luxury toiletries. Highest standard of food, decor and accommodation guaranteed. Ideal touring centre.

B & B from £24pp, Rooms 1 single, 1 double, 1 twin, 1 family, all en-suite, No smoking, Children welcome, No dogs, Closed Xmas & New Year

THE MILL HOUSE Shrewsbury Road, High Ercall, Telford TF6 6BE
Mrs Judy Yates *Tel / Fax:* 01952 770394
Email: mill-house@talk21.com *Web:* www.virtual-shropshire.co.uk/millhouse

Map Ref: 24
B5062

The Mill House is an 18th century converted water mill beside the River Rodew on a nine acre working small holding. There is a wood beamed guest lounge with colour television for relaxing in. Situated between Shrewsbury and Telford and ideally placed to visit Ironbridge, Mid-Wales and Shropshire. Reduced rates for longer stays.

B & B from £20pp, Rooms 1 single, 1 twin, 1 family, all en-suite, No smoking, Children welcome, Dogs by arrangement, Open all year

SHRAY HILL HOUSE Shray Hill, Telford TF6 6JR
Chris Wright
Tel / Fax: 01952 541260

Map Ref: 25
M54

150 year old country house with panoramic views set in four acres of woodland and formal gardens. Easy access to Shrewsbury, Ironbridge, Newport and Telford. All rooms have en-suite, colour television and tea/coffee facilities. Private drawing room with log fire for guests' use together with ample parking. AA 4 Diamonds.

B & B from £25pp, Rooms 1 single, 2 double, 1 twin, all en-suite, No smoking, Children welcome, No dogs, Closed Xmas & New Year

DEARNFORD HALL Tilstock Road, Whitchurch SY13 3JJ
Charles & Jane Bebbington *Tel:* 01948 662319 *Fax:* 01948 666670
Email: dearnford_hall@yahoo.com *Web:* www.dearnfordhall.com

Map Ref: 26
B5476

Handsome William and Mary house in a peaceful, private setting. King-sized en-suite bedrooms are bright and sunny with rich fabrics, deep mattresses, fat duvets and fine linen. Bathrooms have power showers and baths. Play the Steinway in the hall or Jane can arrange fly-fishing, and tuition, on their own trout lake. Stategically placed for Chester, Shrewsbury, the Potteries and the Welsh borders.

B & B £35-£50pp, C-Cards MC VS, Rooms 1 double/twin, 1 twin, all en-suite, No smoking, Children over 12, Dogs by arrangement, Closed Xmas

Somerset

There is no doubt that Somerset is a holiday county; there is so much to enjoy here that one visit could never suffice. The diversity of scenery to the northwest is the high heather-clad moorland plateau of Exmoor bordering the Bristol Channel, giving England's highest sea cliffs. This was once wild and windswept hunting country, changed somewhat during the nineteenth century by a rich ironmaster who converted some 15,000 acres of the moor into farmland and in the process planted miles of beech hedges, many surviving today. This is a glorious region of wild ponies, red deer and lovely combes, an area of prehistoric sites and ancient packhorse bridges. The National Trust owns the vast Holnicote Estate which includes the high tors of Dunkery and Selworthy Beacons that offer staggering views in all directions. Not to be missed by those who enjoy walking in superb scenery is Oare, a pretty and remote hamlet in a wooded valley on the very edge of Exmoor. Its little church was the setting for the wedding of Lorna Doone in R.D.Blackmore's novel. The small harbour of Minehead, developed as a seaside resort during the Victorian era and still retaining much of its Victorian atmosphere, is a grand centre for touring this district. The West Somerset Steam Railway, the longest privately run railway in the country meanders the twenty miles from Minehead to Bishops Lydeard and just two miles from Minehead is the gloriously picturesque and much visited town of Dunster with its fine sixteenth century Yarn Market. Dunster Castle, which is part medieval, part Victorian and the fortified home of the Luttrell family for 600 years, is set in a 28 acre park.

In the east are the Mendips, a range of limestone hills running from Weston-Super-Mare across the county to Frome. Over the centuries the limestone has been deeply eroded producing a large number of underground caves and gorges. The Cheddar Gorge and its associated caves are a great attraction. A road weaves between spectacular cliffs over 400 feet high. Nearby is Wookey Hole, illuminated caverns carved out by the River Axe, housing the famous Wookey Witch. Also within the same area is a 400 year old papermill. The Ebbor Gorge gives wonderful views of the Somerset Levels and in this woodland region badgers are plentiful and buzzards and sparrowhawk may be seen. The Black Rock Nature Reserve is a lovely walking area with plantations, natural woodland, limestone scree

Wells Magnificent Cathedral (SWT)

and dramatic rock faces. At the eastern end of the Mendips stands Wells, England's smallest city, its spectacular limestone streets dwarfed by its magnificent cathedral. The city is an historical and architectural treasure and the wells and springs that give the city its name are in the gardens of the bishop's palace. The Quantock Hills, stretching from near Taunton to the Bristol Channel, at Quantockhead provide the perfect region for the serious walker. The most dramatic parts are Beacon and Bicknoller Hills east of Williton, 630 acres of moorland which includes the ancient monument, Trendle Ring, an Iron Age fort. From the Quantocks are magnificent views over the Bristol Channel, The Vale of Taunton Deane and Exmoor.

At the centre of the county are the Somerset Levels, low-lying flat land. Here the town of Glastonbury, a center of both Christian and atheist beliefs, clusters around the base of the green hillock of Glastonbury Tor, which some say was the Isle of Avalon in the King Arthur legend, crowned with the tower of St Michael's Chapel, visible from far around. The ancient abbey has long been a place of pilgrimage as legend tells that it was here that Joseph of Arimathea buried the chalice used at the Last Supper.

Taunton, the county town of Somerset, has been an important centre of trade and administration since Saxon times. It was in Taunton in 1685 that the Duke of Monmouth was proclaimed king causing the local people to rebel and it was in the Great Hall of Taunton Castle that Judge Jeffreys held his Bloody Assizes in the aftermath of the rebellion. But there is a wealth of interest in this lovely town, much recorded in the excellent Somerset County Museum.

PLACES TO VISIT

This is a small selection of interesting places to visit. Many more are listed in our annual guide to Museums, Galleries, Historic Houses & Sites (see page 448)

Cheddar Caves and Gorge
Cheddar

Two stunning showcaves, Gough's Cave and Cox's cave are both illuminated. The caves were occupied by stone age man 40,000 years ago and there is also a heritage centre with a reconstruction of the dwellings.

Glastonbury Abbey
Glastonbury

Surrounded in myth and legend this is a modern day pilgrimage site set in 36 peaceful acres with the chapel, with its holy water vessel, stone altar and sacred Thorn Tree.

Montacute House
Montacute

This fine Elizabethan house was built by Sir Edward Philips, Speaker of the House of Commons, in 1588. Filled with treasures, especially the Long Gallery, it is set in suitably formal gardens.

Wells Cathedral
Wells

The Cathedral was built incorporating several Gothic styles but it is most famous for its west front, a magnificent sculpture gallery, and its 600 year old clock.

Somerset

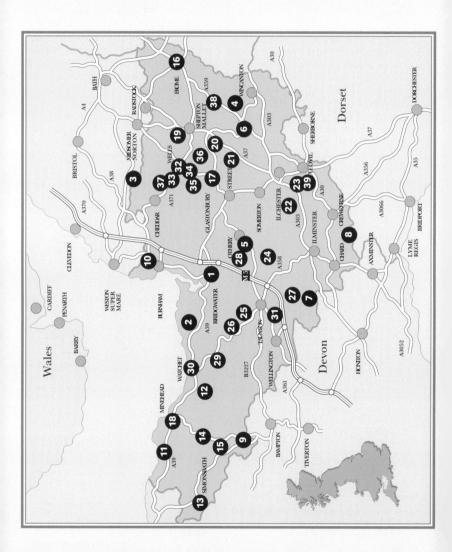

The Red Map References should be used to locate B & B properties on the pages that follow

MODEL FARM Perry Green, Wembdon, Bridgwater TA5 2BA   *Map Ref:* 1
Richard & Carol Wright   *Tel:* 01278 433999   A39
Email: info@modelfarm   *Web:* modelfarm.com

Richard and Carol Wright invite you to share in the peaceful setting of their licensed Victorian farmhouse, set in two acres of garden. Relax in large en-suite bedrooms or enjoy a pre-dinner drink in the lounge by an open fire. Dine by candlelight around an oak refectory table with your hosts, beside a roaring log fire. ETC and AA 4 Diamonds.

B & B £25-£30pp, C-Cards MC VS AE, Dinner from £12, Rooms 1 double, 2 twin, all en-suite, No smoking, Children over 3, Dogs by arrangement, Closed Xmas & New Year

---

FRIARN COTTAGE Over Stowey, Bridgwater TA5 1HW   *Map Ref:* 2
Penny & Michael Taylor-Young   A39
Tel / Fax: 01278 732870

Friarn Cottage stands 500 feet up on the Quantock Hills amid beautiful Somerset countryside. Visitors have a centrally heated self contained wing. Breakfast may be served in the garden which displays a blanket of wild flowers. The bedroom has wonderful views, blankets or duvets to suit. Ponies, sheep, ravens, buzzards and deer abound. Wonderful for bird watching.Nether Stowey is nearby.

B & B from £28.50pp, Dinner from £10, Rooms double/twin en-suite, No smoking, No children, Dogs in car, Open all year

---

HERONS GREEN FARM Compton Martin, Bristol BS40 6NL   *Map Ref:* 3
Sandra Hasell   *Tel:* 01275 333372   *Fax:* 01275 333041   *Mobile:* 07855 745717   B3114
Email: hasell@farmersweekly.net

Set in peaceful surroundings by the side of Chew Valley Lake, this pretty farmhouse features an oak beamed dining room and an original water well. Ideal for walking the Mendip Hills and visiting Chedder, Wells, Weston-super-Mare and Bath. There is central heating, ample parking and a garden for guests.

B & B from £20pp, Rooms 1 double, 1 family, No smoking, Children over 4, No dogs, Closed Nov to Mar

---

GANTS MILL Bruton BA10 0DB   *Map Ref:* 4
Alison & Brian Shingler   *Tel:* 01749 812393   A359
Email: shingler@gantsmill.co.uk   *Web:* www.gantsmill.co.uk

Guests wake to the sound of the waterfall into the millpool by the watermill. They can look out over the professionally designed colour themed garden with its streams, ponds and collections of irises, delphiniums, daylilies and dahlias. The lovely old stonebuilt farmhouse and historic watermill are set in their own valley. There are local walks, gardens, attractions, pubs and restaurants.

B & B from £25pp, C-Cards MC VS, Rooms 1 single with pb, 2 family, 1 en-suite and 1 pb, No smoking, Children over 12, No dogs, Open all year

---

SALTMOOR HOUSE Saltmoor, Burrowbridge TA7 0RL   *Map Ref:* 5
Elizabeth Deacon   *Tel:* 01823 698092   A361
Email: saltmoorhouse@amserve.net

Saltmoor House is a listed Georgian property set in 15 acres in the heart of the Somerset Levels and Moors. Centrally heated house furnished with elegant simplicity with log fires and flagstone floors. Breakfast is served in garden room adjoining guest sitting room and a delicious dinner is also available. Car parking and easy access to M5 Junction 24.

B & B from £45pp, Dinner from £25, Rooms 2 double en-suite with pb, 1 twin en-suite with shower, No smoking, No children or dogs, Open all year

CLANVILLE MANOR Castle Cary BA7 7PJ

Mrs Sally Snook *Tel:* 01963 350124 *Fax:* 01963 350719 *Mobile:* 07966 512732

Email: info@clanvillemanor.co.uk *Web:* www.clanvillemanor.co.uk

Map Ref: 6
A371, B3153

18th century elegance but 21st century comfort. A Georgian farmhouse on a dairy farm, two miles from Castle Cary. Flagstone hall, oriental rugs, old elm floorboards, polished English oak staircase and fully ensuite rooms with all expected comforts. Wonderful Aga breakfasts and outdoor pool in summer. Glastonbury, Wells and lots of National Trust properties nearby. What more could you want?

B & B £25-£27.50pp, C-Cards MC VS, Rooms 1 single, 1 double, 1 twin/family, all en-suite, No smoking, Children welcome, No dogs, Closed Xmas & New Year

---

HILLSIDE Buckland St Mary, Chard TA20 3TQ

Roy Harkness *Tel / Fax:* 01460 234599 *Mobile:* 077 0363 3770

Email: royandmarge@hillsidebsm.freeserve.co.uk *Web:* www.theAA.com/hotels/103591.html

Map Ref: 7
A303

Extended Victorian cottage within spacious gardens and glorious views over Blackdown Hills. Excellently placed for Exmoor, Dartmoor, Quantocks, the stunning Lyme Bay coastline and numerous attractions of the South West. Our comfortable bedrooms have televisions, tea/coffee facilities and hairdryers. The ground floor apartment is fully equipped. We always use local produce and there are pubs and restaurants nearby.

B & B from £22.50pp, Rooms 1 double en-suite, 1 twin, 1 single both pb, 1 s/c apartment, No smoking, Children welcome, Dogs by arrangement, Closed Xmas & New Year

---

HAWTHORNE HOUSE Bishopswood, Chard TA20 3RS

Roger & Sarah Newman-Coburn *Tel:* 01460 234482 *Fax:* 01460 255059

Mobile: 07710 255059 *Email:* info@roger-sarah.com *Web:* www.roger-sarah.co.uk

Map Ref: 7
A303, B3170

In the Blackdown Hills 1 mile off the A303, ideal for overnight stops for Cornwall or the Plymouth Ferries. The coast, Exmoor and NT properties are easily reached. Guests have unrestricted access to their rooms, the garden and lounge with TV. The dining room overlooks the terraces and has views to the garden, the wildlife pond and over the hills. ETB 3 Diamonds.

B & B from £22.50pp, Dinner from £12.50, Rooms 1 twin, 2 double, both en-suite/private, No smoking, Children over 12, Dogs welcome, Open all year

---

MANOR FARM Wayford, Crewkerne TA18 8QL

Austin & Theresa Emery *Tel / Fax:* 01460 78865 *Mobile:* 07767 620031

Web: www.manorfarm.com

Map Ref: 8
B3165

Beautiful Victorian country home in peaceful location with superb views. Easy reach of Lyme Regis coast, Forde Abbey and various National Trust properties. All rooms are en-suite with televisions and tea/coffee facilities and course fishing is available within three ponds located on the property. A self catering flat is also available for renting.

B & B from £25pp, Rooms 1 double, 1 twin, 2 family, all en-suite, No smoking, Children welcome, Guide dogs only, Open all year

---

HIGHER LANGRIDGE FARM Exbridge, Dulverton TA22 9RR

Mrs Gill Summers *Tel / Fax:* 01398 323999

Email: info@langridgefarm.co.uk *Web:* www.langridgefarm.co.uk

Map Ref: 9
B3222

17th century farmhouse overlooking our own peaceful valley on the edge of Exmoor National Park. A real working farm with walks and wildlife in picturesque countryside just four miles south-west of Dulverton. Old beams, log fires and central heating. Double or family rooms with wonderful countryside views.

B & B £21-£24pp, C-Cards MC VS, Dinner from £14, Rooms 2 double, 1 en-suite, 1 family, No smoking, Children welcome, Dogs by arrangement, Closed Xmas & New Year

Wood Advent Farm, Roadwater in Exmoor National Park

SPRINGFIELD FARM Ashwick Lane, Dulverton TA22 9QD
Mrs P Vellacott *Tel / Fax:* 01398 323722
Email: info@springfieldfarms.freeserve.co.uk *Web:* www.springfieldfarms.freeserve.co.uk

Map Ref: 9
M5. B3223

Peacefully situated between Dulverton and Tarr Steps, Springfield Farm has a beautiful view of the Exmoor countryside with much wildlife to be seen. Enjoy delicious meals in the comfort of our farmhouse where 24 hours notice should be given if evening meals are required.

B & B £20-£23.50pp, Dinner from £15, Rooms 1 double, 1 twin/ family, both en-suite, 1 double with pb, No smoking, Children over 4, Dogs by arrangement, Closed Dec to Feb

TOWN MILLS High Street, Dulverton TA22 9HB
Jane Buckingham
Tel: 01398 323124

Map Ref: 9
B3223

Escape for a while to enjoy comfort and peace in our secluded 19th century mill house situated in the centre of Dulverton. We serve full English breakfasts in our attractive and spacious rooms and some have their own log fire. We are an ideal centre for exploring Exmoor.

B & B from £19pp, Rooms 3 double, 2 twin, most en-suite, Children welcome, No dogs, Open all year

KNOLL LODGE Church Road, East Brent TA9 4HZ
Jaqui & Tony Collins
Tel: 01278 760294

Map Ref: 10
M5, A38, A370

Knoll Lodge is a 19th century Somerset house offering comfortable accommodation and quality food in friendly and peaceful rural surroundings. Each room is attractively decorated with antique pine furniture and hand made American patchwork quilts, tea/coffee facilities and colour TV. Two and a half miles from M5, Junction 22. Guest lounge. Ample parking.

B & B from £22pp, Dinner £12, Rooms 2 double en-suite, 1 twin with private bathroom, No smoking, Children over 12, No dogs, Closed Xmas

FERN COTTAGE Allerford, Porlock, Exmoor National Park TA24 8HN
Jean & Ian Hamilton *Tel / Fax:* 01643 862215 *Mobile:* 07989 912394
Email: ferncottage@bushinternet.com *Web:* exmoor.tv/ferncottage

Map Ref: 11
A39

A large 16th century traditional Exmoor cottage set in a tiny National Trust village in a wood fringed vale. Exhilarating walks in dramatic hill and coastal scenery start on the doorstep. Noted for fine classic/bistro cooking and comprehensive cellar. A non-smoking house.

B & B from £29pp, C-Cards MC VS AE, Dinner from £13.75, Rooms 3 double/twin/family, all en-suite, No smoking, Children over 8, Dogs not in public rooms, Closed Xmas

WOOD ADVENT FARM Roadwater, Exmoor National Park TA23 0RR
John & Diana Brewer *Tel / Fax:* 01984 640920
Email: jddibrewer@aol.com *Web:* www.woodadventfarm.co.uk

Map Ref: 12
A39
see Photo on page 273

This is an attractive 19th century Somerset farmhouse and working farm. Peace and tranquillity are offered here in the beautiful Exmoor countryside. Well marked foot paths go for miles. The generously equipped en-suite bedrooms have delightful views. Two large reception rooms with log fires, delicious Exmoor dishes are served in the dining room. Relax by the pool, and enjoy tea in the garden.

B & B from £23pp, C-Cards MC VS, Dinner from £15, Rooms 2 twin, 2 double, 1 family, all en-suite/private, No smoking in bedrooms, Children over 8, Dogs in kennel or car, Closed Xmas

EMMETTS GRANGE Simonsbath, Exmoor National Park TA24 7LD
Map Ref: 13
Tom & Lucy Barlow *Tel:* 01643 831138 *Fax:* 01643 831093 *Mobile:* 07773 239797
B3223
Email: emmetts.grange@virgin.net

Emmett's Grange provides an oasis of friendly civilisation amidst the stunning wild and rugged Exmoor National Park. The graceful Georgian style house is found at the end of a half mile drive at the centre of its own land which stretches to some 900 acres. Lucy and Tom love cooking and the menu often includes local seafood and Exmoor's own Red Devon beef and venison.

B & B £29-£38pp, C-Cards MC VS AE, Dinner from £24, Rooms 2 double, 1 twin, all en-suite, Restricted smoking, Children welcome, No dogs in bedrooms, Closed Xmas & New Year

CUTTHORNE Luckwell Bridge, Wheddon Cross, Exmoor National Park TA24 7EW
Map Ref: 14
Ann Durbin *Tel / Fax:* 01643 831255
B3224
Email: durbin@cutthorne.co.uk *Web:* www.cutthorne.co.uk

Country house in the heart of Exmoor. It is 'off the beaten track,' one can ride and walk in glorious countryside. Exmoor ponies, sheep and red deer can be spied. Visitors are welcome to picnic by the trout pond or wander in the fields. Beautifully presented bedrooms, a four poster and amazing views. English breakfasts. Candlelit fireside dinners. Close to Dunster, Tarr Steps.

B & B £25-£34pp, Dinner from £16, Rooms 1 twin, 1 double, 1 4 poster, all en-suite, No smoking, Children over 12, Dogs welcome, Open all year

LITTLE BRENDON HILL FARM Wheddon Cross, Exmoor National Park TA24 7BG
Map Ref: 14
Shelagh & Larry Maxwell *Tel / Fax:* 01643 841556 *Mobile:* 07813 168174
B3224
Email: info@exmoorheaven.co.uk *Web:* www.exmoorheaven.co.uk

We are proud to have gained English Tourism Council's 5 Diamonds Gold Award for a second year running. Our aim is to give our guests the very best of everything: excellent food prepared with fresh wholesome ingredients, presented on fine china cut glass and silver in the loveliest surroundings. Your comfort is paramount. Log fires, central heating and all rooms ensuite.

B & B from £23pp, C-Cards MC VS AE, Dinner from £16, Rooms 1 double, 1 twin, all ensuite, No smoking, Children over 10, No dogs, Closed Xmas

LARCOMBE FOOT Winsford, Exmoor National Park TA24 7HS
Map Ref: 15
Mrs Val Vicary *Tel / Fax:* 01643 851306
A396
Email: larcombefoot@talk21.com

A charming period house set in its own grounds overlooking the beautiful, tranquil upper Exe Valley, with footpath access to the moor from the doorstep. Comfort is paramount with the pleasantly furnished rooms facing south with views across the valley. The cosy guests' sitting room provides a television and log fire, plus peaceful gardens to relax in make it an ideal base for exploring Exmoor.

B & B from £23pp, Dinner available, Rooms 1 single, 1 double, 1 twin, all en-suite, Children over 6, Dogs welcome, Closed Dec to Mar

GARDEN HOUSE 30 Fromefield, Frome BA11 2HE
Map Ref: 16
Angela & Don Barbour *Tel / Fax:* 01373 301951
A361, A362
Web: www.garden-househotel.co.uk

Our Georgian home is tailored for discerning guests. The Beau Nash Suite includes a dressing room and log fire and The Mozart Room has a private large shower room. All usual facilities plus bath robes, chocolates, fruit and stereo. Georgian style furnishings. Log fires in the vestibule and lounge and a large walled garden with fishponds. Green Tourism Merit Award.

B & B £27.50-£32.50pp, Dinner available, Rooms 2 double, both en-suite, No smoking, Children welcome, No dogs, Open all year

WADBURY HOUSE Mells, Frome BA11 3PA   *Map Ref:* 16
Mrs Sally Brinkmann *Tel:* 01373 812359   A361, A362
Email: sbrinkmann@btinternet.com

Historic country house with galleried hall surrounded by gardens and parkland affording complete peace and quiet. The elegant rooms have magnificent views and all have televisions. There is a heated outdoor pool in summer and there are log fires in the winter. The area abounds with opportunities for outings, Bath, Wells, Glastonbury and Longleat among other local places of interest.

B & B from £28pp, Dinner available, Rooms 1 double, 3 twin, 1 family, all en-suite, Children welcome, Dogs by arrangment, Open all year

MEADOW BARN Middlewick Farm, Wick Lane, Glastonbury BA6 8JW   *Map Ref:* 17
Tel / Fax: 01458 832351   A371
Web: www.smoothhound.co.uk

A grazing cattle and sheep farm, idyllically situated amidst apple orchards and gardens. Meadow Barn has country-style ground floor accommodation with an indoor heated swimming pool. Evening meals can be arranged and children are half price when sharing the family room.

B & B from £23pp, Dinner available, Rooms 2 double, 1 twin, all en-suite, Restricted smoking, Children welcome, No dogs, Open all year

CONYGAR HOUSE 2A The Ball, Dunster, Minehead TA24 6SD   *Map Ref:* 18
Mrs B Bale *Tel / Fax:* 01643 821872   A39
Email: bale.dunster@virgin.net *Web:* http://homepage.virgin.net/bale.dunster

In a quiet road, a step from the main street of the medieval town of Dunster. Wonderful views of Dunster Castle, and to Exmoor. Visitors are invited to enjoy the garden and the patio. There are restaurants, bars and shops a minute's walk away. Dunster beach, Minehead and Porlock, are within easy reach. Conygar is an ideal base from which to explore Exmoor.

B & B £22.50-£25pp, Rooms 2 double en-suite, 1 twin with private bathroom, No smoking, Children welcome, No dogs, Closed 1st Dec to 1st Feb

HIGHER ORCHARD 30 St George's Street, Dunster, Minehead TA24 6RS   *Map Ref:* 18
Janet Lamacraft   A39
Tel: 01643 821915

A relaxed friendly home quietly located 60 yards from Exmoor National Park footpaths. Only a short walk to the village centre where there are pubs, restaurants and shops. This Victorian house built in 1864 has fine views from all en-suite rooms as it looks over the village and church towards the castle. ETB 4 Diamonds.

B & B £20-£22pp, Rooms 2 double, 1 twin, all en-suite, Children welcome, Dogs by arrangement,

THE RED HOUSE Periton Road, Minehead TA24 8DT   *Map Ref:* 18
Mrs Olive Taylor   A39
Tel / Fax: 01643 706519

The Red House is situated on the outskirts of Minehead with easy access to the breathtaking scenery. This smart, detached Queen Ann style property offers high standards of hospitality and accommodation. En-suite bedrooms are neatly presented and furnished for comfort with televisions and tea/coffee facilities and some having views across the town to the sea. Car parking.

B & B from £22pp, Rooms 2 single, 2 double en-suite, No smoking, Children over 12, No dogs, Closed Dec to Feb

PARK FARM HOUSE Forum Lane, Bowlish, Shepton Mallet BA4 5JL
Mr & Mrs J Grattan   *Tel:* 01749 343673   *Fax:* 01749 345279
Email: john.marjorie@ukonline.co.uk

Map Ref: 19
A371

A 17th century house with delightful, peaceful garden. All bedrooms
have en-suite, private bathroom, television and refreshment facilities.
Ideal for Bath, Bristol, Cheddar/Wookey, Longleat, Haynes Motor
Museum, Concord Museum and Clarks Village plus historic houses
and gardens. Many local pubs and restaurants nearby. Secure
parking.

B & B from £18.50pp, Rooms 1 double, 1 twin, 1 family, all
en-suite, Children welcome, No dogs, Closed Xmas week

PENNARD HOUSE East Pennard, Shepton Mallet BA4 6TP
Susie & Martin Dearden   *Tel / Fax:* 01749 860266
Email: m.dearden@ukonline.co.uk

Map Ref: 20
A37

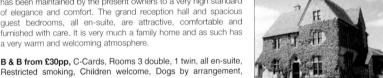

A beautiful Georgian home situated on the south facing slope of the
Mendip Hills. It stands in secluded gardens, surrounded by
meadows, woodlands and cider orchards. There is a grass tennis
court and Victorian spring fed pool. The house is funished with
antiques. Ideally situated for visiting Glastonbury, Wells, Bath and the
houses of Stourhead, Longleat, Montacute and others. Golf and
riding available nearby.

B & B from £30pp, C-Cards MC VS, Rooms 1 single, 2 twin (1 en-
suite, 1 private), 1 double en-suite, Restricted smoking, Children
welcome, No dogs, Closed Xmas & New Year

LYDFORD HOUSE Lydford-on-Fosse, Somerton TA11 7BU
Lynn & Jim Ribbons   *Tel:* 01963 240217   *Fax:* 01963 240413
Email: lynn@jamesribbons.demon.co.uk   *Web:* www.jamesribbons.demon.co.uk

Map Ref: 21
A303, A37

Lydford House was built in 1860 as a Gentleman's Residence and
has been maintained by the present owners to a very high standard
of elegance and comfort. The grand reception hall and spacious
guest bedrooms, all en-suite, are attractive, comfortable and
furnished with care. It is very much a family home and as such has
a very warm and welcoming atmosphere.

B & B from £30pp, C-Cards, Rooms 3 double, 1 twin, all en-suite,
Restricted smoking, Children welcome, Dogs by arrangement,
Open all year

MILL HOUSE Mill House, Barton St David, Somerton TA11 6DF
Michael & Rita Knight   *Tel:* 01458 851215   *Fax:* 01458 851372
Email: KnightsMillHouse@aol.com   *Web:* www.smoothhound.co.uk/hotels/millhouse3.html

Map Ref: 21
A303, A37

Ideally situated and close to Glastonbury and Wells, this beautiful
listed Georgian Mill House lies in peaceful gardens with a stream. All
rooms are en-suite with tea/coffee facilities, televisions and
hairdryers. Luxury accommodation with a warm welcome and
delicious aga cooked breakfasts await you. Good eating available
nearby. ETB 5 Diamonds.

B & B £24-£28pp, C-Cards MC VS, Dinner from £10, Rooms
1 single, 1 double, 1 twin, all en-suite, No smoking, Children
over 10, No dogs, Open all year

EAST LAMBROOK FARM East Lambrook, South Petherton TA13 5HH
Mrs Eeles   *Tel / Fax:* 01460 240064
Email: nicolaeeles@supanet.com

Map Ref: 22
A303

17th century farmhouse in a quiet village position, with a pub nearby.
It is warm and comfortable with antique furniture, central heating and
wood burning stoves. There is a sitting room with television. Guests
are welcome to enjoy the garden and tennis court. Gardens to visit
in the area, Montacute, Tintinhull, Barrington Court (National Trust
properties). Bicycle routes, River Parrett trail and pretty villages.

B & B £23-£25pp, Dinner from £15, Rooms 1 twin, 2 double,
2 private bathrooms, No smoking, Children welcome, No dogs,
Closed Xmas & New Year

COURTFIELD Norton-sub-Hamdon, Stoke-sub-Hamdon TA14 6SG

Richard & Valerie Constable *Tel:* 01935 881246

Email: courtfield@hotmail.com

Map Ref: 23
A303, A356

Comfortable family home in picturesque village one mile off A303. Rooms have handbasins, televisions, sofas and an upstairs kitchen. Relax in the conservatory where breakfast and dinner are served overlooking the lovely gardens and tennis court. The pub serves excellent food and is three minutes walk away. Ideal countryside for walking with many stately homes and gardens nearby.

B & B from £28pp, Dinner from £18, Rooms 1 double, 1 twin, both private bathroom, No smoking, Children over 8, Dogs by arrangement, Closed Xmas & New Year

---

WHITTLES FARM Beercrocombe, Taunton TA3 6AH

Mrs Claire Mitchem *Tel / Fax:* 01823 480301 *Mobile:* 07803 919337

Email: dj.cm.mitchem@themail.co.uk *Web:* www.whittlesfarm.co.uk

Map Ref: 24
A358

Whittles Farm is a dairy beef farm situated at the end of a 'no through road' and surrounded by farmland. The superior 16th century farmhouse is tastefully furnished and the well appointed bedrooms are all en-suite with televisions and tea/coffee facilities. Between Ilminster and Taunton, an ideal stopover point or a relaxing holiday. High standard of accommodation. Dinner by arrangement.

B & B £25-£27pp, Dinner from £16.50, Rooms 1 double, 1 twin, both en-suite, No smoking, Children over 12, No dogs, Closed Dec to Jan

---

THE OLD MILL Bishops Hull, Taunton TA1 5AB

Anne & Bill Slipper

Tel / Fax: 01823 289732

Map Ref: 25
M5, B3227

Grade II listed former corn mill in tranquil riverside setting with two lovely bedrooms both overlooking the weir pool. The Mill Room has a beamed ceiling, stable door and en-suite facilities and the Cottage Room boasts a private bathroom. Enjoy your breakfast from our extensive menu and relax amidst the machinery of a by-gone era. ETC 5 Diamonds, Silver Award.

B & B from £22pp, Rooms 2 double en-suite, No smoking, No children or dogs, Closed Xmas & New Year

---

REDLANDS Trebles Holford, Combe Florey, Taunton TA4 3HA

Elizabeth & Brian Totman *Tel:* 01823 433159

Email: redlandshouse@hotmail.com *Web:* www.escapetothecountry.co.uk

Map Ref: 26
A358

Redlands is a barn conversion peacefully located beside a stream at the foot of the Quantock Hills. A downstairs room is designed for disabled guests [category 3]. Stay and enjoy the West Somerset Railway, Exmoor, gardens and National Trust properties. Excellent local walking, good pubs and a warm welcome make this a relaxing escape to the country.

B & B from £26.50pp, Rooms 1 double, 1 twin, both en-suite, No smoking, Children welcome, Dogs in annexe room only, Closed Xmas & New Year

---

WEST VIEW Minehead Road, Bishops Lydeard, Taunton TA4 3BS

Ann Pattemore *Tel / Fax:* 01823 432223 *Mobile:* 07967 096962

Email: westview@pattemore.freeserve.co.uk

Map Ref: 26
A358

A fine late Victorian house set in pretty gardens on the edge of the peaceful village of Bishops Lydeard. A satisfying, full English breakfast is provided, just right for your day ahead, and there are several local inns, within a short walk, serving meals. At the end of the day, the charming lounge with television is ideal for relaxing in and planning your next day's exploring.

B & B from £25pp, Rooms 1 double en-suite, 2 twin, 1 private bathroom, No smoking, Children over 10, Dogs by arrangement, Open all year

PEAR TREE COTTAGE Stapley, Churchstanton, Taunton TA3 7QA
Pam Parry   *Tel / Fax:* 01823 601224
Email: colvin.parry@virgin.net

Map Ref: 27
M5, A303, A30

Charming south facing thatched country cottage in idyllic rural location, near Somerset/Devon border in an area of outstanding natural beauty. Picturesque countryside, wildlife abounds. Centrally placed for North and South coasts of Somerset/Devon/Dorset. Exmoor, Dartmoor, Torbay. NT and other famous gardens encircle. Traditional cottage garden with lawns, borders, vegetable raised beds, one acre leading to two and a half acre arboretum.

B & B from £15pp, Dinner from £10, Rooms 1 single, 1 double, with pb, 1 family/twin en-suite, No smoking, Children welcome, Dogs by arrangement, Open all year

---

CREECHBARN Vicarage Lane, Creech-St-Michael, Taunton TA3 5PP
Hope & Mick Humphreys   *Tel:* 01823 443955   *Fax:* 01823 443509
Email: mick@somersite.co.uk   *Web:* www.somersite.co.uk

Map Ref: 28
M5 J25

An old converted longbarn on the edge of a quiet village with open views across the Sedge Moor, only five minutes drive from junction 25 on the M5. Suitable for families and business people or short breaks away. Golf, walking, birdwatching and open gardens nearby. Large lounge with television, table tennis, library, large gardens and a patio. Taunton just 10 minutes away.

B & B from £22pp, Dinner from £12.50, Rooms 2 double, 1 en-suite, 1 twin, Restricted smoking, Children welcome, Well behaved dogs, Closed Xmas & New Year

---

NORTHAM MILL Water Lane, Stogumber, Taunton TA4 3TT
Richard Spicer and Kate Butler   *Tel:* 01984 656916   *Fax:* 01984 656144
Mobile: 07836 752235   *Email:* bmsspicercaol.com   *Web:* www.northam-mill.co.uk

Map Ref: 29
A358

Hidden for 300 years, Old Mill House with its 4 acre garden and river. Nestling in a quiet valley between the Quantock and Brendon hills in West Somerset. Idyllic, adult oasis, no children. Beamed library/dining room. Individually furnished en-suite bedrooms, equipped with all essentials. Additionally, self contained beautifully appointed apartment. Five course daily changing menu, own eggs, vegetables, bread and preserves.

B & B £25.50-£37.50pp, C-Cards MC VS AE, Dinner from £22.50, Rooms 1 single, 3 double, 2 twin, most en-suite, Restricted smoking, No children, Dogs in heated kennels, Open all year

---

DOWNFIELD HOUSE 16 St Decumans Road, Watchet TA23 0HR
Tel: 01984 631267   *Fax:* 01984 634369
Web: www.SmoothHound.co.uk/hotels/downf.html

Map Ref: 30
A39, B3190

An attractive Victorian country house with a comfortable lounge and chandeliered dining room. Set in secluded grounds with views over the harbour and town, Downfield House is close to Quantocks and Exmoor. Self catering coach house flat also available. Residential licence. Parking. Brochure available.

B & B £25-£33pp, C-Cards MC VS, Dinner from £22, Rooms 6 double, 2 twin, all en-suite, No smoking, Children over 12, Dogs by arrangement, Closed Jan

---

ESPLANADE HOUSE The Esplanade, Watchet TA23 0AJ
Derek & Rachel Fawcus
Tel: 01984 633444

Map Ref: 30
A39

A listed Georgian former farm house with picturesque garden, situated adjacent to the new Watchet Marina. Very comfortable bedrooms with televisions and tea/coffee facilities. The West Somerset Steam Railway, the museum, sea fishing and riding are all nearby, making Esplanade House a good centre for exploring Exmoor and Quantocks.

B & B from £20pp, Rooms 2 double, 1 twin, all en-suite or private bathroom, No smoking, Children over 10, Dogs by arrangement, Closed Xmas

WYNDHAM HOUSE 4 Sea View Terrace, Watchet TA23 0DF
Susan & Roger Vincent *Tel / Fax:* 01984 631881
Email: rhv@dialstart.net

Map Ref: 30
A39

Grade II listed Georgian home with views over the harbour marina to Bristol Channel and Wales. Extensive gardens bordering steam railway and comfortable bedrooms with television and tea/coffee facilities. Home baking and delicious breakfasts with eating places also nearby. Quantock Hills, Exmoor, Dunster Castle, famous gardens and interesting coastline to explore. Ample parking. ETC 4 Diamonds, Silver Award.

B & B from £25pp, Rooms 1 double with private bathroom, 1 twin en-suite, No smoking, Children welcome, Dogs by arrangement, Closed Xmas & New Year

CAUSEWAY COTTAGE West Buckland, Wellington TA21 9JZ
Lesley Orr *Tel / Fax:* 01823 663458
Email: orrs@westbuckland.freeserve.co.uk *Web:* www.welcome.to/causeway-cottage

Map Ref: 31
M5 J26

200 year old cottage with lovely gardens and views across fields to the lofty village church. Easily reached from J26 of the M5. Bedrooms are en-suite, centrally heated and furnished with antique pine. The smell of homemade bread wafts through the cottage. Lesley runs cookery courses and will gladly prepare you a good supper. Television is in main sitting room.

B & B from £25pp, Dinner from £12, Rooms 2 double en-suite, No smoking, Children over 10, No dogs, Closed Xmas & New Year

THE CROWN AT WELLS Market Place, Wells BA5 2RP
Adrian & Sarah Lawrence *Tel:* 01749 673457 *Fax:* 01749 679792
Email: reception@crownatwells.co.uk *Web:* www.crownatwells.co.uk

Map Ref: 32
A371

The 15th century Crown is situated in the Market Place in the heart of Wells, close to Wells Cathedral and moated Bishop's Palace. Four poster rooms are available and visitors are guaranteed a warm welcome and friendly service. The Crown serves a variety of delicious meals, snacks and refreshments in the Penn Bar and Anton's Bistrot throughout the day.

B & B from £30pp, C-Cards MC VS, Dinner from £15, Rooms 2 single, 8 double, 4 twin, 1 family, all en-suite, Restricted smoking, Children welcome, Dogs by arrangement, Open all year

FURLONG HOUSE Lorne Place, St Thomas Street, Wells BA5 2XF
John Howard *Tel:* 01749 674064
Email: johnhowardwells@cs.com

Map Ref: 32
A371

Peace is assured at this Grade II listed Georgian house, just a five minute stroll from the magnificent Cathedral. Bedrooms are attractively decorated and feature a number of personal touches. The south facing terrace enjoys views of the Cathedral and National Trust woodland. Glastonbury Tor can be seen to the west. There is ample off street parking within the grounds.

B & B £22-£25pp, C-Cards MC VS, Rooms 1 double, 2 twin, all en-suite, No smoking, Children welcome, No dogs, Closed Xmas

INFIELD HOUSE 36 Portway, Wells BA5 2BN
Richard & Heather Betton-Foster *Tel:* 01749 670989 *Fax:* 01749 679093
Email: infield@talk21.com *Web:* www.infieldhouse.co.uk

Map Ref: 32
A371

Beautifully restored Victorian townhouse lovingly appointed with period furnishings, portraits and decor. Bountiful English, continental or vegetarian breakfasts with televisions, tea/coffee facilities and clock radio in every room. Short walk to City Centre with all its amenities then a short stroll to the Cathedral and Bishop's Palace. Wonderful walks on the Mendip Hills and Bath is only a 20 mile drive.

B & B from £21pp, C-Cards MC VS, Dinner from £6.50, Rooms 1 twin, 2 double, all en-suite, No smoking, Children over 10, Dogs welcome, Open all year

MANOR FARM Dulcote, Wells BA5 3PZ
Rosalind Bufton *Tel / Fax:* 01749 672125
Email: rosalind.bufton@ntlworld.com *Web:* www.wells-accommodation.co.uk

Map Ref: 32
A371

This comfortable 17th century farmhouse with lovely views is situated in a pretty village just one mile from Wells with its magnificent Cathedral and Bishops Palace, only five miles from Glastonbury with its Abbey and the Tor. Rosalind will cook you wonderful breakfasts with freshly gathered eggs from her hens and there are sheep, ducks, a goat and friendly cats as well.

B & B £22-£30pp, Rooms 1 single, 3 en-suite double, 1 twin, No smoking, Children over 12, No dogs, Closed Xmas & New Year

THE OLD FARMHOUSE 62 Chamberlain Street, Wells BA5 2PT
Felicity Wilkes *Tel / Fax:* 01749 675058
Email: theoldfarmhouse@talk21.com *Web:* www.plus44.com/oldfarmhouse

Map Ref: 32
A371

Picturesque 17th century farmhouse with secure parking in the centre of Wells. The home of retired diplomat Christopher and his wife Felicity offers a relaxed friendly welcome. Ideal for exploring the city on foot or visiting Bath, Glastonbury, Chedder and the unique Somerset Levels. Dinner by arrangement. Felicity's Cordon Bleu cooking is delicious! AA 5 Diamonds plus Best Breakfast & Dinner Awards.

B & B £25-£30pp, Dinner from £21, Rooms 1 double, 1 twin, both en-suite, No smoking, Children over 12, No dogs, Open all year

BURCOTT MILL GUEST HOUSE Wookey, Wells BA5 1NJ
Lesley & Ian Burt *Tel:* 01749 673118 *Fax:* 01749 677376
Email: theburts@burcottmill.com *Web:* www.burcottmill.com

Map Ref: 33
A371

A working Victorian watermill dating from Domesday, still stonegrinding flour daily. Guests can enjoy a private tour with the miller. Families are especially welcome with a playground, ponies, birds and small animals. Lunches are available in our tearoom and craftshops and opposite is a country pub for evening meals. Ideal for Cheddar, Wells and Glastonbury. Flexible accommodation with a Category 1 disabled suite. ETC 3 Diamond.

B & B from £21pp, C-Cards MC VS, Rooms 1 single, 1 double, 3 triple, 1 family, 5 en-suite, No smoking, Children welcome, Dogs by arrangement, Open all year

GLENCOT HOUSE Glencot Lane, Wookey Hole, Wells BA5 1BH
Tel: 01749 677160 *Fax:* 01749 670210
Email: glencot@ukonline.co.uk *Web:* ukonline.co.uk/glencot

Map Ref: 33
A39, A371

Idyllically set in 18 acres of gardens and parkland this elegantly furnished Victorian mansion offers high class accommodation, good food and friendly service. There is a small indoor pool, sauna, snooker table, table tennis and private fishing. Nearby are many famous tourist attractions and many areas of outstanding natural beauty.

B & B £45-£55pp, C-Cards MC VS AE DC, Dinner from £26, Rooms 3 single, 6 double, 3 twin, 1 family, all en-suite, Restricted smoking, Children welcome, Dogs by arrangement, Open all year

TYNINGS HOUSE Harters Hill Lane, Coxley, Wells BA5 1RF
Jill Parsons *Tel / Fax:* 01749 675368
Email: B&B@tynings.co.uk *Web:* www.tynings.co.uk

Map Ref: 34
A39

Tynings House lies on the edge of a small village in the heart of Somerset. It is surrounded by eight acres of garden and meadow with beautiful views over the unspoilt countryside. Tynings offers a peaceful holiday away from the hustle and bustle of everyday life.

B & B £25-£30pp, Dinner from £20, Rooms 2 double, 1 twin, all en-suite, No smoking, No children or dogs, Open all year

---

SOUTHWAY FARM Polsham, Wells BA5 1RW   *Map Ref:* 35
Naomi Frost *Tel:* 01749 673396 *Fax:* 01749 670373 *Mobile:* 07971 694650   A39
Email: southwayfarm@ukonline.co.uk *Web:* southwayfarm.co.uk

A warm welcome awaits in our Georgian listed farmhouse. Large en-suite bedrooms, all tastefully decorated with wonderful views of open countryside and cider orchards. The rooms are equipped with tea/coffee making facilities, televisions and radio alarm clocks. Quality breakfasts are served with homemade bread and preserves. A friendly cat and dog also reside here and there is a three night special rate.

B & B from £22pp, Rooms 2 double, 1 twin, all en-suite, No smoking, Children welcome, No dogs,

---

RIVERSIDE GRANGE Tanyard Lane, North Wootton, Wells BA4 4AE   *Map Ref:* 36
Pat English   A39
Tel: 01749 890761

Built in 1853, this is a charming converted tannery on the river's edge overlooking cider orchards, set in an area of outstanding natural beauty. Rooms are tastefully furnished and well equipped. North Wootton is a short drive from Wells and Glastonbury, and the factory shopping outlet 'Clarks Village' in street. There is an excellent village Inn within a short walk.

B & B £22.50pp, Rooms 1 twin, 1 double, No smoking, No children or dogs, Closed Xmas & New Year

---

STONELEIGH HOUSE Westbury-sub-Mendip, Wells BA5 1HF   *Map Ref:* 37
Wendy & Tony Thompson *Tel / Fax:* 01749 870668   A371
Email: stoneleigh@dail.pipex.com *Web:* www.stoneleigh.dial.pipex.com

An 18th century farmhouse with wonderful views across open countryside. Excellent accommodation, rooms with TV and tea/coffee facilities. A guests' lounge for relaxation. A generous breakfast is served with homemade preserves and free range eggs. There is a large car park, and a good pub nearby. This is an ideal position for a walking or touring holiday.

B & B £27-£29pp, Rooms 2 double, 1 twin, 2 en-suite, 1 private bathroom, Strictly no smoking, Children over 10, No dogs, Closed Xmas

---

LOWER FARM Shepton Montague, Wincanton BA9 8JG   *Map Ref:* 38
Mrs Susie Dowding *Tel:* 01749 812253   A303
Email: susiedowding@netscapeonline.co.uk *Web:* www.lowerfarm.org.uk

Enjoy the fat of the land in the barn at Lower Farm! The view from the breakfast table is of rural tranquility with hens scratching in the orchard, an inspiring organic vegetable garden and cows wandering over the horizon. Oak floors, beams, lime-washed walls and a stunning end window make a stylish self-contained apartment. Food for healthy appetites!

B & B from £25pp, Dinner from £15, Rooms 1 double en-suite, 1 twin private shower room, No smoking, Children welcome, Dogs not in house, Open all year

---

JESSOPS Vagg Lane, Chilchorne Dorner, Yeovil BA22 8RY   *Map Ref:* 39
Beverley & Richard White   A30, A37
Tel / Fax: 01935 841097 *Mobile:* 07752 704513

Excellent accommodation, set in the countryside offering hearty English breakfasts. Tea/coffee facilities and televisions in all rooms with a four poster en-suite in one room. Yeovil town just five minutes drive, and a short walk to the local pub and good food. Horse riding nearby and Fleet Air Arm Museum, Yeovil.

B & B £22.50-£25pp, Rooms 1 double 4 poster en-suite, 1 double, 1 twin, Restricted smoking, Children welcome, Small dogs by arrangement, Closed Xmas

Suffolk

Suffolk is a delightful county of softly undulating rural landscape, of slow-flowing streams, picturesque villages and the open heath country of the Breckland. The coastline, under constant attack from the eroding sea, nevertheless offers lovely shingle shores, sandy beaches and low cliffs. Dunwich Heath, one of Suffolk's most important conservation areas covers over 200 acres of Sandlings heathland with sandy cliffs and a mile of lovely beach, adjacent is the Minsmere nature reserve run by the RSPB, a refuge for migrating and resident birds.

The glories of this county have been captured on canvas by John Constable and Thomas Gainsborough and the holiday visitor would be well rewarded for following in the footsteps of Constable through a countryside little changed from his day. Sudbury, Gainsborough's birthplace and once one of the largest East Anglian woollen towns is an excellent starting point. Gainsborough's house, an elegant Tudor building with an added Regency facade is now a museum. The narrow twisting streets and medieval houses surround the fine fifteenth century church of St James which contains Constable's painting of 'Christ's Blessing of the Bread and Wine'. Dedham to the east was a favourite subject of Constable, and little wonder, its fine High Street of Tudor and Georgian houses is a delight. Further east at East Bergholt is the birthplace of Constable and a great attraction for tourists, as both Flatford Mill and Willy Lot's Cottage, popular subjects of the master's paintings, are close by.

Lavenham, a medieval wool town is a popular place for tourists who wish to visit the beautiful black and white timbered buildings on market square. Also worth visiting is the fifteenth century Guildhall which has a complete history of Lavenham's wool trade. Lowestoft in the north offers a contrasting variety of pleasures with Lowestoft Ness, the most easterly point of the British Isles, a wild and windswept sanctuary for birds, and Oulton Broad is a popular site for many watersports. There is also Pleasurewood Hills American Theme Park with 50 acres of rides and attractions. Lowestoft was a centre for fishing from the fourteenth century and the fish market is still very much in evidence. South is Aldeburgh, boasting some fine medieval buildings. Much of its ancient history has been devoured by the voracious sea, in fact the handsome sixteenth century Moot Hall, once in the centre of the town, is

Framlingham Castle (EETB)

now at the water's edge. The town is the birthplace of George Crabbe, the eighteenth century writer whose poem, 'The Borough' was adapted by Benjamin Britten to become his opera, 'Peter Grimes', an evocation of life on the Suffolk coast. Aldeburgh is renowned for its music festival held at nearby Snape with the Maltings Proms, venue of the festival, founded by Benjamin Britten.

Ipswich, the county town and inland port on the River Orwell can boast no less than twelve medieval churches and the handsome sixteenth century Christchurch Mansion with its excellent collection of Suffolk antiques and paintings. Cardinal Wolsey was born here, his Tudor brick gate still stands in Fore Street. Bury St Edmunds was once the town of Beodericsworth, a Saxon settlement when the bones of Edmund, the last king of East Anglia who was killed by the Danes for refusing to deny

Christianity, were brought for burial. The settlement changed its name to St Edmundsbury and became an important place of pilgrimage. Except for its two gateways the fourteenth century abbey is in ruins. It was in 1214, at the altar of an earlier abbey on this site that the Barons swore to force King John to honour the Magna Carta. Of course to the west of Bury St Edmunds is Newmarket, the home of the Jockey Club and the historic centre of English horseracing. Before leaving, you must visit the Theatre Royal in Westgate Street, built in 1819 it is a very rare example of a Georgian playhouse boasting a national reputation attracting the foremost touring companies in the country. Also well worth a visit is the eccentric Ickworth House built by the Earl of Bristol in 1795, it is surrounded by a glorious Italianate garden and Capability Brown park,. and contains a superb collection of works by Titian, Gainsborough and Velasquez.

PLACES TO VISIT

This is a small selection of interesting places to visit. Many more are listed in our annual guide to Museums, Galleries, Historic Houses & Sites (see page 448)

Framlingham Castle
Framlingham
One of the first castles to have a curtain wall and several towers instead of one central keep. Mary Tudor spent the summer here waiting to find out if she or Lady Jane Grey was to be declared Queen.

Ickworth House
Horringer, Bury St Edmunds
Discover the Italianate wonders of the house and gardens, an immense oval Rotunda with two large wings with curving corridors, collections of Georgian silver and paintings by Titian and Velasquez.

Kentwell Hall
Long Melford, Sudbury
A mellow red-brick Tudor manor house surrounded by a moat and extensive woodlands. The house has been interestingly restored with Tudor costumes and a mosaic rose maze. The gardens are a delight.

National Horseracing Museums and Tours
Newmarket, Suffolk
A museum displaying the development of horse-racing. There is a display of sporting art and five galleries of loans from major museums and private collections.

Suffolk

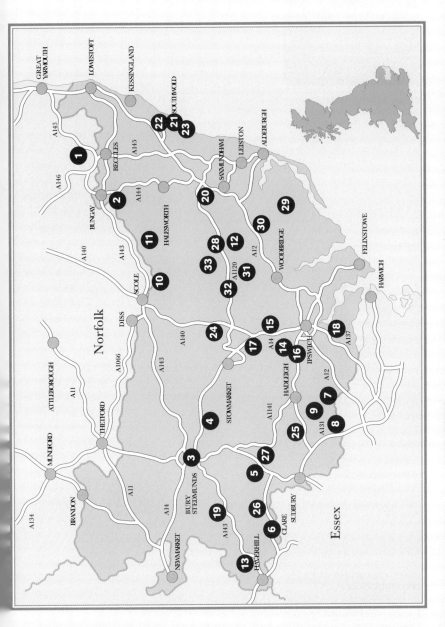

The Red Map References should be used to locate B & B properties on the pages that follow

THE ELMS Toft Monks, Beccles NR34 0EJ　　　　　　　　　*Map Ref:* 1
Richard & Teena Freeland　*Tel:* 01502 677380　*Fax:* 01502 677362　　　　　A143
Email: richardfreeland@btconnect.com　*Web:* www.freelandenterprises.co.uk

Originally a Flax weaver's residence, this beautiful home welcomes guests to enjoy a moated garden, rose walks, lawns and a tennis court, handsome fireplaces, huge sash windows and cast iron baths. Dinner features local produce including fish, game and poultry. The Elms is close to Southwold and other coastal towns. Spectacular local coarse fishing and farm walks, also golf, tennis and riding.

B & B £35-£65pp, Dinner from £22, Rooms 1 twin en-suite, 2 double, 1 private bathroom 1 en-suite, No smoking, Children over 5, No dogs, Closed occasionally

---

EARSHAM PARK FARM Harleston Road, Earsham, Bungay NR35 2AQ　*Map Ref:* 2
Bobbie Watchorn　*Tel / Fax:* 01986 892180　*Mobile:* 07798 728936　　　　A143,A144
Email: bobbie@earsham-parkfarm.co.uk　*Web:* www.earsham-parkfarm.co.uk

Friendly and elegant, this spacious farmhouse stands in a quiet location with panoramic views. It is decorated to a high standard with unique stencilling and paint finishes. Comfort and quality with antique furnishings are complemented by extensive facilities. Delicious breakfasts including our own produce are a feature of this property. Guests receive excellent hospitality here.

B & B from £24pp, C-Cards MC VS, Dinner available, Rooms 2 double, 1 twin, all en-suite, No smoking, Children welcome, Dogs by arrangement, Open all year

---

ASH COTTAGE 59 Whiting Street, Bury St Edmunds IP33 1NP　　*Map Ref:* 3
Elizabeth Barber-Lomax　*Tel / Fax:* 01284 755098　*Mobile:* 07885 038797　　A14, A134, A143
Email: ashcottage@freebie.net　*Web:* www.members.tripod.com/ashcottage

Ash Cottage is situated in the heart of historic and beautiful Bury St Edmunds in a quiet conservation area. You will receive a warm and homely welcome from Elizabeth Barber-Lomax who has lived in Bury St Edmunds for many years. Ash Cottage is a historic medieval house with a lovely garden, heavily beamed and full of ancient character.

B & B from £25pp, Rooms 1 double en-suite, 1 twin with private bathroom, No smoking, Children & dogs welcome, Open all year

---

NORTHGATE HOUSE 8 Northgate Street, Bury St Edmunds IP33 1HQ　*Map Ref:* 3
Joy Fiennes　*Tel:* 01284 760469　*Fax:* 01284 724008　　　　　　　　A14, A134, A143
Email: northgate_hse@hotmail.com　*Web:* www.northgatehouse.com

Hidden behind an imposing Georgian facade, this Grade I house has Medieval origins and is a stone's throw from the historic core. Original spacious en-suite bedrooms are all furnished with antiques and have televisions, radios and tea/coffee facilities. A substantial breakfast is served from the Jacobean panelled room where Norah Lofts wrote most of her books.

B & B £45-£55pp, C-Cards MC VS AE, Rooms 2 double, 1 twin, all en-suite, No smoking, No children or dogs, Closed Xmas & New Year

---

MANORHOUSE The Green, Beyton, Bury St Edmunds IP30 9AF　*Map Ref:* 4
Kay & Mark Dewsbury　*Tel:* 01359 270960　　　　　　　　　　　　　A14
Email: manorhouse@beyton.com　*Web:* www.beyton.com

Relax and unwind at this award winning 15th century timbered longhouse, set in large gardens in the centre of a pretty village with good local inns. Large, luxurious en-suite rooms, excellent breakfasts. Fridge/freezer for guests, televisions, tea/coffee facilities and secure parking. No smoking. Four miles east of Bury St Edmunds. Which? Guide Best Bed & Breakfast.

B & B £25-£28pp, Rooms 2 double/kingsize, 2 twin, all en-suite, No smoking, No children or dogs, Closed Xmas

THE HATCH Pilgrims Lane, Cross Green, Hartest, Bury St Edmunds IP29 4ED
Bridget & Robin Oaten
Tel / Fax: 01284 830226

Map Ref: 5
B1066

A gorgeous thatched listed 15th century house, situated outside Hartest. Surrounded by farmland, the house is very comfortably furnished with fine fabrics and antiques. Guests use the delightful drawing and sitting rooms which have inglenook fireplaces with log fires. A lovely garden to enjoy. Hartest is well placed for visiting West Suffolk, Cambridgeshire and Ely. Great antique hunting, walking and cycling.

B & B from £30pp, Rooms 1 twin, 1 double, No smoking, Children over 9, Closed occasionally

---

SHIP STORES 22 Callis Street, Clare CO10 8PX
Debra & Colin Bowles *Tel:* 01787 277834
Email: shipclare@aol.co.uk *Web:* www.ship-stores.co.uk

Map Ref: 6
A1092

Ship Stores adjoins the village store and tea room in the picturesque small town of Clare. All rooms are en-suite with colour televisions and tea/coffee facilities. There are also deluxe rooms in the converted annexe and main house, with queen size beds and settee. Close to many historic villages.

B & B from £22.50pp, Dinner from £9.50, Rooms 4 double, 1 twin, 1 family, all en-suite, Restricted smoking, Children welcome, No dogs, Open all year

---

OLD VICARAGE Higham, Colchester CO7 6JY
Meg Parker *Tel:* 01206 337248
Email: oldvic.higham@bushinternet.com

Map Ref: 7
A12

Charming 16th century house situated in a beautiful Suffolk village, the fields go down to the river Brets and Stour with boats to watch. There is a swimming pool and tennis court. Much local interest visiting Lavenham and Sudbury showing Gainsborough pictures. The sea is half an hour away. A fine drawing room overlooks the garden, which guests are welcome to enjoy.

B & B £25-£30pp, Rooms 1 twin, 1 double, 1 family, 2 en-suite, Restricted smoking, Children & dogs welcome, Open all year

---

HILL HOUSE Gravel Hill, Nayland, Colchester CO6 4JB
Mrs P Heigham *Tel:* 01206 262782
Email: heigham.hillhouse@rdplus.net

Map Ref: 8
A134

A comfortable 16th century 'hall-house' set on edge of constable village in quiet location. Secluded garden with views over the valley. Good base for touring. Excellent restaurants and good pub food locally. Easy access A12, Colchester 6 miles. Colour TV and tea/coffee facilities. Golf course 1 miles. Good walking country.

B & B from £23pp, Rooms 1 single, 1 double en-suite, 1 twin en-suite, No smoking, Children over 10, No dogs, Closed Xmas & New Year

---

RYEGATE HOUSE Stoke-by-Nayland, Colchester CO6 4RA
Albert & Margaret Geater *Tel:* 01206 263679
Email: ryegate@lineone.net *Web:* www.s-h-systems.co.uk/hotels/ryegate

Map Ref: 9
A12, A134

Situated within the Dedham Vale, in quiet Suffolk village. Ryegate House is a modern property built in the style of a Suffolk farmhouse. Only a few minutes walk from local shops, post office, pubs, restaurants and church. An ideal base for exploring 'Constable Country,' local historic market towns, golf courses and the East coast. Warm welcome, fine food, restful rooms.

B & B £21.25-£26.25pp, Rooms 1 double, 1 twin, all en-suite, No smoking, Children over 12, No dogs, Closed Xmas

GABLES FARM Earsham Street, Wingfield, Diss IP21 5RH
Michael & Sue Harvey *Tel:* 01379 586355 *Fax:* 01379 588058
Email: gables-farm@ntlworld.com *Web:* www.gablesfarm.co.uk
Map Ref: 10
B1118 or A143

A 16th Century timbered farmhouse in moated gardens, Wingfield is a quiet village in East Anglia, convenient for Norwich, Bury St Edmunds, coast and other interesting places. Ideal for cycling and walking, fishing two miles. Bedrooms are en-suite with TV and a hospitality tray. English breakfast with free range eggs is served, and local produce is used. A leaflet is available by request.

B & B from £22pp, Rooms 1 twin, 2 double, all en-suite, No smoking, Children welcome, Dogs by arrangement, Closed Xmas & New Year

CHIPPENHALL HALL Fressingfield, Eye IP21 5TD
Mr & Mrs Sargent *Tel:* 01379 588180
Email: info@chippenhall.co.uk *Web:* www.chippenhall.co.uk
Map Ref: 11
A143

A listed Tudor manor house used as a film location, heavily beamed and with inglenook fireplaces. Chippenhall Hall stands in seven secluded acres and boasts a swimming pool. Fine food and wines are offered. Only two miles south of Fressingfield on B1116. ETC and AA 5 Diamonds and Winner of Johansen Award for Excellence to Country Houses in the UK and Ireland.

B & B from £42.50pp, C-Cards MC VS AE, Dinner available, Rooms 6 double, all en-suite, Restricted smoking, Children over 15, No dogs, Open all year

PRIORY HOUSE Priory Road, Fressingfield, Eye IP21 5PH
Rosemary Willis
Tel: 01379 586254
Map Ref: 11
B1116

A warm welcome awaits in this lovely 16th century farmhouse, in secluded gardens. Comfortable bedrooms are all centrally heated. The house has exposed beams, and is furnished with antiques. There is a guests' lounge and a pleasant dining room. Fressingfield is ideal for a peaceful holiday and as touring base for Norwich, Bury St Edmunds, the Broads, historic buildings and gardens. Excellent village pub.

B & B from £26pp, Rooms 1 twin, 2 double, private bathrooms, Restricted smoking, Children over 10, Dogs by arrangement, Closed Xmas & New Year

WOODLANDS FARM Brundish, Framlingham IP13 8BP
Jill Graham *Tel:* 01379 384444
Email: woodlandsfarm@hotmail.com
Map Ref: 12
A11120, B1116, B1118

Woodlands Farm offers our guests a friendly relaxed atmosphere in a really comfortable old timber-framed farmhouse. There are many original exposed beams with inglenook fireplaces in the dining and sitting rooms. The central heating is backed up with log fires on chilly evenings. We serve excellent home-cooked breakfasts using local produce and our own free range eggs. AA 4 Diamonds.

B & B £20-£22.50pp, Rooms 2 double, 1 twin, all en-suite, No smoking, Children over 10, No dogs, Open all year

THE OLD VICARAGE Great Thurlow, Haverhill CB9 7LE
Jane Sheppard
Tel: 01440 783209 *Fax:* 01638 667270
Map Ref: 13
A1307, A143

Set in mature grounds and woodlands this delightful Old Vicarage has a friendly family atmosphere with peace and comfort and wonderful views of the Suffolk countryside. Open log fires in winter. Guests are welcome to use the garden, and there is ample parking space. Perfectly situated for Newmarket, Cambridge, Long Melford and Constable Country. Evening meals are available with prior notice.

B & B from £28pp, Dinner from £18, Rooms 1 single, 1 twin, 1 double, all en-suite, Restricted smoking, Children over 7, Dogs by arrangement, Closed Xmas

MULBERRY HALL Burstall, Ipswich IP8 3DP   *Map Ref:* 14
Penny Debenham   *Tel:* 01473 652348   *Fax:* 01473 652110   A12, A14, A1071
Email: pennydebenham@hotmail.com

A lovely old farmhouse previously owned by Cardinal Wolsey during 16th century. Prettily situated in a small village only five miles west of Ipswich. Mulberry Hall offers log fires, good home cooking and comfortable rooms, attractively furnished with a lovely garden and tennis court. Ideal venue for sightseeing.

B & B from £25pp, Dinner from £16, Rooms 1 double, 1 twin, No smoking, Children welcome, No dogs, Closed Xmas & New Year

MOCKBEGGARS HALL Claydon, Ipswich IP6 0AH   *Map Ref:* 15
Priscilla Clayton-Mead   *Tel:* 01473 830239   *Fax:* 01473 832989   *Mobile:* 07702 627770   A14
Email: pru@mockbeggars.co.uk   *Web:* www.mockbeggars.co.uk

A grand Grade II listed Jacobean Manor House set in its own grounds and surrounded by rolling countryside. A warm welcome in a relaxing atmosphere awaits our guests. Spacious, comfortable rooms, all en-suite with televisions, welcome trays, hairdryers etc. Good location for exploring Suffolk with a self catering converted coach house available, yacht days sailing and a Therapy Centre. Ample parking.

B & B £22.50-£27.50pp, C-Cards MC VS, Dinner from £15, Rooms 3 double, 1 twin, 1 family, all en-suite, Restricted smoking, Children welcome, Dogs by arrangement, Open all year

COLLEGE FARM Hintlesham, Ipswich IP8 3NT   *Map Ref:* 16
Mrs R Bryce   *Tel / Fax:* 01473 652253   A1071
Email: bryce1@agripro.co.uk   *Web:* www.smoothound.co.uk/hotels/collegefarm

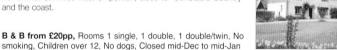

Relax at our peaceful 500 year old beamed farmhouse on a 600 acre arable farm. Comfortable rooms, hearty breakfasts and a warm welcome with good food only half a mile away. The three spacious bedrooms (2 en-suite) all have central heating, television, radio and hot drinks. Six miles west of Ipswich, close to 'Constable Country' and the coast.

B & B from £20pp, Rooms 1 single, 1 double, 1 double/twin, No smoking, Children over 12, No dogs, Closed mid-Dec to mid-Jan

PIPPS FORD Needham Market, Ipswich IP6 8LJ   *Map Ref:* 17
Raewyn Hackett-Jones   *Tel:* 01449 760208   *Fax:* 01449 760561   A14, A140
Email: b&b@pippsford.co.uk   *Web:* www.pippsford.co.uk

Fine and beautiful long, low, black and white timbered house, parts of which date from 1540. There are sloping floors, beams, inglenooks with log fires and historic associations. The cottagey sitting rooms are filled with antique furniture and china, they have a wonderful atmosphere. Well equipped bedrooms are attractive with en-suite bathrooms. More bedrooms in the stables. Excellent, imaginative evening meals.

B & B £28-£37.50pp, C-Cards MC VS AE, Dinner from £19.50, Rooms 4 double, 3 twin, Restricted smoking, Children over 5, Dogs by arrangement, Closed Xmas & New Year

WOOLVERSTONE HOUSE Mannings Lane, Woolverstone, Ispwich IP9 1AN   *Map Ref:* 18
Mrs Jane Cook   *Tel:* 01473 780940   *Fax:* 01473 780959   A12, A14
Email: cooks@enterprise.net

Lutyens designed this Grade II listed house which features a Gertrude Jekyll garden. Surrounded by beautiful countryside on the Shotley Peninsula, it is convenient for Woodbridge, Ipswich, Harwich, Orford and Constable country. Local activities include sailing, walking and birdwatching and Mrs Cook can recommend good haunts for antique collectors. The renovation of the house won an RIBA award for craftsmanship.

B & B £35-£55pp, Dinner from £17.50, Rooms 2 double, both en-suite, 1 twin, private bathroom, No smoking, Children over 12, No dogs, Closed Xmas & New Year

THE OLD BAKERY Farley Green, Wickhambrook, Newmarket CB8 8PX   *Map Ref:* 19
Linda & Brian Lambert *Tel / Fax:* 01440 820852   *Mobile:* 07778 380538   A143
Email: info@theoldbakery.freeserve.co.uk   *Web:* www.theoldbakery.freeserve.co.uk

Experience the tranquility of our 17th century historic home in rural Suffolk. Visit the beautiful towns and villages in the region then return to relax in our large secluded garden. Enjoy the comfort of our spacious rooms with modern en-suites. Awake to a delicious English breakfast including freshly squeezed orange juice and home-made preserves. Exclusively for non-smokers. ETC 4 Diamonds.

B & B from £20pp, Dinner from £10, Rooms 2 double, en-suite, No smoking, Children over 12, No dogs, Closed Jan to Mar

---

CHURCH FARM Yoxford Road, Sibton, Saxmundham IP17 2LX   *Map Ref:* 20
Elizabeth Dixon *Tel:* 01728 660101   *Fax:* 01728 660102   A1120
Email: dixons@church-farmhouse.demon.co.uk   *Web:* www.church-farmhouse.demon.co.uk

Surrounded by glorious countryside this 17th century house is ideal for exploring the Suffolk heritage coast. The bedrooms at Church Farm are elegant, comfortable, light and exceptionally well appointed. The guest dining room has a wealth of beams, the lounge has deep sofas and a wood burning stove. Both overlook the attractive front garden. ETC 5 Diamonds, Silver Award.

B & B £25-£30pp, Rooms 1 twin, 2 double, all en-suite/private, No smoking, Children over 6, No dogs, Closed Xmas

---

PROSPECT PLACE 33 Station Road, Southwold IP18 6AX   *Map Ref:* 21
Tel: 01502 722757   A12, A1095
Email: sally@prospect-place.demon.co.uk   *Web:* www.prospect.place.demon.co.uk

Well appointed, detached Victorian house in the heart of Southwold overlooking common and golf course with fine food and a friendly atmosphere. Spacious, comfortable interior with very attractive bedrooms, some ground floor, all en-suite with television, tea/coffee making facilities, hairdryer. Private car park and large gardens. Ideal location for exploring this beautiful town on the Heritage Coast.

B & B from £20pp, Rooms 3 double, 1 twin, all en-suite, No smoking, Children over 8, Dogs by arrangement, Open all year

---

CHURCH FARMHOUSE Uggeshall, Southwold NR34 8BD   *Map Ref:* 22
Sarah Jupp *Tel:* 01502 578532   *Fax:* 01953 888306   *Mobile:* 07748 801418   A12
Email: sarahjupp@compuserve.com

A lovely 17th century listed farmhouse set in 3 acres of garden and orchard, next to a thatched church. Sympathetically restored, with lovely fabrics, fresh flowers and cotton sheets, it is relaxed here. Sarah cooks wonderful dinners on the Aga. Southwold is four miles away, there are lovely walks, birds, art and music nearby and Sarah has a wealth of local knowledge.

B & B £30-£35pp, Dinner from £20, Rooms 1 single, 1 double, 1 twin, most en-suite, No smoking, Children over 12, No dogs, Closed Xmas day

---

POPLAR HALL Frostenden Corner, Frostenden, Southwold NR34 7JA   *Map Ref:* 22
Anna & John Garwood   A12
Tel: 01502 578549

Minutes from the seaside town of Southwold, Poplar Hall is a 16th century thatched house in a large, peaceful garden. Wonderful walks, coastal or country. Walberswick, Dunwich, Aldburgh, Snape are a short distance. Luxury accommodation, vanity units in all rooms. Guests' library, sitting and dining rooms are delightful, delicious breakfasts of fresh fruit, local fish, sausage, bacon and home made preserves.

B & B from £25pp, Rooms 1 single, 2 double, cot available, 1 en-suite, No smoking, Children welcome, No dogs, Closed Xmas

FERRY HOUSE Walberswick, Southwold IP18 6TH   *Map Ref:* 23
Cathryn Simpson *Tel / Fax:* 01502 723384   A12
Email: ferryhouse.walberswick@virgin.net *Web:* www.ferryhouse-walberswick.com

Ferry House is 200m from the River Blyth, and close to the seashore. Walberswick is a delightful artists' village, this unusual house was built for a playwright. A fireplace surround depicts scenes from one of his plays. This charming home offers a warm welcome with stylish accommodation. Snape Maltings, Minsmere Bird Reserve and Southwold are within easy reach. Good pubs locally.

B & B from £20pp, Rooms 2 single, 1 double, No smoking, Children over 10, No dogs, Closed Xmas & New Year

CHERRY TREE FARM Mendlesham Green, Stowmarket IP14 5RQ   *Map Ref:* 24
Martin & Diana Ridsdale   A140
Tel: 01449 766376

A traditional timber framed farmhouse situated in the heart of Suffolk, where guests are welcomed to warm hospitality. The guests' lounge has an inglenook with a woodburning stove for cool evenings. Meals are served around a refectory table, bread is home baked and seasonal vegetables are garden fresh, traditional puddings are a speciality. Licensed, specialising in East Anglian wines.

B & B from £27pp, Dinner from £17, Rooms 3 double en-suite, No smoking, No children or dogs, Closed Dec to Feb

HURRELLS FARMHOUSE Boxford Lane, Boxford, Sudbury CO10 5JY   *Map Ref:* 25
Carol Deb *Tel:* 01787 210215 *Fax:* 01787 211806   A1071
Email: hurrells@aol.com

A warm welcome awaits you at Hurrells Farmhouse, which is situated on the Suffolk/Essex border, close to many places of historical interest. A Tudor, part Jacobean, timber framed Grade II listed farmhouse with a wealth of exposed beams and full central heating. A variety of local pubs and places to eat within one mile of the house.

B & B from £20pp, Rooms 1 single, 2 double, No smoking, Children over 10, Dogs welcome, Closed Xmas & New Year

THE RED HOUSE Stour Street, Cavendish, Sudbury CO10 8BH   *Map Ref:* 26
Maureen & Brian Theaker *Tel / Fax:* 01787 280611   A1092
Email: bg.theaker@btinternet.com *Web:* www.smoothhound.co.uk/hotels/theredh

A lovely 16th century home standing in a delightful garden overlooking the river Stour. Homemade biscuits and preserves and mouth watering breakfasts. Both bedrooms are comfortably furnished with guests' every need considered. Adjoining cosy, beamed upstairs sitting room with television, books and games. Self contained accommodation with low doorways and narrow stairs. Off road parking. Central for touring. Excellent eating places nearby.

B & B £24-£26.50pp, Rooms 2 twin, en-suite/private, No smoking, Children welcome, No dogs, Closed Xmas & New Year

THE HALL Milden, Lavenham, Sudbury CO10 9NY   *Map Ref:* 27
Juliet & Christopher Hawkins *Tel / Fax:* 01787 247235   A1141, B1115
Email: gjb53@dial.pipex.com

Beautiful Georgianised 16th century hall farmhouse, peacefully surrounded by flower meadows, walled garden, ancient barns and hedged countryside. Woodburner warms large hall and spacious bedrooms. Explore environmentally friendly farm and nature trails around award-winning woodland, castle earthworks, ponds and museum, or nearby Lavenham. Feast on farmyard bantam eggs and bacon, and home grown produce. Relaxed family atmosphere.

B & B £25-£32.50pp, Dinner from £15, Rooms 2 twin, 1 family, No smoking, Children welcome, No dogs, Closed Xmas & New Year

HILL HOUSE FARM Preston St Mary, Lavenham, Sudbury CO10 9LT
Mrs Joy Lloyd Hughes
Tel: 01787 247571

Map Ref: 27
A1141

Beautiful listed Elizabethan farmhouse furnished with antiques in a peaceful rural setting, close to Lavenham. Delightful spacious accommodation with listed medieval wall paintings, wonderful gardens and lake with ornamental ducks and black swans. A delicious evening meal is available. Ideal for exploring the many medieval villages nearby. ETB 4 Diamonds, Silver Award.

B & B from £30pp, Dinner available, Rooms 1 single, 1 twin en-suite, No smoking, Children over 14, No dogs, Open all year

---

LAVENHAM PRIORY Water Street, Lavenham, Sudbury CO10 9RW
Tim & Gilli Pitt　*Tel:* 01787 247404　*Fax:* 01787 248472
Email: mail@lavenhampriory.co.uk　*Web:* www.lavenhampriory.co.uk

Map Ref: 27
A1141, B1115

Winner of the AA guest accommodation of the year award for England and the EETB's regional best B & B. Lavenham Priory, a Grade I listed house provides an unforgettable experience. Bed chambers feature crown posts, Elizabethan wall paintings and oak floors, with four-poster, lit bateau and polonaise beds. Lavenham is one of the finest medieval villages in England with its historic buildings and streets.

B & B £39-£54pp, C-Cards MC VS, Rooms 5 double, 1 twin, all en-suite, No smoking, Children over 10, No dogs, Closed From Xmas to New Year

---

THE RED HOUSE 29 Bolton Street, Lavenham, Sudbury CO10 9RG
Mrs Diana Schofield　*Tel:* 01787 248074　*Mobile:* 07885 536148
Email: redhouse@tag-group.com　*Web:* www.lavenham.co.uk/redhouse

Map Ref: 27
A1141

The Red House is a comfortable friendly home in the heart of medieval Lavenham. It boasts attractively decorated bedrooms, a pretty guest sitting room and a sunny country garden to relax in. Candlelit dinners are also available by prior arrangement. You will have a warm welcome and a restful stay in peaceful surroundings in the centre of the village.

B & B from £25pp, Dinner from £16.50, Rooms 2 double, 1 twin, all en-suite, No smoking, Children welcome, Dogs by arrangement, Closed Xmas & Jan

---

WOOD HALL Little Waldingfield, Lavenham, Sudbury CO10 0SY
Susan T del C Nisbett　*Tel:* 01787 247362　*Fax:* 01787 248326
Email: nisbett@nisbett.enta.net　*Web:* www.nisbett.enta.net

Map Ref: 27
B1115

This Tudor House, modernised in the Georgian period, has large windows and a brick facade. Full of antiques, it has a lovely walled garden to enjoy. Two light and airy well equipped bedrooms for guests. Wood Hall is well placed for Lavenham and nearby medieval villages and Churches. Thomas Gainsborough's house may be found in Sudbury, the area is known as Constable country.

B & B from £30pp, Dinner from £15, Rooms 1 double, 1 twin, both en-suite, No smoking, Children over 10, No dogs, Closed Xmas

---

GRANGE FARM Dennington, Woodbridge IP13 8BT
Mrs E Hickson　*Tel:* 01986 798388　*Mobile:* 07774 182835
Web: www.framlingham.com/grangefarm

Map Ref: 28
A1120

A warm welcome awaits you at our exceptional, medieval moated farmhouse dating from 13th century. Grange Farm is set in extensive grounds and has a superb all weather tennis court. There is a wealth of garden birds to enjoy. The bedrooms have tea/coffee facilities, and the lounges have televisions and log fires. Bread and marmalade are homemade. Fishing available. Snape Maltings and the coast are nearby.

B & B £22pp, Dinner available, Rooms 1/2 double or 1/3 twin (let as single) shared bathroom, No smoking, Children over 12, No dogs, Closed Dec to Jan

BUTLEY PRIORY Butley, Woodbridge IP12 3NR
Frances Cavendish *Tel:* 01394 450046 *Fax:* 01394 450482 *Mobile:* 07889 364710
Email: frances@butleypriory.co.uk *Web:* www.butleypriory.co.uk

Map Ref: 29
A12, B1084

Butley Priory is all that remains of the Augustinian monastery founded in 1171 which Mary Tudor was a frequent visitor of between 1515 and 1527. The dining room and drawing room are available independently and are perfect for concerts, weddings or other social functions. In the bedrooms 20th century comfort is assured with log fires, goose down duvets and a sitting area.

B & B £45-£55pp, Rooms 1 single, 3 double, all en-suite, No smoking, Children welcome, Small dogs only, Open all year

THE OLD RECTORY Campsea Ashe, Woodbridge IP13 0PU
Stewart Bassett
Tel / Fax: 01728 746524

Map Ref: 30
A12

Peaceful Georgian rectory set in mature gardens with a relaxed and homely atmosphere. There are welcoming log fires in the drawing rooms and dining room. All bedrooms are en-suite and well equipped. Delicious home cooked food in the licensed restaurant, to which outside diners are welcome. Local homemade breads, marmalades, jams and honey are a speciality. Well placed for Snape, Woodbridge and coastal areas.

B & B from £30pp, C-Cards VS AE DC, Dinner from £18.50, Rooms 1 single, 4 double, 2 twin, all en-suite, Restricted smoking, Well behaved children, Dogs welcome, Closed Xmas

SHRUBBERY FARMHOUSE Chapel Hill, Cretingham, Woodbridge IP13 7DN
St John & Christine Marston *Tel:* 01473 737494 *Fax:* 01473 737312
Mobile: 07860352317 *Email:* sm@marmar.co.uk *Web:* www.shrubberyfarmhouse.co.uk

Map Ref: 31
A12, A1120

A charming 16th century listed Suffolk farmhouse set in beautiful countryside. Award winning breakfasts. Ideal base for exploring the Heritage coast and walking the Suffolk way. Television and tea/coffee facilities in all bedrooms plus a sitting room, library, music room, gymnasium, tennis court and croquet lawn. Car park.

B & B £29.75-£35pp, Dinner from £14.75, Rooms 1 single, 2 double, all en-suite, No smoking, Children welcome, Dogs by arrangement, Open all year

BRIDGE HOUSE Earl Soham, Woodbridge IP13 7RT
Jennifer Baker *Tel:* 01728 685473/685289
Email: bridgehouse46@hotmail.com *Web:* www.jenniferbaker.co.uk

Map Ref: 32
A1120

Bridge House is an attractive 16th century property close to the Heritage coast. Accommodation comprises of well-appointed bedrooms with tea/coffee making facilities and televisions. Guests have use of own dining, sitting and garden areas. Excellent food and a warm welcome from Jennifer and David await you. ETC 4 Diamonds. Silver Award.

B & B from £25pp, Dinner available, Rooms 2 double, 1 twin, all en-suite, No smoking, Children over 12, Dogs by arrangement, Open all year

GUILDHALL Church Street, Worlingworth IP13 7NS
Mrs Penfold
Tel / Fax: 01728 628057

Map Ref: 33
A140, A1120

16th century thatched, listed Grade II. Set in countryside ideal for bird watching, walking and painting. Heritage coast approx 30 minutes. Southwold, Minsmere, Framlingham, Eye, or Diss a short drive. Beamed rooms, beautifully furnished and centrally heated. Television lounge with inglenook. English breakfast (dinner by previous arrangement) served in a charming dining room or conservatory. Large gardens with summer house to enjoy.

B & B £22-£24pp, Dinner from £12, Rooms 2 double, en-suite/private, No smoking, No children or dogs, Closed Oct to mid-Mar

Surrey

Surrey still remains Britain's most wooded county and is crossed from east to west by the North Downs, whose chalk slopes are broken by the lovely Rivers Wey, Mole and Darent. Its steep scarp slope which faces south is cut by interesting wooded combes ablaze with wildflowers. Box Hill, a highly popular beauty spot, made famous by Jane Austen's Emma, rises four hundred feet from the River Mole on the very edge of the North Downs. This glorious country park consists of over a thousand acres of woods and chalk downland with quite superb views to the South Downs. To the east is a range of sandy hills with Leith Hill being the highest point in south east England. Here the National Trust own the large countryside property which includes a tower dating from 1766 which gives magnificent views across the Surrey Weald and it is claimed that from this tower, 1,029 feet above sea level, you can, on a clear day see no less than eleven counties. Reigate, once an important coaching town, is an ideal centre for exploring this lovely region. The attractive old market town clustered around its Norman castle boasts some fine old houses. To the east near Dorking where the River Mole cuts through the chalk downs is Polesden Lacey, a wonderfully elegant Regency villa set in extensive grounds with a fine walled rose garden and tree-lined walks. The house contains a fascinating collection of paintings, furniture, silver and porcelain and it was here that the Queen Mother and King George VI spent part of their honeymoon.

In the south west corner of Surrey, in the Wey Valley is Frensham Common, now part of a country park managed by Waverley Borough Council. The area is famed for its ponds, Frensham Great and Little Ponds which were dug during the Middle Ages and are the largest in the county. The area is very popular with holiday visitors, having safe sandy beaches, sailing and a wealth of wildlife including wildfowl. To the south at Hindhead are over 1,400 acres of open heathland and woodland covering delightful valleys and sandstone ridges, a great walking region.

Guildford, Surrey's ancient capital, is beautifully sited at the ford where the

Loseley Park, Guildford (SEETB)

River Wey cuts through the North Downs. The town was first mentioned in the will of Alfred the Great, back in 899AD, but its importance was established with the building of its castle (now a ruin), in the twelfth century by Henry II. An important weaving town in Tudor times, today Guildford is a university town, with excellent shopping and a fine venue for the holiday visitor. Dapdune Wharf is being conserved as a focal point for the history of boat building on the River Wey. The Wey is one of the earliest historic waterways in the country. Built in 1651 the waterway was eventually extended by Godalming Navigation to reach the Thames at Weybridge. The eighteenth century watermill on the Tillingbourne at Shalford and Oakhurst Cottage, a small sixteenth century timber-framed cottage wonderfully restored, with its cottage garden, are well worth a visit. To the north of Guildford at West Clandon is Clandon Park, a fine Palladian house with a magnificent two-storeyed marble hall. Clandon is a treasure house of antiques and contains the Ivo Forde collection of Meissen Italian comedy figures.

On the edge of Windsor Great Park, in the north of the county, lies Virginia Water, an artificial lake one-and-a-half miles long, created in the middle of the eighteenth century for the first Duke of Cumberland and contained within four hundred acres of lovely public gardens. At nearby Egham are 188 acres of the historic meadows of Runnymede where in 1215 King John signed the Magna Carta. The American Bar Association built the impressive Magna Carta Memorial, a domed classical temple at the foot of Cooper's Hill. Overlooking the memorial at the top of the hill is the Air Forces Memorial and the John F Kennedy Memorial, an acre of ground given by the people of Great Britain to the people of America as a memorial to their president.

PLACES TO VISIT

This is a small selection of interesting places to visit. Many more are listed in our annual guide to Museums, Galleries, Historic Houses & Sites (see page 448)

Chessington World of Adventures
Leatherhead Road, Chessington
A family theme park, well known for its zoo with penguins, gorillas, tigers and monkeys.

Claremont Landscape Gardens
Portsmouth Road, Esher
Early eighteenth century landscape garden with lake, island, grotto, amphitheatre and views.

Denbies Wine Estate
Dorking
England's largest wine estate set in 265 acres. A tour is provided featuring a 3D time lapse film of vine growing with a tasting in the cellars.

Hampton Court Palace
East Molesey
In peaceful surroundings on the banks of the River Thames, Hampton Court Palace spans 400 years of history and was home to Henry VIII and William III.

Loseley Park
Guildford
A fine example of Elizabethan architecture set in magnificent parkland. Interesting collections of furniture and Christian pictures. Walled garden.

Thorpe Park
Staines Lane, Chertsey
Much to offer for fun seekers of all ages including Europe's highest water ride.

Surrey

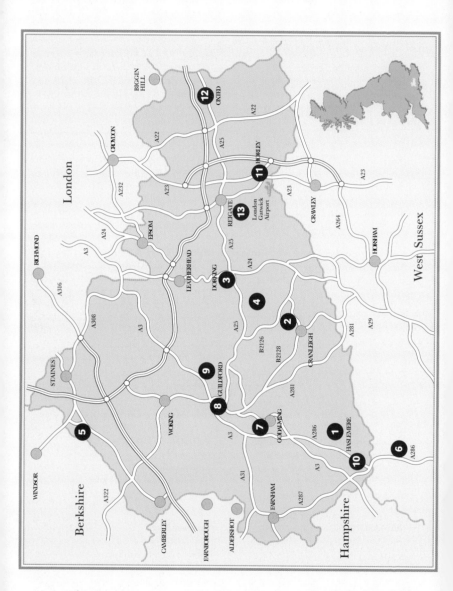

The Red Map References should be used to locate B & B properties on the pages that follow

GREENAWAY Pickhurst Road, Chiddingfold GU8 4TS
Sheila Marsh   *Tel:* 01428 682920   *Fax:* 01428 685078   *Mobile:* 07785 534199
Email: jfvmarsh@nildram.co.uk   *Web:* greenaway.nildram.co.uk

Map Ref: 1
A283

16th century cottage with oak beams and inglenook fireplaces close to the centre of the village. There is a choice of meals within walking distance at the two village hostelries. Television and tea/coffee facilities can be provided if required. Greenaway is run as a family home.

B & B £35-£40pp, C-Cards MC VS, Rooms 2 double, 1 twin, 1 en-suite, No smoking, Children welcome, Dogs by arrangement, Closed Xmas & New Year

---

HIGH EDSER Shere Road, Ewhurst, Cranleigh GU6 7PQ
Carol Franklin-Adams   *Tel:* 01483 278214   *Fax:* 01483 278200   *Mobile:* 0777 5865125
Email: franklinadams@highedser.demon.co.uk

Map Ref: 2
A25

High Edser is a 16th century family home set in area of outstanding natural beauty, surrounded by its own land. A tennis court is available for guests to enjoy, and there is a comfortable lounge for relaxation. The bedrooms are well equipped. The house is 10 miles from Guildford and Dorking, and it is within easy reach of airports and tourist attractions.

B & B £25-£30pp, Rooms 1 twin, 2 double, No smoking, Children welcome, Kennel for dogs, Closed Xmas & Easter

---

PARK HOUSE FARM Hollow Lane, Abinger Common, Dorking RH5 6LW
Ann & Peter Wallis   *Tel:* 01306 730101   *Fax:* 01306 730643   *Mobile:* 07775 861773
Email: Peterwallis@msn.com   *Web:* www.smoothhound.co.uk/hotels/parkhous

Map Ref: 3
A25

Park House Farm is a large spacious house in peaceful park like grounds of 25 acres in an area of outstanding natural beauty with wonderful walks and views. Relaxed and very comfortable accommodation with all bedrooms having televisions, tea/coffee facilities and tastefully decorated with many fine antiques. Convenient for both Gatwick and Heathrow.

B & B £25-£50pp, C-Cards MC VS, Rooms 3 double, 1 twin, all en-suite, No smoking, Children over 12, No dogs, Closed Xmas & New Year

---

BULMER FARM Holmbury St Mary, Dorking RH5 6LG
Gill Hill
Tel: 01306 730210

Map Ref: 4
B2126, A25

A 17th century character farmhouse with beams in a 30 acre beef farm, in the Surrey hills. Choice of twin rooms in the house or double/twin rooms in adjoining converted barn. Very rural, situated at southern end of quiet Victorian village in AONB. Large garden, awarding winning lake, woodland walks, convenient to London, coast, many NT properties, gardens, sports venues. ETC 4 Diamonds.

B & B from £23pp, Rooms 3 double, 5 twin, most en-suite, Restricted smoking, Children over 12, Dogs only in car, Open all year

---

THE OLD PARSONAGE Parsonage Road, Englefield Green TW20 0JW
Peter & Sandi Clark   *Tel / Fax:* 01784 436706
Email: the.old.parsonage@talk21.com   *Web:* www.theoldparsonage.com

Map Ref: 5
A30

A Georgian house in a pretty village on the edge of Windsor Great Park. Accommodation is traditionally furnished and overlooks old fashioned gardens. Bedrooms are well equipped. All meals are freshly prepared, wine is available. Local facilities include a health spa, swimming, golf and horse riding. Conveniently situated for Heathrow (20 minutes), M25, M4, Windsor, Ascot, Wisley Gardens and Egham mainline station (Waterloo 25 minutes).

B & B from £25pp, Dinner from £18, Rooms 1 single, 1 twin, 3 double, 1 family, most en-suite, No smoking, Children welcome, No dogs, Closed Xmas

SHEPS HOLLOW Henley Common, Fernhurst GU27 3HB   *Map Ref:* 6
Elizabeth & Sam Cattell   A286
Tel: 01428 653120

A 17th century cottage, close to beautiful countryside with a television in all rooms and some en-suite. Easy access to London and near Goodwood and Cowdray Park.

B & B from £30pp, Dinner available, Rooms 2 single, 2 en-suite double, Restricted smoking, Children welcome, No dogs, Closed Xmas & New Year

---

LOWER EASHING FARMHOUSE Eashing, Godalming GU7 2QF   *Map Ref:* 7
Gillian & David Swinburn   *Tel / Fax:* 01483 421436   A3
Email: davidswinburn@hotmail.com

This comfortable part 16th century home, situated in a pretty village in a beautiful area, is close to the A3 London - Portsmouth road and convenient for Heathrow and Gatwick airports. An ideal base for touring southern England with an easy train ride to London and pubs nearby. Relax in the walled garden or by a log fire in the guest sitting room.

B & B £27.50-£35pp, Rooms 2 single, 2 twin -1 en-suite,1 private, No smoking, Children welcome, No dogs, Closed Xmas & New Year

---

LITTLEFIELD MANOR Littlefield Common, Guildford GU3 3HJ   *Map Ref:* 8
John Tangye   A3
Tel: 01483 233068   *Fax:* 01483 233686   *Mobile:* 07860 947439

Surrounded by 400 acres of farmland, yet only 35 miles from central London, Littlefield Manor is the perfect setting for both business and holiday visitors. Rooms retain the unique features of this Tudor and Jacobean Manor but have all the convenience of en-suite bathrooms, televisions and tea/coffee making facilities.

B & B from £30pp, C-Cards, Rooms 1 double en-suite, 1 twin with private bathroom, Children welcome, No dogs, Closed Xmas & New Year

---

WAYS COTTAGE Lime Grove, West Clandon, Guildford GU4 7UT   *Map Ref:* 9
Mr & Mrs Christopher Hughes   A25
Tel / Fax: 01483 222454

Ways Cottage is set in a delightful garden on a quiet tree lined road. It is near to several National Trust properties, the M25, A3 and main airports. Breakfast is served in an elegant dining room with the visitors' sitting room adjoining. All rooms have televisions, hairdryers and tea/coffee facilities.

B & B £18-£20pp, Dinner from £12.50, Rooms 2 twin, 1 with pb, 1 with ensuite, No smoking, Children welcome, No dogs, Open all year

---

DEERFELL Blackdown Park, Fernden Lane, Haslemere GU27 3LA   *Map Ref:* 10
Elisabeth Carmichael   *Tel:* 01428 653409   *Fax:* 01428 656106   A286, A3
Email: deerfell@tesco.net

Deerfell lies secluded on the south west side of National Trust Blackdown Hill, with wonderful views towards the South Downs and coast. Rooms are peaceful and comfortable with en-suite bath/shower and tea/coffee/television - one double with separate bath/shower. Comfortable sitting room with open fire. Breakfast served in attractive dining room. Many places of interest. London easily reached from Haslemere Station 4 miles.

B & B from £22pp, Rooms 1 single, 1 twin, 1 double, 1 family, most en-suite, No smoking, Children over 6, Dogs restricted, Closed mid-Dec to mid-Jan

THE LAWN GUEST HOUSE 30 Massetts Road, Horley RH6 7DE   *Map Ref:* 11
Carole & Adrian Grinsted *Tel:* 01293 775751 *Fax:* 01293 821803   A23
Email: info@lawnguesthouse.co.uk *Web:* www.lawnguesthouse.co.uk

The Lawn Guest House, a totally non-smoking establishment, is an attractive Victorian house set in pretty gardens. 2 minutes from town centre, pubs, restaurants, shops and railway station to London and south coast. All rooms are en-suite with tea/coffee/chocolate tray, colour/text TV, hair dryers and direct dial phones. Full English breakfast or healthy alternative is offered. Gatwick airport 5 minutes. On-site parking.

B & B from £27.50pp, C-Cards MC VS AE, Rooms 3 double, 3 twin, 3 triple, 3 family, all en-suite, No smoking, Children & dogs welcome, Open all year

VICTORIA LODGE 161 Victoria Road, Horley RH6 7AS   *Map Ref:* 11
Nikki & Paul Robson *Tel:* 01293 432040 *Fax:* 01293 432042   A23
Email: prnrjr@globalnet.co.uk *Web:* www.gatwicklodge.co.uk

Our family run guest house has many original features and spacious rooms with tea/coffee facilities and hairdryers. Well located for the town centre, rail station, pubs and restaurants. Central London is only 35 minutes by train. Gatwick Airport just five minutes away and holiday parking is available.

B & B from £19pp, Rooms 4 single, 4 twin, 2 double, 2 family, some en-suite, No smoking, Children welcome, No dogs, Open all year

VULCAN LODGE GUEST HOUSE 27 Massetts Road, Horley RH6 7DQ   *Map Ref:* 11
Mrs Karen Moon *Tel:* 01293 771522 *Fax:* 01293 786206 *Mobile:* 07980 576012   A23
Email: karen@vulcan-lodge.com *Web:* www.vulcan-lodge.com

Sitting right in the centre of Horley, Vulcan Lodge is a charming period house, initially built towards the end of the 17th century. Each bedroom is individually decorated and offers a range of thoughtful extras while a delightful lounge is set aside for the exclusive use of our guests. It is regarded as one of the premier establishments in the vicinity of Gatwick Airport.

B & B from £55pp, C-Cards MC VS AE, Rooms 2 single, 1 double, 1 family, all en-suite, No smoking, Children welcome, No dogs, Closed Xmas & New Year

MEADS 23 Granville Road, Oxted RH8 0BX   *Map Ref:* 12
Mrs Helen Holgate *Tel:* 01883 730115 *Mobile:* 07813 268506   M25 J6
Email: holgate@meads9.fsnet.co.uk

Tudor style house on Kent/Surrey border situated within walking distance of town centre with train to London and a good selection of restaurants and pubs. There are televisions and tea/coffee facilities in all rooms and a lovely garden for guests to relax in. Close to Gatwick Airport with off street parking.

B & B from £30pp, Rooms 1 single, 1 double with private bathroom, 1 twin en-suite, No smoking, Children welcome, No dogs, Closed Xmas & New Year

BARN COTTAGE Church Road, Leigh, Reigate RH2 8RF   *Map Ref:* 13
Pat & Mike Corner   A25
Tel: 01306 611347

17th century barn furnished with antiques, large garden with tennis court and pool. Television and tea/coffee making facilities in both rooms. Leigh is a pretty village, the Plough Pub is closeby. Transport provided to Gatwick (15 minutes) and Redhill Station (30 minutes to London, 30 minutes to Brighton). NT properties within reach, including Hever Castle and Chartwell. Introduction to Walton Heath Golf Club available.

B & B from £28pp, Rooms 1 twin, 1 double, 1 with bathroom, Restricted smoking, Children welcome, Dogs by arrangement, Closed Xmas

Sussex

One could be excused for regarding Sussex as very much a seaside county, certainly Rudyard Kipling saw the county as 'Sussex by the sea', but there is considerably more to Sussex than its undoubtedly glorious coastline. The South Downs, that ancient chalk ridge, runs from east to west separating the Sussex Weald from the English Channel, eventually arriving dramatically in the towering form of Beachy Head, the highest cliff on the south coast, and needless to say giving superb views. To explore this area there could be no better starting point than the ancient city of Chichester, although holiday visitors may find it extremely difficult to drag themselves away from the attractions of this fair city! Chichester was a Roman town and there is still evidence of its Roman grid plan, the interesting early sixteenth century market cross indicates the crossing of four of the city's main streets. The Cathedral, early Norman with early English additions, is magnificent, as indeed is its tapestry by John Piper, its painting by Graham Sutherland and its glass by Chagall. The city is blessed with some handsome Georgian houses and an excellent Festival Theatre, plus Chichester Harbour, a fine yachting centre. Nearby is Fishbourne Roman Palace, built for King Cogidubnus, a Roman ally with reconstructed gardens and the original mosaic flooring of the palace, plus the first underground heating system. Petworth House lies to the south, a magnificent seventeenth century palace renowned for its Grinling Gibbons carvings and fine furniture. William Turner worked here for many years during the nineteenth century and a number of his paintings are on exhibition. The house is set in a spectacular 700 acre deer park landscaped by Capability Brown. The glories of Petworth Park are matched by the wonderful Nymans Garden to the east near Haywards Heath, stocked with collections of rare and beautiful plants, trees and shrubs from all over the world. Here is a delightful hidden sunken garden, a walled garden, laurel walk, even romantic ruins! But Sussex is wonderfully endowed with spectacular gardens, in particular Sheffield Park Garden, a hundred acres of landscaped garden with five lakes linked by picturesque waterfalls and cascades. Another Capability Brown masterpiece, and superb whatever the season visited.

Bodiam, in the Rother Valley is an attractive village with a romantic moated castle built in 1385. The castle is extremely popular with children, having a wealth of spiral staircases and battlemented turrets with glorious views from the battlements. To the west of Bodiam is Bateman's, the home of Rudyard Kipling from 1902-36, who loved this county. The house is well worth a visit, the rooms

Great Dixter House & Gardens, Northiam, Rye (SEETB)

and his study are just as they were during the great man's lifetime.

The pride and joy of Sussex however must be its coast, with glorious Brighton at the very centre. The largest town in the county, Brighton was in fact mentioned in the Domesday Book, but it was in 1782 that the Prince of Wales, later to become King George IV arrived, that the town really prospered. The fashionable and famous flocked to Brighton in the wake of the Prince, who built his flamboyant 'Marine Pavilion' here. By 1841 the railway had reached the town and the 'Brighton Belle' brought London to the seaside. Today Brighton offers a delightful warren of narrow pedestrianised streets known as the Lanes, fine shops, restaurants, theatres, the Brighton Festival in May and of course in November the renowned London to Brighton Veteran Car Run. To the east is Brighton's sister resort Eastbourne, developed extensively in 1851 by the Duke of Devonshire to rival Brighton. Here the Eastbourne Sovereign Centre, a massive indoor water leisure complex is a popular attraction, as is the Butterfly Centre on Royal Parade. Hastings, of course holds a special place in the hearts of all Englishmen and was a thriving port even before William the Conqueror arrived. To the north is the attractive town of Battle which grew up around Battle Abbey. The Abbey's high altar marks the spot where Harold is said to have fallen, pierced in the eye with a Frenchman's arrow. There is a fascinating battle-field trail and audiovisual display detailing the whole story of the battle.

PLACES TO VISIT

This is a small selection of interesting places to visit. Many more are listed in our annual guide to Museums, Galleries, Historic Houses & Sites (see page 448)

Arundel Castle
Arundel
Home of the Dukes of Norfolk, the great castle dates from the Norman conquest, containing a very fine collection of furniture and paintings.

Bluebell Railway
Sheffield Park, Uckfield
Bluebell Railway runs standard gauge steam trains through 9 miles of Sussex countryside and has a large collection of railwayana.

Chichester Cathedral
Chichester
The Cathedral was consecrated in 1108 and later much rebuilt and restored. It has the only cathedral spire in England visible from the sea.

Great Dixter House & Gardens
Northiam, Rye
A fifteenth century manor house owned by gardening writer Christopher Lloyd. Lutyens restored both the house and gardens in 1910.

Royal Pavilion
Brighton
Set in restored Regency Gardens, the Royal Pavilion, formerly the seaside residence of King George IV, is an exotically beautiful building with magnificent decorations and furnishings.

Sussex

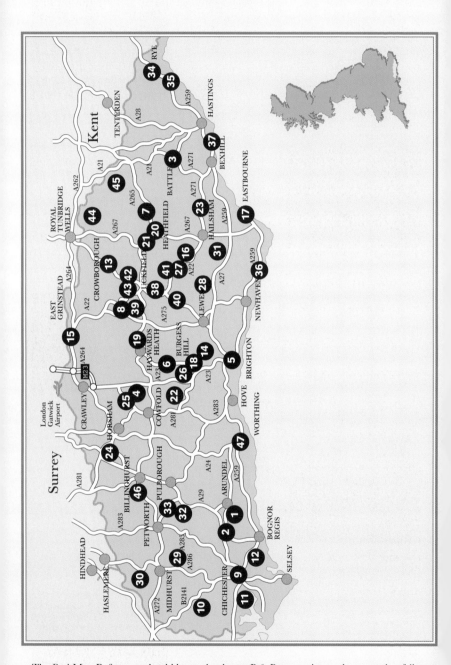

The Red Map References should be used to locate B & B properties on the pages that follow

TODHURST FARM Lake Lane, Barnham, Arundel, W Sussex PO22 0AL
Nigel & Juliet Sedgwick *Tel:* 01243 551959
Email: nigelsedg@aol.com

Map Ref: 1
A27

Attractive period farmhouse close to Chichester, Arundel, Goodwood, South Downs and the coast. Croquet, swimming pool, table tennis, boules, large garden, good walks and evening meal by arrangement.

B & B from £30pp, Rooms 2 double, No smoking, Children welcome, Open all year

---

FELSTED COTTAGE Arundel Road, Walberton, Arundel, W Sussex BN18 0QP
Gloria & Pete Winchester
Tel: 01243 814237

Map Ref: 1
A259

A country cottage set in one and a third acres of gardens and woods, a haven for birds and wildlife. Hearty breakfasts served with fresh eggs from our own hens with tea/coffee facilities in all rooms plus a full suite on ground floor with own sitting room. Easy access for A27, Arundel, Chichester and Goodwood.

B & B from £19.50pp, Rooms 2 double (1 en-suite), 1 twin, Restricted smoking, Children over 10, No dogs, Closed Xmas & New Year

---

BONHAM'S COUNTRY HOUSE Barnham Road, Yapton, Arundel, W Sussex BN18 0DX
Rodney & Judith Dodd *Tel / Fax:* 01243 551301
Email: familydodd@talk21.com

Map Ref: 1
A27

Located halfway between Chichester and Arundel, Bonhams House, built in 1746 offers you luxury away from home. Four large elegant rooms combine quality with the personal attention you can expect at Bonhams. Enjoy breakfast in the oak panelled dining room which adjoins the south facing lounge, overlooking one acre of landscaped gardens. Bonhams offers an indoor pool, tennis, croquet, snooker and basketball. Yacht charter available.

B & B from £25pp, Rooms 1 twin, 2 double, 1 family, all en-suite, Restricted smoking, Children welcome, No dogs in bedrooms, Open all year

---

WOODACRE Arundel Road, Fontwell, Arundel, W Sussex BN18 0QP
Vicki Richards *Tel:* 01243 814301 *Fax:* 01243 814344
Email: wacrebb@aol.com *Web:* www.woodacre.co.uk

Map Ref: 2
A27

Woodacre offers hospitality in a traditional family house with guest accommodation in a separate cottage, joined to the main house. Bedrooms are well presented, well equipped and spacious. Guests are welcome to use the garden. Plenty of parking. We are easy to find from the A27 and conveniently located for Chichester, Arundel, Goodwood and Bognor Regis. Evening meals by arrangement.

B & B from £22.50pp, C-Cards MC VS, Rooms 2 twin, 1 en-suite double, 1 family, Restricted smoking, Children & dogs welcome, Open all year

---

FOX HOLE FARM Kane Hythe Road, Battle, E Sussex TN33 9QU
Paul & Pauline Collins
Tel: 01424 772053 *Fax:* 01424 773771

Map Ref: 3
B2096

A beautiful and secluded 18th century woodcutter's cottage in over 40 acres of rolling East Sussex land. The farmhouse retains its original features, it is beamed with a large inglenook fireplace. Carefully converted to offer three traditionally furnished and well appointed en-suite double rooms. There is a large country garden containing many species of flowers, shrubs, trees and a natural pond.

B & B from £24.50pp, Rooms 3 double en-suite, No smoking, Children over 10, Dogs by arrangement, Closed Xmas & New Year

TIMBERS EDGE Longhouse Lane, off Spronketts Lane, Warninglid, Bolney, E Sussex RH17 5TE
Geoffrey & Sally Earlam *Tel:* 01444 461456 *Fax:* 01444 461813   *Map Ref:* 4
Email: Gearlam@aol.com   A272,A23

Beautiful Sussex country house set in over two acres of gardens and surrounded by woodlands. Breakfast is served in the conservatory overlooking the pool. Within easy reach of Gatwick (15 mins), Brighton (20 mins) and Ardingly the South of England Showground (20 mins). The beautiful gardens of Nymans and Leonardslee (10 mins), Hickstead Show Jumping Ground (10 mins). Bedrooms have TV and beverage facilities.

B & B from £25pp, Rooms 2 twin, No smoking, No dogs, Open all year

ADELAIDE HOTEL 51 Regency Square, Brighton, E Sussex BN1 2FF   *Map Ref:* 5
Paula Hamblin *Tel:* 01273 205286 *Fax:* 01273 220904   A259
Email: adelaide@pavilion.co.uk

Adelaide Hotel is an elegant Regency town house hotel which has been modernised but still retains the charm of yesteryear. It is centrally situated in Brighton's premier seafront square, with NCP parking beneath. There are twelve peaceful bedrooms, individually designed with co-ordinating decor, phone, colour TV etc. A 4 poster bedroom is available. Discounts offered for 2 nights or more.

B & B £35-£46pp, C-Cards MC VS AE, Rooms 3 single, 1 twin, 7 double, 1 family, all en-suite, Restricted smoking, Children over 12, No dogs, Closed Xmas day

TROUVILLE HOTEL 11 New Steine, Brighton, E Sussex BN2 1PB   *Map Ref:* 5
John & Daphne Hansell   A23/A259
Tel: 01273 697384

Grade II listed regency townhouse tastefully restored, situated in a delightful seafront square. The Marina Pavilion Lanes Conference Centre and restaurants within walking distance. Well equipped accommodation is in eight attractive rooms, en-suite and four poster rooms available. Many places of interest in this area including National Trust Properties and gardens, beautiful Downland villages and countryside and historic towns and castle.

B & B from £29pp, C-Cards MC VS AE, Rooms 2 single, 1 twin, 3 double, 2 family, most en-suite, Restricted smoking, Children welcome, No dogs, Closed Xmas & Jan

THE HOMESTEAD Homestead Lane, Valebridge Road, Burgess Hill, W Sussex RH15 0RQ
Tel: 0800 064 0015 *Fax:* 01444 241407   *Map Ref:* 6
Email: homestead@burgess-hill.co.uk *Web:* www.burgess-hill.co.uk   M23/A23, A2300

Quiet, comfortable, friendly home in a peaceful setting of eight acres at end of a private lane. All rooms are en-suite with refreshment facilities and televisions plus two ground floor bedrooms have wheelchair access. Glyndebourne, numerous gardens, National Trust locations and Bluebell steam railway are all nearby. Wivelsfield railway station is one km with Brighton, Gatwick and Lewest 15 minutes, London 50 minutes.

B & B from £25pp, C-Cards MC VS, Rooms 1 single, 1 double, 2 twin, all en-suite, No smoking, Children over 12, No dogs, Closed New Year

ASHLANDS COTTAGE Burwash, E Sussex TN19 7HS   *Map Ref:* 7
Nesta Harmer   A265
Tel: 01435 882207

Pretty cottage may be found in quiet Wealden farmland within area of outstanding natural beauty. Views are glorious, there are beautiful gardens and picnic spots. Kipling's 'Batemans' is 5 minutes walk across the fields and many places of interest nearby. Ashlands Cottage is an ideal location for walking and touring. The bedrooms are comfortable and welcoming, there is a sitting room for relaxing.

B & B from £17pp, Rooms 2 twin, Restricted smoking, Children over 12, Dogs by arrangement, Open all year

JUDINS Heathfield Road, Burwash, E Sussex TN19 7LA
Sandra Jolly   *Tel:* 01435 882455   *Fax:* 01435 883775
Email: sandra.jolly@virgin.net

Map Ref: 7
A265

A delightful 300 year old country house, situated in 1066 countryside with outstanding views across the Rother valley. You are welcome to stroll or relax in the beautiful gardens. Direct walks from Judins to Batemans, former home of Rudyard Kipling. Breakfast is served in the beamed dining room. TV, alarm/radio. hair dryer and hostess tray. Car park. 4 Diamonds Selected.

B & B from £30pp, C-Cards MC VS, Rooms 3 double en-suite, Restricted smoking, Children welcome, No dogs, Open all year

HOLLY HOUSE Beaconsfield Road, Chelwood Gate, E Sussex RH17 7LF
Deidre & Keith Birchell   *Tel:* 01825 740484   *Fax:* 01825 740172
Email: db@hollyhousebnb.demon.co.uk

Map Ref: 8
A275

On the edge of Ashdown Forest stands this 130 year old forest farmhouse. Now converted to form a comfortable family home, in a village with a church, two pubs and a well stocked shop. Guests receive a warm welcome with an inviting lounge, comfortable beds and memorable breakfasts served in the conservatory overlooking the garden. Guests may use the heated pool in summer.

B & B from £25pp, Dinner from £14, Rooms 1 single, 2 twin, 2 double, some en-suite, Children & dogs welcome, Open all year

CEDAR HOUSE 8 Westmead Road, Chichester, W Sussex PO19 3JD
Mel & Judi Woodcock   *Tel:* 01243 787771
Email: mel.judi@talk21.com

Map Ref: 9
A27

Situated within a 15 minute walk from Chichester centre and set within a spacious attractive garden with ample off road parking. The location is perfectly placed for visiting local places of interest such as the picturesque coastal village of Bosham, Fishbourne Roman Palace, Chichester Theatre and Goodwood Race Course. Portsmouth and Arundel lie within a 30 minute drive. Two village pubs within five minute walk.

B & B £22.50-£30pp, Rooms 1 single, 2 double, 1 twin, most en-suite, No smoking, No children or dogs, Closed Xmas & New Year

CHICHESTER LODGE Oakwood, Chichester, W Sussex PO18 9AL
Mr & Mrs Dridge
Tel: 01243 786560

Map Ref: 9
A27, B2178

A charming 1840 Gothic Lodge with wonderful interior design and antiques. Flag stone floors, polished wood, beautiful Gothic windows, wood burning stove in hall way. Two acres of pretty garden with hedges and honeysuckle. En-suite bedrooms are comfortable with nice decorations and furnishings, all rooms have television. There is a garden room with a wood burning stove. Fishing, golf, theatre and Goodwood nearby.

B & B from £25pp, Rooms 2 double, all en-suite, No smoking, No children or dogs, Open all year

FRIARY CLOSE Friary Lane, Chichester, W Sussex PO19 1UF
Brian & Majella Taylor   *Tel:* 01243 527294   *Fax:* 01243 533876
Email: friaryclose@btinternet.com

Map Ref: 9
A27

A large Georgian house set astride an ancient city wall with a walled garden. A City centre location near shops, restaurants and theatre. Televisions and tea/coffee making facilities in each bedroom with a substantial buffet style breakfast. Good base for exploring Sussex and Hampshire. Parking. VISA/Mastercard accepted. 4 Diamonds, Silver Award.

B & B from £25pp, Rooms 3 en-suite twin, No smoking, No children or dogs, Closed Xmas & New Year

THE PROVIDENCE Compton, Chichester, W Sussex PO18 9HD
Juliet & John Diamond   *Tel:* 02392 631880
Email: julietjohn@diamond63.freeserve.co.uk

Map Ref: 10
B2146

Quaint Victorian Grade II listed cottage with pretty garden and orchard. Sitting room with television, tea and coffee available. Compton lies between Petersfield and Chichester in the Downs and close to the South Downs Way, Uppark and other places of interest. Lovely walking and riding country. Field available for visiting horses at £10 per horse per day. Pub for meals and shop in village. On bus route.

B & B £20-£25pp, Rooms 1 double, 1 twin, shared bathroom, No smoking, Children welcome, No dogs, Closed Xmas & New Year

---

THE FLINT HOUSE Pook Lane, East Lavant, Chichester, W Sussex PO18 0AS
Tim & Vivien Read   *Tel:* 01243 773482
Email: theflinthouse@ukonline.co.uk

Map Ref: 11
A286
see Photo opposite

This 19th century house, built by Napoleonic prisoners of war, may be found in a peaceful location on the edge of the South Downs, between Lavant and Goodwood, famous for its racecourse. There are three large, ground floor bedrooms. An wonderful walking area, there are excellent pubs closeby. A twenty minute drive to the sea, and the town of Chichester is within easy reach.

B & B £27.50-£35pp, Rooms 1 king size double & 1 twin, both en-suite, No smoking, Children welcome, No dogs, Closed Xmas

---

WILBURY HOUSE Main Road, Fishbourne, Chichester, W Sussex PO18 8AT
Jackie & Maurice Penfold   *Tel / Fax:* 01243 572953
Email: jackie.penfold@talk21.com

Map Ref: 11
A259

A beautifully kept house, with light airy rooms, all looking out over farm land or the attractive garden. Close to Chichester, Goodwood and Fishbourne Roman Palace. Places to golf and sail are also close by. Jackie and Maurice do their utmost to make you feel at home. Their house is your house with every comfort catered for. AA 4 Diamonds.

B & B from £22.50pp, Rooms 2 double, 1 twin, 1 family, all en-suite, No smoking, Children over 6, No dogs, Closed Xmas & New Year

---

HATPINS Bosham Lane, Old Bosham, Chichester, W Sussex PO18 8HG
Mary Waller   *Tel / Fax:* 01243 572644   *Mobile:* 07778 452156
Email: mary@hatpins.co.uk   *Web:* www.hatpins.co.uk

Map Ref: 11
A259

Mary Waller has combined her artistic talents with a flair for decorating to create delightfully warm and hospitable bed and breakfast accommodation. Bosham is an appealing town and in Old Bosham it is fun to wander to the waterfront and explore. Nearby are Portsmouth and Chichester. A few miles inland is Downland Museum a collection of old cottages and buildings. Honeymoon couples welcome.

B & B £25-£45pp, Rooms 5 en-suite/private bathrooms, No smoking, Children over 10, No dogs, Open all year

---

WHITE BARN Crede Lane, Old Bosham, Chichester, W Sussex PO18 8NX
Christine Reeves & Terry Strudwick   *Tel / Fax:* 01243 573113
Email: whitebarn@compuserve.com

Map Ref: 11
A259

A unique single storey house with timbered interior and a wall of glass in the dining area where memorable dinners and breakfasts are served overlooking the terrace and garden. Located in the Saxon harbour village of Old Bosham. Three delightful, well equipped en-suite bedrooms, charming sitting room with a log fire. NT houses, historic naval ships, Roman Palace and Goodwood House. Warm welcome awaits.

B & B from £28pp, C-Cards MC VS, Dinner from £20, Rooms 2 double, 1 twin, all en-suite, No smoking, Children over 12, No dogs, Open all year

The Flint House, East Lavant, near Chichester

ABELANDS BARN Merston, Chichester, W Sussex PO20 6DY
Mike & Gaile Richardson
Tel: 01243 533826 *Fax:* 01243 555533

Map Ref: 12
A259

Traditional 1850 Sussex Barn converted to a beautiful family home providing spacious and flexible accommodation, with all facilities. A period, flint outbuilding contains large, en-suite bedrooms, and the imposing main Barn offers a ground floor family suite. Attractive gardens overlook the South Downs, a courtyard offers secure, overnight, parking. Abelands Barn is situated two miles from Chichester, with many local attractions.

B & B £25-£35pp, C-Cards MC VS AE, Rooms 1 twin, 2 double, 1 family, en-suite, Children welcome, No dogs, Closed Xmas & New Year

---

HOPE COURT Rannoch Road, Crowborough, E Sussex TN6 1RA
Mrs N L Backhouse *Tel:* 01892 654017 *Mobile:* 07710 289138
Web: www.visitbritain.com/search

Map Ref: 13
A26

A comfortable country house situated in an area of outstanding beauty, facing south over Ashdown Forest. A good touring location for NT gardens, castles and the south coast. Accommodation offered in two well equipped rooms. Private parking. Guests' lounge with Sky television and video. A patio door leads to the garden, there are log fires on chilly days. Good eating places locally.

B & B from £25pp, Rooms 1 double private bathroom, 1 twin en-suite, No smoking, Children over 10, No dogs, Closed Xmas & New Year

---

SOUTH COTTAGE The Drove, Ditchling, E Sussex BN6 8TR
Sonia Stock *Tel:* 01273 846636 *Mobile:* 07788 486315
Email: sonia.stock@amserve.net

Map Ref: 14
M23, M27

A traditional cottage with a pretty garden down a private lane, surrounded by fields, yet is only minutes from the village of Ditchling and its pubs. The cottage is comfortable with tea facilities and TV in each room, it has far reaching views across the fields. Convenient for Gatwick, Newhaven, Brighton and Glyndebourne, a mile from the South Downs Way.

B & B from £25pp, Rooms 1 single, 1 twin with wash basin, 1 double, private bathroom, No smoking, Children & dogs welcome, Closed Xmas & New Year

---

CRANSTON HOUSE Cranston Road, East Grinstead, W Sussex RH19 3HW
Brian & Aileen Linacre *Tel / Fax:* 01342 323609
Email: accommodation@cranstonhouse.screaming.net *Web:* www.cranstonhouse.co.uk

Map Ref: 15
A264 from M23

Each room is well appointed with private facilities, courtesy tray, TV. Care is given to cleanliness. The breakfast choice includes items for vegans. Parking is available. Cranston House is in a quiet residential area within easy walking distance of railway station for London and the town centre with its many restaurants. Gatwick is 15 minutes away by car.

B & B from £22pp, Rooms 2 double, 4 twin, 1 family, all en-suite, No smoking, Children over 6, Dogs by arrangement, Open all year

---

OLD WHYLY Halland Road, East Hoathly, E Sussex BN8 6EL
Sarah Burgoyne
Tel: 01825 840216 *Fax:* 01825 840738

Map Ref: 16
A22

Listed Grade II 17th century manor house with beautiful interior, antiques and pictures. Stunning garden with lake, swimming pool and tennis court. Outstanding cooking with a modern slant; Sarah is famous for her delicious meals and superb breakfasts. Perfect position for Glyndebourne, National Trust houses and gardens where picnics can be ordered. Gatwick only 40 minutes away.

B & B £40-£45pp, Dinner from £22, Rooms 3 twin, 2 en-suite and 1 private, Restricted smoking, Children welcome, Dogs by arrangement, Open all year

BRAYSCROFT HOTEL 13 South Cliff Avenue, Eastbourne, E Sussex BN20 7AH   *Map Ref:* 17
Gerry Crawshaw *Tel:* 01323 647005 *Fax:* 01323 720705 *Mobile:* 07960 187531   A259
Email: brayscroft@hotmail.com *Web:* www.brayscrofthotel.co.uk

This is an elegant, small hotel with a 4 Diamond, Silver Award rating.
The hotel is superbly situated being less than one minute from the
sea front. It is ideally situated for the South Downs, theatres,
restaurants and the town. Elegantly appointed guest rooms have
superb, modern en-suite facilities and well stocked hospitality trays.
There are wonderful walks for outdoor lovers.

B & B from £27pp, C-Cards MC VS, Dinner from £12, Rooms
1 single, 2 double, 2 twin, all en-suite, No smoking, Children over
14, Dogs in bedrooms only, Open all year

THE CHERRY TREE HOTEL 15 Silverdale Road, Eastbourne, E Sussex BN20 7AJ   *Map Ref:* 17
Ann & Michael Henley *Tel:* 01323 722406 *Fax:* 01323 648838   A259
Email: anncherrytree@aol.com *Web:* www.eastbourne.org/cherrytree-hotel

The Cherry Tree is an award winning small, non-smoking, family-run
hotel. Converted from an Edwardian residence it retains all its original
charm, elegance and character. Situated in a quiet location close to
seafront, downlands and theatres. Excellent traditional English
cuisine and holding a full licence. All rooms are en-suite with colour
televisions, clock radios, telephones and welcome trays. ETC 4
Diamonds, Silver Award.

B & B from £28pp, C-Cards MC VS AE DC, Dinner from £13,
Rooms 2 single, 3 double, 4 twin, 1 triple, all en-suite, No smoking,
Children over 7, No dogs, Closed Jan

PINNACLE POINT Foyle Way, Upper Duke's Drive, Eastbourne, E Sussex BN20 7XL   *Map Ref:* 17
Mr & Mrs Peter Pyemont *Tel:* 01323 726666 *Fax:* 01323 643946   A22, A23
Web: www.pinnaclepoint.co.uk

One feels like an honoured guest rather than a paying visitor at
Pinnacle Point. An award winning luxury house used by stars of
theatre, television and international sports stars. It is special and was
featured in the August edition of the Real Homes magazine.
Nominated by the AA for Best Breakfast and RAC for Little Gem
Award. AA RAC & ETC 5 Diamonds, Gold Award

B & B from £50pp, Rooms 2 double, 1 twin, all en-suite,
No smoking, Children over 12, No dogs, Closed Xmas & New Year

DOWER COTTAGE Underhill Lane, Clayton, Hassocks, W Sussex BN6 9PL   *Map Ref:* 18
Chris & Andy Bailey *Tel:* 01273 843363 *Fax:* 01273 846503   A23
Email: andy@dowerbailey.freeserve.co.uk *Web:* www.dowercottage.co.uk

A large country house with beautiful views over Sussex Weald. Ideal
for walking, riding, cycling on South Downs Way. Colour televisions
are fitted in all bedrooms with a library for guests. Off road car
parking. Close to Brighton and only 35 minutes from Gatwick,
Newhaven and Hassocks Station for London 10 minutes away. Also
self catering cottage available.

B & B from £27.50pp, Rooms 1 single, 2 double, 1 twin, 2 family
en-suite, No smoking, Children welcome, No dogs, Open all year

THE PILSTYES 106-108 High Street, Lindfield, Haywards Heath, W Sussex RH16 2HS   *Map Ref:* 19
Roy & Carol Pontifex *Tel:* 01444 484101 *Fax:* 01444 484100   B2028
Email: bnbuk@pavilion.co.uk

Quintessential 16th Century cottage, close to all Lindfield's
amenities. B&B or self catering basis, whichever you prefer.
Romantic four poster bedroom suitable for honeymooners. Gatwick
Airport 15 miles. London 45 minutes by train. Lindfield which is
renowned for its variety of period houses, has brick pavements and
grass verges with lime trees. Pubs, tearooms, shops, village pond
with ducks are nearby.

B & B from £37.50pp, C-Cards MC VS AE, Rooms 1 twin,
1 double, No smoking, Children over 8, No dogs, Open all year

SPICERS BED & BREAKFAST 21 Spicers Cottages, Cade Street, Heathfield, E Sussex TN21 9BS
Valerie & Graham Gumbrell *Tel:* 01435 866363 *Fax:* 01435 868171   *Map Ref:* 20
Email: b+b@spicersbb.co.uk *Web:* www.spicersbb.co.uk   B2096

14th century beamed cottage in the hamlet of Cade Street in an area of outstanding natural beauty on the High Weald of East Sussex. Valerie and Graham offer you a comfortable relaxing night with tea/coffee facilities, televisions, radio/alarms and hairdryers in all rooms with private bathrooms. Our garden sitting room and summerhouse are also for your comfort. ETC 4 Diamonds.

B & B from £22.50pp, C-Cards MC VS, Dinner from £10, Rooms 1 single en-suite, 1 double, 1 twin, No smoking, Children welcome, Dogs by arrangement, Open all year

---

OLD CORNER COTTAGE Little London Road, Cross In Hand, Heathfield, E Sussex TN21 0LT
Cynthia Brown *Tel / Fax:* 01435 863787   *Map Ref:* 21
Email: hamishcjbrown@aol.com   A267

Pretty cottage situated midway between Tunbridge Wells and Eastbourne with a short drive from many National Trust properties and Glyndbourne Opera House. All rooms have en-suite facilities. There is a conservatory for guests to relax in overlooking a pretty garden. An ample breakfast is served in an attractive dining room with an inglenook fireplace. AA 5 Diamonds.

B & B £20-£25pp, Rooms 2 double, 1 twin, all en-suite, No smoking, Children welcome, No dogs, Open all year

---

YEOMANS HALL Blackstone, Henfield, W Sussex BN5 9TB
Alan & Caroline Kerridge *Tel / Fax:* 01273 494224   *Map Ref:* 22
Email: stay@yeomanshall.fsnet.co.uk   A281

Yeomans Hall is a 15th century Hall House situated in a conservation area in the heart of the farming hamlet of Blackstone. Comfortable country style furnishings with beams and inglenook fireplaces, plus an attractive cottage garden. Televisions and tea/coffee facilities are provided in all the rooms. Close to A23, Brighton and fast trains to London and convenient for National Trust properties.

B & B £26-£28.50pp, Rooms 1 single, 2 double, all en-suite, No smoking, Children over 14, No dogs, Closed Xmas & New Year

---

CLEAVERS LYNG COUNTRY HOTEL Church Road, Herstmonceux, E Sussex BN27 1QJ
Tel: 01323 833131 *Fax:* 01323 833617   *Map Ref:* 23
Email: scil@supanet.com *Web:* www.cleaverslyng.co.uk   A271

Photogenic Cleavers Lyng is a small family run hotel adjacent to the west gate of Herstmonceux Castle dating from 1577 with oak beams and an inglenook fireplace. Panoramic views. Good home cooking in traditional English style and full English breakfast served daily. En-suite equipped bedrooms. Fully licensed lounge bar overlooking landscaped gardens and uninterrupted views.

B & B from £30pp, C-Cards MC VS, Dinner from £14.95, Rooms 4 double, 3 twin, Non smoking restaurant, Children & dogs welcome, Closed Xmas & New Year

---

WARTLING PLACE Wartling, Herstmonceux, E Sussex BN27 1RY
Barry & Rowena Gittoes *Tel:* 01323 832590 *Fax:* 01323 831558   *Map Ref:* 23
Email: accom@wartlingplace.prestel.co.uk *Web:* www.countryhouseaccommodation.co.uk   A259, A27

A superb Georgian Grade two listed country house in three acres of gardens, surrounded by magnificent shrubs and trees. Splendidly restored and refurbished, two of the luxuriously appointed bedrooms offer four poster beds. Closeby are some fine restaurants and country pubs. A wealth of stately homes and NT gardens within easy reach such as Sissinghurst, Great Dixter, Hever and Pashley Manor.

B & B £35-£47.50pp, C-Cards MC VS AE, Dinner from £25, Rooms 2 double/king 4 posters, 1 king double/twin, all en-suite, No smoking, Children welcome, No dogs, Open all year

GLEBE END Church Street, Warnham, Horsham, W Sussex RH12 3QW   *Map Ref:* 24
Liz & Chris Cox   *Tel:* 01403 261711   *Fax:* 01403 257572   A24
Email: CoxesWarnham@aol.com

A fascinating medieval house with a sunny walled garden in
Warnham village. Original features include flagstones, curving ships'
timbers and an inglenook fireplace. Bedrooms are charmingly
furnished with antiques, television and drinks trays. Liz is an
excellent cook, breakfasts are delicious. Tennis, swimming, golf and
health club nearby. 20 minutes to Gatwick. Children welcome.
Animals by arrangement. Two excellent Inns nearby. Parking.

B & B from £25pp, Dinner available, Rooms 1 single, 1 double,
1 twin, 1 family, most en-suite, Restricted smoking, Children
welcome, Dogs by arrangement, Open all year

THE VILLAGE PANTRY Handcross Road, Plummers Plain, Horsham, W Sussex RH13 6NU
Mrs Pam Jays   *Tel / Fax:* 01403 891319   *Map Ref:* 25
Email: village-pantry@faxvia.net.   A281, B2110

A comfortable house with a lovely garden offering attractive en-suite
rooms with televisions and courtesy trays. Four miles to Horsham,
five miles from Crawley, and 15 minutes from Gatwick, with London
only one hour away and the coast 30 minutes. Ideal for Nymans,
Leonardslee, Hickstead and Ardingly. Try our warm welcoming
atmosphere. ETC 4 Diamonds.

B & B from £20pp, Rooms 1 single, 2 double, 1 triple, 3 en-suite,
No smoking, Children & dogs welcome, Closed Xmas

CLAYTON WICKHAM FARMHOUSE Belmont Lane, Hurstpierpoint, W Sussex BN6 9EP   *Map Ref:* 26
Mike & Susie Skinner   *Tel:* 01273 845698   *Fax:* 01273 841970   A23
Email: susie@cwfbandb.fsnet.co.uk

Beautifully restored 16th century farmhouse with beams and huge
inglenook. Set in three acres of splendid gardens with tennis court
and lovely views. Quietly secluded, yet convenient for transport
facilities and interesting places. Rooms, including one four poster
en-suite, are generously equipped. Room service for early morning
tea. Truly delicious food with a wide breakfast choice. An excellent
candlelit dinner, or simpler meal available.

B & B from £35pp, Rooms 2 twin/double, 1 double four-poster
en suite, 1 single, Restricted smoking, Children welcome, Dogs by
arrangement, Open all year

WICKHAM PLACE Wickham Drive, Hurstpierpoint, W Sussex BN6 9AP   *Map Ref:* 26
Bill & Joan Moore   *Tel / Fax:* 01273 832172   B2116
Email: accommodation@wickham-place.co.uk

Wickham Place is a large 1920s character house in a lovely quiet
Sussex village. Ideally situated for touring or enjoying a break with
golf, walking, gardens, Brighton and Gatwick all in easy distance.
Hot drink facilities are available in the rooms and the breakfast
selection is from a varied menu and cooked to order.

B & B £22.50-£25pp, Rooms 1 double, 1 twin, 1 family, Restricted
smoking, Children welcome, Dogs by arrangement, Open all year

---

SHORTGATE MANOR FARM Halland, Lewes, E Sussex BN8 6PJ   *Map Ref:* 27
David & Ethel Walters   *Tel / Fax:* 01825 840320   A22
Email: ewalt@shortgate.co.uk   *Web:* www.shortgate.co.uk

Originally an 18th century shepherds cottage on the Earl of
Chichester's estate. It has been enlarged and is now an attractive tile
hung country house with charming landscaped gardens which are
open for the NGS in June every year. Guests have the use of a
private sitting/dining room with wood burning stove for cosy winter
evenings. Perfect location for Glyndebourne.

B & B £27.50-£30pp, Rooms 2 double, 1 twin, all en-suite,
No smoking, Children over 10, No dogs, Open all year

TAMBERRY HALL Eastbourne Road, Halland, Lewes, E Sussex BN8 6PS   *Map Ref:* 27
Rosi Baynham   *Tel / Fax:* 01825 880090   A22
Email: bedandbreakfast@tamberryhall.fsbusiness.co.uk

Set in three acres this beautiful country house has exposed beams and inglenook. Tastefully furnished bedrooms with television, tea/coffee. Elegant dining room. Convenient for touring this Area of Outstanding Natural Beauty, famous gardens, National Trust, golf 3 minutes, Glyndebourne 10 minutes. Restaurant and pub within a short walk, special diets, vegetarian, speciality. Self-catering apartment available. ETC 4 Diamonds.

B & B from £22.50pp, Rooms 2 double en-suite, 1 family/twin en-suite, No smoking, Children welcome, No dogs, Closed Xmas

ECKINGTON HOUSE Ripe Lane, Ripe, Lewes, E Sussex BN8 6AR   *Map Ref:* 28
Sue Tyldsley-Hill   *Tel:* 01323 811274   *Fax:* 01323 811140   *Mobile:* 07720 601347   A27, A22
Email: sue@eckingtonhouse.co.uk   *Web:* www.eckingtonhouse.co.uk

Historic 16th century bailiff's house set in mature gardens. Close to Glyndebourne, Charleston, Lewes and Brighton. Pub serving homemade food nearby. All rooms have en-suite facilities with breakfast served on terrace during warm weather and guests have their own sitting room with inglenook fireplace. Peaceful setting in picturesque village, away from noisy roads.

B & B £25-£30pp, Rooms 1 four poster, 2 double, 1 twin, 1 family, all en-suite, No smoking, Children over 8, No dogs, Closed Dec to Jan

AMBERFOLD Heyshott, Midhurst, W Sussex GU29 0DA   *Map Ref:* 29
Alex & Annabelle Costaras   A286
Tel: 01730 812385   *Fax:* 01730 812842

Amberfold, situated in the scenic hamlet of Heyshott, dates to Tudor times. Miles of woodland walks start on your doorstep, a hideaway for nature lovers. Five minutes drive from Midhurst and local attractions of Goodwood, Chichester and coast. Accommodation comprises: two private self-contained, well equipped annexe, with access all day also electric kettle, cafetiere, toaster, and fridge replenished daily to provide continental breakfasts.

B & B from £27.50pp, Rooms 2 en-suite double, No smoking, No children or dogs, Open all year

REDFORD COTTAGE Redford, Midhurst, W Sussex GU29 0QF   *Map Ref:* 30
Caroline Angela   A272, A3, A286
Tel / Fax: 01428 741242

This attractive, welcoming country house dating to the 16th century, stands in an area of outstanding natural beauty. Comfortable rooms, a self-contained garden suite with a beamed sitting room and en-suite facilities. Tea/coffee facilities, television in bedrooms and drawing room. Convenient to Midhurst, Petworth, Goodwood, Chichester and South Downs. Excellent walks and National Trust properties within easy reach. Ideal for a peaceful stay.

B & B from £35pp, Rooms 3 double/twin, all en-suite, No smoking, Children welcome, No dogs in bedrooms, Closed Xmas & New Year

BATES GREEN Tyhill Road, Arlington, Polegate, E Sussex BN26 6SH   *Map Ref:* 31
Mrs Carolyn McCuthan   *Tel / Fax:* 01323 482039   A22, A27
Web: www.batesgreen.com

Restored 18th century gamekeepers cottage. Bedrooms are individually furnished with own televisions and tea/coffee facilities and a comfortable lounge has log fires in winter. Very quiet location with two acre plantsman's garden to enjoy and a large private oak wood adjoins the working sheep farm. Footpath network leads to South Downs and Arlington Resevoir with Michelham Priory and Charleston Farmhouse close by.

B & B £34-£35pp, Rooms 1 double, 2 twin, all en-suite, No smoking, No children or dogs, Closed Xmas

EEDES COTTAGE Bignor Park Road, Bury Gate, Pulborough, W Sussex RH20 1EZ
David & Jane Hare
Tel: 01798 831438 *Fax:* 01798 831942 *Mobile:* 07703 150022

Map Ref: 32
A29, A283, B2138

Eedes Cottage is a quiet country house surrounded by farmland and is under the personal charge of the proprietors, Jane and David Hare. The house stands in its own grounds of two acres which are maintained to immaculate standards. Children and dogs are welcome. Ideal for easy access to Arundel, Chichester and Sussex coast. Expect a very warm personal welcome.

B & B £22.50-£25pp, Rooms 2 double en-suite, 2 twin, No smoking, Children & dogs welcome, Open all year

THE SWAN INN Lower Street, Fittleworth, Pulborough, W Sussex RH20 1EN
Robert Carey *Tel:* 01798 865429 *Fax:* 01798 865721
Email: hotel@swaninn.com *Web:* www.swaninn.com

Map Ref: 33
A283

All rooms have televisions, tea/coffee facilities, trouser presses and hair dryers with four posters available. Undercover parking. Full on license public lounge, bar and restaurant with a large garden and log fires in winter. Close to Arundel, Chichester, Fontwell and Goodwood Racecourse. Arun Golf courses nearby.

B & B from £30pp, Dinner from £7.95, Rooms 3 single, 8 double, 4 twin, all en-suite, Children welcome, No dogs, Open all year

KING CHARLES II GUEST HOUSE 4 High Street, Rye, E Sussex TN31 7JE
Nicola Fischbach
Tel: 01797 224954 *Fax:* 01797 226615

Map Ref: 34
A259, A268

A fine example of a mediaeval half timbered house. King Charles II Guest House is situated centrally in the ancient and historic town of Rye. Dating back to 1420 it has atmospheric fireplaces, lovely old beams and a wealth of other original features. The rooms are beautifully antique furnished, fully en-suite and combine character and charm with modern conveniences.

B & B £40-£47.50pp, Rooms 3 double with en-suite, No smoking, Children over 6, No dogs, Open all year

LITTLE ORCHARD HOUSE West Street, Rye, E Sussex TN31 7ES
Sara Brinkhurst *Tel / Fax:* 01797 223831
Web: www.littleorchardhouse.com

Map Ref: 34
A259, A268

An informal country house atmosphere in an elegant Georgian town house, which enjoys a quiet, central location. It is presented with antique furnishings throughout. All rooms are en-suite with TV and a hospitality tray. Generous breakfasts feature local/organic produce. There is a large, traditional walled garden for guests' use and a wide selection of good pubs/ restaurants nearby. Off-street parking is available.

B & B £32-£45pp, C-Cards MC VS, Rooms 2 double, No smoking, Children over 12, No dogs, Open all year

LITTLE SALTCOTE 22 Military Road, Rye, E Sussex TN31 7NY
Denys & Barbara Martin *Tel:* 01797 223210 *Fax:* 01797 224474
Email: littlesaltcote.rye@virgin.net

Map Ref: 34
A259

Located just a few minutes walk from the centre of the picturesque town of Rye, Little Saltcote offers a friendly welcome, free parking and acclaimed generous English or vegetarian breakfast cooked to order. There are five comfortable rooms, all with central heating, colour television and well-stocked complimentary beverage tray. Perfect for families, with a large sandy beach three miles away.

B & B from £20pp, C-Cards MC VS, Rooms 2 double, 3 family, 3 en-suite, Restricted smoking, Children welcome, Dogs by arrangement, Closed Xmas

THE OLD VICARAGE 66 Church Square, Rye, E Sussex TN31 7HF
Julia & Paul Masters *Tel:* 01797 222119 *Fax:* 01797 227466
Email: info@oldvicageryе.co.uk *Web:* www.oldvicageryе.co.uk

Map Ref: 34
A259

Charming listed Georgian house in centre of historic Rye overlooking quiet and picturesque church square. Bedrooms beautifully decorated in Laura Ashley prints. All ensuite with television and tea/coffee facilities. Private parking available. 26 restaurants within walking distance. Excellent nature reserves and beaches perfect for walks. Sissinghurst, Bodiam, Leeds and Camber Castle all nearby. AA 5 Diamonds and awarded Best Breakfast In England 2000.

B & B £30-£42pp, Rooms 2 double, 1 twin, 1 family, all en-suite, No smoking, Children over 8, Guide dogs only, Closed Xmas

---

PENDRAGON LODGE Watermill Lane, Pett, Rye, E Sussex TN35 4HY
Mrs Dianna Epton *Tel:* 01424 814051 *Fax:* 01424 812499
Email: pendragon-lodge@hotmail.com *Web:* www.pendragonlodge.co.uk

Map Ref: 35
A259

B&B accommodation of quality and luxury amidst the Sussex countryside. This former old bakery features beautiful bedrooms decorated to the highest standard, the attention given to detail and many thoughtful additions make this establishment an extra special place to stay - antique furnishings, bathrobes, toiletries, lovely flannels and accessories all create an air of luxury. Breakfasts include homemade bread, muesli and preserves.

B & B £25-£30pp, C-Cards MC VS, Rooms 2 double, 1 twin, 1 family, all en-suite, No smoking, Children over 5, Dogs welcome, Closed Xmas

---

THE SILVERDALE 21 Sutton Park Road, Seaford, E Sussex BN25 1RH
Ted & Gilly Cowdrey *Tel:* 01323 491849 *Fax:* 01323 891131
Email: silverdale@mistral.co.uk *Web:* www.mistral.co.uk/silverdale/silver.htm

Map Ref: 36
A259

Friendly town centre house-hotel in a lovely old fashioned seaside town. We are renown for our high standard of attention. Catering is no problem for coeliacs and others with special dietery needs. Experts in single malts and English wines. Ideally situated for those who enjoy walking or touring the local villages. Pets are particularly welcome.

B & B £14-£30pp, C-Cards MC VS AE DC, Dinner from £10, Rooms 6 double, 2 family, most en-suite, Restricted smoking, Children & dogs welcome, Open all year

---

FILSHAM FARM HOUSE 111 Harley Shute Road, St Leonards on Sea, E Sussex TN38 8BY
Barbara Yorke *Tel:* 01424 433109 *Fax:* 01424 461061
Email: filshamfarmhouse@talk21.com *Web:* www.filshamfarmhouse.co.uk

Map Ref: 37
A21, A27

Filsham Farm House is a 17th century listed Sussex farmhouse with old beams and log fires. It is within easy reach of the town centre and the surrounding countryside. The house is furnished with antiques and it provides a high standard of accommodation. All the rooms have colour TV and tea/coffee facilities. There is ample private parking space available.

B & B from £20pp, Rooms 1 twin, 2 double, 1 family, most en-suite, Restricted smoking, Dogs welcome, Open all year

---

NEW GLENMORE Sliders Lane, Furners Green, Uckfield, E Sussex TN22 3RU
Jane & Alan Robinson *Tel / Fax:* 01825 790783
Email: alan.robinson@bigfoot.com

Map Ref: 38
A275

New Glenmore is a spacious bungalow set in six acres of grounds in a rural location close to the bluebell steam railway and Sheffield Park National Trust Gardens. Breakfast comes with our own eggs, honey and home baked bread.

B & B £20-£25pp, Rooms 2 double, 1 twin, 1 family, most en-suite, No smoking, Children welcome, No dogs, Open all year

SLIDERS FARM Furners Green, Danehill, Uckfield, E Sussex TN22 3RT
David & Jean Salmon   *Tel / Fax:* 01825 790258
Email: jean&davidsalmon@sliders.co.uk

Map Ref: 39
A275

Quietly situated, surrounded by fields and woodland within walking distance of Sheffield Park Gardens, the Bluebell Railway and Ashdown Forest. Gatwick, Ardingly Showground, Glyndebourne and Brighton easily reached. London 45 minutes by train. 30 acres of grounds and gardens, swimming pool, tennis court and fishing lakes. Well equipped bedrooms. Lounge and dining room have inglenooks. Self-catering units in 400 year old barn.

B & B from £27.50pp, Rooms 1 twin, 2 double, 1 family, all en-suite, Restricted smoking, Children welcome, No dogs, Closed Xmas & Boxing Day

---

TANYARD HOUSE Tanyard Lane, Danehill, Uckfield, E Sussex RH17 7JW
Mr & Mrs I B Macfarlane
Tel: 01825 740293

Map Ref: 39
A22, A275

Beautifully furnished friendly family home situated in quiet country lane. Breakfast is served in the conservatory overlooking our pretty garden. Excellent pubs nearby and ideally placed for Gatwick, Brighton, The Bluebell Railway, Ashdown Forest and Ravenswood Hotel. Convenient for a great many famous gardens including Wakehurst Place. Ample car parking. AA 4 Diamonds.

B & B £20-£25pp, Rooms 1 double with private bath, extra bed available for 1 child, Restricted smoking, No dogs, Closed Xmas

---

THE FAULKNERS Isfield, Uckfield, E Sussex TN22 5XG
Mrs C Rigby   *Tel:* 01825 750344   *Fax:* 01825 750577
Email: celia.rigby@imagenius.co.uk

Map Ref: 40
A26

The Faulkners, originally a 15th century Wealden Hall house, is set in beautiful gardens with two lakes. The accommodation of one double and two single rooms are furnished to match the age of the house. Glyndebourne, Lewes and many National Trust properties are all close by. The qualities of this house are reflected in our ETC 4 Diamond, Gold Award.

B & B from £28pp, Rooms 2 single, 1 with pb, 1 double with pb, No smoking, Children over 14, No dogs, Closed Xmas & New Year

---

THE OLD FARMHOUSE Honeys Green, Framfield, Uckfield, E Sussex TN22 5RE
Tel: 01825 841054   *Fax:* 0870 122 9055
Email: stay@honeysgreen.com   *Web:* www.honeysgreen.com

Map Ref: 41
A22

Highly commended 16th century farmhouse offering peaceful location in delightful Sussex countryside. It stands in two acres of gardens with a pond plus comfortable rooms, warm hospitality and a full English cooked breakfast. Honey's Green is ideally situated for the South Coast and many local tourist attractions, Glyndebourne and Lewes only three miles. Interior design courses also available.

B & B from £30pp, Rooms 2 double, No smoking, Children over 10, Closed Nov to Mar

---

OLD MILL FARM Chillies Lane, High Hurstwood, Uckfield, E Sussex TN22 4AD
Mrs P Sharpe
Tel / Fax: 01825 732279

Map Ref: 42
A26, A272

Old Mill Farm is situated in the centre of a picturesque village close to Ashdown Forest and many National Trust properties. An ideal retreat.

B & B £24-£30pp, Rooms 1 single with pb, 1 twin en-suite, 1 family en-suite, No smoking, Children welcome, Dogs by arrangement, Open all year

THE OLD OAST Underhill, Maresfield, Uckfield, E Sussex TN22 3AY   *Map Ref:* 43
Mr & Mrs D A Wadsworth   A22
Tel: 01825 768886

Beautiful oast house standing in four acres of gardens and woodland, in an area of outstanding beauty. The carefully restored house offers special hospitality, organic breakfasts, vegetarian and vegan a special feature. Delightful, generously equipped bedrooms, one is situated in the roundel of the oast. There is a comfortable sitting room, with an inglenook fireplace, satellite TV, videos and music. Heated swimming pool.

B & B from £30pp, Rooms 1 double, 2 twin, Children & dogs welcome, Open all year

CHEVIOTS Cousley Wood, Wadhurst, E Sussex TN5 6HD   *Map Ref:* 44
Solvita Field *Tel:* 01892 782952   B2100
Email: b&b@cheviots99.freeserve.co.uk *Web:* www.cheviots99.freeserve.co.uk

On B2100 between Lamberhurst and Wadhurst. Comfortable B&B in modern country house with extensive garden. Convenient for walking and motoring. Close to Bewl Water and many National Trust properties including Scotney Castle, Sissinghurst and Batemans.

B & B from £22pp, C-Cards MC VS, Rooms 2 single, 1 double, 1 twin, some en-suite, No smoking, Children welcome, No dogs, Closed Oct to Mar

CHERRY TREE INN Dale Hill, Ticehurst, Wadhurst, E Sussex TN5 7DG   *Map Ref:* 45
Tel: 01580 201229 *Fax:* 01580 201325   A21, A265
Email: leondiane@aol.com

Cherry Tree Inn is a delightful country pub on the edge of the village of Ticehurst. Bewl Water is within walking distance as is Dalehill Golf Course. All rooms are en-suite and the beamed bar offers a wide range of meals, lunchtime and evenings, together with wines and cask beer. Charming patio and gardens.

B & B from £25pp, Dinner available, Rooms 3 double en-suite, No smoking, No dogs, Open all year

LOWER SPARR FARM Skiff Lane, Wisborough Green, W Sussex RH14 0AA   *Map Ref:* 46
Sally Sclater *Tel:* 01403 820465 *Mobile:* 07971 165517   A272
Email: sally@lowersparrbb.f9.co.uk *Web:* www.lowersparrbb.f9.co.uk

A converted farmhouse in quiet surroundings. All of the bedrooms look out over the large garden, tennis court and pastureland. Although it is in a rural position it is close to several village pubs. Within easy reach of M25, Gatwick and south coast.

B & B from £23pp, Rooms 1 single, 1 double, 1 twin, all with private facilities, No smoking, Children welcome, No dogs, Closed Xmas & New Year

ROSEDALE HOUSE 12 Bath Road, Worthing, W Sussex BN11 3NU   *Map Ref:* 47
Dudley & Joan Nightingale *Tel:* 01903 233181   A259
Email: rosedale@amserve.net

Delightful Victorian house, nestling by a delightful seaside town and run by the friendly Nightingale family. We offer you homely comfort and personal attention in our relaxed guest house. The house is strictly non-smoking and centrally heated. Ideally based for walking and visiting the numerous places of interest including the historic towns of Arundel and Chichester. ETB 4 Diamonds.

B & B from £25pp, Rooms 2 single, 1 double, 1 twin, No smoking, Children welcome, No dogs, Open all year

Warwick & West Midlands

The West Midlands region was once the centre of a vast and complicated canal system, but is now the hub of an equally complicated motorway network. This is one of the most important industrial and manufacturing regions and despite Charles Dickens' description of 'an industrialised realisation of hell', the so called Black Country, Birmingham and Coventry have much to offer the holiday visitor. The towns and cities of the West Midlands provide excellent shopping, theatre, galleries and exhibitions. Brindleyplace is an urban development by the old canal system and contains many shops, bars and restaurants. Birmingham is also the home of the renowned City of Birmingham Symphony Orchestra and the Birmingham Royal Ballet, formally the Sadler's Wells Company, with the City Museum and Art Gallery holding the world's finest collection of pre-Raphaelite paintings. Nearby is Cadbury World, the centre dedicated to the history and making of chocolate, guiding visitors through the discovery by the Aztecs to the origins of the Cadbury family in Bournville.

Nearby Coventry, despite all the appalling bomb damage of 1940, boasts some fine buildings including the medieval Guildhall of St Mary in Bayley Lane, and of course the wonderfully innovative Cathedral of St Michael by Sir Basil Spence, containing Graham Sutherland's enormous tapestry 'Christ in Majesty'. The cathedral was destroyed in 1940 and the ruins left as a reminder with the present cathedral built within the

structure. Just five miles south west of Coventry stands the glorious massive sandstone ruin of Kenilworth Castle built by Geoffrey de Clinton, chamberlain to Henry I in 1125 and later owned by John of Gaunt.

Walsall, to the north of Birmingham and once the nineteenth century, own of a hundred trades' is fascinating, dominated by its parish church perched on a steep limestone hill. Its large open-air markets on Tuesdays and Saturdays attract crowds of shoppers. The birthplace of the humourist Jerome K Jerome whose house is now a museum is only one of the many attractions of a town with a fine country park, arboretum and impressive open spaces. Nearby is Wightwick Manor, a late nineteenth century house much influenced by William Morris, set in a delightful Victorian/Edwardian garden of topiary and yew hedges.

Warwickshire is the quintessential England, one of the country's smallest counties, it is a region rich in history and blessed with some of the country's loveliest scenery. Stratford upon Avon is of course a magnet to the thousands of pilgrims who flock to see the birth and death place of William

Warwick Castle (HETB)

Shakespeare. The town with its many half-timbered buildings is a shrine to The Bard with the Shakespeare Birthplace Trust maintaining five buildings associated with Shakespeare, including Hall's Croft, the home of Shakespeare's daughter Susanna and her husband. Just out of town at Shottery is Anne Hathaway's Cottage, the home of Shakespeare's wife before her marriage and at Wilmcote is Mary Arden's House, once the childhood home of Shakespeare's mother and now a farm and countryside museum. Gloriously sited on the bank of the River Avon is the Shakespeare Memorial Theatre, home of the distinguished Royal Shakespeare Company. Close to Stratford upon Avon is Charlecote Park, the home of the Lucy family since 1247. The present house was built in 1550 and visited by Queen Elizabeth I. It is also claimed that the young Shakespeare poached deer here.

For sheer spectacle little can match wondrous Warwick Castle, one of Britain's most visited stately homes. For centuries it was the grand home of the Earls of Warwick, now brought to life with waxworks depicting the history of the family that lived there. In the summer there are many events, including jousting and other medieval entertainment. The centre of the city of Warwick was rebuilt following a disastrous fire in 1694 and possesses some fine buildings particularly around High Street and Northgate Street. Not to be missed is Leycester's Hospital and the stunning view of the castle from Castle Bridge, where the spectacular castle walls are reflected in the still waters of the Avon. Royal Leamington Spa which is adjacent to Warwick was designated a Royal Spa by Queen Victoria following a visit in 1838. It is a beautiful regency town with the Royal Pump Rooms housing a fascinating museum and art gallery.

PLACES TO VISIT

This is a small selection of interesting places to visit. Many more are listed in our annual guide to Museums, Galleries, Historic Houses & Sites (see page 448)

Birmingham Museum & Art Gallery
Birmingham
Major collections of the fine and decorative arts, archaeology and ethnography, natural history and social history in the Midlands.

Heritage Motor Centre
Gaydon, Warwick
The history of the British motor industry is portrayed from the 1880's to date including rallying, racing and record breaking vehicles.

Shakespeare's Birthplace
Stratford-upon-Avon
Where Shakespeare was born in 1564, a

fascinating insight into what life was like when Shakespeare was a child. The Shakespeare exhibition provides an introduction to his life and background.

Upton House
Banbury
An important collection of paintings and porcelain and an outstanding garden, of interest throughout the season.

Warwick Castle
Warwick
Staterooms, dungeons, torture chambers, armoury are to be viewed. Warwick Castle holds over a thousand years of secrets.

Warwick & West Midlands

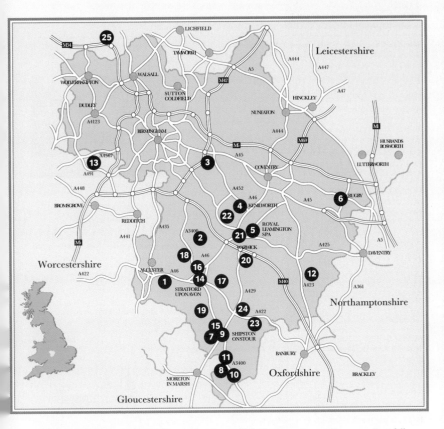

The Red Map References should be used to locate B & B properties on the pages that follow

GLEBE FARM Exhall, Alcester B49 6EA   *Map Ref:* 1
John & Margaret Canning   A46
Tel / Fax: 01789 772202

A quaint old house tucked away beside the church in one of Shakespeare's most unspoiled villages yet convenient for both tourist and commercial centres in south Warwickshire. A quiet refuge for busy people with four poster beds, log fires and early breakfasts if required.

B & B from £20pp, C-Cards MC VS, Rooms 2 single, 1 twin, 2 double, Restricted smoking, Children welcome, Well behaved dogs, Closed Xmas & New Year

---

WOODSIDE Langley Road, Claverdon CV35 8PJ   *Map Ref:* 2
Doreen Bromilow *Tel:* 01926 842446 *Fax:* 01926 843697   A4189
Email: ABO21@dial.Pipex.com

Set in 22 acres of conservation woodland and garden, bedrooms are spacious, well equipped and furnished in a cottage style with antiques and period furniture. Lovely outlook over woodland and garden. Central heating, log fire with television and video in comfortable lounge. A home cooked dinner is served to order. Interesting eating places locally. Doreen and her Burmese mountain dog offer a warm welcome.

B & B £25-£28pp, Dinner from £15, Rooms 2 single/double/family en-suite, 1 double pb, 2 twin, Restricted smoking, Children welcome, Dogs by arrangement, Closed Xmas

---

HOLLIES GUEST HOUSE Kenilworth Road, Hampton-in-Arden B92 0LW   *Map Ref:* 3
Miss Victoria Dickenson *Tel:* 01675 442681 *Fax:* 01675 442941   A452
Email: thehollies@hotmail.com *Web:* www.theholliesguesthouse.co.uk

Excellent accommodation recently refurbished, large, spacious and relaxing. Just three miles from NEC and Birmingham International Airport with ample parking.

B & B from £30pp, Rooms 1 single, 6 double, 4 twin, 2 triple, all en-suite, No smoking, Closed Xmas & New Year

---

ABBEY GUEST HOUSE 41 Station Road, Kenilworth CV8 1JD   *Map Ref:* 4
Trevor & Angela Jefferies *Tel:* 01926 512707 *Fax:* 01926 859148   A452
Email: the-abbey@virgin.net *Web:* www.abbeyguesthouse.com

Our guest house is a cosy licensed Victorian house, located close to the town centre. We are well situated for the NEC, NAC, Coventry and Warwick Universities, Warwick and Stratford-upon-Avon. Our high standards of comfort and hospitality are reflected by our ETC 4 Diamond rating.

B & B from £22.50pp, Rooms 2 single, 3 double, 2 twin, all en-suite, No smoking, Children welcome, No dogs, Closed Xmas & New Year

---

ENDERLEY GUEST HOUSE 20 Queens Road, Kenilworth CV8 1JQ   *Map Ref:* 4
Tel: 01926 855388 *Fax:* 01926 850450   A452
Email: enderleyguesthouse@supanet.com

The Enderley is a quiet, friendly, family owned guest house, where you will receive a warm welcome and enjoy the comfort and cleanliness of our establishment. Nearby is a good range of restaurants serving international cuisine. Kenilworth is conveniently located for Warwick University, the NEC, NAC, Stratford, Warwick, Leamington and has easy access to all Midlands Motorways.

B & B from £22.50pp, Rooms 1 single, 2 double, 1 twin, 1 family, all en-suite, No smoking, Children welcome, No dogs, Open all year

8 CLARENDON CRESCENT Leamington Spa CV32 5NR
Christine & David Lawson *Tel:* 01926 429840 *Fax:* 01926 424641
Email: lawson@lawson71.fsnet.co.uk

Map Ref: 5
A452

A Grade II listed Regency house in a crescent with its own private
dell. Elegantly furnished with antiques with individually designed en-
suite bedrooms and tea/coffee facilities. Situated in a quiet
backwater of Leamington Spa, yet only a five minute walk from the
town centre. Warwick, Stratford, the Royal Agricultural Centre and
the NEC are all within an easy drive.

B & B £27.50-£35pp, Rooms 2 single, 2 double, 1 twin, all
en-suite, Restricted smoking, Children over 4, Dogs by
arrangement, Closed Xmas & New Year

GARDEN COTTAGE 52 Kenilworth Road, Leamington Spa CV32 6JW
Christine Jenkin *Tel / Fax:* 01926 338477
Email: christine@gardencottage.fsworld.co.uk

Map Ref: 5
A452

Warm hospitality awaits you in this charming coach house situated
on the A452, five minutes from the town centre, close to Stratford-
upon-Avon, Kenilworth, Warwick, the Royal Agricultural Centre and
the Birmingham NEC and Airport. The accommodation comprises
one spacious twin bedded room with an adjoining conservatory and
private bathroom, and one double with large a en-suite shower
room. Excellent breakfasts. Off road parking. Garden.

B & B from £22pp, Rooms 1 twin, 1 double, Restricted smoking,
Children welcome, Dogs by arrangement, Open all year

LAWFORD HILL FARM Lawford Heath Lane, Rugby CV23 9HG
Don & Susan Moses *Tel:* 01788 542001 *Fax:* 01788 537880
Email: lawford.hill@talk21.com *Web:* www.lawfordhill.co.uk

Map Ref: 6
A428

We invite you to relax and enjoy our Georgian home set in a
picturesque garden. Our bedrooms, three in the main house and
three in our converted stables, are charmingly decorated and
comfortably furnished. Some en-suite, colour TV and all with tea and
coffee tray. Perfectly placed for touring Stratford, Warwick and the
lovely Cotswolds.

B & B from £21.50pp, C-Cards MC VS, Rooms 1 single, 1 twin,
3 double, 1 family, some en-suite, No smoking, Children & dogs
welcome, Closed Xmas & New Year

BLACKWELL GRANGE Blackwell, Shipston-on-Stour CV36 4PF
Liz Vernon Miller *Tel:* 01608 682357 *Fax:* 01608 682856
Email: staying@blackwellgrange.co.uk *Web:* www.blackwellgrange.co.uk

Map Ref: 7
A429, A3400

Grade II listed farmhouse, part of which dates from 1603, is situated
on the edge of a peaceful village with hill views. Spacious bedrooms
are en-suite and well equipped, ground floor bedroom suitable for
disabled guests. Stone flagged dining room with inglenook, drawing
room with a log fire and deep sofas, a relaxing place to stay. Ground
floor room available for less able guests.

B & B £30-£40pp, C-Cards MC VS AE, Dinner from £15, Rooms
1 single, 1 twin, 2 double, all en-suite, Restricted smoking,
Children over 12, No dogs, Closed Xmas day

LOWER FARM Darlingscott, Shipston-on-Stour CV36 4PN
Jackie Smith *Tel / Fax:* 01608 682750
Email: lowerfarmbb@beeb.net *Web:* www.cotswoldbandb.co.uk

Map Ref: 7
A429

Darlingscott is a pretty hamlet near the Fosseway, here stands
Lower Farm, an 18th century farmhouse where guests receive warm
hospitality. A fine collection of prints and pictures are displayed.
Visitors are welcome to relax in the garden and on the patio.
Perfectly placed for visiting Chipping Campden. Hidcote and
Kiftsgate, also the famous towns of Stratford-on-Avon and Warwick
are within easy reach.

B & B £22.50-£25pp, Rooms 2 double, 1 twin, all en-suite,
No smoking, Children over 8, No dogs, Closed Xmas

LOWER FARM BARN Great Wolford, Shipston-on-Stour CV36 5NQ
Rebecca & Fred Mawle *Tel:* 01608 674435 *Mobile:* 07932 043111
Email: rebecca@greatwolford.freeserve.co.uk

Map Ref: 8
A44, A3400

100 year old barn stands in the small, peaceful village of Great Wolford. The property retains much of its original form, beams and ancient stonework. It is now modernised and very comfortable. Beautifully furnished well equipped bedrooms. A warm welcoming, sitting room with television, for guests' use. A lovely old pub only five minutes walk from Lower Farm Barn, serves traditional home made food.

B & B from £21pp, Rooms 2 double, 1 en-suite (or family room), Restricted smoking, Children welcome, No dogs, Open all year

THE OLD MANOR HOUSE Halford, Shipston-on-Stour CV36 5BT
Jane & William Pusey *Tel:* 01789 740264 *Fax:* 01789 740609
Email: wpusey@st-philips.co.uk

Map Ref: 9
A429, A3400

Eight miles south of Stratford on Avon, dating from the 18th century, the house stands in three acres of gardens, which lead to the River Stour, fishing is available, also tennis. A self contained wing is available, the main house displays beams and oak furniture. A cordon bleu dinner may enjoyed by arrangement, an excellent choice of restaurants locally, and many good Cotswold pubs.

B & B from £30pp, Dinner available, Rooms 1 double, 1 twin, Restricted smoking, Children welcome, Dogs by arrangement, Closed Xmas

ASHBY HOUSE Long Compton, Shipston-on-Stour CV36 5LB
Paul & Charlotte Field *Tel / Fax:* 01608 684286
Email: e.p.field@fieldashby.demon.co.uk

Map Ref: 10
A3400

Ashby House offers a quiet, comfortable and friendly stay, ideally located for Shakespeare's Stratford, Oxford, Blenheim Palace, Warwick Castle and the Cotswolds. Bedrooms and pretty bathrooms are spacious and well equipped. Breakfasts and delicious dinners are served in the 19th century dining room. Good village pub within easy walking distance and the well known Whichford Pottery is a few miles away. Safe parking.

B & B £19-£23pp, Dinner from £12, Rooms 1 twin, 1 double, 1 family, all private bathrooms, No smoking, Children welcome, No dogs, Closed Xmas

WOLFORD FIELDS Shipston-on-Stour CV36 5LT
Richard Mawle *Tel:* 01608 661301 *Mobile:* 07958 649306
Email: richard.wolfordfield@bush.intent.net

Map Ref: 11
A44, A3400

A large Cotswold farmhouse with gardens, built by Lord Campendown in 1857 and farmed by the Mawle family since 1901. Three comfortable bedrooms share two warmly decorated bathrooms which are fitted with power showers. Guests may relax in the television lounge where tea, coffee and chocolate making facilities are available, and stroll in the large garden. Parking. Convenient for Stratford-upon-Avon and the Cotswolds.

B & B from £17.50pp, Rooms 2 double, 1 twin, No smoking, Open all year

CRANDON HOUSE Avon Dassett, Southam CV47 2AA
Deborah Lea *Tel:* 01295 770652 *Fax:* 01295 770632
Email: crandonhouse@talk21.com *Web:* www.crandonhouse.co.uk

Map Ref: 12
M40 J12, B4100, A423

Beautiful country home offering luxury accommodation, set in 20 acres with lovely countryside views. Attractive bedrooms are generously equipped, (one ground floor room.) Guests' dining room and two comfortable sitting rooms one with colour television and woodburning stove. Excellent breakfast menu. Good pubs and restaurants nearby. Situated in Warwickshire within easy reach of Stratford upon Avon, Warwick and other attractions. Winter breaks.

B & B £20-£26pp, C-Cards MC VS, Rooms 3 double, 2 en-suite, 2 twin en-suite, Restricted smoking, Children over 8, No dogs, Closed Xmas

THE WHITE HOUSE   Burton Dassett, Southam CV47 2AB   *Map Ref:* 12
Lisa Foxwell   *Tel / Fax:* 01295 770143   *Mobile:* 07767 458314   B4100
Email: lisa@whitehouse10.freeserve.co.uk

A large country house situated at the top of the Burton Dassett Hills,
the White House was built in 1938 as a farm cottage, it is set in a
rural position enjoying magnificent views over the Warwickshire and
Oxfordshire countryside. Homely and welcoming, guests are offered
en-suite rooms with TV and tea/coffee making facilities. Brochure
available on request.

B & B from £22.50pp, Rooms 2 double, 1 twin, all en-suite,
No smoking, Children welcome, No dogs, Open all year

MARSTON HOUSE   Priors Marston, Southam CV47 7RP   *Map Ref:* 12
John & Kim Mahon   *Tel:* 01327 260297   *Fax:* 01327 262846   A361
Email: seaburne277@hotmail.com   *Web:* www.ivabestbandb.co.uk

Set in a beautiful and historic conservation village Marston House is
a private turn of the 19th century family home. Guests have full use
of the beautiful landscaped garden, private tennis court, croquet
lawn and south-facing terrace. The food is delicious as Kim both
studied and taught at Cordon Bleu in London and dinner can be
arranged for four or more people. Convenient for Warwick Castle,
Stratford and Silverstone.

B & B from £25pp, Dinner from £25, Rooms 1 double, 1 twin,
all with private bathroom, No smoking, Children & dogs welcome,
Open all year

WORMLEIGHTON HALL   Wormleighton, Southam CV47 2XQ   *Map Ref:* 12
Mrs Nicola Burton   *Tel / Fax:* 01295 770234   *Mobile:* 07778 991527   A423
Email: wormleightonhall@farming.co.uk

Stone farmhouse standing in the conservation village of
Wormleighton, at the end of a tree lined drive in extensive grounds
with panoramic countryside views. Bedrooms are spacious and well
furnished, televisions and hostess trays included. Guests can enjoy
the sun lounge, swimming pool, gardens and traditional cooking,
dinner by arrangement. Centrally located for Stratford, Warwick,
Oxford, NEC, NAC and M40 (10 minutes.) Stabling available.

B & B £25-£35pp, Dinner from £15, Rooms 1 double en-suite,
1 double/twin, 1 single, both private, Smoking in sunroom only,
Children over 8, Dogs by arrangement, Open all year

ST ELIZABETH'S COTTAGE   Woodman Lane, Clent, Stourbridge DY9 9PX   *Map Ref:* 13
Mrs Sheila Blankstone   *Tel:* 01562 883883   *Fax:* 01562 885034   A491
Email: st_elizabeth_cot@btconnect.com

Beautiful country cottage in tranquil setting, 6 acres of landscaped
garden with outdoor heated pool. Lovely country walks. TV and
tea/coffee making facilities in all rooms. Residents lounge. Many
pubs and restaurants nearby. Easy access to motorway links, 25
minutes from NEC and Birmingham Airport. Close to Symphony Hall
and Convention Centre, Black Country Museum, Dudley,
Stourbridge Crystal Factories, Severn Valley Railway.

B & B from £28pp, Rooms 2 double, 1 twin, all en-suite,
No smoking, Children & dogs welcome, Open all year

AVONLEA   47 Shipston Road, Stratford-upon-Avon CV37 7LN   *Map Ref:* 14
Irene & Clive Crossley   *Tel:* 01789 205940   *Fax:* 01789 209115   A3400
Email: avonlea-stratford@lineone.net   *Web:* www.avonlea-stratford.co.uk

Avonlea is a large stylish Victorian town house centrally located and
only five minutes walk from the restaurants, theatre and shops. All
rooms are en-suite and furnished to the highest standard with
hospitality trays and telelvisions. Our guests are assured of a warm
and friendly welcome. Full English breakfast is served in our elegant
dining room. Car parking.

B & B £22-£36pp, C-Cards MC VS, Rooms 1 single, 4 double,
1 twin, 1 family, all en-suite, No smoking, Children welcome,
No dogs, Open all year

BRADBOURNE HOUSE 44 Shipston Road, Stratford-upon-Avon CV37 7LP
Ian Gregory *Tel:* 01789 204178 *Fax:* 01789 262335
Email: ian@bradbourne-house.co.uk *Web:* www.bradbourne-house.co.uk

Map Ref: 14
A3400

Bradbourne House is a detached tudor style house, with a beautiful garden, ample parking and only minutes from the town centre. Oue guests are welcome to use the consevatory which overlooks the delightful pond and beautiful garden. The dining room has separate tables and also a view of the garden. All rooms have washbasins, televisions and tea/coffee facilities.

B & B £20-£30pp, C-Cards MC VS, Rooms 2 single, 4 double, 2 twin, 2 family, most en-suite, Restricted smoking, Children over 2, No dogs, Closed Xmas

---

CADLE POOL FARM The Ridgeway, Stratford-upon-Avon CV37 9RE
Mrs Turney
Tel: 01789 292494

Map Ref: 14
A46

In picturesque grounds, with peacocks, ornamental ducks and geese roaming freely, this lovely oak beamed farmhouse is only two miles from Stratford-upon-Avon. Both bedrooms are en-suite and have tea/coffee making facilities. There is an antique oak dining room, and guest sitting room. Ideal touring centre for Warwick, Oxford and Cotswolds.

B & B from £26pp, Rooms 1 double, 1 family, both en-suite, Restricted smoking, Children over 10, No dogs, Closed Xmas

---

CURTAIN CALL 142 Alcester Road, Stratford-upon-Avon CV37 9DR
J Purlan *Tel:* 01789 267734
Email: curtaincall@btinternet.com *Web:* www.curtaincallguesthouse.co.uk

Map Ref: 14
A46

Relax in one of our themed rooms. Enjoy the pleasant atmosphere created by the surroundings and quality, friendly service. Double four-poster beds, family and single rooms are available, most en-suite. Ten minutes from town centre and five minutes from railway station.

B & B £20-£35pp, C-Cards MC VS, Dinner available, Rooms 2 single, 3 double (four poster), 1 twin, 1 family, No smoking, Children welcome, No dogs, Open all year

---

EASTNOR HOUSE HOTEL 33 Shipston Road, Stratford-upon-Avon CV37 7LN
Derek & Barbara Janes *Tel:* 01789 268115 *Fax:* 01789 551133
Email: enquiries@eastnorhouse.com *Web:* www.eastnorhouse.com

Map Ref: 14
A3400

Victorian townhouse with spacious, comfortable rooms, all en-suite. Oak panelling, wide staircases and tasteful furnishings. Centrally located by the River Avon, theatres, shops and restaurants within five minutes pleasant walk. Open all year. A non-smoking hotel with private parking. Great location for visiting Stratford, the Cotswolds and Warwick Castle.

B & B from £25pp, Rooms 3 double, 2 twin, 2 triple, 2 family, all en-suite, No smoking, Children welcome, No dogs, Open all year

---

LINHILL GUEST HOUSE 35 Evesham Place, Stratford-upon-Avon CV37 6HT
Diana Tallis *Tel:* 01789 292879 *Fax:* 01789 299691
Email: linhill@bigwig.net

Map Ref: 14
A46

Linhill is a large Victorian town house, central to town centre and local attractions. A family run guest house where a warm and friendly atmosphere awaits you. Excellent home cooked food and evening meals are available with special diets catered for. Televisions and tea/coffee facilities are in all rooms and babysitting is available if required.

B & B from £18pp, C-Cards MC VS, Dinner from £6.50, Rooms 1 single, 1 double, 3 twin, 3 family, some en-suite, Children welcome, No dogs, Open all year

MOONRAKER HOUSE 40 Alcester Road, Stratford-upon-Avon CV37 9DB
Mr & Mrs Leonard   *Tel:* 01789 299346/267115   *Fax:* 01789 295504
Email: MoonrakerLeonard@aol.com

Map Ref: 14
A46

Moonraker house is family-run and near the centre of Stratford.
Beautifully coordinated decor throughout, some rooms with four
poster beds and a garden terrace is available.

B & B from £24.50pp, Rooms 9 double, 1 twin, 1 triple, all
en-suite, No smoking, Children over 5, Open all year

PARKFIELD 3 Broad Walk, Stratford-upon-Avon CV37 6HS
Roger & Joanna Pettit *Tel / Fax:* 01789 293313
Email: parkfield@btinternet.com   *Web:* www.parkfieldbandb.co.uk

Map Ref: 14
A439

Parkfield is an elegant Victorian town house in a quiet side street.
Conveniently it is only a few minutes walk to the Royal Shakespeare
Theatres and the town centre. There is a large choice on the
breakfast menu including vegetarian options. Visitors are also
welcome to use the private car park.

B & B £22.50-£24pp, C-Cards MC VS, Rooms 1 single, 2 double,
1 twin, 3 family, most en-suite, No smoking, Children over 5,
No dogs, Open all year

PENSHURST GUEST HOUSE 34 Evesham Place, Stratford-upon-Avon CV37 6HT
Karen Cauvin   *Tel:* 01789 205259   *Fax:* 01789 295322
Email: penhurst@cwcom.net   *Web:* www.penhurst.net

Map Ref: 14
A439

An exceptionally warm welcome from Karen and Yannick is offered
at this prettily refurbished, totally non-smoking Victorian townhouse,
situated five minutes walk from the town centre. Bedrooms have
been individually decorated and are well equipped. Delicious English
or Continental breakfasts are served from 7.00am right up until
10.30am. Home cooked evening meals by arrangement. Facilities
for disabled. Brochure available.

B & B from £16pp, Rooms 1 single, 2 twin, 2 double, 2 family,
some en-suite, No smoking, Open all year

STRETTON GUEST HOUSE 38 Grove Road, Stratford-upon-Avon CV37 6PB
Michael & Yvonne Machin   *Tel / Fax:* 01789 268647
Email: skyblues@strettonhouse.co.uk   *Web:* www.strettonhouse.co.uk

Map Ref: 14
A439

Stretton House is a homely guest house situated only three minutes
walk from Stratford-upon-Avon town centre. Very convenient for the
theatres and all local attractions, also close to the station. A warm
welcome, personal attention and very comfortable accommodation
with a pleasant dining room and televisions in all bedrooms.
Vegetarians catered for.

B & B £20-£28pp, Rooms 2 single, 2 double, 2 twin, 1 family, most
en-suite, No smoking, Children over 8, Small dogs only, Open all
year

WILLOW CORNER Armscote, Stratford-upon-Avon CV37 8DE
Trish & Alan Holmes   *Tel:* 01608 682391   *Mobile:* 07803 710149
Email: trish&alan@willowcorner.co.uk   *Web:* www.willowcorner.co.uk

Map Ref: 15
A429, A3400

Willow Corner is a 300 year old thatched and beamed cottage, once
the village smithy, situated in the quiet hamlet of Armscote.
Individually styled luxury en-suite bedrooms feature tea/coffee
facilities, televisions, homemade biscuits and many thoughtful
extras. The full English breakfast includes homemade produce,
served in the main lounge with a magnificent inglenook fireplace.
Close to Stratford and Warwick. ETC AA 4 Diamonds, Silver Award.

B & B £27-£29pp, Rooms 2 double, 1 twin, all en-suite,
No smoking, Children over 12, No dogs, Closed Xmas & New Year

BURTON FARM Bishopston, Stratford-upon-Avon CV37 0RW   *Map Ref:* 16
Eileen & Tony Crook   *Tel:* 01789 293338   *Fax:* 01789 262877   A46
Email: tony.crook@ukonline.co.uk   *Web:* www.stratford-upon-avon/burtonfarm.htm

A 140 acre working farm 2 miles from Stratford. The farmhouse and barns dating from Tudor time, are steeped in the character for which the area is world famous. The accommodation furnished with antiques, has en-suite facilities and is surrounded by colourful gardens and pools which support wildlife, also unusual birds and plants. The friendly atmosphere will ensure a pleasant stay.

B & B from £25pp, Rooms 2 double, 2 twin, 3 with 4 poster, 1 family, all en-suite, No smoking, Children welcome, No dogs, Closed Xmas

GLEBE FARM HOUSE Loxley, Stratford-upon-Avon CV35 9JW   *Map Ref:* 17
Kate McGovern   *Tel:* 01789 842501   *Fax:* 01789 841194   A429, A422
Email: scorpiolimited@msn.com   *Web:* www.glebefarmhouse.com

Glebe Farm is a fine country house set in 30 acres of wonderful countryside, two miles froom Stratford and 10 minutes from Warwick Castle. All rooms enjoy four poster beds, en-suite bathrooms, and rural views. Dinner is served in our candlelit conservatory overlooking the gardens. Glebe Farm is AA 5 Diamonds, Premier status and the Johansens Award for Excellent Service.

B & B from £47.50pp, C-Cards MC VS, Dinner from £22.50, Rooms 4 double en-suite, No smoking, Children over 12, No dogs, Open all year

HOLLY TREE COTTAGE Pathlow, Stratford-upon-Avon CV37 0ES   *Map Ref:* 18
John & Julia Downie   *Tel / Fax:* 01789 204461   A3400
Email: john@hollytree-cottage.co.uk   *Web:* www.hollytree-cottage.co.uk

Holly Tree Cottage is a period cottage with gardens overlooking the countryside. Dating from the 17th century, it has beams, antiques and a friendly atmosphere. The bedrooms have TV, tea/coffee, radio/alarms and hair dryers. Breakfasts, a speciality, include full English and vegetarian. Excellent for Shakespeare country, the theatre, Warwick Castle, the Cotswolds and the National Exhibition centre.

B & B from £25pp, Rooms 1 twin, 1 double, 1 family, all en-suite, No smoking, Children & dogs welcome, Open all year

WINTON HOUSE The Green, Upper Quinton, Stratford-upon-Avon CV37 8SX   *Map Ref:* 19
Mrs G Lyon   *Tel:* 01789 720500   *Mobile:* 07831 485483   B4632, A3400
Email: gail@wintonhouse.com

Historic Victorian farmhouse situated in a rural hamlet, six miles from Stratford. Comforts include four poster beds, log fires and award winning breakfasts including fruit from our organic orchard. Good walking and cycling (Sustian route) with cycles available for hire plus Hidcote Gardens and other National Trust properties nearby. Cottage also available.

B & B £30-£37.50pp, Rooms 2 double, 1 twin, 1 family, 2 en-suite, 2 private, No smoking, Children welcome, No dogs, Closed Xmas

AVONSIDE COTTAGE 1 High Street, Barford, Warwick CV35 8BU   *Map Ref:* 20
Peter & Philippa Wilson   A429
Tel: 01926 624779

17th century property in a peaceful village location, beautifully positioned on the banks of the River Avon, between Warwick and Stratford-upon-Avon. Luxurious, spacious and well equipped guest rooms with en-suite bathrooms and river views, plus a delightful riverside garden. Within walking distance of village pubs. Ample off road parking. ETC 5 Diamond, Gold Award.

B & B £25-£28pp, Rooms 1 double, 1 twin, both en-suite, No smoking, No children or dogs, Closed Xmas & New Year

FORTH HOUSE 44 High Street, Warwick CV34 4AX
Elizabeth Draisey   *Tel:* 01926 401512   *Fax:* 01926 490809
Email: info@forthhouseuk.co.uk   *Web:* www.forthhouseuk.co.uk

Map Ref: 21
A429

Forth House, a rambling Georgian family home within the old town walls of Warwick, offers two guest suites hidden away at the back of the house. They both have private sitting and dining rooms, and they are well equipped with TV, fridge and hot and cold drink facilities. Breakfasts, English or continental, at an agreed time. Ideally situated for business or pleasure.

B & B from £30pp, C-Cards MC VS, Rooms 1 double/twin, 1 family, both en-suite, No smoking, Children welcome, Guide dogs only, Closed occasionally

---

NORTHLEIGH HOUSE Fiveways Road, Hatton, Warwick CV35 7HZ
Sylvia Fenwick   *Tel:* 01926 484203   *Fax:* 01926 484006   *Mobile:* 07774 101894
Web: www.northleigh.co.uk

Map Ref: 22
A4177

A comfortable, peaceful country house, where the elegant rooms are individually designed, each having an en-suite bathroom, television, fridge, kettle and many thoughtful extras. A full English breakfast is freshly cooked to suit each guest. Handy for Warwick, Stratford-upon-Avon and the exhibition centres.

B & B £26-£31pp, C-Cards MC VS, Rooms 1 single, 5 double, 1 twin, all en-suite, No smoking, No dogs in public rooms, Closed Dec & Jan

---

NOLANDS FARM Oxhill, Warwick CV35 0RJ
Sue Hutsby   *Tel:* 01926 640309   *Fax:* 01926 641662
Email: inthecountry@nolandsfarm.co.uk   *Web:* www.nolandsfarm.co.uk

Map Ref: 23
A422

Nolands Farm a working arable farm, is situated in a tranquil valley with woods and wildlife. The well equipped en-suite bedrooms are mostly on the ground floor in tastefully restored annexe stables. There are romantic 4 poster bedrooms with bathroom. A licensed bar adjoins the conservatory, and dinner is by arrangement. Fishing, clay shooting, bicycles for hire and riding nearby. Ballooning in the summer.

B & B from £22pp, C-Cards MC VS, Dinner from £19.95, Rooms 1 single, 4 four posters, 2 double, 1 family, 2 twin, Restricted smoking, Children over 7, Guide dogs only, Open all year

---

DOCKER'S BARN FARM Oxhill Bridle Road, Pillerton Hersey, Warwick CV35 0QB
Carolyn Howard
Tel: 01926 640475   *Fax:* 01926 641747

Map Ref: 24
A422

Idyllically situated barn conversion surrounded by its own land and well placed for Warwick, Stratford, NEC, NAC and the Cotswolds. Junction 12, M40, is six miles. The attractive, beamed en-suite bedrooms are well equipped, the four poster suite has its own front door. Wildlife abounds the walks are lovely. We keep sheep, horses and hens. Friendly service, French and Spanish spoken.

B & B from £21pp, Rooms 1 twin, 2 double, all en-suite, No smoking, Children over 8, Dogs by arrangement, Closed Xmas

---

FEATHERSTONE FARM HOTEL New Road, Featherstone, Wolverhampton WV10 7NW
Tel: 01902 725371   *Fax:* 01902 731741   *Mobile:* 07836 315258
Web: www.featherstonefarm.co.uk

Map Ref: 25
M54

A 17th century farmhouse with listed barns and stables, completely refurbished and open fires for cooler nights. Near M6, M54 and close to Weston Hall. A restaurant offering Indian Cuisine is in a converted Medieval barn on site.

B & B from £35pp, C-Cards MC VS, Dinner available, Rooms 2 single, 3 double, 3 twin, 1 triple, all en-suite, Children welcome, Dogs by arrangement, Open all year

Wiltshire

Following a dispute between the occupants of the royal castle and the cathedral, or more probably because of its bleak, windy and waterless location, the monks of Old Sarum vacated their ancient cathedral, and in the early thirteenth century moved down the valley and built their new cathedral in the pleasant watermeadows where the three rivers, the Avon, Bourne and Nadder meet. And what a building Salisbury Cathedral is! Built between 1220 and 1260 it is the only early English cathedral to be built all in one style and the graceful spire, added in the fourteenth century is 123 metres higher than any other in the country. The Chapter House contains the best preserved of the four manuscripts of the Magna Carta. The cathedral close, England's largest, is contained within walls with medieval gateways and one of the finest houses in the close is Mompesson House, containing the important Turnbull collection of eighteenth century English drinking glasses. Salisbury is packed with interest and is a glorious mixture of inns, churches and fine buildings. The Iron Age hill-fort of Figsbury Ring lies to the north-east giving glorious views of the cathedral and city, as does the seventeenth century folly, a curious octagonal tower on Pepper Box Hill in the south east.

Wiltshire is dominated by the central high chalk plateau of Salisbury Plain, twenty miles by twelve miles, an area of grassy downland from prehistoric times until World War I when large tracts were ploughed. Stonehenge, the country's most famous prehistoric stone circle and a World Heritage Site, attracts visitors from all over the world with the significance of the henge puzzling archaeologists for generations. This impressive monument consists of Sarsen stones from Wiltshire and stones from the Preseli Hills of Wales. It is believed to have been remodeled during the Bronze Age (1600BC) when enormous lintels were added. The National Trust owns 1,450 acres of land surrounding the monument including interesting Bronze Age barrow groups. At Avebury, one of the most important megalithic monuments in Europe, the Trust manages a 28 acre site with stone circles enclosed by a ditch. The site includes the Alexander Keiller Museum and the Wiltshire Life Society's display of Wiltshire rural life in the Great Barn. Just a mile from Avebury is Silbury Hill, the largest prehistoric mound in Europe and remarkably, it has been calculated that it would have taken seven hundred men over ten years to build.

In the south of the county by Warminster are the colourful delights of Stourhead, a

Stonehenge, Wiltshire (SWT)

garden regarded as one of the highest achievements of English landscape gardening. The garden was laid out between 1741 and 1780 with lakes, classical temples, rare trees and plants, inspired by a Grand Tour of Europe by Henry Hoare II, the son of a wealthy banker. The house, built in 1721 by Colen Campbell was one of England's first Palladian mansions with King Alfred's Tower, the red-brick folly built at the edge of the estate in 1772, at 160 feet giving superb views. However, no-one can leave this lovely county without visiting that extravagant palace Longleat, built for John Thynne in 1580 and greatly embellished by the fourth Marquess of Bath on returning from a grand tour. As well as the wonderful grounds landscaped by 'Capability' Brown there is the world's largest maze and the hugely popular safari park.

Malmesbury in the north of the county can boast some of the finest Norman architecture in the country. The ancient settlement grew around its abbey, established in the seventh century, developing in size and importance as a place of pilgrimage to the shrine of St Aldhelm. Marlborough to the south is renowned for its fine wide High Street, and is an excellent centre for exploring the rolling Marlborough Downs and Savernake Forest, at one time a medieval hunting forest, now a glorious walking region. No visitor in this region should miss Lacock Abbey founded in 1232 and converted into a country house some time after 1539. This was the nineteenth century home of William Henry Fox Talbot who invented photography. A museum commemorating his achievement is in Lacock village, one of the prettiest villages in the country.

PLACES TO VISIT

This is a small selection of interesting places to visit. Many more are listed in our annual guide to Museums, Galleries, Historic Houses & Sites (see page 448)

Avebury Stone Circle
Avebury, Marlborough
The site includes the Alexander Keiller Museum which houses one of the most important prehistoric collections of artefacts in Britain

Bowood House
Calne
A Georgian House in a beautiful parkland setting landscaped by 'Capability' Brown. Interesting collections of costumes, watercolours, miniatures and jewellery.

Longleat
Warminster
A great Elizabethan house which includes

many treasures - paintings, tapestries, murals, furniture. Also renowned for its Safari park.

Salisbury Cathedral
Salisbury
The cathedral is unique amongst English medieval cathedrals in that it was designed as a single unit and finished in 1280. It has the tallest spire in England (404ft high) which was added in 1334.

Wilton House
Wilton, Salisbury
Classic example of Palladium style architecture. One of the finest art collections in Europe with over 230 original paintings on display.

Wiltshire

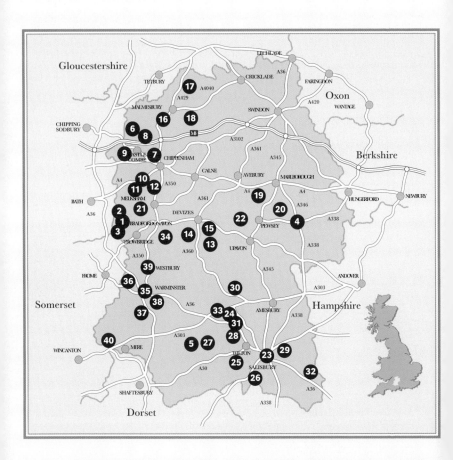

Gloucestershire

Oxon

Berkshire

Somerset

Hampshire

Dorset

LECHLADE
CRICKLADE
A36
FARINGDON
TETBURY
A4040
A429
MALMESBURY
SWINDON
A420
WANTAGE
CHIPPING SODBURY
A3102
A361
AVEBURY
A345
MARLBOROUGH
CALNE
A4
HUNGERFORD
NEWBURY
BATH
A4
A350
A346
A338
A36
A361
DEVIZES
PEWSEY
A338
BRADFORD-ON-AVON
MELKSHAM
M1
CASTLE COMBE
CHIPPENHAM
TROWBRIDGE
A360
UPAVON
A345
WESTBURY
A350
ANDOVER
FROME
WARMINSTER
A303
A36
AMESBURY
A338
WINCANTON
MERE
A303
A30
WILTON
SALISBURY
A36
SHAFTESBURY
A338

17
16
18
6
8
9
7
10
11
12
19
20
4
2
21
1
22
3
34
14
15
13
39
36
35
30
38
37
33
24
31
28
40
5
27
23
29
25
26
32

The Red Map References should be used to locate B & B properties on the pages that follow

330

PRIORY STEPS Newtown, Bradford-on-Avon BA15 1NQ   *Map Ref:* 1
Carey & Diana Chapman *Tel:* 01225 862230 *Fax:* 01225 866248   A363
Email: priorysteps@clara.co.uk *Web:* www.priorysteps.co.uk

Stunning views from all rooms over the beautiful town of Bradford-
on-Avon. Luxury accommodation in en-suite rooms furnished with
antiques. Built in 1690 from locally quarried stone, the house is full
of character, situtated just eight miles from Bath and within 15 miles
of over 30 historic houses, castles and gardens, as well as being
convenient to visit Stonehenge and Avebury.

B & B £37-£42pp, C-Cards MC VS, Dinner from £22, Rooms
3 double, 2 twin, all en-suite, No smoking, Children by
arrangement, No dogs, Open all year

WOODPECKERS Holt Road, Bradford-on-Avon BA15 1TR   *Map Ref:* 1
John & Thelma Jenkins *Tel:* 01225 865616 *Fax:* 01225 865615 *Mobile:* 07941 397970   A36
Email: b&b@wood-peckers.co.uk *Web:* www.wood-peckers.co.uk

Woodpeckers offers a relaxing atmoshere with bright spacious en-
suite rooms with televisions and tea/coffee facilities. There is ample
parking, a large open garden with a patio and a lift is also available.
Bradford on Avon is a quaint town with its canal and river with guests
able to visit the nearby Georgian city of Bath, Longleat, Lacock and
Bowood. ETC 4 Diamonds.

B & B £30-£35pp, C-Cards MC VS, Rooms 1 single, 1 double,
2 twin, 1 family, all en-suite, No smoking, Children over 5,
No dogs, Open all year

MIDWAY COTTAGE Farleigh Wick, Bradford-on-Avon BA15 2PU   *Map Ref:* 2
Mrs Sue Lindsay *Tel:* 01225 863932 *Fax:* 01225 866836   A363
Email: midway_cottage@hotmail.com

A friendly, relaxed cottage with high standards of comfort and
service. Situated on the A363, midway between Batheaston and
Bradford-on-Avon and next door to a country inn serving excellent
food. Easy access to Bath, Cotswolds and many other beautiful
places. Finalist in Landlady of the Year 2000 competition. ETC AA 4
Diamonds.

B & B £22.50-£25pp, Rooms 2 double, 1 twin, all en-suite, No
smoking, Children welcome, Dogs by arrangement, Open all year

---

FERN COTTAGE Monkton Farleigh, Bradford-on-Avon BA15 2QJ   *Map Ref:* 2
Christopher & Jenny Valentine *Tel:* 01225 859412 *Fax:* 01225 859018   A363
Email: enquiries@fern-cottage.co.uk *Web:* www.fern-cottage.co.uk

Delightful cottage dating from 1680, in a quiet conservation Village.
Oak beams, open fire, antiques and family heirlooms. Three
beautifully appointed bedrooms. English breakfast is served at a
large table, there is a lovely conservatory where guests may relax
and look out over a well maintained garden. Ample parking. Local
Inn serves excellent fare. Many interesting places within a few
minutes drive.

B & B from £30pp, Rooms 3 double, all en-suite, No smoking,
Children welcome, No dogs, Open all year

BURGHOPE MANOR Winsley, Bradford-on-Avon BA15 2LA   *Map Ref:* 3
Elizabeth & John Denning *Tel:* 01225 723557 *Fax:* 01225 723113   B3108, A36
Email: burghope.manor@virgin.net *Web:* www.burghopemanor.co.uk

A fine medieval manor house standing in beautiful countryside on the
edge of the village of Winsley, five miles from Bath and close to
Bradford-on-Avon. Steeped in history, yet it is a family home, now
modernised so that the historical features compliment the present
day comforts which include central heating and en-suite bathrooms.
A good selection of pubs within walking and driving distance.

B & B £42.50-£50pp, C-Cards MC VS AE, Rooms 2 double,
3 twin, all en-suite, No smoking, Children over 10, No dogs,
Closed Xmas & New Year

WESTCOURT BOTTOM 165 Westcourt, Burbage SN8 3BW
Felicity Mather *Tel:* 01672 810924
Email: westcourt.b-and-b@virgin.net *Web:* www.westcourtbottom.co.uk

Map Ref: 4
B3087

Large 17th century thatched cottage five miles south of Marlborough in quiet countryside. Half timbered rooms, large garden and swimming pool offer relaxed informal atmosphere. Coffee, tea and biscuits in all rooms. Log fire sitting room with television for guests. Central for Stonehenge, Avebury, Savernake Forest, Ridgeway and Kennet and Avon Canal. Excellent pub food nearby. Ample parking. ETC 4 Diamonds.

B & B from £28pp, Dinner from £15, Rooms 2 double, 1 en-suite, 1 twin, No smoking, Children welcome, No dogs, Open all year

---

THE OLD RECTORY Chilmark SP3 5AT
Scarlet & Edward Leatham *Tel:* 01722 716263 *Fax:* 01722 716159
Email: leathamschilmark@talk21.com

Map Ref: 5
A303 (2 miles)

13th century house in the village, in its own grounds of 20 acres, visitors can relax in the countryside. Library and drawing room with log fires. Dine by candlelight, enjoy locally produced meat and fish, the vegetables and soft fruit are mostly from the kitchen garden. Stourhead and Heale are close by, ideal for visits to Stonehenge, Salisbury and Bath.

B & B £38pp, C-Cards MC VS, Dinner £25, Rooms 2 twin, 1 en-suite, 1 private bathroom, Restricted smoking, Children over 10, Dogs by arrangement, Closed Xmas & New Year

---

MANOR FARM Alderton, Chippenham SN14 6NL
Jeffrey & Victoria Lippiatt *Tel / Fax:* 01666 840271 *Mobile:* 07421 415824
Email: j.lippiatt@farmline.com *Web:* www.themanorfarm.co.uk

Map Ref: 6
B4040

Beautiful 17th century Cotswold family home standing in a charming village near Castle Combe and Badminton. A warm and comfortable house, there are always log fires on chilly days. Breakfasts are delicious, traditional farmhouse fare, or maybe Scottish smoked salmon and scrambled eggs with home baked bread. An ideal place to stay for exploring Bath. The dogs here are lovely. Horses welcome, cosy stables.

B & B from £30pp, Dinner available, Rooms 2 double, 1 twin, all en-suite, Restricted smoking, Children over 12, Dogs by arrangement, Closed Xmas & New Year

---

HOME FARM Harts Lane, Biddestone, Chippenham SN14 7DQ
Audrey Smith *Tel:* 01249 714475 *Fax:* 01249 701488
Email: audrey.smith@homefarmbandb.co.uk *Web:* www.homefarmbandb.co.uk

Map Ref: 7
M4, A4, A420

A traditional family owned and run farm set in 200 acres. The 17th century listed farmhouse is set in a large garden leading down to the village centre, providing peace and quiet but with just a stroll to the pubs or restaurants. Rooms are equipped with all facilities and a full breakfast menu is served in the oak beamed dining room.

B & B £22.50-£25pp, C-Cards MC VS, Rooms 1 single, 1 double, 2 family, all en-suite, No smoking, Children welcome, No dogs, Closed Xmas & New Year

---

CHURCH HOUSE Grittleton, Chippenham SN14 6AP
Anna Moore *Tel:* 01249 782562 *Fax:* 01249 782546
Email: moore@flydoc.fsbusiness.co.uk

Map Ref: 8
M4 J17

Many guests return to enjoy our garden, copper beeches, heated pool, croquet and sheep! Close to the M4, the 'Gateway to the West' offers the delights of Wiltshire, Bath and Malmesbury. Grittleton has a church, pub and cricket club. Bedrooms are well equipped, there is a large drawing room. Dinner by arrangement - 4 courses plus half a bottle of wine per person. Parking.

B & B from £30pp, Dinner from £20, Rooms 2 twin, 1 double, 1 family, Restricted smoking, Children under 2/over 12, No dogs, Open all year

FAIRFIELD FARM Upper Wraxall, Chippenham SN14 7AG

Julie McDonough *Tel:* 01225 891750 *Fax:* 01225 891050 *Mobile:* 07831 292665

Email: mcdonough@globalnet.co.uk

Map Ref: 9
A420

Fairfield farm is a family run farmhouse built of Cotswold stone and set in marvellous countryside. It is an ideal location for visiting Bath, only 10 miles away, Stonehenge, Lacock, Castle Combe and the Cotswolds. There is a lot to do in the area including horse riding and golf, plus there are many restaurants and pubs for evening meals.

B & B from £22.50pp, Rooms 1 double, 1 twin, 1 family, all en-suite, No smoking, Children welcome, No dogs, Closed Xmas & New Year

---

CHURCH FARM Hartham, Corsham SN13 0PU

Mrs Kate Jones *Tel:* 01249 715180 *Fax:* 01249 715572 *Mobile:* 07977 910775

Email: kmjbandb@aol.com *Web:* www.churchfarm.cjb.net.

Map Ref: 10
A4

This is a Cotswold farmhouse on a working farm offering wonderful views. Much wildlife close by, also cycle ways and walks. The bedrooms have TV, tea/coffee making facilities, central heating and super views. Local produce used. Secure parking, and stabling can be arranged. Close to Bath, Castle Combe and Lacock. Good road/rail links. Stonehenge, Avebury,Bowood, Kennet and Avon Canal within easy reach.

B & B £22.50-£25pp, Rooms 1 single, 1 double, 1 family, most en-suite, No smoking, Children over 6 months, No dogs, Closed Xmas & New Year

---

PICKWICK LODGE FARM Guyers Lane, Corsham SN13 0PS

Gill Stafford *Tel:* 01249 712207 *Fax:* 01249 701904

Email: b&b@pickwickfarm.freeserve.co.uk

Map Ref: 10
M4 J17, A4

Beautiful home in wonderful countryside, take a short stroll or longer walk, see rabbits, pheasants and deer, or relax in our garden, 15 minutes from Bath. Ideally situated to visit Lacock, Castle Combe, Avebury, Stonehenge, NT properties, or explore the idyllic villages, have lunch or supper at a pub. Three well appointed bedrooms, refreshment trays with home made biscuits. Delicious breakfasts using local produce.

B & B from £22.50pp, Rooms 1 twin, 2 double, 2 en-suite, 1 with private bathroom, No smoking, Children welcome, No dogs, Closed Xmas & New Year

---

HATT FARM Old Jockey, Box, Corsham SN13 8DJ

Carol & Michael Pope *Tel:* 01225 742989 *Fax:* 01225 742779

Email: hattfarm@netlineuk.net

Map Ref: 11
A365, B3109

An extremely comfortable Georgian farmhouse set in peaceful surroundings. A scrumptious breakfast is served overlooking the rolling Wiltshire countryside. What can be nicer than sitting by a log fire in winter or enjoying the spacious garden in summer? Lovely walks and good golfing nearby. Ideally situated for touring the Cotswolds. Only 15 minutes away is the city of Bath.

B & B from £22.50pp, Rooms 1 twin en-suite, 1 double/family with private bathroom, Restricted smoking, Children welcome, No dogs, Closed Xmas & New Year

---

LORNE HOUSE London Road, Box, Corsham SN13 8NA

Pat Taylor *Tel / Fax:* 01225 742597

Email: LorneHouseBandB@aol.com

Map Ref: 11
A4

Lorne House offers some of the best in comfort and hospitality. Once the home of Rev. Awdrey, author of Thomas the Tank Engine, it sits just 6 miles from Bath city centre. All rooms have colour televisions, tea/coffee facilities and we serve a breakfast to last all day. An outdoor hot tub provides relaxation after a busy day. ETC AA 4 Diamonds.

B & B from £22.50pp, C-Cards MC VS, Rooms 2 double, 1 twin, 1 family, all en-suite, Restricted smoking, Children welcome, No dogs, Open all year

HEATHERLY COTTAGE Ladbrook lane, Gastard, Corsham SN13 9PE   *Map Ref:* 12
Peter & Jenny Daniel   *Tel:* 01249 701402   *Fax:* 01249 701412   A4, A350
Email: ladbrook1@aol.com   *Web:* www.smoothhound.co.uk/hotels/heather3.html

A 17th century cottage in a quiet country lane with two acres and ample parking, overlooking open countryside. Tastefully furnished bedrooms with colour TV and tea/coffee facilities. The cottage is eight miles from the M4 and nine miles from Bath. Ideal for Avebury, Stonehenge, Lacock Abbey, Castle Combe, Corsham and other historic places of interest. Excellent pubs nearby.

B & B from £24pp, Rooms 1 twin en-suite, 2 double en-suite, No smoking, Children over 7, No dogs, Closed Xmas & New Year

---

EASTCOTT MANOR Easterton, Devizes SN10 4PL   *Map Ref:* 13
Mrs Janet Firth   B3098, A342, A360
Tel: 01380 813313

A 16th century manor house, well located between Salisbury Plain and Devizes. Bedrooms have colour TV and tea/coffee making facilities. There is a guest lounge, conservatory and large garden. Dinner is by arrangement with home grown fruit and vegetables. This is excellent country for walking, cycling and riding, also convenient for many historic sites, houses and gardens.

B & B from £23pp, Dinner from £20, Rooms 2 single, 1 double, 1 twin, all en-suite/private, Restricted smoking, Children & dogs welcome, Closed Xmas & New Year

---

BLOUNTS COURT FARM Coxhill Lane, Potterne, Devizes SN10 5PH   *Map Ref:* 14
Mrs Caroline Cary   *Tel:* 01380 727180   A360
Email: blountscourtfarm@tinyworld.co.uk

Situated in a peaceful countryside setting of 150 acres with woodland backdrop. Blounts Court Farm is a traditional stone built farmhouse with ground floor guest accommodation in recently converted stables adjoining the house. Beautifully furnished rooms including four-poster bed and guests' own sitting room. Warm and homely atmosphere. Ideal for exploring this exciting part of Wiltshire. ETC AA 5 Diamonds; Gold Award.

B & B from £25pp, Rooms 1 double, 1 twin, No smoking, Children over 8, Open all year

---

HILL HOUSE Stert, Devizes SN10 3JB   *Map Ref:* 15
Mrs Carol Mitchell   *Tel / Fax:* 01380 722356   A342
Email: caminteriors@yahoo.co.uk

A modern house in one of Wiltshire's prettiest villages, overlooking corn fields and a hill fort. Cosy bedrooms under the eaves have been designed with a' house and garden' feel. A small sitting room with TV and books for guests to enjoy. Dinner, using home grown vegetables by arrangement, there are good pubs nearby. Walking, NT properties and gardens within easy reach.

B & B from £25pp, Dinner from £12.50, Rooms 1 double, 1 twin, both with private bathrooms, No smoking, Children over 12, No dogs, Closed mid-Dec to mid-Jan

---

STONEHILL FARM Charlton, Malmesbury SN16 9DY   *Map Ref:* 16
Edna Edwards   *Tel:* 01666 823310   B4040
Email: johnedna@stonehillfarm.fsnet.co.uk

STOP! You've found us!!! 15th century Cotswold stone farmhouse on a family run dairy farm in rolling countryside on the Wiltshire/Gloucestershire border. Three pretty rooms all with hospitality trays. Wonderful breakfasts, friendly welcome and pets can come too. Ideal for one night, or several days. Oxford, Bath, Stratford-upon-Avon, Stonehenge and the Cotswold hills and villages are within easy reach by car.

B & B from £22pp, Rooms 2 double, 1 twin, Restricted smoking, Children & dogs welcome, Open all year

MANOR FARM Corston, Malmesbury SN16 0HF   *Map Ref:* 16
Mrs Ross Eavis *Tel:* 01666 822148 *Fax:* 01666 826565   A429
Email: ross@manorfarmbandb.fsnet.co.uk *Web:* www.manorfarmbandb.co.uk

Relax and unwind in this charming award winning 17th century farmhouse on a working dairy arable farm. Six tastefully furnished, well equipped bedrooms. A beautiful lounge with inglenook fireplace and a secluded garden for guests' use. Local pub within walking distance. Manor Farm is an ideal base for one night or longer stays for exploring the Cotswolds, Bath, Stonehenge, Avebury, Lacock and stately homes.

B & B from £23pp, C-Cards, Rooms 1 single, 1 twin, 3 double, 1 family, 4 en-suite, No smoking, Children over 10, No dogs, Closed Xmas & New Year

---

MANOR FARMHOUSE Crudwell, Malmesbury SN16 9ER   *Map Ref:* 17
Mrs Helen Carter *Tel:* 01666 577375   A429
Email: user785566@aol.com

The original granary for Malmesbury Abbey was here in the 13th century; now there is this lovely honey-coloured country farmhouse next to the church. It is a peaceful place on a working farm, with a delightful walled garden, offering comfortable accommodation. There is also a hard tennis court which guests may use, plus excellent breakfasts with homemade bread and preserves.

B & B from £30pp, Rooms 1 double en-suite, 1 family with private facilities, No smoking, Children over 12, No dogs, Closed Xmas & New Year

---

WINKWORTH FARM Lea, Malmesbury SN16 9NH   *Map Ref:* 18
Tony & Doi Newman *Tel:* 01666 823267   A429, B4042
Email: doinewman@winkworth89.freeserve.co.uk

Enjoy the warm, friendly atmosphere of our 17th century Cotswold stone farmhouse set in a delightful secluded walled garden - farmhouse almost a mile from the road. Extremely comfortable and beautifully decorated with oak beams and log fires. All rooms have tea/coffee making facilities and televisions. Ideally based for a quiet relaxing holiday or a base for touring. Easy reach of Cirencester, Bath, Avebury and Lacock.

B & B from £25pp, Rooms 2 double with en-suite, 1 family with private bathroom, No smoking, Children & dogs welcome, Closed Xmas & New Year

---

MANBY'S FARM Oaksey, Malmesbury SN16 9SA   *Map Ref:* 17
Ann Shewry-Fitzgerald *Tel:* 01666 577399 *Mobile:* 01666 577241   A429
Email: manbys@oaksey.junglelink.co.uk *Web:* www.cotswoldbandb.com

A warm welcome awaits you in our farmhouse, situated in open countryside, yet only half a mile from village. Ground and first floor rooms are available, all en-suite with tea/coffee facilities, televisions and hair dryers. An indoor heated swimming pool and a full sized snooker table, adult only, are available for guests. Ideal location for visiting Cotswolds, Bath and Oxford. ETC 4 Diamonds.

B & B from £23pp, C-Cards MC VS, Rooms 1 double, 1 family, 1 twin, all en-suite, No smoking, Children welcome, No dogs, Closed Xmas & New Year

---

CLATFORD PARK FARM Clatford, Marlborough SN8 4DZ   *Map Ref:* 19
Christopher & Elizabeth Morgan-Smith   A4, A345
Tel: 01672 861646

Attractive 18th century red brick farmhouse, three miles SW of Marlborough, six miles from Avebury. The house stands on a quiet road, surrounded by fields and bluebell woods. There are sheep, horses, chickens and ducks on this small farm. There is a sitting room with a wood burner and TV. Home grown vegetables, homemade bread and free range eggs. Good pubs/restaurants. Horses welcome.

B & B £22-£26pp, Rooms 1 double en-suite, 1 double with private bathroom, No smoking, Children welcome, Dogs by arrangement, Open all year

CLENCH FARMHOUSE Clench, Marlborough SN8 4NT   *Map Ref:* 20
Clarissa Roe *Tel:* 01672 810264 *Fax:* 01672 811458 *Mobile:* 07774 784601   A345, A346
Email: clarissaroe@btinternet.com *Web:* www.clenchfarmhouse.co.uk

18th century farmhouse with views, and surrounded by farmland. The house has a happy atmosphere and a warm welcome awaits guests. There is a tennis court, heated pool and croquet lawn for guests' use. Delicious dinners cooked by arrangement. We have a two bedroom and two bathroom self catering cottage. Lovely walks, within easy reach of Avebury, Stonehenge, Oxford, Salisbury and Bath.

B & B from £30pp, Dinner from £20, Rooms 1 double, 1 twin/double, 1 twin, 2 en-suite, Restricted smoking, Children welcome, Dogs by arrangement, Open all year

FRYING PAN FARM Broughton Gifford, Melksham SN12 8LL   *Map Ref:* 21
Ralph & Barbara Pullen *Tel:* 01225 702343 *Fax:* 01225 793652   A350, B3107
Email: fr@dial.pipex.com *Web:* www.fryingpanfarm.dial.pipex.com

A cosy 17th century farmhouse overlooking the garden and meadowland. The accommodation is tastefully furnished, the en-suite rooms are well equipped. Guests' own lounge, they are welcome to browse through the well stocked book case. The farm is situated east of Bath. Ideal for visiting Lacock, Bradford on Avon, Caen Hill, flight of canal locks, also National Trust Properties. Good village pub one mile.

B & B from £22pp, Rooms 1 twin, 1 double, both en-suite, No smoking, Children over 2, No dogs, Closed Xmas & New Year

HILCOT FARM HOUSE Hilcot, Pewsey SN9 6LE   *Map Ref:* 22
David & Val Maclay *Tel:* 01672 851372 *Fax:* 01672 851192 *Mobile:* 07836 355801   A4, A345
Email: beds@hilcott.com

A tranquil converted farmhouse in a perfect location for visiting Bath, Salisbury and Winchester. Guests have their own sitting room and dining room. There are excellent local pubs and restaurants nearby with interesting walks and gardens. Horse riding and golf can also be arranged for guests.

B & B £30-£40pp, Rooms 1 single, 2 double, 1 with en-suite, 1 twin, Restricted smoking, Children welcome, Dogs not in house, Closed occasionally

ST CROSS Woodborough, Pewsey SN9 5PL   *Map Ref:* 22
Serena Gore   A4, A345, A342
Tel / Fax: 01672 851346

In the village of Woodborough, close to the Kennet and Avon Canal, stands St Cross. Charming 17th century thatched cottage, which extends warmth to visitors, and is presented to a high standard, the two bedrooms are comfortable and well equipped. Breakfasts are delicious, dinner may be enjoyed, by arrangement. Good village pubs. An ideal base from which to explore the area. Dogs welcome.

B & B from £30pp, C-Cards, Dinner from £12.50, Rooms 1 double, 1 twin, with private bathroom, No smoking in bedrooms, Children over 5, Well behaved dogs, Open all year

THE EDWARDIAN LODGE 59 Castle Road, Salisbury SP1 3RH   *Map Ref:* 23
Richard & Gillian White *Tel:* 01722 413329 *Fax:* 01722 503105   A36, A338
Email: richardwhite@edlodge.freeserve.co.uk *Web:* www.edwardianlodge.co.uk

An Edwardian house, beautifully decorated and fitted with good parking off main road. Only a short walk to city centre, Cathedral and Old Sarum and a beautiful valley drive to Stonehenge.

B & B from £25pp, C-Cards MC VS, Rooms 1 single, 3 double, 2 twin, 1 family, all en-suite, No smoking, Children over 10, No dogs, Closed Xmas

FARTHINGS 9 Swaynes Close, Salisbury SP1 3AE   Map Ref: 23
Gill Rodwell *Tel / Fax:* 01722 330749   A30
Email: farthings@shammer.freeserve.co.uk *Web:* www.shammer.freeserve.co.uk

Farthings is a quiet but central townhouse with parking. It stands a
pleasant stroll away from the city centre. The rooms are comfortable
with tea/coffee facilities, there is a good choice for breakfast. The
guests' lounge has TV and a collection of family photos. The garden
is delightful. An ideal base for visiting Salisbury, Stonehenge and
many other interesting places.

B & B from £22pp, Rooms 2 single, 1 en-suite twin, 1 en-suite
double, No smoking, Children over 12, No dogs, Open all year

THE OLD HOUSE 161 Wilton Road, Salisbury SP2 7JQ   Map Ref: 23
Patrick & Hilary Maidment   A36
Tel: 01722 333433 *Fax:* 01722 335551

The Old House is full of character, old beams and brick walls. After
a restful night, start the day with a hearty breakfast in our cottage
style dining room. All food is freshly prepared and home cooked.
Relax in our large residents lounge after an exciting day or sit in the
attractive garden. All rooms have tea/coffee facilities and televisions.

B & B £22.50-£25pp, Dinner from £15, Rooms 6 double, 2 twin,
1 family, all en-suite, Restricted smoking, Children over 5,
No dogs, Open all year

THE OLD RECTORY BED & BREAKFAST 75 Belle Vue Road, Salisbury SP1 3YE   Map Ref: 23
Trish Smith *Tel:* 01722 502702 *Fax:* 01722 501135   A30, A36
Email: stay@theoldrectory-bb.co.uk *Web:* www.theoldrectory-bb.co.uk

The Old Rectory welcomes you with well appointed rooms and
helpful friendly staff. Situated in a quiet street just a short stroll from
the heart of Salisbury and nestled into a rich green country garden.
Salisbury and its surrounding area is one of the most historically rich
areas of Britain, an ideal base for visiting many of the leading
attractions.

B & B £23-£30pp, Rooms 2 double, 1 twin, 2 en-suite & 1 private
bathroom, No smoking, Children over 10, No dogs, Open all year

STRATFORD LODGE 4 Park Lane, off Castle Road, Salisbury SP1 3NP   Map Ref: 23
Ian & Jacqueline Lawrence *Tel / Fax:* 01722 325177   A30, A36
Email: enquiries@stratfordlodge.co.uk *Web:* www.stratfordlodge.co.uk

Stratford Lodge is an elegant Victorian house which is situated in a
quiet lane overlooking Victoria Park with a short riverside walk to the
city. Delicious breakfasts are served in the conservatory and also
candlelit dinners. All rooms are en-suite and have tea/coffee facilities
and televisions with tasteful furnishings. Superb four poster room.
Discounts for two nights or more.

B & B £30-£35pp, C-Cards MC VS, Dinner from £11.95, Rooms
3 double, 3 twin, 2 family, all en-suite, No smoking, Children
over 5, No dogs, Closed Xmas & New Year

WEBSTERS 11 Hartington Road, Salisbury SP2 7LG   Map Ref: 23
Mary and Peter Webb *Tel / Fax:* 01722 339779   A360
Email: websters.salis@eclipse.co.uk *Web:* websters-bed-breakfast.com

Set on the end of a colourful Victorian terrace of houses in a quiet
cul-de-sac. Computer available for guest use in lounge. Ground floor
room fully accessible for wheelchairs and a small patio available. 15
minute walk to City Centre and Cathedral with only nine miles to
Stonehenge. Scrumptious choices for breakfast with vegetarians
and vegans catered for.

B & B £20-£22pp, C-Cards MC VS, Dinner from £6.50, Rooms
2 single, 1 double, 2 twin, all en-suite, Restricted smoking,
Children over 12, Service dogs only, Open all year

THE MILL HOUSE Berwick St James, near Salisbury SP3 4TS
Diana Gifford Mead
Tel / Fax: 01722 790331

Map Ref: 24
A303, A36, B3083

The Mill House stands in acres of nature reserve. An island paradise with the River Till running through the working mill and beautiful garden. Lovely roses, lovely walks antiquities and houses. Built by the miller in 1785, the bedrooms command magnificent views. Fishing or swimming in the mill pool. Golf and riding nearby. Healthy and organic food. Superb cuisine at Boot Inn, Berwick St James.

B & B £25-£35pp, Rooms 2 single, 2 twin, 4 en-suite double, Children over 5, No dogs, Open all year

MANOR FARM Burcombe, Salisbury SP2 0EJ
Sue Combes   *Tel:* 01722 742177   *Fax:* 01722 744600
Email: s.a.combes@talk21.com

Map Ref: 25
A30

A comfortable farmhouse, warm and attractively furnished, on 960 acre mixed farm in a quiet, pretty village quarter of a mile off A30 west of Salisbury. Ideal base for touring this lovely area where nearby attractions include Wilton House, Salisbury and Stonehenge. Wonderful walks, good riding and a pub with good food nearby. No smoking.

B & B from £22.50pp, C-Cards MC VS AE, Rooms 1 double, 1 twin, both en-suite with shower, No smoking, Children welcome, No dogs, Closed Dec to Feb

SWAYNES FIRS FARM Grimsdyke, Coombe Bissett, Salisbury SP5 5RF
Tel: 01725 519240
Email: swaynes.firs@virgin.net   *Web:* www.swaynesfirs.co.uk

Map Ref: 26
A354

A country farmhouse with en-suite rooms, in a pleasant position on a 11 acre mixed farm with good views. Ancient Roman ditch on farm as well as peacocks, ducks, chickens and horses being reared.

B & B from £22pp, Rooms 2 twin, 1 family, all en-suite, Restricted smoking, Children & dogs welcome, Closed Xmas & New Year

MORRIS' FARM HOUSE Baverstock, Dinton, Salisbury SP3 5EL
Martin & Judith Marriott   *Tel / Fax:* 01722 716874
Email: marriott@waitrose.com

Map Ref: 27
Hindon Road

A 100 year old farmhouse with an attractive garden and set in open countryside. The location is peaceful and the atmosphere is friendly. Guests may use a small sitting room with TV, breakfast is served in a conservatory. There is an excellent pub just two minutes walk away for suppers. Local attractions include Wilton House, Salisbury, Stonehenge and Longleat Safari Park.

B & B from £20pp, Rooms 1 double, 1 twin, shared bathroom, No smoking, Children & dogs welcome, Closed Xmas

WYNDHAM COTTAGE St Mary's Road, Dinton, Salisbury SP3 5HH
Ian & Rosie Robertson
Tel: 01722 716343   *Mobile:* 077 699 116600

Map Ref: 27
A303, A36, B3089

Charming 18th century thatched stone cottage, stands in magnificent National Trust countryside, on the edge of a picturesque village. Bluebells, lambs and calves in Spring, delightful walks with marvellous views of the area. The garden has many interesting plants. Excellent pubs nearby. Ideally situated for sightseeing at some wonderful places, cities and gardens. Stonehenge, Avebury, Salisbury, Bath, Wells, Wilton House, Stourhead, Longleat and more.

B & B from £25pp, Rooms 2 double en-suite, No smoking, Children over 12, No dogs, Closed Nov to Mar

THE OLD POST HOUSE South Street, Great Wishford, Salisbury SP2 0NN
Paulene Patient *Tel:* 01722 790211
Email: paulene@greatwishford.freeserve.co.uk *Web:* www.greatwishford.freeserve.co.uk

Map Ref: 28
A36

Built in 1650, the Grade II listed Old Post House is ten minutes from Stonehenge and Salisbury in a quiet and beautiful village with excellent pubs for evening meals. We have three clean, pretty en-suite rooms with televisions and beverage trays with breakfast cooked to order on a lovely old aga. This is a happy family home in a lovely part of the country.

B & B £24-£30pp, Rooms 1 double, 1 twin, 1 family, all en-suite, No smoking, Children welcome, Dogs by arrangement, Closed Xmas & New Year

LITTLE LANGFORD FARMHOUSE Little Langford, Salisbury SP3 4NR
Patricia Helyer *Tel:* 01722 790205 *Fax:* 01722 790086
Email: bandb@littlelangford.co.uk *Web:* www.dmac.co.uk/llf

Map Ref: 28
A36, A303

Little Langford is a magnificent Victorian gothic farmhouse surrounded by a large pleasant garden with outstanding views. It is a working dairy and arable farm in the beautiful rolling Wiltshire Down with ESA and SSSI land offering glorious walks. The rooms are elegant, spacious and with period furniture including a comfortable lounge and billiard room. Excellent touring to Stonehenge, Salisbury and Bath.

B & B £26-£27.50pp, Rooms 1 double, 1 twin, 1 family, all en-suite or private, No smoking, Children by arrangement, No dogs, Closed Xmas & New Year

1 RIVERSIDE CLOSE Laverstock, Salisbury SP1 1QW
Mary Tucker *Tel / Fax:* 01722 320287
Email: marytucker2001@yahoo.com

Map Ref: 29
A30

This is a charming, well appointed home, in a quiet area not far from Salisbury Cathedral. Tastefully furnished rooms with en-suite bath or shower room, TV and drinks facilities. Salisbury is the centre of an area steeped in antiquity with many places of historical interest. Your hosts are happy to help plan itineraries.

B & B from £25pp, Dinner from £12, Rooms 1 double, 1 family, No smoking, Children & dogs welcome, Open all year

MADDINGTON HOUSE Maddington Street, Shrewton, Salisbury SP3 4JD
Dick & Joan Robathan *Tel / Fax:* 01980 620406
Email: rsrobathan@freenet.co.uk

Map Ref: 30
A360

An elegant family home, this 17th century Grade II listed house with a period hall and dining room, stands in the centre of the pretty village of Shrewton - close to Stonehenge and ten miles from Salisbury. Three attractive, well equipped guest rooms. The village has three pubs within walking distance. A delightful home and the perfect base for a relaxing break.

B & B from £22.50pp, Rooms 1 twin, 1 double, 1 family, all en-suite, Restricted smoking, Children over 7, No dogs, Closed Xmas & New Year

ELM TREE COTTAGE Chain Hill, Stapleford, Salisbury SP3 4LH
Chris & Joe Sykes *Tel:* 01722 790507
Email: jaw.sykes@virgin.net

Map Ref: 31
A36, A303

17th century cottage with inglenook, in a picturesque village. Bedrooms are attractively presented and well equipped. A two storey self contained unit with a kitchen is available for families.It has a garden room and may be used on a self catering basis to sleep up to six or seven people. Good walking, central to Salisbury, Bath, Wilton, Stonehenge, Avebury and Stourhead.

B & B from £25pp, Rooms 2 double, 1 family, all en-suite, Restricted smoking, Children welcome, Dogs by arrangement, Closed Dec to Feb

---

NEWTON FARMHOUSE Southampton Road, Whiteparish, Salisbury SP5 2QL   *Map Ref:* 32
Suzi & John Lanham *Tel / Fax:* 01794 884416   A36
Email: enquiries@newtonfarmhouse.co.uk *Web:* www.newtonfarmhouse.co.uk   *see Photo opposite*

Historic 16th century farmhouse once part of the Trafalgar Estate. Delightfully decorated en-suite bedrooms (5 with genuine four-posters). Beamed dining room with flagstones, bread oven and Nelson memorabilia. Superb breakfasts include fresh fruits, home made bread, preserves and free-range eggs. Extensive grounds with swimming pool. AA, ETC 5 Diamonds.

B & B £25-£30pp, Dinner from £20, Rooms 2 twin, 3 double, 3 family, all en-suite, No smoking, Children welcome, No dogs, Open all year

---

SCOTLAND LODGE Winterbourne Stoke, Salisbury SP3 4TF   *Map Ref:* 33
Jane & John Singleton *Tel:* 01980 620943 *Fax:* 01980 621403 *Mobile:* 07957 863183   A303
Email: scotland.lodge@virgin.net *Web:* www.scotland-lodge.co.uk

Within Scotland Lodge there is a feeling of peace and tranquility and guests exhausted from much travelling often comment on a good night's sleep. We try to provide a respite from the rush of life and offer comfortable surroundings. Each room has a television and tea/coffee facilities with two rooms in the Victorian part particularly large and airy, with comfortable chairs.

B & B £20-£25pp, Rooms 1 single, 1 double, 1 twin, 1 family, all en-suite, No smoking, Children welcome, No dogs, Open all year

---

SCOTLAND LODGE FARM Winterbourne Stoke, Salisbury SP3 4TF   *Map Ref:* 33
Catherine Lockwood *Tel:* 01980 621199 *Fax:* 01980 621188   A303
Email: william.lockwood@bigwig.net

Family run Competition Yard set in 46 acres. Dogs and horses welcome. Lovely views. Stonehenge and Salisbury nearby. Conservatory for guests. Travel cot and highchair available. Good local pubs. French, German and Italian spoken. Wilton House, Longleat, Stourhead, Heale Gardens nearby. On A303 west out of Winterbourne Stoke, past turning on left to Berwick St. James, right immediately after Scotland Lodge. Automatic entry gate.

B & B from £24pp, Rooms 2 double, 1 twin/triple, private bathrooms, No smoking, Children & dogs welcome, Open all year

---

SPIERS PIECE FARM Steeple Ashton, Trowbridge BA14 6HG   *Map Ref:* 34
Jill Awdry   A361
Tel / Fax: 01380 870266

Spiers Piece Farm is a homely and spacious Georgian farmhouse in the heart of the Wiltshire countryside. Bath, Longleat and Stonehenge are within easy reach. There are large, comfortable bedrooms, with washbasins and hospitality trays and a luxury guests' bathroom. There is a comfortable lounge with TV. Generous breakfasts are intended to last you all day!

B & B from £18pp, Rooms 2 double with TV, 1 twin, Restricted smoking, Children welcome, Dogs by arrangement, Closed Nov to Feb

---

BUGLEY BARTON Warminster BA12 7RB   *Map Ref:* 35
Julie & Brian Hocken *Tel:* 01985 213389 *Fax:* 01985 300450   A36, A362
Email: bugleybarton@aol.com

Bugley is a Georgian farmhouse set in a beautiful formal garden. The spacious, comfortable and well equipped en-suite rooms have views overlooking the fountain. The house is traditionally furnished with chandeliers and open fires, homemade cake and a warm welcome. Well situated for trips to Longleat, Bath, Salisbury, Stourhead and Stonehenge. Ample parking and good eating nearby. ETC 5 Diamonds, Silver Award.

B & B £30-£32.50pp, Rooms 2 double en-suite, 1 twin private bathroom, No smoking, Children over 12, No dogs, Open all year

Newton Farmhouse, Whiteparish, near Salisbury

STURFORD MEAD FARM Corsley, Warminster BA12 7QU   *Map Ref:* 36
Lynn Corp   *Tel / Fax:* 01373 832213   A362
Email: lynn_sturford.bed@virgin.net

On A362 halfway between Frome and Warminster, nestling under the historic monument of Cley Hill (National Trust) and opposite Longleat with its safari park, lake and grounds. Stourhead, Cheddar Gorge, Wookey Hole and the prettiest English village of Castle Combe are close by. Convenient also for Bath, Wells and Salisbury. The comfortable bedrooms all with private facilities, are well equipped.

B & B from £24pp, Rooms 2 twin, 1 double, all en-suite/private, No smoking, Children welcome, No dogs, Open all year

---

SPRINGFIELD HOUSE Crockerton, Warminster BA12 8AU   *Map Ref:* 37
Rachel & Colin Singer   A36 A350
Tel / Fax: 01985 213696

In the beautiful Wylye Valley, on the edge of the Longleat Estate, a charming village house, 17th century. Tastefully furnished rooms with garden and woodland views. Grass tennis court. Salisbury, Wells and Bath easily reached, with Stonehenge, Stourhead Gardens, stately homes and castles nearby. Endless walks through woodland or over Salisbury Plain, 2 golf courses nearby. Village pub and lakeside restaurant a few minutes walk.

B & B from £27pp, Rooms 2 double, 1 twin, en-suite/private, No smoking, Children & dogs welcome, Open all year

---

DEVERILL END Deverill Road, Sutton Veny, Warminster BA12 7BY   *Map Ref:* 38
Joy Greathead   *Tel:* 01985 840356   A36
Email: riversgreathead@amserve.net   *Web:* www.suttonveny.co.uk/ForSaleTraders/LocalTraders.htm

In the picturesque Wylye Valley, enjoying magnificent views and wonderfully quiet, we offer a warm welcome, great comfort and delicious breakfasts. Bedrooms are en-suite and well equipped. The pretty garden is invitingly relaxing, whilst cattle graze and ducks forage. Halfway between Bath and Salisbury, an ideal base for visiting Stonehenge, Stourhead's landscaped gardens, the Elizabethan splendour of Longleat and other attractions. Parking.

B & B £23-£25pp, Rooms 1 twin, 2 double, all en-suite, No smoking, Children over 10, No dogs, Open all year

---

GLENMORE FARM The Ham, Westbury BA13 4HQ   *Map Ref:* 39
Rosemary & Stan Painter   *Tel / Fax:* 01373 865022   *Mobile:* 07774 937494   A350
Email: stan@glenmorefarm.freeserve.co.uk   *Web:* www.glenmorefarm.freeserve.co.uk

Glenmore offers a warm welcome with excellent accommodation. All rooms have televisions and tea/coffee facilities and two en-suite rooms have four posters. Glenmore is a farm with many horses and situated in a quiet spot. Within easy reach of many interesting places such as Bath, Longleat, Stonehenge, Salisbury and Avebury.

B & B from £20pp, Rooms 1 single, 2 double, 1 family, most en-suite, No smoking, Children welcome, No dogs, Closed Nov to Mar

---

CORNERWAYS COTTAGE Longcross, Zeals BA12 6LL   *Map Ref:* 40
John & Irene Snook   *Tel / Fax:* 01747 840477   *Mobile:* 07801 282272   A303
Email: cornerwayscottage@btinternet.com   *Web:* www.smoothhound.co.uk/hotels/cornerwa.html

Cornerways is close to attractions such as Longleat and Stonehenge and ideal for visiting Bath, Salisbury and Stourhead. The accommodation comprises of two double en-suite rooms, one with a four poster bed and one twin room with a private bathroom. All bedrooms have tea/coffee facilities.

B & B £19-£21pp, C-Cards MC VS, Rooms 2 double with en-suite, 1 twin with pb, No smoking, Children over 8, No dogs, Closed Xmas & New Year

Yorkshire

Yorkshire is by far Britain's largest county with a vast variation in scenery ranging from the pretty and picturesque to the awe-inspiring and majestic. There is open space aplenty with seaside resorts to suit every possible taste, magnificent stately homes, gardens and parkland of incomparable beauty and history, folklore and legend to entrance the most curious of visitor. This is depicted particularly in York, the city which encapsulates the very essence of Yorkshire. No other city can offer such a concentration of medieval and other historic treasures. The Minster, built between 1240 and 1475 is the largest Gothic cathedral in Britain and contains amongst its many wonders some of the nation's most magnificent stained glass, some dating from 1150. The buildings of this city are a delight with high storeys adjacent to Georgian houses bound together by narrow cobbled roads. York also contains a wide selection of superb museums which between them tell the story of the ancient city and county. The Castle Museum, displaying everyday Victorian and Edwardian life, the Jorvik Viking Centre, a recreation of the ninth century Viking settlement, and the National Railway Museum are all popular tourist attractions.

Near to York is the splendid Castle Howard, recognizable as 'Brideshead' in the television adaptation of Brideshead Revisited. It is the eighteenth century home of the Howard family and is set in 1000 acres of parkland, including a beautiful Rose Garden. This grand manor house also contains a collection of rare china, Felix Kelly murals and an extensive picture gallery.

The grey-white limestone peaks of the Pennine Range, reaching 2,000 feet in places, form the backbone of the county with the Yorkshire Dales National Park covering a vast area of fine walking country. Airedale, with its curious limestone scenery around Malham boasts glorious Gordale Scar waterfall as well as the proud fortress town of Skipton, home of the quite remarkable Lady Anne Clifford who in the seventeenth century restored or built many important buildings. Swaledale is home to the impressive Norman castle at Richmond and the lovely ruin of Easby Abbey with Hardraw Force nearby, the tallest waterfall in England. The Settle to Carlisle railway crosses the high Pennines passing over the spectacular Ribblehead Viaduct in the shadow of

East Window, York Minster (YTB)

Whernside and along the Eden Valley giving memorable views of the Dales landscape. Here the 'Three Peaks', Whernside, Ingleborough and Pen-y-Ghent are a popular challenge to serious walkers. Ingleton is the centre for pot-holers, the whole area being riddled with caves and pot-holes with Gaping Gill renowned as being large enough to contain St Paul's Cathedral.

The North Yorkshire Moors, the largest expanse of moorland in England became a National Park in 1952, including much of the North Yorkshire coastline. Whitby, where Bram Stoker wrote Dracula, was also the point where Captain James Cook set off and is a lovely seaside town with the spectacular monastic site of Whitby Abbey. Staithes, Robin Hood's Bay and Runswick Bay are also resorts of endearing charm and history.

The Vale of York, a magnet to holiday visitors offers a wide variety of attractions. Fountains Abbey and Studley Royal Water Gardens must be one of the most remarkable sites in Europe. A World Heritage Site it encompasses the spectacular ruin of a twelfth century Cistercian Abbey, a Jacobean Mansion and one of the finest surviving examples of a Georgian Green Water Garden. Sheltered in a quiet secluded valley near the historic city of Ripon, there are lakes, avenues, cascades and classical temples. Another sight not to be missed is Rievaulx Terrace and Temples to the north east of Fountains Abbey, two mid-eighteenth century temples on a grass-covered terrace with impressive vistas over Rievaulx Abbey and the Rye Valley to the Hambleton Hills. Harrogate, as well as being a charming town is in its own right an ideal centre for touring the whole Plain of York, with easy access over the Buttertubs Pass to the Yorkshire Dales in the west, and the coastal resorts in the east. Harrogate is a town of elegant Victorian buildings, fine tree-lined avenues, excellent shopping and beautiful municipal gardens, as indeed befits the home of Harlow Carr Botanical Gardens, the headquarters of the Northern Horticultural Society.

PLACES TO VISIT

This is a small selection of interesting places to visit. Many more are listed in our annual guide to Museums, Galleries, Historic Houses & Sites (see page 448)

Castle Howard
Castle Howard, York
This impressive mansion has collections of fabulous paintings, fine furniture, porcelain and sculpture. The gardens are substantial, the walled rose garden must be seen.

Harewood House
Hardwood, Leeds
A fine country mansion with an outstanding art collection, chippendale furniture, and porcelain.

Nostell Priory
Wakefield
The Priory contains one of England's finest collections of Chippendale furniture and an exceptional art collection.

Skipton Castle
Skipton
The last stronghold of the Royalists in the North, one of the most complete and well preserved medieval castles in England.

York Minster
York
The largest Gothic cathedral in England, dating from the 13th century, including a display of a large collection of diocesan church plate.

Yorkshire

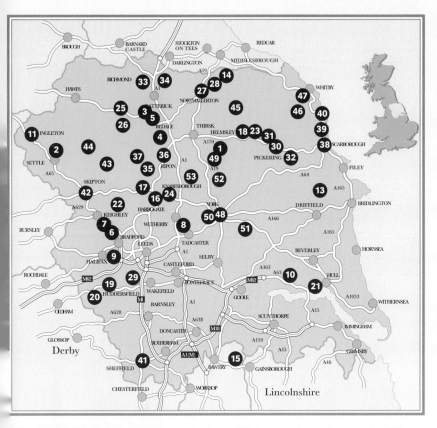

The Red Map References should be used to locate B & B properties on the pages that follow

DALESIDE East End, Ampleforth YO62 4DA
Paul & Pat Williams
Tel: 01439 788266

Map Ref: 1
A170

Daleside, listed for its cruck beams and oak panelling, is the oldest house in this charming stone village. Sympathetic restoration features the two en-suite guests' rooms overlooking the garden and antique furniture includes a Victorian half-tester bed in the double room. There are two inns in the village, other good restaurants nearby, and the beautiful unspoilt countryside offers excellent walking.

B & B £27.50-£31.50pp, Rooms 1 double, 1 twin, both en-suite, No smoking, Children over 11, No dogs, Closed Xmas & New Year

SHALLOWDALE HOUSE West End, Ampleforth YO62 4DY
Phillip Gill & Anton Van Der Horst *Tel:* 01439 788325 *Fax:* 01439 788885
Email: stay@shallowdalehouse.demon.co.uk *Web:* www.shallowdalehouse.demon.co.uk

Map Ref: 1
A170

This is an elegant, modern country house, with an impressive hillside garden, on the southern edge of the North York Moors National Park (20 miles from York). There are wonderful views from every room. Thoughtfully prepared, freshly cooked food, and a quiet and relaxing ambience created by enthusiastic and dedicated proprietors. Reductions for 3 nights or more.

B & B £32.50-£40pp, C-Cards MC VS, Dinner £22.50, Rooms 2 kingsized/twin, 1 double, all en-suite/private, No smoking, Children over 12, No dogs, Closed Xmas & New Year

WOODVIEW GUEST HOUSE The Green, Austwick, Lancaster LA2 8BB
Mrs Jenny Suri
Tel / Fax: 015242 51268

Map Ref: 2
A65

Wood View is a Grade II listed house circa 1700 situated on the pretty village green. The house boasts original beams, open log fires and delicious home cooking. All rooms have televisions, tea/coffee making facilities and hairdryers with Jenny providing a welcome drink on arrival. Children of all ages are welcomed into the family room with cots and highchairs provided on request.

B & B from £26pp, C-Cards MC VS, Rooms 3 double, 1 twin, 2 family, all en-suite, No smoking, Children welcome, Dogs by arrangement, Closed Xmas & New Year

ELMFIELD COUNTRY HOUSE Arrathorne, Bedale DL8 1NE
Jim & Edith Lillie *Tel:* 01677 450558 *Fax:* 01677 450557 *Mobile:* 07802 730027
Email: stay@elmfieldhouse.freeserve.co.uk *Web:* www.countryhouseyorkshire.co.uk

Map Ref: 3
A684

Large house in rolling countryside at the gateway to the Yorkshire Dales. Spacious, comfortable en-suite bedrooms, delightful four poster room available, all rooms include direct dial telephones, colour television with separate movie channel, radio alarms and coffee/tea facilities. Two rooms specifically for disabled guests. English breakfast, and dinner. Lounge bar, conservatory, games room and solarium. Private fishing lake and secure parking.

B & B from £25pp, Dinner from £15, Rooms 3 twin, 4 double, 2 family, all en-suite, Restricted smoking, Children welcome, No dogs, Open all year

THE HALL Newton-le-Willows, Bedale DL8 1SW
Mrs Oriella Featherstone
Tel: 01677 450210 *Fax:* 01677 450014

Map Ref: 3
A684

Enjoy spaciousness and privacy within this glorious listed Georgian hideaway. Come and see the Dales, the Moors, the Castles and ruins. Visit the Georgian theatre at Richmond, or simply relax and enjoy all that this house has to offer. The honour bar and the decanter are at your disposal and whatever the time of day, if hunger strikes, there is always homemade fruitcake to hand.

B & B £45-£50pp, Dinner £25, Rooms 1 double, 1 twin, 1 family, all en-suite, Restricted smoking, Children over 13, No dogs, Open all year

March Cote Farm, Cottingley, near Bingley

UPSLAND FARM Kirklington, Bedale DL8 2PA   *Map Ref:* 4
Mrs C Hodgson   A1
Tel / Fax: 01845 567709

Beautiful stone built house, with log fires, en-suite bedrooms (with brass beds and colour TV) in open countryside surrounded by meadows. The house is built on an historic moated site, situated on land once owned by Katherine Parr, between moors and dales, with stately homes, castles and abbeys within easy reach. Facilities for golf, riding and fishing close by.

B & B from £27.50pp, Dinner from £16, Rooms 2 double, 1 twin, all en-suite, No smoking, Children & dogs welcome, Closed Xmas day

---

MILL CLOSE FARM Patrick Brompton, Bedale DL8 1JY   *Map Ref:* 5
Mrs Patricia Knox *Tel:* 01677 450257 *Fax:* 01677 450585   A684
Email: millclosefarm@btopenworld.com

17th century working farm surrounded by beautiful rolling countryside at the foothills of the Yorkshire Dales and Herriot country. Exceptional en-suite bedrooms with many extras, including jacuzzi, super king-sized beds, toiletries, hairdryers and television with a choice of videos. Enchanting walled garden with pond and waterfall. Delicious breakfasts with homemade bread, scones and preserves. Ideal stopover for Scotland.

B & B £20-£27.50pp, Rooms 1 double, 1 twin, both en-suite, Restricted smoking, Children over 12, Dogs by arrangement, Closed Dec to Feb

---

FIVE RISE LOCKS HOTEL Beck Lane, Bingley BD16 4DD   *Map Ref:* 6
Pat & William Oxley *Tel:* 01274 565296 *Fax:* 01274 568828   A650
Email: info@five-rise-locks.co.uk *Web:* www.five-rise-locks.co.uk

A charming hotel, individual en-suite bedrooms, enjoy the seclusion of the Turret Rooms, the panoramic views from the Studio - each has the same peacefulness. Bistro open daily offering excellent selection of English and European dishes complimented by a pleasing wine list. Tour the Dales, Haworth and Saltaire, shop in the mills, or relax - stroll along the canal and admire the Five Rise Locks.

B & B £29-£32.50pp, C-Cards MC VS, Dinner from £13, Rooms 1 single, 3 twin, 5 double, 2 double/family, all en-suite, Restricted smoking, Children & dogs welcome, Open all year

---

MARCH COTE FARM Cottingley, Bingley BD16 1UB   *Map Ref:* 7
George & Jean Warin *Tel:* 01274 487433 *Fax:* 01274 561074 *Mobile:* 07889 162257   A650
Email: jean.warin@nevisuk.net www.yorkshirenet.co.uk/accgde/marchcote   *see Photo on page 347*

A friendly atmosphere awaits you on our 160 acre livestock farm. This is a 17th century fully modernised farmhouse, but with the character still retained. There are original oak beams and mullions. The accommodation is en-suite throughout. Top quality farmhouse cooking. Beautiful, spacious garden. Long established, with lots of repeat bookings. Professional, business, holiday guests all are welcome.

B & B from £22pp, Dinner available, Rooms 2 double, 1 family suite, all en-suite/private, Restricted smoking, Children welcome, No dogs, Closed Xmas

---

FOUR GABLES Oaks Lane, Boston Spa LS23 6DS   *Map Ref:* 8
David Watts *Tel / Fax:* 01937 845592 *Mobile:* 07941 353202   A1
Email: info@fourgables.co.uk *Web:* www.fourgables.co.uk

Four Gables stands in a lovely half-acre of gardens with its own croquet lawn in a peaceful location. The house has a beautiful interior with original features and log fires in the winter. It is only a few minutes walk to the village of Boston Spa which has many shops and restaurants for guests' convenience.

B & B from £26pp, Dinner available, Rooms 2 double, 1 twin, all en-suite, No smoking, Children over 3, No dogs, Closed Xmas & New Year

ELDER LEA HOUSE Clough Lane, Rastrick, Brighouse HD6 3QH
David & Dawn Collins *Tel / Fax:* 01484 717832 *Mobile:* 07796 178196
Email: elder.lea.house@amserve.net

Map Ref: 9
M62 J24

An elegant Victorian house, built in 1885 and set amidst beautifully landscaped gardens. There is a warm and cosy lounge to relax in after a days sightseeing or business. Delicious homemade food, real Yorkshire cooking at its best. Each bedroom boasts colour televisions, radio alarm clocks, ironing facilities and hospitality trays. We provide an ideal base for touring the scenic beauty spots of Yorkshire.

B & B £24.50-£27.50pp, C-Cards MC VS AE, Dinner from £10, Rooms 3 en-suite double, Restricted smoking, Children over 10, Guide dogs only, Closed Xmas & New Year

---

RUDSTONE WALK South Cave, Brough HU15 2AH
Laura & Charlie Greenwood *Tel:* 01430 422230 *Fax:* 01430 424552
Email: admin@rudstone-walk.co.uk *Web:* www.rudstone-walk.co.uk

Map Ref: 10
B1230, A1034, M62

Set in its own acres on the edge of the Yorkshire Wolds, the house enjoys magnificent views over the Vale of York and Humber Estuary. Luxurious accommodation in a courtyard garden development surrounding the 400 year old Farmhouse, where delicious meals are served. Self catering accommodation is available. Perfect for exploring the historic towns of York and Beverley, the countryside and heritage coastline.

B & B from £29.50pp, C-Cards MC VS AE DC, Dinner from £18, Rooms 6 twin, 7 double, 1 family, all en-suite, Restricted smoking, Children welcome, Dogs by arrangement, Closed Xmas week

---

FERNCLIFFE COUNTRY GUEST HOUSE 55 Main Street, Ingleton, via Carnforth LA6 3HJ
Peter & Susan Ring *Tel:* 015242 42405
Email: ferncliffe@hotmail.com

Map Ref: 11
A65

A warm welcome is assured when you visit our Victorian home, on the edge of the Yorkshire Dales. The house offers comfortable accommodation, with some original features retained. After a hearty breakfast enjoy exploring the surrounding Yorkshire Dales, South Lakes and Forest of Bowland. An ideal location for walkers, biking or car touring. Off road parking and drying facilities available.

B & B from £24pp, C-Cards MC VS, Rooms 1 double, 4 twin, all en-suite, No smoking, Children welcome, Dogs by arrangement, Closed Xmas

---

INGLENOOK GUEST HOUSE 20 Main Street, Ingleton, Carnforth LA6 3HJ
Phil & Carolyn Smith *Tel:* 015242 41270
Email: phillsmith@inglenookguesthouse.fsbusiness.co.uk *Web:* www.nebsweb.co.uk/inglenook

Map Ref: 11
A65

Phil and Carolyn welcome you to their recently refurbished Victorian built guest house. The tastefully co-ordinated bedrooms have colour televisions, tea/coffee facilities and superb views. A ground floor bedroom is available. Attractive patio overlooking river. Picturesque village, ideal base for touring the Dales and Lake District. ETC AA 3 Diamonds.

B & B from £21pp, C-Cards MC VS, Dinner from £10, Rooms 3 double, 2 twin, all en-suite/private facilities, No smoking, Children over 5, Dogs by arrangement, Closed Xmas

---

SPRINGFIELD COUNTRY HOUSE HOTEL Main Street, Ingleton, Carnforth LA6 3HJ
Jack & Kathleen Thornton & Pat Clowes
Tel / Fax: 015242 41280

Map Ref: 11
A65

A detached Victorian villa, with a large garden down to the River Greta. The home cooking is delicious and made with home grown vegetables. The patio overlooks the garden and guests are also welcome to private fishing. Colour televisions are available in all rooms, as well as tea/coffee facilities, hair dryers and radios. ETC AA RAC 3 Diamonds.

B & B from £23pp, C-Cards MC VS AE DC, Dinner from £11, Rooms 1 single, 1 twin, 3 double, 1 family, Restricted smoking, Children welcome, Dogs by arrangement, Closed Xmas

THE WOLD COTTAGE Wold Newton, Driffield YO25 3HL
Mrs Katrina Gray *Tel:* 01262 470696
Email: woldcott@wold-newton.freeserve.co.uk

Map Ref: 13
A64, A165

Spacious Georgian farmhouse set in own grounds, situated away from main roads. We can offer you peace and tranquility and excellent home cooking. All rooms are furnished to the highest standard, overlooking new and mature woodlands and continuous Wold land. Come and relax and forget the pressures of everyday life. Yorkshire's Best Bed & Breakfast finalist 2000. 'Just what you always hope to find.'

B & B from £24pp, C-Cards MC VS, Dinner from £14, Rooms 3 double, 1 twin, 1 family, No smoking, Children welcome, No dogs, Open all year

MANOR HOUSE FARM Ingleby Greenhow, Great Ayton TS9 6RB
Margaret & Martin Bloom *Tel:* 01642 722384
Email: mbloom@globalnet.co.uk

Map Ref: 14
A172

Delightful farmhouse (part 1760) built of Yorkshire stone, in 164 acres of park and woodlands at the foot of the Cleveland hills in the North York Moors National Park. Tranquil and secluded, ideal for nature lovers, relaxing, touring and walking. Accommodation is attractive with beams and interior stonework. Warm atmosphere, guests have separate entrance, lounge and dining room. Fine dinners, special diets, excellent wines.

Dinner B & B from £45pp, C-Cards, Dinner available, Rooms 2 twin, 1 double, all en-suite/private, No smoking, Children over 12, Dogs by arrangement, Closed Xmas

GRINGLEY HALL Gringley on the Hill DN10 4QT
Ian & Dulce Threlfall *Tel:* 01777 817262 *Fax:* 01777 816824
Email: dulce@gringleyhall.fsnet.co.uk

Map Ref: 15
A631

The Hall is set in two acres of beautiful walled gardens which Dulce and Ian have spent many years restoring, redesigning and nurturing. The Hall has delightful reception rooms with spacious comfortable bedrooms all with kingsize beds, televisions and en-suite bathrooms. Breakfast is an experience not to be missed with delicious fresh fruits, organically produced bacon, sausage and egg. Also homemade breads and preserves.

B & B £30-£35pp, Dinner from £22.50, Rooms 3 single, 3 double, 3 twin, 3 family, all en-suite, Restricted smoking, Children & dogs welcome, Open all year

ACACIA LODGE 21 Ripon Road, Harrogate HG1 2JL
Dee & Peter Bateson *Tel:* 01423 560752 *Fax:* 01423 503725
Web: www.smoothhound.co.uk/hotels/acacialodge.html

Map Ref: 16
A61

'Highly Commended', warm, family run Victorian hotel with pretty gardens in select central conservation area. Short stroll from Harrogate's fashionable shops, many restaurants and conference/exhibition facilities. Retaining original character with fine furnishings. All Bedrooms luxuriously en-suite with every comfort and facility. Award winning breakfasts served in oak furnished dining room. Beautiful lounge with open fire and library of books. Floodlit parking. Brochure on request.

B & B from £29pp, Rooms 2 twin, 2 double, 2 triple, all en-suite, No smoking, Children over 10, No dogs, Closed Xmas & New Year

www.stayinstyle.com

All homes listed feature on our Website and those that have their own E-mail address or Website address can be accessed direct

ALAMAH 88 Kings Road, Harrogate HG1 5JX

Map Ref: 16
A1

Tel: 01423 502187

Alamah provides comfortable rooms, personal attention, a friendly atmosphere and a full English breakfast. 300 metres from town centre with garages and plenty of parking.

B & B from £25pp, Rooms 2 single, 2 double, 2 twin, 1 family, all en-suite/private, Children over 5, Open all year

THE ALEXANDER 88 Franklin Road, Harrogate HG1 5EN
Mrs Lesley Toole
Tel: 01423 503348   *Fax:* 01423 540230   *Mobile:* 07860 501107

Map Ref: 16
A1

An immaculately restored Victorian guest house within walking distance of town centre and conference centre. Full central heating, double glazing and beautifully decorated rooms. On street parking is available. Convenient for Yorkshire Dales and shopping in nearby Harrogate, York and Leeds. ETC 4 Diamonds and featured in 'Which' Good Bed and Breakfast Guide.

B & B from £25pp, Rooms 2 single, 2 double, 3 twin, most en-suite, No smoking, Children over 8, No dogs, Closed Xmas & New Year

ASHLEY HOUSE HOTEL 36-40 Franklin Road, Harrogate HG1 5EE
Ron & Linda Thomas   *Tel:* 01423 507474   *Fax:* 01423 560858
Email: ashleyhousehotel@btinternet.com

Map Ref: 16
A1

Close to the town centre, Ashley House is a friendly hotel aiming to give you a memorable stay and value for money. Quality bedrooms, all en-suite and well equipped. Delightful bar with extensive collection of whiskies. Excellent restaurant within walking distance. Tour the Yorkshire Dales and Moors from our convenient location in this lovely spa town.

B & B from £30pp, Rooms 5 single, 5 twin, 5 double, 2 family, all en-suite, Children & dogs welcome, Open all year

FRANKLIN VIEW 19 Grove Road, Harrogate HG1 5EW
Jennifer Mackay   *Tel:* 01423 541388   *Fax:* 01423 547872
Email: jennifer@franklinview.com   *Web:* franklinview.com

Map Ref: 16
M1, A1, A59

Edwardian family home in a tree lined avenue in the heart of Harrogate. Careful preservation has ensured that the original features including the Gothic windows still remain. Each room displays an individual appeal and style. Guests may choose a traditional breakfast or a healthy alternative to suit. A selection of well recommended international restaurants locally. Harrogate has beautiful parks, there are wonderful places to visit.

B & B £24-£27pp, C-Cards MC VS, Rooms 2 double, 1 twin, all en-suite, No smoking, No children or dogs, Open all year

SHANNON COURT HOTEL 65 Dragon Avenue, Harrogate HG1 5DS
Carol & Jim Dodds   *Tel:* 01423 509858   *Fax:* 01423 530606
Email: shannon@hotels.harrogate.com   *Web:* www.harrogate.com/shannon/

Map Ref: 16
A1

A charming Victorian house with eight delightful en-suite bedrooms with every modern comfort including radio/alarm, colour television and tea/coffee facilities. Close to the town centre, we have our own car park. An excellent touring base. Licensed for residents and their guests.

B & B from £25pp, C-Cards MC VS, Rooms 2 single, 3 double, 1 twin, 2 family, all en-suite, No smoking, Children welcome, No dogs, Closed Xmas & New Year

HIGH WINSLEY COTTAGE Burnt Yates, Harrogate HG3 3EP   *Map Ref:* 17
Clive & Gill King   A61, B6165
Tel: 01423 770662

Traditional Dales cottage in Nidderdale in peaceful countryside, lovely views, ideally placed for town and country visiting. Warm welcome, good food and comfort are assured. En-suite, well equipped bedrooms, a choice of sitting rooms with television, books, magazines and maps. Thoughtfully prepared meals, home bred beef, fresh fruit and vegetables from the garden, free range eggs and home baked bread are on offer.

B & B from £24pp, Dinner from £13.50, Rooms 2 double, 2 twin, all en-suite, No smoking, Children over 11, Closed Jan to Feb

---

PLUMPTON COURT High Street, Nawton,, Helmsley YO62 7TT   *Map Ref:* 18
Chris & Sarah Braithwaite   *Tel / Fax:* 01439 771223   A170
Email: chrisandsarah@plumptoncourt.com   *Web:* www.plumptoncourt.com

Built in the 17th century, Plumpton Court stands in the village of Nawton, in the foothills of the North York Moors. Relax by a fire in the lounge, enjoy home cooked food. Well equipped bedrooms, a ground floor room is available. A private car park and a secluded garden to enjoy. Castle Howard, Nunnington Hall, Rievaulx Abbey, and York are a pleasant drive.

B & B £21-£26pp, Dinner from £14.50, Rooms 4 double, 3 twin, all en-suite, No smoking, Children over 12, No dogs, Closed Xmas

---

WEST VIEW COTTAGE Pockley, near Helmsley YO62 7TE   *Map Ref:* 18
Mrs Valerie Lack   A170
Tel: 01439 770526   *Mobile:* 07811 829112

Enchanting 17th century cruck framed thatched Yorkshire long house, situated in a picturesque village on the edge of the North Yorkshire Moors National Park. Cosy lounge and dining room, evening meal may be enjoyed by arrangement. The garden faces south, there is a summerhouse for guests to enjoy. Private parking. Ideal for the Moors, coast, Ryedale, Castle Howard and York. Excellent pubs locally.

B & B from £25pp, Dinner from £15, Rooms 1 double en-suite, 1 twin private bathroom, No smoking, Children over 12, No dogs, Open all year

---

WOODS END BED & BREAKFAST 46 Inglewood Ave, Birkby, Huddersfield HD2 2DS   *Map Ref:* 19
Julie Smith-Moorhouse   *Tel / Fax:* 01484 513580   *Mobile:* 07730 030993   M62, A62
Email: smithmoorhouse@ntlworld.com

Woods End is an elegant modern detached family home, situated in a quiet cul-de-sac, just one mile from Huddersfield town centre. Traditionally furnished to a high standard with a relaxed cosy atmosphere. A private dining room/study is available for guests to use. An ideal base for West Yorkshire's commercial centres but only forty five minutes to the heart of the Yorkshire Dales.

B & B from £20pp, Rooms 1 single en-suite, 1 double, No smoking, No children or dogs, Open all year

---

HEY LEYS FARM Marsden Lane, Cop Hill, Slaithwaite, Huddersfield HD7 5XA   *Map Ref:* 20
Caroline Bower   *Tel:* 01484 845404   *Fax:* 01484 843188   *Mobile:* 07803 744499   M62, A62
Web: www.yorkshireholidays.com

17th century Grade II building with panoramic views of the countryside. Luxurious accommodation with colour televisions and tea/coffee facilities. Extensive breakfast menu including Whitby kippers, smoked salmon and scrambled egg. Water feature garden with summer house. Renowned country inn within walking distance. Easy access to walks and canal restoration scheme. In the area used for 'Last of the Summer Wine'. ETC 4 Diamonds.

B & B from £25pp, Dinner from £10, Rooms 1 single, 1 double, 1 twin, 1 family, most en-suite, Restricted smoking, Children over 5, No dogs, Closed Xmas & New Year

FOREST FARM GUEST HOUSE Mount Road, Marsden, Huddersfield HD7 6NN
May & Ted Fussey   *Tel / Fax:* 01484 842687
Email: mayandted@aol

Map Ref: 20
M62, A62

In the heart of 'Last of the Summer Wine' country, Forest Farm is situated on the edge of Marsden village, overlooking the golf course and moorland. Over 200 years old, a former weaver's cottage constructed in stone, it has been restored to retain its original character. Evening meals and packed lunches are offered. Television room, spring water, free range eggs special diets available.

B & B from £18pp, C-Cards, Dinner from £7, Rooms 1 twin, 1 double, 1 family, Restricted smoking, Children welcome, Dogs by arrangement, Closed Xmas

BOX COTTAGE 2 Hogg Lane, Kirk Ella, Hull HU10 7NU
Martin & Stephanie Hornby   *Tel / Fax:* 01482 658852
Email: Boxcottage2@aol.com

Map Ref: 21
A164

Set within the Kirk Ella conservation area with a delightful enclosed garden, the house is imaginatively decorated and furnished with pictures, photos and flowers. Food is of a high standard. Bedrooms have televisions, tea/coffee facilities, books and magazines. Guests may use the sitting room and garden. Kirk Ella gives easy access to North Sea ferries, the Yorkshire Wolds, Beverley and York.

B & B £28pp, Dinner £18, Rooms 1 double with private bathroom, 1 single (for same party), No smoking, Children over 8, No dogs, Open all year

GROVE HOTEL 66 The Grove, Ilkley LS29 9PA
Tel: 01943 600298   *Fax:* 0870 706 5587
Email: res@grovehotel.org

Map Ref: 22
A65

This attractive Victorian townhouse is family owned and licensed, providing an excellent base for exploring the Yorkshire Dales, Ilkley, Howarth and Bronte country.

B & B from £42pp, Rooms 2 double, 2 twin, 2 triple, all en-suite, Children welcome, No dogs, Open all year

THE CORNMILL Kirby Mills, Kirkbymoorside YO62 6NP
Jeff & Lindsay Lee   *Tel:* 01751 432000   *Fax:* 01751 432300
Email: cornmill@kirbymills.demon.co.uk   *Web:* kirbymills.demon.co.uk

Map Ref: 23
A170

18th Century Watermill & Victorian Farmhouse. Tranquil, luxurious accommodation on the River Dove. Large rooms, powerful showers, four poster and king-size beds, lounge, bar and wood burning stove. Sumptuous breakfasts and pre-booked group dinners served in the Mill with glass viewing panel in the floor. Near to golf and horse riding. Wheelchair friendly. French spoken. ETC 4 Diamonds, Silver Award.

B & B £25-£32.50pp, C-Cards MC VS, Dinner £25, Rooms 3 double, 2 twin, all en-suite, Restricted smoking, Children over 15, No dogs, Closed Nov to Easter

HIGH BLAKEY HOUSE Blakey Ridge, York, Kirkbymoorside YO62 7LQ
Roy & Kath Atherton   *Tel:* 01751 417186
Email: highblakey.house@virgin.net

Map Ref: 23
A170

High Blakey House is six miles north of Hutton le Hole where Farndale, Rosedale and five other valleys converge. There are spectacular views and superb walks and drives. The comfortable spacious rooms have every facility and a fine lounge/diner with picture windows. Cot and high chairs are provided plus a garage-kennel for pet. The renowned and historic Lion Inn is opposite.

B & B £23-£27pp, Rooms 1 single, 3 double, 2 twin, 2 family, most en-suite, Restricted smoking, Children welcome, Dogs by arrangement, Closed Xmas

HOLLY CORNER 3 Coverdale Drive, High Bond End, Knaresborough HG5 9BW   *Map Ref:* 24
Mrs Jan MacLellan   *Tel / Fax:* 01423 864204   A1
Web: www.knaresborough.co.uk/guest-accom/

A Tudor style private house in a quiet private road on town outskirts. Friendly bed and breakfast with personal service guaranteed. Easy access to the town, Dales, riverside and boating, plus close to A1(M) with restaurants and pubs within walking distance. No smoking. Parking available. Plants and preserves for sale. Recommendations freely available. ETC 4 Diamonds.

B & B £24-£28pp, Rooms 1 single, 1 double, 1 twin, No smoking, Children over 12, No dogs, Open all year

ROOKERY COTTAGE 1 East Witton, Leyburn DL8 4SN   *Map Ref:* 25
Ursula Bussey   *Tel / Fax:* 01969 622918   A6108
Email: ursulabussey@aol.com   *Web:* www.rookerycottage.co.uk

Converted from 17th century almhouses, Rookery Cottage is one of the prettiest houses in the village. Formerly the Post Office and before that the tailor's house. The beautifully presented bedrooms enjoy garden views. There are beams everywhere, and painted basins in the bedrooms. Superb breakfasts. This horse training area has much to offer in walking, field sports, towns and abbeys. Excellent local pub.

B & B £22.50-£28pp, Rooms 1 twin, 1 double, sharing luxury bathroom, No smoking, Children & dogs welcome, Open all year

THE PRIORY West End, Middleham, Leyburn DL8 4QG   *Map Ref:* 26
                                                                             A1
Tel: 01969 623279

Friendly, family run business in 200 year old Georgian property, extensively renovated and redecorated throughout. The individual rooms all have beverage tray and many are en-suite with TV. A narrow coaching arch gives access to car parking and we are central for all local amenities and lovely walking country, being opposite the Castle home of Richard III.

B & B from £23pp, Rooms 2 single, 2 double, 2 twin, 2 family, most en-suite, No smoking, Children over 5, Small well behaved dogs, Closed Nov to Mar

PORCH HOUSE High Street, Northallerton DL7 8EG   *Map Ref:* 27
Janet Beardow   *Tel:* 01609 779831   *Fax:* 01609 778603   A684
Web: www.smoothhound.co.uk/hotels/porchhouse1.html

Porch House was built in 1584, still the porch frames the entrance. Historically, the house has offered shelter to travellers including royalty - James (VI of Scotland 1 of England) and Charles I. Bedrooms (one ground floor) are well equipped. English/vegetarian breakfast is offered. Original fireplaces and beams, walled garden, private parking, central position, excellent shopping, ideal for discovering the Yorkshire Dales.

B & B from £26pp, C-Cards MC VS, Rooms 4 double, 2 twin, all en-suite, No smoking, No children or dogs, Closed Xmas & New Year

POTTO GRANGE Potto, Northallerton DL6 3HH   *Map Ref:* 28
Mrs Pauline Kynge   A19, A172
Tel: 01642 700212   *Fax:* 01642 700978

This serene Georgian farmhouse, in the same family ownership for 250 years, has a large leafy garden, a tennis court, croquet lawn and lovely views. The farm and garden are fully organic, and delicious meals reflect this. Bedrooms have all facilities. Guests have an elegant drawing room. Explore the moors, dales, coast and the great cities of York and Durham.

B & B from £28pp, Dinner from £20, Rooms 2 double, 1 twin, all en-suite, No smoking, Children welcome, No dogs, Closed Nov to Mar

HEATH HOUSE Chancery Road, Ossett WF5 9RZ
Jo Holland   *Tel / Fax:* 01924 260654
Email: jo.holland@amserve.net   *Web:* www.heath-house.co.uk

Map Ref: 29
M1

A warm welcome awaits you at Heath House, our family home for over half a century, and which we take great pleasure in sharing with our guests. We aim to provide excellent value at affordable prices. Ideally situated one and a half miles west of M1 junction 40 on the A638. Leeds, Bradford, Wakefield and Dewsbury are easily accessible.

B & B from £24pp, C-Cards MC VS, Rooms 1 single, 1 double, 1 twin, 1 family, all en-suite, Children welcome, Dogs by arrangement, Open all year

---

HEATHCOTE HOUSE 100 Eastgate, Pickering YO18 7DW
Joan & Rod Lovejoy   *Tel / Fax:* 01751 476991
Email: joanlovejoy@lineone.net

Map Ref: 30
A170

A warm, relaxed welcome is guaranteed at this elegant early Victorian house, only minutes from the town centre. Beautifully decorated with very attractive bedrooms, all en-suite. Delicious breakfasts and optional dinners with excellent home cooking. Ideal for walking, cycling and touring the North Yorkshire Moors. Secluded parking. Cycle store.

B & B from £20.50pp, C-Cards MC VS, Dinner available, Rooms 3 double, 2 twin, all en-suite, No smoking, Children over 12, No dogs, Closed Xmas & New Year

---

BURR BANK Cropton, North York Moors, Pickering YO18 8HL
Mrs Julie Richardson   *Tel:* 01751 417777   *Fax:* 01751 417789   *Mobile:* 07768 842233
Email: bandb@burrbank.com   *Web:* www.burrbank.com

Map Ref: 31
A170

Burr Bank is a warm, comfortable and spacious stone cottage in 70 acres with wonderful views in the North York Moors National Park. Burr Bank has a ground floor double and twin bedrooms with colour co-ordinated furnishings. We feel we have thought of most things that will make you feel comfortable and secure. Winner of Guest Accommodation of the Year 2000.

B & B £27pp, Dinner £16, Rooms 1 single, 1 double, 1 twin, all en-suite, No smoking, Children over 12, No dogs, Open all year

---

HIGH FARM Cropton, Pickering YO18 8HL
Mrs Ruth Feaster   *Tel:* 01751 417461   *Fax:* 01751 417807
Email: highfarmcropton@aol.com

Map Ref: 31
A170

Relax in the friendly atmosphere of this elegant Victorian farmhouse surrounded by beautiful gardens, on the edge of a quiet, unspoilt village and overlooking North York Moors National Park. Peaceful base for walkers, and nature and garden lovers. Steam railway and Castle Howard nearby and the village inn has own brewery. A warm welcome awaits. Yorkshire Tourist Board 4 Diamonds, Silver Award.

B & B from £22pp, C-Cards MC VS, Rooms 3 double, all en-suite, No smoking, Children over 10, No dogs, Open all year

---

WILDSMITH HOUSE Marton, near Sinnington, Pickering YO62 6RD
Chris & Malcolm Steele   *Tel:* 01751 432702
Email: wildsmithhouse@talk21.com   *Web:* www.pb-design.com/swiftlink/bb/1102.htm

Map Ref: 31
A170

Charming farmhouse originating from 1720, set on village green in pretty village at the edge of North Yorkshire Moors. High quality en-suite accommodation with televisions and tea/coffee facilities in rooms. Delicious home cooked breakfasts using local produce. Ideally based for exploring the area with the Moors, Heritage coast and York close by. Many delightful inns and restaurants within easy distance.

B & B £22-£26pp, Rooms 2 twin en-suite, No smoking, Children over 12, No dogs, Closed Nov to Mar

FOX & HOUNDS COUNTRY INN Sinnington, Pickering YO62 6SQ   *Map Ref:* 31
Tel: 01751 431577   *Fax:* 01751 432791   A170
Email: foxhoundsinn@easynet.co.uk

Eighteenth century Coaching Inn set in one of Yorkshire's prettiest villages. Riverside and woodland walks close by. Central for Castle Howard, Heartbeat, York and Whitby. Renowned for our food and friendly service.

B & B from £25pp, C-Cards MC VS AE, Dinner from £15, Rooms 1 single, 7 double, 2 twin, all en-suite, Restricted smoking, Dogs welcome, Open all year

---

ALLERSTON MANOR HOUSE near Thornton-Le-Dale, Pickering YO18 7PF   *Map Ref:* 32
Tess & Rupert Chetwynd   *Tel / Fax:* 01723 850112   A64, A170
Email: red@allerston-manor.com   *Web:* www.allerston-manor.com

Three hundred years old, built around the remains of a 14th century Knight's Templar Hall with wonderful views to the Vale of Pickering. Excellent walking, Allerston borders the North York Moors National Park. Bedrooms look onto the 'ancient field' grazed by sheep or cattle. Informal party style candlelit dinners. Guests are welcome to bring their wine. Historic properties within easy reach.

B & B £35-£42.50pp, C-Cards MC VS, Dinner from £20, Rooms 2 double, 1 double/twin, all en-suite, No smoking, Children over 12, No dogs, Open all year

---

THE HIGH HALL Hurrell Lane, Thornton le Dale, Pickering YO18 7QR   *Map Ref:* 32
Richard & Tuppie Craven   *Tel:* 01751 474371   *Fax:* 01751 477701   A170
Mobile: 07803 161064   *Email:* CravenGriffin@aol.com

A warm welcome awaits at The High Hall. Built in 1767 of mellow Yorkshire stone in one of North Yorkshire's prettiest villages. An air of quiet repose with period furniture, lovely drawing room, nice garden and patio. Close to North Yorkshire Moors with many places of interest to visit. Good local pubs with the coast only 15 miles away.

B & B from £30pp, Rooms 1 double, 1 twin, 1 single, all private bathrooms, No smoking, Children welcome, No dogs, Closed Xmas & New Year

---

OLD BREWERY 29 The Green, Richmond DL10 4RG   *Map Ref:* 33
Mrs Y F Mears   A1
Tel: 01748 822460   *Fax:* 01748 825561

Nestling on the green, close to the river Swale with marvellous views of Richmond Castle, Old Brewery was once an old inn. It has en-suite rooms, a four poster bed and television and tea/coffee facilities. Needlepoint, puzzle, games and books available in the lounge. Homemade muffins along with local produce at breakfast. Patio garden.

B & B from £23pp, C-Cards MC VS, Rooms 4 double, 1 twin, all en-suite, No smoking, Children over 8, No dogs, Closed Dec & Jan

---

BROOK HOUSE Middleton Tyas, Richmond DL10 6RP   *Map Ref:* 34
Mr & Mrs John Harrop   A1(M), A66
Tel / Fax: 01325 377713

A Georgian period former farmhouse surrounded by mature oaks, tranquil pastures and secluded game coverts. Elegantly furnished, well proportioned rooms with individual bathrooms, log fires and central heating. Minutes from the A1, near Richmond and Barnard Castle, placed for exploring the Yorkshire Dales and Moors, plus the Cathedral cities of Durham, Ripon and York. A peaceful stop on the way to Northumbria and Scotland.

B & B from £35pp, Dinner from £25, Rooms 1 double, 1 twin, both with private bathroom, Restricted smoking, Children over 16, Dogs by arrangement, Closed Xmas & New Year

MALLARD GRANGE Aldfield, Nr Fountains Abbey, Ripon HG4 3BE
Maggie Johnson *Tel / Fax:* 01765 620242 *Mobile:* 07720 295918
Email: mallard.grange@btinternet.com

Map Ref: 35
B6265

Rambling 16th century farmhouse, full of character and charm, in glorious countryside near Fountains Abbey. Welcoming, spacious and offering superb quality and comfort. En-suite bedrooms, 2 on ground floor, have large, comfortable beds, warm towels, colour TV, hair dryer and refreshments tray. Delicious breakfasts! Pretty walled garden. Safe car parking.

B & B £27.50-£30pp, C-Cards MC VS, Rooms 2 double, 2 twin, all en-suite, No smoking, Children over 12, No dogs, Closed Xmas & New Year

BISHOPTON GROVE HOUSE Bishopton, Ripon HG4 2QL
Susi Wimpress *Tel:* 01765 600888
Email: wimpress@bronco.co.uk

Map Ref: 36
A61

An informal, friendly atmosphere and a peaceful, secluded setting attractive features of this restored Georgian house in a lovely rural corner of Ripon, near the River Laver and Fountains Abbey. All rooms are generously proportioned with tea/coffee making facilities and televisions. Breakfast offers a good choice to suit all tastes. The Dales are easily accessible.

B & B from £20pp, Rooms 2 double, 1 twin, 2 en-suite, Children welcome, Open all year

ST GEORGE'S COURT Old Home Farm, Grantley, Ripon HG4 3EU
Sandra Gordon *Tel / Fax:* 01765 620618
Email: stgeorgescourt@bronco.co.uk

Map Ref: 37
B6265

Enjoy the warm hospitality of St George's Court, a listed farmhouse, situated in the Yorkshire Dales, near Fountains Abbey in 20 acres of peaceful farmland. Our en-suite rooms in a renovated farm building, offer comfort and all modern facilities, whilst retaining character and charm. Delicious breakfasts are served in the lovely farmhouse conservatory dining room. Lots of parking. Peace and tranquillity are our passwords.

B & B £25-£27.50pp, C-Cards MC VS, Rooms 1 twin, 3 double, 1 family, all en-suite, Restricted smoking, Children & dogs welcome, Closed Xmas

RICHMOND PRIVATE HOTEL 135 Columbus Ravine, Scarborough YO12 7QZ
Brian & Janet Shaw
Tel: 01723 362934

Map Ref: 38
A64, A165

The resident proprietors guarantee a warm welcome and comfortable accommodation. There are colour televisions and tea/coffee facilities in all rooms with a separate guest lounge, licensed bar and good home cooking. Convenient for town centre, cricket ground, indoor bowls complex, North Bays sandy beaches, swimming pools and many more attractions. Discounted golf available when you book with us.

B & B from £15.50pp, Dinner from £7.50, Rooms 1 single, 3 en-suite, 1 double, 2 family, Restricted smoking, Children welcome, Dogs by arrangement, Open all year

WELLINGTON LODGE Staintondale, Scarborough YO13 0EL
Ruth & Bruce Wright *Tel:* 01723 871234
Email: b&b@llamatreks.co.uk *Web:* www.llamatreks.co.uk

Map Ref: 38
A171

Nestled in the National Park, Wellington Lodge has sea and country views towards the Heritage Coast. Ideally situated for visiting nearby picturesque villages on the North Yorkshire Moors. English breakfasts with local produce, and homemade preserves are served in the sun lounge. Newly furnished bedrooms have usual facilities. Guests can join a trek, leading friendly llamas who carry their champagne lunches.

B & B £24-£26pp, C-Cards MC VS AE, Rooms 2 double en-suite, No smoking, No children or dogs, Closed Xmas

HARMONY COUNTRY LODGE Limestone Road, Burniston, Scarborough YO13 0DG   *Map Ref:* 39
Sue & Tony Hewitt   *Tel:* 0800 2985840   A171
Email: harmonylodge@cwcom.net   *Web:* www.spiderweb.co.uk/harmony

A comfortable peaceful retreat with an unusual octagonal design having superb panoramic views overlooking sea and National Park. TV and tea/coffee facilities in all rooms. Guests lounge, conservatory and massage available. Licensed, ample parking. Ideal for walking or motoring and only two miles from Scarborough. Personal service and warm welcome guaranteed. Also self-catering caravan. ETB 4 Diamonds.

B & B £22.50-£29.50pp, Dinner available, Rooms 1 single, 5 double, 1 twin, 1 family, most en-suite, No smoking, Children over 7, Dogs by arrangement, Open all year

BIDE-A-WHILE 3 Loring Road, Ravenscar, Scarborough YO13 0LY   *Map Ref:* 40
Beryl & Bill Leach   A171
Tel: 01723 870643   *Fax:* 01723 871577

A small guest house offering clean, comfortable accommodation in a homely atmosphere. Home cooking with fresh produce, beautiful sea views from all rooms. On the edge of North York Moors and ideal for exploring the Dales. Ideal for walking, 11 miles from Scarborough, 11 miles from Whitby. ETB 3 Diamonds.

B & B £16.50-£21.50pp, Dinner available, Rooms 2 double, 1 twin, 1 family, all en-suite, Children welcome, No dogs, Open all year

THE BRIARY 12 Moncrieffe Road, Nether Edge, Sheffield S7 1HR   *Map Ref:* 41
Mr & Mrs Daji   *Tel:* 0114 255 1951   *Fax:* 0114 249 4746   M1
Email: briaryguesthouse@hotmail.com

The Briary is an imposing detached Victorian residence of character set in lovely gardens. Recently refurbished, it is centrally heated and antique furniture is found throughout. Superior quality bedrooms are all equipped with televisions, hairdryers, radio alarms and hospitality trays. Imaginative cuisine with a choice of breakfasts. RAC 5 Diamonds.

B & B from £26pp, C-Cards MC VS AE, Rooms 1 single, 3 double, 2 twin, 2 family, all en-suite, No smoking, Children & dogs welcome, Open all year

LOW SKIBEDEN FARM HOUSE Harrogate Road, Skipton BD23 6AB   *Map Ref:* 42
Mrs Heather Simpson   *Tel:* 01756 793849   *Fax:* 01756 793804   *Mobile:* 07734 64316   A59, A65
Email: skibhols.yorkdales@talk21.com   *Web:* www.lowskibedenfarmhouse.co.uk

At Low Skibeden a warm and friendly reception awaits you from Heather and Bill Simpson. On arrival you will be served with tea or coffee and cakes. There is a visitors lounge with television, separate dining room, central heating and electric over blankets, run from October to May. There is ample parking and is the ideal base for touring the Dales.

B & B £20-£24pp, C-Cards MC VS AE, Rooms 1 double, 1 twin, 3 family, most ensuite, No smoking, Children over 10, No dogs, Closed Xmas & New Year

KNOWLES LODGE Appletreewick, Skipton BD23 6DQ   *Map Ref:* 43
Pam & Chris Knowles-Fitton   *Tel:* 01756 720228   *Fax:* 01756 720381   *Mobile:* 07860 617641   B6170
Email: chris.knowlesfitton@totalise.co.uk   *Web:* www.knowleslodge.com

Set in 18 acres of garden, woodland and pasture, Knowles Lodge enjoys breathtaking views while overlooking both the 'Dales Way' and River Wharf. Three imaginatively decorated twin/double bedrooms offer luxurious bed and breakfast each with its en-suite bathroom. Pam and Chris Knowles-Fitton do their utmost to pamper their guests whether walking the Dales Way or just relaxing and enjoying the Dales.

B & B from £28pp, C-Cards, Dinner from £15, Rooms 2 double, 1 twin, all en-suite, Restricted smoking, Children welcome, Dogs by arrangement, Open all year

TENNANT ARM HOTEL Kilnsey, Skipton BD23 5DS
Norrie & Dilly Dean
Tel: 01756 752301

Map Ref: 44
A65

A 17th century coaching inn, family owned and run, with 10 en-suite rooms, colour televisions and tea/coffee facilities. Pine panelled restaurant with bar meals served every lunch and evening in the heart of Yorkshire Dales. Ideal for fishing and walking. ETB 3 Crown commended.

B & B from £27.50pp, Dinner from £6.75, Rooms 5 double, 3 twin, 2 family, all en-suite, Children welcome, Dogs by arrangement, Closed Xmas

---

LASKILL FARM Hawnby, Thirsk YO62 5NB
Mrs S Smith *Tel / Fax:* 01439 798268
Email: suesmith@laskillfarm.fsnet.co.uk

Map Ref: 45
B1257

Laskill Farm is a 60 acre mixed farm in a peaceful setting within the North York Moors National Park. Ideal for stately homes and walking. Own natural spring water. Peace and tranquillity in idyllic surroundings and every comfort. York 45 minutes. Laskill Farm has earned its reputation from attention to detail, friendly, personal service and, most of all value for money.

B & B from £28.50pp, Dinner from £13.50, Rooms 1 single, 3 double, 2 twin, most en-suite, Open all year

---

WHITFIELD HOUSE HOTEL Darnholm, Goathland, Whitby YO22 5LA
Adrian & Sue Caulder
Tel: 01947 896215

Map Ref: 46
A169

Quietly situated in the heart of the North York Moors National Park, once a 17th century farmhouse, now carefully modernised to provide every comfort, yet retaining its charm. Superb country cooking, personal attention and a friendly atmosphere. Licensed. Ideal base for walking or touring the North York Moors, steam railway and the coast. Goathland is 'Aidensfield' in Yorkshire TV's 'Heartbeat'.

B & B from £31pp, Dinner from £12.95, Rooms 1 single, 2 twin, 6 double, all en-suite, Restricted smoking, Children over 5, Dogs by arrangement, Open all year

---

NETHERBY HOUSE 90 Coach Road, Sleights, Whitby YO22 5EQ
Barry & Lyn Truman *Tel / Fax:* 01947 810211
Email: netherby_house@hotmail.com

Map Ref: 47
A165

Elegant Victorian Villa set in 1.5 acres of garden with superb views over the Esk Valley. Very attractive en-suite bedrooms with television, tea/coffee facilities and some available on the ground floor. Good food served in attractive dining room. Licensed and private car park. Ideal base for the coast, moors and North Yorkshire.

B & B £24-£29pp, C-Cards MC VS, Dinner from £14, Rooms 1 single, 6 double, 2 twin, 2 family, all en-suite, No smoking, Children welcome, No dogs, Closed Xmas day and Boxing day

---

ALCUIN LODGE 15 Sycamore Place, Bootham, York YO30 7DW
Susan Taylor *Tel:* 01904 632222 *Fax:* 01904 626630
Email: alcuinlodg@aol.com

Map Ref: 48
A19

A fine Edwardian House situated in a quiet cul de sac overlooking a bowling green, five minutes walk through the beautiful Museum Gardens to the heart of the city. A warm welcome is assured. Alcuin Lodge is within walking distance of York train station. Rooms are well equipped with tea/coffee facilities and central heating. Guests have access to rooms at all times. Ample parking.

B & B from £20pp, C-Cards MC VS DC, Rooms 1 twin, 3 double, 1 family, all en-suite, No smoking, Children over 12, No dogs, Closed Xmas

ARNOT HOUSE 17 Grosvenor Terrace, Bootham, York YO30 7AG   *Map Ref:* 48
Kim & Ann Sluter-Robbins *Tel / Fax:* 01904 641966   A19
Email: kim.robbins@virgin.net *Web:* www.arnothouseyork.co.uk

Arnot House is a family run guest house overlooking Bootham Park, five minutes walk from York Minster. The four guest bedrooms are furnished in a Victorian style with antiques and paintings, brass or wooden beds. There is a guest lounge and car parking. Breakfast includes cereals, fruit juices, fresh fruit salad, English or vegetarian breakfast or even scrambled eggs with smoked salmon!

B & B from £25pp, C-Cards MC VS, Dinner available, Rooms 1 twin, 3 double, all en-suite, No smoking, Children over 12, No dogs, Closed Xmas & Jan

ASCOT HOUSE 80 East Parade, York YO31 7YH   *Map Ref:* 48
June & Keith Wood *Tel:* 01904 426826 *Fax:* 01904 431077   A64
Email: j+k@ascot-house-york.demon.co.uk

A family run 15 bedroomed Victorian Villa, built in 1869, with en-suite rooms of character and many fourposter or canopy beds. There is a spacious Residents Lounge to relax in and delicious Traditional English or Vegetarian breakfasts are served in the dining room. Fifteen minutes walk to City Centre, Jorvik Viking Museum, Castle Museum or York Minster. Residential licence, Sauna and private enclosed car park.

B & B £22-£30pp, C-Cards MC VS DC, Rooms 1 single, 8 double, 3 twin, 3 family, most en-suite, Restricted smoking, Children welcome, Well behaved dogs, Closed Xmas

AVONDALE 61 Bishopthorpe Road, York YO23 1NX   *Map Ref:* 48
Ian & Berni Addyman *Tel:* 01904 633989 *Fax:* 01904 633951   A153 from M62
Email: addyman@avondalehouse.freeserve.co.uk *Web:* www.avondalehouse.co.uk

A 5 minute walk to the City centre, the atmosphere at Avondale House is one of restful comfort. Rooms are individually decorated, fitted with pine furniture and quality fabrics. A wide choice of breakfast menus including vegetarian, traditional and healthy options.

B & B from £23pp, Rooms 1 single, 3 double, 1 twin, 1 triple, all en-suite, Children welcome, No dogs, Open all year

BARBICAN HOUSE 20 Barbican Road, York YO10 5AA   *Map Ref:* 48
Michael & Juliet Morgan *Tel:* 01904 627617 *Fax:* 01904 647140   A19
Email: info@barbicanhouse.com *Web:* www.barbicanhouse.com

Friendly welcome in this delightful Victorian residence, carefully restored to retain original features. Bedrooms are en-suite and have TV and tea/coffee facilities. One ground floor room. Traditional or vegetarian breakfast is served, also a fresh fruit platter, scones, muffins and yoghurt. Central York is a five minute walk and the Barbican Leisure centre a 100 yards. Private car park.

B & B from £28pp, C-Cards MC VS, Rooms 1 twin, 6 double, all en-suite, No smoking, Children over 12, No dogs, Closed Xmas & New Year

THE BENTLEY 25 Grosvenor Terrace, Bootham, York YO30 7AG *Map Ref:* 48
Will & Penny Lefebve *Tel / Fax:* 01904 644313 *Mobile:* 07860 199440 A19
Email: bentley.ofyork@btinternet.com *Web:* www.bentleyofyork.co.uk

The Bentley offers friendly value-for-money accommodation, only 10 minutes walk from York Minster. This elegant Victorian property contains spacious en-suite rooms overlooking parkland, with the Minster nestling beyond. It is furnished with quality, care and comfort in mind. The hall and stairways reflect the owner's lifetime in horse racing, providing turf enthusiasts with the opportunity to wallow in nostalgia. ETC 4 Diamonds.

B & B £21-£27.50pp, Rooms 1 single, 4 double, 1 twin, 1 family, most en-suite, No smoking, Children over 10, No dogs, Closed mid-Dec to mid-Jan

BOWEN HOUSE 4 Gladstone Street, Huntington Road, York YO31 8RF
Mrs Valerie Wood   *Tel / Fax:* 01904 636881
Email: info@bowenhouse.co.uk   *Web:* www.bowenhouse.co.uk

Map Ref: 48
A64

Small, family-run, Victorian guesthouse with period furnishings throughout. Excellent traditional and vegetarian breakfasts, with free range eggs and home made preserves. Short stroll to York city centre. Private car park. Non-smoking in all rooms. Brochure available.

B & B from £19pp, C-Cards MC VS, Rooms 1 single, 2 double, 1 twin, 1 family, most en-suite, No smoking, Children & dogs welcome, Closed Xmas

---

BRONTE HOUSE 22 Grosvenor Terrace, Bootham, York YO30 7AG
David & Yvonne Copley   *Tel:* 01904 621066   *Fax:* 01904 653434
Email: reservations@bronte-guesthouse.com   *Web:* www.bronte-guesthouse.com

Map Ref: 48
A19

Award winning Victorian guesthouse 5 minutes walk to City Centre. Free parking. All rooms are individually decorated with many antiques. Remote control Colour TV, tea/coffee, hair dryer, alarm clock radio and thermostats are standard facilities. Please see our website for more details. York Tourism Bureau 'Guesthouse of the Year' winners and recommended by Which? Holiday magazine. ETC 4 Diamonds.

B & B from £26pp, C-Cards MC VS, Rooms 2 single, 1 double, 1 twin, 1 family, all en-suite, No smoking, Children welcome, No dogs, Open all year

---

CLAXTON HALL COTTAGE B&B Malton Road, York YO60 7RE
Carol & Martin Brough   *Tel / Fax:* 01904 468697
Email: claxcott@aol.com   *Web:* claxtonhallcottage.com

Map Ref: 48
A64

Carol and Martin welcome you with homebaked cake to their peaceful 18th century cottage, set in one acre of gardens with panoramic views. It boasts beams and log fires and is the perfect setting for a romantic candlelit dinner, available on request. York is four miles away and Castle Howard, six miles. Easy access for Moors, Dales and the coast. ETC 4 Diamonds.

B & B £22.50-£27.50pp, C-Cards MC VS, Dinner from £12.50, Rooms 2 double, 1 twin, all en-suite, No smoking, Children welcome, No dogs, Closed Xmas & New Year

---

CROSSWAYS GUEST HOUSE 23 Wigginton Road, York YO31 8HJ
Mary Sutherland   *Tel:* 01904 637250
Email: crossways@tinyonline.co.uk   *Web:* crosswaysguesthouse.freeserve.co.uk

Map Ref: 48
A64

Crossways Guest House is situated only ten minutes' walk from city centre. All en-suite rooms have colour television with residents welcome to relax in the garden. Warm welcome and hearty breakfast. Offers visitors the perfect base for exploring some of York's most famous attractions, the Minster, Railway Museum and City Wall.

B & B from £20pp, C-Cards MC VS, Rooms 4 double, 1 twin, all en-suite, No smoking, Children welcome, No dogs, Open all year

---

DAIRY GUEST HOUSE 3 Scarcroft Road, York YO23 1ND
Phillip Hunt & Chris Andrade
Tel: 01904 639367

Map Ref: 48
A64

Once the local dairy, now a beautifully appointed Victorian town house, Dairy Guest House features a flower filled courtyard. Rooms are well equipped in a cottage style, they are prettily presented, one room has a four poster bed. English, or wholefood vegetarian breakfast, the atmosphere is relaxed and informal. Within walking distance of the city centre, and 200 yards from the medieval city walls.

B & B from £20pp, Rooms 1 single, 1 twin, 2 double, 1 family, some en-suite, Children welcome, Dogs by arrangement, Closed mid-Dec to Jan

FOSS BANK GUEST HOUSE 16 Huntington Road, York YO31 8RB   *Map Ref:* 48
K Jervis   A64
Tel: 01904 635548

Foss Bank is an ideal base to visit York, the East Coast and the surrounding countryside. Overlooking the river Foss this Victorian town house provides comfortable accommodation in individually furnished rooms. Leave your car in our private car park and take a 5 minute stroll into the City via Monkgate Bar, one of the stone gateways through the City Walls.

B & B £21-£26pp, Rooms 2 single, 3 double, 1 twin, No dogs, Open all year

---

FRIARS REST GUEST HOUSE 81 Fulford Road, York YO10 4BD   *Map Ref:* 48
Tel / Fax: 01904 629823   A19, A64
Email: friarsrest@btinternet.com   *Web:* www.friarsrest.co.uk

Friars Rest is a small, family-run guest house, with a friendly atmosphere. Only 10 minutes' walk to the town centre and local attractions. We have a car park so you can leave your car and take a short riverside walk into York's centre. Stay with us and enjoy what York has to offer.

B & B £18-£27pp, C-Cards MC VS, Rooms 4 double, 2 triple, 1 family, all en-suite, Children welcome, No dogs, Open all year

---

GRANGE LODGE 52 Bootham Crescent, Bootham, York YO3 7AH   *Map Ref:* 48
Jenny Robinson   *Tel:* 01904 621137   A19
Email: grangeldg@aol.com

The Grange Lodge offers a warm welcome to all who stay. Seven comfortable and attractively presented bedrooms are well equipped, many of them have en-suite facilities. This guest house is ideally placed for visiting all of the city's attractions, the famous York Minster is just 10 minutes away. An ideal base from which to explore this most beautiful region.

B & B £18-£25pp, C-Cards, Dinner from £8, Rooms 3 double, 2 family, 1 twin, 1 single, most en-suite, Children welcome, No dogs, Open all year

---

THE HAZELWOOD 24/25 Portland Street, York YO31 7EH   *Map Ref:* 48
Tel: 01904 626548   *Fax:* 01904 628032   Gillygate
Web: www.thehazelwoodyork.com

The Hazelwood is perfectly situated being just 400 yards from York Minster in a quiet side street with its own car park. There is a friendly atmosphere in our lovely Victorian townhouse. Individually styled en-suite bedrooms have been refurbished to the highest standards using designer fabrics. A wide choice of high quality breakfasts including vegetarian, ranging from traditional English, to croissants and Danish pastries.

B & B £35-£50pp, C-Cards MC VS, Rooms 1 single, 3 twin, 8 double, 2 family, all en-suite, No smoking, Children over 8, No dogs, Open all year

---

HOLLY LODGE 204-206 Fulford Road, York YO10 4DD   *Map Ref:* 48
Mr & Mrs Gallagher   *Tel:* 01904 646005   A19, A64
Web: www.thehollylodge.co.uk

Beautifully appointed Georgian Grade II listed building with quiet en-suite rooms overlooking garden or terrace. A pleasant 10 minutes riverside stroll to the city. Conveniently situated for all York's attractions. An ideal venue for a stay where you are assured of a warm welcome and on site parking. Booking recommended. 4 Diamonds, AA, RAC and ETC.

B & B from £29pp, C-Cards MC VS, Rooms 3 double, 1 twin, 1 family, all en-suite, No smoking, Children welcome, No dogs, Open all year

HOLMWOOD HOUSE HOTEL   114 Holgate Road, York YO24 4BB   *Map Ref:* 48
Rosie Blanksby & Bill Pitts   *Tel:* 01904 626183   *Fax:* 01904 670899   A59
Email: holmwood.house@dial.pipex.com   *Web:* www.holmwoodhousehotel.co.uk

Listed building built in the 19th century, backs onto one of the
prettiest squares in York. Lovingly restored, it retains the ambience
of a private home with elegant rooms. En-suite bedrooms have
shower, bath or spa-bath, TV, coffee and tea facilities and direct dial
telephone. With parking, we are 7-8 minutes walk from the City
Walls, the railway station and centre 15 minutes.

B & B £32.50-£52.50pp, C-Cards MC VS, Rooms 3 twin,
8 double, family suites, all en-suite, No smoking, Children over 8,
No dogs, Open all year

MIDWAY HOUSE   145 Fulford Road, York YO10 4HG   *Map Ref:* 48
Annette & Ian Roberts   *Tel:* 01904 659272   M1/A1, A64, A19
Email: midway.house@virgin.net   *Web:* www.s-h-systems.co.uk/hotel/midway

A welcoming, family run, detached, non-smoking, Victorian guest
house with comfortable en-suite bedrooms. Four poster and ground
floor available. Guests Lounge. Guaranteed private on-site parking.
Pleasant riverside stroll to historical city centre, university and
racecourse. Delicious, freshly prepared breakfasts. Three/seven
night and winter break rates - please contact us.

B & B £22-£32pp, C-Cards MC VS, Rooms 1 single, 7 double,
2 twin, 2 triple, No smoking, Children welcome, No dogs, Closed
Xmas

NUNMILL HOUSE   85 Bishopthorpe Road, York YO23 1NX   *Map Ref:* 48
Russell & Cherry Whitbourn-Hammond   *Tel:* 01904 634047   *Fax:* 01904 655879   A59/A64
Email: info@nunmill.co.uk   *Web:* www.nunmill.co.uk

Nunmill House is a splendid Victorian house which has been lovingly
restored to enhance all the original features. Each bedroom is
individually furnished, some have 4 poster beds. This is an ideal
place to stay for those looking for comfortable, yet affordable en-
suite accommodation. Easy walk to all attractions. ETC 4 Diamonds,
Silver Award. SAE for colour brochure. Please visit our website.

B & B £27-£35pp, Rooms 1 twin, 6 double, 1 family, 7 en-suite,
1 private bathroom, No smoking, Children welcome, No dogs,
Closed Dec & Jan

ST GEORGE'S HOTEL   6 St George's Place, York YO24 1DR   *Map Ref:* 48
Brian & Kristine Livingstone   *Tel:* 01904 625056   *Fax:* 01904 625009   A1036, A64
Email: sixstgeorg@aol.com   *Web:* www.members.aol.com/sixstgeorg/

A Victorian house in a quiet cul-de-sac by York's racecourse. The
comfortably furnished en-suite bedrooms have television and
tea/coffee trays. Excellent access from the A64 from the south and
A19 from the north, it is well placed for Castle Howard,
Scarborough, Herriot country, the North Yorkshire Moors and York.
A ten minute walk to the City walls. Pets very welcome. Private
enclosed parking.

B & B from £24pp, C-Cards MC VS AE DC, Dinner from £7,
Rooms 5 double (2 four posters),5 family, all en-suite, Children &
dogs welcome, Open all year

OLDSTEAD GRANGE   Oldstead, Coxwold, York YO61 4BJ   *Map Ref:* 49
Mrs Anne Banks   *Tel:* 01347 868634   A19
Email: anne@yorkshireuk.com   *Web:* www.yorkshireuk.com

17th century features with superb comfort in a beautiful situation
amidst 160 acres of fields, woods and valleys near Byland Abbey in
the Moors National Park. Spacious bedrooms with comfortable
king-size beds, television, warm towels and robes, fresh flowers and
refreshment tray with homemade chocolates and biscuits. Breakfast
choice of teas, coffees, fruit and traditional and speciality dishes.
Renowned eating places in pretty villages.

B & B £28-£35pp, C-Cards MC VS, Rooms 1 twin, 2 double,
all en-suite, No smoking, Children over 10, No dogs, Open all year

CURZON LODGE & STABLE COTTAGES 23 Tadcaster Road, Dringhouses, York YO24 1QG
Richard & Wendy Wood *Map Ref:* 50
Tel / Fax: 01904 703157 A64, A1036

A delightful 17th century former farmhouse and stables overlooking York Racecourse. 10 comfortable and well equipped en-suite rooms, some with 4-posters. Country antiques, books, prints, fresh flowers and complimentary sherry in our cosy sitting room lend English house ambience. Friendly and informal. Parking in grounds. Restaurants close by. RAC, AA, WHICH?, ETC Highly Commended.

B & B £25-£35pp, C-Cards MC VS, Rooms 1 single, 5 double, 3 twin, 1 family, all en-suite, No smoking, Children welcome, No dogs, Closed Xmas

---

FIFTH MILESTONE COTTAGE Hull Road, Dunnington, York YO19 5LR *Map Ref:* 51
Karen & Alan Jackson A1079
Tel: 01904 489361

Situated in the countryside, close to York city, three spacious rooms, all have television, hospitality tray and central heating, they are in ground floor converted stables with an antiques theme, you can unwind in our conservatory or landscaped gardens. Private car park. A convenient base from which to tour James Herriot's Yorkshire Dales, Heartbeat's North York Moors and the Heritage coast with Whitby.

B & B from £16.50pp, Rooms 1 twin, 1 double en-suite, 1 family en-suite, Restricted smoking, Children & dogs welcome, Open all year

---

ALDERSIDE Thirsk Road, Easingwold, York YO61 3HJ *Map Ref:* 52
Daphne Tanner Smith *Tel / Fax:* 01347 822132 A19
Email: john.TSmith@tinyonline.co.uk

A comfortable Edwardian family home quietly situated in large gardens, secluded, yet only ten minutes walk from Easingwold market place and within easy reach of York, the Moors and coast. Bedrooms are comfortable and well equipped. An additional room is for accompanying relatives or friends. Traditional English breakfast is served using local produce and home made preserves. Excellent eating places nearby. Private parking.

B & B from £21pp, Rooms 2 double en-suite/private, No smoking, Children over 10, No dogs, Closed Nov to Apr

---

PRIMROSE COTTAGE Lime Bar Lane, Grafton, York YO51 9QJ *Map Ref:* 53
Tony & Tricia Styan *Tel / Fax:* 01423 322835 *Mobile:* 07801 300886 A1, A168
Email: primrosecottage@btinternet.com

A warm welcome awaits in our country cottage in picturesque Grafton. Situated in an acre of garden and paddock between York and Ripon, one mile east of A1. Three comfortable bedrooms with wash basins and tea/coffee facilities and a spacious well furnished television lounge. Excellent food served in 16th century inn only five minutes walk away.

B & B from £20pp, Rooms 1 double, 2 twin, both with private bathroom, Children welcome, Dogs by arrangement, Closed Xmas & New Year

---

www.stayinstyle.com

All homes listed feature on our Website and those that have their own E-mail address or Website address can be accessed direct

Scotland

The regions of Scotland have through the centuries maintained their differences, the Highlanders, largely Gaelic speaking were mobile cattle farmers, while the Lowlanders, English speaking, were firmly planted arable farmers. The Lowlands is the most densely populated region, an area of impressive castles, palaces and medieval burghs. Edinburgh is a stunning city renowned for its castle, which represents the origin of the city where from the battlements the whole city can be seen. Greyfriars historic church stands not far from the castle, with the most famous memorial of a canine, Greyfriars Bobby, who when his owner died in 1858 followed his master to his grave where he then refused to leave for the next 14 years, becoming a popular tourist attraction. Edinburgh is also renowned for its festival in August where people come from all over the world to join in with the fringe. The architecture of the city is displayed at its best in New Town, the most impressive area of Georgian architecture in the whole of Europe. Glasgow has gradually become the second favourite city to visit in the whole of Britain. The cathedral is the central point of the oldest part of the city, founded by St Mungo, patron saint of Scotland and displaying spectacular pre-Reformation Gothic architecture.

The Southern Uplands consist of the wild western hills of Dumfries and Galloway and the Borders, a region that has experienced turmoil and conflict since Roman times and now a glorious place of rolling hills, bracing moors and fine border towns. Ayrshire is a holiday region with two parts, North Ayrshire with its rugged coastlines and South Ayrshire with its rolling pastures and small villages. However, Ayrshire is most known for being the birthplace of Robert Burns in 1759 at Alloway. Thanks to the Burns National Heritage Park visitors to this area are able to almost walk in his very footsteps with many buildings which were associated with him now turned into museums. Nearby is Culzean Castle, the most visited property belonging to the National Trust of Scotland. It was built by Robert Adams in 1777 and houses a stunning oval staircase and circular saloon. Stirling Castle is also a popular place for tourists and has been the site of many infamous battles including at Stirling Bridge where William Wallace beat the English in 1297 and Robert the Bruce who fought at Bannockburn in 1314.

The boundary between the Lowlands and Highlands is emphasised by The Great Glen, a series of interlinked lochs representing a geological fault zone. The lochs of Linnhe, Lochy, Oich and Ness make up the Caledonian Canal of which Loch Ness is the most famous, being the

Head of Loch Shiel, Glenn Finnan (SCTB)

legendary home of the Loch Ness Monster. The loch sinks down to 800 feet and in its murky depths is said to contain many underground caverns where Nessie resides. The first sighting stretches back to 1871, but the legend was at its most popular in the thirties when the loch became the tourist attraction that it is today. The Highlands and Islands present a back cloth of awesome mountains and majestic coastal scenery. The perfect example of this is Fort William, an excellent site for exploring Ben Nevis, the highest mountain in Britain at 4406 feet with its name meaning 'cloudy mountain'.

The Jacobite Rebellions of the 'Fifteens' and the 'Forty-fives' resulted in the loss of the power of the Clan Chiefs and the accompanying highland way of life. One might associate the Scottish islands with remoteness but these days they are easily accessible; the Western Isles are a 130 mile long chain of islands rich in culture. There are long sandy beaches to enjoy in the height of summer and is an area of unspoilt natural beauty with nature reserves and the famous Standing Stones of Calanais. The Shetland Islands, though renowned for unpredictable weather and scenery can offer either a peaceful holiday or an action packed adventure. The wildlife cannot be surpassed with a variety of migratory birds and regular sightings of whales and dolphins. There are several Neolithic sites in the Scottish Isles but the most impressive is that of Skara Brae on the Orkney Islands, the remains of a Stone Age fishing village preserved from 3000BC.

PLACES TO VISIT

This is a small selection of interesting places to visit. Many more are listed in our annual guide to Museums, Galleries, Historic Houses & Sites (see page 448)

Blair Castle
Pitlochry, Perthshire
A picture of Scottish life from the 16th century to date with fine collections of furniture, paintings, arms and armour, china, embroidery and other treasures. Set in extensive parkland.

Bowhill House and Country Park
Bowhill, Selkirk
Internationally renowned art collection, superb French furniture, silver, porcelain and tapestries. Relics of the Duke of Monmouth, Queen Victoria and Sir Walter Scott.

Gallery of Modern Art
Queen Street, Glasgow
The gallery is on four floors each themed on one of the elements - fire, water, earth and air. Collection of predominantly living artists.

Inveraray Castle
Inveraray, Argyll
Home of the Duke and Duchess of Argyll, built in the late 18th century in French chateau-style, the great hall, armoury and staterooms are open to view.

The National Gallery of Scotland
The Mound, Edinburgh
Outstanding collection of paintings, drawings and prints by the greatest artists from the Renaissance to Post-Impressionism shown alongside the National Collection of Scottish Art.

Edinburgh, Glasgow & Southern Scotland

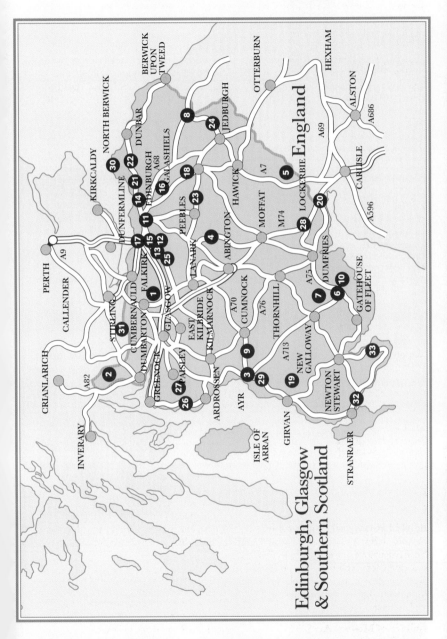

The Red Map References should be used to locate B & B properties on the pages that follow

EASTER GLENTORE FARM Slamannan Road, Greengairs, Airdrie ML6 7TJ   *Map Ref:* 1
Elsie Hunter   *Tel / Fax:* 01236 830243   *Mobile:* 07715 738323   B803
Email: hunter@glentore.freeserve.co.uk   *Web:* www.glentore.freeserve.co.uk

Enjoy warm Scottish hospitality in our 18th century groundfloor farmhouse. Panoramic views, good home cooking, baking and an evening tea tray. Near the unique Falkirk Wheel linking Central Scotland's canals and an ideal base for exploring Glasgow, Falkirk, Stirling and Edinburgh. Member of Scotland's Best Bed and Breakfasts and recommended by Which Good Bed and Breakfast Guide. AA 4 Diamonds, STB 4 Stars.

B & B £21-£25pp, C-Cards MC VS, Rooms 1 double pb, 1 double en-suite, 1 twin en-suite, No smoking, Children over 12, No dogs, Closed Xmas & New Year

---

THE OLD SCHOOL HOUSE Gartocharn, Alexandria G83 8SB   *Map Ref:* 2
Lizzie Armstrong   *Tel / Fax:* 01389 830373   A811
Web: www.the-old-school-house.co.uk

The Old School House provides top class accommodation, spacious and inviting public rooms, fine food and the very warmest of welcomes. Lizzie is proud of her breakfasts, which will get you off to a fine start, and you can round off your day with a delicious dinner served in a warm relaxed atmosphere. The half-acre garden provides panoramic views over farmland towards Loch Lomond.

B & B from £25pp, C-Cards MC VS, Dinner from £18.50, Rooms 2 double, 1 twin, all en-suite, No smoking, Children over 12, Dogs by arrangement, Closed Xmas & New Year

---

BELMONT GUEST HOUSE 15 Park Circus, Ayr KA7 2DJ   *Map Ref:* 3
Andrew Hillhouse   *Tel:* 01292 265588   *Fax:* 01292 290303   A713
Email: belmontguesthouse@btinternet.com   *Web:* www.belmontguesthouse.co.uk

A Scottish town house built in 1877 in a quiet tree-lined conservation area. All bedrooms are equipped with television, radio/alarm, hair dryer and hospitality tray. Guest lounge and car parking. AA 3 Diamonds, STB 2 Stars, Scotland's Best, Welcome Host and current fire certificate held. Member of Ayrshire and Arran Tourist Board.

B & B from £20pp, C-Cards MC VS, Rooms 2 double, 3 family, all en-suite, Children welcome, Dogs by arrangement, Closed Xmas & New Year

---

THE CRESCENT 26 Bellevue Crescent, Ayr KA7 2DR   *Map Ref:* 3
Caroline McDonald   *Tel:* 01292 287329   *Fax:* 01292 286779   *Mobile:* 07808 778690   A77, A719
Email: carrie@26crescent.freeserve.co.uk   *Web:* www.26crescent.freeserve.co.uk

Victorian terrace house situated in the heart of Ayr. Individually styled bedrooms offer the guest every luxury and one room has a four poster bed. Good location for golf, Culzean Castle and Burns Heritage. 50 minutes drive from Glasgow Airport and 10 minutes drive from Prestwick. A warm Scottish welcome awaits you at The Crescent.

B & B from £25pp, C-Cards MC VS, Rooms 4 double, 2 twin, all en-suite, No smoking, Children welcome, No dogs, Closed Jan to Feb

---

DOONBRAE 40 Alloway, Ayr KA7 4PQ   *Map Ref:* 3
Mr & Mrs John Pollok-Morris   *Tel / Fax:* 01292 442511   B7024
Email: doonbrae@aol.com   *Web:* aboutscotland.com

Doonbrae, built in 1810, is situated on the banks of the River Doon in the heart of Burns country. Surrounded by a two acre garden it is close to championship golf courses, Turnberry, Troon and Prestwick. The house has been in the family since 1920 and had much family history. All rooms are freshly decorated and the atmosphere is happy and relaxed.

B & B from £35pp, Rooms 1 double with private facilities, 1 twin en-suite, No smoking, Children over 12, No dogs, Closed Xmas & New Year

DUNDUFF HOUSE Dunure, Ayr KA7 4LH

John & Agnes Gemmell *Tel:* 01292 500225 *Fax:* 01292 500222

Email: gemmelldunduff@aol.com *Web:* www.gemmelldunduff.co.uk

Map Ref: 3
A719

Perfect for relaxing, situated in the coastal village of Dunure, it is ideal for walks, Culzean Castle, Burns Cottage, Turnberry, Galloway Forest, and many more. Accommodation is excellent, bedrooms have panoramic coastal views and all facilities. Breakfast has something for all appetites, our 'Dunduff Grand' will set you up for the day, also our home baked soda bread and locally smoked kippers.

B & B from £20pp, Rooms 1 twin, 2 double, 1 family, all en-suite, No smoking, Children over 10, No dogs, Closed Nov to Feb

---

THE GLENHOLM CENTRE Broughton, Biggar ML12 6JF

Dr Fiona Burnett and Neil Robinson *Tel / Fax:* 01899 830408

Email: glenholm@dircon.co.uk *Web:* www.glenholm.co.uk

Map Ref: 4
A701

Fiona and Neil aim to make your visit to their guesthouse, set in a peaceful glen, as pleasant and relaxing as possible. Set on a 1000 acre upland farm with plenty of walking opportunities, home cooking and comfortable accommodation. Friendly staff create an informal and homelike atmosphere with telephones, televisions and fridges in the bedrooms. A small computer training centre adjoins the guesthouse.

B & B from £25pp, C-Cards MC VS, Dinner from £12.50, Rooms 1 double, 2 twin, 1 family, all en-suite, No smoking, Children & dogs welcome, Closed Jan

---

KIRKLANDS Canonbie DG14 0RA

Archie & Elizabeth Findlay *Tel:* 01387 371769 *Fax:* 01387 371784

Email: irvineho@aol.com *Web:* www.aboutscotland.com/south/kirklands.html

Map Ref: 5
B6357 Just off A7

A charming Georgian House on the banks of the border Esk river, beside the pretty village of Canobie. Spacious, elegant rooms with south facing views. Pleasant riverside and woodland walks. Ideally situated for an over night stop on North/South journeys. Bedrooms with en-suite or private facilities, are light and sunny with extensive views. Dinner available. Good pub food locally. Excellent for exploring Dumfries and Galloway.

B & B £30-£35pp, C-Cards MC VS, Dinner from £20, Rooms 1 double en-suite, 1 single en-suite, 1 double/twin, No smoking, Children over 8, No dogs in the house, Closed Xmas & Easter

---

SMITHY HOUSE The Buchan, Castle Douglas DG7 1TH

Maureen & Bill Carcas *Tel:* 01556 503841

Email: enquiries@smithyhouse.co.uk *Web:* www.smithyhouse.co.uk

Map Ref: 6
A75, B736

Traditional Galloway cottage in lovely gardens overlooking Carlingwark Loch on the outskirts of Castle Douglas with its excellent shops and restaurants. Comfortable bedrooms with full facilities and guest sitting room. Close to Threave Garden and centrally situated to explore the region. Weekly rates available. STB 4 Stars.

B & B £22.50-£27.50pp, C-Cards MC VS, Rooms 2 double en-suite, 1 twin with private bathroom, No smoking, Children over 16, No dogs, Closed Xmas & New Year

---

CHIPPERKYLE Kirkpatrick Durham, Castle Douglas DG7 3EY

Willie & Catriona Dickson *Tel / Fax:* 01556 650223

Email: dickson@chipperkyle.freeserve.co.uk *Web:* www.sawdays.co.uk

Map Ref: 7
B794

Chipperkyle is a beautiful eighteenth century Scottish Georgian house. The bedrooms have a cast-iron bed, elegant linen, excellent furniture and masses of light and good books. There are 200 acres of grazing land, a dog, cat, donkey and free-ranging hens. An enjoyable and sociable place to stay.

B & B from £36pp, Rooms 1 double en-suite, 1 twin private bathroom, Restricted smoking, Children welcome, No dogs, Closed Xmas

RUTHVEN HOUSE Coldstream TD12 4JU
Elizabeth & Francis Gradidge *Tel:* 01890 840771 *Fax:* 01890 840680
Email: gradidge@gradidge.worldonline.co.uk *Web:* www.bordersovernight.co.uk

Map Ref: 8
A1/A698

A fine Victorian residence standing 3 miles north of Coldstream. It is south facing and is set in grounds amidst beautiful countryside with stunning views to the Cheviot Hills. An ideal place to stay as a half way house between the South of England and the North of Scotland. The house offers hospitality to fishing, golfing or shooting parties.

B & B from £29pp, Dinner from £20, Rooms 3 twin, private bathrooms, No smoking in bedrooms, Children welcome, Dogs by arrangement, Open all year

LOW COYLTON HOUSE Manse Road, Coylton KA6 6LE
Anne & George Hay *Tel / Fax:* 01292 570615
Email: xy122@dial.pipex.com

Map Ref: 9
A70

A spacious, comfortable and quiet country house (OldManse 1820) in an attractive garden. Well equipped bedrooms offer television and tea and coffee facilities and a private bathroom. A golfer's paradise, there are several courses nearby, including Ayr, Troon and Turnberry. Six miles away are safe, sandy beaches. Visitors may go hill walking, 15 miles. Culzean Castle (national Trust). Glasgow 35 miles. Edinburgh 70 miles.

B & B from £25pp, Rooms 2 twin, 1 double, all private/en-suite, Well behaved children, Well behaved dogs, Closed Xmas & New Year

AUCHENSKEOCH LODGE Dalbeattie DG5 4PG
Christopher & Mary Broom-Smith *Tel / Fax:* 01387 780277
Email: brmsmth@aol.com *Web:* www.auchenskeochlodge.com

Map Ref: 10
B793

A Victorian shooting lodge of considerable character set in 20 acre grounds. Peaceful rural setting with high quality accommodation in spacious well-equipped en-suite bedrooms. Traditional furnishings throughout with an interesting collection of books and pictures. Billiard room, croquet lawn, fishing on own loch and candlelit dinners, utilising much home grown produce. Licensed.

B & B £28-£33pp, C-Cards MC VS, Dinner from £17.50, Rooms 2 double, 1 twin, all en-suite, Restricted smoking, Children over 12, Dogs not in public rooms, Closed Nov to Easter

AILSA CRAIG HOTEL 24 Royal Terrace, Edinburgh EH7 5AH
Cathie Hamilton *Tel:* 0131 556 6055/1022 *Fax:* 0131 556 6055
Email: ailsacraighotel@ednet.co.uk *Web:* www.townhousehotels.co.uk

Map Ref: 11
A1, A702

Elegant Georgian town house in city centre with tastefully decorated bedrooms, some compact, situated in quiet residential area overlooking landscaped public gardens. Front facing top floor bedrooms have views across Edinburgh to the Firth of Forth and the Fife Coast, but due to the architectural nature of the building there is no lift. Evening meals on request.

B & B from £22.50pp, C-Cards, Dinner available, Rooms 4 single, 4 double, 4 twin, 5 family, most en-suite, Children welcome, No dogs, Open all year

1 ALBERT TERRACE Churchill, Edinburgh EH10 5EA
Clarissa Notley
Tel: 0131 447 4491

Map Ref: 11
A702

An elegant house, with views to the Pentland Hills, standing in a quiet street near to bus routes into the city centre, it is about a 20 minute walk. Bedrooms are en-suite, the attractive double room has an American four poster bed. Guests have the use of a study/television room and a beautiful back garden. Excellent local restaurants, Edinburgh is steeped in history.

B & B £30-£40pp, Rooms 2 double, 1 en-suite, No smoking, Children welcome, No dogs, Closed Xmas

Ellesmere House, Edinburgh

THE AVENUE HOTEL 4 Murrayfield Avenue, Edinburgh EH12 6AX   *Map Ref:* 11
Adrian & Jackie Hayes   A8
Tel: 0131 346 7270   *Fax:* 0131 337 9733

In a quiet tree lined avenue this imposing Victorian villa is situated west of, and minutes from the city centre. It is ideal for the business traveller and the tourist, with easy access to the motorway links to both the north and west of Scotland. Individually designed rooms are en-suite and generously equipped. Ample free parking. Full Scottish breakfast is included.

B & B from £30pp, Rooms 2 single, 2 twin, 3 double, 2 family, all en-suite, Children & dogs welcome, Closed Xmas

---

BEN CRUACHAN 17 McDonald Road, Edinburgh EH7 4LX   *Map Ref:* 11
Nan & Eden Stark   *Tel:* 0131 556 3709   A1
Email: nan@bencruachan.com   *Web:* www.bencruachan.com

A friendly welcome awaits you at Ben Cruachan. The house is centrally located, and offers high standards. Within walking distance of the Castle, the Royal Mile, Holyrood Palace and Princes Street, one of Britain's most picturesque shopping venues. Many varied restaurants within a five minute walk. En-suite rooms are tastefully decorated and thoughtfully equipped. An excellent breakfast is served. There is unrestricted street parking.

B & B from £25pp, Rooms 1 twin, 1 double, 1 family, all en-suite, No smoking, Children over 10, No dogs, Closed Nov to Mar

---

60 BRAID ROAD Edinburgh EH10 6AL   *Map Ref:* 11
Iola & Michael Fass   *Tel:* 0131 446 9356   *Fax:* 0131 447 7367   *Mobile:* 07957 602889   A68
Email: fass@dial.pipex.com

60 Braid Road is a family home where you will receive a warm welcome, lovely quiet rooms with comfortable beds and beautiful bedlinen. Breakfasts are continental or full Scottish with free-range eggs, homemade bread and jam. There is free on-street parking outside and frequent buses from just around the corner to the heart of fascinating Edinburgh.

B & B £26-£30pp, C-Cards MC VS, Rooms 1 double, 2 twin, all with private bathrooms, No smoking, Children welcome, No dogs, Closed Xmas

---

DUNSTANE HOUSE 4 West Coates, Haymarket, Edinburgh EH12 5JQ   *Map Ref:* 11
Shirley & Derek Mowat   *Tel:* 0131 337 6169   *Fax:* 0131 3376169   A68
Email: reservations@dunstanehousehotel.co.uk

Impressive listed Victorian mansion retaining many original features enjoying imposing position within large grounds on the A8 airport road (major bus route). Only 10 minutes walk from the city centre and close to Edinburgh Conference Centre, Murrayfield and Edinburgh Zoo. Private secluded car park. New seafood restaurant/bar and function facilities opening January 2001.

B & B from £33.50pp, Rooms 4 single, 6 double, 2 twin, 4 family, all en-suite, No smoking, Children welcome, No dogs, Open all year

---

ELLESMERE HOUSE 11 Glengyle Terrace, Edinburgh EH3 9LN   *Map Ref:* 11
Celia & Tommy Leishman   *Tel:* 0131 229 4823   *Fax:* 0131 229 5285   A702
Email: celia@edinburghbandb.co.uk   *Web:* www.edinburghbandb.co.uk   *see Photo on page 371*

A city centre, Victorian town house facing south over park. Castle, Royal Mile and Princes Street are all within walking distance. Also close to International conference centre, theatres, restaurants and pubs. All rooms are en-suite and well equipped with everything for your comfort in mind. 'Your home away from Home'

B & B £28-£38pp, Rooms 1 single, 2 twin, 2 double, 1 family, all en-suite, Children over 10, Dogs welcome, Open all year

GREENSIDE HOTEL 9 Royal Terrace, Edinburgh EH7 5AB *Map Ref:* 11
Alan Maguire *Tel / Fax:* 0131 5570022 A1
Email: greensidehotel@ednet.co.uk *Web:* www.townhousehotels.co.uk

Personally run hotel in traditional Georgian terraced house. Quiet location, close to Prices Street, Waverley train station, Edinburgh Castle and The Playhouse Theatre combining traditional features with modern facilities, the hotel offers superb views, private gardens and friendly atmosphere together providing the perfect blend of history and hospitality.

B & B from £22.50pp, C-Cards MC VS AE DC, Dinner from £9.50, Rooms 3 single, 3 double, 2 twin, 8 family, all en-suite, Children welcome, No dogs, Open all year

---

27 HERIOT ROW Edinburgh EH3 6EN *Map Ref:* 11
Andrea & Gene Targett Adams *Tel:* 0131 225 9474 *Fax:* 0131 220 1699 Heriot Row
Email: t.a@blueyonder.co.uk

Built in 1804 in Edinburgh's premier residential street and only three streets away from Princes Street and the world famous Edinburgh Castle, your stay here will be luxurious also quiet and relaxing. Rooms are furnished to the highest deluxe standard and are generously equipped. Your hosts will be delighted to help plan your sightseeing. French, German and Spanish are spoken.

B & B from £45pp, Rooms 1 single, 1 twin, 1 double, all en-suite, No smoking, Children welcome, No dogs, Open all year

---

HOPETOUN 15 Mayfield Road, Edinburgh EH9 2NG *Map Ref:* 11
Rhoda Mitchell *Tel:* 0131 667 7691 *Fax:* 0131 466 1691 City by-pass
Email: hopetoun@aol.com *Web:* http://members.aol.com/hopetoun

A small, friendly, family-run guest house close to Edinburgh University, 1 1/2 miles from Princes Street, with an excellent route into the city. It offers very comfortable accommodation in a smoke-free environment. Bedrooms with private facilities, central heating, wash basins, colour TV and tea/coffee facilities. Parking. Which? Books - Good B&B Guide. 3 Stars.

B & B £20-£30pp, C-Cards MC VS, Rooms 1 twin, 1 double, 1 family, 2 en-suite, No smoking, Children welcome, No dogs, Closed Xmas

---

INTERNATIONAL GUEST HOUSE 37 Mayfield Gardens, Edinburgh EH9 2BX *Map Ref:* 11
Mrs Niven *Tel:* 0131 6672511 *Fax:* 0131 667 1112 A701
Email: intergh@easynet.co.uk *Web:* www.accommodation-edinburgh.com

Attractive Victorian house south of Princes Street on the A701. Parking. Luxury well equipped bedrooms. Magnificent views across the extinct volcano of Arthur's seat. Scottish breakfast served. International has received many accolades for its quality. A 19th century setting with 21st century facilities. ' In Britain' magazine rated the International as their 'find' in all Edinburgh. Ground floor room for guests with limited disability.

B & B £20-£45pp, C-Cards MC VS, Rooms 3 single, 2 double, 1 twin, 3 family, all en-suite, Restricted smoking, Children welcome, No dogs, Open all year

---

INVERMARK 60 Polwarth Terrace, Edinburgh EH11 1NJ *Map Ref:* 11
Mrs H Donaldson A68
Tel: 0131 337 1066

A semi-detached Victorian villa with private parking in quiet suburbs on the main bus route into city with easy access from bypass. Bedrooms have television and tea/coffee making facilities and a friendly welcome is assured. A canal walk and park behind house local hotels provide evening meals.

B & B from £20pp, Rooms 1 single, 1 twin, 1 family, No smoking, Children & dogs welcome, Closed Dec & Jan, open New Year

THE LODGE HOTEL 6 Hampton Terrace, West Coates, Edinburgh EH12 5JD   *Map Ref:* 11
George & Linda Jarron *Tel:* 0131 3373682 *Fax:* 0131 3131700   A8
Email: thelodgehotel@btconnect.com *Web:* www.thelodgehotel.co.uk

An elegant family run hotel situated 1 mile from the city centre and the major attractions. Rooms are beautifully furnished throughout, each with personal touches for guests' comfort. Relax in the cocktail bar or lounge after a day exploring Scotlands' capital. Our menu offers well prepared dishes with a good selection of wines. Car parking available. A good bus service from outside the hotel.

B & B £30-£45pp, C-Cards MC VS AE, Dinner from £16.50, Rooms 1 single, 2 twin, 6 double, all en-suite, Restricted smoking, Children welcome, Guide dogs only, Closed most of Dec

22 MURRAYFIELD GARDENS Edinburgh EH12 6DF   *Map Ref:* 11
Tim & Christine MacDowel *Tel:* 0131 3373569 *Fax:* 0131 3373803   A8
Email: mac@number22.co.uk *Web:* www.number22.co.uk

Safe in a leafy suburb, less than 10 minutes due west of the city centre, the house stands in its own grounds surrounded by ornamental trees and shrubs. Accommodation is provided on first floor level where rooms are grandly comfortable with wonderful beds and glorious views to the Pentland Hills. Private parking is available in the drive or on the unrestricted road.

B & B from £40pp, C-Cards MC VS, Rooms 2 double, 1 twin, all en-suite or private facilities, No smoking, Children & dogs welcome, Open all year

NEWINGTON COTTAGE DELUXE GUEST HOUSE 15 Blacket Place, Edinburgh EH9 1RJ
Frank & Freda Mickel *Tel:* 0131 668 1935 *Fax:* 0131 667 4644 *Mobile:* 07968 783241 *Map Ref:* 11
Email: mickel@newcot.demon.co.uk *Web:* www.newcot.demon.co.uk   A7, A701

A historic Regency cottage tastefully furnished, awarded both AA 5 Diamonds and STB 5 Stars, offering superior bed and breakfast in a quiet, leafy conservation area in the 'Heart of Edinburgh'. Ideally situated for visits to the University, theatres and all the main tourist attractions. We provide all the little extras, quality and comfort you would expect from the 'best'.

B & B £40-£55pp, C-Cards MC VS, Rooms 2 double, 1 twin, all en-suite, No smoking, No children or dogs, Closed Xmas

ROWAN GUEST HOUSE 13 Glenorchy Terrace, Edinburgh EH9 2DQ   *Map Ref:* 11
Alan & Angela Vidler *Tel / Fax:* 0131 667 2463   A7, A701
Email: angela@rowan-house.co.uk *Web:* www.rowan-house.co.uk

An elegant 19th century Victorian home in a quiet, conservation area. It has free parking, only a ten minute bus ride to the centre. The castle, Royal Mile, Holyrood Palace, University, Theatres, restaurants and other amenities are easily reached. Bedrooms are charmingly decorated and have television, tea/coffee and biscuits. A hearty Scottish breakfast is served including porridge and freshly baked scones.

B & B £23-£35pp, Rooms 3 single, 2 twin, 3 double, 1 family, some en-suite, Restricted smoking, Children welcome, Dogs by arrangement, Closed Xmas

www.stayinstyle.com

All homes listed feature on our Website and those that have their own E-mail address or Website address can be accessed direct

ST VALERY GUEST HOUSE 36 Coates Gardens, Haymarket, Edinburgh EH12 5LE   *Map Ref:* 11
George & Sheila Gardner   *Tel:* 0131 337 1893   *Fax:* 0131 346 8529   A68
Email: thestvalery@cs.com   *Web:* www.stvalery.com

A traditionally pleasant, family run business, newly refurbished and
situated one mile from the famous Royal Mile and half a mile from
Princes Street (station 100 yards). A full cooked Scottish breakfast is
served every morning and all rooms are en-suite with heating, 60
channel satellite televisions, direct dial telephones and tea/coffee
facilities.

B & B £22.50-£38pp, C-Cards MC VS AE, Dinner from £5, Rooms
5 single, 2 twin, 7 double, 5 family, all en-suite, Restricted
smoking, Children welcome, Dogs by arrangement, Open all year

SPYLAW BANK HOUSE 2 Spylaw Avenue, Colinton, Edinburgh EH13 0LR   *Map Ref:* 11
David & Angela Martin   *Tel:* 0131 441 5022   A70
Email: angela@spylawbank.freeserve.co.uk   *Web:* www.spylawbank.freeserve.co.uk

Spylaw Bank House is an elegant Georgian house in secluded
grounds situated within the city. Luxurious en-suite bedrooms with
period furnishings and modern bathrooms. Original drawing and
dining rooms. Ideal for Edinburgh sightseeing and touring Scotland.
Close to the motorway, the airport, and fifteen minutes by bus to an
historic centre. Local restaurants and pubs nearby. Ample parking.

B & B £25-£35pp, C-Cards MC VS, Rooms 1 twin, 2 double, all
en-suite, No smoking, Children welcome, No dogs, Closed Xmas

THE STUARTS 17 Glengyle Terrace, Edinburgh EH3 9LN   *Map Ref:* 11
Jon & Gloria Stuart   *Tel:* 0131 229 9559   *Fax:* 0131 229 2226   A702
Email: tomorrow@the-stuarts.com   *Web:* www.the-stuarts.com

5 Star accommodation in quiet location in City Centre. Easy walking
distance to world heritage site of Castle and Old Town. Also
University, Conference Centre, theatres, concert halls, restaurants
and shops nearby. 25 years of talking with our guests enabled us to
incorporate all requested facilities. Significant off season discounts
allow comfortable voyages of discovery in and around Edinburgh.

B & B from £52.50pp, C-Cards MC VS AE, Rooms 3 double/twin
en-suite, No smoking, Children welcome, No dogs, Closed Xmas

THE TOWN HOUSE 65 Gilmore Place, Edinburgh EH3 9NU   *Map Ref:* 11
Susan Virtue   *Tel:* 0131 2291985   A702, A1
Email: susan@thetownhouse.com   *Web:* www.thetownhouse.com

An attractive, Victorian house, located in the city centre. Theatres
and restaurants are a few minutes walk away. The Town House has
been fully restored and tastefully decorated, retaining original
architectural features. En-suite bedrooms are tastefully furnished
generously equipped and individually decorated. As well as a full
Scottish breakfast, there is porridge, kippers and smoked salmon
fishcakes. Parking to the rear.

B & B £28-£38pp, Rooms 1 single, 1 twin, 3 double, all en-suite,
No smoking, Children over 10, No dogs, Closed Xmas

TUDORBANK LODGE 18 St John's Road, Corstorphine, Edinburgh EH12 6NY   *Map Ref:* 11
William & Eleanor Clark   *Tel:* 0131 334 7845   *Fax:* 0131 334 5386   A8
Email: tudorbank@yahoo.co.uk   *Web:* www.tudorbanklodge.co.uk

Tudorbank Lodge is set in private gardens, it is well placed for many
local attractions in Edinburgh. A Tudor style house it is listed as an
historic building. The Edinburgh festival, fringe and tattoo are within
easy reach. It is near to Murrayfield which is home to Scottish rugby.
Breakfasts are a feature, and vegetarians are well catered for. Plenty
of parking.

B & B from £25pp, C-Cards MC VS, Rooms 1 single, 2 twin,
2 double, 2 family, some en-suite, Children welcome, No dogs,
Open all year

NEWMILLS COTTAGE 472 Lanark Road West, Balerno, Edinburgh EH14 5AE   *Map Ref:* 12
Mrs Elizabeth Linn   *Tel / Fax:* 0131 449 4300   M8, A70, A71
Email: newmillscottage@blueyonder.co.uk   *Web:* www.newmillscottage.co.uk

Delightful house in grounds with private parking. A member of 'Scotland's Best Bed and Breakfasts' offers charming accommodation in peaceful surroundings close to the city, airport, and Heriot Watt University. Three extremely spacious bedrooms available with their own sitting area, television, hairdryer and tea/coffee facilities. Perfect base for exploring Edinburgh and beyond. Excellent bus service to City Centre.

B & B £25-£35pp, C-Cards MC VS, Rooms 3 twin, all en-suite, No smoking, Children over 12, No dogs, Open all year

---

ASHCROFT FARMHOUSE East Calder, Livingston, Edinburgh EH53 0ET   *Map Ref:* 13
Derek & Elizabeth Scott   *Tel:* 01506 881810   *Fax:* 01506 884327   *Mobile:* 07788 926239   A71
Email: ashcroft30538@aol.com   *Web:* www.ashcroftfarmhouse.com

Ashcroft is a modern, tastefully decorated farmhouse with co-ordinating fabrics complementing the smart pine furnishings. The house has a golfing theme with the bedrooms named after Scottish Championship golf courses and our spacious dining room has a fine collection of golf memorabilia. Our beautifully landscaped and spacious garden is available for picnics and alfresco dining, or for simply relaxing in peace and quiet.

B & B from £30pp, C-Cards MC VS, Rooms 1 double, 3 twin, 2 family, all en-suite, No smoking, Children over 5, No dogs, Open all year

---

DELTA HOUSE 16 Carberry Road, Inveresk, Musselburgh, Edinburgh EH21 7TN   *Map Ref:* 14
Judith & Harper Cuthbert   *Tel:* 0131 665 2107   *Fax:* 0131 665 2175   *Mobile:* 07809 044774   A1, A720
Email: Karmarcla@aol.com

Victorian house situated in a conservation village seven miles east of Edinburgh. Overlooking fields and close to river walks and the seaside with a harbour. Buses from door to city, near the sports centre with swimming pool, close to golf courses. Spacious accommodation with central heating. Two large bathrooms adjacent. Full breakfast included. Parking in a quiet side road or within the walled garden.

B & B £18-£25pp, Rooms 3 double, 1 family, 2 en-suite, No smoking, Children over 7, No dogs, Closed Xmas & New Year

---

CRAIGBRAE Kirkliston, Edinburgh EH29 9EL   *Map Ref:* 15
Michael & Louise Westmacott   *Tel:* 0131 331 1205   *Fax:* 0131 319 1476   A90
Email: westmacott@compuserve.com   *Web:* www.aboutscotland.com/central/craigbrae

In beautiful countryside near Dalmeny village, an 18th century stone house, family run bed and breakfast. Bedrooms are well presented, pretty and comfortable, each has a basin. The dining room with country views displays family paintings, it enjoys country views. There is a log fire in the drawing room, and satellite TV to enjoy. Craigbrae is well located for touring and golfing.

B & B £25-£30pp, C-Cards MC VS, Rooms 1 double, 2 double/twin, No smoking, Children welcome, No dogs in house, Closed Xmas

---

RATHO HALL 51 Baird Road, Ratho, Edinburgh EH28 8QY   *Map Ref:* 15
Janet & Freddie Small   *Tel:* 0131 335 3333   *Fax:* 0131 335 3035   M8, M9, A8
Email: ratho.hall@btinternet.com   *Web:* www.countrymansions.com

Ratho Hall is a beautiful classical Georgian mansion house built in 1798 set in 22 acres of gardens and paddocks. The house has many fine period features in generously proportioned rooms. The gardens include a tennis court and croquet lawn. Ratho Hall is 20 minutes from the centre of Edinburgh and five minutes from the Airport.

B & B £45-£50pp, C-Cards MC VS, Dinner from £20, Rooms 1 double ensuite, 2 twin/Kingsize, 1 pb, 1 en-suite, No smoking, Children welcome, Dogs by arrangement, Closed Xmas

CARLETHAN HOUSE Wadingburn Lane, Lasswade, Edinburgh EH18 1HG
Margaret Dunlop *Tel:* 0131 663 7047 *Fax:* 0131 654 2657
Email: carlethan@aol.com *Web:* www.carlethan-house.co.uk

Map Ref: 16
A7

Listed Georgian home recently extensively refurbished. Set in an
acre of mature landscaped garden with water feature. Six miles from
Edinburgh City Centre, one mile from city bypass and 20 minutes
from airport and train station. All bedrooms have televisions and
tea/coffee facilities, also a guest sitting room. Off street parking and
good local restaurant half a mile away.

B & B from £23pp, C-Cards MC VS, Rooms 1 double, 1 twin,
1 family, all en-suite, Restricted smoking, Children welcome, Dogs
by arrangement, Closed Nov

PRIORY LODGE 8 The Loan, South Queensferry, Edinburgh EH30 9NS
Calmyn Lamb *Tel / Fax:* 0131 331 4345 *Mobile:* 07885 083478
Email: calmyn@aol.com *Web:* www.queensferry.com

Map Ref: 17
A90

Priory Lodge is a four star guest house situated in the beautiful and
historic town of Queensferry which has good restaurants and ale
houses, plus excellent visitor attractions on the doorstep. Edinburgh
is only 12 minutes by train or 20 by bus and both services run
efficiently. Edinburgh Airport and main motorways are only 10
minutes from this wonderful central location.

B & B £27-£30pp, C-Cards MC VS, Rooms 1 double, 1 twin,
3 family, all en-suite, No smoking, Children welcome, No dogs,
Closed Xmas

OVER LANGSHAW Langshaw, Galashiels TD1 2PE
Sheila Bergius *Tel / Fax:* 01896 860244
Email: bergius@overlangshaw.fs.net.co.uk

Map Ref: 18
A7, A68

Enjoy the charm of our farmhouse in this beautiful area. Cows and
sheep are the mainstay of the farm. Log fires and hearty breakfasts
to sustain. Melrose is delightful, Edinburgh a must. Find Traquair or
walk the 'Southern Upland Way'. From A7 1 mile north of Galashiels
take Langshaw road, follow the signs. Over Langshaw is the white
house on the hill. Two pretty, comfortable bedrooms.

B & B from £22pp, Rooms 1 double, 1 family, both en-suite, No
smoking, Children welcome, Dogs by arrangement, Open all year

---

GLENGENNET FARM Barr, Girvan KA26 9TY
Mrs V Dunlop *Tel / Fax:* 01465 861220
Email: vsd@glengennet.fsnet.co.uk

Map Ref: 19
B734

A Victorian shooting lodge on hill farm with lovely views over Stinchar
Valley and neighbouring Galloway Forest Park. All bedrooms are en-
suite with tea trays, television in guests' lounge. The farm is near a
conservation village with hotel for evening meals. A good peaceful
base for Glentrool Culzean Castle and Country Park, Burns country
and Ayrshire coast. STB 4 Stars.

B & B £21-£25pp, Rooms 1 double, 1 twin, both en-suite,
No smoking, Children welcome, No dogs, Closed Nov to Mar

RAEBURNHEAD Kirkpatrick Fleming, Gretna Green DG11 3BA
Mrs R M Lane *Tel / Fax:* 01461 800201 *Mobile:* 07719 505967
Web: www.b&bscotland.co.uk.dumfrieshtm/raeburnhead

Map Ref: 20
A74(M)

A lovely period country house in a quiet location, very accessible to
the A74. Large tasteful rooms with beautiful views and good
Scottish/English food. Perfect base for the Solway Coast, Lake
District, Scottish Borders and Edinburgh. Raeburnhead, built in
1891, stands amidst its own farmland and is also home to the
Rosslayne stud of show ponies. STB 4 Stars.

B & B from £25.50pp, Dinner from £15, Rooms 3 double, 1 twin,
all en-suite, No smoking, No children, Dogs by arrangement, Open
all year

Innerleithan Hotel: 01896 830229 - Traquair Arms Hotel

FAUSSETTHILL HOUSE 20 Main Street, Gullane EH31 2DR
George & Dorothy Nisbet
Tel / Fax: 01620 842396

Map Ref: 21
A1, A198

George and Dorothy Nisbet welcome you to their delightful home which stands in well tended gardens in the picturesque village of Gullane. Immaculately maintained, the house is both comfortable and inviting with the bedrooms attractively decorated. Gullane has a beautiful beach and is only 30 minutes by car to Edinburgh. There are 19 golf courses in the area including Muirfeild.

B & B £26-£30pp, C-Cards MC VS, Rooms 1 double, 2 twin, all en-suite, No smoking, Children over 12, No dogs, Closed Nov to Mar

ABBEY MAINS Haddington EH41 3SB
David & Joyce Playfair
Tel: 01620 823286   *Fax:* 01620 826348

Map Ref: 22
A1

Abbey Mains is situated in the beautiful farmland of East Lothian and has superb views of the Lammermuir Hills. It is two miles from the historic town of Haddington and 35 minutes from Edinburgh. East Lothian has excellent golf courses and other attractions include a bird sanctuary, the Scottish Seabird Centre, the Museum of Flight and Glenkinchie, the only Lowland distillery.

B & B from £40pp, Rooms 2 double, 1 twin, all en-suite, No smoking, Children welcome, Dogs by arrangement, Open all year

TRAQUAIR HOUSE Innerleithen EH44 6PW
Catherine Maxwell Stuart   *Tel:* 01896 830323   *Fax:* 01896 830639
Email: enquiries@traquair.co.uk   *Web:* www.traquair.co.uk

Map Ref: 23
A72

Visited by 27 kings, the oldest inhabited house in Scotland. A chapel, an old laundry, spacious en-suite bedrooms, furnished with antiques. Guests are invited to a tour of the house. They are welcome to relax in the lower drawing room. A maze is seven feet high and a quarter of a mile long! Dinner is available, there is a good local hotel in Innerleithen.

B & B from £75pp, C-Cards MC VS, Dinner from £35, Rooms 2 double, both en-suite, No smoking in bedrooms, Children welcome, Dogs by arrangement, Closed Xmas & New Year

WHITEHILL FARM Nenthorn, Kelso TD5 7RZ
Betty Smith   *Tel / Fax:* 01573 470203
Email: besmith@whitehillfarm.freeserve.co.uk   *Web:* www.whitehillfarm.freeserve.co.uk

Map Ref: 24
A6089

A Victorian farmhouse on a mixed farm in a wonderful location with marvellous views of the Cheviot Hills, carefully renovated to provide a comfortable atmosphere in which to relax. A sitting room is available to guests with a log fire. Abbeys, historic houses, golf, walking, fishing and the coast within easy reach. Edinburgh is one hour away. Four pretty bedrooms.

B & B from £22pp, Dinner from £14, Rooms 2 single, 2 twin, 1 en-suite, Restricted smoking, Children & dogs welcome, Closed Xmas & New Year

HIGHFIELD HOUSE Kirknewton EH27 8DD
Jill & Hugh Hunter Gordon   *Tel:* 01506 881489   *Fax:* 01506 885384
Email: HHunterGordon@compuserve.com   *Web:* highfield-h.co.uk

Map Ref: 25
A71

Dating from the 1600s, the house is a former Scottish Manse furnished in traditional style and set in lovely gardens with room for parking. The en-suite bedrooms are spacious and well appointed. A full Scittish breakfast is served around a large table in an elegant dining room. Ideally placed for visiting Edinburgh, the train station is only 5 minutes away.

B & B £25-£30pp, C-Cards MC VS, Rooms 3 double/twin, all en-suite or private bathroom, No smoking, Children welcome, No dogs, Closed Xmas & New Year

SOUTH WHITTLIEBURN FARM Brisbane Glen, Largs KA30 8SN
Mary Watson *Tel:* 01475 675881 *Fax:* 01475 675080
Email: largsbandb@southwhittlieburnfarm.freeserve.co.uk   www.smoothhound.co.uk/hotels.whittlie.html

Map Ref: 26
A78

Enjoy a great holiday at South Whittlieburn Farm and a warm
welcome from Mary Watson. Friendly hospitality with enormous
delicious breakfasts and lovely peaceful views on our working sheep
farm. Only five minutes drive from the popular tourist resort of Largs
with ferries to the islands and just 40 minutes to Glasgow Airport.

B & B £20.50-£25.50pp, Rooms 1 double, 1 twin, 1 family, all
en-suite, Restricted smoking, Children welcome, No dogs,

EAST LOCHHEAD Largs Road, Lochwinnoch PA12 4DX
Janet Anderson *Tel / Fax:* 01505 842610
Email: eastlochhead@aol.com *Web:* www.eastlochhead.co.uk

Map Ref: 27
A760

You will receive a warmth and every comfort at East Lochhead. The
100 year old farmhouse has spectacular views over Barr Loch and
the Renfrewshire hills. Wander around the landscaped gardens,
explore the Paisley/Irvine cycle track which passes close to the
house. An enthusiastic cook Janet would be delighted to prepare
you dinner with prior notice. Both rooms are beautifully furnished
and equipped.

B & B from £32pp, C-Cards MC VS AE, Dinner from £18, Rooms
2 double, 1 twin, all en-suite, Restricted smoking, Children
welcome, Dogs by arrangement, Open all year

KNOCKHILL Hoddom, Lockerbie DG11 1AW
Rupert & Yda Morgan *Tel:* 01576 300232 *Fax:* 01576 300818
Email: morganbellows@yahoo.co.uk

Map Ref: 28
M74

A pretty Georgian house that lives up to the motto over the front
door, 'too small for envy, for contempt too great.' Knockhill has a
friendly though gracious ambience. The food is excellent and there
are a variety of restaurants within five miles. Plenty of golf nearby.
This is a perfect stop off en-route to the Highlands.

B & B £25-£30pp, C-Cards MC VS, Dinner from £18, Rooms
2 twin, both with private facilities, Restricted smoking, Children
welcome, Dogs by arrangement, Closed Xmas & New Year

THE EISENHOWER APARTMENT Culzean Castle, Maybole KA19 8LE
Jonathan & Susan Cardale *Tel:* 01655 884455 *Fax:* 01655 884503
Email: culzean@nts.org.uk *Web:* www.culzeancastle.net

Map Ref: 29
A719

Culzean Castle, Robert Adam's final masterpiece, perched on a cliff
with superb views to Arran and Kintyre, offers something special.
The Eisenhower Apartment in the top floor of the castle was given to
Eisenhower in 1945 from Scotland. It offers self-contained country
house accommodation in six bedrooms, a charming round sitting
room and the best of Scottish food in an elegant little dining room.

B & B from £100pp, C-Cards MC VS AE, Dinner inc wine £45,
Rooms 4 twin, 2 double, all en-suite, No smoking, Children over
10, No dogs, Closed Nov to Mar

THE GLEBE HOUSE Law Road, North Berwick EH39 4PL
Jake & Gwen Scott *Tel / Fax:* 01620 892608
Email: J.A.Scott@tesco.net *Web:* www.aboutscotland.com/glebe/house

Map Ref: 30
A1, A198

The Glebe House is a listed Manse built in 1780, situated in secluded
grounds yet in centre of North Berwick. Edinburgh half an hour drive,
or regular train service. Edinburgh airport 40 minutes away. Beach a
two minute walk as is High Street with shops and restaurants. Gwen
keeps sample menus and will happily book you a table. Haven for
golfers - several courses within 20 minutes drive.

B & B £30-£40pp, Rooms 2 double, 1 twin, all en-suite, Restricted
smoking, Children welcome, Dogs not in house, Closed Xmas &
New Year

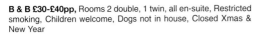

KAIMEND Hamilton Road, North Berwick EH39 4NA
Charlotte & Nigel Souter *Tel / Fax:* 01620 893557
Email: souter@kaimend.freeserve.co.uk

Map Ref: 30
A198

Kaimend is spacious and bright with stunning views over golf course, beach and sea. 13 golf courses within 20 minutes including Gullane and Muirfield with Edinburgh only 30 minutes by train and car, airport 40 minutes. Wonderful beaches, castles and museums nearby, also good restaurants and pubs. Souters enjoy spoiling guests, two twin rooms and two singles with lovely food too.

B & B from £45pp, Rooms 2 single, 2 twin, all with private bathrooms, Restricted smoking, No children, Dogs by arrangement, Closed Dec to Feb

THE STUDIO Grange Road, North Berwick EH39 4QT
Mrs M Ramsay *Tel:* 01620 895150 *Fax:* 01620 895120
Email: johnvramsay@compuserve.com *Web:* www.b-and-b-scotland.co.uk/studio.htm

Map Ref: 30
A198

Refurbished and extended historic building, tastefully decorated and furnished, situated within a walled garden. Guests enjoy a high degree of privacy in rural surroundings yet convenient for town and railway station. All rooms have private patios with garden furniture. Parking. Regret no smoking.

B & B £25-£30pp, Rooms 2 double, 1 twin, all en-suite, No smoking, No children or dogs, Open all year

CULCREUCH CASTLE & COUNTRY PARK Fintry, Stirling G63 0LW
Laird Andrew Haslam *Tel:* 01360 860555 *Fax:* 01360 860556
Email: reservations@culcreuch.com *Web:* www.culcreuch.com

Map Ref: 31
B822

The ancient castle of Galbraith dates back to 1296 and today, over 700 years later, it has survived intact and in remarkable condition. The castle has thirteen individually decorated and furnished bedrooms (some four poster). All have en-suite facilities, colour television, direct dial telephone and hot drinks facilities. Furthur accommodation is available in our eight self-catering lodges.

B & B £40-£70pp, C-Cards MC VS AE, Dinner from £25, Rooms 7 double, 2 double/twin, 4 family all en-suite, Restricted smoking, Children welcome, Dogs by arrangement, Closed Jan 4 to Jan 16

CHLENRY FARMHOUSE Castle Kennedy, Stranraer DG9 8SL
Ginny Wolseley Brinton *Tel:* 01776 705316 *Fax:* 01776 889488 *Mobile:* 07718 049910
Email: WolseleyBrinton@aol.com

Map Ref: 32
A75, A77

'Another gem for my collection', wrote a delighted guest. This comfortable old farmhouse offers peace and tranquility in its own private glen with superb walks, golf and gardens to visit. Delicious home cooked dinners are available by request. It is graciously furnished: comfortable bedrooms with fresh fruit and flowers, spacious, well equipped bathrooms and a sitting room with television and open fire.

B & B from £27.50pp, Dinner from £23.50, Rooms 1 double, 1 twin, both with private bathroom, Restricted smoking, Children welcome, Dogs in car or kennel, Closed Xmas & New Year

CRAIGMOUNT GUEST HOUSE High Street, Wigtown DG8 9EQ
David & Pat Taylor *Tel:* 01988 402291
Email: taylorpat1@talk21.com

Map Ref: 33
A714

A former manse, a listed building with a guests lounge with television, alcohol license and tea/coffee facilities. Ample car parking and easy access to ferries for Northern Ireland from Stranraer. Walking in the Galloway Hills, wild fowling, sea and river fishing, many golf course and beaches nearby.

B & B from £20pp, Rooms 1 single, 1 double, 1 twin, 2 family, most en-suite, Restricted smoking, Children & dogs welcome, Closed part of Oct

Central, East & Northeast Scotland

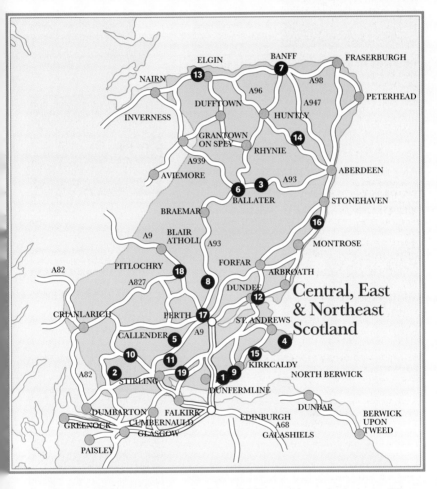

FORTH VIEW HOTEL Hawkcraig Point, Aberdour KY3 0TZ   *Map Ref:* 1
Pauleen Norman *Tel:* 01383 860402 *Fax:* 01383 860262   A921
Email: forthviewhotel@btinternet.com

Located on Hawkcraig Point, this small secluded hotel on the seashore with a high standard of comfortable accommodation commands impressive views across the Forth to Edinburgh. Numerous leisure facilities include award winning Silver Sands Beach and 18 Hole Golf Course; with Edinburgh and St Andrews accessible from Aberdour Station.

B & B from £19pp, Rooms 1 single, 1 double, 2 twin, 1 family, most en-suite, Restricted smoking, Children welcome, Dogs by arrangement, Closed Nov to Apr

THE BARNS OF SHANNOCHILL by Aberfoyle FK8 3UZ   *Map Ref:* 2
Val & George Willis *Tel:* 01877 382878 *Fax:* 01877 382964 *Mobile:* 07774 823232   A81
Email: shannochill@aol.com *Web:* thebarnsofshannochill.co.uk

A tranquil haven set amidst spectacular countryside. An ideal base for central Scotland, with lochs, mountains and history all on the doorstep. Self-contained guest wing sleeps four with own sitting area and full panoramic views of Lake of Menteith. Large selection of aga made breakfasts with homemade jams. Dinner made to requirements and a kitchen is also available for self catering use.

B & B from £30pp, C-Cards MC VS, Dinner from £15, Rooms 2 double/twin, 1 family, all en-suite, No smoking, Children welcome, Dogs by arrangement, Open all year

MIGVIE HOUSE by Logie Coldstone, Aboyne AB34 4XL   *Map Ref:* 3
Carole & Bruce Luffman *Tel:* 013398 81313 *Fax:* 013398 81635   A97
Email: migviehouse@yahoo.co.uk *Web:* www.b-and-b-scotland.co.uk/migvie.htm

Off the beaten track in Royal Deeside, Migvie House provides a refuge of comfort and tranquility within our enchanting farmhouse. Lovingly restored with antiques, country furnishings and wood fires. An idyllic setting with glorious mountain views amidst a small highland estate. Meals are taken around the huge old pine table with our own eggs, homemade bread and spring water.

B & B from £25pp, C-Cards MC VS, Rooms 1 double, 2 twin, all en-suite, No smoking, Children over 14, Dogs by arrangement, Closed Nov to Mar

BEAUMONT LODGE GUEST HOUSE 43 Pittenweem Road, Anstruther KY10 3DT   *Map Ref:* 4
Julia Anderson *Tel / Fax:* 01333 310315   A917
Email: reservations@beau-lodge.demon.co.uk *Web:* www.beaumontlodge.co.uk

Beaumont Lodge Guest House is an immaculately maintained home, situated just a two minute walk from the shoreline and Anstruther's golf course, Saint Andrews is nine miles away. This family run guest house offers affordable excellence, guests receive warm hospitality. The en-suite rooms are spacious, tastefully decorated and have thoughtful extras. Your host is a keen and accomplished cook. Private parking.

B & B from £25pp, C-Cards MC VS, Dinner from £15, Rooms 2 twin, 2 double, all en-suite, No smoking, Children over 4, No dogs, Open all year

THE SPINDRIFT Pittenweem Road, Anstruther KY10 3DT   *Map Ref:* 4
Ken & Christine Lawson *Tel / Fax:* 01333 310573   A917
Email: info@thespindrift.co.uk *Web:* www.thespindrift.co.uk

The Spindrift is an imposing, stone-built victorian home. Many original internal features have been carefully restored. Elegantly furnished public rooms. The bedrooms are generously proportioned, individually and tastefully furnished with en-suite bathroom, colour television and direct dial telephone. The cuisine is freshly prepared using the best local produce. The area boasts a wide variety of activities, including golf, boat trips and surfing.

B & B £26.50-£31pp, C-Cards MC VS, Dinner from £13.50, Rooms 4 double, 4 twin, all en-suite, No smoking, Children over 9, Dogs by arrangement, Closed Xmas

DUNEARN HOUSE High Street, Auchterarder PH3 1DB
June & Gerrard Elrick *Tel:* 01764 664774 *Fax:* 01764 663242
Email: dunearnhouse@talk21.co.uk

Map Ref: 5
A9

'The Perthshire Experience' a Victorian country house hotel. Quiet, sympathetically restored throughout, with spectacular views. Gleneagles and many other stunning golf courses on the doorstep. En-suite well equipped rooms with TV. Fully licensed with restaurant, cosy lounge and bar. We are well used to caring for your needs and we are able to provide a relaxing environment for you to unwind in.

B & B from £35pp, C-Cards MC VS, Dinner from £7, Rooms 2 single, 1 twin, 3 double, 1 family, all en-suite, No smoking in bedrooms, Children welcome, No dogs, Open all year

---

THE BELVEDERE Station Square, Ballater AB35 5QB
Bill & Flora Ingram *Tel:* 013397 55996 *Fax:* 013397 55110
Email: flora-ingram@freeuk.com

Map Ref: 6
A93

A Victorian town house situated in the heart of Royal Deeside. Perfect base for touring the whisky and castle trails. Two minutes walk to award winning restaurants. All bedrooms have television, tea/coffee making facilities and many thoughtful extras. Ten minutes to Balmoral Castle, two minutes to local golf course. Cooked or Continental breakfast served. AA 4 Diamond, STB 4 Stars.

B & B from £22pp, Rooms 2 double, 1 twin, 1 family, all en-suite, No smoking, Children over 5, Guide dogs only, Closed Xmas & New Year

---

INVERDEEN HOUSE 11 Bridge Square, Ballater AB35 5QJ
Mark Nelson *Tel:* 013397 55759 *Fax:* 013397 55993 *Mobile:* 07970 812382
Email: info@inverdeen.com *Web:* www.inverdeen.com

Map Ref: 6
A93

Beautifully restored Georgian townhouse in the rural village of Ballater, famous for its royal connection. Excellent breakfasts, comfortable beds and spacious rooms. Tea/coffee facilities, hairdryers and colour televisions in every room. Drying facilities also available. Close to all amenities including several excellent dining establishments.

B & B £25-£35pp, C-Cards MC VS, Rooms 1 single, 3 double, 1 twin, 1 family, with en-suite or pb, No smoking, Children welcome, No dogs, Open all year

---

RAVENSWOOD HOTEL Braemar Road, Ballater AB35 5RQ
Cathy & Scott Fyfe *Tel:* 013397 55539 *Fax:* 013397 56313
Email: cathy.fyfe@virgin.net *Web:* www.ravenswoodhotel.co.uk

Map Ref: 6
A93, A939

Ravenswood Hotel has a Victorian ambience, discreetly modernised. Personally run by Cathy and Scott, ensuring all guests a warm, friendly service and high standards. Ideal for relaxing in comfort with good wholesome food. A homely base to explore Royal Deeside, walking, fishing or touring.

B & B from £25pp, C-Cards MC VS AE, Dinner available, Rooms 1 single, 4 double, 3 twin, 2 family, some en-suite, Children welcome, Dogs by arrangement, Closed Nov to Jan

---

THE ORCHARD Duff House, Banff AB45 3TA
Jim & Anne Mackie *Tel / Fax:* 01261 812146 *Mobile:* 07712 045777
Email: jma6914291@aol.com *Web:* www.strathdee.com/orchard.html

Map Ref: 7
A98

The Orchard is a traditional house enjoying complete privacy due to the surrounding woodland area. It is aptly named as the large, sheltered garden hosts various fruit trees. Breakfast times are flexible with homemade preserves and honey from our own apiary. The warm and comfortable sitting room is available at all times for our guests. Ample private parking.

B & B from £25pp, Rooms 2 single, 1 double, 2 twin, all en-suite, No smoking, Children over 10, No dogs in the house, Closed Dec to Jan

MARLEE HOUSE Kinloch, Blairgowrie PH10 6SD   *Map Ref:* 8
Kenneth & Nicolette Lumsden   A923
Tel: 01250 884216

A pretty 16th century manor house set in extensive gardens and grounds by Marlee Loch. The house offers an informal country house atmosphere with log fires in winter. The charming bedrooms have televisions and en-suite bathrooms. There are excellent restaurants nearby and is an ideal base for golf, fishing and ski-ing or simply to rest in comfortable and elegant surroundings.

B & B £35-£45pp, Rooms 1 double, 1 twin, both en-suite, Restricted smoking, Children over 12, Dogs by arrangement, Closed Xmas & New Year

---

GRUINARD 148 Kinghorn Road, Burntisland KY3 9JU   *Map Ref:* 9
Mrs Jean Bowman *Tel:* 01592 873877 *Mobile:* 07798 738578   A921
Email: gruinard@dircon.co.uk *Web:* www.gruinardguesthouse.co.uk

Gruinard is a charming and tastefully decorated house, situated on the outskirts of quiet coastal town of Bruntisland. It is renowned for hospitality, comfort and fine food and quality en-suite rooms overlook the interesting and colourful garden. Scenic views can be enjoyed across the River Forth to the Edinburgh skyline, accessible by road or rail in 35 minutes. STB 4 Stars.

B & B £21-£26pp, C-Cards, Rooms 1 double, 1 twin, both en-suite, No smoking, No children, Dogs by arrangement, Closed Dec to Feb

---

LENY HOUSE Leny Estate, Callander FK17 8HA   *Map Ref:* 10
Mrs F Roebuck *Tel / Fax:* 01877 331078   A84
Email: res@lenyestate.com *Web:* www.lenyestate.com

Historic Leny House is a family country mansion in parkland, mountains and glens with abundant wildlife. We offer spacious Victorian four poster beds in luxury en-suite bedrooms with antiques, tapestries, grand piano, baronial surroundings and open fires throughout the house. A pub, restaurant and ceilidh music also on the estate. Winner of AA Best Accommodation in Scotland and Northern Ireland. Tranquil retreat to unwind.

B & B £50-£55pp, C-Cards MC VS, Dinner available, Rooms 3 double, 1 twin, all en-suite, No smoking, Children over 12, No dogs, Closed Nov to Mar

---

ROKEBY HOUSE Doune Road, Dunblane FK15 9AT   *Map Ref:* 11
Richard Beatts *Tel:* 01786 824447 *Fax:* 01786 821399 *Mobile:* 07890 305553   A9
Email: rokeby.house@btconnect.com *Web:* www.aboutscotland.com/stirling/rokeby.html

Fine period Scottish country house set on the outskirts of delightful village with beautifully furnished rooms. Gardens lovingly restored, lovely cooking and fine wines. A wonderful retreat for that 'Get away from it' holiday. Ideal for touring Stirling Trossachs and Edinburgh. A peaceful setting and a private residents parking. A superb and comfortable house providing every comfort in luxurious surroundings.

B & B from £45pp, C-Cards MC VS, Dinner from £25, Rooms 2 double, 1 twin, all en-suite, No smoking, No children or dogs, Open all year

---

WESTWOOD Doune Road, Kilbryde, Dunblane FK15 9ND   *Map Ref:* 11
Liz Duncan *Tel:* 01786 822579 *Fax:* 01786 825929   M9, A9
Email: lizduncan.westwood@scotland.com *Web:* www.westwoodbanb.co.uk

Westwood is set in over one acre of lovely gardens in quiet country location, yet convenient for A9/M9. Ground and first floor rooms with en-suite and private bathroom. Rooms equipped with television, radio, hairdryer and tea/coffee facilities, plus guests' own lounge. Ideally situated for touring Trossachs and central Scotland. Good choice of eating places nearby. STB 4 Stars, AA 4 Diamonds.

B & B from £22pp, Rooms 2 double en-suite, 1 twin with private facilities, No smoking, Children over 7, Guide Dogs only, Closed Nov to Mar

HOMEBANK GUEST HOUSE 9 Ellieslea Road, Broughty Ferry, Dundee DD5 1JH   *Map Ref:* 12
Pat & John Moore   *Tel / Fax:* 01382 477481   M90, A90, A92, A930
Email: pat.moore.homebank@bushinternet.com   *Web:* www.scotland2000.com

Homebank is a splendid Victorian mansion house, lovingly restored by owners Pat and Sean Moore, having a host of original architectural features. The house creates its own quiet charm and ambiance set with an unusually spacious interior set in a beautifully walled garden. We are situated in a very prestigious area of Tayside, three miles from Dundee, within walking distance of Broughton Ferry.

B & B £25-£27.50pp, Rooms 2 single, 2 double en-suite, No smoking, Children over 8, Guide dogs only, Closed Dec to Feb

---

BROUGH HOUSE Milton Brodie, Forres IV36 2UA   *Map Ref:* 13
Mrs Rosemary Lawson   *Tel / Fax:* 01343 850617   *Mobile:* 07740 681816   A96
Email: marklawson@public-relations.freeserve.co.uk   *Web:* www.wolsey-lodges.co.uk

Situated in the beautiful Scottish countryside, only 40 minutes from Inverness, the house is within easy reach of Brodie and Cawdor Castles. Rosemary's cooking is lovely and based on traditional Scottish recipes with local game, fish and fresh produce from the garden. One mile to beautiful forest walks with the Malt Whisky Trail nearby as well as 15 golf courses.

B & B from £30pp, Dinner from £15, Rooms 1 double, 2 twin, all en-suite, Restricted smoking, Children welcome, No dogs, Closed Xmas & New Year

---

KNOCKOMIE LODGE Forres IV36 2SG   *Map Ref:* 13
Olga Foran   *Tel / Fax:* 01309 676785   *Mobile:* 07713 903324   A96
Email: welcome@knockomie.com   *Web:* www.knockomie.com

All rooms are equipped with television, clock radio and beverage tray. Located one mile outside Forres on A940 Grantown Road, five miles away from Findhorn Bay for fishing, etc. Ideally situated for visiting castles and the distillery trail and there are ten golf courses within 12 miles.

B & B £18-£21pp, C-Cards MC VS, Rooms 2 double en-suite, 1 triple with private bathroom, No smoking, Children welcome, No dogs, Open all year

ARDENT HOUSE 43 Forsyth Street, Hopeman IV30 5SY   *Map Ref:* 13
Hamish & Norma McPherson   *Tel / Fax:* 01343 830694   A9, B9040
Email: normaardent@aol.com   *Web:* www.Ardent-House.co.uk

Local stone built house of character with conservatory overlooking large secluded rose garden. Special breakfasts include our own smoked fish, homebaking and fruit from the garden. The host was a finalist twice in AA Landlady of the Year. Good touring base for the Castle, coastal trails and whisky trails. Excellent golf courses around the area and a sandy beach on the doorstep. Car parking.

B & B £17-£28pp, Rooms 1 double en-suite, 1 double, 1 twin shared facilities, No smoking, Children ove 10, No dogs, Closed Xmas & New Year

---

FRIDAYHILL Kinmuck, Inverurie AB51 0LY   *Map Ref:* 14
Shena McGhie   *Tel / Fax:* 01651 882252   *Mobile:* 07712 005044   A96
Email: fergusmcgh@aol.com   *Web:* www.b-and-b-scotland.co.uk/fridayhill.htm

At Fridayhill we offer unique comfortable accommodation in a tranquil picturesque setting with four poster bedroom, en-suite shower room and dressing room plus double room with private bathroom. An ideal location for exploring Castle and Whisky trails, stone circles, Royal Deeside and our magnificent varied coastline, with Aberdeen Airport only eight miles away. Non-smoking house. STB 4 Star.

B & B £25-£29pp, C-Cards MC VS, Rooms 2 double, 1 en-suite, 1 private bathroom, No smoking, Children over 14, No dogs, Open all year

MONTURPIE GUEST HOUSE Monturpie, Upper Largo, Leven KY8 5QS
Mrs Linda Law **Tel:** 01333 360254 **Fax:** 01333 360850 **Mobile:** 07850 735446
Email: enquiries@monturpie.co.uk **Web:** www.monturpie.co.uk

Map Ref: 15
A915

A friendly welcome awaits at Monturpie Guest House, a family run traditional stone built farmhouse. Modernised to a high standard, it has magnificent views over Firth of Forth. Ideally suited for golfing in the 'East Neuk' and not forgetting the 'Old Course.' Many pubs and restaurants in the area.

B & B £20-£25pp, C-Cards MC VS, Rooms 2 single, 2 double, 2 twin, 1 family, all en-suite, No smoking, Children over 5, No dogs, Closed mid-Dec to mid-Jan

ELLINGTON Station Place, Johnshaven, Montrose DD10 0JD
Margaret Gibson **Tel:** 01561 362756
Email: ellington13@supanet.com

Map Ref: 16
A92

Modern family home in old fishing village. The en-suite and centrally heated rooms have televisions, shaver points, hairdryers and radio/cassette alarm. The twin room is on the ground floor and tea is served on request in the lounge. Only one minute walk away is a pub serving food and the house is ideally situated for 14th century Dunnottar Castle, coastal walks and golf.

B & B £20-£22pp, Rooms 1 double, 1 twin, both en-suite, No smoking, No children or dogs, Open all year

ABERCROMBIE 85 Glasgow Road, Perth PH2 0PQ
Mr David D Dewar
Tel / Fax: 01738 444728 **Mobile:** 01738 444728

Map Ref: 17
A9

This beautiful Victorian town house is superbly furnished with your comfort foremost in mind. Ideally situated near rail and bus stations with a few minutes walk from the leisure pool, ice rinks and town centre. Rooms have tea/coffee facilities, hairdryers, colour televisions and a decanter of sherry. Most rooms have trouser press.

B & B £25-£30pp, C-Cards MC VS, Rooms 2 single, 1 double, 1 twin, most en-suite, No smoking, Children over 12, No dogs, Open all year

EASTER DUNFALLANDY COUNTRY HOUSE Logierait Road, Pitlochry PH16 5NA
Sue Mathieson **Tel:** 01796 474128 **Mobile:** 07990 524219
Email: sue@dunfallandy.co.uk **Web:** www.dunfallandy.co.uk

Map Ref: 18
A9, A924

Welcome to Easter Dunfallandy House. A Victorian house set in an elevated position two miles outside Pitlochry with views over the town, Ben-y-Vrackie Mountain and Tummel Valley. A perfect base to explore the Central Highlands and convenient for the famous Festival Theatre. A short drive to Blair Castle, Queens View, Balmoral and many more beautiful locations.

B & B £25-£29pp, C-Cards MC VS, Dinner from £20, Rooms 1 double, 2 twin, all en-suite, No smoking, Children over 8, No dogs, Open all year

WESTBOURNE HOUSE B & B 10 Dollar Road, Tillicoultry, Stirling FK13 6PA
Jane & Adrian O'Dell **Tel:** 01259 750314 **Fax:** 01259 750642
Email: odellwestbourne@compuserve.com **Web:** www.westbournehouse.co.uk

Map Ref: 19
A91

Fascinating Victorian mill owner's mansion within wooded grounds, beneath the Ochil Hills. Friendly atmosphere with log fires, and a croquet lawn. Off road parking. Located amid glorious countryside in central Scotland, with The Trossachs, Loch Lomond, Edinburgh and Glasgow one hour away. Motorway connections within 15 miles. Sight seeing in historic Stirling, numerous golf courses, fishing and hill walking in Braveheart country.

B & B from £22pp, Rooms 2 double en-suite, 1 family, No smoking, Children welcome, Dogs by arrangement, Closed Xmas & New Year

Highlands & Islands

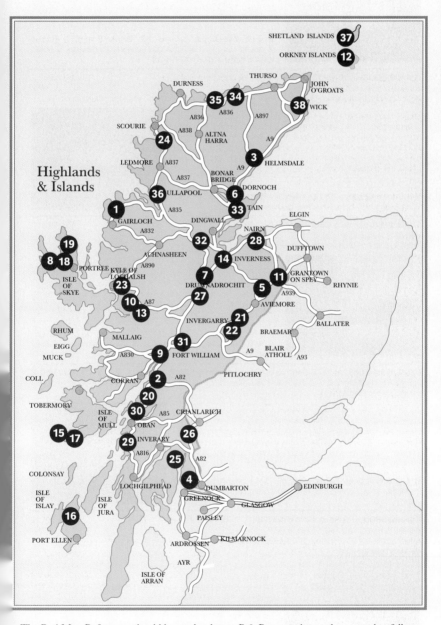

The Red Map References should be used to locate B & B properties on the pages that follow

MELLONDALE   47 Mellon Charles, Aultbea IV22 2JL   *Map Ref:* 1
Mrs A Macrae   *Tel / Fax:* 01445 731326   A832
Email: mellondale@lineone.net   *Web:* www.host.co.uk

Come and enjoy home cooked meals in a relaxed atmosphere, overlooking Lochewe. Mellondale is an ideal base for a quiet restful holiday in an area that is not only renowned for its scenic beauty, but also the world famous tropical Inverewe Gardens. All bedrooms are en-suite with televisions, tea/coffee facilities and hairdryers. STB 4 Stars, AA 4 Diamonds.

B & B £24-£25pp, C-Cards VS, Dinner from £13, Rooms 2 double, 2 twin, all en-suite, Restricted smoking, Children welcome, No dogs, Closed Nov to Feb

CAMUS HOUSE LOCHSIDE LODGE   Onich, Ballachulish PH33 6RY   *Map Ref:* 2
Tel / Fax: 01855 821200   A82
Email: Young@Camushouse.Freeserve.co.uk   *Web:* www.smouthhound.co.uk/hotels.camushouse/html

Large well appointed house set in extensive lochside gardens with superb views of the sea loch and mountains. Situated 10 miles south of Fort William and midway between Ben Nevis and Glencoe. An ideal base for touring, walking, mountain biking, climbing and skiing. Highland hospitality at it's very best with hotel standard of comfort at affordable prices.

B & B from £23.50pp, Dinner available, Rooms 3 double, 2 twin, 2 family, most en-suite, No smoking, Closed Nov to Jan

FERN VILLA   Loanfern, Ballachulish PH49 4JE   *Map Ref:* 2
Ken & June Chandler   *Tel:* 01855 811393   *Fax:* 01855 811727   A82
Email: BBD@fernvilla.com   *Web:* www.fernvilla.com

A warm welcome awaits you in this fine Victorian granite built house in the lochside village amidst spectacular scenery. One mile from Glencoe and convenient for Fort William. Home baking and Natural Cooking of Scotland features on our dinner menu, we also have a table licence. The perfect base for walking, climbing or touring in the West Highlands. Private parking.

B & B £20-£23pp, C-Cards MC VS, Dinner available, Rooms 3 double, 2 twin, all en-suite, No smoking, No dogs, Open all year

LYN-LEVEN GUEST HOUSE   West Laroch, Ballachulish PH49 4JP   *Map Ref:* 2
John & Priscilla Macleod   *Tel:* 01855 811392   *Fax:* 01855 811600   A82
Email: Lynleven@amserve.net

A very warm Highland welcome awaits you at our award winning guest house. Situated within attractive, well cared for gardens overlooking Loch Leven in the heart of some of Scotland's most spectacular scenery. Traditional home cooking and ample parking. Glencoe is only one mile away, an ideal base for ski-ing, walking, climbing and fishing. STB 4 Stars, AA RAC 4 Diamonds.

B & B from £21pp, C-Cards MC VS, Dinner available, Rooms 3 double, 3 twin, 2 family, all en-suite, Children welcome, Closed Xmas

GLENAVERON   Golf Road, Brora KW9 6QS   *Map Ref:* 3
Alistair Fortune   *Tel / Fax:* 01408 621601   A9
Email: glenaveron@hotmail.com   *Web:* www.glenaveron.co.uk

Glenaveron is a luxurious Edwardian House set in mature gardens in a quiet area of Brora, a few minutes walk from the golf course and beautiful beaches. All rooms are en-suite with televisions and full facilities. An ideal base for touring the Northern Highland and going to Orkney. Non smoking and disabled facilities are available. AA 5 Diamonds.

B & B from £26pp, C-Cards MC VS, Rooms 1 double, 1 twin, 1 family, all en-suite, No smoking, Children welcome, No dogs, Closed Xmas & New Year

LYNWOOD Golf Road, Brora KW9 6QS   *Map Ref:* 3
Adam & Kitty Cranston   A9
Tel / Fax: 01408 621226

Enjoy a warm welcome and relaxed atmosphere at this elegant Edwardian house situated close to the Brora Golf Club. Lynwood overlooks the harbour and River Brora and guests can relax in the large secluded garden or take one of the many interesting local walks. Our enthusiasm for good food is reflected in the imaginative way we prepare dishes from local Highland produce.

B & B from £25pp, C-Cards MC VS, Dinner from £15, Rooms 2 double, 1 twin, all en-suite, No smoking, Children welcome, Guide dogs only, Closed Xmas & New Year

KIRKTON HOUSE Darleith Road, Cardross, Dumbarton G82 5EZ   *Map Ref:* 4
Stewart & Gillian Macdonald   *Tel:* 01389 841951   *Fax:* 01389 841868   A814
Email: GBBB@kirktonhouse.co.uk   *Web:* www.kirktonhouse.co.uk

Kirkton House is a 19th century converted farmstead, set in a tranquil country setting with wonderful views of the Clyde, Loch Lomond, Glasgow city or the airport. The rooms offer full amenities including bath/shower, television, telephone, tea/coffee tray, desk and hair dryer. Dine by oil lamplight. Wine, draught beer and spirits available. Extensive daily menu for home cooked dinners.

B & B from £30.50pp, C-Cards MC VS AE DC, Dinner from £16.25, Rooms 2 twin, 4 family, all en-suite, Restricted smoking, Children & dogs welcome, Closed Dec to Jan

CARRMOOR GUEST HOUSE Carr Road, Carrbridge PH23 3AD   *Map Ref:* 5
Michael & Christine Stitt   *Tel / Fax:* 01479 841244   A9
Email: christine@carrmoorguesthouse.co.uk   *Web:* www.carrmoorguesthouse.co.uk

Carrmoor is a family run Licensed Guest House and is centrally located for touring the Spey Valley and Highlands of Scotland. The restaurant is well known for its excellent cuisine and serves a Table d'hote Menu as well as an A la Carte Menu. Carrbridge is the original ski village. However there is also a nine hole golf course and pony trekking.

B & B £20-£22pp, C-Cards MC VS, Dinner from £12.75, Rooms 3 double, 2 twin, 1 family, all en-suite, Restricted smoking, Children welcome, Dogs by arrangement, Open all year

PARFOUR Embo Street, Dornoch IV25 3PW   *Map Ref:* 6
Mrs Sandy Young   *Tel / Fax:* 01862 810955   A9
Email: parfourdornoch@talk21.com   *Web:* http://freespace.virgin.net/parfour.dornoch

Parfour was built in 2000 and is situated approximately one mile from the centre of Dornoch and five minutes by car to Royal Dornoch Golf Course. It has panoramic views to the Dornoch Firth and an open outlook at the rear of the house to Ben Bhraggie. We offer a relaxing environment where guests can feel totally at home.

B & B from £24pp, C-Cards MC VS, Rooms 2 twin en-suite, No smoking, Children welcome, Dogs by arrangement, Closed Xmas & New Year

GLEN ROWAN HOUSE West Lewiston, Drumnadrochit IV63 6UW   *Map Ref:* 7
Sheila Harrod   *Tel:* 01456 450235   *Fax:* 01456 450817   A82
Email: glenrowan@loch-ness.demon.co.uk   *Web:* www.loch-ness.demon.co.uk

Family run Highland village house with large gardens running down to river. Plenty of off road parking. En-suite ground floor level bedrooms all individually decorated and furnished with colour televisions, hostess tray and all comforts of home. Two lounge areas, one overlooking hills and river. Ideal location for touring, walking, fishing, horse riding nearby. Near Urquart Castle, Loch-Ness Monster Centre.

B & B £17-£26pp, C-Cards VS, Rooms 1 double, 2 twin, all en-suite, No smoking, Children welcome, No dogs, Closed Nov to Feb

ROSKHILL Roskhill, Dunvegan IV55 8ZD   *Map Ref:* 8
Gillian Griffith *Tel:* 01470 521317 *Fax:* 01470 521761   A863
Email: stay@roskhill.demon.co.uk *Web:* www.roskhill.demon.co.uk

Cottage style rooms and relaxing atmosphere coupled with four star quality and an affordable price. Gillian prepares old fashioned farmhouse food; hot, fresh and plenty of it. No pictures on plates that leave you wanting more. Alice Beer of BBC television said, 'A wonderful night, I wish I could stay longer and carry on eating and sleeping.' An ideal base to tour this magical island.

B & B £27-£35pp, C-Cards MC VS, Dinner from £14.50, Rooms 1 single, 3 double with en-suite, 1 twin, No smoking, Children over 10, Dogs welcome, Closed Nov to Feb

ASHBURN HOUSE Achintore Road, Fort William PH33 6RQ   *Map Ref:* 9
Alexandra Henderson *Tel:* 01397 706000 *Fax:* 01397 702024   A82
Email: ashburn.house@tinyworld.co.uk *Web:* www.highland5star.co.uk

A completely refurbished Victorian house only 500 yards from the town centre. Ashburn House is quietly located, and overlooks Loch Linnhe. Central heating, delicious Scottish breakfasts, tea making facilities and TV. Close to all Highland visitor attractions, yet only two and a half hours from Glasgow. Off road parking. The house holds the highest commendations. A truly restful holiday. 6 feet wide Super King beds.

B & B £30-£40pp, C-Cards MC VS, Rooms 3 single, 4 double, all en-suite, No smoking, Children welcome, No dogs, Closed Nov to Feb

GLENLOCHY GUEST HOUSE Nevis Bridge, North Road, Fort William PH33 6PF   *Map Ref:* 9
Margaret & Donnie Macbeth *Tel:* 01397 702909   A82
Email: glenlochyguesthouse@hotmail.com

Situated in its own extensive grounds, midway between the town centre and Ben Nevis. 10 of 12 rooms are en-suite with colour televisions and tea/coffee facilities. Special rates are available for three or more night bookings. Large private car park. Recommended by Which and Best Bed & Breakfast Guide. Colour brochure available.

B & B £16-£27pp, C-Cards MC VS, Rooms 6 double, 4 twin, 2 family, most en-suite, Restricted smoking, Children welcome, Open all year

THE GRANGE Grange Road, Fort William PH33 6JF   *Map Ref:* 9
Joan Campbell *Tel:* 01397 705516 *Fax:* 01397 701595   A82
Email: jcampbell@grangefortwilliam.com *Web:* www.grangefortwilliam.com

Tucked away in its own grounds overlooking Loch Linnhe, The Grange offers luxury accommodation with log fires, antiques and fresh flowers. All rooms have a loch view and breakfast is served surrounded by beautiful scenery. Previous award winner of Best Bed & Breakfast in Scotland, this truly is a special place to stay in the magnificent Scottish Highlands.

B & B £38-£46pp, C-Cards MC VS, Rooms 4 double en-suite, No smoking, No children or dogs, Closed Nov to Mar

LOCHVIEW HOUSE Heathercroft, Argyll Road, Fort William PH33 6RE   *Map Ref:* 9
Mrs Kirk *Tel:* 01397 703149 *Fax:* 01397 706138   A82
Email: info@lochview.co.uk *Web:* www.lochview.co.uk

Lochview is situated in a quiet location on Hillside above the town with panoramic views over Loch Linnhe. All rooms are en-suite with tea/coffee facilities and televisions. Lochview is a non smoking house with private off-street parking and a large mature garden.

B & B £22-£26pp, C-Cards MC VS, Rooms 1 single, 4 double, 1 twin, all en-suite, No smoking, No dogs, Closed Oct to Apr

WEST END HOTEL Achintore Road, Fort William PH33 6ED
C C Chisholm   *Tel:* 01397 702614   *Fax:* 01397 706279
Email: welcome@westend-hotel.co.uk

Map Ref: 9
A82

A family run hotel that enjoys breathtaking views of Loch Linnhe and the Ardgour Mountains. All rooms are en-suite with televisions, telephones and tea/coffee facilities. An ideal base for touring Scotland and with a relaxed and friendly atmosphere any stay is sure to be enjoyed.

B & B from £20pp, Dinner from £12.50, Rooms all en-suite, Children welcome, No dogs, Closed Jan

DUICH HOUSE Letterfearn, Glenshiel IV40 8HS
Anne Kempthorne   *Tel / Fax:* 01599 555259
Email: duich@cwcom.net   *Web:* www.milford.co.uk/go/duich.html

Map Ref: 10
A87

There are spectacular views across Loch Duich to the mountains of Kintail from our 1830s home, which lies half an hours drive from the ferry to Skye. Two individually decorated bedrooms each having private bathrooms. Homemade preserves and fruit juice from the garden served with serious cooked breakfasts. Dinners are imaginatively presented with seafood and Scottish beef being specialities. Taste of Scotland.

B & B £34-£40pp, Dinner from £30, Rooms 2 double with private facilities, No smoking, Children over 16, No dogs, Closed Oct to Mar

ARDCONNEL HOUSE Woodlands Terrace, Grantown-on-Spey PH26 3JU
Michel & Barbara Bouchard   *Tel / Fax:* 01479 872104
Email: enquiry@ardconnel.com   *Web:* www.ardconnel.com

Map Ref: 11
A95

An elegant and comfortable Victorian house furnished with antiques and pine. All bedrooms are en-suite offering colour televisions, hairdryers and tea/coffee facilities. Excellent 'Taste of Scotland' dinner prepared by French owner/chef. Ideal base for fishing, golfing, the Whisky Trail and visiting Royal Deeside and castles. AA Accommodation of the Year for Scotland 2001. STB 5 Star, AA 5 Diamonds, RAC 5 Diamonds.

B & B from £30pp, C-Cards MC VS, Dinner from £22.50, Rooms 1 single, 3 double, 2 twin, all en-suite, No smoking, Children over 8, No dogs, Closed Oct to Easter

RICKLA Harray, Orkney KW17 2JT
Jacky Anderson   *Tel / Fax:* 01856 761575   *Mobile:* 07884 353730
Email: jacky@rickla.com   *Web:* www.rickla.com

Map Ref: 12
A986

Rickla has luxury en-suite accommodation set in 50 acres of own land and practically in the centre of Western Europe's richest area for pre-historic remains. The rooms have beautiful panoramic views over the hills and countryside scenery. A quiet and peaceful location, far from the madding crowd, yet still situated close to restaurants. STB 5 Stars.

B & B £28-£33pp, C-Cards MC VS, Rooms 1 double, 1 double/twin, both en-suite, No smoking, No children or dogs, Closed Nov to Jan

CRAIGARD HOUSE Invergarry PH35 4HG
Robert & Barbara Withers   *Tel / Fax:* 01809 501258
Email: bob@craigard.saltire.org   *Web:* www.craigard.saltire.org

Map Ref: 13
A87

Set in breathtaking Highland splendour, this large country house on the western outskirts of Invergarry is the perfect base for a relaxing holiday. Well furnished bedrooms are equipped with washbasin, tea/coffee facilities and TV. Guests may enjoy a drink in the residents' lounge with a log fire for chilly evenings. The magnificent scenery makes Craigard an ideal point for touring.

B & B from £18pp, C-Cards MC VS, Dinner from £15, Rooms 1 single, 5 double, 1 twin, shower and bathroom, No smoking, Children over 12, No dogs, Open all year

SKIARY Loch Hourn, Invergarry PH35 4HD
John & Christina Everett
Tel: 01809 511214

Map Ref: 13
A87

Originally a fisherman's cottage, Skiary accommodates six guests in three twin rooms. Its unique setting and absence of mains services make it truly a world apart from everyday life, yet it is cosy and comfortable, heated with log fires and lit by oil lamps. The food is calculated to satisfy the heartiest and most discerning of appetites. Guests are invited to indicate any personal preferences. No road access, collection by boat.

Dinner B & B £80pp, Rooms 3 twin (1 shared bathroom), Restricted smoking, Children by arrangement, Dogs by arrangement, Closed Oct to Mar

---

ACORN HOUSE 2A Bruce Gardens, Inverness IV3 5EN
Dugie & Fiona Cameron   *Tel:* 01463 717021   *Fax:* 01463 714236
Email: enquiries@acorn-house.freeserve.co.uk   *Web:* www.acorn-house.freeserve.co.uk

Map Ref: 14
A9, A82

Acorn House is the premier guest house in Inverness where you will find a truly Highland welcome. All rooms are en-suite with Sky television and tea/coffee facilities. All of the food is freshly prepared by the hostess and a residents lounge is available for putting your feet up. Sauna, jacuzzi and ample car parking. Central to town and theatre plus the Aquadrome Sports centre. AA 4 Diamonds.

B & B from £27.50pp, C-Cards MC VS AE DC, Dinner from £10, Rooms 1 twin, 3 double, 3 family, all en-suite, Restricted smoking, Children & dogs welcome, Open all year

---

BALLINDARROCH Aldourie, Inverness IV2 6EL
Alison Parsons & Philip Alvy   *Tel:* 01463 751348   *Fax:* 01463 751372
Email: ali.phil@ntlworld.com   *Web:* www.milford.co.uk/go/ballindarroch.html

Map Ref: 14
B862
see Photo opposite

Built as a shooting lodge circa 1850, Ballindarroch stands in ten acres of woodland gardens above the Caledonian Canal. The house offers peace and relaxation, the animals here help to create a family atmosphere. Spacious bedrooms enjoy garden and woodland views. Generous breakfast may include natural smoked kippers, finnan haddock and white pudding. Numerous golf courses, also many local attractions of historical interest.

B & B £20-£30pp, Rooms 1 family, 1 double, 1 twin, 1 single, 2 private bathrooms, Restricted smoking, Children & dogs welcome, Open all year

---

CLACH MHUILINN 7 Harris Road, Inverness IV2 3LS
Jacqi & Iain Elmslie   *Tel:* 01463 237059   *Fax:* 01463 242092
Email: jacqi@ness.co.uk   *Web:* www.ness.co.uk

Map Ref: 14
A9, A82

Explore the magnificent Highlands from Clach Mhuilinn. Two delightful en-suite bedrooms, one double and one twin suite with sitting room, have all facilities and many extra touches to enhance your stay. Delicious breakfasts served overlooking the beautiful garden. No smoking. Convenient for golf course, Loch Ness, Culloden, Cawdor Castle. Scottish Thistle Awards Website Winner 2000. STB 5 Star Bed and Breakfast.

B & B £29-£35pp, C-Cards MC VS, Rooms 1 double, 1 twin suite, both en-suite, No smoking, Children over 14, No dogs, Closed Nov to Mar

---

LYNDALE GUEST HOUSE 2 Ballifeary Road, Inverness IV3 5PJ
Mrs F McKendrick   *Tel:* 01463 231529   *Fax:* 01463 710003
Email: Invcomps@aol.com

Map Ref: 14
A9, A82

Delightfully situated in an exclusive residential area close to River Ness, the Cathedral and Eden Court Theatre. Only eight minutes walk from the town centre with the Loch Ness cruise departure point and golf course nearby. All bedrooms have colour televisions and tea/coffee facilities plus one en-suite family room. Private parking in grounds.

B & B from £20pp, Rooms 1 single, 2 double, 2 twin, 1 family en-suite, Children & dogs welcome, Closed Xmas & New Year

Ballindarroch, Aldourie, Inverness

ARGYLL HOTEL Isle of Iona PA76 6SJ   *Map Ref:* 15
Claire Bachellerie & Daniel Morgan   *Tel:* 01681 700334   *Fax:* 01681 700510   Ferry
Email: reception@argyllhoteliona.co.uk   *Web:* www.argyllhoteliona.co.uk

A small and friendly seashore hotel with plant and book filled lounges and open fires. The bedrooms are cosy with electric blankets and tea/coffee facilities and all overlook the Sound of Iona. Excellent home-cooking features organic meats and vegetarian dishes are always available. Very interesting and affordable wine list.

B & B £20-£50pp, C-Cards MC VS, Dinner from £15, Rooms 6 single, 3 twin, 5 double, 1 family, 1 small double, Restricted smoking, Children & dogs welcome, Closed Oct to Apr

---

KILMENY COUNTRY GUEST HOUSE Ballygrant, Isle of Islay PA45 7QW   *Map Ref:* 16
Mrs Margaret Rozga   *Tel / Fax:* 01496 840668   *Mobile:* 07796 197811   A846
Email: info@kilmeny.co.uk   *Web:* www.kilmeny.co.uk

Said to be the most beautiful of all the Hebridean islands, Islay is best known for its stunning scenery and varied wildlife. Kilmeny offers exclusive accommodation and superior dining in a peaceful country house atmosphere. Small and elegant, warm and friendly with many malt whisky distillaries, stone circles and peace and quiet.

B & B from £38pp, Dinner from £24, Rooms 2 double, 1 twin, all en-suite, No smoking, Children over 5, Dogs by arrangement, Closed Xmas & New Year

---

RED BAY COTTAGE Deargphort, Fionnphort, Isle of Mull PA66 6BP   *Map Ref:* 17
John & Eleanor Wagstaff   A849
Tel: 01681 700396

Red Bay Cottage is a modern house built on an isolated shoreline position overlooking Iona. John and Eleanor have built up a good reputation for the quality of the food in their adjoining restaurant and guests can eat in the pleasant dining room overlooking Iona Sound. This is an excellent centre for exploring Mull, Iona and the Treshnish Islands. Wonderful walking and beaches.

B & B from £16.50pp, Dinner from £7.50, Rooms 2 twin, 1 double, Restricted smoking, Children welcome, Dogs by arrangement, Open all year

---

LYNDALE HOUSE Edinbane, Isle of Skye IV51 9PX   *Map Ref:* 18
Linda & Marcus Ridsdill-Smith   *Tel:* 01470 582329   A850
Email: linda@lyndale.free-online.co.uk

Hidden at the end of a long wooded driveway, Lyndale is an elegant house in a wonderfully secluded position, overlooking the sea. The house has been painstakingly restored to its original 18th century style and is now a beautiful family home, offering tranquility and seclusion with magnificent views and stunning sunsets. Ideally situated for exploring the rest of the island.

B & B from £40pp, Rooms 1 double en-suite, 1 twin with private bathroom, No smoking, Children welcome, Dogs by arrangement, Closed Xmas & New Year

---

GLENVIEW INN & RESTAURANT Culnacnoc, Staffin, Isle of Skye IV51 9JH   *Map Ref:* 19
Paul & Cathie Booth   *Tel:* 01470 562248   *Fax:* 01470 562211   A855
Email: enquiries@glenview-skye.co.uk   *Web:* www.glenview-skye.co.uk

This charming inn nestles between mountains and sea. Ideally situated for exploring the majic of North Skye. Pretty country style bedrooms with private facilities and tea and coffee facilities. A cosy lounge with television and a peat fire. A lovely place to relax after supper in our restaurant which is licensed and offers fresh Skye seafood, also traditional, ethnic and vegetarian specialities.

B & B £20-£30pp, C-Cards MC VS, Dinner from £12.95, Rooms 1 twin, 3 double, 1 family, all en-suite, Restricted smoking, Children & dogs welcome, Closed Nov to Feb

ARDSHEAL HOME FARM   Kentallen, Duror in Appin PA38 4BZ   *Map Ref:* 20
Flavia MacArthur   A828
Tel / Fax: 01631 740229

A charming Scottish hill farm of 1,000 acres, surrounded by breath
taking views on the shores of Loch Linnhe, overlooking the Morven
Hills. A warm welcome is assured. Three attractive bedrooms are
comfortable and well furnished with electric blankets and tea and
coffee facilities. The farm is convenient for touring the inner Isles.
There is a private one mile beach with spectaluar sunsets.

B & B £18-£19pp, Dinner from £13.50, Rooms 1 twin, 1 double,
1 private bathroom, No smoking, Children welcome, Guide dogs
only, Closed Oct to Mar

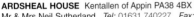

ARDSHEAL HOUSE   Kentallen of Appin PA38 4BX   *Map Ref:* 20
Mr & Mrs Neil Sutherland   *Tel:* 01631 740227   *Fax:* 01631 740342   A828
Email: info@ardsheal.co.uk   *Web:* www.ardsheal.co.uk

Ardsheal House, which was originally built in the early 16th century,
was destroyed by fire as a result of the 1745 uprising and rebuilt
around 1760. The house is steeped in history and provides unique
accommodation, the hill on which the house stands, drops away
sharply providing an open outlook with wonderful views. We offer
delicious food and luxurious accommodation.

B & B from £50pp, C-Cards MC VS AE, Dinner from £27, Rooms
1 single, 5 double, 1 twin, 1 family, all en-suite, Restricted
smoking, Children & dogs welcome, Closed Xmas

BALCRAGGAN HOUSE   Feshiebridge, Kincraig PH21 1NG   *Map Ref:* 21
Helen Gillies   A9, B970
Tel: 01540 651488

Balcraggan House is situated in the foothills of Glenfeshie, where
pine marten, buzzard, osprey, roe deer and red squirrel abound.
Miles of cycle routes and walks, or use your car to explore the
magnificent Highlands. Spacious bedrooms are tastefully furnished.
There are log and peat fires in the drawing and dining rooms, perfect
for relaxing beside after a day exploring this wonderful area.

B & B from £25pp, Dinner from £15, Rooms 1 twin, 1 double, both
en-suite, No smoking, Children over 10, No dogs, Open all year

THE HERMITAGE   Spey Street, Kingussie PH21 1HN   *Map Ref:* 22
David & Marie Taylor   *Tel:* 01540 662137   *Fax:* 01540 662177   A9
Email: thehermitage@clara.net   *Web:* www.thehermitage-scotland.com

Enjoy the splendour of the Highlands and make Kingussie your
base, letting us help you plan your daily itinerary. Wonderful walking
and mountain bike trails. In easy reach of skiing, fishing, bird
watching, heritage centres and whisky trail. Situated two minutes
from the main street in a quiet location, The Hermitage is very
convenient for the railway station. A warm welcome awaits you at
the Hermitage which is fully licensed.

B & B from £22pp, C-Cards MC VS, Dinner available, Rooms
3 double, 1 twin, 1 family, all en-suite, No smoking, No dogs, Open
all year

ROWAN HOUSE   Homewood, Newtonmore Road, Kingussie PH21 1HD   *Map Ref:* 22
Susan Smiter & David Jackson   *Tel:* 01540 662153   A9, A86
Email: info@rowanhousescotland.com   *Web:* www.rowanhousescotland.com

Rowan House is a modern split level villa situated in a hillside
location with uninterrupted views of the Spey Valley and Cairngorm
mountains. Kingussie is surrounded by spectacular countryside and
the area is famed for summer and winter leisure activities including
walking, golf, fishing and birdwatching. Accommodation includes a
self-contained two bedroomed suite ideal for family or friends. STB
4 Stars.

B & B £19-£24pp, Rooms 2 double, 1 twin, all en-suite, No
smoking, Children welcome, Dogs by arrangement, Closed Xmas

CONCHRA HOUSE Ardelve, Kyle of Lochalsh IV40 8DZ
Tel: 01599 555233   *Fax:* 01599 888433
Email: enquiries@conchra.co.uk   *Web:* www.conchra.co.uk

Map Ref: 23
A87, A890

Former seat and ancestral home of the Macraes of Conchra dating from 1760 in a secluded and tranquil lochside setting. Warm West Highland hospitality, in a comfortable country house and a family environment, personally run by proprietors.

B & B from £25pp, Dinner available, Rooms 1 single, 3 double, 2 twin, most en-suite, Children welcome, Closed Xmas & New Year

KYLESKU HOTEL Kylescu IV27 4HW
Tel: 01971 502231   *Fax:* 01971 502313
Email: kylesku.hotel@excite.co.uk   *Web:* www.smoothhound.co.uk/hotels/kylesku.html

Map Ref: 24
A837, A894

A converted former ferry house at the water's edge with spectacular views over Loch Glendhu to the mountains beyond, and is ideal for serious climbers and hill walkers. The unspoilt terrane is also home to a wide variety of wildlife. Handa Island is only a short distance away. Lovely meals made with fresh produce, seafood is a speciality. Annexed room available and some rooms have televisions.

B & B from £27.50pp, Dinner available, Rooms 6 double, 2 twin, 1 family, most en-suite, Dogs welcome, Closed Nov to Mar

NEWTON LODGE Kylesku IV27 4HW
Tel / Fax: 01971 502070
Email: newtonlge@aol.com

Map Ref: 24
A837, A894

A large modern and comfortable private hotel, surrounded by an inspiring panorama of mountains and lochs. Here you will find a warm welcome, comfort and home cooking. The hotel holds a residents' licence for wines or spirits. The lounge is peaceful and relaxing and here one is able to unwind with an after dinner coffee or drink. Ample car parking available.

B & B from £28pp, C-Cards MC VS, Dinner available, Rooms 4 double, 3 twin, all en-suite, No smoking, Children over 13, Dogs by arrangement, Closed Oct to Apr

WATERS EDGE COTTAGE Duck Bay, Arden, Loch Lomond G83 8QZ
Colleen Robertson   *Tel:* 01389 850629   *Mobile:* 07788 920062
Email: watersedge99@hotmail.com   *Web:* www.watersedgecottage.co.uk

Map Ref: 25
A82

Experience the romantic ambience and natural beauty surrounding you in our Victorian lochside cottage. Quaint and charming, furnished with antiques and imaginatively decorated rooms. Delicious breakfasts and stunning views, together with an air of peaceful tranquility guarantee a memorable and relaxing visit. Stroll to quality restaurants and there is also an international golf course nearby.

B & B £27.53-£32.50pp, C-Cards MC VS, Rooms 3 double en-suite, No smoking, No children or dogs, Open all year

LOMOND VIEW COUNTRY HOUSE Tarbet, Arrochar, Loch Lomond G83 7DG
Grace & George Brown   *Tel / Fax:* 01301 702477
Email: lomondview@talk21.com   *Web:* www.lomondview.co.uk

Map Ref: 26
A82

A warm friendly Scottish welcome is assured at our home on the bonnie banks of Loch Lomond. Magnificent scenery and picturesque Loch views from your en-suite room. Ideal touring base and also romantic and stress free breaks. Relaxing strolls, energetic hill walks and Loch cruises minutes away. Breakfast at your own table overlooking the Loch. Enjoy a complimentary sherry in guests' lounge.

B & B £25-£30pp, C-Cards MC VS, Rooms 2 double, 1 twin, all en-suite, No smoking, No children or dogs, Closed Xmas & New Year

FOYERS BAY HOUSE Lower Foyers, Loch Ness
Mr & Mrs O E Panciroli *Tel:* 01456 486624 *Fax:* 01456 486337
Email: panciroli@foyersbay.freeserve.co.uk *Web:* www.foyersbay.freeserve.co.uk

Map Ref: 27
A82, A9

Standing in magnificent grounds of wooded pine slopes abundant rhododendrons and an apple orchard with fabulous view of Loch Ness, is the splendid Victorian villa, Foyers Bay House. The grounds are set amid beautiful forest, nature trails, and adjoin the famous Falls of Foyers. Tastefully and luxuriously refurbished, rooms are generously equipped and offer thoughtful complimentary extras. The house has a table licence.

B & B from £23pp, C-Cards MC VS AE, Dinner from £10.50, Rooms 3 double, 2 twin, No smoking in bedrooms, Children welcome, No dogs, Open all year

---

GREENLAWNS 13 Seafield Street, Nairn IV12 4HG
Sheelagh Southwell *Tel / Fax:* 01667 452738 *Mobile:* 07890 405379
Email: greenlawns@cali.co.uk *Web:* www.greenlawns.uk.com

Map Ref: 28
A96

Victorian villa, lovingly restored, full of antique furniture. Award winning patio garden. Close to all amenities. Seven en-suite rooms, some with large bathtubs, king size beds and a 'wee dram.' Car parking, residents lounge, real fires and small bar. Genealogy help and good value home cooking.

B & B £19-£28pp, C-Cards MC VS AE, Dinner from £10, Rooms 1 single, 3 double, 3 twin, all en-suite, No smoking, Children & dogs welcome, Closed Xmas & 10-25 Jan

---

LOCH MELFORT HOTEL Arduaine, Oban PA34 4XG
Tel: 01852 200203 *Fax:* 01852 200214
Email: imhotel@aol.com *Web:* www.loch-melfort.co.uk

Map Ref: 29
A816

Family run hotel located 20 miles south from Oban in a magnificent location overlooking the Sound of Jura and many small islands. Spectacular views from all bedrooms, lounge and restaurant. Emphasis on locally caught seafood and shellfish and enjoying an excellent reputation for home cooking and fresh produce. Arduanle Gardens adjacent with many other glorious gardens in the area. Pony trekking and water sports available.

B & B from £38pp, Dinner available, Rooms 1 single, 7 double, 18 twin, all en-suite, Children welcome, Open all year

---

HAWTHORN 5 Keil Crofts, Benderloch, Oban PA37 1QS
Will & June Currie *Tel:* 01631 720452 *Fax:* 01631 720240
Email: junecurrie@hotmail.com *Web:* www.hawthorncottages.co.uk

Map Ref: 30
A828

Family run croft where highland cattle are bred and graze. Comfortable bungalow furnished to a high standard, supreme en-suite bedrooms with a small lounge area. Peacefully located 15 minutes from Oban. An ideal base for touring West Coast. Daily sailings to Mull and Iona. Wonderful for hill walking, fishing, sailing, pony trekking, Sea Life Centre and Rare Breeds Park nearby. Dinner available, delicious home cooking.

B & B £18-£21pp, C-Cards MC VS, Dinner from £10, Rooms 1 twin, 1 double, 1 family, all en-suite, Restricted smoking, Children over 3, No dogs, Open all year

---

CORRIECHOILLE LODGE Spean Bridge PH34 4EY
Justin & Lucy Swabey *Tel / Fax:* 01397 712002
Email: enquiry@corriechoille.com *Web:* www.corriechoille.com

Map Ref: 31
A82

18th century fishing lodge in a peaceful and secluded setting above the River Spean. Magnificent mountain view with all rooms en-suite. Our evening meals are carefully prepared using fresh local and home grown produce whenever possible.

B & B £23-£27pp, C-Cards MC VS, Dinner from £16, Rooms 2 double, 1 twin, 2 family, all en-suite, No smoking, Children over 7, No dogs, Closed Nov to Mar

INVERGLOY HOUSE Spean Bridge PH34 4DY   *Map Ref:* 31
Mrs Margaret Cairns *Tel:* 01397 712681   A82
Email: cairns@invergloy-house.co.uk *Web:* www.invergloy-house.co.uk

A warm welcome to peaceful stables and coach house in beautiful Great Glen. A guests' sitting room overlooks Loch Lochy, the house enjoys superb views in 50 acres of attractive woodland. The en-suite bedrooms are tastefully furnished, and they have hospitality trays. Excellent meals nearby. Invergloy House is just five and a half miles north of Spean Bridge. SAE for details.

B & B £23-£25pp, Rooms 3 twin, all en-suite, No smoking, Children over 8, No dogs, Open all year

---

CRAIGVAR The Square, Strathpeffer IV14 9DL   *Map Ref:* 32
Margaret Scott *Tel:* 01997 421622 *Fax:* 01997 421796 *Mobile:* 07808 406241   A9, A835, A834
Email: craigvar@talk21.com *Web:* www.craigvar.com

Craigvar is beautifully situated, overlooking the Square in a charming Victorian spa village. This distinctive Georgian house offers superb luxury facilities with en-suite rooms and one four poster bed. It is a most comfortable and attractively furnished house with spacious rooms and original fireplaces. A unique and memorable breakfast menu with many personal touches. Superb touring base for the Highlands.

B & B £21-£28pp, C-Cards MC VS, Rooms 1 single, 1 double, 1 twin, all en-suite, No smoking, Children welcome, No dogs, Closed Xmas & New Year

---

ALDIE HOUSE Tain IV19 1LZ   *Map Ref:* 33
Chris & Charles De Decker *Tel / Fax:* 01862 893787   A9
Email: info@aldiehouse.co.uk *Web:* www.aldiehouse.co.uk

The owners, Chris and Charles invite you to Aldie House, a late Victorian country house set in its own grounds, which offers you a special stay. The rooms are nicely decorated with views over the garden and fields. Guests are recommended to use Aldie House as a base to explore this unique area of Scotland, The Highlands.

B & B £24-£26pp, C-Cards MC VS, Rooms 1 double, 1 twin, 1 family, all en-suite, No smoking, Children welcome, Guide dogs only, Open all year

---

THE SHEILING GUEST HOUSE Melvich, Thurso KW14 7YJ   *Map Ref:* 34
Joan & Hugh Campbell *Tel / Fax:* 01641 531256 *Mobile:* 07715 662010   A836
Email: thesheiling@btinternet.com *Web:* b-and-b-scotland.co.uk/thesheiling.htm

Warm hospitality, great comfort and excellent food can be guaranteed at The Sheiling, along with peace and quiet. Rooms have tea/coffee facilities and there is also two charming lounges and a regency dining room, all boasting splendid views. Day trips to Orkneys can be arranged as well as interesting walks, beautiful beaches and bird watching. AA 4 Diamonds. STB 4 Stars.

B & B £24-£26pp, C-Cards MC VS, Rooms 2 double, 1 twin, all en-suite, No smoking, Children over 12, No dogs, Closed Oct to Mar

---

CATALINA Aultivullin, Strathy Point, Thurso KW14 7RY   *Map Ref:* 34
Jane & Peter Salisbury *Tel:* 01641 541395 *Fax:* 0870 124 7960   A836
Email: jane@catalina72.freeserve.co.uk

Situated between John O'Groats and Cape Wrath, on the far north Scottish Atlantic coastline, Catalina enjoys fantastic scenery. We accept only two visitors who have their own private suite which comprises a twin bedroom and shower room, a lounge and a dining room. Delicious meals to include Scottish venison, salmon and vegetarian dishes are served at a time to suit our guests.

B & B from £17pp, Dinner from £9, Rooms 1 en-suite twin, No smoking, No children or dogs, Open all year

THE BEN LOYAL HOTEL Main Street, Tongue IV27 4XE
Paul & Elaine Lewis *Tel:* 01847 611216 *Fax:* 01847 611212
Email: benloyalhotel@btinternet.com *Web:* www.benloyal.co.uk

Map Ref: 35
A836

A quiet and peaceful haven with grand views over mountains and
sea in a comfortable family-run hotel. All rooms are en-suite with
colour terrestrial televisions and tea/coffee facilities available. Very
good food - AA single rosette for several years.

B & B from £38pp, C-Cards MC VS, Dinner available, Rooms
2 single, 4 double, 5 twin, all en-suite, Restricted smoking,
Children & dogs welcome, Open all year

THE SHEILING GUEST HOUSE Garve Road, Ullapool IV26 2SX
Duncan & Mhairi Mackenzie *Tel / Fax:* 01854 612947
Web: www.thesheiling.ullapool.co.uk

Map Ref: 36
A835

A warm welcome is assured at the Mackenzies' comfortable home.
Set in one acre of landscaped gardens with wonderful views of Loch
Broom and the mountains beyond. All rooms are en-suite and
facilities include sauna, laundry, drying room and 40 square miles of
wild Brown Trout fishing, free to residents. Strictly non-smoking.

B & B £24-£27pp, C-Cards MC VS, Rooms 4 double, 2 twin,
all en-suite, No smoking, No children, Guide dogs only, Closed
Xmas & New Year

TANGLEWOOD HOUSE Ullapool IV26 2TB
Anne Holloway *Tel / Fax:* 01854 612059
Email: tanglewoodhouse@msn.com *Web:* www.tanglewoodhouse.co.uk

Map Ref: 36
A835

The house is perched on its own heather covered headland above
Loch Broom. Every room has panoramic views of the water and
mountains. It is furnished with antique furniture, comfortable beds
and interesting modern pictures. The area has sandy beaches,
challenging mountains and outstanding scenic drives along the
craggy sea coast roads. The village has a nine hole golf course and
swimming pool.

B & B from £35pp, C-Cards MC VS, Dinner £25, Rooms 1 double,
2 twin, all en-suite, No smoking, Children over 5, Dogs not in
house, Closed Xmas & New Year

BUNESS HOUSE Baltasound, Unst, Shetland ZE2 9DS
Mr & Mrs David Edmondston *Tel:* 01957 711315 *Fax:* 01957 711815
Email: buness-house@zenet.co.uk *Web:* www.users.zetnet.co.uk/buness-house

Map Ref: 37
A968

Listed seventeenth century house by the sea on Unst, Britain's most
northerly island. Excellent dinners using local land and sea produce,
usually in the conservatory (no nights in summer). Fine views. Otters
on shoreline. Splendid walking country. Historic remains.
Spectacular cliffs and beaches. Two Nature Reserves, teeming bird
and plant life (puffins are almost tame! One flower is unique to Unst).

B & B from £31.50pp, C-Cards MC VS, Dinner £25, Rooms
2 double, 1 twin, both en-suite, Restricted smoking, Children by
arrangement, Dogs by arrangement, Closed Xmas & New Year

BILBSTER HOUSE Bilbster, Wick KW1 5TB
Ian Stewart *Tel / Fax:* 01955 621212
Email: ianstewart@bilbster.freeserve.co.uk *Web:* www.accommodationbilbster.com

Map Ref: 38
A882

Bilbster House is an attractive listed country house dating from
before the 1700s in five acres of garden and woodland. Furnished to
a high standard, all bedrooms have traditional bedding with electric
blankets. Situated five miles west of Wick on A882 and central for all
Caithness attractions such as John O Groats, day trips around
Orkney Isles and Wicks. Award winning heritage museum.

B & B £18-£19pp, Rooms 2 double, 1 twin, most ensuite,
No smoking, Children & dogs welcome, Closed Xmas & New Year

Wales

A proud and independent nation where the Welsh language is the first language of many, particularly in the north and west. There is a strong tradition here of choral singing, and the Welsh love of music in all its forms. Literature and poetry is also manifest in the large number of eisteddfods. The decline in the Welsh mining industry has now resulted in the most important industry being tourism.

The land bordering on England, known as the Marches and formed by the gorge of the lower Wye gives a glorious introduction to South Wales. The coastline improves as you proceed westwards with the Gower Peninsular jutting fourteen miles out into Carmarthen Bay, declared in 1956 the first official Area of Outstanding Beauty, and Pembrokeshire, an old favourite destination of seaside holiday makers. Mid Wales represents glorious unspoilt border country with little traffic and was described in the Times as "one of the last wildernesses of Britain". It is relatively unknown to the holiday visitor offers the glorious Brecon Beacons National Park, the Black Mountains, a wild ridge to the west rising to 2,630 feet at Fan Brycheiniog, and the Cambrian Mountains. North Wales contains the Snowdonia National Park including the highest mountains in England and Wales. The north coast boasts the 'Queen of the Welsh Resorts', Llandudno, gloriously situated between the

Lake Vyrnwy, Powys, Mid-Wales (WTB)

Cwmystwyth, Ceredigion, Mid-Wales (WTB)

Great Orme and the Little Orme. The town retains much of its Victorian charm

The Isle of Anglesey is a delight, with fine beaches and a remarkable number of neolithic remains. The Menai Strait between the island and the mainland is spanned by Telford's suspension bridge.

Wales is a country of spectacular sights, of magnificent National Parks and wonderful mountain scenery with well over a hundred medieval castles. In 1284 at Caernarfon Castle, Edward I presented his son to the Welsh people as Prince of Wales. HRH Prince Charles was similarly invested in 1969.

PLACES TO VISIT

This is a small selection of interesting places to visit. Many more are listed in our annual guide to Museums, Galleries, Historic Houses & Sites (see page 448)

Caernarfon Castle
Caernarfon
The castle was begun by Edward I in 1283, and is the most famous and one of the most impressive castles in Wales. Prince Charles was invested here in 1969.

Glynn Vivian Art Gallery
Swansea
Swansea porcelain and pottery, works by Welsh and UK artists, glass including time paperweights, European and Oriental china.

National Museum and Gallery
Cardiff
Founded in 1907 to preserve Welsh heritage, the museum's collections include works of major impressionists, national sciences, archaelogy and geology.

Powis Castle and Garden
Welshpool
The medieval castle contains one of the finest collections of paintings and furniture in Wales. The garden is famous for its clipped yew trees and herbaceous borders.

St Davids Bishop's Palace and Cathedral
St Davids, Dyfed
The 12th to 14th century cathedral is one of Britain's finest. Nearby is the 14th century Bishop's Palace, unoccupied for the past 300 years.

South & Southwest Wales

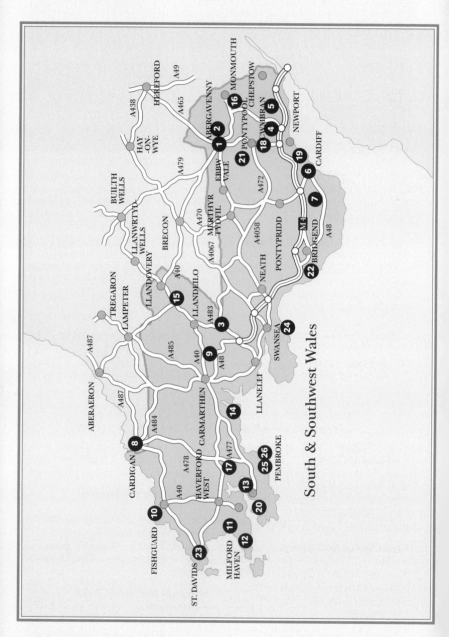

South & Southwest Wales

The Red Map References should be used to locate B & B properties on the pages that follow

LLANWENARTH HOUSE Gofilon, Abergavenny NP7 9SF
Mrs A R Weatherill   *Tel:* 01873 830289   *Fax:* 01873 832199
Email: amanda.bbdq@welsh-hotel.co.uk   *Web:* www.welsh-hotel.co.uk

Map Ref: 1
A465

The house stands in its own tranquil and beautiful grounds within the Brecon Beacons National Park. King Charles is said to have kept reserve horses and arms here during the Civil War, yet none of the character of the house has been lost through the ages. Dinner is served by candlelight and Amanda, a Cordon Bleu cook, makes full use of local game and fish. Award Winning Welsh Country House of the Year, AA 4 Diamonds

B & B £42-£45pp, Dinner from £25, Rooms 4 double, 1 twin, all en-suite, Restricted smoking, Children over 8, Dogs by arrangement, Closed Xmas & Feb

---

THE WENALLT Abergavenny NP7 0HP
B L Harris   *Tel / Fax:* 01873 830694
Email: wenallt@ukworld.net   *Web:* www.ukworld.net.wenallt

Map Ref: 1
A465

15th century longhouse in the rolling hills of the Brecon Beacons, described by some as the perfect peace and tranquillity. Small, quiet hotel offering comfort, personal service and excellent home cooking. Ideal location for country walks, or for relaxing on the spacious lawns. A perfect place for artists or photographers with its panoramic views. En-suite bedrooms. Inglenook log fires in winter. Restaurant licensed.

B & B from £19.50pp, Dinner from £12, Rooms 4 single, 1 twin, 5 double, 1 family, all en-suite, Restricted smoking, Children welcome, Dogs by arrangement, Open all year

---

LLANVAPLEY COURT Llanvapley, Abergavenny NP7 8SG
Countess Flavia Stampa Gruss
Tel: 01600 780250   *Fax:* 01600 780520

Map Ref: 2
B4233

Llanvapley Court is a Georgian manor house in Wye Valley with tea/coffee facilities in each room. There is a Michelin starred Walnut Tree restaurant nearby and also good food pubs. The house has recently been a location for films with local abbeys and castles to visit. There is also fishing available by prior arrangement. Private drive and ample parking.

B & B £35-£40pp, Rooms 1 single, 2 double, 1 twin, private bathrooms, No smoking, Children over 12, No dogs, Closed Xmas & New Year

BRYNCOCH FARM Llandyfan, Ammanford SA18 2TY
Mary & Graham Richardson   *Tel:* 01269 850480   *Fax:* 01269 850888
Email: robrich@ntlworld.com

Map Ref: 3
A483

Bryncoch Farm, built in the 17th century, is situated high above the Amman Valley in the Brecon Beacons National Park. Large comfortably furnished en-suite bedrooms and the Botanic Gardens mere minutes away.

B & B from £18pp, Rooms 1 double, 2 twin, all en-suite, Children welcome, Dogs by arrangement, Open all year

---

GREAT HOUSE Isca Road, Old Village, Caerleon NP18 1QG
Dinah Price   *Tel:* 01633 420216   *Fax:* 01633 423492   *Mobile:* 07977 261687
Email: price.greathouse@tesco.net   *Web:* www.visitgreathouse.co.uk

Map Ref: 4
M4 J25, B4596

Great House is a Grade II 16th century attractive old village house. I welcome guests to my riverside home with its clematis garden, wood burning stoves and beams which help to maintain its original character. The Celtic Manor Golf Resort is within walking distance and Caerleon Roman Amphitheatre is nearby. It is ideal as a stopover for those travelling through Wales.

B & B £22.50-£25pp, Rooms 1 single, 2 twin, No smoking, Children over 10, Very small dogs only, Closed Xmas

PENYLAN St Brides, Netherwent, Caldicot NP26 3AS   *Map Ref:* 5
Mrs Anne Arthur   M4 J23a
Tel: 01633 400267   *Fax:* 01633 400997

Penylan is a fine Elizabethan farm house set in half an acre of beautiful gardens looking out over the peaceful St Brides Valley. The lounge has a fine inglenook fireplace and visitors are welcome to use our large heated indoor swimming pool. In all rooms there are tea/coffee facilities and televisions. Very good local eateries in easy reach. Two miles from M4.

B & B from £25pp, Rooms 2 single, 1 twin with en-suite, 1 family, No smoking, Children welcome, No dogs, Closed Dec to Feb

---

THE GUEST HOUSE 160 Richmond Road, Roath, Cardiff CF24 3BX   *Map Ref:* 6
Pete & Maggie Bird   M4, A48
Tel: 029 20483619

A small, friendly family run guest house with a private car park. Conveniently situated with a 15 minute walk to the town centre or three minute drive, on the main bus route. The Castle, shops, parks all very close. All rooms are centrally heated with washbasins, colour televisions and hospitality trays. M4 junction 29.

B & B from £15pp, Rooms 2 single, 3 twin, 3 double, 2 family, 2 en-suite, No smoking, Children over 5, No dogs, Closed Xmas

---

LLANERCH VINEYARD Hensol, Pendoylan, Cardiff CF72 8JU   *Map Ref:* 7
Peter & Diana Andrews *Tel:* 01443 225877   *Fax:* 01443 225546   M4 J34
Email: enquiries@llanerch-vineyard.co.uk *Web:* www.llanerch-vineyard.co.uk

Featured on the BBC, television 'Holidays Out' programme, this beautifully converted, fully modernised farmhouse overlooks the six acre vineyard and farmland. En-suite rooms offer central heating, tea facilities and TV. Guests can tour the vineyard and winery, taste the award winning wines and follow trails through woodland and lakes. Ideal for touring South Wales, 15 minutes from Cardiff. Parking. Golf, fishing and riding nearby.

B & B from £25pp, C-Cards MC VS, Rooms 2 twin, 1 double, all en-suite, self contained double suite, No smoking, Children over 8, No dogs, Closed Xmas & New Year

---

THE OLD VICARAGE Moylgrove, Cardigan SA43 3BN   *Map Ref:* 8
Patricia & David Phillips *Tel:* 01239 881231   *Fax:* 0870 1362382   A487
Email: stay@old-vic.co.uk *Web:* www.old-vic.co.uk

Spacious Edwardian home set in an elevated position in the National Park with large gardens and glorious sea view. Close to dramatic section of the Pembrokeshire Coast Path at Ceibwr Bay, with the Preseli Hills, Gwaun and Teifi valleys nearby. Enjoy imaginative home-cooking and interesting wine list. Relax in the timeless and leisurely tranquility of North Pembrokeshire - Bluestone Country.

B & B £30pp, Dinner £18, Rooms 2 double, 1 twin, all en-suite, No smoking, No children, Closed Dec to Feb

---

PLAS ALLTYFERIN Pontargothi, Nantgaredig, Carmarthen SA32 7PF   *Map Ref:* 9
Charlotte & Gerard Dent *Tel:* 01267 290662   *Fax:* 01267 290919   A40
Email: dent@altyferin.fsnet.co.uk

A classic Georgian country house in the hills above the Towy Valley, overlooking a Norman hillfort, the River Cothi, and private cricket pitch. Two spacious twin bedrooms, with private bathrooms and stunning views, for guests welcomed as family friends. Antiques, log fires. Excellent local pubs and restaurants. Marvellous touring country for castles, beaches and Welsh speaking Wales. Total peace, under four hours from London.

B & B from £25pp, Rooms 1 twin en-suite, 1 twin private bathroom, Children over 12, Dogs by arrangement, Closed Xmas & New Year

BRYNAWEL COUNTRY HOUSE/ANNEXE Llanwnda, Goodwick, Fishguard SA64 0HR   *Map Ref:* 10
Rhian C Lloyd   *Tel / Fax:* 01348 874155   A40
Email: brynawel@amserve.net

A Victorian guest house sited on a small holding. Self catering with
tea/coffee facilities and televisions in all rooms and a private, secure
lit car park. Half a mile from coastal path. Ferry to Ireland only five
minutes with fishing, horse riding and golf within five miles. Winners
of 1998 Welcome Host of Year Award. Free transport for coastal
path walkers (2 nights or more).

B & B from £18pp, Dinner from £9, Rooms 2 double, 2 twin,
1 private family, Restricted smoking, Children over 4, Dogs
welcome, Open all year

LION ROCK Broad Haven, Haverfordwest SA62 3JP   *Map Ref:* 11
Anthony & Jane Main   *Tel:* 01437 781645   *Fax:* 01437 781203   *Mobile:* 07970 426505   B4341
Email: lion.rock@btinternet.com   *Web:* www.stayatlionrock.co.uk

Our single storey house occupies a cliff top position overlooking St
Brides' Bay, with our own access to the coast path. We are well
situated for walking, bird watching, water sports and visiting
Pembrokeshire's islands. All our rooms have television, tea/coffee
making facilities, and either en-suite or private bathrooms. There are
good pubs and restaurants locally.

B & B £24-£32pp, Dinner from £12.50, Rooms 2 double, 1 twin,
2 single, most en-suite, No smoking, Children over 8, Dogs by
arrangement, Closed Nov to Jan

POST HOUSE HOTEL Dale, Haverfordwest SA62 3RE   *Map Ref:* 12
Laurence & Christine Riley   B4327
Tel: 01646 636201

Family run licensed hotel in coastal village of Dale in an Area of
Outstanding Natural Beauty. Bedrooms all tastefully furnished with
resident's lounge, conservatory, dining room and bar.

B & B from £25pp, Dinner available, Rooms 5 en-suite, Restricted
smoking, Closed Mar to Jan

KNOWLES FARM Lawrenny, Kilgetty SA68 0PX   *Map Ref:* 13
Virginia Lort Phillips   *Tel / Fax:* 01834 891221   A4075
Email: ginilp@lawrenny.org.uk   *Web:* www.lawrenny.org.uk

Come and relax at our lovely south facing family home overlooking
the Milford Haven Estuary. Our organic farm is on the edge of this
beautiful winding estuary in the heart of the National Park. The coast
is minutes away and within a short distance there is birding, boating,
castles and gardens. Pets are also welcome.

B & B £23-£25pp, Dinner from £10, Rooms 2 double, 1 twin,
1 family, all en-suite, No smoking, Children welcome, No dogs
downstairs, Closed Nov to Mar

LAUGHARNE CASTLE HOUSE B & B Castle House, Market Lane, Laugharne SA33 4SA
Amanda & Charles Mitchell   *Tel:* 01994 427616   *Map Ref:* 14
Email: amanda@laugharne.co.uk   *Web:* www.laugharne.co.uk   A4066
Beautiful Grade II* listed Georgian house dating from 1730s in
ancient township of Laugharne. Situated next to Norman Castle with
lovely gardens overlooking estuary. Large attractively furnished
rooms with en-suite or private bathroom have tea/coffee making
facilities. Family room available. Restaurants/pubs close by. Pendine
Beach, National Botanical Aberglasney Gardens within easy reach.
Walks, fishing, riding, and sailing locally. Ideal quiet break.

B & B £25-£35pp, C-Cards MC VS, Rooms 3 double, 1 twin,
1 family, most en-suite, Children & dogs welcome, Open all year

MOUNT PLEASANT FARM Llanwrda SA19 8AN
Sue & Nick Thompson
Tel / Fax: 01550 777537   *Mobile:* 07770 993588

Map Ref: 15
A40, A482

Anyone looking for complete tranquility will find it in this 200 year old farmhouse that unashamedly boasts the most beautiful view in the country. Aberglasney and the Botanic Gardens are within 30 minutes drive and all around there are wonderful walks. Sue, an interior designer, and her daughter, Alice, love cooking using organic and local produce with outstanding results.

B & B from £25pp, Dinner from £12.50, Rooms 1 single, 2 double/twin, all en-suite, No smoking, Children over 12, No dogs, Closed Xmas

---

CHURCH FARM GUEST HOUSE Mitchel Troy, Monmouth NP25 4HZ
Rosey & Derek Ringer
Tel: 01600 712176

Map Ref: 16
A40

A spacious and homely 16th century former farmhouse with oak beams and inglenook fireplaces. Set in one acre of grounds with stream with easy access to A40 and only two miles from historic Monmouth. Large car park, terrace and barbecue. Most rooms en-suite. WTB 2 Star guest house. AA 3 Diamonds.

B & B £20-£24pp, Dinner from £13, Rooms 1 single, 2 twin, 3 double, 2 family, most en-suite, No smoking, Children welcome, Dogs by arrangement, Closed Xmas

---

THE PEACOCK GUEST HOUSE Hoarstone, Martletwy, Narberth SA67 8AZ
Mrs R E Mooney   *Tel / Fax:* 01834 891707
Email: ros@peacockguesthouse.co.uk   *Web:* www.peacockguesthouse.co.uk

Map Ref: 17
A40, A477, A4075

Visitors can be assured of peaceful nights and warm hospitality. This attractive house stands in the beautiful Pembrokeshire Coast National Park . The gardens in a tree lined glade, are home to some peacocks, guests are welcome to relax and enjoy the atmosphere. Individually styled bedrooms with lovely views, offer either en-suite or private facilities. Picnics, packed lunches and dinners by arrangement.

B & B £20-£25pp, C-Cards MC VS, Dinner available, Rooms 1 double en-suite, 1 twin with private bathroom, Restricted Smoking, Children over 12, No dogs, Closed Oct to Mar

---

THE GLEBE Croes-Y-Ceiliog, Cwmbran, Newport NP44 2DE
Mrs Beryl Watkins
Tel: 01633 450251/450242

Map Ref: 18
M4 J25A, A4042

The Glebe is an ideal spot from which to explore this historic region of rural Wales with its numerous castles and abbeys and the book shops of Hay-on-Wye. Your friendly and helpful host is only too happy to help you plan if need be. Cardiff is only 20 minutes. In the evening good pub fare is a pleasant country stroll away.

B & B from £22pp, Rooms 1 single, 2 double, 1 with en-suite, No smoking, Children welcome, No dogs, Closed Xmas & New Year

---

WEST USK LIGHTHOUSE St Brides, Wentloog, Newport NP1 9SF
Frank & Danielle Sheahan *Tel:* 01633 810126/815860
Email: lighthousel@tesco.net *Web:* www.westusklighthouse.co.uk

Map Ref: 19
M4 J28, B4239

Stay in a distinctly different Grade II listed lighthouse built in 1821. West Usk Lighthouse has wedge-shaped rooms, water and four poster beds, also a flotation tank for deep relaxation. Champagne breakfasts, therapies and a Rolls Royce ride to a local restaurant are all on offer here, this is a romantic and peaceful setting. Many amenities and attractions nearby.

B & B from £40pp, C-Cards MC VS AE DC, Rooms 3 double en-suite, No smoking, Children welcome, Dogs by arrangement, Open all year

---

BOWETT FARM Hundleton, Pembroke SA71 5QS
Ann Morris
Tel / Fax: 01646 683473

Map Ref: 20
B4320

Bowett is a lovely spacious old farmhouse set in it's own grounds with a natural stream running through. Bedrooms have tea/coffee making facilities, radios and hairdryers. We are within a mile of ancient Pembroke town on the South Bank of Milford Haven Waterway and close to the spectacular Pembrokeshire Coast National Park.

B & B £23-£25pp, Rooms 1 double, 1 twin, both with private bathroom, No smoking, Children over 12, No dogs, Closed Nov to Mar

---

CRESSWELL HOUSE Cresswell Quay, Pembroke SA68 0TE
Philip Wight *Tel:* 01646 651435
Email: phil@cresswellhouse.co.uk *Web:* www.cresswellhouse.co.uk

Map Ref: 20
A4075

On the edge of the Cleodale Estuary this Georgian Quay Masters' House has an enviable location as all rooms have river views. Your host, Phil, produces imaginative and memorable food for both breakfast and dinner. Situated within an eight mile radius of Tenby, Pembroke, historic castles and the coastal path. There is also a fine old fashioned inn 50 yards away.

B & B £25-£30pp, Dinner from £25, Rooms 2 double, 1 twin, all en-suite, Restricted smoking, Children over 7, No dogs, Closed Xmas & New Year

---

TY'R YWEN FARM Lasgarn Lane, Mamhilad, via Trevethin, Pontypool NP4 8TT
Susan Armitage *Tel / Fax:* 01495 785200
Email: susan.armitage@virgin.net *Web:* http://freespace.virgin.net/susan.armitage/webpage3.htm

Map Ref: 21
A472

A remote 16th century Welsh longhouse high on the Gwent Ridgeway in the Brecon Beacons National Park. Breathtaking views down the Usk Valley and across the Bristol Channel. The house retains many original features, inglenooks, and comfortable bedrooms. One room has a four poster bed, and a jacuzzi. Pets welcomed. 2 stables and grazing for horses. 30,000 acres of upland moor, numerous bridleways.

B & B £20-£30pp, C-Cards MC VS, Rooms 3 double (4 poster beds), 1 twin, all en-suite, No smoking, Children over 14, Dogs welcome, Closed Xmas & New Year

---

MICHAELSTON 11 West Drive, Porthcawl CF36 3LS
Clark & Bennie Warren *Tel:* 01656 783617 *Fax:* 01656 789162
Email: clrkbenwaraol.com *Web:* www.michaelston.sagenet.co.uk

Map Ref: 22
M4, A4229

Michaelston overlooks the seafront with a lovely private garden and heated swimming pool. It boasts three beautifully appointed suites with exceptional food in the Ballymalde style, using only the finest ingredients. Ideal coastal situation, only 30 minutes drive to Cardiff and Gower Coast with Royal Porthcawl only one mile away. WTB 5 Star.

B & B £35-£40pp, C-Cards, Dinner from £25, Rooms 2 double, 1 twin, all en-suite, No smoking, Children over 10, Dogs by arrangement, Closed Xmas, New Year & Easter

RAMSEY HOUSE Lower Moor, St Davids SA62 6RP   *Map Ref:* 23
Mac & Sandra Thompson *Tel:* 01437 720321 *Fax:* 01437 720025   A487
Email: info@ramseyhouse.co.uk *Web:* www.ramseyhouse.co.uk

Ramsey House caters exclusively for adults. Six delightfully appointed en-suite bedrooms, some with sea view, all with remote control colour television and hospitality tray. Award winning dinners with Welsh emphasis featuring fresh local produce. Quiet location ideally situated for St David's Cathedral, Pembrokeshire Coast Path, beaches and attractions. Private parking.

B & B £32-£34pp, C-Cards MC VS, Dinner from £16, Rooms 3 double, 3 twin, en-suite, No smoking, No children, Dogs by arrangement, Closed Xmas

---

TIDES REACH 388 Mumbles Road, Mumbles, Swansea SA3 5TN   *Map Ref:* 24
Mrs Jan Maybery *Tel:* 01792 404877 *Fax:* 01792 404775   A4067
Email: tidesreachmumbles@yahoo.com *Web:* www.tidesreachguesthouse.co.uk

Tides Reach was originally built as the Bath House Hotel in 1855 and retains elegant Victorian surroundings with period furniture and beautiful fabrics and furnishings. Pleasantly situated on the Sea Front overlooking the Bay. Attractive bedrooms have colour television, tea/coffee making facilities and are centrally heated, a sea-view four poster bedroom is available. Breakfast is served in a cheerful and welcoming Welsh dining room.

B & B £25-£35pp, Rooms 3 double, 1 twin, 2 family, all en-suite, No smoking, Children over 10, Dogs by arrangement, Closed Nov to Feb

---

FERNLEY LODGE Manorbier, Tenby   *Map Ref:* 25
Jane Cowper *Tel:* 01834 871226   B4585
Email: fernleylodge@yahoo.com

Fernley Lodge is in the centre of the beautiful coastal village of Manorbier. The Pembrokeshire coastal path and superb beach, are a quarter of a mile away. This wonderfully restored imposing house is classically decorated with antique furnishings. Bedrooms have TV and tea making facilities. The guests' lovely drawing room overlooks the croquet and tennis lawn, there is an open fire on cooler evenings.

B & B £20-£25pp, Rooms 2 double, 1 en-suite family, No smoking, Children & dogs welcome, Closed Xmas

---

THE OLD VICARAGE Manorbier, Tenby SA70 7TN   *Map Ref:* 25
Jill McHugh *Tel / Fax:* 01834 871452 *Mobile:* 07974 109877   A4139
Email: old_vic@manorbier@yahoo.com

The Old Vicarage is set in a peaceful coastal location. It offers gracious accommodation with glimpses of Barafundle Bay. Guests are welcome to enjoy the gardens or log fires. There are two spacious en-suite rooms with tea/coffee facilities. Manorbier is famous for its Norman Castle, sandy beach and stunning scenery. Irish ferries from Pembroke (20 minutes) or Fishguard (45 minutes).

B & B from £22.50pp, Rooms 1 twin, 1 double, en-suite, No smoking, No children or dogs, Closed Xmas

---

WYCHWOOD HOUSE Penally, Tenby SA70 7PE   *Map Ref:* 26
Lee & Mherly Ravenscroft *Tel:* 01834 844387 *Mobile:* 07815 678812   A4139
Email: wychwoodbb@aol.com

An elegant country house with sea views, secure parking and well appointed bedrooms, which are equipped with televisions and tea/coffee facilities. Wychwood House is situated in the National Park with lovely walks and fishing plus two golf courses nearby. Penally is a quiet village only a 20 minute walk along a path to Tenby. The beach is a 10 minute walk.

B & B from £25pp, C-Cards MC VS, Dinner from £17.50, Rooms 2 double (4 poster beds), 1 family, all en-suite, No smoking, Children welcome, Dogs by arrangement, Open all year

Mid-Wales

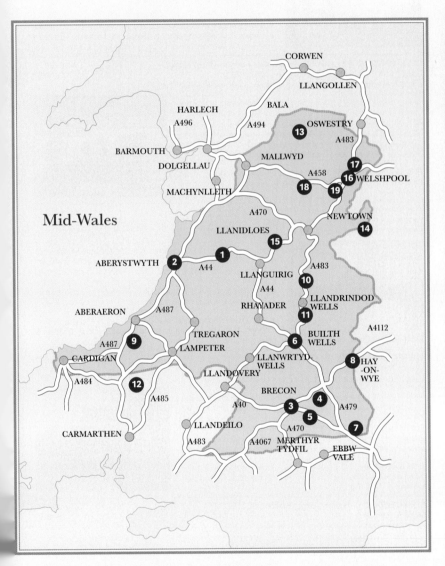

The Red Map References should be used to locate B & B properties on the pages that follow

THE GEORGE BORROW HOTEL Ponterwyd, Aberystwyth SY23 3AD — *Map Ref:* 1
John & Jill Wall *Tel:* 01970 890230 *Fax:* 01970 890587 — A44, A487
Email: georgeborrow@clara.net *Web:* www.george-burrow.co.uk

A famous hotel overlooking Rheidol Gorge in the foothills of the Cambrian Mountains. All rooms have televisions, tea/coffee facilities and are central heated. Lounge overlooking beautiful countryside with log fires and good food and beer. Ideal for walking, fishing, bird watching (Red Kite) or exploring Mid Wales.

B & B from £25pp, C-Cards MC VS, Dinner from £5.25, Rooms 2 single, 2 double, 3 twin, 2 family, all en-suite, Restricted smoking, Children welcome, Dogs by arrangement, Open all year

GLYN-GARTH GUEST HOUSE South Road, Aberystwyth SY23 1JS — *Map Ref:* 2
Louis Evans *Tel:* 01970 615050 *Fax:* 01970 636835 — A44, A487
Email: glyn-garth@southroad88freeserve.co.uk *Web:* www.glyngarthgh.cjb.net

A guaranteed warm welcome awaits you at Glyn-Garth, run by the Evans family for 40 years. Renowned for excellent service and accommodation with televisions, tea/coffee facilities in every room. Situated adjacent to the south promenade near the harbour and Castle. A perfect base to explore the delights of Mid-Wales. RAC 4 diamonds, AA 4 diamonds, Welsh Tourist Board 4 star.

B & B £21-£27pp, Rooms 1 single, 5 double, 2 family, most en-suite, No smoking, Children welcome, No dogs, Closed Xmas & New Year

THE BEACONS 16 Bridge Street, Brecon LD3 8AH — *Map Ref:* 3
Mr & Mrs P E Jackson *Tel:* 01874 623339 — A40, A470
Email: beacons@brecon.co.uk

The Beacons is a recently restored 17th/18th century house which retains many original features. There are well appointed, standard, en-suite and luxury period rooms. Enjoy a drink in the original meat cellar before our award winning chef spoils you with our outstanding cuisine. There is a car park and cycle store. Ring Peter and Barbara Jackson for more information.

B & B from £18pp, Dinner from £9.95, Rooms 1 single, 3 twin, 4 double, 6 family, most en-suite, Restricted smoking, Children & dogs welcome, Closed Xmas

TREFECCA FAWR Brecon LD3 0PW — *Map Ref:* 3
Miles & Patricia Park *Tel:* 01874 712 195 *Fax:* 01874 712 196 — A40, B4560
Email: lodge@trefecca.zx3.net *Web:* www.trefeccafawr.co.uk

Without doubt the most comfortable and well appointed private country house accommodation in the National Park. The Grade I listed medieval and 17th century house with fine plaster ceilings is perfect for a short break among the lakes and mountains of mid-Wales. Hay-on-Wye, book lovers paradise, is nearby; ancient castles, priories and gardens abound with plenty of local restaurants.

B & B £38-£48pp, C-Cards MC VS, Rooms 2 double, 1 twin, all en-suite, No smoking, Children over 12, No dogs, Closed Dec to Feb

SHIWA LODGE Llangorse Village, Brecon LD3 7UG — *Map Ref:* 4
Marie & John Gray — B4560
Tel: 01874 658631 *Fax:* 01874 658144

Overlooks Llangorse lake and is decorated in African style. The house is set in lovely grounds with parking and within walking distance of village pubs. Rooms are en-suite with tea/coffee facilities. 1 bedroom has facilities for the disabled. Within the Brecon Beacons National Park are many activity centres catering for riding, climbing, sailing or walking to soak up the glorious scenery.

B & B £20-£25pp, Rooms 1 double, 1 twin, 1 family, all en-suite, No smoking, Children welcome, No dogs, Closed Xmas & New Year

Glangrwyney Court, Crickhowell

DOLYCOED Talyllyn, Brecon LD3 7SY   *Map Ref:* 4
Mary Cole   A40
Tel: 01874 658666

This Edwardian house stands in a sheltered spot in the Brecon Beacons National Park, just five miles from Brecon. There are mature gardens for guests to enjoy with the house offering warmth and home comforts. Disabled guests are welcome. From Brecon A40/A470 take the A40 for Abergavenny, then B4558 to Llangorse, first right, next right, house is on right at next T junction.

B & B from £20pp, Rooms 1 twin, 1 double with shower, Children & dogs welcome, Closed Xmas

---

CAMBRIAN CRUISERS Ty Newydd, Pencelli, Brecon LD3 7LJ   *Map Ref:* 5
Mrs Nicola Atkins *Tel / Fax:* 01874 665315   A40, B4558
Email: cambrian@talk21.com *Web:* www.cambriancruisers.co.uk

Our accommodation is just three miles south of Brecon at Ty Newydd - a farmhouse which has changed little in appearance since it was built in around 1720. Its location is quite superb with open views to Pen-y-Fan, the highest point of the Brecon Beacons just a few miles away, and adjacent to the Monmouthshire and Brecon Canal.

B & B £23-£28pp, C-Cards MC VS, Rooms 3 double, 1 twin, all en-suite, No smoking, No children or dogs, Closed Nov to Mar

---

RHYDFELIN GUEST HOUSE Builth Road, Builth Wells LD2 3RT   *Map Ref:* 6
Alan & Liz Moyes *Tel:* 01982 552493   A44
Email: liz@rhydfelinguesthouse.freeserve.co.uk *Web:* www.rhydfelinguesthouse.freeserve.co.uk

An 18th century stone farmhouse on the A470 in Wye Valley. Easy access to 'Heart of Wales' attractions with Builth Wells only three miles away. Licensed restaurant, cosy bar and television lounge. Bedrooms with tea/coffee facilities and hot and cold water. Cream teas served in summer. Adequate car parking. WTB 3 Stars.

B & B from £19.50pp, Dinner from £12, Rooms 2 double, 1 twin, 1 en-suite family, No smoking, Children welcome, Dogs by arrangement, Closed Xmas

---

TRERICKET MILL VEGETARIAN GUESTHOUSE Erwood, Builth Wells LD2 3TQ   *Map Ref:* 6
Nicky & Alistair Legge *Tel:* 01982 560312 *Fax:* 01982 560768   A470
Email: mail@trericket.co.uk *Web:* www.trericket.co.uk

Trericket Mill has a unique, informal and historic atmosphere complete with original milling machinery, log fires, books, games and a riverside garden. All the catering is vegetarian using wholefoods, organic, free range and fair trade produce wherever possible. The bedrooms are accessed via a wooden spiral staircase, have original fireplaces, handcrafted beds and views across the River Wye.

B & B £21-£24pp, Dinner from £12.75, Rooms 2 double, 1 twin, all en-suite, No smoking, Children welcome, No dogs, Closed Xmas

---

GLANGRWYNEY COURT Crickhowell NP8 1ES   *Map Ref:* 7
Christina Jackson *Tel:* 01873 811288 *Fax:* 01873 810317   A40
Email: glangrwyne@aol.com *Web:* www.walescountryhousebandb.com   *see Photo on page 411*

A Grade 2 Listed Georgian mansion in four acres of garden, surrounded by parkland. Centrally heated, with log fires in winter, the bedrooms are well equipped. The house is furnished with antiques there is a residents' lounge with television. There is tennis, croquet and bowls. Golf and pony trekking can be arranged. Walking in the Brecon Beacons National Park is minutes away. Parking.

B & B from £22.50pp, C-Cards, Dinner from £20, Rooms 1 single, 2 twin, 2 double, 1 family, all en-suite, Restricted smoking, Children & dogs welcome, Open all year

YORK HOUSE Hardwicke Road, Cusop, Hay-on-Wye HR3 5QX
Peter & Olwen Roberts *Tel / Fax:* 01497 820705
Email: roberts@yorkhouse59.fsnet.co.uk

Map Ref: 8
B4348

This elegant, late Victorian residence is quietly situated at the edge of Hay-on-Wye, a small but ancient market town, with a beautiful, large, southerly garden. Since 1985 we have lovingly refurbished York House, which happily retains many of its original features, to create a haven of comfort and convenience. All rooms are furnished to a fine standard in period style.

B & B £27-£29pp, C-Cards MC VS AE, Dinner from £16, Rooms 1 double, 3 double/twin, all en-suite, No smoking, Children over 8, Dogs by arrangement, Closed Xmas

---

GWYNFRYN Llanarth SA47 0PA
Paul & Delyth Wilson and Peter Grey-Hughes *Tel:* 01545 580837 *Fax:* 01545 580212
Email: delyth.wilson@virgin.net *Web:* www.privateprincipality

Map Ref: 9
A487

Built in 1895 for a retiring bishop Gwynfryn is a typical house of its time but now a handsome family home. Decorated with traditional furnishings, fine paintings and antique furniture, it offers every possible comfort. Set in five acres of gardens it is within easy reach of the coastal paths and fishing villages of Cardigan Bay as well as the mountains of Mid-Wales.

B & B from £40pp, Dinner from £23, Rooms 1 double, 1 twin, both en-suite, No smoking, No children or dogs, Closed Dec to Feb

---

GUIDFA HOUSE Crossgates, Llandrindod Wells LD1 6RF
Tony & Anne Millan *Tel:* 01597 851241 *Fax:* 01597 851875
Email: guidfa@globalnet.co.uk *Web:* www.guidfa-house.co.uk

Map Ref: 10
A44, A483

Stylish Georgian guest house with an enviable reputation for its comfort, award winning food and service. Superior accommodation, all en-suite, including a ground floor room. Imaginative meals using fresh local produce prepared by 'Cordon Bleu' trained Anne and accompanied by excellent wines. Ideally located for touring Wales and the Borders. Selected by Wales Great Little Places and recommended by Which.

B & B from £26.50pp, C-Cards MC VS, Dinner from £17.50, Rooms 1 single, 3 double, 2 twin, all en-suite, Restricted smoking, Children over 12, Only guide dogs, Open all year

---

HOLLY FARM Holly Farm, Howey, Llandrindod Wells LD1 5PP
Ruth Jones *Tel / Fax:* 01597 822402
Web: www.ukworld.net/hollyfarm

Map Ref: 11
A483

Tastefully restored Tudor farmhouse on working farm in peaceful location. Pretty bedrooms, some with exposed beams and breathtaking views over fields and woods, televisions and tea/coffee facilities. Lounge with cosy log fire, dining room with separate tables. Traditional farmhouse cooking using farm's own lamb, beef and vegetables when available. Wonderful area for wildlife, walking and cycling and near Red Kite feeding station.

B & B £20-£26pp, C-Cards MC VS, Dinner from £11, Rooms 2 double, 2 twin, 1 family, most en-suite, Restricted smoking, Children welcome, Dogs not in house, Closed Xmas

---

BRONIWAN Rhydlewis, Llandysul SA44 5PF
Mrs Carole Jacobs *Tel / Fax:* 01239 851261
Email: broniwan@compuserve.com

Map Ref: 12
B4334

A small peaceful farm just 10 minutes from the coast with wonderful views of the Preseli Hills. Carole and Allen unfussily draw you into their home, warm with natural colours in paintings and tapestries. Food comes form their organic farm. Vegetarian menus available. Broniwan's ivy covered walls look over a pretty garden with grassy terrace. Aberglasney within easy reach.

B & B from £25pp, Dinner from £17, Rooms 1 single, 2 double with en-suite, No smoking, Children over 11, Dogs by arrangement, Open all year

PLAS CERDIN Ffostrasol, Llandysul SA44 4TA   *Map Ref:* 12
Judith Hicks   A486
Tel: 01239 851329

This impeccably maintained split level house stands in its own landscaped garden and enjoys some breathtaking views down the Cerdin Valley. Bedrooms have tea/coffee facilities and televisions and guests have use of a comfortably furnished lounge. Only ten miles from the coast of Cardigan Bay. From Llandysul take A486 to New Quay through Bulchy Groes, turn right into private drive.

B & B from £22pp, Dinner available, Rooms 1 double, 1 twin, 1 family, all en-suite, Restricted smoking, Children over 3, Dogs by arrangement, Open all year

BRON HEULOG Waterfall Street, Llanrhaeadr YM Mochnant SY10 0JX   *Map Ref:* 13
Karon & Ken Raines   *Tel:* 01691 780521   B4396, A483
Email: kraines@enta.net   *Web:* www.kraines.enta.net

Built in 1861, this beautiful Victorian house stands in a two acre garden. The house features a magnificent curved staircase, there are original fireplaces in every room. The bedrooms enjoy views to the garden with a pond and waterfall, or to the mountains or village, there are good places to eat, plus general stores. A perfect location for birdwatching, cycling, and other outdoor pursuits.

B & B £22-£25pp, C-Cards MC VS, Rooms 2 double, 1 twin, all en-suite, No smoking, Children welcome, Dogs must sleep in car, Open all year

DREWIN FARM Churchstoke, Montgomery SY15 6TW   *Map Ref:* 14
Mrs Ceinwen Richards   *Tel / Fax:* 01588 620325   B4385
Email: ceinwen@drewinfreeserve.co.uk

Ceinwen, Robert and family offer you a warm welcome to their home. Drewin Farm overlooks a beautiful panorama of the Welsh borderlands, a landscape steeped in history and rich in wildlife. Our 17th century farmhouse lies in an area of quiet lanes and small market towns. Traditional home cooking is served in the dining room and a separate lounge is available for your comfort.

B & B £40-£44pp, Dinner from £10, Rooms 1 twin, 1 family, both en-suite, No smoking, Children welcome, Dogs outside only, Closed Nov to Mar

DYFFRYN FARMHOUSE Aberhafesp, Newtown SY16 3JD   *Map Ref:* 15
Dave & Sue Jones   *Tel:* 01686 688817   *Fax:* 01686 688324   B4568
Email: daveandsue@clara.net

Lovingly restored 17th century farmhouse, set in the heart of a 200 acre working sheep and beef farm. An abundance of wildlife and flowers along the stream outside the door, woodland and lakes nearby. Close to golf, fishing and glorious walks. Luxury en-suite rooms with full central heating. Traditional farmhouse fare, vegetarian specialities. Garden, and banks of stream to enjoy.

B & B from £25pp, Dinner from £12, Rooms 1 twin, 2 double, 1 family, all en-suite, No smoking, Children welcome, No dogs, Closed Xmas & New Year

www.stayinstyle.com

All homes listed feature on our Website and those that have their own E-mail address or Website address can be accessed direct

TYNLLWYN FARM Welshpool SY21 9BW
Jane Emberton *Tel:* 01938 553175 *Fax:* 01983 553054
Email: caroline@tynllwyn.fsnet.co.uk *Web:* www.tynllwynfarm.co.uk

Map Ref: 16
A458, A483

Tynllwyn is a family run farm with a warm friendly welcome, good
farmhouse food and service. Only one mile from the lovely market
town of Welshpool on the A490 - north - standing on a hillside, very
quiet and pleasantly situated with beautiful views of the Severn
Valley.

B & B from £18pp, Dinner from £10, Rooms 2 single, 2 double,
2 twin, Children welcome, Dogs by arrangement, Open all year

BUTTINGTON COUNTRY HOUSE Buttington, Welshpool SY21 8HD
Brian & Jean Thomas *Tel / Fax:* 01938 553351
Web: www.country-house-accommodation.co.uk/buttington/index.html

Map Ref: 17
A458

A late Georgian Country House near Welshpool with lovely views of
Severn Valley. En-suite luxury accommodation in the elegant period
residence. Ideal centre for touring mid Wales borders, Powis Castle
and walking Offa's Dyke. WTB 4 Stars, RAC 5 Diamonds.

B & B from £40pp, Dinner from £25, Restricted smoking, Children
welcome, No dogs, Open all year

LOWER TRELYDAN FARMHOUSE Guilsfield, Welshpool SY21 9PH
Graham and Sue Jones *Tel / Fax:* 01938 553105
Email: stay@lowertrelydan.com *Web:* www.lowertrelydan.com

Map Ref: 17
A490, B4392

Graham and Sue welcome you to their beautiful listed house on this
working farm. Attractive en-suite rooms freshly decorated, with
colour television, licensed bar and beverage tray. Delicious cuisine
served every night in elegant beamed dining room. Relax afterwards
in the beamed and panelled lounge. Enjoy quiet luxury in a relaxed,
friendly family atmosphere. Lovely situation - Welshpool two miles.

B & B from £26pp, Dinner from £14, Rooms 1 single, 2 double,
1 twin, 1 family, all en-suite, No smoking, Children welcome,
No dogs, Closed Xmas & New Year

CWM LLWYNOG Llanfair Caereinion, Welshpool SY21 0HF
Joyce Cornes
Tel / Fax: 01938 810791

Map Ref: 18
A458

This is a genuine working farm which Roger Cornes tends to while
his wife Joyce provides a warm welcome. Joyce's 17th century
farmhouse, with its low ceilings, beams, cosy rooms, wood panelling
and inglenook fireplace is rich in character. Joyce is a keen gardener
and her hanging baskets are a delight, as is her lovely garden leading
down to a brook.

B & B £20-£25pp, Dinner from £10, Rooms 2 double, 1 twin,
all en-suite, No smoking, Children welcome, Dogs by
arrangement, Closed Xmas

DYSSERTH HALL near Powys Castle, Welshpool SY21 8RQ
Mrs Marriott
Tel / Fax: 01938 552153

Map Ref: 19
A490

The friendly Georgian family home of Paul and Marion Marriott
situated in superb peaceful setting close to Powys Castle with
hanging gardens and deer park. Relax in the old world atmosphere.
Rooms individually and attractively decorated. Candlelit dinners
sometimes arranged. The Morning Room with television is available
in the evening. Your hosts and their labradors will welcome you.

B & B £23-£25pp, Dinner from £16, Rooms 1 single, 1 en-suite
twin, 1 private, 1 family, No smoking, Children over 8, Dogs in car,
Closed Nov to Mar

North Wales

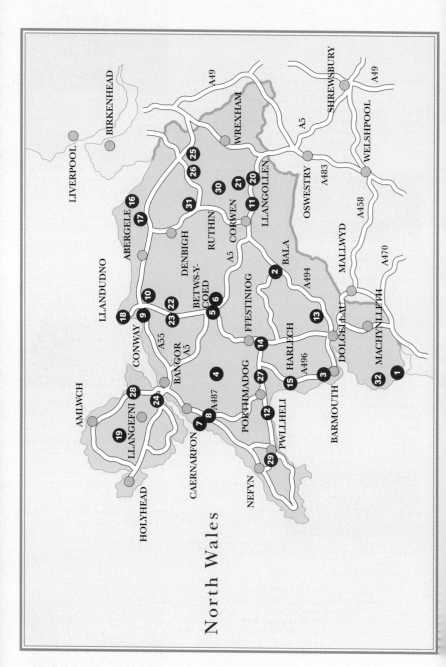

The Red Map References should be used to locate B & B properties on the pages that follow

CARTREF GUEST HOUSE Penrhos, Aberdovey LL35 0NR
William & Julie Moeran *Tel:* 01654 767273 *Fax:* 01654 767000
Email: moeran@globalnet.co.uk

Map Ref: 1
A493

Cartref is an attractive Edwardian family run guesthouse, decorated to a high standard. We offer a friendly and flexible service to ensure that you have a relaxing and enjoyable stay with us. Like many of our guests we would like you to return again and again to enjoy this area of outstanding natural beauty of Snowdonia's scenic mountains and sandy beaches.

B & B £20-£25pp, C-Cards MC VS, Rooms 1 single, 3 double, 2 twin, 2 family, most en-suite, No smoking, Children & dogs welcome, Closed Xmas & New Year

---

FRONDDERW GUEST HOUSE Stryd-y-Fron, Bala LL23 7YD
Norman & Janet Jones *Tel:* 01678 520301
Email: GB&B@thefron.co.uk *Web:* www.thefron.co.uk

Map Ref: 2
A494

Whilst the occasional owl may break the silence, the peace and tranquility of this magnificent 16th century mansion will captivate you. With spectacular views across to the Berwyn Mountains and the North of Bala Lake, this is the perfect setting for a relaxed break. Ideal for touring North/Mid Wales. 5 minutes walk from Bala town. CTV all rooms. WTB 3 stars.

B & B from £21pp, C-Cards MC VS, Dinner from £14, Rooms 1 single, 2 twin, 2 double, 3 family, most en-suite, No smoking, Children welcome, No dogs, Closed Dec to Feb

---

MELIN MELOCH near Llanfor, Bala LL23 7DP
Richard & Beryl *Tel:* 01678 520101
Email: theoldmill@mac.com *Web:* www.melochmill.co.uk

Map Ref: 2
B494, B4401

This picturesque former watermill close to Bala stands in two acres of beautiful waterscaped gardens, a delight for garden lovers. En-suite rooms in granary and mill with own front doors with televisions and hot drinks trays. The spectacular galleried interior of the mill is furnished with antiques and paintings. Here breakfast is served in a friendly relaxed atmosphere. Two minutes drive to Bala Lake and town, excellent for touring. Parking.

B & B from £22pp, Rooms 2 single, 2 twin, 2 double, 1 family, most en-suite, No smoking, Children welcome, Dogs by arrangement, Closed Nov to Feb

---

LLWYNDU FARMHOUSE Llanaber, Barmouth LL42 1RR
Peter & Paula Thompson *Tel:* 01341 280144 *Fax:* 01341 281236
Email: Intouch@llwyndu-farmhouse.co.uk *Web:* www.llwyndu-farmhouse.co.uk

Map Ref: 3
A496

A delightful 16th century house in a spectacular location with panoramic views over Cardigan Bay, north of Barmouth. A real historic farmhouse with inglenooks, oak beams, nooks and crannies. Seven very comfortable en-suite bedrooms, a fully licensed restaurant and imaginative cuisine by candlelight make a stay here one to remember. A very beautiful area to explore. For more details, ring Peter or Paula.

B & B from £32pp, C-Cards MC VS, Dinner from £14.95, Rooms 1 twin, 4 double, 2 family, all en-suite, No smoking, Children welcome, Dogs by arrangement, Closed Xmas

---

CWM CAETH Nantmor, Beddgelert LL55 4YH
Gay & Tim Harvey *Tel:* 01766 890408
Email: timharvey@ukonline.co.uk

Map Ref: 4
A498, A4085

Situated in the heart of Snowdonia and south facing with magnificent mountain views. Part of the film 'The Inn of the Sixth Happiness' was filmed here. Snowdon, the sea, castles, copper and slate mines are all close by. Cwm Caeth, a typical Welsh farmhouse, is noted for its peaceful tranquility and hospitality. WTB 3 Stars.

B & B from £20pp, Rooms 1 double en-suite, Children over 8, Dogs by arrangement, Closed Dec to Feb

SYGUN FAWR COUNTRY HOUSE Beddgelert LL55 4NE
Ian Davies and Chris Jennings *Tel / Fax:* 01766 890258
Email: sygunfawr@aol.com *Web:* www.sygunfawr.co.uk

Map Ref: 4
A498, A4085

Spectacular scenery awaits you at this former Welsh Manor House dating from 1644. Set in 20 acres of mountainside and gardens, peace and tranquility are assured at this ultimate mountain retreat. Set in the oldest part of the building the restaurant with its antique furniture and cosy atmosphere provides a relaxed and informal place to dine. It is the perfect place to walk and explore Snowdonia.

B & B £29.50-£37pp, Dinner £16, Rooms 6 double, 2 twin, 1 family, Restricted smoking, Children & dogs welcome, Closed January

---

ABERCONWY HOUSE Lon Muriau, Betws-y-Coed LL24 0HD
Kevin & Dianne Jones *Tel:* 01690 710202 *Fax:* 01690 710800
Email: welcome@aberconwy-house.co.uk *Web:* www.aberconwy-house.co.uk

Map Ref: 5
A470

Aberconwy is a large Victorian house nestling in a quiet elevated position overlooking the picturesque village of Betws-y-Coed. There are beautiful views of the Llugwy Valley, surrounding mountains and the Conwy River. Situated in Snowdonia National Park, Betwys-y-Coed is an ideal centre for touring and walking, yet is within easy reach of the fine coastlines. WTB 4 Stars.

B & B £44-£50pp, C-Cards MC VS, Rooms 4 double, 4 twin, 1 family, No smoking, Children over 8, No dogs, Open all year

---

BRYN AFON GUEST HOUSE Pentre Felin, Betws-y-Coed LL24 0BB
William & Marion Betteney *Tel:* 01690 710403 *Fax:* 01690 710989
Email: wbetteney@aol.com

Map Ref: 5
A5, A470

A Victorian stone house overlooking the river and historic stone bridge. All rooms have beverage trays, televisions, radio/alarms and central heating. There is also a lounge and dining room where special diets are catered for. Ideal situation for forest walks, golf, fishing, historic sites, beaches and museams. Restaurants and pubs all within a few minutes walk.

B & B £21-£25pp, Rooms 1 single, 3 double, 3 twin, most en-suite, No smoking, Children welcome, No dogs, Closed Xmas

---

THE FERNS GUEST HOUSE Holyhead Road, Betws-y-Coed LL24 0AN
Ian & Deborah Baxter *Tel / Fax:* 01690 710587
Email: ferns@betws-y-coed.co.uk *Web:* www.betws-y-coed.co.uk/accommodation/ferns

Map Ref: 5
A5, A470

A substantial Victorian stone house in a good location in the heart of this attractive village in the Snowdonia National Park. All en-suite bedrooms tastefully furnished with televisions, beverage trays and central heating. A delightful breakfast room and cosy guest lounge. Many restaurants in easy walking distance. Private parking. AA 4 Diamonds.

B & B £20-£24pp, C-Cards MC VS, Rooms 6 double, 1 twin, 2 family, all en-suite, No smoking, Children over 7, No dogs, Closed New Year

---

FRON HEULOG COUNTRY HOUSE Betws-y-Coed LL24 0BL
Jean & Peter Whittingham *Tel:* 01690 710736 *Fax:* 01690 710920
Email: jean&peter@fronheulog.co.uk *Web:* www.fronheulog.co.uk

Map Ref: 5
A5, A470, B5106

'The Country House in the Village,' an elegant Victorian stone-built house has excellent comfort, food and facilities, with hosts' personal hospitality and local Snowdonia knowledge in a friendly atmosphere. A5 road; Pont-y-Pair Bridge (B5106), immediately left. The WTB 3 Star award-winning house with private parking is 150 metres up ahead on quiet peaceful wooded riverside.

B & B £22-£28pp, Rooms 2 double, 1 twin, all en-suite, No smoking, No small children, No dogs, Open all year

TAN-Y-FOEL COUNTRY HOUSE Capel Garmon, Betws-y-Coed LL26 0RE *Map Ref:* 6
Mr & Mrs Pitman *Tel:* 01690 710507 *Fax:* 01690 710681 A5/A470
Email: enquiries@tyfhotel.co.uk *Web:* www.tyfhotel.co.uk

Snowdonia's only 5 star Country House, dating from the 17th century, built in Welsh stone, beautifully decorated in a traditional modern style providing visitors with outstanding accommodation and cuisine. Set high in the hillside just outside Betws-y-Coed with magnificent views of the Conwy Valley. No traffic or busy clamour, relaxing, romantic location. Perfect base to explore Snowdonia's National Park attractions.

B & B £45-£75pp, C-Cards MC VS AE DC, Dinner from £30, Rooms 4 double/twin, 2 king/double, all en-suite, No smoking, Children over 7, No dogs, Closed Xmas & some of Jan

THE WHITE HOUSE Llanfaglan, Caernarfon LL54 5RA *Map Ref:* 7
Richard Bayles *Tel:* 01286 673003 A487
Email: rwbayles@sjms.co.uk

Modern country house, splendid views of the Menai Straits and Snowdonia. Superb for bird watchers and walkers. Outdoor pool available. Caernarfon Golf Club, two miles. Access to The White House is via the A487 Caernarfon/Porthmadog, on leaving Caernarfon, across roundabout, right for Saron/Llanfaglan. Set mileometer to zero, 1.6 miles, right signposted to Sea shore. The White House is on the left, last house before the sea.

B & B £20-£22pp, Rooms 2 double, 2 twin, all en-suite/private, Restricted smoking, Children welcome, Dogs by arrangement, Closed Nov to Mar

HAFOTY Rhostryfan, Caernarfon LL54 7PH *Map Ref:* 8
Mari & Wil Davies *Tel:* 01286 830144 *Fax:* 01286 830441 A487, A4086
Email: hafoty@btinternet.com *Web:* www.hafotyfarmguesthouse.co.uk

This peaceful 18th century farmhouse, with a large courtyard and converted barns, is set in 17 acres of land where guests are allowed to walk freely. The lounge has retained its farmhouse cosiness with open oak beams and a large inglenook fireplace. Hafoty is only ten minutes drive from Caernarfon. It also boasts having been voted by the Wales Tourist Board the award of The Best Farmhouse and Accommodation in Wales.

B & B £24-£26pp, C-Cards MC VS, Rooms 1 single, 2 double, 1 twin, 1 family, all en-suite., Restricted smoking, Children welcome, No dogs, Closed Nov to Mar

PENGWERN FARM Saron, Caernarfon LL54 5UH *Map Ref:* 8
Gwyndaf & Jane Rowlands *Tel:* 01286 831500 *Fax:* 01286 830741 A487
Email: Pengwern@talk21.com

A charming spacious farmhouse of character, beautifully situated between mountains and sea with unobstructed views of Snowdonia. Well appointed en-suite bedrooms with televisions, luggage racks and tea/coffee facilities. Jane has a cookery diploma and provides excellent meals with farmhouse fresh food including local produce. Near Snowdonia National Park and lovely beaches of Anglesey and Lleyn Peninsula.

B & B from £24pp, Dinner available, Rooms 3 en-suite, No smoking, No dogs, Closed Dec & Jan

SYCHNANT PASS HOUSE Sychnant Pass Road, Conwy LL32 8BJ *Map Ref:* 9
Bre & Graham Carrington-Sykes *Tel / Fax:* 01492 596868 A55
Email: bre@sychnant-pass-house.co.uk *Web:* www.sychnant-pass-house.co.uk

Inside Snowdonia National Park, two miles from Conwy Castle and the beach, our Victorian House stands in three acres of gardens. Big sitting rooms with cosy sofas and log fires. A candlelit restaurant, ensuite bedrooms, some with terraces and four poster beds, are just a few of the lovely treats awaiting you in our home. Children and dogs warmly welcomed.

B & B from £30pp, C-Cards MC VS, Dinner from £16.95, Rooms 5 double, 3 twin, 3 family, all en-suite, No smoking in bedrooms, Children & dogs welcome, Closed Xmas

THE OLD RECTORY COUNTRY HOUSE Llanrwst Road, Llansanffraid Glan Conwy LL28 5LF
Michael & Wendy Vaughan *Tel:* 01492 580611 *Fax:* 01492 584555 *Map Ref:* 10
Email: info@oldrectorycountryhouse.co.uk *Web:* www.oldrectorycountryhouse.co.uk A470

This idyllic country house stands in large gardens overlooking the Conwy Bird Reserve. Wendy is a 'Master Chef of GB' and she features in all of Britain's premier good food guides. Welsh mountain lamb, locally reared Welsh black beef and locally landed fish are on her menu. The house displays a sense of elegance coupled with a delight in old paintings, antiques and opulent furnishings. The bedrooms are luxuriously appointed and generously equipped.

B & B £49.90-£84.90pp, C-Cards MC VS, Dinner from £29.90, Rooms 4 double, 2 twin, all en-suite, No smoking, Children over 5, Dogs in coach house only, Closed Dec to Jan

---

RHAGATT HALL Carrog, Corwen LL21 9HY *Map Ref:* 11
John & Frances Bradshaw *Tel:* 01490 412308 *Fax:* 01490 413388 A5
Email: fjcb01@aol.com

Georgian mansion overlooking the River Dee and the Berwyn Mountains. Surrounded by trees and gardens, there are beautiful walks through bluebell woods to the river. Spacious bedrooms, garden views. The sitting room has a log fire and french windows. Frances has a Cordon Bleu Diploma. The Grouse pub is a mile away, interesting places can be reached from here via the steam railway.

B & B from £34pp, C-Cards MC VS, Dinner from £12, Rooms 1 double, 1 twin, all en-suite, No smoking in bedrooms, Children over 12, No dogs, Closed Xmas & New Year

---

MIN-Y-GAER HOTEL Porthmadog Road, Criccieth LL52 0HP *Map Ref:* 12
Mrs Rita Murray *Tel:* 01766 522151 *Fax:* 01766 523540 A497
Email: info@minygaerhotel.co.uk *Web:* www.minygaerhotel.co.uk

This is a pleasant, licensed hotel which is conveniently situated being near to the beach. It has delightful views of Criccieth Castle and the scenic Cardigan Bay coastline. There are ten comfortably furnished bedrooms which are equipped with colour TV and beverage facilities. A lounge and licensed bar are available for guests and there is a private car park on the premises.

B & B £22-£26pp, C-Cards MC VS AE, Rooms 1 single, 2 twin, 4 double, 3 family, all en-suite, No smoking in bedrooms, Children welcome, No dogs, Closed Nov to Feb

---

MOR-HELI Min-y-Mor, Criccieth LL52 0EF *Map Ref:* 12
Eirwyn & Carolyn Williams A487
Tel: 01766 522802 *Fax:* 01766 522878

Overlooking the coast line from Aberdaron to Aberdyfei, all en-suite bedrooms have a sea view, television and hospitality trays. Established over 20 years by Williams Family 'Croeso Cynnes Gymreig,' noted for good food and atmosphere. Close to Snowdonia, Portmeirion, Llyn Peninsula and Ffestiniog Railway.

B & B from £20pp, Dinner from £12, Rooms 1 single, 2 double, 2 twin, 2 family, all en-suite, Restricted smoking, Children & dogs welcome, Open all year

---

CORS-Y-GARNEDD Llanfachreth, Dolgellau LL40 2EH *Map Ref:* 13
Merle Gibbs *Tel:* 01341 422627 *Fax:* 01341 421062 A470
Email: merle@welshmountain.demon.co.uk *Web:* www.welshmountain.demon.co.uk

The house has been renovated and decorated to offer the best in modern comfort but still preserving the character of this important house. Traditional home cooked meals served in the spacious main hall which boasts authentic decorative beams, an enormous inglenook fireplace with wood burning fire as well as a hidden stone spiral staircase. Also a lounge where guests can relax. Cot available for under 1 year.

B & B from £25.50pp, C-Cards MC VS, Dinner from £15, Rooms 1 single, 1 double en-suite, 1 twin en-suite, No smoking, Children over 10, Dogs by arrangement, Closed Dec to Feb

TYDDYN DU FARM Gellilydan, Ffestiniog, near Porthmadog LL41 4RB

Mrs Paula Williams *Tel / Fax:* 01766 590281 *Mobile:* 07867 577522

Email: paula@snowdonia-farm.com *Web:* www.snowdonia-farm.com

Map Ref: 14
A470, A487

Set amidst spectacular scenery in a superb central Snowdonia location, enchanting 400 year old farmhouse has a special charm and character. Suites have jacuzzi baths, fridges and microwaves. Delicious candlelight dinners. Patio window gardens overlooking the beautiful countryside. Working sheep farm, feed chickens, ducks and lambs. Ideal base for walking, visiting Portmeirion and Ffestiniog railway. Weekly B&B rates available.

B & B £25-£35pp, Dinner from £15, Rooms (suites) double/twin/family en-suite, No smoking, Children welcome, Dogs by arrangement,

GWRACH YNYS COUNTRY GUEST HOUSE Talsarnau, Harlech LL47 6TS

Deborah Williams *Tel:* 01766 780742 *Fax:* 01766 781199

Email: gwrachynys@btinternet.com *Web:* www.gwrachynys.co.uk

Map Ref: 15
A496

Enjoy a peaceful break in a glorious rural setting close to mountains and the sea. Ideal base for walking and touring the Snowdonia National Park and North Wales. Close to Portmeirion, Ffestiniog Railway and many other popular attractions. En-suite bedrooms individually decorated and furnished to a high standard. A warm Welsh welcome awaits you. WTB 4 Stars Country House. AA 4 Crowns.

B & B £22-£28pp, Dinner from £15, Rooms 2 double, 1 twin, 3 family, 1 single, all en-suite, No smoking, Children welcome, No dogs, Closed Nov to Mar

NODDFA GUEST HOUSE Ffordd Newydd, Harlech LL46 2UB

Jane & Richard Salter *Tel:* 01766 780043

Email: noddfa@welshnet.co.uk *Web:* www.noddfa.welshnet.co.uk

Map Ref: 15
A496

Noddfa overlooks the Royal St David's Golf Course, with splendid views of the Snowdon mountain range and Tremadog Bay. Extensively rebuilt in 1850 it provides comfortable bedrooms with en-suite or private bathrooms. The historic town of Harlech offers restaurants, swimming pool, theatre and spectacular sandy beach. Central for the attractions of Wales. Residential licence, evening meals on request.

B & B from £24pp, C-Cards, Rooms 1 single, 5 double, some en-suite, Restricted smoking, Children over 5, No dogs, Open all year

GOLDEN GROVE Llanasa, Holywell CH8 9NA

Nigel, Mervyn, Ann & Ann Steele-Mortimer *Tel:* 01745 854452 *Fax:* 01745 854547

Email: goldengrove@lineone.net

Map Ref: 16
A548, A5151

A beautiful Grade I Elizabethan manor, with extensive gardens, set in 1000 acres of pasture and woodland; close to Chester, The Vale of Clwyd, Bodnant Gardens, several fine National Trust properties, Snowdonia and en-route to Holyhead and Dublin. The menu features home produce, interesting wine and home baking. The friendly and informal atmosphere makes this the ideal spot for relaxing in North Wales.

B & B from £37pp, C-Cards MC VS, Dinner from £22, Rooms 1 double, 2 double/twin, en-suite or private bathroom, Restricted smoking, Children over 12, No dogs, Closed Dec & Jan

GREENHILL FARM GUEST HOUSE Bryn Celyn, Holywell CH8 7QF

John & Mary Jones *Tel:* 01352 713270

Email: mary@greenhillfarm.fsnet.co.uk *Web:* www.greenhillfarm.co.uk

Map Ref: 17
A55

Our 16th century farmhouse, set in beautiful gardens, boasts an impressive panoramic view across the Dee estuary and beyond. The oak beamed house includes a bedroom with an inglenook and a panelled dining room. All rooms include televisions and tea/coffee facilities with two en-suite rooms. Guests are offered a warm welcome and fresh locally produced foods.

B & B from £19.50pp, Dinner from £8, Rooms 1 double, 1 twin, 2 family en-suite, Children welcome, No dogs, Closed Dec to Feb

ABBEY LODGE 14 Abbey Road, Llandudno LL30 2EA　　　　*Map Ref:* 18
Geoff & Trish Howard　*Tel / Fax:* 01492 878042　　　　　　　　　A470
Email: enquiries@abbeylodgeuk.com　*Web:* www.abbeylodgeuk.com

Abbey Lodge is quietly situated only a few minutes walk from the centre of the Victorian resort town of Llandudno with its wide bay and gracious promenade. It was built as a gentleman's residence around 1870 and has been refurbished to combine every modern comfort with its original Victorian charm and character, elegant yet homely. AA 5 Diamonds, WTB 4 Stars.

B & B £25-£35pp, Dinner from £15, Rooms 3 double, 1 twin, all en-suite, No smoking, Children over 12, No dogs, Closed Xmas

LYMPLEY LODGE Colwyn Road, Craigside, Llandudno LL30 3AL　　*Map Ref:* 18
Patricia Richards　*Tel:* 01492 549304　*Fax:* 0870 138 3370　　　B5115
Email: clive@lympleylodge.co.uk　*Web:* www.lympleylodge.co.uk

A beautiful Victorian House set beneath the headland known as Little Orme, it overlooks Llandudno bay. Generously equipped bedrooms display their indvidual characters, the elegant Orme room, the Marina with its Medtierranean charm. Fresh and preserved fruits, locally cured bacon and sausages and free range eggs are offered. An excellent local choice of restaurants and bistros. Ideal for exploring North Wales.

B & B £27.50-£30pp, Rooms 3 double, all en-suite, No smoking, Children over 12, No dogs, Closed mid-Dec to mid-Jan

DRWS Y COED FARM Llanerchymedd LL71 8AD　　　　　*Map Ref:* 19
Jane Bown　　　　　　　　　　　　　　　　　　　　A55, A5, A5025
Tel / Fax: 01248 470473　*Mobile:* 07971 827184

Guests are welcomed by Tom and Jane to this beautifully appointed farmhouse on a 550 acre working farm. Enjoy wonderful panoramic views of Snowdonia, excellent hospitality, food and tranquil surroundings. Inviting spacious lounge with log fire. Bedrooms are tastefully decorated and offer en-suite facilities. Full central heating. Centrally situated to explore Anglesey. 25 minutes to Holyhead for Irish Sea crossings.

B & B £23-£25pp, C-Cards MC VS, Rooms 1 twin, 1 double, 1 family, all en-suite, No smoking, Children welcome, No dogs, Closed Xmas day

LLWYDIARTH FAWR LLanerchymedd LL71 8DF　　　　　*Map Ref:* 19
Mrs Margaret Hughes　*Tel:* 01248 470321/470540　　　　　A55, B5111
Email: llwydiarth@hotmail.com

Beautiful Georgian house with quiet luxury, superior standards, beautiful antiques, delicious food and a warm welcome. Bedrooms are furnished to a high standard, with colour television, tea/coffee making facilities and full central heating. Mealtimes are a special occasion, using farm and fresh local produce. An ideal base to explore all of Anglesey.

B & B from £25pp, C-Cards MC VS, Dinner from £15, Rooms 1 double, 1 twin, 1 family, 1 single, all en-suite, No smoking, Children welcome, No dogs, Closed Xmas

OAKMERE Regent Street, Llangollen LL20 8HS　　　　　*Map Ref:* 20
Lyndsey Knibbs　*Tel:* 01978 861126　　　　　　　　　　　A5
Email: oakmeregh@aol.com　*Web:* www.oakmere.llangollen.co.uk

Oakmere is a large, faithfully restored Victorian house set in its own grounds, just a few minutes' walk from Llangollen's town centre. The terraced gardens offer magnificent views across the valley and include an all-weather tennis court. Accommodation is either en-suite or with private facilities providing a relaxing atmosphere of spacious comfort. All rooms have televisions and tea/coffee facilities. AA 4 Diamonds, WTB 4 Stars.

B & B £22.50-£25pp, Rooms 2 double, 2 twin, 2 family, all en-suite, No smoking, Children welcome, No dogs, Open all year

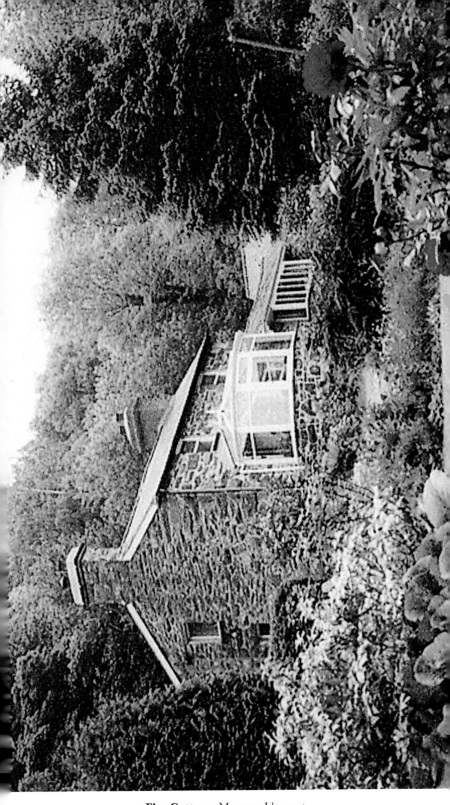

Firs Cottage, Maenan, Llanrwst

TYN CELYN FARMHOUSE Tyndwr, Llangollen LL20 8AR
Mrs Janet Bather   *Tel:* 01978 861117
Email: j.m.bather-tyncelyn@talk21.com   *Web:* www.SmoothHound.co.uk/hotels/tyncelyn.html

Map Ref: 20
A5

A spacious oak beamed country house on the outskirts of Llangollen. Situated in a peaceful valley, Tyncelyn is over 300 years old and enjoys outstanding views of Dinas Bran Castle and the surrounding majestic hills of Llangollen. All bedrooms have en-suite bathrooms, there is a ground floor room and a four poster bedroom. Wholesome breakfasts and secure off road parking.

B & B from £22pp, Rooms 1 double, 1 twin, 1 family, all en-suite, No smoking, Children welcome, No dogs, Closed Xmas & New Year

---

DEE FARM Rhewl, Llangollen LL20 7YT
Mrs Mary Harman   *Tel / Fax:* 01978 861598
Email: harman@activelives.co.uk

Map Ref: 21
A5, A542

18th century farmhouse in the most glorious and peaceful setting on the River Dee. Very comfortable accommodation which includes two guest sitting rooms with television. All rooms have tea/coffee facilities. The Sun Inn is only 400 yards away. It is four miles to Llangollen and there is plenty to do as National Trust Chirk Castle and Erddig are nearby. Safe parking.

B & B £21-£24pp, Dinner from £12, Rooms 1 single, 2 twin with en-suite, No smoking, Children welcome, Dogs by arrangement, Closed Nov to Mar

---

FIRS COTTAGE Maenan, Llanrwst LL26 0YR
Jack & Mary Marrow
Tel: 01492 660244   *Mobile:* 0775 1058051

Map Ref: 22
A470
see Photo on page 423

17th century comfortable cottage family home, situated in the Conway Valley, enjoying wonderful hill views. It stands away from the A470, in a quiet area with a beautiful garden and patio. Bodnant Garden, Conwy Castle, Llandudno and Snowdon are within easy reach. Excellent choice of places to eat. Three well furnished cottage bedrooms and a Welsh breakfast with homemade bread, jams and marmalades.

B & B from £17.50pp, Rooms 2 twin/double, 1 double, Restricted smoking, Children welcome, Dogs by arrangement, Closed Xmas

---

CRAFNANT GUEST HOUSE Trefriw, near Llanrwst LL27 0JH
Mike & Jan Bertenshaw   *Tel:* 01492 640809
Email: crafnant@tesco.net   *Web:* www.trefriw.co.uk

Map Ref: 23
A5

An ideal peaceful base in a picturesque village. All rooms have gas central heating, tea and coffee, colour televisions and are furnished to high standards including cast iron beds with fresh white linen. Two real village pubs both serving excellent food on the doorstep. Three mountain lakes within three miles. Private parking. Two guest lounges. WTB 3 Stars.

B & B from £20pp, C-Cards MC VS, Rooms 3 double, 1 twin, 1 family, most en-suite, No smoking, Children welcome, No dogs, Closed Dec & Jan

---

GLANDWR Trefriw, Llanrwst LL27 0JP

Tel: 01492 640431

Map Ref: 23
A5

A spacious country house on the outskirts of Trefriw village, close to Llanrwst, Betws-y-Coed and Swallow Falls and nine miles from A55. A good touring centre with golf, fishing and riding locally. Glandwr has a guests' lounge with television, a bathroom, shower room and downstairs cloakroom with toilet and wash basin. Bedrooms also have washbasins. Guide dogs and owners especially welcome.

B & B from £18pp, Rooms 1 single, 2 double, 1 twin, 1 family, Children & dogs welcome, Closed Oct to Apr

WERN FARM Pentraeth Road, Menai Bridge LL59 5RR
Peter & Linda Brayshaw   *Tel / Fax:* 01248 712421
Email: wernfarmanglesey@onetel.net.uk   *Web:* angleseyfarms.com/wern.htm

Map Ref: 24
A5025

Wern is a lovely 18th century farmhouse set in 250 acres of countryside, where hosts Peter and Linda Brayshaw have resided for over 30 years. Guest accommodation is spacious and well equipped. Award winning breakfasts are served in the Victorian style conservatory, where guests can enjoy breathtaking views of the beautiful garden and the Snowdonia mountain range.

B & B £23-£28pp, C-Cards MC VS, Rooms 1 double, 1 twin, 1 family, all en-suite, No smoking, Children welcome, Dogs not allowed in house, Closed Dec to Feb

PLAS PENUCHA Caerwys, Mold CH7 5BH
Nest Price
Tel: 01352 720210   *Fax:* 01352 720881

Map Ref: 25
A55, B5122, A541

A 16th century comfortable farmhouse, in the same family for 450 years, although altered over generations, retains a sense of history. Large gardens overlook the Clwydian Hills. A spacious lounge and library, the bedrooms are well equipped. Central heating and log fires. Ideal for walking and exploring. All North Wales and Chester in easy reach, two miles from A55 Expressway.

B & B £21-£25pp, Dinner from £11.50, Rooms 2 twin, 2 double, some en-suite, Restricted smoking, Children welcome, Dogs by arrangement, Open all year

TOWER Nercwys Road, Nercwys, Mold CH7 4EW
Wendy Wynne-Eyton
Tel: 01352 700220   *Mobile:* 07714 155267

Map Ref: 26
A494

The Mayor of Chester was hanged in Tower in 1465. A warmer welcome now awaits visitors to this beautiful, fortified border house, Grade I listed, set in tranquil grounds. Despite its antiquity, Tower offers visitors all the comforts of the 21st century with tea/coffee facilities and televisions in all bedrooms. Relax in tranquility or explore North Wales and Chester.

B & B from £35pp, Rooms 2 double, 1 twin, all en-suite, Children welcome, Dogs by arrangement, Closed Xmas & New Year

PENTRE CERRIG MAWR Maeshafn, Mold CH7 5LU
Ted & Charmian Spencer   *Tel / Fax:* 01352 810607
Email: charmian.sunbeam@care4free.net   *Web:* www.pentrecerrigmawr.com

Map Ref: 26
A494

Beautiful house, two acres of walled gardens, dating from Elizabethan times, peaceful, with beams and open fires. Spacious bedrooms have fine cotton sheets, thick towels, a hospitality tray and spectacular valley views. Four miles from Mold, perfect for touring Snowdonia, Welsh National Park, the coast. 40 minutes from Manchester and Liverpool, en-route for Holyhead. Interesting pubs, lovely walks, good food and a warm welcome.

B & B from £37pp, C-Cards MC VS, Dinner from £25, Rooms 2 double, 1 double/twin, all en-suite, No smoking, Children over 8, Dogs by arrangement, Closed occasionally

Y WERN Llanfrothen, Penrhyndeudraeth LL48 6LX
Tony Bayley   *Tel / Fax:* 01766 770556
Email: bbwern@btinternet.com

Map Ref: 27
A4085, B4410

A 16th century stone built farmhouse situated in beautiful countryside within the Snowdonia National Park. 'Wern' abounds with oak beams and inglenook fireplaces, and the large comfortable well equipped bedrooms have delightful views. An excellent centre for walking, it is well placed for beaches and attractions such as Portmerion, Castles and the Ffestiniog Railway. Dinner by arrangement.

B & B from £19pp, Dinner from £12.50, Rooms 2 twin, 2 double, all en-suite/private, No smoking, Children over 5, No dogs, Closed part Dec

PARC-YR-ODYN Pentraeth LL75 8UL   *Map Ref:* 28
Mrs Helen Thomas   *Tel:* 01248 450566   A5025
Email: parcyrodyn@yahoo.com

Private farmhouse, rural location, convenient to local attractions. Beautiful property, delightfully decorated. Warm welcome and ideally located for quiet breaks or for touring North Wales. AA 5 Diamonds, WTB 5 Stars.

B & B from £25pp, Rooms 2 double en-suite, No smoking, No children or dogs, Open all year

---

THE OLD RECTORY Boduan, Pwllheli LL53 6DT   *Map Ref:* 29
Gabrielle & Roger Pollard   A497
Tel / Fax: 01758 721519   *Mobile:* 07974 786261

The Old Rectory is a delightful country house which has been extensively and sympathetically renovated over time. It now welcomes guests to enjoy modern and well equipped accommodation. There is an elegant lounge for guests to enjoy, and dinners are available by arrangement. This is a warm and relaxing place to stay.

B & B from £35pp, Dinner from £17.50, Rooms 2 double, 2 twin, all en-suite, No smoking, Children welcome, Dogs by arrangement, Closed Xmas

---

EYARTH STATION Llanfair D C, Ruthin LL15 2EE   *Map Ref:* 30
Jen & Bert Spencer   *Tel:* 01824 703643   *Fax:* 01824 707464   A525
Email: eyarthstation@amserve.net   *Web:* www.smoothhound.co.uk/hotels/eyarth

A former railway station now converted country house with six en-suite bedrooms, TV lounge, swimming pool, car park and magnificent views. Eyarth Station is located in beautiful countryside just 3 minutes drive to the castle with its Medieval banquets, and the town. Central for Chester, Snowdonia and Llangollen Bala and the coast. BTA commended. AA. B&B Winner 96.

B & B £23-£25pp, C-Cards MC VS, Dinner from £12, Rooms 2 twin, 2 double, 2 family, all en-suite, Restricted smoking, Children & dogs welcome, Closed Nov, Jan & Feb

---

THE OLD BARN Esgairlygain, Llangynhafal, Ruthin LL15 1RT   *Map Ref:* 31
Mrs I Henderson   B5429
Tel: 01824 704047/704993   *Fax:* 01824 704047

Sleep in the haylofts, breakfast in the Shippon where the cows were once milked. Our barn has been sensitively converted for guests with sloping ceilings and beams. Lovely views, spectacular sunsets. Direct access to Clwydian Hills, Offa's Dyke and mountain bike tracks. Horse riding available nearby. Central for Llangollen, Chester, Snowdonia, Castles and coast with National Trust properties. Refreshments and welcome on arrival.

B & B from £20pp, Rooms 1 double, 1 family, both en-suite, Restricted smoking, Children & dogs welcome, Closed Nov to Feb

---

CEFN COCH COUNTRY GUEST HOUSE Llanegryn, Tywyn LL36 9SD   *Map Ref:* 32
David & Anne Sylvester   *Tel / Fax:* 01654 712193   A493
Email: david@cefn-coch.co.uk   *Web:* www.cefn-coch.co.uk/

A former coaching inn with spectacular views of the Dysynni Valley and Cader Idris. Retaining original features; stone walls, slate floors, beamed ceilings, Cefn Coch provides comfortable accommodation. Enjoy excellent home cooked food in our candle-lit dining room. A good place to explore Snowdonia National Park and Cardigan Bay.

B & B £21-£25pp, Dinner from £15, Rooms 2 double, 3 twin, all en-suite, No smoking, Children over 14, No dogs, Closed Xmas & New Year

Property Index

Property Index

Property Index

Property Index

Property Index

Property Index

Property Index

Property Index

Property Index

Property Index

Property Index

Town Index

Town Index

Town Index

Town Index

Town Index

Town Index

Report Form

Please photocopy and use this form to let us know about your stay.
We value your comments, good or bad, and we will take the
appropriate action where necessary.

Property Name: _____

Address: _____

_____ Postcode: _____

Comments:

_____
_____
_____
_____
_____
_____
_____
_____
_____
_____
_____
_____
_____
_____

From:

Name: _____

Address: _____

_____ Postcode: _____

Please send the completed form to:
The Editor (BBD), Tomorrow's Guides, PO Box 7677,
Hungerford RG17 0FX *or email*: editor@tomorrows.co.uk

Recommendations

Please photocopy and use this form to tell us about any other Homes that you would recommend for listing in future editions.

Property Name: _____

Address: _____

_____ Postcode: _____

Comments:

_____
_____
_____
_____
_____
_____
_____
_____
_____
_____
_____
_____
_____
_____

From:

Name: _____

Address: _____

_____ Postcode: _____

Please send the completed form to:
The Editor (BBD), Tomorrow's Guides, PO Box 7677,
Hungerford RG17 0FX *or email*: editor@tomorrows.co.uk

Notes